Understanding China

The series will provide you with in-depth information on China's social, cultural and economic aspects. It covers a broad variety of topics, from economics and history to law, philosophy, cultural geography and regional politics, and offers a wealth of materials for researchers, doctoral students, and experienced practitioners.

Jun Zhang

Reform, Transformation and Growth

Observation and Interpretation

北京师范大学出版集团
BEIJING NORMAL UNIVERSITY PUBLISHING GROUP
北京师范大学出版社

Springer

Jun Zhang
School of Economics
Fudan University
Shanghai, China

Translated by
Qiuhai Wang
School of Economics
Fudan University
Shanghai, China

ISSN 2196-3134 ISSN 2196-3142 (electronic)
Understanding China
ISBN 978-981-99-5711-8 ISBN 978-981-99-5712-5 (eBook)
https://doi.org/10.1007/978-981-99-5712-5

Jointly published with Beijing Normal University Press (Group) Co., Ltd.
The print edition is not for sale in China (Mainland). Customers from China (Mainland) please order the print book from: Beijing Normal University Press (Group) Co., Ltd.

Funded by Chinese Fund for the Humanities and Social Sciences

This Springer imprint is published by the registered company Springer Nature Singapore Pte Ltd.
The registered company address is: 152 Beach Road, #21-01/04 Gateway East, Singapore 189721, Singapore

Preface I

The Beijing Normal University Press published the collection of my essays, titled "Reform, Transformation and Growth: Observation and Interpretation" 10 years ago. The collection belongs to the "Contemporary Chinese Economists Series" of Beijing Normal University Press. I was greatly honored that the press invited me to edit the collection of my academic papers for the series. In this collection, I've selected 12 papers from my hundreds of papers that were published in different periods with different themes. These papers can be classified into five categories, including the research of traditional socialist economic structure, the China's transformation from planned economy to market economy, the reform of China industrial economy, economic growth and political economy. Currently, I still carry out research into these fields and they are really drawing for me.

When the collection was published, I wrote a preface for the book to review the time span covered by these papers. At that time, I was engaged in many international academic activities and cooperated with many foreign economists to do some research. I also carried out research in some foreign academic institutions and universities and many papers were the result of these collaborative research work.

Since the early 1990s, I've studied the China's economic development for almost three decades. At first, I was very interested in how the country ran the scheme of planned economy. I was very curious why China's planned economy was so different from that run in the Soviet Union. Why China's ministry of industry only could divide such a little amount of goods and products. These questions drew me to research the relationship between central and local government in terms of economic development. China's market-oriented reforms, which were started since 1980s, began with the further decentralization of power and benefits from the central government to local governments. After that, I began to watch closely on China's economic development and the process of economic reform. And I focused on important issues in different fields at different stages.

The 12 papers selected present readers with my researches in the past 30 years. Initially, I mainly focused on the research of the property rights under different economic schemes, as well as institutional arrangements and institutional change theories. With the furthering of my research, I gradually shifted to study many important areas of China's economic transformation, economic development and growth. These areas include strategies for economic transformation, dual-track pricing, industrial transformation and enterprise reform, capital formation and economic growth, structural changes and productivity growth, macroeconomics, fiscal relations between central and local governments, and the political economy of growth. Specifically, these papers reflect my main research work and achievements.

Let me give you a summary.

(1) In my papers, I systematically analyze the changes in the distribution of profitability of three-digit industries brought by China's industrial reforms, find the pattern of losses in the state-owned enterprises, identify the determinants and changes in the total profit rate of the industrial section, and use different hypotheses to check the reasons for the deteriorating trend of profit rates in different stages.
(2) Based on the empirical analysis towards China and Russia's economic transition, I developed the theory about economic transformation. Through conducting an economic analysis based on the perspective of industrial organization on the dual-track price system implemented by China in the 1980s, I made contribution to the transitional economics literature.
(3) I systematically assessed China's provinces' material capital stock values and subsequent other provincial panel data from 1952 to 2005, which provided an important data basis for domestic and foreign scholars to fit China's total production function and was widely used by domestic and foreign economists. With the data, I studied the changes in productivity (TFP) of China's economic sub-sectors and provinces, estimated the main characteristics of productivity changes in the industrial sector, especially the state-owned sector in the post-reform period, providing an important basis for decomposing and evaluating the sources of economic growth.
(4) I systematically studied the relationship between China's capital formation, investment efficiency and economic growth after 1978, which has become the basic knowledge for economists to understand China's economic growth pattern since the Reform and Opening up and carry out research in forecasting and analyzing future growth trends.
(5) Under the framework of intergovernmental fiscal relations and horizontal competition between local governments, I systematically studied the determinants of public capital formation, especially the infrastructure investment, and researched into the mechanism of China's economic development. I also included the evaluation of officials, promotion incentives and local government competition mechanisms into a growth model, which constructs a dynamic general equilibrium model. This theory of economic growth, which mainly focuses on the governmental economic decision, can not only explain China's past high-speed growth mechanism, but also explain the structural slowdown

in China's economy in recent years. These researches, along with other similar researches carried out by domestic and foreign counterparts, have constituted the mainstream international literature on China's economic development and growth in the post-reform period.

Over the past decade, I was committed to summarizing and disseminating the experience, gains and losses of China's economic transformation and development, and I have published many articles on world-known journals. "Piece by Jun Zhang of Fudan is perhaps the best account of the China Miracle I have ever read," commented Professor Edmund Phelps, winner of the 2006 Nobel Prize in Economics, after reading my article on the analysis of China's economic development.

The large-scale international biennial event "Transformation and Economic Development" (TED) founded by me and organized at Shanghai's Fudan University has achieved good results in the past 10 years. And I was invited to publish special columns of the event in foreign economics journals, for the purpose of spreading the Chinese experience. It is noticeable that Journal of the Asia Pacific Economy, one of the prestigious journals in the Social Sciences Citation Index devoted the length of entire journal to publish the special issue "The Political Economy of China's Robust Performance," which was finished by me as the guest editor. The special issue published a set of high-quality research papers including my paper, which was regarded as great efforts to stimulate empirical research on China's economic development in the international academic community.

In 2018, the famous economist Justin Yifu Lin and I were invited by Dr. Arkebe Oqubay, Special Advisor to Ethiopian Prime Minister and development economist to work together to write the paper about China's economic development experience "China: Learning to Catch up in a Globalized World." The article was included into the collection *How Nations Learn: Learning to Catch Up and Lessons for Late Latecomer* edited by Kenichi Ohno and Arkebe Oqubay and published by Oxford University Press in 2019. At the same year, I cooperated with my colleagues to write the chapter "Industrial Hubs in Sphinx China" for the book *The Oxford Handbook of Industrial Hubs and Economic Development.*

In recent years, especially after 2013, China's economy has shown a sign of sustained slowdown. As for the reasons, it should be ascribed to the external economic environment and some long-term structural factors, like the decline of birth rate. But I think that the government itself should also give an explanation towards the situation. To my bold speculation, if the central government does not use the GDP growth as the main standard to evaluate local officials' performance and considers factors like environmental protection, risk prevent and control and poverty relief as the assessment criteria, local governments, under the influence of Yardstick Competition, will deliberately slow down the effective investment required for economic growth and constantly lower the local GDP growth target. Recently, I theorized this conjecture with my collaborators and confirmed it statistically. This theory can well explain and predict the continuous decline in China's economic growth after 2013, and it can also help evaluate the social welfare impact of this phenomenon.

Besides, it is noteworthy that the current global economy is undergoing major changes unseen in nearly a century, and China and the United States, the two largest economies are in the most tense relationship in the past 40 years. Under such a background, what's the future of China's economy? How will China adjust the development strategy to keep a sustained growing momentum? These questions have become the research topics that I am increasingly interested in. I hope that my new researches can come out in a few years later and I believe that they are carried out on the basis of the theory and studies mentioned in this book.

At last, I am very delighted and honored that the book's English version can be published after its Chinese version was published 10 years ago. I hope that the English version can better share the results of my research on Chinese economy in the English-speaking world, and it will also enable more people in the world to understand the successful development of China's economy.

I want to express my heartfelt thanks to editors of the Beijing Normal University Press and the friends who provided direct or indirect help for the English version's publishing. Without their efforts, the English version of this book cannot be presented to Western readers. I also want to convey my thanks to my family for their selfless support and dedication to my long-term research work.

Shanghai, China
October 2020

Jun Zhang

Preface II[1]

It should be said that from 1988 (the year I got my master's degree in Fudan University) to early 1994 when I finished my postdoctoral study and research at University of Sussex's AFRAS College, my interest was focused primarily on the general theory of property rights economics and institutional change. I not only published the *Modern Property Rights Economics* (1991), but also translated and published *Public Option* (1990) and *Law and Economics* (1991), as well as published many research papers related to this field in the journals such as *Economic Research.*

In late autumn of 1994, I was awarded the research grant offered by the US-Sino Academic Exchange Committee (CSCC), and began doing research with Dr. William Hallagan on China's economic reform at the Economics Department of the State University of Washington. After that, my interest began to gradually shift to the "transitional economics" that aimed at explaining the way of transition in Chinese and other transitional economies. In 1997 and 1998, my *Double Track Economics: China's Economic Reforms from 1978 to 1992* and *Review* and *Analysis of Economic Reform in China* were published by Shanghai Joint Publishing Company Ltd., Shanghai People's Publishing House and Shanxi Economic Publishing House.

When I came back from the United States to Fudan University in the summer of 1995, my focus was gradually narrowed down on the reform of industrial sectors in China. I was really interested in the change of industrial organizations, profit margins, productivity and economic growth model theories and experience. In particular during this period, I was lucky enough to get the support of Dr. Athar Hussian, former director of the China Project Team of the London School of Economics' STICERD Research Center. Under his recommendation, I got the K. C. Wong Research Fellowship of British Academy/The Royal Society at the end of 1996 which allowed me to engage in research for half a year at the STICERD Research Center of the London School of Economics in the autumn of 1997. My interest then was large-scale losses

---

[1] This preface used, revised and supplemented some portions of the *Introduction to China's Industrial and Economic Growth: Problems and Explanations* (Jun Zhang, Shanghai Joint Publishing Company Ltd. and Shanghai People's Publishing House, 2003) which generally describes the author's main research experience since the 1990s.

of the China's industrial sectors and I completed a paper on the loss model of the state-owned enterprises. During that period, I was also invited to be a researcher by the Department of Economics of the University of London's SOAS (School of Oriental and African Studies) where I had more opportunities to meet and discuss problems with Dr. Lu Di, because China's industrial reform and its performance evaluation were his main interest at that time.

After finishing my research in London, I was invited by the Department of Economics and East Asian Studies Center of University of Aarhus in Denmark for a week in March 1998 where I gave three speeches including one on the paper about the losses of the state-owned enterprises written in London. The dean of the School of Social Sciences (we met earlier at Fudan University), Prof. Sidenius, made thoughtful arrangement for my visit, and provided generous funding (salary) for me in the name of lecture professor. The visit let me get to know Prof. Clemens and Prof. S. Clauson, two experts on Chinese studies of that school. Half a year later, in November 1998, I was invited to attend the Wilton Park Conference at Wilton House in England on the theme of "China in the New Century," where I made a speech entitled "China's Policy on the Reform of State-Owned Industrial Enterprises and Its Outlook," detailing my research results on China's industrial reform during my stay in the London School of Economics.

In addition, almost at this time, Prof. Naoki Murakami of the Economics Department of the Tokyo Metropolitan University began academic exchanges with me and through him I came to know a lot of Japanese economists and a number of Chinese economists working in Japan. Of course, prior to this, I have noticed many papers written by Prof. Murayama and others on the industrial reform in China. At that time, Prof. Murakami, Prof. Keijiro Otsuka and Prof. Liu Deqiang were going to publish their findings, *Industrial Reform in China*, in Oxford University Press and I was lucky enough to read the book's typescript in advance and made efforts for the book's publication in China.

At the end of 1998, I was offered the recruit fund from the Tokyo Metropolitan University with the help of Professor Murakami and went to the Economics Department of that university to work with Murakami and to discuss questions about China with Japanese famous economist, Prof. Keijiro Otsuka. One of the results of this visit was a paper on the profit margins of China's industrial enterprises in cooperation with Murakami and Dr. Liang Jian. At the same time, I started to be interested in measuring the changes in China's industrial enterprise efficiency and economies of scale and made these topics my focus in the following 2 years.

During that period, I visited Hitotsubashi University and two economic research institutes of Kyoto University where I met Prof. Yukihiko Kiyokawa, then Director of the Economics Institute of Hitotsubashi University and Prof. Hiroshi Sato, a China expert, Professor Shimizu Yoshinori, Dean of the School of Business of the Hitotshubushi University and Renowned Economist, Prof. Ryoshin Minami, of the Tokyo University of Economics. At Hitotsubashi University, I gave a report on my research on the profit margins of China's state-owned enterprises in English. In addition, I also visited the Asian Economics Research Institute (IDE) in Tokyo (now it has moved to Chiba Prefecture), where I came to know two research fellows on Chinese economy,

Dr. Imai Kenichi and Dr. Marukawa Tomoo, both of whom became my friends. The visit let me see the strengths of Japanese economists on empirical research.

In the summer of 1999, I was invited by the Aoyama Gakuin University in Tokyo to teach a short course for a month at the International Economy and Politics Department titled "Globalization and East Asia Economy." During that time, I went back to Tokyo Metropolitan University where I gave a speech about the influence of transition velocity and initial conditions on economic growth, a research done by Dr. Hallagan and me. Later I also delivered two reports on China's industrial reform at Sophia University in Tokyo. In June the following year, I went back to Tokyo again at the invitation of Prof. Katsuji Nakagane, the famous economist from the Economics Department of the Tokyo University, to take part in a seminar on the reform of the state-owned industrial enterprises in China held in Tokyo University. The guest speakers at the seminar were Prof. Tom Rawski from the University of Pittsburgh, Dr. Imai Kenichi from Asian Economics Research Institute in Japan and me. Renowned Japanese economist, Prof. S. Ishikawa, also attended the seminar and made comments. My report at the meeting was about the loss model of China's state-owned enterprises and its significance. After the event, Prof. Rawski and I had a long chat on the train going from Tokyo to Chiba where we were going to visit the new location of the Asian Economic Research Institute. Due to the chat, I begin to pay close attention to the efficiency of investment and capital formation in China's economy.

In the summer of 2000, I also received a grant from the "Sino-European Higher Education Cooperation Program" of the European Union Commission and, with the help of Prof. David Wall, returned to SOAS of the University of London to engage in research for a month. I took this opportunity to use the library of the SOAS College and acquired a lot of techniques and knowledge about the efficiency measurement of China's industry, economies of scale and total investment through reading documents. During this time, apart from Mr. Wall, the Director of the China Research Center, Dr. Michael Hochx and Dr. Lu Di of the Department of Economics gave me a lot of help. I also went to Cambridge University as well as its East Asia Center and University of Wales with Prof. Wall where we met many colleagues. One of the colleagues was Prof. Peter Norlan from the Jesus College, Cambridge with whom I had a very interesting talk.

As soon as my visit to London was ended in August 2000, I made a hurried journey to Harvard University. As a guest assisted financially by the Yenching Institute of Harvard, my main research work there was still the economic growth and industrial reform in China. One year at Harvard gave me plenty of time to sort out a lot of research literatures and train of thought I had accumulated and composed three papers involving the reduced margin model of China's industrial enterprises, economy of scale, capital formation and economic growth in China. This year I also had a chance to pay a visit to Prof. Dwight Perkins, Prof. Janos Kornai and Prof. Oliver Hart, all from the Department of Economics as well as Stanford University Prof. Paul Milgrom who was then visiting Harvard. Other professors I met with included Tom Rawski, Qian Yingyi and Hu Yongtai.

During the 2 months before I left Harvard in September 2001, Prof. Gary Jefferson from the Brandeis University in Boston and I met once a week at the Fairbank Center to discuss the research and development problems of the industrial enterprises in China. Aided by some of his funding, I looked over a large number of literatures on research and development. Professor Rosicky also invited me to fly to the University of Pittsburgh in Pennsylvania to speak about my paper about the changing pattern of Industrial profit margins at the Department of Economics. And another paper of mine about the excessive investment and economic growth of China was first read at the Asia Business Club of Harvard Business School. My paper about the profit margin decision of state-owned enterprise was briefly reported at the international conference on China's economy and enterprise reform at Wilton House in the UK in November 2001.

From September 2002 to January 2003, I was employed by the Kyungpook National University of South Korea to teach for a whole semester at its Economics and Business Institute. Using my relatively abundant spare time, I not only finished a paper on total factor productivity (TFP), but also wrote an article to explain again China's investment efficiency and growth. At the time when the first draft of the paper was written, the School of Economics and Business held a Special Lectures on China's Economics for me, so I took the chance to elaborate on the main content of this paper which aroused great interest and drew many comments from South Korean economists. Before long, I was invited to read this paper again by Yeungnam University of South Korea at a conference hosted by the university's Center for Chinese Studies. As South Korea's economic growth and industrialization has a lot of similarities with China's current economic development pattern, I undoubtedly had a better understanding of the South Korean economy and the growth experience of the east Asian economies by staying in South Korea for a few months.

In the years 2005–2008, my main research was focused on the aspect of the political economics of economic growth. During this period, I was engaged in the research of China's financial deepening and productivity problems from June to September in 2005 at the United Nations University World Institute for Development Economics Research (UNU WIDER) in Helsinki, Finland. From May to August 2007, I was a Visiting Researcher at the Policy Research Institute of the Queen's University in Canada where I thoroughly prepared the materials of the experience of China's economic reform and 30 years of transformation. I also started to write some of the chapters for The *Reform Not Known to the Public* (Zhongxin Publishing House, 2010 edition), and completed several papers including Term of Office and Exchanges of Chinese Officials in Different Places and Economic Growth Since the Reform: Evidence from Provincial Experience and Separation of Powers and Growth: The Story of China.

Another by-product of my stay in Canada was the two-volume collection of papers in English edited by Prof. Arthur Sweetman and me and published in Canada entitled *Economic Transition with Chinese Characteristics: Thirty Years of Reform and Opening Up* (McGill Queen University Press, 2008). Its Chinese version is going to be published in China soon.

After the Spring Festival of 2008, I was assigned by Fudan University to Yale University to talk about developing cooperation with its Economic Growth Center. While in Yale I carried out the empirical research on structural reform experience and re-centralization of fiscal power in China since 1994. In the 10 months after I returned to Shanghai from Yale University, apart from being busy with teaching and doing research, I was invited to participate in the project *Collection of Research Books of 30 Years of Economic Reform in China* launched by the Shanghai Century Publishing Group and the New Political Economics Research Center of Fudan University. My job was to preside over the writing of *The Transformation of the Chinese Enterprises*. The English version of the book was also published (Cengage Learning, 2009) and displayed at the Frankfurt Book Fair in Germany in October 2009.

When reviewing the past 10 years of my research, I found my research interest has always been the theory and empirical experience of China's economic reform, transformation, governance and economic growth. In my own academic biography, I summed up my research achievements over the past years as follows: ① Systematically studied and measured the impact of China's industrial reform on productivity and profitability of the enterprises, including the decision and changes of profit margins and scale effect that belong to the areas of industrial organization or market structure. I also studied Chinese industrial sectors, especially the main characteristics of productivity (TFP) changes of the state-owned sectors in the wake of reform; ② has carried on theoretical and empirical researches on the mode of the transformation of Chinese economic system and mechanism of enterprise privatization; ③ studied capital formation and the relationship between the investment efficiency and economic growth since 1978 in China by using panel data of Chinese provinces. This study is mainly focused on the evolution of the investment mode since the reform and opening up in China and its sustainable impact on the existing and future economic growth of China; ④ estimated the material capital stock of the Chinese provinces from 1952 to 2005 and other provincial panel data, which provided an important database for domestic and foreign scholars to match China's total production function. This estimate has been quoted extensively both in China and overseas.

In the past 2 years, I had a strong interest in the empirical research on China's political system and the relationship between governance and economic growth and therefore organized a large international meeting held every 2 years at the Fudan University's China Center for Economic Research. On the basis of this, in August 2008 I edited a special issue, *The Political Economy of China's Robust Performance*, for the *Journal of Asia Pacific Economy*, a SSCI publication. A group of research papers including mine were published in this issue, making a meager contribution to promoting the political economics research in China's economic transformation experience.

I must mention that over the past years, I have been supported and helped directly or indirectly in my main research by many economists as well as my graduate students at home and abroad and benefited greatly through exchanges and discussions with them. My research activities were also done at the same time with the funding provided by a number of research projects and foundations. In fact, frequent participation in academic exchanges and cooperative research both at home and abroad over the years has broadened my horizons and promoted my research. There is no doubt that this collection of articles contains many suggestions and inspirations generated in a variety of ways from my exchanges with my counterparts both at home and abroad and my graduate students I have supervised. It is through these persistent exchanges and discussions that have enabled me to constantly improve my understanding of the Chinese economy and ability of explaining it.

Shanghai, China
2010

Jun Zhang

Contents

Part I
Socialist Economic System and Its Changes

Chapter 1
Information Costs, Limited Reasoning Ability and Simplifying Planning: A Theoretical Explanation of Traditional Chinese Planning Structure

1.1 Introduction

Over the past 40 years, the development of modern economics has been promoted thanks to many basic assumptions being modified. Two of the striking aspects are:

(1) Information is no longer presumed to be an item for free. To gain access to information needs to pay a price and in many cases, it is wise and economical to give up searching for information. Because of the existence of information costs, information needed for decision-making can no longer be fully complete for all policy makers, so to pursue perfection in decision-making is not an economical act.

(2) Man's reasoning ability is extremely limited. No matter what kind of a policy maker one might be, the extent of his knowledge, experience and the education is not perfect and his ability to receive, analyze and process information as well as his power of estimating rational action is limited. No one can avoid committing errors.

The above two propositions can also be applied to the planning organizations or planners of the central government. Not only the information conditions required for fully centralized planning cannot be satisfied, but the central planners' ability to process information and calculate rational behavior is also extremely limited. That is to say, a planner's rationality is limited. On the basis of this, this paper proposes the following hypothesis: the formation of the traditional socialist planning structure is a response to the information costs and planners' limited rationality. This paper further breaks down this reaction into the constant process of "streamlining" of the central planning. Under various working conditions, the results of streamlining lead to multilevel structures and diverse planners in planning.

However, with regard to the China's traditional planned economy investigated in this article, the simplified or streamlined planning adopted a reasonable and haphazard approach. This means that the regional simplification was done according

J. Zhang, *Reform, Transformation and Growth*, Understanding China,
https://doi.org/10.1007/978-981-99-5712-5_1

to the existing administrative divisions, and the department streamlining gave rise to the central administrative agencies. This not only resulted in an overlapping planned management system, but also defined the scopes of property rights of central and local administrative governments over the state-owned property (mainly state-owned enterprises and institutions). As a result, the planning of China's economy cannot extricate itself from the dilemma of being managed by governments at all levels which often caused overlapping and competitions. In fact, many confusions or problems in the comprehensive economic reforms started more than a decade ago all had something to do with this phenomenon. We will discuss these problems later on. What this article tries to do is to give a theoretical explanation to the special structure and planning management system formed in the past 30 years after the founding of new China and makes an empirical examination of it within a certain scope.

1.2 Information Costs and Limited Rationality

To look for the socialist economic system established by classical writers or a large number of assumptions within the "classical context" (explicit and implicit) is the best starting point for studying the difference between the traditional central planned economy and classical models. But considering that theoretical study only needs (and should need) the "principle of moderation" with very few assumptions, we will only focus on the most critical and most strict assumptions for our discussions. You can list a large number of assumptions different from those listed by others, but I think only two assumptions can truly reflect the most basic premise of the classical modes: one is the zero information cost; second, the central planners have an unlimited reasoning ability. The first one means that information is a kind of a complimentary gift and there is no price for searching it, so any private information can be fully known to planners and the central planning authorities can obtain the completely sufficient information including each enterprise's production function, quality of labor, capital stock, constraints and production possibilities of its social resources, consumer's preferences and demand quantities. However, even if such an amount of complete information is available, to effectively, reasonably and timely process and assemble tens of thousands of information and calculate a rational choice can only rely on the implicit assumptions of the infinite capacity or unlimited rationality of planners. So obviously, in the classical mode, along with the hypothesis of the zero information costs, there is inevitably a presumption that the planners have a unlimited reasoning ability. To put it simply, in the face of such a large information flow, the central planning authorities are supposed to have a limitless understanding capacity, processing capacity and computing power.

Of course, the vulnerability of the second assumption is no less serious than the assumption of complete information or zero information cost. Information is not a free item; in order to obtain information needed for decision-making, one must pay a price for searching it and, in order to guarantee the authenticity of information, one needs to further spend a lot of additional resources. Nor is the reasoning ability of planners infinite. And the central planning authorities are made of institutions that implement planning functions and personnel engaged in the work of planning. Neither ordinary people nor planners have boundless rationality. Although they may always try to give full play to their intelligence in their work, their cognitive, analytical abilities and computing power are always limited and their behavior is inevitably situated between reasonable thinking and limited rationality or between irrational behavior and super reasonable calculation. In other words, they are quite limited in their ability in processing and computing information. In this sense, a person's ability is uncertaint. In that case, the planning authority's ability to process information and the computing power fundamentally depends on the limited rationality of an individual planner.

Richard Judy (1967) noted when he talked about the Soviet planning authorities' ability of processing information in an article titled: Information, Control, and Economic Management of the Soviet Union: "The increase of the amount of information in economy is about the square (sometimes cube root) of the increase of production, and... so more and more people needed to be recruited into the field of planning and management. According to the estimation of Glushenkov, director of the Institute of Control Theory of the Academy of Sciences of the Ukrainian Soviet Socialist Republic, in order to maintain the existing economic planning and management system, by 1980, all adults in the country will have to be hired...".[1]

But, can we solve the problem of limited rationality with computer? An affirmative answer to this question used to be a core hypothesis of the absolute centralized planning mode. A detailed analysis about this problem is beyond the topic of this article, but as to whether we can solve the problem of planners' limited rationality by computer, it would be enough to mention the comments by Neuberger (1976). When talking about "computer utopia", Neuberger wrote: "The practical barriers of computer utopia comes from the difficulty of sorting out and organizing data, or the difficulty of designing a kind of economic model to develop a mathematical calculation system model of managing such a complex mode, create a language suitable for central agencies and enterprises to pass on information and obtain the accurate information about the future that can input this pattern. According to the existing status of knowledge, it is only a pipe dream to design a very detailed economic model that can very accurately reflect all the interactions. A lack of complete knowledge about all the relevant variables, the value of all parameters and function relations of countless decisions, as well as the gap between the time to design a model and the time to put it into use suggests that there are significant differences between models and reality. In addition, only in fields where all the necessary parameters can be measured, written into programs and controlled can a model produce good results. Therefore, it is difficult to solve some basic problems such as product quality and application of technological innovation in the computer utopia mode."[2]

[1] [US] Egon Neuberger, William Duffy, et al. (1985a).

[2] [US] Egon Neuberger, William Duffy, et al. (1985b).

1.3 Simplification of Planning

The basic reason for the existence of the multi-level control structure of planning under the traditional planned economy system is that it is impossible for the above mentioned conditions of the two most fundamental assumptions in the classical model to realize. Information is not free and to access it one must pay a resource cost. For some information, the searching costs may be so high and reach a prohibitive level that the planning authorities have to give up their search. For example, the information-search costs for consumer preferences and their fickle demand for goods, as well as for product quality and the disposition of laborers may be so high as to stop the authorities from continuing their searching intention. Under the existing resource constraints it is simply impossible for planning authorities to obtain such information. Even for the information available within the possibility of resources, the flow of information that will be delivered to the central planning authorities may still be beyond the maximum value that the planners' limited rationality can cope with. For example, in the early 1960s in the Soviet Union, in order to make plans, an enterprise contained 13,000 to 40,000 items of data which called for at least 6 million times of calculation per year. If the superiors wanted to know about an enterprise's situation, they probably needed at least 4,400 pieces of information, although this amount only account for 12~15% of the total amount of information needed.[3] What's more, in the Soviet Union at that time, there were about 46,000 industrial enterprises, 66,000 transportation enterprises, 11,000 construction and design enterprises, 50,000 agricultural enterprises, 600,000 retail outlets, 163,000 public restaurants, 175,000 warehouses.[4] In 1980, China had about 83,000 state-owned enterprises and about 7 million collective enterprises (including rural production teams).[5] For any central planning authorities, such a large information flow is a fatal shock for the limited rationality.

Under such circumstances, the central planning authorities need to respond to this problem. The first response is to simplify the planning within the scope of various constraints faced by the planners and satisfying the preferences of the government. The simplification must be done in such a way that the information the planners have to deal with will not go beyond the scope of their limited rationality. The first step is to simplify the entire national economy into "two sectors"—one is controlled and the other uncontrolled. In order to make the analysis clearer, an input–output matrix of a production plan is used here to help explain this point.[6] In the matrix, each square represents the output quantity flowed from one enterprise to another. If an economy contains m enterprises and n products, then the matrix contains.

mn-dimensional vectors of input–output relations among various enterprises. They constitute the planning index numbers that need to be worked out by the central

[3] Ibid, pp.192–193.

[4] Ibid, pp.192–193.

[5] Lyons (1987).

[6] For the matrixes used here and later on, I consulted works of input–output economics and T. Lyons' work mentioned above.

planning authorities and the rows and columns where each enterprise is placed in the matrix shows all the instructions or index numbers that central planning authorities send to the enterprise. Limited by space, let us assume that the economy has 6 enterprises and 4 kinds of products. X_{ij}^k refers to the number of k product provided by enterprise i to enterprise j. Of course, $k = 1, 2, 3, 4$; $i = j = 1, 2, 3, 4, 5, 6$; $X_{ij}^k \geq 0$. As a result, a matrix for the whole economic planning can be written as follows:

$$\begin{bmatrix} X_{11} & X_{12} & X_{13} & X_{14} & X_{15} & X_{16} \\ X_{21} & X_{22} & X_{23} & X_{24} & X_{25} & X_{26} \\ X_{31} & X_{32} & X_{33} & X_{34} & X_{35} & X_{36} \\ X_{41} & X_{42} & X_{43} & X_{44} & X_{45} & X_{46} \\ X_{51} & X_{52} & X_{53} & X_{54} & X_{55} & X_{56} \\ X_{61} & X_{62} & X_{63} & X_{64} & X_{65} & X_{66} \end{bmatrix}$$

In the matrix, the planning control that each enterprise is subject to can be determined by the row and column the enterprise is in. For example, the first line where enterprise 1 is placed represents the output and inflow (i.e. allocation) instruction and its numbers to other five enterprises, while the first column represents the output and inflow (ration) instructions and its numbers of the five enterprises to enterprise 1, and so on.

However, if we reduce the scope of planned control to three enterprises, for example and designate the the rest of the 3 enterprises as outside the planned control, then, for the planning authorities, the production of the first three enterprises only represents the "export" or "import of the departments controlled by planning. If we use E to refer to the department not controlled by planning, the model for the two departments both controlled and not controlled by planning in the simplified economy can be written as:

$$\begin{bmatrix} X_{11} & X_{12} & X_{13} & X_{1E} \\ X_{21} & X_{22} & X_{23} & X_{2E} \\ X_{31} & X_{32} & X_{33} & X_{3E} \\ X_{E1} & X_{E2} & X_{E3} & \end{bmatrix}$$

The part surrounded by X_{ij} (i=1, 2, 3; j=1, 2, 3) is controlled by planning whereas the part outside of it is not controlled by planning. Now for part controlled by planning, X_{E1} X_{E2} and X_{E3} represent the "import" vector quantity from the part outside planning to the part controlled by planning, and $X_{1E}X_{2E}$ and X_{3E} represent the "export" vector quantity from the part controlled by planning to the part outside planning.

The above abstract analysis of a simplified model of planned economy seems to suggest that to simplify the economy into a part controlled by planning and a part not controlled by planning is done in an arbitrary way. Actually it is not true because which departments should be under planning control is very important. First of all, the basic principle of streamlining planning is to reduce the information load and workload of planning authorities and give full play to the planner's rationality so as to ensure the feasibility, continuity and quality of plans. This point can be seen from the above matrix. For planning authorities, the connection of the part under planning control must be minimized with the "external" (E) factors; because the closer the contact between the controlled part and the uncontrolled part is and the larger the amount of information the planning authorities have to handle, the heavier the work of planning will be, which does not accord with the logic of simplifying planning. At the same time, the more connections of this kind there are, the greater the likelihood of interference will be for the part under planning control, which in turn will increase the cost of planning and disrupt the continuity of planning. In addition, the streamlining of the two sectors will also be inevitably affected by the preference of the central authorities. That is to say, the streamlining may be influenced by the dominant economic development strategic thinking and guiding ideology of the central government (including the ruling party) in a certain period of time. The above-mentioned two factors are likely to influence the scope of the department that will be controlled by planning. There are maybe more factors such as the system of ownership. But strictly speaking, the factor of system of ownership is not decisive because, at least from experience, the determination of which part should be under planning control is not carried out in strict accordance with the degree of public ownership or the structure of ownership. As shown from China's experience, the sectors controlled by planning have long included collectively-owned enterprises whereas those outside the control of planning also included small and medium-sized state-owned enterprises and institutions.[7]

If we take into consideration the preference that the central government (as well as the ruling party) has given priority to the development of means of production under the guideline of rapid industrialization in a certain period of time, results would be that the sector that produces means of production is most likely to be placed under the planning control. Likewise, if the war and national security considerations are dominant over a given period of time, as in the case of "be prepared for war and natural disasters" in the 1960s in China, military and defense industries will surely be included in the centralized planning control. Seen from the production correlation among departments, those sectors that have a fixed input and output coefficient, use more specialized equipment and mainly depends on their own sectors for the vast majority of input products are most likely under the planned control. The most typical example is the heavy industry or machine building industry.

[7] This paper can also assume that ownership is an "exogenous variables" of simplification of planning. How to decide the scope of the state ownership cannot be explained by the theory of simplification of planning of this paper.

1.4 Regional and Departmental Simplification of Planning

It is only the first step to simplify the central planning into two parts–one within the control of planning and one outside. It is also the first response to information costs and planners' limited rational power. However, it is still not possible if the parts under the planned control be all put within the level of centralized planning authorities because of the constraints of planners' reasoning ability and the information costs. Particularly for the economy of a big country, this part under the control of planning still needs to be further simplified. Obviously, for the convenience of economic management, the part not controlled by planning also needs to undergo simplification along with the further simplification of the part under the planned control. Through re-simplification, the two parts at each simplified level will be under the management of the agencies of the same level, only one part being controlled by planning. But our analysis is limited only to the re-simplification of the part under the planned control.

Let's still use the matrix we have used above to continue our discussion. The aim of re-simplification of the part under planned control is to classify all enterprises under the planned controlled into groups of the same kind, making every group to be controlled by a corresponding planning sub-agency (i.e., a branch agency under the central planning authorities). If there are M numbers of such branch agencies, there will be M number of input–output matrixes with each matrix containing m number of vector quantities. They represent the input–output relations among all the enterprises within the same kind of group and the similar relations between the enterprises of this group and those in other groups. In this case, the plan of the central authority only shows an added transfer relationship representing various branch agencies as well as representing an input–output correlation matrix of the part not controlled by planning. So this process of re-simplification will greatly reduce the planning work of the central authorities, because now the M number of planning branch agencies will be responsible for M number of input–output matrix, while what the central planning authorities will do is only to add a planning matrix on top of M number of matrixes. This added matrix can determine and coordinate and balance the input–output relationship among the M number of the branch agencies. However, whether it is possible to achieve such a balance on the input–output among these planning agencies depends on whether the central planning authorities may find a feasible solution including a $(M + 1)$ matrix, in order to satisfy the dual conditions of the input–output within the part under the planned control. And this last condition further depends on whether the part not controlled by planning exists and whether it is willing to use specific "export" to meet the need of its "import". When the link between the vector of various matrixes and the "external" vector becomes more frequent, the coordination and balance process of the central planning will become very complicated accordingly.

Suppose the four enterprises originally controlled by central planning are now controlled by two branch agencies, A and B, under the central planning authorities after re-simplification with each agency controlling two enterprises. Let us ask

$X_{i(B+E)}$ to represent the output vector flowed from enterprise i ($i = 1, 2$) to all enterprises outside A; and $X_{i(B+E)}$ to represent the output vector flowed from enterprises outside A to enterprises i within B. Now we order $X_{i(A+E)}$ and $X_{(A+E)i}$ to represent the output vector flowed from enterprise i ($i = 3, 4$) to all the enterprises outside B and the output vector flowed all enterprises outside B to enterprises i within B. Of course here we have $X_{i(B+E)}, X_{(B+E)i} \geq 0$ ($i = 1, 2$); $X_{i(A+E)}, X_{(A+E)i} \geq 0$ ($i = 3, 4$). At this time, the matrix for planning agency A is:

$$\begin{bmatrix} X_{11} & X_{21} & X_{1(B+E)} \\ X_{12} & X_{22} & X_{2(B+E)} \\ X_{(B+E)1} & X_{(B+E)2} & \end{bmatrix}$$

The matrix for planning agency B is:

$$\begin{bmatrix} X_{33} & X_{34} & X_{3(A+E)} \\ X_{43} & X_{44} & X_{4(A+E)} \\ X_{(A+E)3} & X_{(A+E)4} & \end{bmatrix}$$

If we further designate X_{AB} as the vector flowing from branch agency A to branch agency B; X_{BA} as the vector flowing from B to A, X_{AE} (or X_{BE}) as the vector flowing from A (or B) to all the enterprises outside A and B, and $X_{EA}, X_{EB}, X_{AE}, X_{BE} \geq 0$, then, what the central planning needs is to add a coordinating and balancing matrix between A and B, namely:

$$\begin{bmatrix} X_{AA} & X_{AB} & X_{AE} \\ X_{BA} & X_{BB} & X_{BE} \\ X_{EA} & X_{EB} & \end{bmatrix}$$

In this case, the task of the central planning authorities is look for a group of X_{AE}, X_{BE}, X_{EA} and X_{EB}, so that the plan of planning agency A coincides with the plan of planning agency B. This job is also commonly known as the "comprehensive balance". Of course, for the central planning agency, it is not easy to truly achieve this balance.

However, the planning work of the central authorities will become more simplified in the following situation: many zeroes appear in the input–output-related vector among the various branch agencies in the above-mentioned matrix. In other words, the "cooperative relationships" among various branch agencies are relatively few, which will reduce the work of the central planning authorities in coordination and comprehensive balance. In this sense, the approach of re-simplification of planning is crucially important.

It is not hard to find that so long as the re-simplification can be done according to geographical regions or specific industrial sectors, the above conditions can basically be met. This is because cooperation can easily be achieved within a geographical regions and without needing much external help, especially when an area is basically self-sufficient economically. But to streamline the central planning according to specific industrial sectors needs stricter conditions. Only those sectors that have less external connections in their production but are more dependent on the input provided by their own industries are the most suitable for re-simplification of planning. In this regard, heavy industry is more typical than other industries.

By looking at the historical experience of streamlining the central planning since the 1950s in China, we found that guided by the basic principle of "unified planning but hierarchical management", a multi-level planning agency system with the planning of ministries and local governments playing the major role has been gradually established. It shows that the traditional Chinese planning structure or management system has its legitimacy of existence. But further analysis also let us discover its accidental side, which is mainly reflected in the fact that regional simplification in China is carried out in strict accordance with the administrative divisions (all administrative levels). Of course, streamlining central planning according to administrative divisions does not run counter to the rules of streamlining in local areas. Although administrative division is a way of defining geographical areas, it is not the only way, nor is it the best way for graded planning the reasons of which we will discuss in the sixth section. What we need to point out is that the purpose of regional simplification of the central planning is to achieve efficiency (namely overall balance) of central planning through deregulating the scope and power of planning control. The hierarchical planning units after the streamlining are but the branches of central planning authorities with their target and behavior subject to the central planning authorities. However, the local planning agencies set up through streamlining according to administrative divisions are designated as departments under local governments at various levels. As a result, they are more subject to local governments rather than the central authorities in carrying out their duties. Thus, planning became a so-called "separation of power" problem as the central government has to devolve the control power over grassroots units (mainly enterprises owned by the whole people) to local governments at all levels. As planning streamlining based on departments does not involve local governments, only those enterprises outside the planning units owned by the whole people are under the central control.

What's interesting is that in every administrative region, the simplification of local planning is also carried out in two ways-according to administrative divisions and departments, resulting in the so-called provincial, municipal, even prefectural and county enterprises. On the one hand, even though the enterprises are all owned by the whole people, they in fact have different levels of subordinate relations; on the other hand, both the central planning authorities and local planning agencies at all levels have direct control of the enterprises' planning under their regions; they also control the planning of the various units at a lower level. In China, therefore, the streamlining of the central planning evolved into a configuration of isomorphic structure or planning management system (see Fig. 1.1).

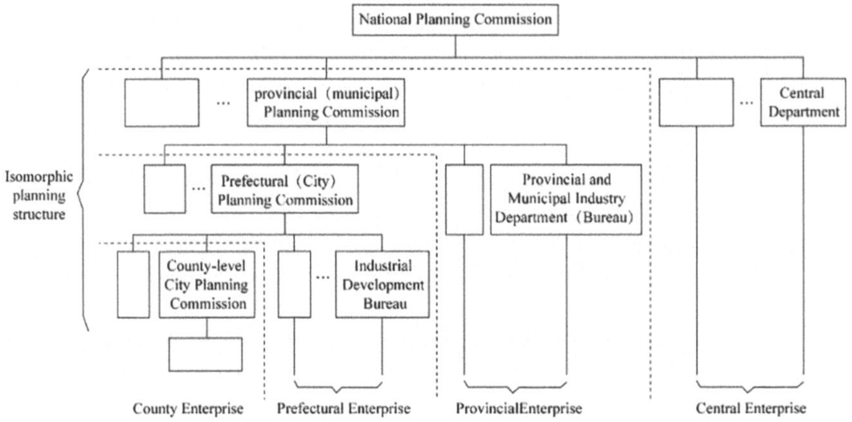

Fig. 1.1 A simplified isomorphic planning structure (an example in China)

1.5 Instability of Departmental Simplification

According to the basic rules of regional and departmental simplification, the requirement that there has to be a minimum correlation among industrial sectors when they undergo streamlining is very demanding. It is not easy to even meet the condition of "minimum correlation" alone.

From the point of view of the central planning authorities, if the division of each industrial sector is not carried out according to the principle of seeking minimal correlation among industries, but for the pursuit of a target of developing comprehensive industrial sectors, the simplification of departments may not necessarily streamline the complexity and difficulty of the central planning, but instead bring about pressure on the coordinating and balancing work of the central planning authorities. Faced with this situation, the central planning authorities may take the following options: one is to reduce the number of so-called grassroots planning units controlled by the central departments and delegate the enterprises of the central government to the management of local governments so as to alleviate the complexity and pressure of the planning of the central authorities; second is to readjust the number of departments, merge or divide the structure of industrial sectors and try to reduce the correlation and friction among various departments, so that it would be easier for the central planning authorities to coordinate the planning work of various departments.

When we examine the several adjustments of the planning management system of China from 1957 to the late 1970s, apart from noticing that delegating the enterprises under the central government and ministries may help to stimulate the enthusiasm of the local regions, we should also note that this series of large scale decentralization of enterprises was also a response to the fact that the simplification of planning of departments failed to reduce the planning burden of the central planning authorities. Otherwise it would be difficult to fully explain why the ministries decentralized their enterprises to lower levels and took back control over them again for six times in the

20 years from 1957 to late 1970s. We know that though the central enterprises were delegated to local governments, their profits were not for the central authorities still retained the claim to most of the earnings of these enterprises. For example, even during the period of the blind campaign, "the great leap forward", the central government still controlled 80% of the profits made by the enterprises delegated to the local governments. This illustrates that handing over profit was not the main reason for taking back the control over enterprises by the central government for three times. Rather, it was a reaction to the instability resulted from streamlining planning based on departments in planning management. Another reaction of the central government to this instability, namely, the adjustment of the scope of the functions of various departments of the central government, was also supported by experience. Allow us to elaborate this by taking machine building industry as an example. In early 1958, the former First Ministry of Machinery Industry was merged with the Second Ministry of Machinery Industry and Ministry of Motor Manufacturing Industry. Thus, the locomotive and medical equipment departments formerly under the First Ministry of Machinery Industry were incorporated into the Ministry of Railways and Ministry of Health respectively. In September 1959, agricultural machinery manufacturing department of the First Ministry of Machinery Industry became an independent ministry—Ministry of Agricultural Machinery. In 1960, the Third Ministry of Machinery Industry was set up by incorporating some departments from the First Ministry of Machinery Industry followed by the establishment of the fourth, fifth and the sixth and seventh ministry of machinery Industry. The year 1961 saw the centralized management again through the merger of institutions. From 1979 to 1980, the Ministry of Agricultural Machinery and State Instrument Industry Administration came into being by separating from the First Ministry of Machinery Industry. In early 1982, the First Machinery Industry, Ministry of Agricultural Machinery, State Administration of Instruments and Meters, State Bureau of Complete Sets of Mechanical Equipment were merged into the Ministry of Machinery Industry.[8]

Of course, while we notice the instability in the simplification of departments, we should also consider the opposite trend that may play a role as well. For any planning organization that has been streamlined, reducing the external uncertainties that may influence its planning, enhance the continuity of the planning and reduce the cost of planning mistakes are all in line with the rational thinking of planners at all levels. In each level, therefore, planners objectively have the motivation and tendency to minimize the relevance and dependence between their own planning units and external planning units, which may lead to each unit tending to be self-sufficient even within the same department. Whether this trend is strong or weak depends on the preferences of the central government towards the industry standard and its guiding ideology. Local planning units, by contrast, are less restricted in this respect which naturally leads to their self-sufficiency.

In China, we found that there exists the trend of pursuing self-sufficiency by departments. Almost every industrial department under the central authorities more or less has the machinery manufacturing capacity of its own. Data show that in 1962,

---

[8] Zhou (1984a).

the central government had about 25 departments responsible for the machinery enterprises nationwide, and in 1977, the number of the departments reached 41. The enterprises controlled by the First Ministry of Machinery Industry only accounted for 1/10, yielding 1/3 output value.[9]

1.6 Interaction Between Planning Power Structure and Property Rights Structure

In the fourth part of this article we illustrate that once the simplification of planning in regions were carried out according to administrative divisions, the structure of simplification of planning is in tune with the power structure of the governments at all levels that leads to the following two results: ① planning simplification conducted based on regions and departments defines the scope of property rights of governments at all levels to state-owned property (mainly referring to the state-owned enterprises), which results in the creation of local enterprises and enterprises directly affiliated to the central government; ② regional simplification in accordance with administrative divisions inevitably turns the separation of power of planning into separation of administrative power and gives considerable "free disposal power" to the local government. As a result, the nature of the simple administrative relationship between central and local governments also changes from what it is previously. Although the central government or a higher level department is still in the leading position administratively and has the power of leadership, they can't afford not to consider the possible response of the local government when making decisions. So, the simplification of planning transforms the original administrative relationship of subordination into a relation of tug-of-war between the central and the local governments or the superiors and subordinates.

Under a centrally planned economy, both the central government or local governments were trying to maximize their fiscal revenues. And fiscal revenue comes from two main sources: one is from the property rights, which mainly are the profits of the enterprises; the second from power, coming mainly from taxes. Under the mechanism of planning power, the revenue from property rights for the central authorities relies mainly on the profits of enterprises directly under the central government and the amounts of profits depend on the number of enterprises directly under the central government and the extent to which the central planning is implemented. In general, an enterprise would make a negative reaction to, and adverse selection of, the tautness of the mandatory planning target set by the central government, so to expand the the number of enterprises managed by the central authorities should become the main option of increasing revues from the source of property rights. But, as we have talked about in the previous section, this option is inevitably constrained by rationality of streamlining the central planning. On the other hand, due to regional planning simplification, the revue or taxes gained by the central authorities through

[9] Zhou (1984b).

power depends, to a considerable extent, on the result of the "bargaining" between the central government and local government. The impact from the interaction of these two aspects is manifested in many ways. Due to the limited control of the allocation of resources by the central authorities, to expand the number of enterprises directly under the central and local governments can actually increase the bargaining counters of the local government in negotiations. The more enterprises the central authorities have in local regions and the higher the friction costs are in planning and supply distribution between central and local governments, the more adverse the position the central government will find itself in bargaining with local governments in terms of gaining revenues through administrative power. But the opposite may not always be true. When the central authorities delegate its enterprises to regions, it has to give a small amount of profits to the local government. Though the profits are not sufficient enough to threaten the finance of the central authorities, they cannot necessarily increase the revenues that stem from the administrative power. If it is the case, even though the central government can still retain most of the claims to the profits of the enterprises it has delegated to different regions, its fiscal revenue may still be severely weakened. This analysis has been proved to be true by the following experience: In 1958, after 8100 (88%) centrally controlled enterprises were delegated to local regions, the finance of the central authorities was badly affected, falling down to 50% from 75% on average during the first "five-year-plan" period. At the same time, non-budgetary funds of the local governments and enterprises surged sharply from 8.5% of the budgetary revenue in 1957 to 20.6% in 1960.[10]

Another aspect of interaction between planning power structure and property rights structure is reflected in the shared property rights of the central and local governments over some large enterprise. In most cases, this shared right is a reaction to the friction and interaction between an enterprise's planning power structure and property rights structure. Sometimes, it requires the central government and local government at a certain level to redefine the property rights to enterprises before the friction can be overcome, or the central and local governments at two levels make a response, resulting in a multiple property rights structure where an enterprise is under the control of governments at three levels. The Anshan Iron and Steel Works, for example, was once under the control of the central, provincial and municipal governments at the same time. The friction of planning power structure and the property rights structure is constant. When a certain portion of supplies needed by the central enterprises have to be solved by local planning authorities, this frictions will occur. The causes of friction are diverse, but some frictions can be solved without the need to adjust or redefine the property rights. One common friction is caused by the fact that electricity, water, or other services needed by the central enterprises must be provided by the regions they are located in, which is usually solved by "bargaining" rather than by adjusting the property rights structure.

Sharing enterprise's property rights is likely to mean that the reason that the central and local governments jointly divide the financial revenues or material products of enterprises may also be that the two sides have different stakes for the production of

[10] Zhou (1984c).

the enterprise. For the central government, the main content constituting the common property rights is its control over the enterprise's products and possession of the enterprise's financial revenue. But it is not enough to just rely on its planning power in order to realize this kind of property rights. For the enterprises whose property rights are shared with the central authorities, the local government can also put pressure on them through output plans and profit plan quota. In fact, the local government can share enterprise's products with the central authorities by imposing output pressure on the enterprise via financial planning target. It should be noted that the concrete rules dividing the portions of the property rights shared by the central and local governments are not unified and many contents of property rights are inseparable, thus it is difficult to determine the extent of their respective scope. As a result, "bargaining" between central and local governments plays a very important role.

If the planning power used by the central and local governments in their "tug-of-war" for adjusting the boundary of property rights is regarded as the control vectors of their respective planning, we use $P_C\left(P_C = \left\{p_C^1, p_C^2, p_C^3, \cdots\right\}\right)$ to represent the planning control vector of the central government and $P_L\left(P_L = \left\{p_L^1, p_L^1, p_L^3, ...\right\}\right)$ to present the planning control vector of the local government. We then further use P_I as the response vector of the enterprise and $\cup$ as the sum, then the reaction model of the bargaining between the local and central governments can be described as:

Choose $P_L | P_I (P_C \cup P_L)$ to maximize the local interests.

Of course the more control levels an enterprises is subject to, the stronger the response strategies it will have. In other words, the more intense a competition environment an enterprise find itself in, the more likely that it will hide its production capacity. As further discussion on this problem is beyond the purpose of this article, I will elaborate on it exclusively in another article. But even so, the brief analysis presented here has already reflected the general outcome resulted from the conflicts and interaction in planning power structure and property rights structure between the central and local governments.

1.7 Conclusion

This paper offers a theoretical explanation to the multi-layered planning structure formed in a centrally planned economy structure with a view of the hypothesis of information costs and the limited rationality and mainly examines the planning system and its characteristics of the Chinese socialist economy. We find that the planning management system in China has its reasonable aspect, which is made possible by simplifying the administrative department and regional governments–a response to the information costs and limited rationality of planners.

But, according to the theory of this article, it seems that we are still unable to explain, with enough reason, why China streamlined its regional planning in accordance with regional administrative divisions. From this point, we argue that the formation of the multi-layered planning structure with the governments at all levels as the main body in China is also accidental. This choice led to a situation where the central and local governments as well as enterprises in a planned economy are trying to compete and interact with each other over the control of the planning power and property rights structure. This not only got the overall economic development bogged down in an extremely unfavorable institutional environment, but also brought about many serious obstacles to the institutional reform in the future.

Admittedly, for a long time we haven"t had a good understanding of our planning management system. We only see the necessity of "unified planning and management by various levels" but ignored the property rights problem caused by the multi-level management, thus naively interpreting the reform of the management system as "separation of powers" only. However, instead of solving the problems inherent in planning management, "separation of powers" exacerbated the barriers between the ministries and the local governments which finally resulted in the centralized control again. When we examine the repeated decentralizing and taking back power in planning management system in our country, it should not be difficult for us to perceive the property rights relation hidden deeply behind the planning management system.

This discovery will enable us to further explore the reason why this relation exists. We found that it is not accidental that the multi-layered structure of planning power corresponds to the multi-layered structure of property rights. Rather, it is the inevitable result of simplifying administrative regions in the process of developing the multi-layered planning structure, although we still can't explain the reason for streamlining planning according to administrative divisions. After we have found out the root cause of the property rights relationship behind the planning power structure, we are clear about the many inveterate problems in the planning management system, i.e. the way of planning simplification, especially the simplification based on administrative divisions.

Based on this, we argue that whether we should change the way planning is simplified has become a criterion of assessing the reform of planning system. Using this criterion, we found that in our country only two planning system reforms and the measures taken complied with this standard.

The first one was the plan to develop a three-level planning management system in cooperative areas established in June 1958. The plan was aimed to divide the country into seven big cooperative zones–northeast, north, south, east, central, southwest and northwest. Various provinces and autonomous regions were required to complete the national plan and establish the industrial system in those zones. Although the plan was not really implemented because of the "great leap forward", it was an attempt to overcome the conflict between the planning power structure and the property rights structure of governments at all levels and to avoid simplifying planning power according to local administrative divisions.

Another case was the reform plan of "independent planning" to be implemented in several cities and a number of large industrial enterprises initiated by the State Council during the period of 1983 to 1989. From February 1983 to February 1989, the State Council approved 15 cities including Chongqing, Wuhan, Shenyang and Dalian to work out their own planning. The cities were regarded as units at the provincial level, so their planning was accordingly incorporated into the national planning to be considered in a comprehensive way. Enterprises affiliated to various ministries and provinces were devolved to these cities for management. In March 1987, the State Council also approved and issued a document submitted by the State Planning Commission titled Provisional Rules on Independent Planning by Large Industrial Consortium in the State Planning Commission. Under these rules, more than ten corporate groups such as the Liberation Car Joint Companies were approved to formulate independent planning within the framework of the national planning. At the same time they were also given the power to examine and approve (equal to the power of a ministry) investment in fixed assets, importing technology by using foreign capital and self-owned foreign currencies. These reform measures were meant to change the traditional way of streamlining planning with a view of overcoming localism, barriers between central ministries and local governments and overlapping control. Although these efforts were not comprehensive and need to be fully implemented, we can be sure that, if they represent the basic direction of reform of the planning management system, they will help overcome the shortcomings in the traditional planning management system and provide a good institutional framework for the reform of comprehensive economic system. Only on the basis of the reform on narrowing down the scope of planning, reducing the planning target and strengthening the market mechanism can we expect to combine the effectiveness of the national macroeconomic regulation and micro economic vitality.

Author's Note

I explained in this paper, starting from the information-saving perspective, why the planned economy system in the Soviet Union is characterized by the vertical management structure with industrial sector playing the major role (commonly known as "bars") while in China it is characterized by a horizontal management structure with the local government playing the major role (commonly known as "blocks"). In this sense, I discussed, much earlier than others, about what was later called the logic of "U" and "M" structures in various documents.

This article was written in the second half of 1991. During 1989–1991, I had a strong interest in the comparative economic systems, mainly focusing on the central planning economic system. When this article was finished, the first issue of the journal *Economic Development Research* was launched by the Institute of Economic Development of the East China University of Science and Technology, so in this paper, as the first article, was published on its no. 3 issue in 1992. Unfortunately, the publication of the journal was stopped before long.

References

[US] Egon Neuberger, William Duffy, et al: Comparative Economic System – A Comparison from the Viewpoint of Decision, tr. Wu Jinglian, pp. 192, Beijing, Commercial Press, 1985.
[US] Egon Neuberger, William Duffy, et al: Comparative Economic System – A Comparison from the Viewpoint of Decision, tr. Wu Jinglian, pp. 90, Beijing, Commercial Press, 1985.

T. Lyons, Economic Integration and Planning in Maoist China, Columbia University Press, New York, 1987, pp. 206-207.
Zhou Taihe: Economic Institutution Reform in Contemporary China, pp. 295–308, Beijing: Chinese Social Sciences Press, 1984.
Zhou Taihe: Economic Institutution Reform in Contemporary China, pp. 298, Beijing: Chinese Social Sciences Press, 1984.
Zhou Taihe: Economic Institutution Reform in Contemporary China, pp. 74–75, Beijing: Chinese Social Sciences Press, 1984.

Chapter 2
Socialist Government and Enterprise: An Analysis from the Perspective of "Exit"

2.1 Introduction

Any possible relationship between two or more than two economic entities can be described by a (explicit or implicit) contract. A contract is a commitment, which is a swapping of rights.[1] And from the point of view of a contract, the efficiency problem is not only how to define the rights, but also whether the contract can be effectively implemented, which is known as "enforceability problem".

The reason that enforceability can be problematic is mainly due to the high costs of supervising the execution of contract and inadequate information. As one or several parties in a contract tend to take countermeasures to deal with the contract, they inevitably resort to cheating and breach the contract. In such cases, the best punitive measure the other party of the contract can use is to suspend the contract relationship.[2] In this article, this kind of behavior is called "exit".[3] Although the meanings of this term vary slightly with the types and contents of a contract, they are the same as a punitive strategy in protecting one's rights and interests from the harm of others.

It appears that even though scholars of the property rights school in economics have not touched upon the problem of "keeping an agreement" and "exit" in their research on defining rights and contract, the problem of "exit" is actually included in their definition of rights because the voluntary, tradable rights are fully stressed by them. They simply did not deal with the problem of "exit" as an aspect of their

---

[1] Mutual commitment could be seen as a bartering of rights, because once a commitment is made, the party involved has to give up certain rights.

[2] Telser (1980).

[3] Within the category of economics, Hirschman studied the "exit" (or "vote with one's feet") problem in his book *Exit, Voice, and Loyalty*. In the book, exit is a way to show preference. See: Hirschman (1970). In addition, in terms of the theory of industrial organization, Baumol and others, in their theory of contestable markets, highlight the theoretical significance of the potential possibility of "entering-exit" to maintain the contestability of a monopoly market. Zhang (1987).

J. Zhang, *Reform, Transformation and Growth*, Understanding China,
https://doi.org/10.1007/978-981-99-5712-5_2

research.[4] The focus of property rights school is mainly on the stage "signing up an agreement".[5] By contrast, Williamson, in his *Transaction Cost Economics*, shifted his research focus to "keeping an agreement", although he regarded the exclusive use of assets rather than rights—a non-asset aspect–as his key research target, so the feasibility of "exit" was weakened.[6] Implicit contract theory provides a systematic analysis of the structure and nature of committed contract which, by combining the modern game theory, has achieved considerable research results. For example, the theory of "self-honoring a contract" has been greatly developed and successfully applied in many fields (such as labor market, collective bargaining, principal-agent relationship, etc.) (Carmichael 1989, Telser 1989).[7] However, it seems that the problem of "exit" is still not dealt with as a clear theoretical issue within the framework of the implicit contract theory.

In 1968, economist Zhang Wuchang laid stress on the major significance of exit conditions in his theory in his paper, Private Property Rights and Divided Tenancy, and in his published doctoral thesis titled Divided Tenancy Theory (1969).[8] In 1990, in his explanation of the agricultural cooperative movement in the 1950s and the agricultural crisis of 1959–1961 in China, Lin Yifu regarded the "exit rights" of the members of people's commune as an explanatory variable. For him, the exit problem is explicitly included in the theory of implicit contract. Although the problem and its corresponding contract structure discussed by Zhang Wuchang and Lin Yifu is different (Zhang Wuchang discussed the problem of keeping an agreement within the framework of principal-agent relationship while the problem Lin Yifu dealt with is in the structure of a collaborative labor contract), the significance of the "exit" problem in ensuring the honoring of an agreement was recognized and emphasized. I will give a simple review and summary of their theory in the second part of this article.

In fact, the problem of "exit" is more prominent in the relationship between state and enterprises under the central planned economy. Now more and more economists began to use the long-term implicit contract theory to deal with the special relationship between a socialist country and its state-owned enterprises.[9] When describing this relationship, the concept of "soft budget constraint" is thought to be very important. However, soft budget constraint cannot be seen as an exogenous variable–itself can be included in the theoretical framework of implicit contracts to be regarded as a "violation of an agreement" of an enterprise. It shows that the existence of the soft

---

[4] Maybe there is an exception. In modern company theory, to protect one's own property rights by "exit" on the part of a shareholder and prevent the transferable shares caused by the divergent behavior of the company agents is greatly emphasized.

[5] Wiliamson (1985).

[6] Williamson mentioned this point when comparing the theoretical difference between "transaction cost economics" and Baumol's "competitive market theory".

[7] Carmichael (1989).

[8] Zhang Wuchang: Private Property Rights and Divided Tenancy (Chinese version), see Liu et al. (1991).

[9] Kornai (1993).

budget constraint cannot be attributed to the fact that the state's rights over enterprise property are blurred, but can prove that the state's rights to the state-owned assets of the enterprise is not adequately respected and protected. The research of this paper will show that the low efficiency of traditional socialist state-owned enterprises, including the explicit and implicit decapitalization of state-owned assets, can be explained by the fact that the state cannot "exit" from the implicit contract relationship with the enterprise. When the state cannot allow enterprises to go bankrupt and workers to lose their job, the long-term implicit contract between the state and enterprises tends to become a special kind of "safe contract" that can last for a long time. The third part of this article will give a theoretical explanation of this problem.

As a way of promoting theory, I will give a brief comment on some theoretical questions concerning the economic reform from the perspective of exit in the fourth part of this article. The final part is a conclusive note.

2.2 Theoretical Review

In order to prevent the discussion from deviating from generality, it is necessary for us to give a simple definition of the problems involved here. First of all, we will regard the contractual relationship discussed here (whether cooperative labor contracts or principal-agent contract) as implicit, because in these contractual relations, there are always some variables that cannot be observed, such as the degree of a person's effort, the extent of concern for others' property, etc. These variables cannot be written in the terms of the contract because of their unrecognizable nature. Second, if both sides to the contract are asymmetrical in relation to relevant information, there will be potential dangers such as opportunism, moral hazard and the free-riders in the process of honoring a contract. Finally, suppose that the costs of supervision by a third party for the contract is very high, so the possibility of relying on a third party to solve the problem of keeping a contract is ruled out. In this case, to maintain the contractual relationship requires the self-enforcing of the contract itself. This kind of contractual relationship is defined as the "sub game perfect equilibrium" in the game theory.[10]

In 1990, Lin Yifu put forward and discussed the significance of exit rights as a condition of "self-enforcing" within the framework of the cooperative labor contract.[11] In his Collectivization and Chinese Agricultural Crisis in the Years of 1959–1961, he wrote:

[10] For the definition ad meaning of the concept of "sub-game perfect equilibrium", see: Fudenberg and Tirole (1991), or the introductory article written by Yang (1993).

[11] I made a short review in my article: Echo of the Theory of Self-Enforcing of Contract: Comment on An International Debate on China's Agricultural Cooperatives and Agricultural Crisis (1959–1961), See Zhang Jun: Echo of the Theory of Self-Enforcing of Contract: Comment on An International Debate on China's Agricultural Cooperatives and Agricultural Crisis (1959–1961), in *Economics News Daily,* 1994–04-21.

> The cost is extremely high to carry out effective supervision in agricultural production; therefore, the success of an agricultural cooperative undoubtedly depends on a tacit understanding of self-discipline reached by its members. However, a self-enforcing contract cannot be maintained unless the cooperative members have the right to exit the cooperatives if other members don't abide by the agreement.[12]

In Lin's theoretical logic, for the cooperative agreement, the "exit" of members means the disintegration of the cooperative. This threat will ensure that those who are willing to stay in the cooperative will have to honor their commitments. Therefore, in this game, the exit of members is a solution to the problem of keeping a contract.

In fact, even before Lin Yifu, Zhang Wuchang has already touched upon the "exit" problem in his excellent research on sharecropping theory.[13] No one seemed to have noted this question before Zhang. It is worth mentioning that the contribution of Zhang's sharecropping theory also includes his deep analysis of contractual structure and terms of rights trading, something rarely found in the literature of the economics of property rights. In addition, although sharing contract can be an explicit contract, it can also be partially regarded as a kind of implicit contract given the fact that it is difficult to observe the efforts of the tenants and the degree at which they make use of the land.

The best way to know the main significance of the condition of "exit" in Zhang Wuchang's study of the sharing system theory is to read his paper Private Property Rights and Divided Tenancy (1968) or his book *Theory of Shared Tenancy* (1969). We can only briefly say something about his argument here. We know that since Marshall, the following views have always been held by economists on shared system: compared with farming the land by a land owner himself or by hiring farmhands, the system of sharing the output with tenants cannot lead to intensive use of land resources but to low efficiency. The reason is that under the sharecropping system, a part of the yields produced in each unit is taken away by the land owner, which is equivalent to "paying a tax" on the output. As a result, laborers are not willing to work hard or make a long-term investment. Nonetheless, Zhang Wuchang points out that this view of low efficiency is an "illusion". He wrote:

The error of viewing it as an equivalent to paying a tax is that there is a lack of clear analysis of the terms of the shared contract concluded. When the shared contract is reached, the parties involved must abide by the contract by agreement. Under the fixed lease and wage lease by salary, the contractual terms of factor payment is subject to change and are determined by the market which in turn decides the income distribution and allocation of resources of both sides to the contract. There is no exception to contract of shared system, though its terms are expressed in different ways.

After giving a standard mathematical analysis of the above argument,[14] Zhang Wuchang continues.

---

[12] Lin (1990).

[13] S. Cheung, *The Theory of Share Tenance*, University of Chicago Press, 1969.

[14] For this mathematical analysis and proof, see Zhang Wuchang: Private Property Rights and Divided Tenancy (Chinese version), and see: Liu (1991).

In fact, under the condition of private property rights, given that the right to land can be freely transferrable (marketization), a land owner does not have to know the details of the farming, for the competition of the ownership of resources will lead to a valid contract. If the value of crops grown by tenant farmers isn't very high, the rent rate is too low, the land size that each tenant farmer is required to plow is too big, or the tenant farmers put too little effort in their job, then the annual rental rate for land owners will be lower than the interest rate. In this case, on the one hand, the land owner may make proper adjustment by renting the land to other tenants so as to opt for a different contract arrangement; or he can directly sell the ownership of the land. On the other hand, if the earnings of a tenant farmer are less than his other options of income, other land owners will pay a high price for his labor.

Because there is competition among landowners, the competition among tenants will ensure that they complete the amount of effort stipulated in the contract. In fact, just by examining the output, the land owners will know whether tenants have abode by the terms of the contract, so as to decide whether they should continue the shared contracts.[15]

The above analysis of Zhang Wuchang's theory implies a very interesting point, i.e., as long as there is a potential possibility that a land owner can decide whether to continue to maintain the original contractual relationship (assuming, of course, the tenant farmers are not monopolists), the tendency that the enthusiasm of peasants in labor work and investment in the shared system tends to reduce can be suppressed. Obviously, the "exit right" of land owners is expressed by the freedom (rights) of land owners' decision whether to suspend or continue to keep the contract. Thus, just like Lin Yifu's argument, the landowners' freedom to exit (a potential threat is enough), as a punitive strategy, is the necessary condition to ensure that tenants honor the contractual terms as well as maintain effective investment enthusiasm in the land.[16] At the same time, the implications of this condition is that in dealing with the tenants regarding the rights, the possibility of exit on the part of land owners becomes a strategic choice to protect their rights and interests.

2.3 Theoretical Analysis

Socialist state-owned enterprises, in many cases, cannot effectively (often excessively and carelessly) use the state-owned property of enterprises. This is attributed to the fact that an enterprise's behavior lacks necessary and self- constraints, or the constraints tend to be "softened". Within the theoretical framework of Kornai, the

---

[15] Zhang Wuchang: Private Property Rights and Divided Tenancy (Chinese version), see: Liu (1991).

[16] In this sense, we may be able to further revise the following point of view which believes that under the current household contract responsibility system in rural China (which is actually a kind of divided system), the collective ownership of land failed to provide incentives for the long-term investment by farmers who leased the land, because under the collective ownership of land the expected earnings for farmers' investment would be reduced. This view is correct only in the absence of a competitive market where land property rights transfer is permitted.

concept of soft budget constraint is explained by the "paternal love" relation that exists between the state and the enterprise.[17] There is no doubt that this explanation is profound. The concepts of "soft budget constraint" and "paternalism" seems to become the "exogenous variables" that most scholars used to explain the low efficiency syndrome of socialist state-owned enterprises: although these concepts are used to explain the low efficiency of state-owned enterprises, this couple of concepts themselves has not been satisfactorily explained. But when people start to study socialist economic theory from the perspective of property right economics, the above problems have been solved step by step even though the explanations seem to be incomplete. For example, one view holds that the soft budget constraint actually shows the government's rights to the state-owned property have not been clearly defined (Yang 1989).Thus it seems that the concept can be explained away with the ambiguity of rights. However, this view is vulnerable to doubt, because the fact is that the various rights of the state to the state-owned property are defined very clearly in the Constitution[18] So, at least from the fact that the state's right to the state-owned property has been clearly defined, the existence of the soft budget constraint cannot be fully attributed to the ambiguity of rights.

However, the softening of the budget constraint of state-owned enterprises is enough to prove that the rights of the owner of state assets have not been adequately respected and protected.[19] The losses, deficit and fiscal subsidies of state-owned enterprises have becoming more and more serious, and man-made depreciation rate as well as bad, dead debts led to the obvious and implicit loss of a large number of properties of the state-owned enterprises.[20] Even though the reform to expand the autonomy of enterprises in China, especially the combination of "contract system" (divided system) promoted in 1987 with the soft budget constraint, was helpful to stimulate the intensity of labor, it has produced a series of profound "internal contradictions".[21] So, the question is no longer whether the rights have been clearly defined, but rather why these state rights cannot be protected and respected.

We have pointed out that it seems we cannot offer a perfect solution to these problems by the general theory of property right economics. The reason is that while laying too much emphasis on the clearly defined rights and impact on resource allocation efficiency through voluntary trade, the property rights economics ignored providing a detailed explanation of the contractual framework of rights deal. Therefore, possible countermeasures such as breaking a contract in the rights deal have not been taken into account and analyzed. If seen from the point of view of "keeping the contract", the fact that the state right to state-owned assets of enterprises cannot be

[17] (Hungarian) Kornai (1986).

[18] Article 12 of the Chinese Constitution stipulates: "Socialist public property is inviolable. The state protects socialist public property and all organizations or individuals shall be prohibited from occupying or damaging the property of the state or the collective by any means."

[19] What is worthy thinking deeply is that when many scholars called for legislation to prevent the property of the individual and private economy from being violated, they failed to see that the property of the state-owned enterprises' properties have not been effectively protected.

[20] Di (1992).

[21] Du and Guo (1992).

effectively respected and protected apparently means that there is a lack of effective monitoring system or the choice of other effective punitive measures in the implicit contractual relation between the state and state-owned enterprises. It also means that the state cannot maintain its property rights by "exiting" this contractual relation (such as allowing enterprise to go bankrupt, not giving the enterprise cross fiscal subsidies and external aid, etc.). We need now to analyze the costs of exit. The existence of exit costs refers to the damage caused when the state takes ways to suspend the contractual relationship to maintain its rights to property by allowing enterprises to go bankrupt and not giving fiscal subsidies and external aid to enterprises that suffer great losses.

The reason that the state, as a stakeholder, is constrained by the potential costs of exit in its implicit contractual relationship with the state-owned enterprises can be explained by the so-called implicit "social contract" between the state and its citizens (that is, the social commitment). As is known to all, under the centrally planned economy of the Soviet style, it was taken for granted that citizens have the "right to work". Naturally, to make the greatest effort to provide employment opportunities and job security has become the obligation of the state in the "social contract". Late Professor David Granick, famous for his study of the Soviet economy, did a systematic research on this issue in his book titled *Job Rights in the Soviet Union: Its Consequences* (1987). His hypothesis of job rights-over employment (shortened as JROE) has been proved by experience. His research suggests that in the social welfare objective function in the Soviet-style socialist countries, job rights-over employment is a variable that is given priority to before the pursuit of other goal variables, or in other words, when the state's social welfare function does not contain JROE variable, it will become an absolutely necessary constraint imposed on a country. In this case, it is taken for granted that the state, as a stakeholder, cannot quit just as citizens must have the right to work. In fact, under the traditional system, it is unnecessary for the country to exit because, given the fact that the social welfare functions of the state, including job rights-over employment variable, are satisfied, maintaining existing contractual relationship cannot be considered as inefficient.[22]

Of course, this article is not going to offer an explanation of "social contract" in terms of the theory of economics; on the contrary, I deem the problem of social contract to be outside the field of economics which can only be explained by political and moral philosophies of a country.[23] However, the job right-over employment hypothesis proposed by Granick can be used to explain why a country lacks the penalty policy by withdrawing from the contractual relation to protect the state-owned property rights in its implicit contractual relation with the state-owned enterprises.

Given the precondition that the country lacks the choice to exit, we can give an explanation for the low efficiency of state-owned enterprises and decapitalization of state-owned assets on the basis of game theory. First, we regard the relation

[22] Granick (1987).

[23] I made a brief analysis of the implicit "social contract" between the socialist countries and their citizens in Fragmented Theory about Social Contract, see Zhang (1993). For systematic theoretical books, see collections of papers edited by Lessnoff.

between socialist countries and the state-owned enterprises as an implicit long-term contractual relationship (Kornai 1993).Then we interpret the implicit contract as a series of commitments by the state and enterprises. For example, the state will use the guarantee for employment as a commitment to barter for a promise of enterprises to provide labor and concern for the state-owned assets at a level not lower than their private labor and their own assets. If both sides could fulfill their implicit commitments, it is possible to maintain this "perfect equilibrium of sub-game". In this case, the efficiency of state-owned enterprises is secured. However, according to the research of Lin Yifu (1990), this equilibrium is difficult to maintain in the following situations. The first one is that one of the parties cannot use exiting the contractual relationship as a countermeasure choice to protect its rights and interests. If so, the threat or punitive tactics of this party is untrustworthy to the other party which results in making use of other's "weakness" to seek gains by "breaking a contract" or "cheating".

Therefore, we can probably offer a theoretical assumption now. The low efficiency syndrome of socialist state-owned enterprises (Kornai, Chinese version 1986; Hu 1992) seems to demonstrate that it is impossible for socialist countries to exit from their long-term implicit contractual relationship with the state-owned enterprises.[24] When this happens, the state's commitment to providing job security and the public distribution of physical assets that can be explained by the goal of maximizing employment tends to lead to the decreasing effort of enterprise labor and "moral hazard" in asset management. The original transaction contract between the state and enterprises will actually become a kind of special "insurance contract" under which the state assumes the full (unlimited) responsibility (Kornai 1993). According to this interpretation, Kornai 's concept of "soft budget constraint" can be "internalized". The explanation for the softening of budget constraint of state-owned enterprises given by the game theory is that the state's threat to enterprises (such as not granting subsidies and assuming responsibility for the risk of bankruptcy) is not credible.[25] Therefore, the soft budget constraint concept of Kornai can be perfectly embraced into the "strong- weak" model proposed by Kreps and Wilson—the state is weak.[26] And I will offer an alternative explanation here for the weak state: for the state-owned enterprises, the investor who cannot exit is weak. As long as the enterprise assumes that it does not have the complete information that the state can punish them for their behavior of "breaking the contract" by exiting the contractual relationship, the enterprise will make use of this information to its advantage.

Thus, this article has theoretically incorporated the concepts of Kornai's "soft budget constraint" and "paternalism" into the "model of exit", and given explanations within this model. Because people tend to regard these two concepts as "exogenous variables" and the questions discussed are often eventually attributed to them, the fact that they have been internalized to a theoretical model where they are explained will help us deepen our empirical research on the socialist economic theory.

---

[24] Hu (1992).

[25] Schaffer (1989).

[26] Kreps and Wilson (1982).

2.4 Extension of Some Theories

The theoretical analysis and the meanings therein can be extended to the following aspects from which certain thought-provoking views can be obtained.

(1) Way of Reform

We have pointed out that in traditional socialist economy, the state cannot maintain the efficiency of the enterprise by the potential threat of "exiting" the contractual relationship with the state-owned enterprises. This is because in the social welfare objective functions of the socialist countries, job rights-over employment is a variable that must be satisfied as a priority. It can probably be attributed to the "social contract" that exists implicitly between the state and citizens. The rights of the state are not in line with its obligations as defined by the "social contract" and shown by some scholars.[27] If this is true, then there can be no commitments including "bankruptcy law" in a country under the traditional system. So the economic reform shows that in a country's social welfare function, the "efficiency" variable should claim precedence over the "job rights-over employment".

If priority is given to "efficiency" variable rather than the job rights-over employment" variable, the efficiency of state-owned enterprises and the use of state-owned assets will inevitably become a "core" problem of socialist economic reform. And it is required, according to the theory of this article, that the state, as an investor of the state-owned assets, must change its traditional concept and ideology of not being able to exit owing to its commitment to providing job security in the long-term contractual relationship with state-owned enterprises.[28]

However, awareness of the need for change is one thing, how to put them into practice is another. And the latter is closely related to the cost–benefit calculation of a state. In theory, allowing the enterprise to go bankrupt and workers to lose their jobs not only causes direct internal costs, but also affects departments and industries concerned, bringing about a negative external effect. So the social cost is huge, but the cost for "exit" by the state may be a one-off. On the other hand, the loss for continuing to maintain and comply with the traditional "social contract" could be endless for the state (such as continuous fiscal subsidy and external assistance to enterprises that suffer losses), for the expected value in losses in the future may be enormous. It seems we can't answer for sure which cost is more tremendous. Therefore, we need to introduce the concept of "discount rate". Discount rate is the preference rate for time, that is, a "time horizon". Only after a corresponding assumption is given on the time horizon of a state, can a rational calculation of the costs and benefits mentioned above produce a clear-cut result.

---

[27] From the angle of economics of property rights, there exists an "externality" in the relationship between the state and enterprises by the fact the state cannot exit: the state bears the "social costs" imposed by the company's "job rights". For the general analysis of this type of externality, see Zhang (1993).

[28] The concept of "ideology" was taken from North. See Douglass (1991).

In general, it is possible to get a higher estimates for the future losses only if the time horizon is long enough, or the discount rate for the future is not high. According to the general conclusion of the centrally planned economy, socialist countries in general tend to make very high discount rate for the future (Schaffer 1989). Due to the fact that discount rate represents the degree of impatience, it can be actually assumed that socialist countries often lack patience. Although the long-term loss of interests may be greater if the state continues to maintain the original relationship with the state-owned enterprises, it tends to consider too much the consequences of prompt exit, so that it is reluctant to make sudden changes in state-owned enterprises. If the government in a country that is undergoing economic reform has this type of time preference rate, the country will tend to choose an incremental way of reform to transform the state-owned enterprises. And if a higher discount rate in the future is anticipated,[29] it may tend to adopt a radical reform path to rebuild the system of enterprise. Therefore, assuming that other conditions remain unchanged, the way and strategic choices of reforming state-owned enterprises can be explained by the time preference rate of the government in a country that is undergoing economic reform.

Therefore, only after the assumption of the rate of time preference on policy is made, can a corresponding discussion about the social costs of exit and the way of reforming state-owned enterprises be conducted. Different evaluations on bankruptcy of enterprises and the social costs of employed workers will lead to different, specific ways of reform. This problem has been discussed theoretically by Schmidt and Schnitzer in their paper.[30]

(2) Evaluation of Reform Path for China's Enterprises.

The reform of state-owned enterprises in China has lasted for more than 15 years, from enterprise fund system in 1978, profit-keeping system in 1981, replacement of profit delivery by taxes in 1983 and 1984 and the enterprises' "contract system" that was widely promoted in 1987. The main goal of the reform of state-owned enterprises is obviously still to increase productivity and management as well as expand corporate autonomy. There is no doubt that the improvement of the enterprise's labor incentive structure and "decentralization and transfer of profits" played a big role in raising the productivity of workers and managers. However, they cannot make the level of constraints of an enterprise become more effective. Fischer and Gelb have suggested that the combination of separation of power and the limited corporate ownership will lead to "self-management" of assets by enterprises.[31] This problem becomes more obvious after the state and enterprises signed a formal contract (shared). And theoretical analysis of this article shows that under the circumstance that the state cannot protect its rights and interests as a stakeholder by the potential threat of "exit", the terms of the contract are not binding, the enterprise's commitment cannot

[29] Time preference rate is affected by many factors such as political structures, change of leaders, and even the personalities of main rulers. So, it is a complex problem to explain why there are differences in time preference rate in countries that are undergoing economic reforms.

[30] Schmidt and Schnitzer (1993).

[31] Fischer and Gelb (1991).

be trusted, the negotiations between the state and the enterprise is difficult to avoid, and the overt and implicit losses and erosion of state-owned assets would become more serious.

Although it seems that the theoretical framework of this article cannot give a sufficient explanation to the rationality of the path to the reform of state-owned enterprises, there may be a possibility for the following explanation within this framework. Experience shows that the incremental reform in China aimed at developing a variety of non-state economies and phasing out planned control has helped state-owned enterprises oriented to the market to a great extent. Even though the goal of production is for the market, it does not necessarily lead to the effective use of state-owned assets. Nonetheless, for the traditional state-owned enterprises, it is a process of "learning" through which the knowledge of competition and the evolution of natural selection has been spread. Spread of knowledge is a social process whose value of discontinuing the original implicit contracts and giving way to a new type of "social contract" cannot to be underestimated, for it would help reduce the costs of "change of role".

The future of the reform of state-owned enterprises in China was basically decided in the Resolution of the Central Committee of the Communist Party of China to Some Issues Regarding the Establishment of the Socialist Market Economic System approved at the third plenary session of the 14th National Congress of the Communist Party of China held in 14 November 1993. From the point of view of this article, the theoretical meaning of the "resolution" is profound, for it proposed to restructure the state-owned enterprises with a modern enterprise system to ensure the protection of the rights and interests of the stakeholders, and that the state will no longer be subject to the unlimited liability of not being able to exit in its relationship with the enterprise, which is consistent with the "exit" theory expounded in this article.

(3) Macroscopic Consideration

In the market-oriented reforms of the traditional planned economy, macro stabilization was proposed to be the priority choice.[32] One of its meanings shows that macro instability in "transitional economy" is inevitable. One of the main reasons for the adverse effect on the macro-economy in the transitional period is the failure to reform the state-owned enterprise successfully. Thus, constantly providing cross-subsidy to enterprises, especially those that suffer losses is bound to bring adverse impact on the government budget deficit in the transitional period. Moreover, the credit that the state-owned banks were compelled to loan to enterprises suffering from losses will cause huge amount of "quasi-deficit" in the forms of bad debt and bad loans.[33] Therefore, macro instability in transitional economy has an inseparable relationship with the fact that the state cannot truly implement bankruptcy law against the state-owned enterprise with the result that there is still a fair degree of softening of constraints of enterprise's budget.

---

[32] Fischer (1994).

[33] I benefited from my discussions with Ms. Francis Perkins of Australian National University for this view.

In the transitional period, monetary policy is an important policy tool to stabilize the macro-economy. But the materialized assets of state-owned enterprises and a lack of counterparts of financial assets make the financial flow occur only in the current payment behavior. In corporate assets, liquidity loans from banks constitute a high proportion resulting in the monetary policy working directly on the enterprise's production activities.[34] But if the state as an investor fails to allow the unprofitable enterprises to close down and tolerate unemployment, the monetary policy will not be carried out successfully. Therefore, in the transitional economy, there seems to be an alternative relationship between macroeconomic stability and social stability which, at some stage, represents a "tension". All the signs indicate that China's current economic reform process has reached this "tension" stage and, if it can survive, it will provide a favorable social environment for the future reform of state-owned enterprises.

2.5 Conclusion

This paper discusses the relationship between socialist countries and their enterprises in a highly formal contract framework, without considering the differences of exit costs and possible results in terms of enterprise scale, production nature and type. Nor does it discuss the significance of the internal organizational structure and labor incentive structure of an enterprise in explaining enterprise's efficiency. Moreover, the analysis of the paper from the "exit" angle only stresses the importance of the exit rights and threat the state has as an investor in maintaining the enterprise efficiency and the rights and interests of state-owned assets, but does not touch upon the role of the "entry-exit" threat of management personnel and general workers of an enterprise in keeping the "activities of an enterprise". In this regard, the existence of a competitive career market and labor market is very important. For an economy with an excess of labor, their potential must not be overlooked.

Although this paper only deals with the problem of "exit" from one perspective, there is no doubt that In the theoretical study of the transition from the traditional centrally planned economy to the market economy, "exit" is a theoretical problem rich in implications. In fact, many scholars have noticed the profound contradictions and a series of problems caused by the state's commitment to employment security (such as Fischer and Gelb (1991), Hinds (1990), etc.).[35] But the theoretical analysis of the problem is still unsatisfactory. This article is only a preliminary attempt, and the improvement of the theory remains to be done by more economists.

Author's Note

This is another article on my early reflection about the socialist economic system and its reform. Since I began to contact the game theory from 1992 to 1994, I

[34] Thank Dr. Yuan Zhigang for providing me with this argument.

[35] Hinds (1990).

gradually came up with a game theory framework to study the socialist system. In this article, I interpret the socialist system as an "implicit contract" between the state and its citizens, and the purpose of the reform is for the state to "withdraw" from the original contract and commitment and re-sign the contract. In this framework, I have discussed the mode of reform and examined the experience of China's economic reform. The article, published in the no. 9 issue of *Economic Research* in 1994, was widely cited in the following years.

References

H. Carmichael, Self Enforcing Contracts, Shirking and Life Cycle Incentives, Journal of Economic Perspective, 1989, 3 (4), pp. 65-83.

S. Cheung, The Theory of Share Tenance, University of Chicago Press, 1969.

Di Na: The Hidden Losses of the State-Owned Enterprises are Shocking, in Economic Research Reference, 1992 (22), pp. 2 ~ 8.

Douglass C. North: *Structure and Change in Economic History*, Chen Yu, Luo Pinghua, et al. tr. Shanghai, Shanghai Joint Publishing Company Ltd., 1991.

S. Fischer, A. Gelb, The Process of Socialist Economic Transformation, Journal of Economic Perspective, 1991, 5 (4), pp. 91-105.

(U.S), S. Fischer: Socialist Economic Reform - Experience and Lessons of the First Three Years, in Comparison of Social and Economic Institutions, 1994 (3), pp. 30 ~ 34.

D. Fudenberg, J. Tirole, Game Theory, MIT Press, 1991

D. Granick, Job Rights in the Soviet Union, Their Consequences, Cambridge University Press, 1987.

Du Haiyan, Guo Jingang: Autonomy, Incentive Mechanism and Enterprise's Efficiency and Behavior, in Economic Research Reference, 1992 (157), pp. 39-47.

M. Hinds, Issues, in the Introduction of Market Forces in Eastern European Economies, EMTTF, World Bank, 1990.

A. Hirschman, Exit, Voice and Loyalty, Harvard University Press, 1970

J. Kornai, The Evolution of Financial Discipline Under the Postsocialist System, KYKLOS, 1993, pp. 315–336.

Janos Kornai: *Economics of Shortage*, tr. Gao Hongye, Beijing: Economics Science Press, 1986.

D. Kreps, R. Wilson, Reputation and Imperfect Information, Journal of Economics, 1982, 27 (2).

J. Lin, Colectivization and China's Agricultural Crisis in 1959–1961, Journal of Political Economy, 1990 98(6) pp. 1228–1252.

Liu Shouying et al: Property Rights and Institutional Changes, Shanghai: Shanghai Joint Publishing Company Ltd., 1991.

Hu Ruyin: Economics of Low Efficiency, Shanghai, Shanghai Joint Publishing Company Ltd., 1992.

M. Schaffer, The Credible Commitment Problem in the Center–Enterprise Relationship, Journal of Comparative Economics, 1989, 13 (3), pp. 359-382.

K. Schmidt, M. Schnitzer, Privatization and Management Incentives in the Transition Period in Eastern Europe, Journal of Comparative Economics, 1993 (2), pp. 264-287.

L. Telser, A Theory of Self Enforcing Agreements, Journal of Business, 1980, 53 (1), pp. 27-44.

O. Wiliamson, The Economic Institutions of Capitalism, Free Press, 1985.

Yang Xiaokai (Yang Xiaokai: New Development of Economics on the Basis of Theory of Countermeasures, in Finance Monthly, 1993 (3), pp. 83–86.

Zhang Jun: New Theory of Monopoly and Competition, in Collection of World Economy, 1987 (3), pp. 29–33.

Zhang Jun: Property Rights and Institutional Change Theory under the Centrally Planned Economy, in Economic Research, 1993 (5), pp. 72–72.
Zhang Jun: Echo of the Theory of Self-Enforcing of Contract: Comment on An International Debate on China's Agricultural Cooperatives and Agricultural Crisis (1959–1961), in Economics News Daily, 1994-04-21.

Chapter 3
Monetary Incentive and Property Rights Structure of Socialist Enterprises: China's Experience

3.1 Introduction

During the ten years from the pilot reform of enterprise distribution system in 1978 to the contracted responsibility system promoted across the country in 1987, China's state-owned enterprises have experienced a series of decentralization of power and transfer of profits reforms aimed at expanding the autonomy of enterprise management and encouraging the employees to work hard. All these institutional changes were trying to relax or even free enterprises from the constraints of the centralized, unified revenue and expenditure distribution system, and to give full play to the role of material incentives through setting and expanding the funds that an enterprise is entitled to retain and reward funds while strengthening the ideological education. The fact that statistics shows that the annual corporate profits are increasing is a reflection of the original intention of reform.

However, a series of so-called "micro issues" such as whether the enthusiasm of the employees has been truly mobilized or the state-owned enterprises have become vigorous cannot be directly revealed in statistics. So, we don't really know much about it. Most of our understanding is still perceptual experience, so it is urgent for us to analyze and judge it theoretically. But we still lack a theoretical model of incentive mechanism of the state-owned enterprise.

This paper tries to provide a theoretical model of monetary incentive for state-owned enterprises[1] to examine the incentive effect in reward design or distribution system of the state-owned enterprises. Finally, it proposes the further direction of the reform of incentive system. Because the model described in this paper is only

[1] The monetary income of employees of state-owned enterprises is divided into wage income and bonus income. Generally speaking, however, the wage variable is predetermined by the state outside the state-owned enterprises. Therefore, this model regards salary as an exogenous variable and examines only bonus income. Of course, in the reform of state-owned enterprises, if wages and benefits of enterprises are linked together, then this salary has a bonus nature, so it belongs to the research object of this paper.

J. Zhang, *Reform, Transformation and Growth*, Understanding China,
https://doi.org/10.1007/978-981-99-5712-5_3

limited to bonus-type monetary incentives which can better describe and explain the monetary incentive problems of state-owned enterprise, one should not expect the model to have the same effect on other institutional arrangements of state-owned enterprises such as wage incentive, mental incentive and management participation. In this sense, this article is only a research on one aspect of the topic.

3.2 Theoretical Model of Monetary Incentives

An effective monetary incentive mechanism is achieved by indirectly controlling the events that have a decisive effect on the consequences without changing the target function of the persons receiving the incentive.[2] Therefore, our model will start with defining the objective function of an enterprise worker.

Generally speaking, a person, whether he is a worker employed by capitalists, a member of a cooperative enterprise, or a worker in a state-owned enterprise, can always be characterized by utility function. The variables that affect or determine his utility can also be summed up as monetary income (y) and the price paid for labor (called effort e in this article). Since y and e are considered as variables, it is more reasonable to see y as a bonus than a fixed salary when we use them to describe the goals of employees of state-owned enterprises. In fact, for the employees of state-owned enterprises, now that the wage income has been fixed, it cannot become a variable affecting the effectiveness of workers.

To make things easier, let us assume that monetary income is expressed by the effort production function $Y(e)$, and that the capital stock remains the same. In general, the rules governing the allocation of y_i have at least one of the following three attributes, which represent different reward structures between remuneration and effort:

(1) $y_i = Y(e)/N$
(2) $\mathrm{y_i = S_i Y(e)}$
(3) $y_i = \omega e_i$

Here, y_i represents the remuneration (income) of the i employee, Y presents the total output or total products of the labor of all employees, N stands for all employees, e is the total labor of all employees, S_i represents the ratio of the labor quantity of the i employee to the total amount of labor of all the workers, that is, the "allocation weight" for employee i. ω is the market equilibrium wage rate, and e_i is the amount of labor of the i employee.

It is not difficult to see that the first distribution rule has typical equalitarian characteristics. It shows that the remuneration of employee i is $1/N$ of the total products. Since N is the total number of employees, this distribution rule is essentially "per capita income". This is one of the basic characteristics of the cooperative enterprise

[2] (US) Egon et al. (1985).

model of Benjamin Ward's (1958) "Illyrian Labor Management",[3] later known as the "pure mode" of cooperation.

The second distribution rule takes the individual's share of labor as the distributional weight, where $S_i = y_i / Y(e)$. It is very clear that this distribution is no longer equalitarian, but "to each according to his work" which has been deemed to be one of the essential characteristics of the socialist enterprise system.

The third distribution is what is known as "the market wage system", which is based on the so-called theory of marginal productivity or market equilibrium theory of labor factor. As it is characterized by employing labor and market competition, it reflects the institutional characteristics of private enterprises in the market economy.

The above analysis shows that, in its pure form, the decision or allocation of remuneration is subject to the enterprise's system and can reflect the characteristics of the enterprise's system to some extent. Therefore, the incentive effect of different enterprise's systems and reward rules can be compared through the calculation of the "marginal income of effort" under various rules.[4] Here, the labor incentives of employee i under the above three distribution rules can be calculated with "marginal income of effort" ($\partial y_i / \partial e_i$) respectively as follows:

(1) If $y_i = \frac{1}{N} Y(e)$, then $\partial Y_i / \partial e_i = \frac{1}{N} \frac{\partial Y(e)}{\partial e_i} = \frac{1}{N} Y'(e)$. This equation shows that under the egalitarian distribution rule, the labor incentive obtained by employee i is only equal to $\underline{1}$ of the marginal product of labor. If the number of employees is large, the labor incentive of each employee can only account for a small share of marginal output on a measurable basis. This shows that egalitarian distribution greatly reduces labor incentives.
(2) if $y_i = (\frac{e_i}{e}) Y(e)$, then $\frac{\partial y_i}{\partial e_i} = \frac{e_i}{e} Y'(e)(1 - \frac{e_i}{e}) \frac{Y(e)}{e}$. Here, $Y'(e)$ and $\frac{Y(e)}{e}$ are marginal outputs and average outputs for effort respectively. This shows that if employee i is paid according to his efforts (i.e., distribution on the basis of labor), the incentive effect of this distribution will be equal to the weighted mean of the average output and marginal output, of which the weight is S_i ($\frac{e_i}{e}$).
(3) if $y_i = \omega e_i$, then $\frac{\partial y_i}{\partial e_i} = \omega = Y'(e)$. Just as stated by the theory of marginal productivity, the reward for labor equals the marginal output of labor. The equation illustrates that the incentive effect of employee i is exactly equal to the market wage rate or marginal output.

By comparing the above three incentive effects, we find that if other conditions remain the same, within the normal production range of average descending of products, there must be[5]:

$$S_i Y'(e) + (1 - S_i) \frac{Y(e)}{e} > Y'(e) > \frac{1}{N} (Y'(e)) \tag{3.1}$$

According to inequality (1), we derive the following propositions:

---

[3] Ward (1958).

[4] Bonin (1980).

[5] "A normal range" is defined as the stage where a marginal product is less than the average product or the average product is decreasing. The term is usually explained in textbooks on microeconomics.

Proposition 1 : different distribution rules produce different incentive effects. If other conditions remain the same, the incentive effect of distribution according to work is not only greater than equalitarianism, but also greater than the market wage system.

But it should be pointed out that, as indicated by "assuming that other things remain the same", what is actually hidden here is the basic assumption that the labor share of a single worker can be distinguished and measured. That is to say, the greater incentive effect of distribution according to work is based on the condition which can determine and measure the contribution share of a single worker, but it is not easy to satisfy this condition.

Broadly speaking, the clearer the link between effort and compensation, the greater the incentive effect; but this relationship is often difficult to establish. Although the piecework system could establish a clear link between effort and reward, it is not applicable in many types of production, because most of the production set higher requirements on the quality of products, and production activities often cannot be broken down to such minute level. So, for most of the large-scale industries, because of the inseparability of production factors or their interdependence, it is less likely to distinguish and determine the contribution of an individual from the total output. The unit of "team" in modern production has made it very difficult to measure the effort of an individual worker resulting in laborers loafing on the job or the "free rider" behavior. It is the existence of this "moral hazard" that makes it necessary for the supervision of full-time managers. In order to overcome the difficulty of measuring the contribution of individuals and establish a clear link between pay and effort, it requires managers to make the greatest efforts in oversight and management. However, it is equally necessary to provide managers with incentives for them to work hard to monitor and manage employees. Therefore, in our monetary incentive model, the incentive effect analysis of managers is also an essential component. The purpose of incentive study on manager is to investigate by what kind of incentives the optimal degree of supervision can be achieved; or, to what extent the managers are willing to provide supervision and effort in order to achieve their objectives.

3.3 Residual Claim and the Objective of Manager

The goal of managers of state-owned enterprises has always been one of the focuses of comparative institutional economics (especially the socialist economy). Although we cannot say that there is a consistent objective function of managers in state-owned enterprises, there is hardly any big difference in incorporating bonus and other related variables such as social status, occupation development and promotion into the utility function of managers. All of these variables will become the-called discounted lifetime earnings that the managers pursue. Although it is reasonable to assume that the target of managers is to maximize the discounted lifetime income, we will, due to the need of this model, choose the bonus as a motivating variable for managers to supervise and manage. To do so is to take into account the weak relationship between monetary incentive explained by our model and other variables associated with social status, occupation development and the promotion. But what is more important is that in China, restoration of the bonus system is treated as an important element in economic reform, especially reform on enterprises. Bonuses are the most stimulating given the current constraints and circumstances faced by managers. Based on this, the research on the incentive effect of bonus on managers has become an important part of the theory of monetary incentive in state-owned enterprises.

The source and nature of the manager's bonus is undoubtedly the main aspect of the manager's motivation. And the sources of bonuses are often directly related to the assessment indicators of managers. In fact, a carefully designed bonus system must include the following aspects: ① the performance target to be completed; ② bonus coefficient, which shows whether each target is completed and how much money can be rewarded as a bonus; ③ the source of bonuses; ④ the ways bonuses are awarded. We will focus on the assessment of managers by their superiors and planning departments as well as the sources of incentive funds.

The evaluation index of managers is an important institutional factor that influences managers' behavior and motivation. However, because the performance of enterprises can be shown by different indicators, the selection of indicators for an enterprise's success depends on or reflects the preference function of the higher authorities (including planning authorities). It is interesting to note that, from the experience of most socialist countries, profits have never been paid enough attention to as a sign of enterprise's success. On the contrary, the output or output value, as the basic assessment criterion, has always been used as an important indicator to measure the performance of the traditional state-owned enterprises at the beginning. This is clearly due to the vertical dependence of the state-owned enterprises on the higher authorities or the government in the traditional centralized planning system. In this relationship, the appointment of managers is largely dependent on the views of the higher-ups rather than through the "professional market". This is a special kind of "agent relationship" without the need to use incentive means to prevent the client from deviating from the intention of the agent. So, there is no doubt that the managers' goal of the state-owned enterprise is to go all the way to complete the performance evaluation in order to please the superior, though, of course, this is not to say that the manager lacks interest in profits. The problem lies in the fact that when the profits and the soft budget constraint are combined together, the floodgates will be open wide for managers to manipulate financial variables, raise prices, and seek more financial funding from the state. And that's what the higher authorities are trying to avoid which has been supported by the practical experience of socialist countries. What we want to emphasize in particular is that even under the traditional system, the bonus may still be awarded to enterprise managers,[6] but its role is at

[6] For example, in the Soviet Union in the 1950s, business managers and professionals could earn bonuses which were about 12~19% of their earnings. But in China, according to a survey of enterprises in mid 60 s, although ordinary workers may receive a bonus, a factory director and deputy

most a reward for enterprise managers to achieve the target of the authorities, rather than encourage them to effectively supervise and manage the work and effort of employees.

Profit indicator is considered the broadest indicator of success, which reflects the outcomes of all decision-making on inputs and outputs. It is not difficult to find that the economic reforms undertaken by socialist countries tend to take this broad indicator in place of other local indicators. Of course, the degree of this replacement varies with the reform intensity of the vertical dependence of enterprises. In general, the extent to which the motivation of managers of state-owned enterprises will be changed by using profit index to assess them depends on how many profits they can set aside to be placed at their disposal. According to the theory of Alchian and Demsetz (Alchian & Demsets, 1972), if the profits retained by managers is the remainder deducted from the profit quota handed over to the country, the managers actually become "residual claimants", which will greatly stimulate them to work hard in supervision and management. This answers the question we put forward at the end of the last section about by what kind of incentive may the optimum degree of supervision be achieved. Unfortunately, under the state-owned enterprise system, this is almost impossible to be realized because all the business risks will have to be assumed by managers, who, in fact, are risk averters.[7] Therefore, the profits retained by an enterprise is actually divided into fixed, proportional projects such as production development fund, welfare spending funds and reward funds etc. by the higher authorities or the state. Obviously, in this case, monetary incentives for managers come mainly from the incentive fund.

Most of the bonuses for managers come from two different sources, as in the case of some Eastern European countries where bonus may come from a fund of a particular department. This bonus is issued not based on any specific assessment index of the personnel, but on the subjective evaluation of the managers by authorities.[8] Another common source comes from parts of a profits retained by the enterprise, namely, the aforementioned incentive fund which is the same in nature as the bonus of enterprise workers.[9] The total amount of incentive funds (bonus pot) is defined as a fixed percentage or the growth proportion of the profits retained by the enterprise. It can be expected that the manager's goal is to maximize the base of the firm's retained profits. If the number of enterprise employees is fixed, or the managers have

---

director and party secretary of an enterprise had no bonus at all. It was only after the reform that the enterprise reward fund was gradually restored.

[7] For discussion of this problem, see Jean Tirole, *The Theory of Industrial Organization*, The MIT Press, 1990, pp. 35–56.

[8] Detailed discussion can be found in Maurice Bernstein's article titled Economic Reform in Eastern Europe. Other scholars have concluded that in Germany and Romania in the 1970s, bonuses for senior managers had been awarded out of the preferences of higher authorities and were not linked to certain indicators of successful performance.

[9] According to some documents, in some Eastern European countries, the bonuses of workers and staff were drawn from the special departments of enterprise's wage funds for quite a long time. The reason is that the action of a single worker rarely affects a company's performance, so a typical way of motivating workers is to give bonuses to those who were "role models".

no power to change the number of employees, the maximization of the total sum of retained profit is the same thing as the per capita retained profit. Motivated by bonus, enterprise managers will naturally pursue the per capita income of bonus. Thus, as we have stated in proposition 1, while managers receive this form of monetary incentive, monetary incentives for workers are greatly weakened. From this we can draw the following propositions:

Proposition 2 : under the modern enterprise property rights structure, the policy and practice of establishing the enterprise incentive fund and linking the incentive funds with corporate earnings as the goal of corporate reform cannot achieve "incentive compatibility" within an enterprise.

Proposition 3 : in essence, there exists a paradox of monetary incentive within state-owned enterprises under the existing property rights structure. The paradox is that within a state-owned enterprise, since managers cannot become residual claimants, it is therefore impossible that the best monetary incentives for employees will be compatible with the best supervision and management from managers. A further analysis indicates that not only expanding incentives fund will create difficulties mentioned above, but the managers' incentive would be weakened because their bonus and that of the workers come from the same reward fund and the government may not tolerate the income gap if the managers have a much higher ratio of bonuses than employees. Hungary, for example, has dramatically reduced the maximum bonuses available to managers when workers were unhappy with the high income of managers in the reform of bonus system.[10] If so, the "equalitarian" principle is not only reflected in "per capita" distribution in workers' bonus, but also in the equalization trend in the division of reward fund between managers and employees: on the one hand, workers will receive a small monetary incentive; on the other hand, it is difficult to stimulate the optimal degree of supervision from the managers. This is what "incompatibility" means.

3.4 Examination of Chinese Experience

As the title suggests, the monetary incentive model is used to describe and explain the monetary incentive effect of state-owned enterprises. In this respect, we have encountered two assumptions: First, it is assumed that the manager's maximized

[10] This is actually a kind of "ceiling" phenomenon frequently encountered by socialist countries in economic reform. The government is likely to constantly revise its original rules in order to reduce objections after hearing opposition from the grassroots. Some scholars call it "changing rules throughout the game.".

behavior determines the objectives of the business; second, it is assumed that business goal is to maximize the income of workers.[11] As for the first hypothesis, we have pointed out that the greatest effort of managers to supervise is motivated by the managers' pursuit of the maximization of personal bonus income. However, this is often accompanied by more complex factors. If the incentive fund of a company is the source of bonus for managers, the above two assumptions are virtually unrecognizable. That is to say, it is unclear whether managers are guided by individual bonuses or by the maximization of per capita income. Because the managers do not have the right to control the scale of labor, the pursuit of maximum bonus base is tantamount to the pursuit of per capita (profit) maximization. Therefore, there must be a quota problem, that is to say, how can the proportion between the manager's bonus and that of the workers be subject to a "fair" moral constraint.[12]

The bonus system of enterprises in China began in 1983 when the system of profits retention was implemented in state-owned enterprises nationwide. In 1978, the "enterprise fund" system had been tried out, which stipulated that the state-owned enterprises can extract this fund from their profits according to 5% of the total amount of the annual wage of workers on the condition that the enterprises had completed the production, quality and profit targets. Some part of this fund can also be drawn from the exceeded profits. In 1979, the fund was extracted from the new growth in profits. The enterprise fund was mainly used for the welfare of workers and development of production—a first time reform on the unified revenue and expenditure allocation system of state-owned enterprises. According to statistics, in 1979, this fund had accounted for about 12% of the profits of that year, indicating that state-owned enterprises could enjoy part of their own financial resources.

Since the implementation of the profit retention system was carried out by state-owned enterprises, enterprises began to draw more retained funds from the profit made according to proportion mainly for the establishment of enterprise development funds, welfare funds and bonuses funds. In order to further expand the autonomy of enterprises, replacing profit delivery with tax payments was implemented in state-owned enterprises in June 1983, which was to tax profits first before dividing the surplus. In October 1984, the second round of replacing profit delivery with tax payments was implemented, changing the profits paid by the enterprise into tax revenues according to the prescribed tax rates with all the remaining profits placed at the disposal of the enterprise. Three years later in 1987, the contract management responsibility system was introduced across the country including the allocation principle of "guaranteeing fixed base, ensuring paying profits, retaining more surplus if production goes head of schedule and responsible for one's own losses" in order to

[11] For private enterprises, corporate goals are determined only by the pursuit of top managers, and the workers' goals have little impact on the firm's behavior. This is mainly because workers'goals and behaviors are determined by the "labor market" and the competition mechanism outside the enterprise. Therefore, the second hypothesis does not hold true for private enterprises.

[12] Hungarian economist Kornai, in his article titled Efficiency and Socialist Moral Principle, investigated the binding of this moral principle and the choice made by socialist governments between efficiency and fairness of morality, see (Hungary) Janos Kornai: *Contradictions and Difficulties*, tr. Shen Lisheng, pp. 103– 116, Beijing, China Economic Publishing House, 1978.

further expand the profit margin of independent operation of enterprises. During the ten years from 1978 to1988, the total profits and extent of profits reserved by state-owned enterprises in various distribution reforms increased year by year. It proved the government's original intention of the reform of trying to mobilize the initiative of workers and management personnel of enterprises through expanding delegating powers and transferring profits (see Table 3.1).

However, what we are interested in now is whether the incentive effect has satisfied the original purpose of reform or delegating of power and transferring of profit while the level of the profits kept by state-owned enterprises is increasing every year. It is a bit arbitrary to judge whether an enterprise is invigorating or not only from the yearly increase of retained profits in Table 3.1. We still need a deeper analysis of the internal bonus incentives of the enterprise by using the theoretical model of this article. As the incentive fund is drawn from the retained profits of the enterprise, we can infer that with the increase of enterprise profits, the incentive fund base is expanding as well. But the factors influencing the incentive effect of enterprise still lie in whether there is a "per capita" tendency in income distribution, how great this tendency is, and whether managers have sufficient sensitivity towards bonus income.

The "equalitarianism" in income distribution in Chinese state-owned enterprise has existed for long time, which was evolved from the government prescribed fixed levels of wages of employees (eight levels). These wage levels are based on factors other than the effort variable (such as age, skills, etc.). Therefore, although the wages of workers and staff members have been generally raised over the past ten years, their equalitarian nature is still the same, lacking a clear relationship. Since 1978, the bonus system has been established by enterprises owing to the retained profits and resumption of the bonus mechanism. However, the bonus payment soon followed the wage path with the result that the relation between bonuses and effort or contribution still remained ambiguous. In fact, bonuses have been awarded equally as a wage supplement because the only reason why a worker can't get or get less bonuses is staying away from work without reason (or sick leave).

On the other hand, the monetary income of managers and employees' income tend to be "equal". According to international standards, the average income earned by the top managers of state-owned enterprises in China is very low compared with the average income of employees in their enterprises. According to a survey conducted by the Shanghai Academy of Social Sciences, the average income of factory directors

Table 3.1 Profits retained by state-owned enterprises (1978–1987)

Year	1978	1979	1980	1981	1982	1983	1984	1985	1986	1987
Amount (billion *yuan*)	28	87	144	168	216	291	365	431	489	589
Retention rate (%)	4	12	21.5	26.1	34.2	42	45	47	50	51

Note The retention rate refers to the retained profit ratio of profit fulfilled in a year. The figures of 1978 and 1979 refer to enterprise fund

Source Han Yongwen, Jin Ping: Changes and Analysis of Financial Distribution Pattern, in *Economic Research References*, 1989 (103)

Table 3.2 "Three Funds" distribution (amount drawn) of 2,200 enterprises unit: %

	1986	1987
Total	100	100
Production & development fund	23.4	21.8
Collective welfare fund	23.0	28.0
Staff bonus fund	26.1	23.5
	(two item total: 49.1)	(two item total: 51.5)

Source Hu Tingzhao, Cai Xuchu: Macro Environment, Economic Behavior and Countermeasures in the Development of Enterprises, in *Economic Research References*, 1989 (98)

(managers) in Shanghai was only about 1.25 times the average income of employees in 1986, which is less than 25% of the workers' income.

It is worth emphasizing that the contract system fully implemented in state-owned enterprise in 1987 seems to have strengthened the trend of "flattening of income". Moreover, in investigating the effect of currency incentives of the state-owned enterprises after the contract system was introduced, it was noted that even if the contract system would increase efforts for more profits for the enterprise, the enterprise managers remained unchanged as agents who prefer avoiding risks. As a result, these managers will not become "residual claimants" and redouble their efforts in supervision and management. Instead, they would add fuel to the realization of the goal of maximizing per capita income. This inference has been supported by a long-term follow-up survey (1985 to September1988) of 200 large and medium-sized enterprises in Shanghai. The investigation tracked the changing trends in labor distribution rate and profit distribution rate in 200 enterprises which found that the labor distribution rate kept rising from January to September during 1985 -1988, reaching 9.2%, 11.7%, 12.4% and 13.2% respectively. At the same time the profit distribution rate decreased to 48.4%, 49.7% 43.9% and 41.2% respectively.[13] The two reverse trends show that the pursuit of employee income outweighs other goals by enterprises in their added value. What is even more interesting is that since the priority of enterprises is to maximize the incomes of their employees, we can further infer that the enterprise will be inclined to change the structure of using the retained profits and crowd out fund for productive development by various means. This inference has again been supported by experience (see Table 3.2).

And analysis of these experiences indicates that although the distribution system of state-owned enterprises has undergone various reforms, the tendency of "egalitarianism" and "big pot" in income distribution inside the state-owned enterprise still exists. With the help of the incentive model of this article, we can conclude that the problem of motivation of workers and management personnel of the state-owned

[13] The target of this survey is 200 enterprises, of which the large and medium-sized state-owned enterprises are the main ones. On average, 74.5% of the enterprises have adopted the contract system. Among them, the contracting rate of state-owned enterprises is 97.3%. See Hu Tingzhao, Cai Xuchu: Macro Environment, Economic Behavior and Countermeasures in the Development of Enterprises, in *Economic Research References*, 1989 (98).

enterprise behind the statistics has not been resolved—presumably the real reason for the lack of vitality in large and medium-sized state-owned enterprises.

3.5 Conclusion

The above analysis clearly shows that in the past ten years, the reform of the distribution system of state-owned enterprises in China has basically not eliminated the tendency of equalitarianism. Instead, there has been a possibility to strengthen this tendency in institutional arrangements. Therefore, monetary stimulus, the best source of efficiency, is still not put in good use which is a very important conclusion drawn from the analysis of the contract system. If we rely on this model to recognize that the "equalitarian" allocation rules will bring the minimum incentive effect; we have no reason to be satisfied with the statistics that the state-owned enterprises fulfill or overfulfill the evaluation index required by the higher authorities. In fact, our model has the implicit assumption that if the state-owned enterprises in socialist countries can truly implement "to each according to his work", they will have greater monetary incentive effect than private enterprises of capitalism. However, the model tells us that this requires managers to perform the best possible oversight and management, or that managers are required to be sensitive enough to bonuses. Unfortunately, it is impossible in the existing structure of property rights, that is, the state (or government) ownership system: on the one hand, managers must have the right to get a sufficient proportion of the surplus of the enterprise; on the other hand, they are inclined to escape risks under the current property rights structure of state-owned enterprise, so it is impossible to provide the best incentive to managers. This paradox, in fact, is what Kornai called the conflict between the fact that socialist state-owned enterprises are subject to the principle of distribution on the basis of labor and the socialist fair morality.

It is exactly because of this that the direction of institutional reform has become clear: since the current enterprise property rights structure cannot provide the best incentive to managers which, in turn, will not guarantee the optimal degree of supervision and management of the work of workers, it is natural to establish a mechanism whereby workers would have the motivation for self supervision. And to do this, we must allow workers to share the "residual claim" as well. This obviously means a change in the system which is not new to us. It has been a universally acknowledged fact that the huge institutional reform in 1979 of turning production teams in rural China into the household contract responsibility system greatly aroused the enthusiasm of farmers and increased agricultural productivity.

According to the theoretical model of this paper, it is not difficult to understand the "internal causes" of this institutional change in rural production units in China. As everyone knows, the production team, as an industrial structure of the "collectivization" and "people's commune" campaigns in the 1950s, has been the basic unit of agricultural production China in the following 20-odd years. The distribution system adopted in the production team was "work-point", which was equivalent to the second distribution principle (distribution according to work) mentioned in this article. However, it has been proved that the high incentive effect of this distribution principle has not been brought into full play for decades. The reason is not complicated. The model tells us that the incentive of "work-point" can only become effective if the labor share of each farmer in a production team can be reasonably calculated. However, as many scholars have pointed out that in agriculture, especially traditional agriculture, due to natural climate conditions plus the temporal and spatial span of crops and other factors, it is difficult to monitor and calculate the contribution of each farmer in production. So it can be expected that in the production team, the supervision degree of labor by management personnel (captain) was at a very low level, resulting in minimal incentive effect on payment according to work points. Agricultural production was thus greatly fettered as well.

More importantly, the theoretical model used in this paper can also explain why the family responsibility system introduced in1979 greatly stimulated the enthusiasm of farmers and improved agricultural productivity. The reason is that since the supervision and measurement by production team managers were rather difficult, we must rely on the self supervision of farmers. The re-arrangement of the system was meant to motivate farmers for self supervision.

The traditional means of agricultural production in China made it possible for agricultural activities to be broken down into families and individuals. In the family responsibility system, the production process was broken down from the production team to family members, turning individuals into "residual claimants" and eliminating the need for external supervision and measurement of labor share.

The fundamental difference between industrial production and agricultural production is not only the difficulty of supervision in agriculture due to natural factors, but also the fact that industrial production cannot be broken down into families and individuals. This shows that, in order to improve the incentive effect, or to make the workers have self supervision motivation, the institutional reform of state-owned enterprises cannot proceed like the agricultural production teams where the production was subcontracted to each family and individuals while still reserving the collective land ownership. It must transform the property rights, from the state-owned system to a workers' cooperative share system (also called the community system), so that each worker can enjoy the residual claim. Only in this way can external supervision be internalized.

At present, the generally approved shareholding system seems to be a way to carry out this institutional reform. But further analysis shows that it is not a viable option. Perhaps it would be enough to cite one of the problems lurking in the stock sharing business. I once wrote in an article, Structure of Property Rights, Ownership and Socialist Enterprise System, that: "One of the main disadvantages is that it is pregnant with the danger of destruction. D. Ellerman has studied the fatal dilemma of the form of ownership of workers' cooperative and he concluded that if the cooperative fails, it will go bankrupt. But if it does succeed–he cited the Pullywood cooperatives in northwest of the Pacific Ocean to illustrate his point–the value of its stocks will be so high as to make the new members often find it difficult to buy. In successful Pullywood cooperatives, an ordinary stock can sell as high as 80,000 or 90,000 dollars. On the other hand, those who retire from the co-operatives prefer to sell their shares to the highest bidder who does not belong to the cooperative. As a result, this process will eventually cause enterprises to be taken over by outsiders and even bring them to ruin. And, as long as the enterprise's stock price is so high as to prevent potential new members from entering, the enterprise will slowly change for the worse, because its members don't want (and it is impossible to them to intend) to lower their stock prices resulting in potential new members not able to join them. In that case, these partners will have to start hiring wage earners outside the co-operatives and treat them as "second-class citizens" in the enterprise.[14]

In view of this, the reform of the property rights system can only be based on the sharing system of the non-transferrable rights of the residual claim, and on the internal account of the workers as the evidence of their residual claim. Because of the non-transferability of the internal account, it can avoid the dangers and abuses brought about by the stocks used as the residual claim certificate mentioned above. At the same time, the internal account can also simulate the function of the stock in solving the problem of clarity of ownership and efficiency, which has been supported by the experience from the Mondragon Industrial Cooperative in the province of Basque, Spain.

The internal account can bring about changes in pay structure of workers. In addition to earning the current basic wages, each employee also acquires the "basic interest" (calculated by referring to the bank interest rate) according to the balance of his internal account. These two items are included in the cost of the accounting, which are used to calculate the surplus of the enterprise. After the enterprise's accumulation fund is deducted from this surplus, the rest is allocated according to the proportion of the basic income of the individual (including basic salary plus basic interest). The major part of the annual surplus allocated to an individual is credited to each employee's internal account (of course, if the enterprise loses money, it should be debited according to the same proportion).The account cannot be transferred, but employees can draw the money if he leaves or retire from the company. If the efficiency of the enterprise is high, the balance of each employee's internal accounts increases accordingly. Therefore, the internal account, serving as the evidence of the residual claim, can motivate workers for self-monitoring without the need of external supervision. The difficulty of measuring the contribution of an individual's labor has also been overcome. This method solves the problem of the low incentive effect of state-owned enterprises from the basic system of property rights. This is also the significance of the property rights theory presented in this article in the reform of the incentive mechanism.

Author's Note

This is one of the few articles I've written about business reform in the early days. The main idea of this article is that if there is no change in the structure of property rights of the state-owned enterprises and a redefining of the right of control, the reform

[14] Zhang Jun (1989).

aimed at "transferring profits" to enterprises cannot solve the insufficient incentive and incentive incompatibility issues in the production of enterprises.

From mid 1980s to early 90 s, the reform of state-owned enterprises has been following the policy of decentralization of power and transfer of profits. My article discusses theoretically the relationship between monetary incentive and ownership structure of enterprises, and presents some important propositions. Based on theoretical analysis, I examine the expansion of incentive fund and "per capita" tendency of state-owned enterprises since the reform in the latter part of the article, pointing out that without redefining the problem of ownership, it would be difficult to really set up the monetary incentive mechanism of enterprises. This article was published in the 6th issue of *Shanghai Economic Research* in 1991.

References

Armen Alchian, Harold Demsetz: Production, Information Costs, and Economic Organization. *American Economic Review*, 1972, 62 (5), 777–795.

(US) Egon Neuberger, William Duffy, et al: Comparative Economic System -- Comparison from the Perspective of Decision Making, tr. by Wu Jinglian, p. 71, Beijing: Commercial Press, 1985.

B. Ward, The Firm in Ilyrian, Market Syndicalism, American Economic Review, 1958, 58, 58. pp.566, 589.

J. Bonin, Work Incentives and Uncertainty on a Collective Farm, Journal of Comparative Economics, 1977, pp.77, 97.L.Israelson, Collectives, Communes and Incentives, Journal of Comparative Economics, 1980, 4, pp.99, 124.

Zhang Jun: Structure of Property Rights, Ownership and Socialist Enterprise System, in Economic Studies, 1989 (8).

Chapter 4
Privileges Sustained by Central Planning: An Analytical Method of Property Rights

4.1 Problem of Concept

One of the fundamental features of the centrally planned economy (CPEs) is that its operation is fully based on initial definition of distribution of privileges maintained by executive order, which is the basic system arrangement of central economic planning: urban and rural separation, the household registration system, farmers cannot change their identity, favorable planned price, unemployed professions, welfare subsidized by government, regions and industries that are given priority for development and resource allocation dictated by administrative orders, etc., are the various forms of privileges stemmed from the central planning. We call this type of privilege "planning privilege".[1] These privileges were created by the planned economy which, in turn, created vested interest. And the vested interest induces people to maintain the privileges, a phenomenon that the rent-seeking theory can make good use of. But I do not intend to use the rent-seeking theory to analyze and study this problem in this article. My analysis will be related with the theory of property rights economics. I regard planning privilege as a property rights and the distribution of this privilege as an initial allocation of property rights. Planning privilege is a right by which one can get some resources and benefits without the permission of others. However, this property rights is not granted through market transactions and competition, but defined and maintained via force by the state or planners which naturally cannot be traded. This is one of the reasons this right is called "planning privilege".

[1] In the research literature about the economics of central planning, the system's features are often stressed. In fact, as a fact of experience, these features are probably known to all. However, there are not many research literatures directly about these privileges. As far as I know, Jan Winiecki is probably a more prominent scholar who analyzed the impact of these privileges in her many literatures discussing reform on the economic system of the Soviet Union. For example, we may refer to her latest book, *Obstacles to Economic Restructuring in the Soviet Union: A Property Rights Approach.* In China, literatures on this problem mainly include Cheng Hong's *Seeking A Stable Approach to Reform and Conditions, Limitations and Forms of Marketization*, Jun Zhang's *Theory of Property Rights and Institutional Change under Centrally Planned Economy.*

J. Zhang, *Reform, Transformation and Growth*, Understanding China,
https://doi.org/10.1007/978-981-99-5712-5_4

There are many forms of planning privileges. We will use a typical one for the sake of analysis: state-owned enterprise A has the right to obtain products (input) from enterprise B at the state-set price, or city residents can buy foods cheaply from farmers, all of which are typical of this planning privilege. Some scholars have used the concept of "planning rights" to illustrate the same meaning, regarding enterprise A or the city residents described above as recipients of the planning rights and enterprise B or farmers as "bearers of the planning obligation".[2] I think the description of the above relation is appropriate, and I also have borrowed the two concepts to analyze the external problems of planned economy.[3] Therefore, the planning privilege used here is equivalent to the planning rights used in the past. But when we use the concept of planning rights, we must avoid a misunderstanding that we need to explain.

As far as I am concerned, the concepts of "planning rights and "planning obligations were borrowed from Cheng Hong. Like Cheng Hong, I also used these concepts to describe a specific arrangement of property right or a specific profit and loss boundary of the centrally planned economy. I believe that in the centrally planned economy, there is, in fact, a profit and loss boundary of each party defined by a mandatory imperative. Specifically, a right embodying a particular interest is arranged or defined for a particular party concerned. It can be argued that the initial allocation of such property rights is not efficient, because it is not the result of voluntary contracting between parties, but is maintained by administrative directives. I use the concepts of "planning rights owner" in my paper to refer to the party of the transaction who enjoys a particular interests, and "bearer of planning obligations" to refer to the party whose interests are harmed. Since I studied both sides of a particular "transaction", I only consider the profits and losses of the two parties in the "transaction" relationship. Therefore, the relationship between the two parties can be defined as the "planning rights-planning obligations" relation.

However, the two concepts of "planning rights-planning obligations" now seem to be bad ones, because it is very easy to link them with the inseparable concept and meaning of rights and obligations. In particular, it is easy to treat these two concepts with specific meanings as having the general sense of the rights-obligation relationship. In this way, you may argue that there is almost no such a person who only has planning obligations without enjoying planning rights under the planned economy; selling grain to the government at a planned price below the market equilibrium price is a farmer's planning obligation while buying products used for farming at a price below the market equilibrium price is his planning right. Yes, the statement is alright. But this is not what we want to discuss. In the centrally planned economy, if we consider the rights and obligations of an individual or a party only in their general sense, and claim each one or party is equal because he or she is entitled to planning rights and should fulfill the planning obligations, what can we say about the "externality"? The objects of our study are both sides of a "transaction", or the sides bound together by the planning directives, rather than a single person or a party. As far as the interests of the two parties in the transaction are concerned, as the "transaction"

[2] Sheng (1991, 1992).

[3] Zhang (1993).

is not voluntary but planned by the order, there is a kind of externality caused by the prohibition of negotiations. For example, in the food issue, according to this way of thinking, it is easy to regard farmers in the "transaction" between farmers and urban residents as "the bearer of planning obligation" while the latter as the owner or recipients of "planning rights". Similarly, between the two state-owned enterprises, if one party can obtain a product from the other at state-set price, then the former enjoys the rights of planning while the latter assumes the obligations of planning. In other words, a kind of property rights reflected in the government-controlled price is defined in favor of the former. As for the possibility that the former (owner of planning rights) may also sell his products to another company at state-set price according to planning instructions, or farmers may also obtain agricultural inputs with state-set price, it is a different matter. One can investigate the externality between the two in the same way. However, it is not appropriate to mix together all the "transaction" relationships that may exist at the same time, nor consider the relationship between the rights and obligations of a single person or party only from the general sense of the two terms; otherwise the "externality" behind the specific relation between planning rights and planning obligations would be covered up.

4.2 General Theory About Property Rights and Externality

If we look at the allocation of resources from a trading point of view, we must turn our attention to the allocation of rights in various resources (tangible and intangible). In any economic system, "in addition to resource ownership, many other rights are also created by law, such as the right to use a man's land in some way, the right to extricate oneself from suffering, the right to be compensated in an event of a fraud or the right to perform a contract.[4] The concept of "property rights" is used by economists in this broader sense. From this point of view, the concept of property rights used by economists has a deeper and broader meaning than that used by lawyers. The meaning of this concept involves tort law, contract law, common law, statute law, civil law, criminal law and civil rights.[5] The modern property right economics takes the definition and exchange of legal rights as its target of research which, starting from Coase, has extended the traditional theory of resource exchange and effective allocation.[6]

The legal rights prescribed by law or administrative regulations that have legal effect essentially determine the behavior boundary—what can be done or cannot be done—of economic agents, thus containing the distribution of rights of one or other

---

[4] Cot: Coase Theorem, see: *New Palgrave Dictionary of Economics* (English Edition), vol. 1, MacMillan Publishing Company, 1987.

[5] Economist J. Stephen expressed this view in *Legal Economics* which was published in 1988 by Wheatsheaf Press. The book is a useful reference to know economics of property rights and an introduction to economics of law.

[6] For modern property right economics, see Zhang (1991).

persons concerned who have been harmed. However, if such rights allocation is built on the basis of voluntary negotiation, the property rights not only define how people can gain benefit or be harmed, but also imply who must provide compensation to correct the actions taken. It is easy to see the relationship between property rights and externalities by recognizing this point. I will try to illustrate this point with "external cost".

External cost is a kind of social cost, or a kind of damage caused by an individual action to others or borne by others. However, turning the impact of a personal activity on the gains and losses to others into an externality is conditional, which can be brought about by one of the following two situations. An external cost may be caused by the inevitable "spillover effect" of an activity. If the cost of preventing such spillover effect is too high to be worth trying, externality comes into being. For example, externality appears when the sparks from a train cause fire in the farmland, when lost cattle destroy nearby crops, or the machine noise of a candy maker seriously disturbs the work of next-door doctors.[7] Obviously, this kind of externality has nothing to do with the initial definition of the property right because the definition does not cause it to happen. Another externality is caused by legal reasons, precisely because of the legal prohibition of voluntary negotiations. Once this kind of externality appears, the definition of the property right contains the content that compels one party to undertake and fulfill the obligations involuntarily. Examples often cited include hiring slave labor and compulsory conscription. Such externalities are formed by the prohibition of freedom of negotiations in the initial definition of property rights.[8]

Because freedom of negotiations by one party is prohibited by law, it is believed that an enterprise that uses slave labor has not borne all the costs of its production, because slave labor can be obtained by this enterprise by only paying the minimum living wage under this law. However, if the law allows freedom of negotiation, the situation would be different, because the slaves can legally pay a ransom to the enterprise to free themselves from slavery. In this case, the enterprise, in order to obtain the slave labor, has to include the ransom that the slaves are willing to pay for their freedom in its labor cost calculation of using slave labor. Thus, external costs are internalized.

According to Demsetz's analysis, compulsory conscription has the same property right arrangement that leads to the same externality. Under the compulsory conscription system, the taxpayers do not assume the full cost of recruiting the army. The cost that the taxpayer escaped is equal to the added total amount of payment required to make the voluntary enlistment, or equal to the total amount of the ransom the volunteers are willing to provide to the taxpayer in order to avoid the duty of enlistment. In any case, the taxpayers escape this cost due to the ban on negotiations and voluntary transaction. However, if negotiations are allowed, the full costs for enlisting

[7] R. Coase's study mainly focuses on these externalities or social costs. See Coase (1960).

[8] This externality caused by the prohibition of negotiations was discussed by Demsetz. See (US) Demsetz (1967).

troops will be borne by the taxpayers whether in the voluntary enlistment system, i.e. buy-him-in system, or in the let-him-buy-his-way-out system.[9]

This is exactly what the Coase theorem means. The theorem asserts that if the parties can carry out successful voluntary negotiation and transaction on property rights, no matter which side the initial definition of property rights is on, i.e. whether it is a "buy-in" system (the definition of property rights is on the side of draftees), or a "buy-out" system (the definition of property rights is on the side of taxpayers), the results of resource distribution are the same, that is to say the final result of the combination of military and civilians is identical. It is because the army men recruited by taxpayers in the "buy-in" type of property rights system must be the same men who do not pay the ransom, for they are unwilling to be exempted from the enlistment obligations in the "buy-out" type of property rights system. The highest bidder under the "buy-out" property right system must be the person after the last volunteer under the "buy-in" system.[10]

Obviously, it is important to allow negotiations or the trading of property rights if we want to internalize external costs. The so-called internalization of external effects, according to Demsetz's definition, "refers to the process of making all the interacting people bear these effects (to a greater extent), which is usually the process of change of property rights."[11] Here, the essence of property change is to change property right from non-tradable to tradable, because it is the prevention of adjustment of property rights and the right of exchange that hampers the internalization of externalities. The tradability of property right means that the parties can negotiate about their rights voluntarily, or the parties have the freedom to negotiate on such rights. If the provisions and protection of the legitimate rights of a party is based on free transaction, rather than being maintained by imposing a mandatory order on the other party, it is deemed to be a tradable property rights. Tradable property rights will provide effective incentives for both parties to internalize externalities. For example, a legal provision stipulating that a person has the right to freedom will make those enterprises or taxpayers who wish to utilize the labor of others to pay all the costs of labor, so that all the costs will be considered in the decision-making of enterprises or taxpayers. In the same token, a law allowing enterprises or taxpayers to use slave labor will make slave owners take into account the willingness of slaves to free themselves by paying a ransom, with the result that the external cost to use slaves will also be included in the enterprises' or the taxpayers' decision-making. Therefore, as long as negotiations are allowed and property rights are tradable, the initial definitions of the two different rights may internalize externalities. However, different initial definitions of rights will determine the direction of wealth transfer of property rights transactions.

---

[9] Demsetz's expression of Coase theorem from the point of view of "buy-in" and "buy- out" is very brilliant to me. For details, see (US) Demsetz (1967).

[10] Demsetz's expression of Coase theorem from the point of view of "buy-in" and "buy- out" is very brilliant to me. For details, see (US) Demsetz (1967).

[11] Demsetz's expression of Coase theorem from the point of view of "buy-in" and "buy- out" is very brilliant to me. For details, see (US) Demsetz (1967).

Coase theorem does not consider the change of a right arrangement to another arrangement. It only considers conditions and possibility of the same result that can be achieved under the optional right arrangement of another assumption. Demsetz also pointed out this point by saying, "It is important to recognize that Coase did not consider the changes in the arrangement of rights. He is talking about the hypothetical, alternative rights arrangements."[12] Take the use of slave labor and conscription mentioned above as an example, according to Coase's principle, if negotiation is allowed, whether it is "buy-in" or "buy-out" right arrangement, it will tend to lead to the same result of Pareto. However, the theorem does not show how negotiations are possible under the conscription system, and whether or why it is possible that slaves were allowed to redeem their identity in societies where slavery was legalized.

A relevant empirical observation shows that in the late nineteenth century or early twentieth century in North America and other places, there were indeed a few case of slave redemption although it was not a common phenomenon. Then a question was raised: under a system in which a law permitted the use of slaves and the owners of slaves had the absolute legal rights over slaves, how or why could slaves have the right to redeem their liberty?

Y. Barzel answered this question by turning to oversight and examination fees.[13] Basel believes that because the law defines the legitimate rights of slaves as belonging to the slave owner, the slaves, along with their labor fruits, are completely and legitimately owned by the slave owners. This will produce a serious shortage of supply of slave labor. Under such circumstance, the slave owners not only need to appeal to the state to help them prevent slaves from escaping, but also pay a large amount of money to supervise and assess the slave labor. If the cost of supervision and assessment of the slave owners increases progressively, then full supervision will not be possible. Because of this, there is a gap between the potential supply of the slave labor and the actual supply, which is essentially the "property" of the slaves. Therefore, if we recognize that the protection of a property right system is cost effective, we will find that such property rights are often difficult to be fully defined and protected. We then can imagine that, for the sake of their own interest and saving the cost of supervision and assessment, the slave owners will consider transferring certain rights to slaves in exchange for the labor supply of slaves. As a result, slaves may have the right to govern part of their free time and their labor. According to Barzel, it is the only way for slaves to accumulate personal wealth by gaining part of the right in a slavery society. Relying on personal wealth accumulation to finally redeem the slave identity is called "self purchase".

To gain freedom by buying back the compulsory slavery contract through self purchase can be regarded as the "buy-out" institutional change mentioned above. "Self purchase", of course, occurs only to those who have been forced to become slaves, because only those who are forced to perform their slave duties are willing to "buy out" their slave contracts. Except for the mandatory slave contract, there are

[12] (US) Demsetz (1991).

[13] (US) Barzel (1989). This book is a successful study on the historical and institutional changes (especially slavery) by using property rights economics and has some impact on Western academia.

voluntary slave contracts whereby debts can be paid back by forced labor. According to the Coase theorem, we know that under the "buy-out" arrangement of property rights, as long as the slaves can negotiate on their rights, the slaves who are willing to redeem themselves must be those who are forced into slavery. And similar to the result of the arrangement of "buy-out" type of property rights, slaves used by slave owners must be voluntary ones who do not want to redeem the slave contract under the arrangement of the "buy-out" property rights. However, slavery almost disappeared at the beginning of the twentieth century, and both the compulsory slave contract and the voluntary slavery contract were abolished by law. This fact means that the disappearance of slavery is not the result of the change of "buy-out" system by which slaves can redeem their freedom through "self-purchase", because, if that was the case, the voluntary slavery contract system would have been preserved. But in fact it was abolished. Why?

Barzel points out that although the voluntary slave contract is a kind of arrangement that is beneficial to both sides, due to the fact that existence of slavery is permitted by law, that is to say that the legitimate rights are defined initially in favor of the slave owners, even voluntary slave contracts will make the country pay an additional price. These costs are related to preventing slaves from escaping and looking for slaves that have run away. In a society that allows the existence of slavery legally, free people will spend resources to protect themselves from suffering the misfortune of becoming slaves; on the other hand, those who have become slaves would find it extremely difficult to prove they have been forced to become slaves. So it can be inferred that in such a society, the gains one gets by escaping is higher than in a society where slavery is prohibited by law; in the latter, the risk for a free person to become a slave is relatively low. So, Barzel says, "The fear of the free man to suffer the misfortune of becoming a slave can partially explains the abolition of slavery."[14] Because in a society where slavery is permitted by law, the frequency of slave flight must be very high, so is the cost of protecting slavery. As the cost of protecting slavery is borne by the state, we can draw the following proposition: if the costs of protecting a property rights system are too expensive compared with private benefits, the state will abolish this system of property rights.

The abolition of slavery shows that property rights have changed from "buy-out" to "buy-in" arrangement in what we call the "buy-in" institutional change. It differs from the "buy-out" type of institutional change, for it restores or acknowledges the legal rights of slaves over their personal freedom and labor, changes the initial definition of legal rights to slaves from slave owners, relieves the slaves from their obligations and internalizes the external cost of using slaves. This change in property rights will inevitably lead to the redistribution of wealth to the slaves. By contrast, the change in the "buy-out" system will lead to the transfer of wealth to slave owners, because this change is achieved through the self-purchase process of slaves from slave owners to regain their freedom. However, just as the analysis we have done shows, the probability of occurrence of the changes of "buy-out" system depends on the following: ① How much personal wealth can slaves accumulate and to what

[14] Barzel (1989), p. 83.

extent can they effectively protect their wealth? ② Whether the cost of protecting and maintaining slavery is increasing too fast compared with private benefit? Although there are a few "redemption" cases, the historical fact that slavery is prohibited by the state law shows that in a society where slavery is allowed to exist, it is quite difficult to witness large-scale "buy-out" type of institutional changes. Perhaps it has a lot to do with the fact that property right was initially defined on the side of slave owners.

4.3 Planning Privilege and Coase Theorem

Under the traditional planning system, the government sets the boundaries of interests for almost all economic parties, and does not allow free transaction between individuals afterwards. Therefore, the government's decisions can be regarded as the initial definition of property right. Favorable planned price, exclusive monopoly, legitimate losses, occupations without the risk of unemployment, welfare supported by government subsidies, etc. can all be regarded as a kind of implicit privilege or "planned rights"; adverse planned price, identity that cannot be changed (such as farmers) can all be regarded as an implicit obligation, or "planned obligations". These rights and obligations are interwoven with the overt rights and obligations, constituting the established arrangement of the property rights of each party.

The existence of planned obligations itself shows that under the planning system, rights are not exchangeable and negotiations are prohibited, because tradable property rights do not contain obligations. Due to the rejection of the right transaction, the rights and obligations mentioned above are maintained and performed by the command-obedience mechanism, so the planning system will inevitably lead to widespread externalities caused by the prohibition of negotiation: owners of planned privilege benefit through escaping from some extra cost under the protection of the planning system, while the bearers of the planned obligation under the planning system suffer damages due to external costs. This is a typical externality. Therefore, fundamentally speaking, the reform of the centrally planned economy is essentially the process of "internalizing" the above externalities. And marketization means internalization. Because the internalization of externalities is a process of property rights change, the real goal of market-oriented reform of planned economy is to eliminate the above-mentioned externalities and the change of property rights of planned privileges.

According to the theory of property right, the key of property right change is to change the definition and arrangement of property right from the principle of command-obedience to the principle of voluntary trading, allowing equal and voluntary negotiation among economic parties. Coase theorem shows that as long as the transaction of legitimate rights and voluntary negotiations between the parties are allowed, and as long as the transaction or negotiation is successful, no matter which side the initial definition of rights is on, externality caused by the initially defined rights will always be considered by the parties concerned in their decision-making and calculation. This is "internalization", the gist of Coase theorem. If we include the two possibilities of initial definition of property rights into our consideration of property right change, we can come up with a way of institutional changes by two different means from the Coase theorem. One of the changes takes place in the way that the harmed person "buys back" the right (or redeem the obligations) from the privilege owners, or what I call the "Buy-out" change. Another possible change takes place in the way that the original owner of privilege must now pay an additional cost to "buy in" the agreement of the original harmed party or bearer of obligations (i.e. voluntary transactions), which usually requires the third party (state) to abolish the "collective action" of the original property rights system. I call this a "buy-in" change. The results of these two modes of change are completely equivalent under the guarantee of Coase theorem, but the wealth transfer in property right change goes in different directions.

In fact, the Coase theorem only states its conclusion under the assumption of two alternative definitions of property rights, and does not actually consider the changing process of property rights. Since property changes usually lead to transfer or redistribution of wealth, especially when one party can only eliminate externalities by "redeeming" obligations from the other party due to reasons of the initial definition of property rights, the Coase theorem may need to be supported by an assumption of compensatory wealth change, if the bearer of obligation lacks necessary accumulation of wealth.

The implications of the wealth allocation effect used here are the same as those used by Demsetz.[15] As Demsetz pointed out, Coase did not consider the wealth effect when discussing social costs. He only assumes that when the transaction cost is zero, no matter what party the original definition is strictly made for, externality can always be internalized through voluntary transaction of rights. Demsetz stresses that Coase's conclusion could only be guaranteed under another additional condition—"the zero income (wealth) allocation effect". If the wealth effect is to be considered, on which side the office of initial property right will be located becomes important, because the property right itself represents wealth. And this wealth effect affects the party concerned in its demand for and valuation of rights. In particular, if the initial definition of the right has an adverse effect on one side, it may not be able to conclude a transaction in the voluntary negotiation due to a lack of basic accumulation of wealth. In fact, Demsetz clearly pointed out that in Coase's examples, if the rights are defined for the cattle breeder, and the land of farmers is marginal, the farmers will not be able to persuade the cattle breeder to reduce the number of cattle owing to a lack of enough wealth to compensate the latter.[16]

Therefore, Demsetz believes that it calls for a compensatory wealth allocation hypothesis to guarantee the reliability of the Coase theorem. By the way, Demsetz mentions somewhere that Coase fails to take into account the wealth effect of the property rights initial office because he simple regards the two sides that influence each other as producers rather than demanders; nor did he consider the effect caused

[15] For the wealth distribution effect in this contex, see Zhang (1993).

[16] This externality caused by the prohibition of negotiations was discussed by Demsetz. See (US) Demsetz (1967).

by the change of wealth distribution of producers on the mode of demand. He assumes that the fact that wealth effect does not exist means that the demand for corresponding item (rights) will not be influenced by redistribution of wealth between the farmers as producers and herdsmen.[17]

The above analysis aims to show that the planned privilege defined in a non-voluntary way leads to an externality or social cost, the internalization of which is essentially a process of change in property rights. If we put the process of property right change into the system of "Coase theorem", we can make a distinction between the "buy-in" and "buy-out" changes. Although these two are exactly equivalent under the guarantee of Coase theorem that does not have the wealth effect, our purpose to assume the zero wealth effect is to study more complex change processes that have the wealth effect which I discussed in my article Theory of Property Rights and Institutional Change under Centrally Planned Economy.[18] A basic conclusion drawn by me is that the existence and maintenance of the planned privilege is very unfavorable to the party of "planned obligation" to accumulate wealth. This preliminary view is that if the wealth effect brought by the planned privilege is taken into account in the process of change of rights, it may make the previously discussed "buy-out" change become more difficult and even impossible. I also analyzed the maintenance costs of the planned privileges and drew a conclusion in the same article mentioned above. Under the planned economy, the existence of planned privileges makes the society bear a great deal of maintenance costs.[19] Based on these analyses, I believe that in order to eliminate the planned privilege, it is possible for us to embark on a path of "buy-in" type of property right change.

There are different views in the discussion on how to eliminate the planned privilege through economic reform. One view holds that on the premise of maintaining the planned privilege, buying and selling of planned quota can be adopted to eliminate the planned privileges. The following example is a good illustration of this view.

Under the planned economy system, the market-oriented reform can proceed in this way: the boundary of interests of all economic parties stipulated by the government and based on the command-obedience relationship is regarded and protected as the initial definition of a property right. Then, equal and voluntary transactions between the parties involved are allowed in a legal form on these initial definitions of "planned rights" and "planned obligations" in order to gradually realize the market reform. A hypothetical example can be used to illustrate this process: the planned price of certain steel is 1,000 yuan per ton, and the market price is 2,000 yuan, which represents the market price of the planned rights. If an enterprise should acquire 100 tons of steel at the state-set price, such market price arranged by property rights is the difference between the market price and planned price of the steel multiplied by 100. If the plan requires that an enterprise should turn over 100 parity cars, the value of its property right is the parity difference of the cars multiplied by 100, plus a minus sign, on the basis of which voluntary transactions between people can be

[17] (US) Demsetz (1991).

[18] Zhang (1993).

[19] Zhang (1993).

conducted on equal terms. An enterprise that has a certain quota of steel of parity price can sell the steel at the market price or sell the steel quotas obtained at the parity price. As long as the evaluation of steel by the buyer is higher than the market price, the efficiency of resource allocation can be improved and mutual benefits achieved. The beauty of the market reform in such a way is to protect the established property rights under the planned system through government and to trade these property rights with the form of market. Through the sale of the property rights, the traces of the initial definition of the property rights–command-obedience relationship and shortage under the traditional planned economy–will gradually disappear.[20]

Obviously, the main point of this idea is that the initial definition of the planned privilege and pattern of interests do not have to change but need to be legally protected. As long as the parties are allowed to engage in voluntary transactions on the planned quota gained by planned privileges, externalities can be naturally eliminated. Although it looks like what I call the "buy-out" type of change, it is not that simple. What I call the change of "buy-out" type, like the change of "buy-in" type, is still a changing process of initial property. But the premise of the so-called trading of planned right mentioned above is to keep the initial privilege arrangement unchanged, or to still retain the allocation of planned quota. In this case, the transaction of privilege is conceived as the owner of planned privilege selling his products or quota obtained at state-set price at the market price. However, if the buyers of the quota or products sold at the market price are persons rather than the corresponding bearers of the planned obligations, this is no longer the "transaction of rights", but "illegal reselling" or "rent-seeking" activities. So, I think it can only be assumed that the one who buys the parity quota is the undertaker of planned obligations. Such a circuitous process essentially amounts to the bearer of planned obligation subsidizing the owner of planned privilege with a parity price difference so that the latter can buy the former's products at the market price. Since the process is purely voluntary, the subsidy must be provided by the undertaker of planned obligations. For example, it is like farmers paying money to subsidize urban residents so that the latter can buy food at market prices without damaging their original interests. I have pointed out that the possibility of this subsidy is problematic. At the same time, this is not consistent with the China's economic reform whereupon the government is trying to increase the purchasing price of grain while subsidizing the urban residents.

However, in theoretical analysis, under the premise that the allocation of the original privilege cannot be changed, the planned privileges cannot be eliminated by trading planned quota. Since the planned privileges have existed and are legalized, the planned quota can be "reproduced" continuously, so that the amount of rent brought by the planned privilege will keep flowing to the owner of planned privilege. Isn't this a typical practice of "trading power for money"? To say the least, even if we assume that there is a possibility of market transactions of privileges, this idea has a series of theoretical problems if the initial definition of privilege remains unchanged. Suppose the transaction is a "one-time affair", the trading of privilege means the change of the initial definition of property rights, which contradicts the prerequisite that the initial

[20] Cheng (1992).

property rights are not subject to change. If the transaction is "repeated infinitely", the rules for defining property rights will continue indefinitely, the original relationship of planned privilege-planned obligations will be reproduced in an unlimited way, the original margin of profit and loss and the externality will still exist and transaction of planned quota will not internalize the externality. According to Coase theorem, the transaction of planned quote can only improve the allocation efficiency of the planned quota (regardless of the initial allocation), but does not lead to the demise of planned quota.

Even if an agreement or contract has been reached on the sale of planned privileged between the party owning the planned privilege and the party bearing the planned obligation, from the practical point of view, this contract is hardly binding if the centrally planned economic system (as well as the rules for the initial definition of property rights) remains unchanged. Moreover, there is not a "contract law" in the planned economic system that protects and enforces the sale of such rights. Because of this, it will certainly provide a strong incentive for the breach of contract committed by the party of the planned rights. Finally, even if, in the normative sense, the above problems are overcome, such a contract law will also need transaction costs. Because in reality, the problem we face does not involve an individual's contracting behavior only, but two or more than two very large groups. Apart from the "free rider" issue inherent in a collective action, the negotiation costs and performance expenses of such a large-scale signing of the sale of planned rights is likely to be prohibitive.

4.4 Chinese Experience: Change of "Buy-In" Model

The experience of economic reform in China over the past ten years has greatly demonstrated that China has actually undergone a property rights transformation of "buy-in" rather than "buy-out" model. Conversely, if the change of "buy-out" model and "buy-in" model are equivalent in reality, what we should have observed is the voluntary contracting behavior of the parties of planned rights and planned obligations for the elimination of externality, particularly (though it may be an individual phenomenon) the "compensation" offered by the party bearing planned obligations to the party owning planned rights. However, the experience after 1984 shows a different picture: outside the planned control, there appeared a "local market",[21] where transaction was conducted for planned products that have been deregulated. The transaction was also taking place between those who had a demand for the products, rather than between the parties of planned privilege and planned obligations. The local market and the deals for certain products obviously has a marginal regulating effect on the inefficiency of the original planned distribution or on improving

[21] About formation and analysis of local market, see Pan and Luo (1988).

the efficiency of allocation,[22] but, without affecting the planned system, product transactions through such a local market cannot internalize the externalities of the planned privileges.

However, the appearance of the local market has proved the sustained efforts made by the government to deregulate (relax and share profits), which is what I call an institutional change process of "buy-in" model. This process means that the external costs borne by the bearer of planned obligations will be gradually considered (internalized) in the decision-making of the owner of planned privileges, or the process of "decentralizing power and transferring profits" to the bearer of planned obligations. In essence, the process of "delegating power and transferring profits" is one that recognizes and restores the legitimate rights of the "freedom" and "achievements" of the bearer of planned obligations. It is obvious that the Chinese style reform since 1978 has fully demonstrated its "buy-in" feature.

In order to describe more clearly the institutional change of "buy-in" model in China's reform, let me cite an interesting study done recently by Yang Xiaokai and others. In an essay titled The Growth of Rural Economy of China, Commercialization and Institutional Change: 1979–1987, Yang and others not only try to prove that in rural areas, the definition and implementation of efficiency increase in property rights has led to the increase in division of labor and commercialization, as well as the per capita income of the peasants, but also provide a large number of official documents on the structural changes in property rights in the countryside which can be well used to describe the "buy-in" features in the Chinese economic reform. The authors wrote: "In rural China, the basic characteristics of the changes in government policy, legal system and other institutional arrangements since 1978 is as follows: as the government has relaxed the direct control over economic activities, farmers have gained more property rights. In other words, with the process of liberal reform, Chinese peasants have acquired the increasing freedom of using and transferring different types of their properties and exclusively enjoying the income brought by their properties."[23] In table 5 In the article, the authors laboriously compiled (with indexation) a record of institutional changes with focus on property rights change from 1979 to 1987 from 12 aspects of property rights change totaling 108 pages. As many as 80 official documents were consulted for this record. What's more interesting is that an analysis of the chronological order of these documents testifies that farmers' property rights are "increasing", which was emphasized by the authors.

The so-called "increasing property rights" reflect the progressive effort in the adjustment of property rights in favor of the bearer of planned obligations and also the gradual institutional change in the reform in China. The main difference between the radical reform and gradual reform is whether the rate of transformation of property right takes a shock or mild approach, rather than what someone said if it changes or only modifies the original vested interest. Some criticized the

[22] An empirical study proved the role of this marginal adjustment. See *Comprehensive Investigation Team of Chinese Institute of Economic Restructuring: Reform: Challenges and Choices We Face*, pp. 45–57, Beijing, China Economic Press, 1986.

[23] Yang et al. (1992).

"shock therapy" approach of radical reform saying that, in a sense, it did not take into account the damage to the vested interests caused by the reform of the wealth distribution, thus claiming it as a product "irrelevant to income distribution".[24] This criticism is specious, for a gradual reform will also affect (though perhaps in a milder way) the vested interests of the beneficiary of planned privilege. Take raising food prices as an example, in order to try to curb the effects of the redistribution of wealth in reform, the government gives urban residents a price subsidy. But the subsidy is only to mitigate, to some extent, the impact of reform on vested interests of the beneficiary of planned privileges rather than the result of the so-called "planned privilege" transaction. Because of this, the economic reform, apart from gradually eliminating externalities caused by the planned economy, also created a new social cost: the price compensation for urban residents, the financial subsidies for enterprises and subsidies and allowances for the placement of laid-off workers. Whether the reform is radical or gradual, as long as we want to reduce the wealth redistribution effect of reform so as to mitigate the resistance to reform, the government has to bear this huge cost. Generally speaking, development costs money, so does reform! Therefore, the shortage of funds is naturally the most prominent problem in a "transitional economy". In this sense, whether it is Russia's demand for foreign aid or China's intensified use of foreign investment, they can all be regarded as fund-raising activities for this cost.

Author's Note

This article, written when I was a postdoctoral fellow at the University of Sussex in England (1992–1993), represents a useful attempt to apply the Coase theorem to the analysis of the socialist planned economic system. Since I came into contact with modern property rights economics in 1988 and published the first book on property economics in China in 1991, I have written several articles on economic reform from the perspective of property rights theory, one of which is this one. In this article, I use the idea of Coase theorem to re-analyze the "institutional change process" of property right structure and the redistribution of rights under the centrally planned economy. The basic idea is that the "planned privilege" defined and protected by the planned system can be monetized and, through trading (buy out rights), subject to re-allocation of rights, thus eliminating the difference between "planned obligation" and "planned privilege" and leading to the redefinition of property rights and institutional changes.

When published in the 5th issue of *Economic Studies* in 1993, the title was changed to Theory of Property Rights and Institutional Change under the Centrally Planned Economy. As I criticized Cheng Hong's idea about market-oriented planning rights in the last part of my article, it caused some controversy and discussions among scholars. Later, this article was included in *Chinese Transitional Economics* edited by Cheng Hong (Shanghai SDX Joint Publishing Company edition, 1994).

[24] Cheng (1993).

References

Coase: Social Costs Issue, in *Journal of Law and Economics*, 1960 (10), pp. 1–44.
Cheng Hong: Conditions, Limitation and Forms of Marketization, in *Economic Studies*, 1992 (11).
Cheng Hong: Correlation of Income Distribution, Transaction Costs and Others, in *Economy Studies*, 1993 (11).
Pan Zhenmin, Luo Shouchu: *Equilibrium Theory of Socialist Micro-Economy*, pp. 88–107, Shanghai, Shanghai SDX Joint Publishing Company, 1988.
Sheng Hong: Conditions, Limitations and Forms of Marketization, in *Economic Stuides*, 1992 (11).
Sheng Hong; Seeking A Stable Way for Reform, *in Economic Studies*, 1991 (1).
(US) Demsetz: Toward A Theory of Property Rights, in *The American Economic Review*, 1967 (5), pp. 347–359.
(US) Demsetz: A Framework for the Study of Ownership, in *Property Rights and Institutional Changes*, pp. 179–200, Shanghai, SDS Joint Publishing Company, 1991.
(US) Barzel: *An Economic Analysis of Property Rights* (English Edition), Cambridge, University of Cambridge Press, 1989.
Yang Xiaokai, Wang Jianguo, Hui Ersi: Economic Growth, Commercialization and Institutional Changes of Chinese Agriculture, in *Chinese Economic Review*, 1992 (1), pp. 1–37.
Zhang Jun: Theory of Property Rights and Institutional Change under Centrally Planned Economy, in *Economic Studies*, 1993 (5).
Zhang Jun: *Modern Property Right Economics*, Shanghai, SDX Joint Publishing Company, 1991.

Part II
Transitional Economics

Chapter 5
The Growth of China's Industrial Output Since the Reform: Double-Track Pricing and Border Competition

5.1 Introduction

Since the reform, especially the reform of local industrial sectors since the 1980s, the industrial production in China has maintained a good growth momentum, avoided the bitter experience of production landslide and collapse (the so-called "L" growth curve) in the early transitional period in Russia and Eastern European countries and realized the smooth transition and industrial production growth in transition. Moreover, the state-owned industrial sectors continue to maintain its dominant position in industrial growth activities, making great contributions to both industrial output and industrial output growth.

However, as the output of state-owned sector grows, there is a divergence between economic efficiency (as measured by TFP) and profit rate (measured by the rate of capital, profit and tax). While the total factor productivity of the state-owned industrial sectors has increased markedly, its profitability has deteriorated. We found that this decrease of profitability does not seem to be an individual or accidental incidence, but a general trend. At the same time, the statistical data show that the non-state industrial sector, mainly rural and urban collective segments, has developed very rapidly since the middle of 80 s, with a growth rate (18.4%) significantly higher than that of the state-owned sectors (7.8%). By 1992, the output of the non-state sector, including private enterprises, surpassed that of the state-owned sector for the first time, constituting half of China's industrial production. Among them, the share of the collective industrial sectors accounts for about 40%, while the share of the private and other forms of enterprise is negligible. In fact, the production of private sector performed unsatisfactorily during the 80 s and did not pick up markedly until the 90 s.

These features raise a lot of questions for us to explain. First of all, compared with the "L" type growth curve of industrial production in the radical reform of the "Big Bang" program in Russia and Eastern European countries, why can China's industrial production achieve a smooth transition and growth at the same time? Secondly, how

J. Zhang, *Reform, Transformation and Growth*, Understanding China,
https://doi.org/10.1007/978-981-99-5712-5_5

did growth in state owned industrial sectors happen? Although it seems that the institutional structure of China's industrial economy still has important flaws contrary to the classic model of the free market system, growth is still developing rapidly. In addition, how do we explain the fact that growth of the output, improvement of efficiency and decrease of profitability coexist in the state-owned sectors? Is there a relationship among the three? Also, although the institutional structure of the private sector is closer to the classical model with characteristics of higher efficiency, why was the growth there so slow?

5.2 A Modified Model of Dominant Sector

In order to explain the production response model (production behavior) under the dual price system of traditional state-owned sector, we need to establish or construct a method of theoretical analysis. One of the most convenient starting points for the analysis is clearly to use micro economics or the basic principle and the analytical model about the manufacturers in industrial organization theory, but we need to alter or modify this classic model by introducing the dual price system conditions. Specifically, we will use the dominant manufacturer theory here to study the state sector rather than a single state-owned enterprise, and will consider an additional "planning constraints" condition in the framework of the "standard model" of the dominant manufacturer theory. On the basis of this, we will analyze the production balance of state-owned sectors.

In the standard model of industrial organization theory, the production equilibrium of a dominant firm is characterized by the output-price combination (or profit maximization) that satisfies the equality of marginal revenue and marginal costs.[1] We use *MR* to stand for the marginal revenue and *MC* for the marginal cost of manufacturer, then the marginal equivalent condition (first order condition) of profit maximization is:

$$MR = MC \tag{5.1}$$

As we know, the marginal revenue (*MR*) on the left the Eq. (5.1) has the following relationship with the manufacturer's demand curve:

$$MR = AR(1 - 1/e^d) \tag{5.2}$$

Here, *AR* is the manufacturer's demand curve, and e^d is the price elasticity of demand. Equation (5.2) shows that, unless $e^d \rightarrow \infty$ (which means an "atomic manufacturer"), generally, $(1 - 1/e^d) < 1$; therefore, in general, $MR < AR$.[2] As such, we can

[1] This standard model can be found in any textbook of microeconomics.

[2] The argument about the relationship between the average revenue (*AR*) and the marginal revenue (*MR*) is very simple, which can be found in any textbook of microeconomics.

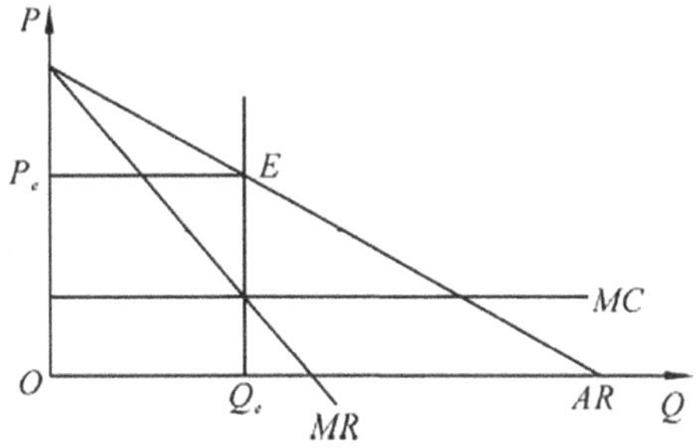

Fig. 5.1 Standard model of dominant manufacturer's equilibrium

express the equilibrium and condition (Eq. (5.1)) of this manufacturer in Fig. 5.1, of which $MR = MC$ determines the output quantity of manufacturers, and the price is determined by the demand curve *AR*. The price level decided in this way is price P_e represented by *E* on the demand curve.

In such a standard analysis, if we want to consider the production and partial equilibrium problem under the conditions of the double track pricing system in traditional state-owned enterprises, we need to make the following assumptions.

(1) The state-owned enterprises in the reform have been partially liberalized. On the one hand, the enterprise is partially restricted by planning; on the other hand, it is also market-oriented. In order to facilitate the analysis, we call the planned constraint of the state-owned sector as "planned production" while the production for the market as "unplanned production". The dual track pricing system means that the state-owned sector is subject to the planned target and prices within the planned production, while its production beyond planning is entirely subject to market demand.
(2) We assume that the traditional state-owned sector in the reform is the biggest profit maker. Generally speaking, in the economic reform, the traditional state-owned enterprises, due to institutional structure adjustment and reform and the significant changes in the distribution of income and wealth between them and government, are far more concerned about the profit than other targets. Therefore, here we will define the post-reform objective function of the state-owned sector with the assumption of profit maximization.
(3) For the sake of analyzing and dealing with the problem more easily, we assume that the planned price for the state sector is relatively low and equal to the marginal cost of production. On the one hand, the serious distortion over prices in the planned economy is characterized by the assumption that the planned price is relatively low; on the other hand, assuming that the planned price equals the marginal cost is purely for a simple analysis. Although we have no reason to think the planned price is set according to the marginal cost of enterprises, assuming the two are equal does not affect the conclusion of our analysis.
(4) Within the "planning", the target assigned for the state-owned sector is smaller than its production capacity. The aim of assumption of "relaxing the planning" is to reflect the government's efforts to allow room for market adjustment and

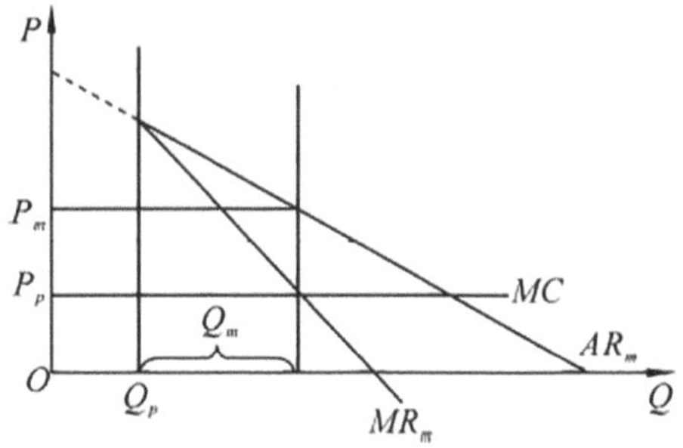

Fig. 5.2 Equilibrium of leading sectors under dual price system

introduce market mechanisms by gradually reducing the planned targets in the process of economic reform.

(5) As in the standard model, we assume that the state-owned sector faces a downward sloping demand curve in an unplanned market.

(6) Market demand remains unchanged.

Under these assumptions, we can modify the standard model of the dominant manufacturer equilibrium in order to consider the production behavior and equilibrium in the state-owned sector under the dual price system. Specifically, we can take the following steps to establish a simple model of production theory of the leading state sector under the dual price system (see Fig. 5.2) by using the standard model of Fig. 5.1.

Step One: based on assumption 1, we can set an output level Q_p on the horizontal axis (i.e. the Q axis) of Fig. 5.1, and use Q_p to represent the planned output index of the enterprise, and take the Q axis on the right side of Q_p as the possible unplanned output of the state sector.

Step Two: based on assumption 4, we put the position of Q_p near the original point or on a position towards the left.

Step Three, based on assumption 3, we determine a lower planned price level P_p on the vertical axis (i.e. the P axis) and make $P_p = MC$.

Step Four: by the above steps we know that now the state sector faces two "markets". One is the "market" within the plan where the state sector must produce Q_p according to planned target with P_p as the planned price. And beyond the planning, i.e. on the right side of Q_p, is the real market the state sector faces. Based on assumption 5, the unplanned market demand curve slides downward, so we get a downward sloping AR_m curve.

Step Five: according to Eq. (5.2) of standard model, we can see that there is a corresponding marginal revenue line, AR_m, below the demand line MR_m.

Step Six: based on assumption 2, because the state-owned sector pursues profit maximization, so its marginal equivalence condition of profit maximization also satisfies Eq. (5.1) of the standard model, i.e. $MR_m = MC$.

Thus, the balance of the dominant state sector under the dual price system was established. According to the dual price system, the state-owned sector will face a planned quota output, Q_p, which will be traded within the state-owned sectors according to the planned control price P_p. However, the surplus beyond the planned output can be sold at market prices. Therefore, a state-owned sector will face two separate "markets", one is the planned "market" defined by the planned output quota Q_p and the planned price P_p. The other is the unplanned market, the part of the market demand represented by the demand line AR_m on the right side of Q_p. But for the state-owned sector, it is only the unplanned market that makes sense. In fact, its production behavior is entirely regulated by this surplus market.

As shown in Fig. 5.2, due to the control of the planning, only the market of the state sector beyond planning is facing a downward sloping marginal income line MR_m. And, again, only in this market can a decision be made as to how much products should be produced to maximize profits from surplus output in accordance with the marginal principle, $MR_m = MC$. Since the marginal cost is assumed to be MC in Fig. 5.2, we can determine the optimal output Q_m of the sector in the unplanned market in Fig. 5.2, and, accordingly, the unplanned selling price is p_m. Thus, under the dual track system, the total output of the state-owned sector is $Q_p + Q_m$, in which the unplanned output Q_m is sold at the planned price P_m. This shows that, under the dual pricing system, the state-owned sector faces two separate markets and two completely different (average) income curves. Specifically, within the planning, the average income obtained by the state-owned sector was P_p, while the average income earned beyond planning was P_m. Apparently, $P_m > P_p$. Therefore, the production behavior of the state-owned sector is entirely regulated by the unplanned market demand.

Here, we can also simplify the above analysis into a mathematical model. For the convenience of analysis, as shown in Fig. 5.2, we still assume that the demand function of the state sector is linear:

$$P_m = a - b(Q - Q_p) \tag{5.3}$$

P_m is the price set by the state-owned sector in the unplanned market; $(Q - Q_p)$ is the unplanned output, and a and b is the coefficient greater than zero. At this point, the marginal revenue function of the state sector will be:

$$MR_m = a - 2b(Q - Q_p) \tag{5.4}$$

Then, let's assume that the cost function of the state sector is a general primary function:

$$C = \delta(Q - Q_p) \tag{5.5}$$

In the formula, C is the cost of production, and δ is also a coefficient greater than zero, so that its marginal cost is equal to its average cost, both of which are δ. Of course, according to the hypothesis, $\delta = P_p$. To set the cost function this way is purely for the purpose of linking the analysis here with Figs. 5.1 and 5.2. In fact, Fig. 5.2 can be considered as a geometric illustration of the Eqs. (5.3) and (5.4). Obviously, as shown in Fig. 5.2, the equilibrium condition of the state-owned sector in the unplanned market satisfies $MR_m = \delta$, that is:

$$Q = \frac{1}{2b}(a - \delta) + Q_p \tag{5.6}$$

Now let's consider the planned target and price control of the planned output. The price control of planned output means that whenever the state-owned sector produces a unit output within the planning, the sector assumes a "cost", which is equal to the difference between the unplanned price and planned price of the output, i.e. $P_m - P_p$. Therefore, the profit function π of the state-owned sector at this time will be:

$$\pi = P_m(Q - Q_p) - \delta(Q - Q_p) - (P_m - P_p)Q_p \tag{5.7}$$

Here, Q_p is the planned target of the state sector, that is, the amount of planned output to be completed. Due to the assumption that the planned price P_p is equal to the marginal cost of the state sector, namely,$P_p = \delta$, formula (5.7) may be reorganized as:

$$\pi = (P_m - P_p)(Q - Q_p) - (P_m - P_p)Q_p \tag{5.8}$$

or

$$\pi = (P_m - P_p)(Q - 2Q_p) \tag{5.9}$$

Formula (5.9) represents the maximum real profit of the state-owned sector under the condition of dual price system. I would like to point out that from Eq. (5.9) we can infer an important conclusion. That is, in the dual system arrangement, if the state sector intends to obtain positive real profits, the unplanned output must be no less than the planned quota, or, the total output must be two times greater than the planned quota. In Fig. 5.2, this means that the total output of the state sector under planned control will be greater than the total output without planning. In other words, the state-owned sector will produce more in a dual price system than in a completely liberalized market. We will postpone our discussion of the problem to the next part. We will make a comparative analysis of the reform characterized by double track price system and the reform of "Big Bang" price, so as to make a microeconomic explanation for the serious decline of production in Russia after the big bang reform. But now, let us first make a further expansion of the simple model of the dual track price system that has been set up to consider the more realistic situation.

5.3 An Extension of the Model: Subsidies and Price Regulation Ability

The previous analysis shows that, under the dual price system, planned output is controlled by the planned price of the state, while the unplanned output is traded freely at market prices. Since the average yield of unplanned production is greater than planned price, the production behavior of the state-owned sector will be entirely determined by the demand and supply of the market outside the planning under the dual track system. As we have seen in Fig. 5.2, the state-owned sector has become a typical monopolist in the market outside the planning.

However, China's experience in the early years of economic reform does not fully conform to the conclusions drawn from such a simple analytical model. The reason is that China's experience in the early stages of economic reform has not taken into account at least three aspects in the above models.

First, the continuing subsidies to the state sector. As a matter of fact, China has never abolished the government subsidies to the state sector in the course of the reform of state-owned industries. State owned enterprises, for example, continue to have access to cheap credit provided by government banks and "par" products produced by other state-owned enterprises as non-labor inputs. In addition, the labor cost within the state-owned enterprises has the nature of "fixed costs" to a great extent, because their labor force is non-liquid, that is to say, enterprises cannot fire or lay off workers, and the labor remuneration, in a large part, is paid to employees by providing them with free housing, health care and other non-wage forms of social welfare. This means that in the early stages of the reform, the production of the state-owned sector has a lower "marginal cost". But it should be pointed out that a low marginal cost does not mean that state-owned enterprises have a strong capacity to make profit, for the welfare spending the state-owned sector bears constitutes an important part of its fixed costs, which in turn will make the state-owned sector has a higher "average cost" for its production.

Second, regulation of pricing capacity. In the unplanned market, the government carefully controls the pricing capacity of the state sector. Although the market economy in China is being developed by the gradual process of "control the planning sector while openning up the part outside the planning", in the early stage of the reform, the government still cautiously controlled the price of market outside the planning to a certain degree and within a certain scope. For example, for the unplanned output produced by state-owned enterprises, the government generally stipulated an increasing range of free pricing (such as 20% or 30%). For the relatively tight production goods in particular, the policy of floating price control was generally adopted for output beyond planning before the unplanned price was completely lifted. Of course, one of the purposes of doing so was perhaps to prevent the excessive monopoly prices for many production goods in the unplanned market at the beginning of the implementation of the dual price system.[3]

[3] In the late 1980s, in response to macroeconomic problems, the government once more carefully controlled the pricing power of the enterprise, especially the control over the price ceiling of

Third, "entry" of non-state sector. The analytical model we established earlier has actually assumed that the state-owned sector faces a downward sloping demand curve in an unplanned market, which means that the state-owned sector is a monopolist in the market. A more realistic assumption, however, is that the state-owned sector is a "dominant firm" in the unplanned market. It is because on the one hand, in the early stages of reform the share of total output of state-owned sector had an absolute advantage, thus making its production a major source of growth in the industrial sector; on the other hand, with the progress of the reform, the increasing output of collective sector (including the rural township enterprises), plus the share of private economy and other non-state-owned economic sector (although the share was not significant throughout the 1980s), undoubtedly constitutes the so-called "competitive fringe" that the state sector cannot ignore in the unplanned market.[4] Based on these considerations, when we created the enterprise equilibrium model under the condition of dual price system, it seems to be more reasonable to regard the state-owned sector as the "dominant manufacturer" in the unplanned market and the non-state sector as the "border manufacturer".

In order to clarify our way of thinking, let us put aside the "non-state sector entry" issue for the time being and mainly consider and analyze the first two issues. We will exclusively discuss the non-state sector entry problem later. We will then introduce the "competitive fringe" into the industrial organization theory under the dual pricing system that has been established, with a view of considering the impact on the production and the balance of output of state-owned sector due to the entry of non-state-owned sector.

With regard to the influence of government subsidies to the state sector on the production behavior of state-owned enterprises in the unplanned market during the reform process, our main consideration is that, when market assessment has already existed outside the planning, subsidies to the state sector will make the marginal cost of production of the latter move downward. To illustrate this effect, let's consider only the unplanned section in Fig. 5.2 (the diagram on the right side of Q_p), because the analysis here is not related to production within the planning. What we are concerned about is the effect of subsidies on unplanned production. For a clear analysis, we have moved this part of the diagram to establish the following Fig. 5.3.

According to Fig. 5.3, because the subsidy has the effect of reducing the marginal cost of production, the marginal cost MC of the state sector will move downward to MC'. With the demand curve faced by the state sector (AR_m) and the corresponding marginal revenue (MR_m) curve remaining unchanged, the condition of the production equilibrium (profit maximization) of state sector will be changed to $MR_m = MC'$ when the MC moves downward. In Fig. 5.3, the change is shown in this way: the equilibrium output moves to the right and increases from Q_m to Q'_m;

production goods. In the most stringent time, 90% unplanned price-limited production of steel and non-ferrous metal was under control. See Chen Gongyan, Qiao Gang: Formation of Product Market and Price Reform, in Fang Gang, Li Yang, Zhou Zhenhua: *Toward Market* (1978–1993), Shanghai, Shanghai People's Publishing House, 1994.

[4] "Competitive fringe" is a standard concept frequently used in the theory of industrial organization.

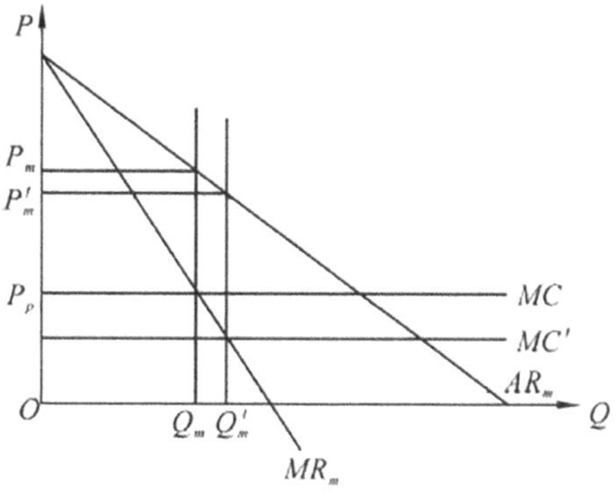

Fig. 5.3 Unplanned production under subsidy

accordingly, the unplanned price has gone down from P_m to P'_m. Therefore, we can say that the existence of subsidies will induce the state-owned sector to produce more unplanned products at lower prices. This conclusion is intuitively consistent with our observations of the situation in the early years of China's reform.

Next, we will consider the impact of the limited price controls imposed by the government on the production behavior of the state sector in the unplanned market. Unlike the effect of continuing to enjoy a variety of subsidies by the state sector, when the state-owned sector faces a downward, sloping demand curve in the unplanned market, the government's control over the pricing ability of the enterprise will change the average profits and marginal revenue of state sector in the market, thus further changing its production equilibrium. We can assume that the government, in the initial stage of reform, permitted the state-owned sector to freely sell their products at a price limit no higher than a certain percentage of the planned price, indicating that the government imposed a certain amount of control over the pricing power of the state sector in the unplanned market in order to avoid the relatively high market monopoly price. For example, in the early stages of China's economic reform, the state limited the increase range of the market price of production goods to 20% of the planned price.

In order to capture this feature, we assume that the degree of control of the government over the pricing ability of the state sector in the market is ρ, $\rho \in (0, 1)$, $\rho = 0$ means that the state-owned sector can freely set a price for its unplanned products while $\rho = 1$ means that the state-owned sector must sell its unplanned output according to the official, planned price which does not accord with the precondition of our dual price system. So here $0 \leq \rho < 1$ is more realistic. The government's regulation of the autonomous pricing ability of the state sector in the unplanned market will change the average income function of the state-owned sector in the market. Specifically, the average income function of the state-owned sector will be changed from the original $P_m = a - bQ_m$ to the piecewise linear form:

$$(1 - \rho)P_m + \rho P_p \tag{5.10}$$

P_m is the original average revenue function, P_p is the planned price and ρ is the degree of the government's regulation of the enterprise's pricing power. From (10), the following can be obtained:

$$(1-\rho)P_m + \rho P_p = \begin{cases} P_m, & when\ \rho = 0 \\ P_p, & when\ \rho = 1 \end{cases} \tag{5.11}$$

The above formula (5.10) and (5.11) tell us that the average income function of the state-owned sector has been changed when it faces the local regulation of the government on its pricing power in the market. In Fig. 5.3, for example, this new average revenue curve can be derived from the original average revenue curve, which is centered around P_p and rotates at a certain angle downward on the left. By this rotation, the steeper demand curve of the state sector has now leveled off. We use Fig. 5.4 to illustrate intuitively the effectiveness of controlling the pricing power of an enterprise. In Fig. 5.4, the dotted line represents the original solid line of Fig. 5.3. When the free pricing power of the state-owned sector is limited, the average income curve it faces is situated in the flatter section below the original AR_m curve on the upper left of point A. If we represent this new average income curve with AR'_m, then the marginal revenue curve corresponding to AR'_m is MR'_m.

As can be seen from Fig. 5.4, at this time, the profit maximization of the state-owned sector in the market is Q''_m and pricing is the relatively low P''_m. This shows that when the monopoly of the state-owned sector in the unplanned market is regulated by the government, the sector will produce more than it does in a fully monopolized market and at a lower price. In fact, Fig. 5.4 is a comprehensive analytical diagram of both the effects of subsidy and regulation of pricing power. It tells us that under the dual price system, when the state-owned sector gains the free pricing right outside the planning, to continue giving the state-owned sector a certain amount of subsidy and limiting at the same time its free pricing power will induce the monopolist to produce more and lower the price further.

Take the reform experience of China as an example. When the state sector was allowed to trade their output produced outside the planning by market channels, the

Fig. 5.4 Production equilibrium under regulatory pricing power

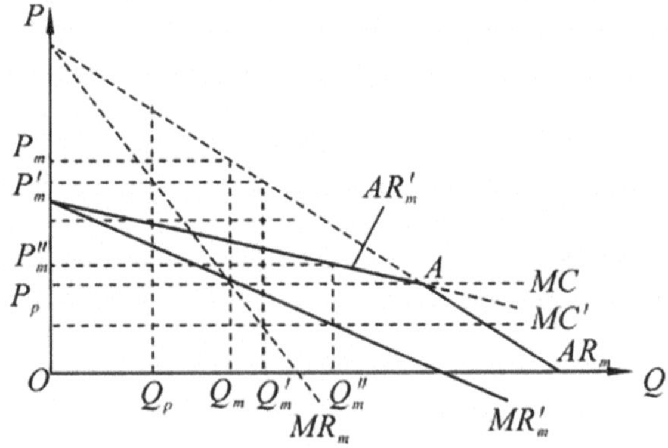

government began cautiously to impose certain restrictions on the pricing ability of state-owned enterprises in the market, allowing unplanned price to float freely in a scope no higher than 20% of the planned price. This regulation, plus the hidden subsidies in credit and other forms provided by the government to the state-owned sector, undoubtedly induced the state sector to expand production and a smooth transition of the price level, which played a positive role in avoiding the sudden rise in the prices of means of production and inflation in the early stages of reform.

5.4 Effect of Competitive Fringe

Our analysis of the production behavior of the state-owned sector under the dual track system does not consider the entry and competition of non-state industrial sectors, so the analysis is incomplete. The experience of China's economic reform shows that the entry and expansion of the non-state sector plays an important role in the growth of industrial output. From the existing literature, most economists have emphasized the contribution made by the non-state sector's expansion and growth to China's economic growth after the reform, so a large part of their attention has been shifted to the research on non-state sector (mainly township enterprises), but the focus here is on in the state sector, with a view of considering the effect on the state sector production caused by the entry and expansion of the non-state sector. To this end, we need to introduce "competitive fringe" to the model of monopoly firm to expand its analytical capabilities.

In Fig. 5.5, the supply curve of non-state sector is represented by $S^F(P)$, which is equal to the horizontal sum of supply lines of all the boundary enterprises, i.e. $S^F(P) = n \cdot qf(P)$ (n is the number of enterprises). We call this supply line the "competitive fringe". After the introduction of this competitive fringe, the demand line of the dominant state sector (i.e., the average revenue line) will change further, adjusted from the original market demand line *ECBF* to the kinked *DBF*.

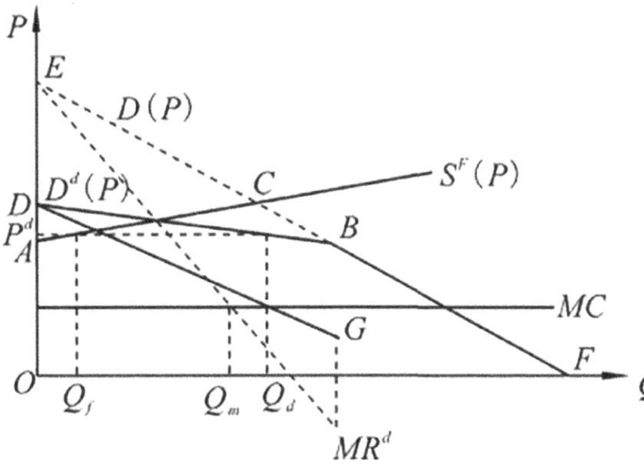

Fig. 5.5 Entry and competition of non-state sector (the part within the planning is omitted)

The reasons that the demand line of dominant sector is kinked at point *B* and becomes flat in the upper left part of point *B* are as follows: as shown in Fig. 5.5, if the competitive fringe is $S^F(P)$, we can see that when the price level is *A* or below *A*, the boundary sector will withdraw from the market, so its supply is zero. At this moment, the demand line of the dominant sector is equal to the market demand *D*(*P*) on the right of point *B*. When the demands of the unplanned market are all supplied by the boundary sector, that is, when $S^F(P)$ and *D*(*P*) intersect at the point *C*, the demand of the dominant sector is zero. Therefore, *D* must be a point on the new line of demand of the dominant sector. With the price level rising from *A*, the supply of the border sector will move from *A* to *C*, while the demand line of the dominant sector will move gradually from *B* to *D*. Thus, the line between *B* and *D* represents the demand line of the dominant sector at a price level above *A*. Because the demand line of the dominant sector is equal to the market demand line *D*(*P*) when the price level is below *A*, a breaking point will emerge at *B* on the demand line of the dominant sector when confronted with the entry of the border sector.

Another deduction method is as follows: the demand line of dominant sector can be acquired through the broad-wise subtraction in geometry of the market demand line *D*(*P*) and the border sector supply line $S^F(P)$ at different prices, namely $D^d(p) = D(p) - S^F(P)$. When the price level is higher than *A*, because $S^F(P) > 0$, $D^d(P) < D(P)$, that is, the demand line of dominant sector becomes flatter (*DB*) than the market demand line *D*(*P*) in segment *EB*. And when the price level is lower than *A*, the border sector withdraws out of the market, i.e. $S^F(P) = 0$, so $D^d(P) = D(P)$, which means that when the price level is below *A*, the demand of the dominant sector is equal to the demand of market.

As can be seen from Fig. 5.5, for the dominant sector, the marginal revenue line MR^d corresponding to the kinked demand line $D^d(p)$ must be broken at *G* and divided into two parts. Given the level of marginal cost we have given, we do not have to consider the *MR* below the horizontal line, but only the marginal revenue line of the *DG* segment only. At this time, the output of the maximum profit of dominant sector is Q_d (determined by $MR = MC$), and the price level is P_d. Since we have assumed that the border sector is the price recipient, its output is Q_f (that is, the aggregate supply level at the price level of P_d). In this way, the total output level in the unplanned market is $Q_d + Q_f$, and the price level is P_d. We can also infer from Fig. 5.5 that because the dominant sector demand line $D^d(P)$ is flatter than the demand line of market in the *DB* section and, as we have discussed earlier, the marginal cost of the dominant sector is generally lower than that of the boundary sector, the dominant sector, when faced with the entry and competition of the border sector, will produce more than if it has no competition from the border sector. This conclusion can be explained by comparing Q_d in Fig. 5.5 with the original Q_m. Q_m is the unplanned output of state sector when there was no competition from the non-state sector–the maximum profit output of the state sector under the original market demand *D*(*P*) and its corresponding marginal income line (MR^d represented in dotted line in Fig. 5.5). Also, as the demand line of dominant state-owned sector is now flatter, it can be inferred that the price level is, at present, much lower than prior to the entry of border sector.

In our model, access and supply of the non-state sector depend entirely on the output price of the leading sector in the unplanned market. As long as the price is higher than point A, the entry of the non-state sector will occur, namely: $S^F(P) > 0$ when $P > A$. In Fig. 5.5, point A corresponds to the kinked B of demand line of the dominant sector. Under A, the border sector has withdrawn from the market, so it looks like that the production behavior of the dominant sector on the unplanned market will be restored to the situation in Fig. 5.2, maintaining the unplanned output at the level of Q_m in Fig. 5.5 and keeping a higher prices. However, according to the assumption, maintaining such a high price level will prevent the entry of the non-state sector and lead to the reduced market share of the dominant sector. So, from a dynamic point of view, owing to the entry and competition pressure of the border sector, the production behavior of the dominant sector will be limited to the DB segment of its demand line. Despite of this, we still have not considered the expansionary effect of competitive fringe, that is to say, the impact of the growth in the number of non-state sectors on the production of the dominant sector. In fact, we can imagine that in the early stages of reform, the number of non-state sector was not very large; therefore, the supply line $S^F(P)$ of the border sector was steeper than it is in Fig. 5.5. Accordingly, the demand line $D^d(P)$ of dominant sector in the DB section was also steeper than it is now, so is the marginal revenue line in the DG section. As a result, the output of the dominant sector must be on the left-hand side of Q_d.

Reversing this logic exactly illustrates the expansion effect of competitive fringe. The analysis done here is only from a static or comparatively static angle, the dynamic effect of further expansion of competitive fringe is more complex. For example, we still have not taken into account the deepening of market and expansion (or shrinking) of market demand driven by this competition, all of which are beyond the scope of discussion of our simple model. However, the analysis of the model has at least helped demonstrate that the entry of the non-state sector can create a competitive environment, promote expansion and deepening of the market and weaken the market power of traditional state-owned sector on the unplanned market. This point has become an accepted fact in the interpretation of the success of the reform of China's industrial problem. Norton, for example, has pointed out that:

> The emergence and rapid entry of emerging economies is a feature of almost all transitional economies. Growth in the emerging private sector is widely regarded as a successful example of the transition in a socialist economy. Therefore, the growth of China's township enterprises is only a variant of a more general process. Ironically, this process is often referred to as 'privatization from grassroots' in other transitional economies, while in China, the same process of entry is largely dependent on collective enterprises. China's case shows that the key feature of this process is entry, not privatization: entry promotes competition and market development, leading to the weakening of state control and monopoly.[5]

This is the positive role of the entry process of non-state sector in promoting market competition. However, what this author did not emphasize is that China experience further shows that the prerequisite of entry is the dual system of the state sector.

[5] Naughton (1994a, 1994b, 1994c).

Under the dual system, as the market and liberalization occur only in the unplanned production of state sector, the increase of market competitive power will only come from the boundary outside the planning and only when the non-state sector "enters" the unplanned market.[6] On the contrary, if without the dual system, the liberalization of the state sector in fact would mean the "entry" of the state-owned sector, which may lead to a process contrary to the one mentioned above, resulting in the state sector manipulating the market. This point has been proved by Russia's experience. We will discuss this question in the next section.

Moreover, the above model does not consider the changes within the planning. In fact, our analysis of unplanned market is based on the assumption that the planned output remains unchanged; therefore, the model naturally cannot reflect the influence on the output on the unplanned market if the planned quota is reduced. If, like this model, we assume that market demand remains unchanged, we can see then that when the planned quota Q_p is reduced, the total output may decrease, but obviously on a lesser degree than if under the full liberalization scheme. When the entry of boundary enterprises and the growth of market competition produce an effect that can offset the negative impact of planned production cuts on total output, the total output may not necessarily decline. Of course, this needs to take specific conditions into consideration, but the implications at least show that it is advisable to continue to maintain a larger share of planned production before boundary firms enter in large numbers. This also means that if the proportion of planned control departments in the dominant sector is not to be reduced until the entry and supply of border sector (non-state enterprises) reach a certain scale, a large-scale reduction of overall output may be avoided. Intuitively, we have found that this is basically consistent with the experience of China's industrial reform.

[6] The dual price system in the state-owned sector clearly provides favorable conditions for non state-owned sectors to enter the market. Lin Yifu and others in Chinese Miracle: Development Strategy and Economic Reform also mentioned this view, believing that in the 1980s the increasing resource allocation and price system were intended to improve the allocation efficiency of products and materials of state-owned enterprise, yet they also provided the conditions for township enterprises to enter the market. The survey done by the Development Office of the Institute of Economic Research of the Chinese Academy of Social Sciences (1987) shows that 72.1% of the main raw material supplies of township enterprises was purchased from the state-owned sector at a high price. In addition, we should also see that the production liberalization outside the planning of state sector provided the township enterprises with another way to enter, that is, the "joint venture" between the two sides. Township enterprises, especially those located in developed areas and urban fringe, were often allied with state-owned enterprises which became an important way for state-owned enterprises to expand their production capacity and increase profits. See Center for Economic Research, Fudan University: *Enterprise Reform and New Path of Development -- A Collections of Surveys of Horizontal Integration of Industrial Enterprises in Shanghai*, Shanghai, Fudan University Press, 1988.

5.5 Form of Border Entry

A significant change that Chinese economic growth experienced in the early stage of the reform is that while the state sector production continued to grow, the collective enterprises, especially the rural township enterprises, grew with an unusual speed that was faster than that of the state-owned sector. As our previous analysis shows, in the course of China's economic reform, the traditional state-owned sector, as the leading sector, has encountered the entry and competition from the non-state sector. As a matter of fact, the theoretical model of production behavior of the state-owned sector is based on the context of entry and competition of the non-state sector. Now, we will further study the ways of entry of the non state sector (that is, the competitive border), in order to better characterize China's reform experience and the pattern of industrial growth after the reform.

First of all, the main reasons for non-state sector to enter are: ① the price structure of the planned economy is severely distorted by which processing industry of the state-owned sector gained the "false" monopoly profits. Coupled with the protection of the government policy, the state sector acquired a large number of monopoly rents. After the economic reform, with the decentralization of economic decision-making and the loosening of control, the local government (including township government) had a strong motivation to actively participate in the market and share the rents monopolized by the state-owned sector. The local governments at all levels (especially at the grass-roots level) begun to intervene and organize production activities on a large scale. ② The former management system under the planned economy made the scale distribution of industrial enterprises seriously distorted. For this problem, Kornai made a comparative study when he analyzed the market structure of the socialist economy after the reform.[7] He found that the scale distribution of industrial enterprises in planned economy was in the shape of an "inverted pyramid", just the opposite of the "pyramid" shape of the scale distribution of enterprises in market economy. Taking Hungary and Denmark as an example, he cited data that show that enterprises with more than 500 employees accounted for 37% of the total number of enterprises in Hungary, and in Denmark this kind of enterprises accounted for only 1%; on the other hand, enterprises with 5 to 19 workers in Denmark account for 47% of all enterprises in that country, while enterprises of the same size only account for 1% in Hungary.[8] Such a distortion of scale distribution will inevitably provide the small-and medium-sized enterprises with the opportunity and space to enter the market when the reform started.

Strictly speaking, the two points mentioned above exist in varying degrees in all the centrally planned economies. Take the latter case as an example, when the scale distribution of production units is seriously distorted, the growth and development of a large number of small enterprises can also be seen in other countries of market economy. Therefore, with regard to the non-state sector's "entry" into production

---

[7] (Hungary) Kornai (1985).

[8] To be exact, Kornai did his comparison in his paper by quoting the data from Schweitzer's book *Scale of Enterprise*.

areas dominated by state-owned sector and competing with the latter, China is no exception except that this general phenomenon is manifested in different ways in different economies. However, China is not the same as other economies in the following point: for other transitional economies (such as Hungary, Russia, Poland, etc.), the entry of the non-state sector in the early stage of the reform is often the quick and agile response of families or individuals to the potential market opportunities. If, in the planned economy period, families or individuals are willing to sacrifice personal leisure to engage in self-employed production, this trend will be further strengthened in the wake of the reform. But in China, although business operated by families and individual also "entered" and grew rapidly in the early stages of reform like other transitional economies, the main force was the township collective enterprises (TVEs) from rural areas.

Although Chinese township enterprises made contribution to the development strategy of solving the rural mechanization funds problem and implementing the "two legs development" policy (they were then called "collective enterprises") in the 1970s, their scale was very limited, and being mainly confined to local rural areas, they failed to truly enter the "market". In fact, until 1978, the time prior to reform, the output value of collective enterprises accounted for only about 7% of the total output value of the whole society. With the implementation of economic reform in the early 80 s, the township enterprises in rural areas achieved rapid growth and extraordinary development. Figure 5.6 depicts the development of the output value of township enterprises in the years of 1978–1991. According to other information, from 1981 to 1992, the number of township enterprises increased by 26.6% year on year, and the number of their employees increased by 11.2% annually. During this period, the average annual growth rate of total output value was as high as 29.6%.[9]

The extraordinary entry and development of township enterprises have aroused the interest of many economists. As a result, they began to try to find out the deep reasons why township enterprises were more "vigorous" than traditional state-owned enterprises (Nee, (1992a), (1992b)[10]; Whiting, 1993[11]; Weitzman & Xu, 1994[12]). In their view, Chinese township enterprises seem to have a unique, delicate organizational structure and property rights structure, which can help them adapt to the market conditions and government regulation in the transitional period. In short, as a hybrid, it has a strong and resilient institutional function of absorbing the advantages of the market and administration. However, these views and interpretations have also been criticized by other economists.[13] These economists argue that the institutional structure difference between state-owned and township enterprises is not as significant as some scholars think of, because they are all owned by the government, subject to government intervention, as well as have equally vague property rights. Norton also

[9] Lin et al. (1994).

[10] Nee (1992a, 1992b).

[11] The Whiting (1993).

[12] Weitzman and Xu (1994).

[13] Naughton (1994a, 1994b, 1994c); Jefferson, Rawski (1994).

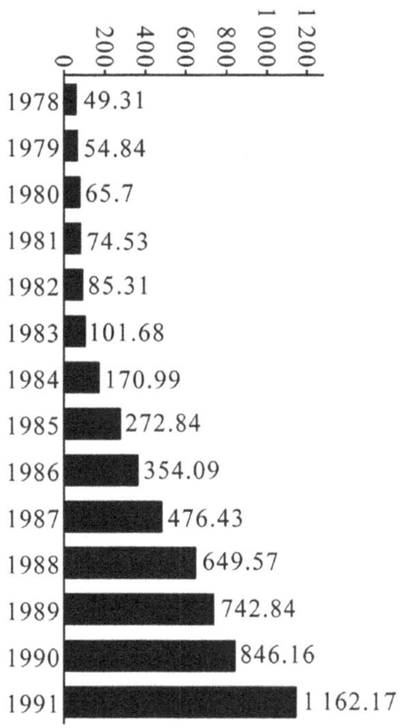

Fig. 5.6 Evolution of total output value of township enterprises in China (1978–1991). *Note* the unit is 100,000 RMB, and all the output data are calculated according to the current price. *Source* National Bureau of Statistics: *China Statistical Yearbook*, Beijing, China Statistics Press, 1992

found that the change (declining) trend of the profitability of township enterprises is in full accord with that of the state-owned enterprises.[14]

However, another problem Norton ignored is that the township enterprises are risking the "survival of the fittest" in the process of growth, while the state-owned enterprises have a complete "risk function". According to statistics, although the total growth of township enterprises in Jiangsu, Shanghai areas increased several times over since the reform, this growth was achieved at the expense of the elimination of about 40% of the township enterprises. Especially in the period of economic austerity in 1989, about 3 million township enterprises went bankrupt, closed or were merged with other companies.[15] Of course, research on the institutional structure of Chinese township enterprises and the differences (if any) between them and state-owned enterprises will continue and I have no intention of being involved in this research field in this article. However, regardless of the differences between township and state-owned enterprises in terms of organizational structure and property right structure, it is important to notice that township enterprise, as a newly emergent production enterprise sponsored by the village and town government in the reform, has gained a high-speed development space and market opportunities. Therefore, the inevitable question is why township enterprises can achieve a faster growth than other non-state-owned enterprises?

[14] Naughton (1994a, 1994b, 1994c).

[15] Zhou Zhenhua (1994).

To answer this question, we need to study the mode of reform in China and the market conditions in the early stage of its reform. At least three conditions should be met for any non-state enterprise to enter the market. The first one is that factors of production can be easily obtained, especially investment funds. Generally speaking, a complete capital market is needed for capital which, of course, could not be satisfied in the early stage of reform. The second condition is that the state-owned enterprises should leave some "niches" for non-state enterprises to enter. Owing to the reasons we mentioned above, these two conditions already existed, that is to say, the scale distribution of state-owned enterprises is seriously distorted, which provides a lot of "niches" for the production of non-state-owned enterprises. Therefore, for the niches left by the state- owned enterprises, it is clear that whoever can enter depends, to some extent, on who can meet the first condition.

In fact, in all transition economies, due to the fact that the factors of production market, especially the capital market, is not perfect, those who can occupy these "niches" are mostly small family or private businesses, most of which are not directly involved in production activities. It is difficult for large-scale production businesses to enter. In China, the entry of large-scale production activities has indeed occurred, not mainly from the private sector, but from the development of rural township enterprises. This is certainly not because China had developed a relatively complete capital market at the beginning of the reform, but because of the role played by the township government in overcoming the defects of the capital market for the township enterprises. The participation and intervention of local governments helped solve the problem of capital demand for township enterprises to enter the market to a great extent.[16] The third condition is related to cost. Regarding the entry of the non-state sector, we find in further analysis that, because the state-owned enterprises monopolize or occupy a dominant position in the production of many products, the advantages of the cost conditions of potential entrants often facilitate their entry. We have analyzed this problem in the previous theoretical model. That analysis means that even if the second condition has been met, who can really enter will depend on whether the cost is advantageous. Because of the dual price system in the state sector, coupled with continued subsidies to the state sector and imposition of certain regulation on the pricing capacity of unplanned production of the state-owned enterprise, the state sector has to set a low price in the unplanned market, which will not only reduce the speed of non-state sector to enter the market, but also constitute another kind of "barriers to entry" to many potential entrants.

During the period of 1978–1990, China witnessed the slow entry of large-scale private production sectors (such as private enterprises, foreign-funded enterprises) the growth of which, compared with the entry and growth of rural township enterprises, was not significant. This can be partially explained by the low price barriers caused by the dual price system of the state-owned sector, the continued subsidies and local liberalization process it was entitled to. Compared with the private production sector, the township enterprises became the beneficiaries of China's gradual reform due to the average low cost advantage caused by their employment and production

[16] Nee (1992a, 1992b).

cost structure. We can prove the cost advantages of township enterprises from the segments that they "entered".

To illustrate this problem, please see Table 5.1 which clearly reflects the regular pattern of output value changes of the large, medium and small enterprises not only among different types of ownerships but also among enterprises of different scales. We should notice in the table that in the "large enterprise" category (commonly known as the "large and medium-sized enterprises"), the monopoly of state-owned enterprises (represented here by the proportion of output or market share) has basically not changed, and the non-state (namely "other") sectors basically failed to "enter" this area. Generally speaking, large and medium-sized state-owned enterprises are highly concentrated in capital and technology with increasing returns to scale; therefore, the failure of township enterprises to enter this area means that they do not have technical and cost efficient strengths in this segment. On the contrary, we can see from Table 5.1 that the entry of township enterprises mainly comprised small and medium-sized enterprises which, by 1991, provided output that accounted for over 20% of the total output of industry. As experience shows, the majority of small and medium-sized enterprises in China are labor-intensive such as clothing, textile, toys, plastic industry, etc. It can be inferred that the main fields township enterprises entered are of labor intensive ones, which in turn shows that township enterprises obviously have a better cost condition than state-owned and private enterprises in labor-intensive industries, because they saved a lot of cost in terms of production land and use of labor force. Township enterprises, unlike state-owned enterprises, do not need to bear a heavy burden of welfare. Because of this, they quickly entered and developed rapidly in the labor intensive industries. Take the garment industry as an example, according to the National Bureau of Statistics, in 1990, the clothing industry accounted for 2% of the output value of entire manufacturing industry, of which 40% of clothing was manufactured by the rural township enterprises. The entry of township enterprises brought competition pressure to the state-owned sector, and the intensified market competition greatly reduced the average profit margin of the industry. In 1980, for example, the ratio of profit and taxes on funds of textile industry was 69%, but decreased to 7% in 1991 also according to the National Bureau of Statistics.

The simple discussion on the entry of township enterprises demonstrates that in the gradual reform of China, due to the reform approach of partial liberalization (dual system transition) implemented in the traditional state sector, coupled with the immature capital market in the early stage of reform, made the entry of typical private production sector very slow, and township enterprises arguably became the lucky dog of the incomplete liberalization mode and capital market. This reminds us of Marx's remark on the relationship between gold and silver and money in *Das Kapital*: "Gold and silver are not naturally currencies, but money is naturally gold and silver."[17] It seems appropriate to apply this sentence to the township enterprises.

The rise and large-scale entry of township enterprises in the early stage of reform in China means that there was a relatively large "competitive fringe" in the early stages

[17] Marx (1975).

Table 5.1 Changes in industrial output broken down by firm size and ownership

Percentage of total industrial output (%)		
	1978	1991
Large enterprises	41.5	43.6
(State-owned)	(41.5)	(40.7)
(Others)	(0.0)	(2.9)
Urban medium/small businesses	49.4	25.1
(State-owned)	(35.8)	(12.1)
(Collective)	(13.6)	(13.0)
Rural medium/small enterprises	8.7	20.6
(Town)	(4.8)	(10.3)
(Village)	(3.9)	(10.3)
Other medium/small businesses	0.0	2.9
Small businesses	0.4	7.8
Total	100.0	100.0

Note the output value data for 1978 are calculated at constant prices in 1970, while the data for 1991 are calculated at prices of that year. "Large enterprises" include large and medium-sized enterprises in China, namely, the medium-sized enterprises with more than 500 people are regarded as large enterprises according to international standards. The output of "other medium/small enterprises" refers to that of foreign-funded enterprises (43%), plus the output of domestic joint ventures (57%)
Source Naughton, B., *Growing Out of Plan: Chinese Economic, Reform*, 1978–1993, Cambridge University Press, New York, 1994

of reform, which shows that China differed from other transformational economies in terms of initial conditions. However, whether the existence of this "competitive fringe" is the decisive factor in explaining Chinese reform experience and achievements, or the main reason for the different reform performances between China and Eastern Europe and Russia cannot be answered until further study is done. What we want to emphasize here is: ① with regard to the initial conditions in the economy in the reform, we not only need to see the differences in the initial conditions, but also the common problems they are faced with and the similar logic in the traditional economic system; ② if there were not a feasible reform policy and a dual track system approach to keep the continued growth of the state-owned sector in the early period of reform (i.e. continued control within the plan, continued subsidies and the liberalization on the fringe of planning and market reform), but only a relatively large competitive fringe, it would be impossible for Chinese economy to avoid the "L" type growth curve after the reform.

5.6 Full Liberalization of Price of Monopoly of State Sector: Different Effects on Industrial Output

In the simple model developed previously, the production equilibrium problem under the dual price system has been analyzed and explained in detail. But in that same model, we can further discuss the production response mode of the state-owned sector under the condition of complete price liberalization. In fact, if we change the double track conditions of the price system into complete price liberalization, then our previous model can provide a simple theoretical framework of micro-analysis for the response pattern of the state sector under the "big bang" reform approach.

In order to consider the possible effect of the complete liberalization of price on the production behavior of the state-owned sector in the transitional economy, we need to go back to Fig. 5.2 which is a simple schema for analyzing the balanced production of the state sector under the dual price system. By breaking down the market conditions that the state-owned enterprises face in the figure into "planned" and "unplanned" separate markets, we include the price system conditions into a general equilibrium problem of a manufacturer. Of course, we omitted many complex details in establishing such a model, but by doing so we have identified the most important features of dual price system, so Fig. 5.2 is a useful theoretical framework for the analysis of the dual price system.

Now, let's copy Fig. 5.2 place it in Fig. 5.7. According to our previous analysis of the dual price system, we can infer that when price is completely freed from the control of planning, the state sector in transition will directly face the whole market, rather than the two divided "markets" under the dual price system, meaning that the revenue function of the state-owned sector will change. Without considering the entry of the non-state sector, the complete liberalization of prices will make the state-owned sector a monopolist in the market which can be illustrated by Fig. 5.7.

Figure 5.7 provides us with a schema of the balanced production of the state sector under the conditions of complete price liberalization. It is shown that if there are no dual pricing arrangements, the enterprises of the state sector will no longer face constraints of planned control, which means, in Fig. 5.7, that there is no longer a plan-controlled output, Q_p, which is expressed here with the dotted line. The lifting of planned control means that the state-owned sector is now faced with an entire

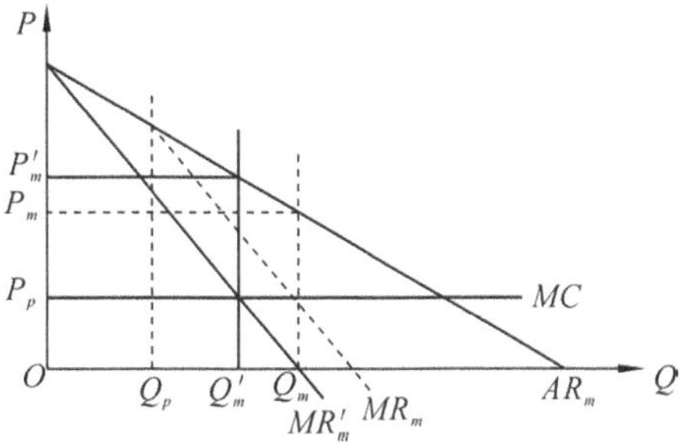

Fig. 5.7 Monopoly of the state sector under the condition of complete liberalization of prices

unified market need, AR_m, instead of two separate "markets". Therefore, its production behavior is regulated now by a unified market demand, and no longer by the demand of the unplanned market (that is, the average income line AR_m on the right side of Q_p). Because in this unified market, the marginal income line of the sector is adjusted to MR'_m from MR_m, it will, seen from Fig. 5.7, reduce the output level to Q'_m to the left according to the marginal principle of profit maximization $MR'_m = MC$, and the output price will rise to P'_m accordingly. This allows us to draw a preliminary conclusion: compared with the equilibrium level (Q_m, P_m) under the two-tier pricing arrangement, a complete price liberalization will probably make the state sector produce less and set a higher prices, i.e., $\left(Q'_m, P'_m\right)$. The mode of production reaction of the state-owned sector is obviously characterized by monopoly. Moreover, from Fig. 5.7 we can also infer that the steeper the demand line MR_m that the state-owned sector faces, namely, the more monopolistic the traditional state-owned industrial sector is, the more significantly its output will decrease and more fiercely its price will rise under the radical reform of complete price liberalization.[18]

The above simple discussion actually raises a very important question, namely, the problem of industrial organization in the transition or the structure of the market. The relationship between the plan and the market is not a simple one characterized by fluctuation and correspondence. The abolition of planned control does not mean the emergence of a competitive market. Our model shows that the way in which planned control is cancelled is critical to the market process of a reformed economy. In this regard, the absolute size of the traditional state-owned sector will undoubtedly become the most important force in the market structure of emerging markets.

Whether a market structure is competitive or monopolistic depends largely on the pricing power of the industry sector on the market. In the early stage of the reform on Chinese industrial sector, the reformers correctly noted that due to the relative shortage of means of production, to impose price control to a certain degree on enterprises that manufacture means of production is necessary to gradually relax the planned distribution and introduce a competitive market structure. The complete liberalization of a huge state-owned sector is tantamount to giving the state sector absolute monopoly power, a problem that is particularly prominent in the early stages of reform. The economic experience of some reforms in Russia and Eastern Europe has proved it.[19]

As a matter of fact, the analysis of the complete price liberalization based on the above model is in agreement with the conclusion of the analysis of other scholars. Some scholars have made analysis of the serious decline in production that could be caused by radical effort such as the complete price liberalization from different perspective. John Ross,[20] for example, compared the huge difference in

[18] For example, in the case of Russia, the production of some important means of production has fallen particularly badly.

[19] Mackinnon made a deep analysis of the consequences of Russia's complete liberalization program. See: McKinnon, R., Gradual versus Rapid Liberalization in Socialist Economies: The Problem of Macroeconomic Control, Proceedings of the World Bank Annual Conference on Development Economics, 1993, the World Bank, 1994.

[20] Ross (1994).

industrial concentration between the centrally planned economy and the Western market economy.[21] He found that in the Soviet Union, Eastern Europe and China, the scale of enterprises in industrial sector is relatively large. In the West, the total number of workers in enterprises with more than 1,000 employees accounts for only 20~33% of all employed workers; even in the most capital intensive industries, such as semiconductor industry, Japan's top five enterprises can only provide 60% of all semiconductor production. In the Soviet Union, the total number of employees in enterprises with more than 1,250 workers accounted for 85% of the total employment, and 30~40% of industrial products was often provided by one enterprise. The size and structure of such an industry are naturally closer to total monopoly which, more importantly, actually existed at the level of production, rather than an institutional monopoly only. Therefore, the privatization of state-owned industrial enterprises itself cannot eliminate the monopoly of state-owned enterprises. On the contrary, the complete price liberalization will provide the state-owned enterprises with the opportunity to control the market and manipulate the pricing power. Ross (1994) wrote in his article, Economic Reform: China's Success and the Failure of Eastern Europe:

> In the system of the Soviet Union, the monopolist (referring to the traditional state sector—note by me) engages in production in order to complete the planned targets and, because they are restricted by the price control, they can only rely on increased output instead of limiting production to increase profits. But, with the transition to 'free market', the best strategy for these monopolists freed from government control is to reduce production and raise prices to maximize profits. In fact, this is the way things are done in Russia and Eastern Europe, which in itself explains their economic decline to a large extent.

Zhou Huizhong also studies the possible monopolistic behavior of the traditional state-owned industrial sector in the transitional economy from the analytical framework of "two-stage game"[22] He constructed a "two-stage game" model in a paper entitled Behavior of State Enterprise in a Hybrid Economy with Imperfect Market. In the first stage, because of the lifting of central planning control, the traditional state sector will use political leverage to engage in non productive activities to influence and gain market power. In the second stage, when the state-owned sector faces market competition, they will use their market power to manipulate the market and increase profits by cutting production as monopolists do. Therefore, the downward trend in production in the transitional economy can be explained by the manipulation of the market by the state sector and the monopolistic forces. He wrote:

> We find that if the state-owned sector is fairly large.... competition pressure from the private sector is insignificant to the market power of state-owned enterprises. Specifically, although private firms will increase output when state-owned enterprises cut theirs, the overall output of a weak private sector is negligible. Therefore, by cutting output, state-owned enterprises can significantly reduce the total supply and increase the market price accordingly to increase profits. This market manipulation can help explain why there appeared a continuous and in

[21] Thanks to Dr. J. Donnely of Washington State University for providing me with this document.

[22] I would like to express my gratitude to Dr. Zhou Huizhong for offering me his paper. See Zhou, H., Behavior of State Enterprise in a Hybrid Economy with Imperfect Market, *Economic Systems*, 1994, 18 (1).

some cases even serious shortage under the centrally planned economy during the market-oriented reform period. Now, if the decrease in output actually increases their profits, the SOEs will excessively engage in unproductive activities. As a result, one can observe a large number of influencing activities in the early stages of the transition period, some of which are even illegal.

The above theoretical research done by scholars is consistent in logic with mine in this article, for we are all using monopoly theory to explain the possible behavior that the state sector may exhibit in economic transition, although the research methods we use are not exactly the same. Strictly speaking, the decline of industrial production in a transitional economy may be caused by many factors, and the monopoly of the state sector may be just one of them. But the model developed here combines the mode of reform with the emergence of monopolies. Our logic is that the production decline and economic recession in early transitional period can be explained by the state-owned sector monopoly which, in turn, has been interpreted as a rational response of state-owned enterprises under the condition of complete liberalization of prices. The model of this paper proves that under the dual price system, the state-owned sector will produce more and set a lower price than under the complete liberalization of price. In fact, this conclusion tells us that in the context of thorough price liberalization reform, the production decline is the rational micro-reaction of the state sector to the changes of external conditions (as shown in Fig. 5.8), rather than the consequences of bankruptcy or closure of a large number of enterprises caused by industrial restructuring of the state sector in the transition period. In other words, if our conclusion is correct, it means that for an economy undergoing radical reform, its production decline should mainly be explained by the monopoly of the state sector and not by the bankruptcy and large-scale closure of state-owned enterprises. Therefore, it is possible for us to test this "monopoly hypothesis" from experience.

According to the information we have, the experience of Poland in the wake of implementing the "shock therapy" provides a good example of this "monopoly hypothesis". In the early 1990, a radical reform strategy was implemented by the Solidarity Union-controlled government to transition to the market economy. Similar to other countries in Eastern Europe and the Soviet Union, Poland's "shock therapy" or the reform package includes the following aspects: complete price liberalization

Fig. 5.8 Rational response of state sector to macroeconomic stability plan

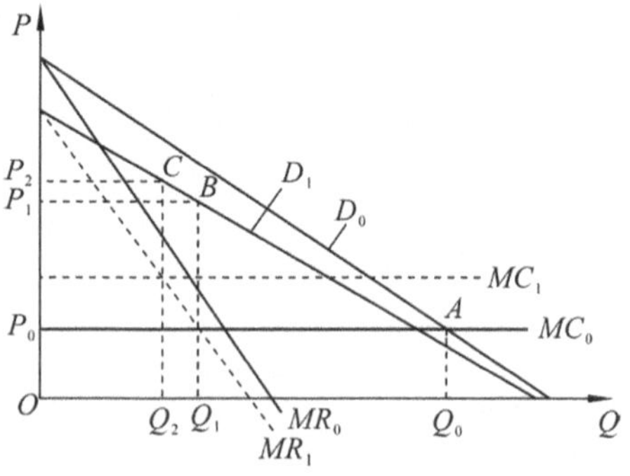

and privatization, rapid cuts or suspension of government subsidies, free trade, free currency convertibility, wage control, budget balance and substantial cuts of soft loans provided by government to state owned enterprises. However, in the first two years following the implementation of the "shock therapy, Poland's economy was in deep recession. Compared with 1989, GDP fell by 11% in 1990, industrial production dropped by 35%, and investment spending by 10%. In 1991, there was hardly any large-scale bankruptcy and closure of enterprises in Poland.

According to data provided by the Central Planning Office (CPO) in Poland, from 1990 to 1991, only 18 state-owned enterprises, which accounted for about 0.2% of the total number of enterprises of their kind, began to enter bankruptcy proceedings. This shows that the industrial production decline and economic recession after the "Big Bang" reform in Poland were not mainly caused by the large-scale bankruptcy and closure of state-owned enterprises. However, how should we explain production decline of Poland's industrial sector under the conditions of the price liberalization? In fact, Dutch economists Zajicek and Heisler[23] made an analysis similar to ours in their article titled Economic Transformation in Eastern Europe: The Case of Poland-Comment.[24] They point out:

> "These results (referring to the recession and hyperinflation in Poland after the implementation of shock therapy—note by me) can be easily explained by economic theory. The response of highly monopolistic state sector to these reform measures is a classic example of a monopolist's reaction to free prices and the high tax burden on inputs found in textbooks: industrial output decreased while price level increased. The decline in industrial output is not due to the bankruptcy of enterprises or large-scale closure of a series of workshops—these can be caused largely by economic restructuring—but due to a rational microeconomic response of enterprises to the changes of the macroeconomic environment."

We can use the simple analytical schema we developed previously to explain the monopolistic production behavior of the state-owned sector under the condition of the complete liberalization of prices and the high tax burden on enterprise inputs. Let us copy the previous analytical schema in Fig. 5.7 into Fig. 5.8. According to the analysis of Zajicek and Heisler, due to the impact of imports, the state sector, as a monopolist, will face a shrinking and more elastic market demand curve is (D_1 in Fig. 5.8). But even so, the state sector does not need to increase output. The reasons are twofold. First, because of the stable reform program of the macro-economy, the price was fully liberalized, so the pricing power of the state-owned sector was granted. At this time, the state-owned sector will reduce output to maintain maximum profit at the equilibrium price level (shown in the figure as moving from A to B). Second, in addition to the change in the demand structure, the state-owned sector has to face a very severe wage fund progressive tax under the macro stable scheme, which is paid by the enterprise's profits. This tax structure significantly distorts the cost structure of the state sector and greatly increases the variable cost of production, shown in Fig. 5.8 as the marginal cost MC_0 curve moving upward. The joint effects

---

[23] Zajicek and Heisler (1995).

[24] From the title of their paper, it is clear that the author is clearly commenting and discussing Sachs'article, The Economic Transformation of Eastern Europe: The Case of Poland.

of these two aspects make the state-owned sector still play the role of monopoly even in the face of import competition. As a result, the production balance shifts to the *C* point and even moves further to the left.

Our microeconomic analysis of the monopoly model of the traditional state sector under the radical reform has clearly questioned or challenged the basic hypothesis of radical reform theory. While advocating "shock therapy" approach to reform, Western advisers to the Soviet Union and Eastern European countries deeply believed that relying solely on the strength of emerging markets will change an economy under reform from the traditional planning mode to a market model in a very short period of time. In the words of Sachs and Lipton, "shock therapy" will quickly creates domestic competition and a realistic price structure similar to that of Western Europe.[25]

In a word, the theory of radical reform is logically considered to have an advantage similar to neo-classical economics. According to this logic, a planned economy, as long as it quickly adopts the privatization program, completely removes control over price, allows trade liberalization, substantially reduces or suspends financial subsidies to enterprises, allows free exchange of currencies and relies on a price mechanism and competition, will automatically evolve into a competitive market structure. In this market, the supply and production will increase and, under the conditions of such a competitive market, Darwin's "survival of the fittest" (the so-called "positive elimination") mechanism will enable efficient enterprise survive in the market and inefficient ones be expelled from the market, finally realizing the reorganization of a planned economy to a market economy by relying on market forces.

Such a reform theory ignores many important features of the transitional economy, especially its excessive underestimation of the significance of the transition time in the process of economic transformation. In regard to the way of reform, although you can choose a radical strategy and quickly put reform policy in place, the institutional change is generally gradual and a substantial time is needed to allow a system to take shape and become effective. If we look at and analyze the theory of radical reform from the microeconomic perspective, it would not difficult to see why an economy undergoing reform will inevitably experience a "L"-shaped growth curve at the beginning of the transition. Even if the "J" growth appeared in such an economy in the end, we think the price of "L" in return for "J" is too costly. Isn't this price unavoidable?

We study transitional economics in order to search for a path that will minimize the cost of transition. A comparative study of the theory of progressive reform and the theory of shock therapy or radical reform is also based on the concept of transitional costs. Many people believe that such a comparative study may be meaningless, because a country faces many constraints in the choice of reform modes such as knowledge, initial economic conditions and the political factors. In our view, this view exaggerates the power of these constraints. Any country will consider the constrained conditions in its choice of the way of reform.

However, constraints are not absolute factors. In fact, for the centrally planned economy, their economic system, production system structure, industry structure

---

[25] Lipton and Sachs (1990).

and the rational behavior of microcosmic agent all follow the same or similar logic. These "commonalities" alone are enough to guarantee the significance of studying different ways of reform and seeking a universal transitional strategy. Now, let's make a brief comment on Sachs' arguments on the two years of economic transformation in Poland.

Sachs, in his Economic Transformation in Eastern Europe: The Case of Poland, expresses view that the experience of Poland in the wake of "shock therapy" seems to indicate that "shock therapy" also needs time and patience. Radical reform will also have a positive effect if only sufficient time is given to the new system.[26] In theory, the real problem of shock therapy, as a form of reform, is not whether it will work, but whether it will work faster than the gradual change. Many, including Sachs himself, have to admit that under the condition of market monopoly by the traditional state-owned sector, the entry of emerging enterprises did not really happen. On the other hand, Poland did see the emergence of new sectors entering the market, but most of them were engaged in retail business and trade, having an obvious speculative nature. People engaged themselves in foreign exchange, tobacco and even sale of cars, with the result that the accumulation of personal wealth did not create new production capacity but was used for the import of luxury consumption (Zajicek & Heisler, 1995). Although you may say that the emergence of these non-productive sectors is a rebound to the original repressed sectors, thus having a positive effect, the productive segments (including the oppressed light industry, food industry and production industry) failed to get a real expansion and competition in the market, which in any case is a "falsification" of the "shock therapy".

5.7 Conclusion

On the basis of differentiating the different price liberalization schemes, this paper attempts to analyze the path and characteristics of China's industrial reform from the angle of microeconomics or industrial organization theory and emphasize, through the establishment of an analytical model, the theoretical significance of the dual pricing arrangement in China's industrial economic growth after the reform. In the analysis, this paper first emphasizes the difference of the methods of the reform in order to understand the significance of different reform paths and reform results. Secondly, the analysis shows that the dual pricing arrangement, as a partial price liberalization plan, can lead to the growth of state-owned enterprises' production. Finally, through the establishment of a simple "dominant sector-competitive fringe" analysis model, the article also discusses the production reaction of the state sector under the dual system as well as the effect of entry of the non-state sector and the competitive market structure, which, to a certain extent, have explained why Chinese industrial reform can maintain a output growth pattern in a longer period of time from the angle of industrial organization.

[26] Sachs (1992).

In explaining the different results of economic transition in China and Russia (as well as Eastern Europe), previous studies often show the following characteristics: in the interpretation of Russia's economic recession, some scholars tend to find the reasons in the state sector attributing the economic recession, especially serous industrial production decline, to excessive regulation on the traditional state-owned sector in the economy in transition (the gradual reform period) and to the monopoly gained (radical reform period); in the interpretation of economic growth of China after the reform, they turn their attention to the non-state sector, and try to explain what makes the non-state-owned sector grow. The difference between our theoretical analysis and the previous literature is that, while dealing with the growth of China's industrial production during the transition period, our attention and research focus are placed on the traditional, state-owned sector. In fact, the question I am trying to ask is why China's state-owned industrial sector can sustain the growth of production during the transition period. The theoretical models of this paper have, on a large degree, answered this question.

Although my analysis is focused only on the state-owned industrial sector, in general, the theory of this article supports the guiding ideology and strategic choice of Chinese economic reform to a great extent, because the path of industrial reform inherited the dual track strategy of agricultural reform started earlier, i.e. while continuing to maintain the control of the plan, the liberalization reform outside the plan is also actively promoted. To sum up, the theoretical analysis of this article contains the following implications of the gradual reform in China.

First, in the early stages of economic reform, in order to maintain the post-reform economic growth, it is necessary to continue maintaining the traditional planned control system instead of rapidly eliminating it. To borrow a famous sentence from Shakespeare's play *Hamlet*, "to be or not to be, this is a question" can be said about the planning controlled system in the early stages of reform.

Second, actively promoting the liberalization reform at outer boundary of the plan while continuing to retain planning control in the traditional state-owned sector is not only helpful to maintain growth and gradually pass the whole economy to the market, but also costs less.

Third, it has been proved that allowing the state-owned economy to face the growth of competitive power on the unplanned border instead of the border of the ownership is more conducive to the growth of production than putting the entire sector on a purely commercial basis.

Fourth, the experience of "boundary reform" featuring dual track system shows is that it s faster for the state-owned sector to seize profit opportunities by responding to price signals at the unplanned border than for privatized state-owned sector to respond to economic distortions and shortage. The theoretical analysis of this paper at least illustrates that all of these have played a very important role in the performance of Chinese economy in the initial stage of transition.

Author's Notes

Under the framework of a simple two-sector industrial organization, this paper discusses how the dual track reform strategy has helped to achieve the growth of total industrial output. The framework of this analysis is consistent with the article Starting Point and Path of Reform: A Feasible Simulation. Unlike the latter which discusses general theories, though, this article mainly explains China's experience and practice. It is the contribution of this paper to have integrated the experience of China's industrial reform into the analytical framework of "dual price system" and "dominant firm-border competition".

This article was probably written in the second half of 1995. At that time I was writing the book, *Dual-Track Economics: Economic Reform in China 1978–1992* (Shanghai SDX Joint Company and Shanghai People's Publishing House, 1997 edition), so I revised the article and included it in the book. Since the publication of the article was considered to be too long, I cut it short and had it published in the 3nd issue of the *Economist*, 1996 under the title of Why China's Gradual Reform Was Successful? Therefore, the original version of this article has not been formally published. The inclusion of it in this book has finally had my wish fulfilled.

References

(Hungary) Kornai: Dual Reliance of State-Owned Enterprises-Hungarian Experience, in Economic Studies, 1985 (10).

Jefferson, Rawski: China Industry's Internal Innovation, Competition and Property Rights Reform Model, in Chinese Industrial Economic Research, 1994 (8).

Lin Yifu, Cai Chuang, Li Zhou: Chinese Miracle: Development Strategy and Economic Reform, Chinese Center for Economic Research of Peking University, working paper, 1994.

Lipton, D., Sachs, J., Creating a Market Economy in Eastern Europe: the Case of Poland, Brookings Institute Papers on Economic, Activity, 1990, 1.

Marx: Das Kapital, vol. one, Beijing, People's Press, 1975.

Naughton, B., Chinese Institutional Innovation and Privatization from Below, American Economic Review, 1994, 84 (2), p.266.

Naughton, B., Growing out of the Plan: Chinese Economic Reform 1978–1993, Cambridge University Press, New York, 1994.Rawski, T., Chinese Industrial Reform: Accomplishments, Prospects, and Implications, American Economic Review, 1994, 84 (2).

Naughton, B., What Is Distinctive about China's Economic Transition? State Enterprise Reform and Overall System Transformation, Journal of Comparative Economics, 1994, 18.

Nee (1992) Discussed the relation between township enterprise and local government in detail. See Nee, V., Organizational Dynamics of Market Transition: Hybrid Forms, Property Rights, and Mixed Economy in China, Administrative Science Quarterly, 1992, 37 (1).

Nee. V., Organizational Dynamics of Market Transition: Hybrid Forms, Property Rights, and Mixed Economy in China, Administrative Science Quarterly, 1992, 37 (1)

Ross, J., Economic Reform: Success in China and Failure in Eastern Europe, Monthly Review, 1994, 5.

Sachs, J., The Economic Transformation of Eastern Europe: The Case of Poland, The American Economist, 1992, 36 (2)

The Whiting, S., Contract Incentives and Market Discipline in China s Rural Industrial Sector, Paper Presented at Conference on the Evolution of Market Institutions in Transition Economies, University of California, 1993.

Weitzman, M., Xu, C., Chinese Township Village Enterprises as Vaguely Defined Cooperatives, Journal of Comparative Economics, 1994, 18.

Zajicek, E., Heisler, J., The Economic Transformation of Eastern Europe: The Case of Poland-Comment, The American Economist, 1995, 39 (1)

Zhou Zhenhua: Cultivate the Main Body of the Market Economy: Development of Non-State Economy and Reform of State-Owned Economy, in Fang Gang, Li Yang, Zhou Zhenhua: Toward Market (1978-1993), Shanghai, Shanghai people's Publishing House, 1994.

Part III
Industrial Reform

Chapter 6
Technology, Classification of Scale and Industrial Organization: Why Can China's "Large Enterprises" Make Higher Profit Margins?

6.1 Introduction

In the past several decades, economists made a lot of research on the Chinese industrial reform and changing patterns of productivity with the purpose of better understanding the impact of reform policy on improving the performance Chinese industry.[1] At the same time, we have also noted that the relatively high productivity and profitability of large enterprises are becoming the special focus recently in these research literatures.[2] Indeed, since the industrial transition, although the profitability of the state-owned sector has been significantly lower than that of the non-state sector, large enterprises (mostly state-owned enterprises) performed slightly better if the profitability is broken down by scale. The existing studies often interpret this observation as the "scale economy". This could be attributed to the government's "good treatment" for big enterprises, and the result of it.

However, it is still not clear whether we should attribute the slightly better profitability performance of large enterprises in the transition period to the government's

[1] Zhang and Shi (2003) made a systematic and analytical review of the empirical research literatures on the change of efficiency of China's state-owned industry in the post-reform period. Moreover, Keijiro Otsukam, Li Deqiang and Murakami also did a review on these research literatures in their latest work, on the basis of which, they revised many existing research conclusions and conducted an in-depth analysis of the efficiency differences between state-owned and non state-owned enterprises by using more detailed methods and direct survey data.. In addition, recent studies on the performance of state-owned enterprises in China also include *Reform of State-Owned Enterprises of China* compiled by Jefferson and Xin Ge.

[2] For example, Jefferson (1990)'s research on China's iron and steel industry is probably the earlier literature on economies of scale. The related literature later on include Cao (1994)'s research on iron and steel enterprises, Lo (1999)'s study on the overall state sector, as well as research done by. Murakami and others (1996) and Zhang (1997).

J. Zhang, *Reform, Transformation and Growth*, Understanding China,
https://doi.org/10.1007/978-981-99-5712-5_6

favorable policy, the institutional reform of industrial enterprises and rational evolution of industrial organizations or to other aspects. From the existing research literatures, there are three basic related viewpoints: first, The improvement of the profitability ability of large enterprises is the result of organizational innovations that China has undergone since the reform, and a source of improving the efficiency of Chinese industry and corporate competitiveness (Nolan 1996); second, the excellent performance of large enterprises reflects the effect of industrial policy and the rational evolution of market organization since the transition (Lo 1999); third, the higher profit rate of large enterprises indicates that the state-owned enterprises have a comparative advantage in the segments with remarkable economies of scale (Perkins 1994[3]; Naughton 1995[4]).

The scholars who hold the first view think that it is an important strategy for China's industrial reform and development to set up internationally competitive large enterprises and corporate groups (so-called organizational innovation). The implementation of this strategy has gradually enabled large enterprises to focus on the upstream sector, thus realizing the industrialization model of balanced development between heavy and light industries. However, this view of organizational innovation is clearly problematic, because the operational effect of a corporate group with a strong government backing is obviously exaggerated. More importantly, this argument relies more on the description of experience, lacking a formal theoretical framework and a careful empirical examination.

The second view concerns the debate over the choice of technology and the structure of factors in the Chinese state sector. It is generally believed that because the technology choice of state-owned sector was out of the need of the "catching-up strategy" since the 50s, the capital/labor ratio of the state sector in China has excessively deviated from the natural essential factor structure. This is considered to be the main reason of the lack of competitiveness and profitability of the state sector since the reform and opening up.[5] Like the debates involving development economics, One possible challenge to this kind of "comparative advantage" hypothesis completely based on "natural factors" comes from the formation of economies of scale that hedges against the artificially distorted structure of factors. Therefore, in the view of economists of "post-developing school", or at least partially proved by the experience of East Asia, if the natural structure of artificially distorted factors can breed "economies of scale" of the industry and other dynamic efficiency, then the productivity and profitability of an enterprise will probably increase rather than worsen.[6]

---

[3] Perkins (1994).

[4] Naughton (1995).

[5] Lin et al. (1994, 1997).

[6] The research in this field is very rich in the literatures of development economics. See the review of literatures provided by Lo (1995). Topic studies on countries are mainly targeted at South Korea, because from the 60s to 80s, economic development strategy in South Korea is typical of the "catching-up strategy"—the government's industrial and trade policies, to a great extent, were aimed at "natural" ratio of twisted factors and changing the given "comparative advantage" so as to achieve "competitive advantage" through creating the scale economy.

The third view is that the non state-owned enterprises not only entered the small business sector and showed remarkable profitability there, but also gradually made the state-owned sector enterprises concentrated on capital intensive large sectors with increasing returns to scale. Such observations are often implicit in many qualitative theoretical discussions. But Perkins (1994, p. 43) has made this implicit argument explicit. He noted, "Some people think that the state-owned sector will end up in failure because of the competition from the flexible township and local enterprises. But this is unlikely to happen. Economies of scale in iron and steel, automobile, petrochemical, railway and electric power will ensure that large enterprises will continue to exist." The implication is clear: the existence of economies of scale will probably maintain the division and coexistence of enterprises with different ownerships for a considerable length of time in China.[7] It is obvious that if the argument of scale economy can be established, the coexistence of state-owned and non state-owned systems is not entirely due to ideological reasons, but may be purely the outcome to meet the requirement of economic efficiency.

However, a further problem is that not only the proof of existence of economies of scale is often unreliable in experience, but more importantly, the existing literatures have not given a clear reason as to whether large firms may achieve economies of scale. The conclusion of most empirical research is that large enterprises have higher "technical efficiency" than small- and medium-enterprises, but there is no research on the possible factors that lead to the difference of technical efficiency. We think it indiscreet to simply attribute the result to the realization of economies of scale. For this conclusion, we can actually have different interpretations, such as the degree of access to capital and the difference in technical levels. In this article, we will explain why some existing studies have found that large enterprises tend to be more "technical efficient" than small- and medium-enterprises.

As for economies of scale, we believe that its realization should be a result of significant changes in industrial organizations. However, there is not enough evidence to suggest that significant changes have taken place in the industrial structure of China's economy since the reform. For example, the third national industrial census data show that there is still a positive correlation between the average size of enterprises and the levels of government the state-owned enterprises are affiliated to.[8] A possible explanation of this organizational characteristics is that the scale of the enterprise still seems to be decided by the degree of closeness to capital rather than the differences in productivity, because the government at higher levels often means that it is easier to gain capital (this fully reveals that the capital market is highly incomplete). Moreover, a great deal of empirical observations show that, even in

[7] In a fairly long period of time, many economists in China have also linked the economies of scale with the ownership system. One version is that in the so-called "natural monopoly" industries with remarkable economies of scale, the state ownership of enterprises should be kept unchanged. However, there is a great deal of disagreements among economists about the fate of state-owned enterprises in competitive industries. Some propose that state-owned enterprises should "withdraw partially", allowing coexistence of a variety of ownerships while others argue that state-owned enterprises should "completely withdraw" from the competitive industries.

[8] The Third National Industrial Census Office (1997).

many capital intensive manufacturing sectors, industrial organizations still exhibit a high degree of production diversification and differentiation of productivity levels.

Based on the above considerations, we believe that the existing literatures' attempt to understand China's large state-owned enterprises from the perspective of economies of scale is problematic. In theory, the profitability of enterprises can be improved by the reasonable change of industrial organization structure (such as integration or decentralization of production), or maybe purely as the result of technological innovation. Since the vast majority of large enterprises are state-owned ones, we cannot expect them to make a difference in technological innovation (R&D). We believe that in the economic transition in China, the structure of industrial organization, decided by the property ownership, often typically exhibits a relatively "sticky" nature, for even vertically integrated large enterprises in industrial sectors with increasing returns to scale are often unable to fully realize the integration of production to improve their profitability. Therefore, there is no sufficient reason to use scale economy to explain the better profitability capability of large enterprises displayed on statistics.

Not only that, generally speaking, because capital is more expensive than labor based on the theory of the technological choices in economics, the profitability of large enterprises in developing economy with a relatively high rate of capital equipment will inevitably deteriorate because of the higher cost and their capital productivity is often lower than that of small- and medium-sized enterprises. Therefore, there should be other reasons for the higher profit margins generally displayed by "large enterprises". As we have found in this article, the reason may actually be that the way the "large enterprise" is defined statistically has created a higher profit margin for "large enterprises".

The structure of this paper is as follows: in the second part, we will make a brief review and comment of the existing research literature and put forward the need for further studies. In the third part, we will briefly describe the present situation and characteristics of the industrial organization structure of China's economy since the reform. The fourth part will provide an enlightening conceptual framework. In the fifth part, we will explain the main reason why the technical efficiency of large enterprises is slightly higher than that of small and medium-sized enterprises, and analyze the different mechanisms through which technological efficiency has been improved under different scales of enterprises. In the sixth part we will discuss once more the question of scale economy. We did a general empirical analysis of whether we can confirm the presence of economies of scale by using the scale classification data of 1990–1991 of 40 industrial sectors classified by their fixed assets and labor scale provided by the *Statistical Yearbook of Chinese Industrial Economy*.[9] Then, in the seventh section, we will give a possible explanation of why the profitability of large business sector is statistically higher than that of small and medium enterprises. The final part is the main conclusion of this paper.

[9] National Bureau of Statistics (1992, 1994).

6.2 Literature Review and Comments

China's industrial reform has had a profound impact on the profitability of the state-owned industrial sector. Official statistics show that, first, since the reform, profits rate of the state-owned sector has shown a downward trend and even worsened since the 1990s; second, the proportion and amount of losses of state-owned enterprises in the aftermath of the 1980s declined but increased sharply in late 80s.[10] Thus, early literature was mainly focused on: ① to explain the decline of the state-owned sector's profit margins in general[11]; ② to give an in-depth analysis and empirical test of the growth of non state-owned sector's profitability and relative efficiency. In the opinion of most economists, constrained by traditional institutions, the efficiency of state-owned sector is not worth mentioning even if it improved somewhat since the reform, the efficiency and profitability of state-owned enterprises have been and continue to be surpassed by non state-owned enterprises, the economic reform and industrial transition will make state-owned enterprises (especially large and medium sized enterprises) lose their competitive ability and gradually replaced by small and medium-sized non-state-owned dynamic enterprises.[12] In China, the rapid expansion of the non state sector and its contribution to China's post reform economic growth seem to be in line with the expectations of mainstream economists.

But further observation makes the above problem seem complicated. As shown in Fig. 6.1, since the reform, the statistics show that the large enterprises are slightly better in its profitability than small and medium-sized enterprises The profit margins of large enterprises (mostly state-owned enterprises) are not only higher than the average profit margins of all industrial sectors, but no less than that of the collective sector. Compared with the small and medium enterprises, large enterprises also maintained a high level of profitability and, the profit rate gap between large enterprises and small- and medium-sized enterprises gradually widened at the end of the 1980s. In addition, some empirical research confirming the excellent performance of large state-owned enterprises in recent years also found that within the state-owned sector, the profitability of large enterprises is not weaker than that of the non state-owned enterprise sector (Lo 1999).

Indeed, the relative performance of China's large enterprises has puzzled us since the reform. For most economists, the performance of large enterprises is often inferior to that of small- and medium-sized enterprises in less developed economies, This is mainly because most large enterprises are the product of the traditional "catch-up" development strategy. Under the traditional development strategy, they chose

[10] Jun Zhang offered a logically consistent explanation of the changing loss patterns of the state-owned sector in China since the reform, see Zhang (1998, 2000).

[11] Early studies of the changing patterns of the profitability of the state sector can be found in Naughton (1995). Also, Lo (2000) provided a review and comments on the existing research literatures. Zhang (2001) made further revisions to the existing explanations of the decline in the profitability of the state sector and proposed an explanation more consistent with empirical observation, see Zhang (2001).

[12] Otsuka et al. (2000).

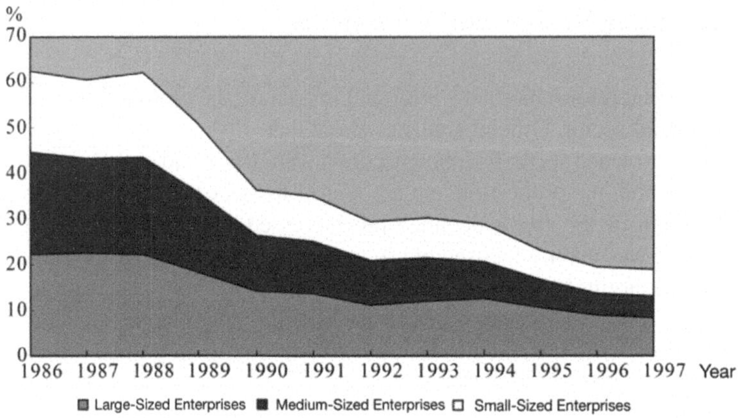

Fig. 6.1 Differences in profit margins between large and small and medium-sized enterprises (1986–1997)

technology type not suitable for them, and their excessive capital intensity did not conform to the overall economic comparative advantage (Lin et al. 1997; Otsuka et al. 1998[13]). Therefore, after the economic transition, the profitability of large enterprises is expected to deteriorate rather than improve in the latter part of the reform.

With regard to the higher profitability of China's large enterprises, one potential explanation may be that large state-owned enterprises are still the firms of monopoly in the product market, and its relatively good profit margins are only a kind of monopoly rents. However, this explanation does not agree with empirical observations because the existence of monopolies should be accompanied by a production decline of these sectors rather than an increase. In fact, the study found that industries dominated by state-owned sector almost all grew fastest in terms of output since the reform,[14] Not only that, large enterprises, in terms of pricing, may actually be subject to more institutional constraints than small- and medium-sized enterprises.[15]

Another possible explanation is that since the industrial transition, large enterprises have gradually shown their scale advantages. Although a lot of studies seem to confirm that there may exist the so-called scale economy in some of the industrial sectors in China (for example, Jefferson 1990; Cao 1994), this conclusion was often reached in the absence of controlling other variables that affect the production efficiency of large enterprises. Therefore, we can have different ways to explain the fact that the technical efficiency of large enterprises is higher than that of the small- and medium-sized enterprises. We insist that economies of scale is a problem that must be understood from the point of view of changes in industrial organizations, yet the "stickiness" of the structure of Chinese industrial organizations seems to be a well-known phenomenon. Therefore, it is not enough to prove the existence of

[13] Otsuka et al. (1998).

[14] Jiang (1999).

[15] Cao (1994).

economies of scale by simply discovering the higher technical efficiency of large enterprises.

On the contrary, some research on machine tools and steel industries even revealed the scale of large enterprises is uneconomical (Murakami et al. 1996, Otsuka et al., Chinese version, 2000). They think that in accordance with the standards of the division of labor theory (Arrow 1951), the concept of scale economy should be the result of high degree of (horizontal) specialization and a deepening division of labor but, under the planned economy system, the state-owned sector has not developed a system of high division of labor and professional cooperation. Moreover, the state-owned enterprises (especially large enterprises) tend to evolve into a typically vertical and integrated organizational structure.[16] It is often the case that some large state-owned enterprises not only produce the final product, but also the spare parts and intermediate products, so their scale is relatively large and their capital intensive. When the division of labor is restricted, the vertical integrated structure of large state-owned enterprises often leads to insufficient utilization of production capacity and inadequate utilization of resources. Therefore, it seems that the scale of state-owned enterprises is not economical instead of economies of scale. The problem with these documents, however, is that they have not provided a theoretical explanation for the higher profitability shown by large firms.

At the same time, some studies on the positive evaluation of China's large state-owned enterprises have a strong "development" bias. For example, some scholars pointed out that since the reform, the national policy quickly shifted the focus to activities that other forms of ownership cannot carry out, which include natural monopoly and industries related to energy and basic means of production where large state-owned enterprises occupy the absolute share (Nolan 1996). They noted: "Heavy industry products usually require greater amount of capital per unit of output, more factories, more skills rather than entrepreneurial ability (e.g., marketing, product selection, distribution capacity), and longer digestion period than light industry. In the uncertain environment of the transition economy, it is very important that the state should play a central role in these sectors. The relation between segments has shifted from unbalanced heavy industry growth to balanced growth mode instead of emphasizing light industry and ignoring heavy industry." (Nolan and Wang 1999).

At the same time, the usual explanation in these documents for the economies of scale that the large enterprises may have depends largely on their views on the East Asian capitalist industrial policy that China's industrial transition is following. In their view, similar to the East Asian model, the development of the market and the government's implementation of industrial development strategies and industrial organization policies have helped large enterprises achieve the economies of scale (Lo 1999).

---

[16] In China, this vertically integrated structure is commonly known as "big or small, it is all inclusive". Of course, in fact, this kind of structure is still typical of state-owned large enterprises. We have carried on a thorough analysis of the shaping logic of this structure of the state-owned enterprises under the planned economy system. See Zhang (1992).

Thus, there are actually two entirely different views in the existing literature. A mainstream view holds that, during the Chinese industrial transition, state-owned enterprises will gradually be replaced by more efficient small- and medium-sized non state-owned enterprises, which is the inevitable result of market oriented economy and the change from the import substitution strategy to the development strategy of comparative advantage. Another defensive view insists that since the government has adhered to the balanced development strategy, the large state-owned enterprises will continue to exist at least in industrial sectors with significant economies of scale (especially the "upstream" sector and heavy industry) (Perkins 1994; Naughton 1995).

6.3 An Enlightening Conceptual Framework

In this section, we will use a simple analytical schema to illustrate our ideas for explaining the profitability and its changes in the transition from a planned economy to a market economy. Our basic ideas stem from our empirical observations of industrial organizations in the state-owned sector. First of all, we know that large state-owned enterprises usually have a significant vertically integrated structure. The typical case is that they not only produce the final product, but also produce intermediate products and components.[17] Second, we believe that the vertically integrated structure may be a response of state-owned enterprises to the high uncertainty of products and factor markets, or the inherent requirement of the increasing returns to scale of the sector. Finally, the process of industrial transformation has led to the entry and expansion of non-state-owned enterprises.

The basic logic is that if the high transaction cost caused by uncertainty tends to encourage enterprises to favor the vertical integration in industrial production, then the original uncertainty will decline sharply with the expansion of the scale of market exchange after the reform. This result should be manifested in the improvement of division of labor and expansion among enterprises, and the improvement of specialization of production. In this sense, the decentralization of production should gradually improve the profitability of enterprises. On the other hand, in a sector with potential economies of scale, the production integration of an enterprise can save costs, so the improvement of enterprise's profitability should depend on the centralization rather than the scattering of production. However, it is important that no matter what kind of situation and experience happens, the fragmented and centralized of production demonstrates significant changes in present industrial organization structure: expansion of division of labor will gradually make the enterprise become more

[17] For example, the state-owned iron and steel enterprises not only produce steel, but also iron ore, pig iron and steel. Large state-owned machine tool enterprises not only produce machine tools, but also machine tool parts. The state-owned chemical enterprises not only produce chemical raw materials, but also chemical consumer goods. State-owned TV enterprises not only produce TV sets, but also supporting equipment and intermediate products such as picture tubes. We rarely see highly specialized manufacturers producing only one product among large state-owned enterprises.

and more specialized and its scale smaller; while the centralized production will make an enterprise highly integrated, thus the enterprise tends to expand its scale.

Unfortunately, we do not seem to have any strong evidence that China's industrial organizations are experiencing such changes. On the contrary, what we do see is that in most labor intensive industries, the division of labor and development of specialization are quite slow. In fact, there are still many large and medium-sized enterprises in these sectors. On the other hand, in most capital intensive industrial sectors with potential economies of scale, production is rather fragmented. A typical situation is that in the manufacturing sector, there often appears an industrial organization pattern where enterprises of different ownerships and sizes coexist. For example, in the automotive industry, state-owned large enterprises, SMEs as well as enterprises of collective ownership exist together. But it is worth noting that almost all of the enterprises produce complete vehicles, which not only failed to develop an effective system of division of labor and specialization cooperation among enterprises, nor a highly concentrated production (Marukawa 1995). This is probably the most remarkable institutional feature left in the industrial organization since the industrial transition. This feature partly reflects the multi ownership property rights structure of China's state-owned industrial sector before the reform,[18] as well as the result of a highly imperfect factor market (especially the capital market) in the industrial transition period. In this article, we characterize this feature of organization as the structural "stickiness" of industrial organization.

The above basic empirical observation has important implications for us to discuss the profitability of large enterprises during the industrial transition period. In theory, the capability of an enterprise for making profit depends on the following factors: ① the size of the market or the nature of the demand; ② the structure of the industrial organization (decentralization or centralization of production); ③ the shape of the unit cost curve. In order to make it clearer, we will illustrate our basic ideas with Fig. 6.2. In this figure, we use horizontal n to indicate the degree of diversification of production, so the movement towards the original point can be interpreted as integration of production. Considering the universality of the problem, we divide the manufacturing sector into two parts: increasing returns to scale and diminishing returns to scale. The nature of the sector's remuneration is reflected in the unit cost curve of the enterprise, pc. Besides, just as we have emphasized, let us assume that the structure of industrial organizations in each sector is "sticky" and that large enterprises exist in every sector. Finally, assume the price is given by pp.

First of all, let us look at the sector with increasing returns to scale as shown in Fig. 6.2a. We move the production cost of pc of an enterprise upward, which reflects the "scale effect" of production integration on the unit cost of an enterprise. We then define the difference between the price pp and the unit cost pc as the profit margin which, in Fig. 6.2a, can be obtained by the "vertical subtraction" of price

[18] Granick (1990) made an in-depth analysis of this structure of property rights, see Granick (1990). Qian and Xu (1993a and b) further treated this structure as a "M-type" structure and believed that the existence of such a structure became a good starting point for the rapid entry and expansion of the non-state sector after the reform.

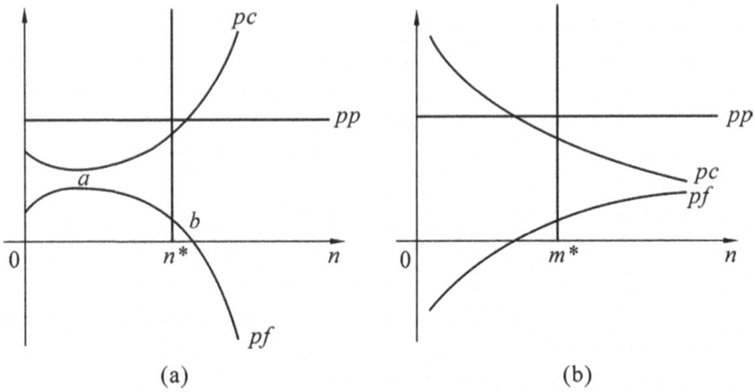

Fig. 6.2 Analytical figure of the change of industrial organization and profitability of enterprise

line pp and cost curve pc (i.e. curve pf). If the production of a sector is integrated into a large enterprise, the unit cost will reach the lowest point (point a), and the profit margin will be maximized. This means that the integration of production will be more economical than scattered production. Here, we present the meaning of economies of scale which refers to the cost saving effect produced by the change (integration) of industrial organizations. Therefore, in order to achieve a full scale economy, changes in industrial organizations should be shifted along the horizontal axis to the left. However, according to our assumptions, the industrial organization structure in this sector is sticky (given by point n^*) which means that the profit margin of large enterprise is on point b, thus profitability has not been fully realized.

As far as a sector of decreasing returns to scale is concerned, the unit cost curve pc of large enterprises should slope downward, which makes its profit margin curve pf thrust upward, see Fig. 6.2b. This signifies that as long as the structure of industrial organizations can be significantly improved–for example, if large enterprises can easily delegate the specialized manufacturing of spare parts and intermediate products to small businesses, or if large enterprises downsize their sizes (which is simply manifested by the production moving along the horizontal axis n to the left)—its production cost can be greatly reduced, and large enterprises can improve their profitability through downsizing and decentralized production. In the same way, as the "stickiness" (point m^*) of the structure of industrial organization makes division of labor and specialization very difficult, the profitability of large enterprises remains very low, because, again due to this "stickiness", large enterprises' production capacity cannot be fully utilized with the result that the vertical integration within large enterprises would become a "luxury".[19]

[19] But, in theory, as shown in Fig. 6.2, one possibility that large enterprises' profitability will be improved when the structure of industrial organization is "sticky" is the profit margin curve moving upward, rather than moving along the given curve of profit margin. The emergence of this situation is often the result of technological innovation. But it is obvious that China's large enterprises do not

We hope that such a simple conceptual framework will help us understand the basic characteristics of changes in profitability of China's industrial enterprises during the transition period. Next, we will review the structure and characteristics of China's industrial organizations since the reform.

6.4 A General Review of Structure of Industrial Organization Since the Reform

In general, the structure of the industrial organization and its changing patterns can reflect whether or not the existing capacity in an economy is showing or moving toward a more efficient distribution or structure. In some industries, if the concentration of production is helpful to improve the production efficiency and profitability, the enterprise scale will be enlarged; and if the improvement of efficiency and profit margins can be achieved through the fragmentation of production and miniaturization, then the scale of the enterprise should be changed in the opposite direction. Therefore, changes of industrial organization can help companies improve productivity and profitability. At the industry level, the adjustment of the organizational structure should be shown as an equal productivity or an increase in average productivity. The effect of this improvement on productivity and profitability is often referred to as "economies of scale", and because of this, people tend to see the existence of large enterprises as a result of economies of scale.

Now let's first take a look at the basic situation of large enterprises in China's industry. Figures 6.3 and 6.4 provide the distribution of large enterprises in 1991 in the Chinese manufacturing sector based on their original value of fixed assets of 100 million yuan or more (definition 1) and on the number of 5,000 employees or more (definition 2). From the information provided by these two diagrams, we can draw the following conclusions:

(1) With regard to the proportion of large enterprises in industries, light industry, mining industry and heavy industry are almost the same, especially measured in accordance with definition 2 of large enterprises. If judged by the definition 1 of large enterprises, the proportion of large enterprises in the heavy and chemical industries is slightly higher than that in extractive and light industries, if we do not include the oil and gas industry.

(2) If the definition of large enterprises is converted from definition 1 to definition 2, the proportion of large enterprises of coal mining, timber harvesting and processing and the textile industries will significantly increase. This shows that the large enterprises in these four industries are mostly large enterprises with a relatively large labor force, but the density of capital is not high.

---

have the inherent mechanism of technological innovation. So the movement of the profit margin curve itself will hardly happen in China's large enterprise sector.

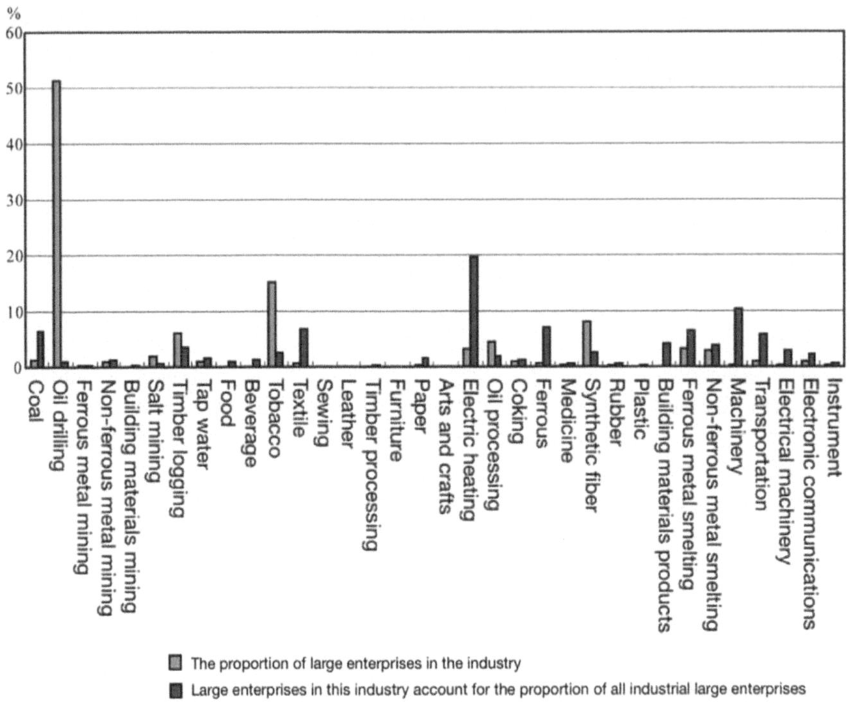

Fig. 6.3 Sector distribution of large enterprises (defined 1) (1991) of China's manufacturing industry

(3) Let us turn from definition 1 to definition 2, the proportion of large enterprises in this sector among the total industrial enterprises has risen significantly in extractive industries, but there is a significant decrease in the heavy chemical industry. In the light industry sector, about half of the industry increased while half decreased. This means that most large enterprises in mining and light industry sectors are ones with a large-scale labor force, while most large enterprises of heavy chemical industry have a lot of capital, further reflecting the fact that there is a significant difference between different sectors in terms of capital density.

(4) Large enterprises in the textile industry are the most prominent among the light industries. Turning from definition 1 to definition 2, we found that the proportion of large enterprises in this industry increased slightly, while the proportion of large enterprises in this industry among the total industrial large enterprises increased by 10 percentage points, proving once again that large enterprises in textile industry are mostly labor-intensive ones. In addition, according to definition 2, large textile enterprises are second to none in the total number of large enterprises in all industrial sectors. By definition 1, although the electricity and steam industries have the highest proportion of large enterprises of all

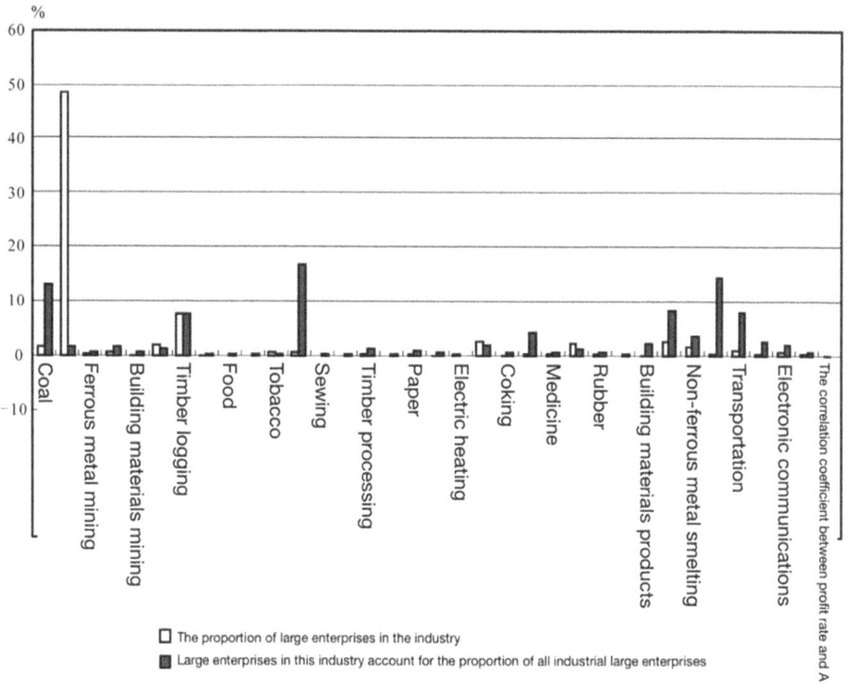

Fig. 6.4 Sector distribution of large enterprises (defined 2) (1991) of China's manufacturing industry

industries, this proportion dropped to 0.01% in accordance with definition 2, indicating large enterprises in the electricity and steam industries are capital intensive enterprises.

(5) In the heavy chemical industry, according to definition 1, chemical fiber enterprise has the highest proportion of large enterprises in this sector, but in accordance with definition 2, the proportion dropped by nearly 6 percentage points (from 8.12% down to 2.27%), which indicates that the chemical fiber industry is dominated by large capital intensive enterprises.

In a word, seen from the organizational structure of the given industry, large enterprises occupy a significant proportion in oil drilling and oil processing, timber harvesting, tobacco processing, chemical fiber, ferrous and non-ferrous metal smelting, electric heating and other sectors. Among them, the proportion of large enterprises in oil mining and tobacco processing sectors account for 51.4% and 15.2% respectively. In terms of proportion of large enterprises compared with their counterparts in the entire industrial sectors, large enterprises are mainly found in machinery, textile, chemical, building materials, coal, ferrous and non-ferrous metal smelting equipment, transportation and other sectors. This means that although in such sectors as textiles and machinery, small and medium-sized enterprises account

Table 6.1 Proportion of China's total industrial output value divided by the size of enterprises (1980–1993)

	1980	1985	1991	1993
L Enterprise	25.1	25.3	28.1	29.3
MS enterprise	18.1	17.0	15.5	16.5
S enterprise	56.8	47.5	38.3	35.4
Others	–	10.2	18.1	18.8

Source National Bureau of Statistics: *China Statistical Yearbook* (1994), Beijing, China Statistics Press, 1994

for the majority proportion, the absolute number of large enterprises is very large, totaling 122 and 186 respectively.[20]

It is worth noting that since the industrial transition, although the non-state sector represented by township enterprises has achieved rapid entry and expansion, the industrial organization structure of Chinese manufacturing sector does not seem to have undergone any significant changes on the whole, exhibiting an "organizational sitickiness". Table 6.1 shows the changes in the relative proportion of the total industrial output value of 1980–1993 by the size of the enterprises. We find that the proportion of large enterprises has shown no sign of decrease. Furthermore, in the state-owned sector, the change in the scale of output share shows a steady growing trend for large enterprises. As shown in Table 6.2, during 1978–1993, the output share of large state-owned enterprises in the total industrial output of China was basically at the 40% level, while the small state-owned enterprises' share of output decreased significantly, from 35.8% in 1978 to 12.1% in the early 90s. At the same time, the output share of township enterprises rose from 8.7% in the early transition period to over 20%. Therefore, the production expansion of non-state sector is mainly characterized by the growth of small non-state-owned enterprises, among which the output of enterprises of township and lower levels and of other ownerships grew the fastest. In our opinion, this deviation of entry is mainly due to the highly imperfect capital market in the transition period where the non state-owned enterprises found it difficult to obtain capital.

Because of the "stickiness" of industrial organizations, the structure of industrial organizations seems decentralized in many industrial sectors. Seen from the subsector, in 1990, the number of township enterprises entering the black metal and non-ferrous metal smelting and rolling processing industry were 5,648 and 3,839, the number entering transportation equipment manufacturing industry and electronic and communication equipment manufacturing enterprises were 7,603 and 3,506.[21]

[20] If definition 1 for large enterprises changed from the original value of fixed assets of 100 million to 50 million yuan (i.e., definition 2), the number of large enterprises in textile and machinery industries would soar to 471 and 491. See National Bureau of Statistics (1992).

[21] Calculation is based on the township and village industrial sub-sector index data provided by the *Statistical Yearbook of Chinese Industrial Economy* (1991) on pages 397 and 399. Among them, the data of township enterprises only include the data of independent accounting township enterprises.

Table 6.2 Total industrial output value of china in terms of ownership and enterprise size (1978–1993)

	1978	1991	1993
Large state-owned enterprise	41.5	40.7	41.4
Small state-owned enterprise	35.8	12.1	7.9
Township enterprise	8.7	20.6	–
Other enterprise	14	36.6	–

Source National Bureau of Statistics: *China Statistical Yearbook* (1994), Beijing, China Statistics Press, 1994

In the iron and steel industry dominated by state-owned enterprises with increasing returns to scale, small-scale township enterprises also occupy a considerable proportion. These village and township enterprises mainly produce the final products (steel products). *China's Statistical Yearbook* (1995) shows that in 1994, 17,455 township enterprises produced steel, which provided 26% of the total output value of iron and steel industry.[22] Even in the state-owned sector, there were as many as 1,598 steel enterprises in 1990. Among them, only 4 had an annual output capacity of more than 3 million tons, and 16 had an annual output of more than 1 million tons according to data provided by Gu Zhiming. In the automotive industry, 124 companies produced complete vehicles with four wheels in 1993 with an average annual output of around 10,000 vehicles per enterprise. There were 32 enterprises with an average annual output of only 1,000 vehicles (Murakawa 1995).

The research report[23] on the reform of Chinese enterprises published by the World Bank provides some background information of the structural features of China's industrial organizations since the reform. For example, China's textile industry typically exhibits a pattern of coexistence of enterprises of multiple ownerships and different sizes. Although there was a large number of state-owned large enterprises, up to the early 1980s, among 17,100 textile enterprises, 2/3 were small local enterprises and only 1/3 belonged to the Ministry of Textile Industry and the textile industry bureau of local government. Among these, there were 3,261 state-owned enterprises, 2,314 urban collective enterprises, and 66 joint ventures between state and collectives and with Hong Kong enterprises.[24] In the clock and watch industry, although the largest producer was the Shanghai Watch Company, there were actually more than 100 enterprises producing watches and spare parts in 1982, and there were only 6 provinces that did not produce clocks and watches, showing a highly dispersed industrial organization structure (Byrd and Tidrick 1992).

With regard to the iron and steel industry which is considered as having an increasing returns to scale, the characteristics of large iron and steel enterprises and large smelting equipment is of high output, low energy consumption and high productivity, so the production should have a centralized trend. However, due to the stickiness of industrial organizations, China's steel industry has experienced the trend

---

[22] Otsuka et al. (2000).

[23] Byrd (1992).

[24] Sabin (1992).

of decentralized production since the reform. Gu Zhiming found in his studies that in late 1980s, the construction of a large number of small blast furnaces, converters and small rolling mills with backward technology in local regions seems to have greatly reduced the productivity of the iron and steel enterprises in China. According to data provided by him, 1,130 blast furnaces were built in 1990 compared to 561 in 1985, an increase of 101%, while the average volume of each blast furnace dropped from 145.9 to 103.2 m^3, down 31%. BOF increased from 126 to 171, a rise of 36%, but their average volume increased by only 8.8%; rolling mills increased from 1,056 sets to 1,888 sets, a growth of 78%, while the average per mill production capacity decreased from 47 thousand tons down to 39 thousand tons. Owing to the small size of the enterprises, the construction of a large number of small enterprises with backward technology restricted the improvement of productivity of China's iron and steel enterprises. In 1988, a China's steel worker produced 29.5 tons of steel per year on average, 1/25 of a Japanese worker, 1/14 of an American worker and 1/13 of a South Korean worker in the same year according to Gu Zhiming.

Furthermore, the problem of the structure of China's industrial organizations may not lie in the excessive decentralization of production, but in the fact that the difference in productivity levels and costs among different enterprises within the sector can be maintained for a long time. Because of this, we call it the "stickiness" of industrial organization structure. We still use the watch sector as an example to illustrate the problem. Byrd and Tidrick (1992) pointed out sharply in their research report: "In China's watch industry.... An unusual feature is a large number of producers with large differences in efficiency. In the early 80s, China had the world's largest number of independent and completely integrated watch manufacturers. In 1980, 21 small businesses accounted for 21% of the country's annual output with each one producing less than 500,000 pieces. The proportion of small businesses increased since then.... The cost of production, labor productivity and capital/labor ratio difference became very significant. The present data show that the difference in the cost of the enterprise is 4 to 1, and, if some of the unplanned enterprises are included, the difference is as high as 7:1. The difference in labor productivity is 12 or 13:1, while the difference in capital productivity is 12 to 1."[25]

The stickiness of the industrial structure has had an adverse effect on the labor productivity of the industry. According to data provided by Byrd and Tidrick, in 1981, the labor productivity of China's watch and clock enterprises produced 524 watches per person per year, much lower than that in India and Japan. They (Byrd 1992) wrote: "The productivity of India's two watch enterprises is 909 watches per person per year, some enterprises in Japan can produce 16,500 pieces per person, 30 times more than the average level of China. Although this does not necessarily mean that China's watch enterprises are inefficient, there is indeed a huge difference in the labor productivity and costs in China's watch industry. The per capita output of Shanghai Watch Factory (whose output is more than that of India's two watch enterprises) was 1,052 in 1980 and 1,220 in 1981. However, the average per capita

[25] Firms with too large productivity gaps existing in the same sector without being integrated are typically found in China's steel sector. See Otsuka et al. (2000).

output of China's remaining watch enterprises in 1981 was only 377 pieces. In 1980, the productivity of an enterprise was so low that only 89 pieces were produced…. So, at least in part, China's watch industry has shown a high degree of inefficiency."

In a word, it is inaccurate to describe the industrial organization structure of China's economy simply by the word "dispersed". From an efficiency point of view, the decentralization of production can improve efficiency in an increasing cost sector. In fact, the problem of the structure of Chinese industrial organization is not about the decentralization of production (such as iron and steel, machinery, etc.) or too centralized (such as clothing, food, etc.), but lies in the "differentiation" that can be maintained: in a given sector, enterprises with a huge difference between costs and technical conditions can exist side by side. This sustainable differentiation is particularly prominent in sectors with a higher capital/labor ratio. In our opinion, the long-term maintenance of differentiation is undoubtedly the main reason leading to the structural stickiness of industrial organizations.[26]

6.5 Explanation of Differences of Technical Efficiency of Enterprises of Different Scales

In the early days of industrial transition, one of the most widely observed and basic observations was that the level of technology shows an interesting sequence among enterprises with different ownerships. On the whole, the level of technology and equipment of state-owned enterprises may be lower than that of foreign/joint ventures, but higher than that of township enterprises. Rawski and Jefferson (Chinese edition, 1994), based on the similar observation, have constructed a dynamic process on technology diffusion among enterprises with different ownerships. At the beginning of this process, township enterprises made significant technical progress by absorbing technologies of state-owned enterprises (Chen 1999[27]; Otsuka et al. 1998).

---

[26] It is obvious that the fact that enterprises with significant differences in productivity can exist in the same sector is the product of the property right system of state-owned enterprises and the centralized capital formation system under the planned economy. Since the 1980s, although the decision-making of investment has been decentralized, the property rights system of enterprises has not changed. Therefore, the basic characteristics of corporate investment and the formation of state-owned capital have not changed as well. The extraordinary growth of demand scale at the beginning of the reform has further encouraged and strengthened this differentiation.

[27] Chen (1999). Chen (1999) provides a detailed analysis of the technological acquisition methods and technical choices of Chinese township enterprises. He pointed out that in the early stage of industrial transition, township enterprises obtained technical input mainly through state-owned enterprises (make use of the obsolete equipment of state-owned enterprises and hire their technical personnel) and achieved growth by producing labor-intensive products. But since the late 80s, due to the change of market demand, township enterprises began to invest in the production of technology or capital intensive products, resulting in a gradual increase in capital/labor ratio of township enterprises. This choice of the technology may not be caused by the rapid rise in labor prices, but may reflect the nature of collective property rights of township enterprises in their mode of investment.

However, it is certain that the technological level of large enterprises is still higher than the overall level of other types of enterprises. Let's still take China's steel enterprises as an example. Tan Chengdong and Tang Fuxiao's research[28] shows that, based on the technical indicators, large iron and steel enterprises are generally better than small and medium-sized ones. By the end of 1984, there were more than 1,100 small and medium-sized iron and steel enterprises at the county level or above in China which produced 8.77 million tons of steel, accounting for 20% of the country's steel production. The energy they consumed was equal to 24 million 80 thousand tons of standard coal, accounting for 33% of the energy consumed for iron and steel. So, small and medium-sized iron and steel enterprises were significantly higher than large enterprises in respect with the general energy consumption per ton of steel. According to the estimates they provided, in 1984, the key steel and iron enterprises consumed 17.93 tons of standard coal for an average output value of 1 million yuan, and the comprehensive energy consumption per ton of steel was 1.332 tons of standard coal. Regional backbone small and medium-sized steel enterprises consumed 22.21 tons of standard coal for an average output value of 1 million yuan, and their comprehensive energy consumption per ton of steel was 1.747 tons of standard coal, about 30% higher than that of key enterprises. The utilization coefficient of blast furnace, comprehensive coke ratio, ratio of putting coke into furnace and utilization coefficient of BOF of small and medium-sized enterprises are all inferior to those of the large iron and steel enterprises (Tan and Tang 1986).

Since the average technological level of large enterprises is higher than that of small and medium enterprises, the proportion of net industrial output value of large enterprises in total industrial output should be higher than that of small and medium-sized enterprises. Net industrial output value is the difference between total industrial output value and material consumption. In Fig. 6.5, based on the data provided by the *Statistical Yearbook Chinese Industrial Economy* (National Bureau of Statistics 1992), we found that large enterprises' net output ratio is always higher than that of small and medium enterprises, which confirms the judgment that the technical level of large enterprises is generally higher than that of small and medium enterprises.

In our opinion, an important reason for the higher level of technology of state-owned enterprises, especially large enterprises, is that it is easier for them to access the country's capital and they are the main beneficiaries of the country's technological transformation. Indeed, in China's industrial transition, state-owned enterprises, especially large and medium-sized ones, are more likely to receive government's protection and capital support. The state owned banking sector still has a bias in granting credit in terms of ownership.[29] If we look at the evolution of policy for enterprise reform, the large and medium-sized state-owned enterprises, in programs such as "establishment of modern enterprise system", "optimizing capital structure", "ten, hundred and thousand project", "foster large enterprise and let go of the development of small and medium-sized business", "establishment of corporate group"

[28] Tan and Tang (1986).

[29] Chow and Fung (1998).

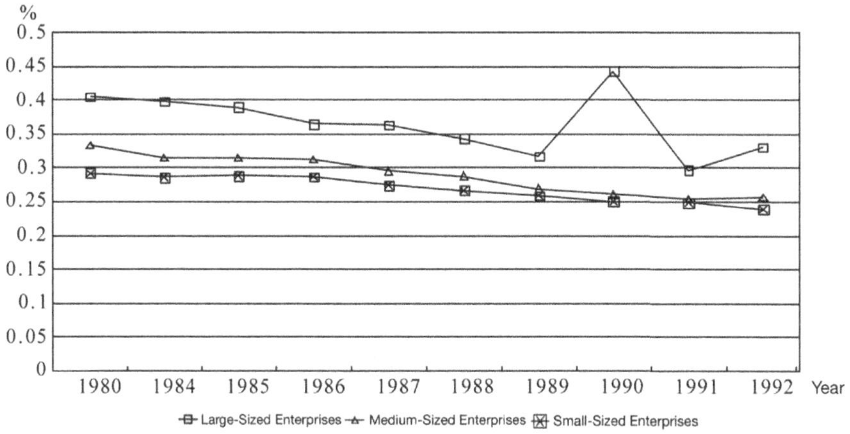

Fig. 6.5 Ratio of industrial net output value by the scale of enterprise (1980–1992)

and "increase investment and the pace of reform"(double increase),[30] have always enjoyed the preferential treatment of the government in capital support.[31]

We see that since the 1980s, although the focus of the government's policy shifted from encouraging basic construction investment in new enterprises to upgrading and renovation investment in technological innovation and progress, most of the investment funds in renovation investment were still used for the purchase of new equipment, improving the equipment level and the so-called technical content. Moreover, the technical level of large enterprises also benefited from the introduction of technologies and equipment from abroad. Chinese technology import mainly included three areas: complete sets of equipment, key technology and technology licensing, out of which complete sets of equipment and key equipment accounted for more than 80%. And in the emerging technology and manufacturing sector with high-speed growth, large and medium-sized enterprises were the main beneficiaries (Jiang et al. 1999).

In fact, the degree of proximity to capital alone has explained the "identity" of China's large enterprises. In China, although small enterprises must grow and expand gradually through their effort in the market to eventually become large enterprises, a typical large state-owned enterprise is usually not evolved from a small firm through its own growth and expansion, but is launched as a large enterprise in the first place. The difference in the growth of the size of firms itself has reflected a very significant difference in the extent to which the firms with different identities have access to capital. We can find the difference in the results of the third national industrial

[30] The "double increase project" is a program initiated and implemented by the State Economic and Trade Commission at the end of the 8th "five-year-plan" to increase the technical transformation investment in key enterprises and industries as well as accelerate the pace of enterprise reform.

[31] Jun Zhang provided a comment on the evolution of the reform policy of large and medium enterprises.

Table 6.3 Average scale of state-owned enterprises under different subordinate relations

	Gross output value (10,000 yuan)	Employment (person)
Total average	2275	504
Central enterprises	12552	2289
Provincial enterprises	3494	871
Local enterprises	2501	599
County enterprise	826	224

Source Dpt. of Industrial and Transportation Statistics of National Bureau of Statistics: *Big Trends: Changes in Ownership Structure*, Beijing, China Statistics Press, 1999

census conducted in 1995. In China, for example, the size of state-owned enterprises is positively related to the level of government they are subordinate to (see Table 6.3).

As large enterprises enjoy relative advantages in gaining the government capital support and the introduction of advanced technology, the level of technology has a gradient structure among enterprises with different sizes and ownerships. Considering that the purchase and installation of more advanced technical equipment can increase the capital density or the capital/labor ratio, the higher capital/labor ratio will have a negative impact on capital productivity and profit rate unless large enterprises can achieve significant economies of scale, or enjoy a protected domestic market (such as steel).[32] However, the higher technological level of large enterprises may be the reason for its relatively high technical efficiency compared with small and medium-sized enterprises. In other words, when we compare the technical efficiency of large enterprises with small and medium-sized enterprises by using the fitting method of production function, we may find that the large enterprise sector with a higher capital/labor ratio will exhibit higher technical efficiency.[33] And there are indeed many studies in the literature that confirm the greater technological efficiency of large enterprises than small and medium-sized enterprises.

Cao (1994), for example, used the method of estimating stochastic frontier production functions to study changes in the efficiency of China's steel industry. Among them, he made an estimate of the technical efficiency of the steel industry from 1980 to 1988. He found that although the steel industry still has considerable room for further improvement in technical efficiency, technical efficiency has improved significantly. In 1980, the average technical efficiency of all the sample enterprises was 0.46 (assuming that the technical efficiency level of firms on the boundary of production possibilities is 1). By 1985, the technical efficiency increased to 0.49 and 0.53 in 1988. In 8 years, technical efficiency increased by an average of 1.8% per year. In particular, he further discovered that the technical efficiency of large enterprises is consistently higher than that of small and medium-sized enterprises. According to his

[32] With regard to this conclusion, one can see the empirical study on the determinants of the profitability of Chinese state-owned enterprises based on the third national industrial census data done by Jun Zhang and others.

[33] As to the meaning of technical efficiency, see Farrel's distinction method proposed in his classic paper of 1957.

estimation results, the technical efficiency levels of large, medium-sized and small enterprises in 1980 were 0.55, 0.47 and 0.25; 0.59, 0.51 and 0.29 in 1985; and 0.62, 0.55 and 0.33 in 1988. Thus, during 1980–1988, the average technical efficiency of large enterprises is about 2 times that of small enterprises and nearly 20% higher than that of medium-sized enterprises.

Yao Yang[34] also got the same conclusion. Unlike Cao, he used data from the third national industrial census. He sampled 14,670 firms from 12 major industries. He first fitted the production functions of the 12 industrial sectors by using the stochastic frontier production function model, then calculated the technical efficiency of each enterprise, and finally made a multi-factor regression analysis of the technical efficiency of all the enterprises sampled. In the regression based on the scale of the enterprise as explanatory variables, he found that although overall, the technical efficiency of collective sector and private sector (including joint ventures and private enterprises, etc.) is higher than that of state-owned sector by 22% and 30% on average respectively, the technical efficiency of small enterprises is 49% lower than that of large enterprises, and 20% lower than that of medium-sized enterprises. The result demonstrates that the technical efficiency and the enterprise scale showed a positive correlation: the average TE (i.e. the vertical drop of the estimated production possibility boundary and the actual production possibility boundary—the smaller the drop, the higher the technical efficiency) of large enterprises (1844) was 0.68; 1.06 for medium-sized enterprises (3,221); and 1.15 for Small enterprises (9,605).

However, we would like to point out that Cao (1994) has wrongly attributed the higher technical efficiency of large enterprises to "economies of scale". In fact, as the above research failed to control the technological differences, management skills of enterprises and other factors of reforms, his conclusion could not confirm whether there really exists economies of scale or whether this existence was remarkable. At the same time, we should also point out that the difference in technical efficiency between large enterprises and small and medium-sized enterprises does not necessarily determine their differences in speed of improvement on technical efficiency. According to our existing empirical observation and the conclusion of the research on total factor productivity, we believe that although the technical efficiency of large enterprises is higher than that of small and medium enterprises because of the special "identity" of the former, the overall technical efficiency of small and medium enterprises should be improved faster than that of large enterprises, for the small and medium-sized enterprises are facing a more adverse market environment, and it is especially not easily for them to get official capital support. Therefore, it would be difficult for them to grow and survive without continuously improving their competitive ability. We might as well summarize our idea in Fig. 6.6, where we make a distinction between the different technological efficiency improvement mechanisms that large enterprises and small and medium enterprises may have.

As we have mentioned, because large firms are more likely to receive support of capital and equipment replacement, their technical efficiency curve is not a smooth rise, but ladder-shaped, each technical step upward is the result of a major investment

[34] Yao (1998).

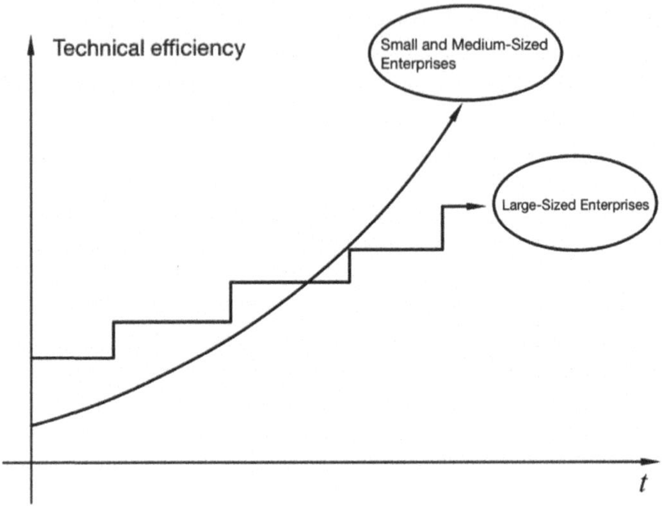

Fig. 6.6 Different mechanisms for improving technical efficiency in large and small and medium-sized enterprises

and a project of equipment renewal. We have emphasized before, in particular, that large enterprises are not the result of their own growth and expansion from small enterprises, but were started as large firms. The special "identity" of large enterprises in China has determined their different technological efficiency improvement mechanisms. In large enterprises, we often use the so-called "phase-one project", "phase-two project" or "phase-three projects" to refer to this mechanism. One of such typical cases is Baoshang Iron and Steel Corporation. For small and medium-sized enterprises, because it is not easy for them to obtain capital support, their technical efficiency improvement can be achieved by mainly relying on the existing technologies and making use of the most efficient way of production. This process is shown as an increasingly upward curve.

The scenario described in Fig. 6.6 is basically in line with the actual situation of China's industrial enterprises. We can observe the different changing patterns of actual labor productivity in different enterprises since the reform. We know that the growth of labor productivity can be theoretically divided into contribution to changes in capital density and contribution to changes in TFP. We have been convinced that large enterprises and small and medium-sized enterprises have significant differences in capital density, that is to say, the capital density growth of large enterprises is much faster than small enterprises. Therefore, if the labor productivity of large enterprises is growing slower than that of small enterprises, then the growth of their technical efficiency is actually slower than that of small enterprises. By using the original data offered by D. Lo,[35] Fig. 6.7 shows the growth curve of labor productivity of China's industrial enterprises in 1980–1996 calculated according to actual

[35] Lo (1999).

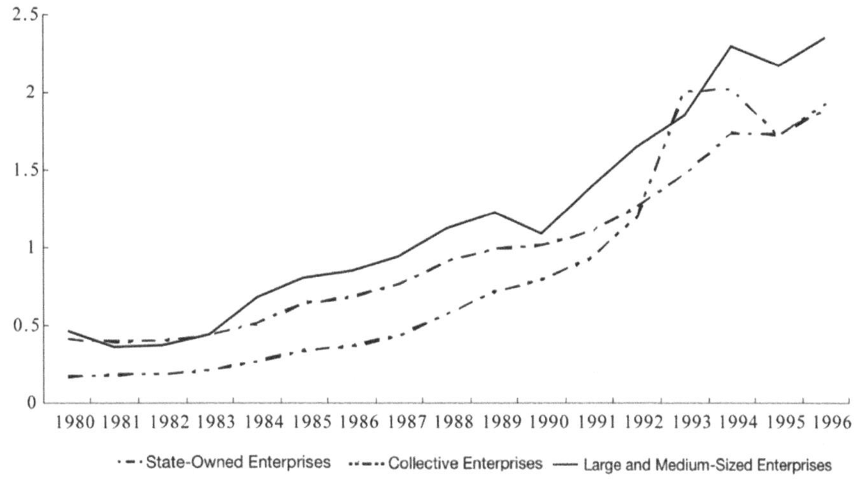

Fig. 6.7 Growth curve of actual labor productivity of state-owned enterprises, collective enterprises and large and medium-sized enterprises (1980–1996)

net industrial output.[36] The labor productivity curve calculated on the basis of ownerships shows that although the labor productivity of collective enterprises in the 1980s was lower than that of the state-owned enterprise as well as large and medium-sized enterprises, it surpassed the state-owned enterprises and large and medium-sized enterprises around 1992, indicating collective enterprises (mainly small and medium sized enterprises) had a superior mechanism to improve their efficiency faster.

6.6 Review of Economies of Scale Hypothesis

Indeed, the fact that the profitability of large enterprises is higher than that of small and medium-sized enterprises can easily remind one of the possible existence of "economy of scale" in the industrial sector. However, in the existing research literature, scholars who hold this view tend to rely on the profit margin indicators of "large and small and medium-sized enterprises" (Lo 1999; Nolan 1996[37]) given in the statistics. Of course, there are also individual studies of economies of scale. Indeed, as we have seen in the table, statistics show that the profitability of "large enterprises" is consistently higher than that of small and medium-sized enterprises at the aggregate level rather than the level of sector. Other empirical studies, however, do not seem to have found enough evidence to prove that there are significant economies of scale in

[36] In calculating the actual labor productivity, we use the price index of industrial net output value provided by Lo (1999).

[37] Nolan (1996).

some manufacturing sectors in China.[38] And in the theoretical level, most economists do not believe that the performance and efficiency of big business will be better than that of the small and medium-sized enterprises, because large enterprises often use capital intensive technology, thus in terms of profitability, they usually are not as good as small and medium-sized enterprises with comparative advantages (Otsuka et al. 1998; Lin et al. 1997). In short, the financial performance of China's large corporate sector leaves us with a "big business puzzle" to unravel.

Even many empirical studies using formal measurement methods have different interpretations of the existing conclusions. For example, Jefferson (1990[39]) found in his study on China's iron and steel industry that the output elasticity of capital and labor of iron and steel enterprises are 0.649 and 0.523, which means that there are economies of scale in the steel sector (the estimated scale parameter is 0.172). However, Otsuka and others (2000) argue that if the relationship between reform variables and characteristics variables uniquely possessed by enterprises cannot be well controlled and dealt with, or the potential effects of difference in product components of enterprises on efficiency are not fully considered, estimation error might not be avoided. In their view, Jefferson failed to control the variable of the enterprise reform, so the economy scale in his estimation is likely to be the effect of the reform of enterprise system. They used "number of employees" of the sampled enterprise as representing variables of the enterprise scale in their own study. After fitting the Cobb–Douglas production function by using the panel data of 1980, 1985, 1991 and 1994, they found that from the beginning of the reform to 1994, no economies of scale existed in China's iron and steel industry, nor did they find diseconomies of scale.

What is interesting is that before 1992, the *Statistical Yearbook of Chinese Industrial Economy* continuously provided the main data of the so-called "scale economy of Chinese industry". It is indeed commendable because these valuable data cover 40 Chinese (38 or 37 in some years) industries, and in each industry, the data also provide 9 (6 or 7 in some industries) grouped data on enterprise scales. The size of the enterprise is defined in accordance with the total output value, fixed assets, the number of employees and total pre-tax profit. Based on each scale category, we can obtain detailed data regarding the number of enterprises, total profit, total capital and the number of workers. These off-the-shelf data provide us with another possibility to validate the hypothesis of economies of scale from the two aspects of productivity and profitability.

According to the theory of industrial organization, the hypothesis of scale effect can be easily tested by the changing relation between profit margin and scale. O Keijiro, Murakami Naoki and Liu Deqiang used the data of 1991 provided in "scale economy of Chinese industry" by the *Statistical Yearbook Chinese Industrial Economy* (1992). They chose fixed assets as the representative variables of the firm size, and then gave a simple definition of the following regression equation: (total

[38] Murakami et al. (1996).

[39] Jefferson (1990).

profits-tax/sum of net value of fixed assets and circulating assets) $= a + b \cdot Ln$ (net value of fixed assets).

This simple regression becomes possible because the *Statistical Yearbook Chinese Industrial Economy* (1992) publicized the main data of 9 scale blocks of 40 industrial sectors grouped on fixed assets with each scale block corresponding to the average profit rate level. Therefore, they weight-regressed the scale coefficient (b) of the equation by using the intersecting data of these 9 firm size bocks and corresponding profit rate margins. According to their understanding, if there is a significant scale economic effect in an industry, the correlation coefficient (b) between profit margins and firm size should be positive, and vice versa.

Table 6.4 presents the results of their estimation. As can be clearly seen, in the 35 industries they estimated, none of the scale coefficient is greater than zero, and the gap between the scale coefficient of 28 industries and zero is obviously negative at the 5% level. Since large enterprises basically are state-owned, the change (expansion) of the scale of enterprise asset itself does not seem to lead to better profit margins on the whole; or, there does not seem to be a simple linear relationship between asset size and profitability. This, at the very least, does not support the hypothesis of economies of scale. In other words, the higher profit margins sustained by Chinese big business may not be the result of greater corporate size. Based on this result, they came to such a conclusion:

> As far as the scale of most industries that can be observed is concerned, the advantage of the enterprise size does not exist. What we should pay attention to here is that because we have not received information about the proportion of township enterprises in all the industries, this result contains the institutional effect of township enterprises. Therefore, the negative scale factor may reflect the high efficiency of township enterprises. In industries where township enterprises account for a small proportion such as printing and mechanical transportation, the proportion of township enterprises only accounts for 10.5% and 6.8%, though the scale coefficient of the two industries is still negative and obvious in statistics. In the machine tool industry, small-scale state-owned enterprises have higher production efficiency than large-scale state-owned enterprises. Therefore, it is difficult to find statistical evident to support the view that large state-owned enterprises will continue to be dominant in many industries on the ground of scale economy. (O Keijiro et al.)

Similar to their views, we have also used this data to test the hypothesis of economies of scale. What we used is the classification data for 1991 and 1992 under the title Scale Economy of Chinese Industry in the *Statistical Yearbook of Chinese Industrial Economy*. We have combined the production functions of China's industrial sectors to test whether the scale "factor" has a positive effect on the change of industrial labor productivity which is a supplement to O Keijiro's estimate. For each given industry, we can get up to 18 sample data at most (that is, two sets of data grouped by 9 scale blocks). Considering that the provided data mainly includes the average number of employees (L), the total industrial output value (Y) and the original value of fixed assets (K) of each industrial sector according to 9 scale block subgroups, we decided to use the changes of number of workers (L) to pinpoint the changing effect of enterprise scale. To this end, we assume a linear logarithm of the standard Cobb Douglas production function as:

Table 6.4 Estimated coefficients of firm size in profit margins and profit margin equation (Classified by industries, 1991)

Industry category	Average profit margin	b	Standard deviation	R^2
Mining and smelting				
Coal mining	−2.9	−5.96**	1.12	0.80
Black metal ore	8.1	−9.61**	1.06	0.92
Nonferrous metal ore	6.0	−7.25**	1.17	0.85
Building materials and other non metal mining	9.7	−9.54**	1.51	0.85
Salt mining	8.9	−9.64**	1.82	0.80
Timber and bamboo logging	6.6	−12.64**	1.79	0.88
Tap water	6.5	−0.66**	0.17	0.68
Light industry				
Food manufacturing	8.1	−2.05**	0.57	0.65
Beverage	16.2	−2.29	0.99	0.43
Feed	13.7	−1.50*	0.46	0.64
Textile	5.1	−1.10**	0.26	0.72
Sewing	10.1	−1.49*	0.58	0.48
Leather and fur	4.8	−3.15**	0.50	0.87
Timber processing	2.6	−5.97**	0.73	0.90
Furniture	5.4	−3.76**	0.65	0.85
Paper and its products	8.4	−2.58**	0.48	0.80
Printing	12.5	−3.42**	0.65	0.85
Stationery and sporting goods	13.8	−1.97**	0.50	0.69
Arts and crafts	10.5	−3.39**	0.49	0.89
Chemical industry				
Petroleum processing	23.0	−1.63	0.94	0.30
Coking and gas	0.8	−4.41**	0.55	0.30
Chemistry	11.2	−2.27**	0.49	0.76
Medicine	15.9	−0.29	0.29	0.12
Synthetic fiber	15.8	−1.46	1.11	0.20
Rubber products	17.7	−1.78*	0.69	0.49
Plastic products	7.5	−3.11**	0.64	0.77
Building materials	8.6	−3.18**	0.65	0.77
Heavy industry				
Ferrous metal smelting	11.9	−1.57	0.98	0.27
Nonferrous metal smelting	8.2	−3.42**	0.92	0.67

(continued)

Table 6.4 (continued)

(Classified by industries, 1991)				
Industry category	Average profit margin	b	Standard deviation	R^2
Metal products	9.0	−2.57**	0.43	0.84
Machinery industry	12.6	−2.84**	0.52	0.81
Transportation equipment	9.5	−2.85**	0.64	0.74
Electrical machinery	9.5	−2.44**	0.46	0.80
Electronic communication equipment	7.2	−2.42**	0.42	0.83
Instrument manufacturing	7.4	−2.88**	0.25	0.95

Note * means obvious at 5% level, ** means obvious at the 1% level
Source O Keijiro, Liu Deqiang, Murakami Naoki: *Industrial Reform in China*, Shanghai SDX Joint Publishing Company, Shanghai People's Publishing House, 2000

$$\text{Ln}Y = a_0 + a_K\text{Ln}K + a_l\text{Ln}L,$$

When both sides of the upper formula is divided by L, we get:

$$\text{Ln}\left(\frac{Y}{L}\right) = a_0 + a_K\text{Ln}\left(\frac{K}{L}\right) + (a_K + a_L - 1)\text{Ln}(L).$$

We set the parameter $c = a_K + a_L - 1$. So, when $a_K + a_L > 1, c > 0$; this way, the regression equation we created that contains the scale factor is changed into:

$$\text{Ln}(Y/L) = a + b\text{Ln}(K/L) + c\text{Ln}(L) + \varepsilon$$

Among them, (Y/L) is the labor productivity, and (K/L) is the capital-labor ratio, which represents the level of equipment. The size of the enterprise is identified by the employment scale (L) of the workforce. Because the logarithmic form is used, b and c represent the impact of changes in equipment levels and the size of the firm's employment on labor productivity. ε is the error term.

In theory, the capital-labor ratio (K/L) has a positive effect on labor productivity (Y/L), so the parameter b is expected to be positive. The sign of parameter c depends on whether there is a positive effect of scale change on labor productivity. If there is a positive effect of scale change, then parameter c is expected to be greater than zero, and test value t to be relatively high; otherwise, if parameter c is less than zero and test value t is higher, no effect of scale change is expected to exist. Here, we use the total industrial output value, the original value of fixed assets and the number of workers to regress the above equation.

After deleting some of the unsatisfactory results due to data problems in some industries, the regression results for 35 industries are also given in Table 6.5. Of these 35 industries, at least 10 of them revealed remarkable diseconomies of scale, the scale coefficients of 12 industries are significantly greater than zero, while the scale coefficients of 23 industries either tend to be near zero or cannot be confirmed to have an obvious positive or negative effect of scale because their test value t is not high.[40]

In general, at the industry level, whether using the number of workers or the scale of fixed assets of enterprises as a representative variables for the scale of enterprise certainly cannot confirm the existence of increasing returns to scale in Chinese industrial sectors. We mentioned in the beginning of this article that in the official version of the profit rate data of "large, small and medium-sized enterprises", the profit margins of large corporations are always significantly higher than that of small and medium enterprises. And, as shown in Fig. 6.1, although the overall profit ability of enterprises have declined since the 80s, the difference in profitability capability between large enterprises and small and medium-sized enterprises has not changed. Obviously, the fact that the profitability of "large enterprises" is consistently higher than "small and medium enterprises" does not mean (nor does the existing literature seem to have discovered) that there is economies of scale in Chinese industry. So, what message has the official profit rate data of the large and small and medium-sized enterprises conveyed to us?

6.7 One Possible Explanation of Higher Profit Margins of "Large Enterprises"

Our aforementioned review of the relevant literature on economies of scale and preliminary empirical investigation did not find any strong evidence to prove that China's large enterprise sector is the product of economies of scale. Moreover, from the financial performance point of view, because large enterprises have a high density of capital, usually their profit margins may not be higher than that of small and medium-sized enterprises. Moreover, as the vast majority of China's large enterprises are state-owned, the soft budget constraints in these enterprises are more common than in small and medium-sized enterprises. Therefore, the profit margins of large enterprises should not be higher than those of small and medium-sized enterprises.

But why the official statistics showed that the profit rate of large enterprise is always higher than that of the small and medium-sized enterprises? We believe that this statistic result may be due to the wrong official definition of "large enterprises" which distorts the true profitability of large enterprises. Why is that possible? First of all, we need to understand the meaning of "large enterprises" defined in China's statistical publications. In order to understand the official statistical standards of

[40] Our conclusion is similar to that reached by Zhang (1997) in his earlier studies. His measurement results show that there are different degrees of increasing returns to scale in textile/garment, light industry, petrochemical and chemical industry, building materials industry and other industrial sectors. In his research, the other 4 sectors have different degrees of diminishing returns to scale, but the return of scale of all the enterprises exampled is basically unchanged.

Table 6.5 Estimated results of scale effect of China's industrial sectors (1990–1991)

Sector	c	Test value t	R^2
Coal mining	−0.0648426	−3.4704906***	0.887502
Oil and gas extraction	n.a	n.a	n.a
Ferrous metal mining	−0.1366429	−2.6162530**	0.663654
Nonferrous metal mining	−0.0742740	−2.9964216***	0.789516
Construction materials and other non-metallic mining	−0.0823230	−2.2542755**	0.764812
Salt mining	−0.0576743	−1.1959000	0.764084
Other mining	n.a	n.a	n.a
Timber and bamboo	−0.2211561	−5.4523807***	0.759257
Tap water production and supply industry	n.a	n.a	n.a
Food manufacturing	−0.0447828	−1.0982968	0.980525
Beverage manufacturing	0.0692195	0.6991359	0.966562
Tobacco processing	0.2994359	2.5772552**	0.898712
Feed industry	−0.3364982	−1.7344644	0.961224
Textile industry	0.0976930	2.6210341**	0.940238
Sewing industry	0.2361133	6.6223221***	0.969409
Leather, fur and products	0.0642550	0.5633522	0.837087
Wood processing and bamboo, rattan, palm and straw products	−0.1548840	−2.6522856**	0.650969
Furniture manufacturing	−0.0363298	−0.4555514	0.906071
Paper and its products	0.0591276	1.8512996*	0.926058
Printing	−0.3351905	−2.0145064*	0.968470
Stationery and sporting goods	n.a	n.a	n.a
Arts and crafts	−0.1110854	−0.8986785	0.915107
Electricity, steam, hot water production and supply	0.0343683	0.6265814	0.978039
Petroleum processing	0.0547220	0.7191712	0.874502
Coking, gas and coal products	0.1938571	15.135043***	0.938542
Chemical industry	0.1482437	3.5399572***	0.966831
Pharmaceutical industry	0.0959805	1.9678109*	0.967077
Chemical fiber industry	0.2998186	11.095204***	0.884978
Rubber products industry	0.0624817	0.8180478	0.983974
Plastics industry	0.1168166	0.6818542	0.956556
Building materials and other non-metallic mineral products	0.0080294	0.0861029	0.989056
Ferrous metal smelting and rolling processing industry	0.0915174	1.7291888*	0.876832
Non ferrous metal smelting and rolling process	−0.0393796	−0.9328429	0.869802

(continued)

Table 6.5 (continued)

Sector	*c*	Test value *t*	R^2
Metal products	−0.1427416	−3.2261693***	0.981559
Machinery industry	0.0908560	2.4328797**	0.958151
Transportation equipment manufacturing	0.2245125	21.912267***	0.971466
Electrical machinery and equipment manufacturing	0.1561554	1.5609000	0.938518
Electronic and communication equipment manufacturing	n.a	n.a	n.a
Instrumentation and other measuring instruments manufacturing	−0.0277458	−0.2516503	0.387580
Other industries	−0.1265800	−1.4709690	0.961280

Note the sample scale of each industry is 18. * is the significant level of 10%, ** is the significant level of 5%, and *** is the significant level of 1%. n.a indicates that the fitting is not ideal
Source National Bureau of Statistics: *Statistical Yearbook of Chinese Industrial Economy* (1991, 1992), Beijing, China Statistics Press, 1991, 1992

large, small and medium-sized enterprises in China, we found the "standards for categorizing large, small and medium-sized industrial enterprises" in the appendix of *Statistical Yearbook of Chinese Industrial Economy* (1994). This is probably the only information that has appeared in China's official statistics publication about the division of enterprise size. This information is very detailed, because the "categorization standard" specifically stipulates how large, small and medium-sized enterprises are divided in each of the 4-digit industry which is the very root of the problem.

Specifically, the "categorization standard" provides us with the dividing methods and indicators of large, small and medium-sized enterprises in 12 major categories of sectors. In each major category, single products of 4-digit sector are classified and then, the large, small and medium-sized scale standards of producers of each single product (or main product) are given. For example, under the "black metal industry", "categorization standard" specifically provides the classifying standards for "large, small and medium-sized enterprises" in sectors such as iron and steel complex, special steel enterprises, independent steel rolling enterprises, independent steelmaking enterprise, independent iron ore and other ferrous metals enterprises. In "machinery industry", it maps out the classifying standard for "large, small and medium-sized enterprises" in 31 4-digit industries including metallurgical and mining equipment, textile machinery, automobile manufacturing enterprises and motor enterprises. In addition, in "large" and "medium-sized" enterprises, large and medium-sized enterprises are divided into "large I" and "large II" and "medium I" and "medium II" according to different standards. The scale of the firm's fixed assets is not taken as one of the most important and direct indicators in the data. Of course, in some sectors such as mechanical industry, the scale of some enterprises is classified on the basis of enterprises' "original value of fixed assets for production", although the scale of a large number of enterprises is classified based on the "annual production capacity" for their products. In the machinery sector, industries whose scale is classified by "original value of fixed assets for production" include textile machinery, building material machinery and medical machinery enterprises; those classified by "annual production capacity" include motor and diesel engine enterprises, petrochemical equipment enterprise. We also found that in some sectors, some industries and enterprises have to satisfy the two targets of "annual production capacity" and "original value of fixed assets production" before they can be categorized as "large enterprises".

Thus, the definition of large business in this way is very different from our usual definitions. The official definition clearly does not rank the size of the business, which is different from the classification of the size of the enterprise we obtained in other ways. For example, we can carry out a scale ranking of all industrial enterprises from highest to lowest in accordance with the enterprise's single index such as total profits, sales income or the size of fixed asset. Under the concept of this ranking chart, the scale of an enterprise is independent of the specific industry where the enterprise is located. Often, under the official definition, a large firm defined in an industry is likely to be smaller in size than a medium-sized or even small firm in another industry. This is because, at the 4-digit industry level, the nature or portfolio of the products are quite different, so that at the industry level, companies that are classified as "large" ones are entirely different in sizes. That is to say, the "large enterprises" defined in this way does not cover the largest enterprises in their sectors whose fixed assets have reached a certain scale, but the total sum of enterprises whose production capacity of different products has met a certain index. In such aggregate "large enterprises", their actual firm size (asset size) is uneven which will lead to an interesting "aggregate effect". We will take the building materials industry as an example to illustrate this point.

In the industry of building materials, we know from the "large, small and medium-sized industrial enterprise classification standards" that, cement enterprises with an annual capacity of 1.2 million tons and above is classified as large enterprises (large I), those with an annual capacity of 300,000–600,000 tons are medium-sized enterprises (medium I); and with respect to "glass fiber enterprises", the standard for classifying large enterprises (large I) are those with an annual production capacity of 80 million tons and above, those with 30–50 million tons are "medium (medium I) enterprises". The large (large I) "new type building material enterprises" refer to those with "original value of fixed assets for production" at 120 million yuan or more, but other building material enterprises can be classified as "large enterprises"(large I) if they can meet the standard of having 100 million yuan or more of "original value of fixed assets for production. Moreover, "large II" enterprises that have also been included in the "large enterprises" are much smaller than "large I" enterprises both in the "annual production capacity and "fixed assets". For example, cement enterprises with an annual production capacity of over 600,000 tons and below 1.2 million tons of cement have been classified as "large II enterprises". Therefore, even in the same industry, the so-called "large enterprises" classified in this way can vary greatly in the size of the real assets or the number of employed workers.

Under these circumstances, once we try to analyze the total data of these large and medium-sized enterprises by using the fixed assets or the number of workers as parameters, we will find that there is a lot of "overlapping" in large and medium-sized enterprises in terms of their actual scale. The results of this breaking-down analysis are given in Table 6.6. In the table, we can see clearly that once enterprises are classified into different scales in accordance with the original value of fixed assets, there would be a lot of overlapping in total amount in large and medium-sized enterprises: in the scale range with fixed assets from 500 million to 10 billion yuan, we found 41 large enterprises, 6 medium-sized enterprises; in the scale range with fixed assets from 100 to 300 million yuan, there are 220 large enterprises and 88 medium-sized enterprises; in the scale range of the fixed assets below 100 million yuan, there are 1,239 large enterprises and 3,772 medium-sized enterprises. We obtained similar results according to the number of employees in the enterprise scale. For example, in the scale range of 10,000–30,000 employees, there are 133 large enterprises and 71 medium-sized enterprises. In the scale range with less than 10,000 workers, there are 1,418 large enterprises and 3,803 medium-sized enterprises.

The distribution characteristics of large, small and medium-sized enterprises in total amount clearly show that, because the difference among large, small and medium-sized enterprises is mainly divided based on the production capacity of main products of the 4-digit industries, even in a given industry, the so-called "large enterprises" in fact contain enterprises that have a great difference in fixed assets or the number of employees. It is entirely possible that within a same sector, a "large enterprise" in an industry (such as watch-making in light industry) is even smaller than a "medium-sized enterprise" in another segment (such as bicycle manufacturing in light industry) in asset size or number of employees.

Only after we have understood the official standard of classifying large, small and medium-sized enterprises can we know the true meaning of large, small and medium-sized enterprises in Fig. 6.1 at the beginning of this article. The so called "large enterprise" mentioned in the figure, in fact, is the total sum of "large enterprises" defined in such a way for the whole Chinese industrial sectors. In this total picture, the large enterprises are not necessarily (and not always) larger than small and medium enterprises in asset scale. A large enterprise in an industry is likely to be smaller than a small and medium enterprise in another industry. For example, if a large enterprise's asset scale is not always as large as that of a small and medium-sized enterprise, even smaller, then, even if the total profits of the "large enterprise" may be smaller than that of the small and medium-sized enterprise, the calculated rate of profit of the "large enterprise" is likely to appear higher than that of the small and medium enterprise because the scale of assets is the denominator for calculating "profit margins ". If so, it is only a selective error caused by the definition.

6.8 Conclusive Comment

It is not normal for large companies to maintain higher profit margins than that of small and medium sized enterprises in such a fast developing emergent industry as that in China. In theory, as the market process advances and the gradual rationalization of factor prices, the difference between the original profitability of China's

Table 6.6 Number of "Large and Medium-Sized Enterprises" according to original value of fixed assets and number of workers

	No. of enterprise units					No. of enterprise units			
	L enterprises		M enterprises			L enterprises		M enterprises	
	Absolute no	Proportion (%)	Absolute no	Proportion (%)		Absolute no	Proportion (%)	Absolute no	Proportion (%)
Total	1611	100	3887	100	Total	1611	100	3887	100
More than 1B yuan	58	3.6	–	–	More than 100000P	7	0.43	–	–
500M–1B yuan	41	2.54	6	0.16	50000–100000P	27	1.68	1	0.02
300–500M yuan	53	3.29	21	0.54	30000–50000P	26	1.61	12	0.31
100–300M yuan	220	13.66	88	2.26	10000–30000P	133	8.26	71	1.83
Below 100M yuan	1239	76.91	3772	97.04	Below 10000P	1418	88.02	3803	97.84

Source National Bureau of Statistics: *Statistics of Chinese Industrial Economy* (1949–1984), pp. 254–255, Beijing, China Statistics Press, 1985

industrial enterprises will gradually disappear. We have proved in another study that the difference in profitability between China's industrial enterprises is mainly due to differences in ownership, rather than in scale.[41] Therefore, China's industrial reform, especially the reform of ownership, should enable SMEs to show their relative advantages in terms of profitability. However, our official statistics have provided a different scenario: in the period of economic transition, although the profitability of large enterprises, similar to the whole industry, also experienced a significant downward trend since the transition, the fact that the profit margins of large enterprises are greater than that of small and medium enterprises still has not changed significantly, and the difference is even widening which has attracted our research interest in Chinese large enterprises and industrial organization issues.

Our study seems to have supported our previous conclusions that Chinese industrial organization still lacks a flexible structure adjustment mechanism, and the differentiation is still the structural characteristics of industrial organization. Therefore, it is difficult to prevent profit margins of industrial sectors from continuously declining since the reform. In many industries, the structure of industrial organizations has not changed significantly. In other words, although the entry and development of small and medium-sized enterprises are very fast, there have been no significant changes in the industries or sectors where large enterprises are distributed. Large state-owned enterprises still remain entrenched in the main capital intensive industrial sectors, which fully reflects the defects of China's capital allocation system. In many sectors where efficiency and profitability can be significantly improved, SMEs are unable to share financial resources and find it difficult to access these areas because of the serious shortcomings of the financial system. Chinese enterprises' "identity" and the "differential treatment" they enjoy to access financial resources is an important institutional reason for the continued deterioration of overall profitability during the transition period of Chinese industry since the reform. Therefore, from the point of view of policy, our research argues that, to completely eliminate discrimination against corporate ownership in financial system, improve the allocative efficiency of the financial system, especially the thorough reform of the existing state-owned banking system and encourage the development of non state-owned banking sector is the key to further improving the industrial organization structure of China and significantly increasing the overall profitability of the industrial sector.

Author's Notes

This article was originally drafted in the first half of 2001 when I was a visiting scholar at Harvard University. I made many revisions and supplements after returning to China but, as a complete article, it has not yet been published. The article was later incorporated into my book, *China's Industrial Reform and Economic Growth.*

I studied the impact of industrial reform policies on corporate profitability and productivity during that time, in order to evaluate the effect of industrial reform. When I studied industrial reform, I found an interesting phenomenon–China's official statistics show that the profitability of large enterprises has consistently been higher

---

[41] Liang et al. (2000).

than that of small and medium enterprises. I always asked myself: does this mean that there is a significant scale economy in the industrial sector? Because if not, how will we explain the performance of "large enterprises"?

In my article, I described and analyzed the evolution of China's industrial organization structure since the reform and its pattern of decentralization and centralization. In particular, I pointed out that the most striking characteristics of China's industrial organizations is that companies with very high different efficiencies coexist in the same industry or sector. This differentiation has not only led to the structural "stickiness" of industrial organizations, but in fact has become an important factor leading to continued deterioration in the profitability of the industrial sector as a whole. On the basis of this, I further studied the technical efficiency differences between large enterprises and small and medium enterprises. I found that the fact that the technical efficiency of large businesses is, on average, higher than that of small and medium-sized businesses (such as the net industrial output value of large enterprises rate is always higher than that of small and medium enterprises) does not mean that large enterprises are more efficient, but mainly because they are using more advanced and complex production technologies than small and medium-sized enterprises to achieve a technical effect. This phenomenon is obviously caused by the imperfect capital market and the defects of the financial system. I have also examined whether there is a scale economy in the industrial sectors and found that there are no obvious economies of scale in most industries.

References

Arrow, Kenneth J.: Social Choice and Individual Values. (1951).

W. Byrd, *Chinese Industrial Firms under Reform*, Oxford, Oxford University Press, 1992.

Byrd, William A., Gene Tidrick: The Chongqing Clock and Watch Company. In Chinese Industrial Firms under Reform, ed. William A. Byrd. New York, Oxford University Press, 1992, pp. 58–119.

I. Y. Cao, The Impact of Partially Introduced Market Mechanisms on the Efficiency of Chinese Industry: The Case of Iron and Steel Industry, *Economic Systems*, 1994, 18, pp. 335–362.

Chen Jianbo: Technical Acquisition and Technical Choice of Township Enterprises in the Evolution of Market Economy, in *Economic Studies*, 1999 (4).

Chow C.K.W., Fung M.K.Y., Ownership Structure, Lending Bias, and Liquidity Constraints: Evidence from Shanghai' s Manufacturing Sector, *Journal of Comparative Economics*, 1998, 26, pp. 301–316.

D. Granick, *Chinese State Enterprises: A Regional Property Rights Analysis*, University of Chicago, 1990.

G. Jefferson, China's Iron and Steel Industry: Source of Enterprise Efficiency and the Impact of Reform, *Journal of Development Economics*, 1990, 33, pp. 329–355.

Jiang Xiaojuan: *Industrial Policy in the Period of Economic Transition*, Shanghai, SDX Joint Publishing Company, Shanghai People's Publishing House, 1999.

J. Liang, J. Zhang, N. Murakami: The Determinates of Profitability in China's Manufacturing Industry: Evidence from the Census Data, working paper, Tokyo Metropolitan University, 2000.

Lin Yifu, Cai Chuang, Li Zhou: *Chinese Miracle: Development Strategy and Economic Reform*, Shanghai: SDX Joint Publishing Company, 1994.

Lin Yifu, Cai Chuang, Li Zhou: *Sufficient Information and Reform of State-Owned Enterprises*, Shanghai, SDX Joint Publishing Company, Shanghai People's Publishing House, 1997.

D. Lo, Reappraising the Performance of China 's State-Owned Industrial Enterprises, 1980–1996, *Cambridge Journal of Economics*, 1999, 23 (6), pp. 693–718.

Lo, Dic: Techno-economic paradigm versus the market: on recent theories of late industrialization. *Economy and Society*, 1995, 24 (3), pp. 443–470.

Lo, Dic, Cheng, Y-S: Explaining the financial performance of Chinese industrial enterprises. *Economic Research Journal*, 2000, 7, pp. 39–47.

N. Murakami, D. Liu, K. Otsuka, Market Reform, Division of Labor and Increasing Advantage of Small Scale Enterprises: The Case of Machine Tool Industry in China, *Journal of Comparative Economics*, 1996, 23, pp. 256–277.

T. Marukawa: Industrial Groups and Division of Labor in China's Automobile Industry. *Developing Economies*, 1995, 33, 353–355.

National Bureau of Statistics: *Statistical Year Book of Chinese Industrial Economy* (1992, 1994), Beijing, China Statistics Press, 1992, 1994.

B. Naughton, *Growing out of the Plan: Chinese Economic Reform*, Cambridge University Press, Cambridge, 1995.

P. Nolan, Large Firms and China's Industrial Reform, Cambridge, *Journal of Economics*, 1996.

P. Nolan, W. Xiao-qiang: Beyond privatization: Institutional innovation and growth in China's large state-owned enterprises. *World Development*, 1999, 27 (1), pp. 169–200.

Keijiro Otsuka, Liu Deqiang, Murakami: *China's Industrial Reform*, Shanghai SDX Joint Publishing Company, Shanghai People's Publishing House, 2000.

K. Otsuka, D. Liu, N. Murakami, *Industrial Reform in China: Past Performance and Future Prospects*, London, Oxford University Press, 1998.

Keijiro Otsuka, Liu Deqiang, Murakami Naoki: *Industrial Reform in China*, Shanghai SDX Joint Publishing Company, Shanghai People's Publishing House, 2000.

D. Perkins, Completing China' s Move to the Market, *Journal of Economic Perspectives*, 1994, 8, pp. 23–46.

Yingyi Qian, Chenggang Xu: Why China's Economic Reforms Differ: The M-Form Hierarchy and Entry/Expansion of the Non-State Sector. *Economics of Transition*, June 1993, 1 (2), pp. 135–170.

Yingyi Qian, Chenggang Xu: M-Form Hierarchy and China's Economic Reform. European Economic Review, Papers and Proceedings, April 1993, 37, pp. 541–548.

L. Sabin, The Qinghe Woolen Textile Mill, in W. Byrd, *Chinese Industrial Firms under Reform*, Oxford, Oxford University Press, 1992.

Tan Chengdong, Tang Fuxiao: *A Study on the Structure of China's Iron and Steel Industry*, Taiyuan, Shanxi People's Publishing House, Beijing, Chinese Social Science Press, 1986.

The Third National Industrial Census Office: *Collected Data of the Third National Industrial Census of 1995 of the People's Republic of China: Volume of State-Owned, Foreign-Funded and Township Enterprises*, Beijing, China Statistics Press, 1997.

Yao Yang: Effects of Non State-Owned Economic Components on the Technical Efficiency of Industrial Enterprises in China, in *Economic Research*, 1998 (12).

Zhang Jun, Information Cost, Limited Rationality and Simplified Planning: Analysis of the Structure of the Planned Economic in China, in *Economic Development Studies*, 1992 (2).

Zhang Jun: Demand, Scale Effect and Loss Making Patterns of Chinese State-Owned Industry, in *Economic Studies*, 1998 (8).

J. Zhang, Market Size, Scale Economies, and the Pattern of Loss Making in China's Industry: 1978–1997, *East Asian Review*, 2000 3, (3), pp. 1–27.

Zhang Jun: Changing Pattern of Profit Rate of Chinese State-Owned Industrial Sector (1980–1998), in *Economic Studies*, 2001 (3).

Zhang Jun: *Double Regulation Economics: China's Economic Reform 1978-1992*, Shanghai SDX Joint Publishing Company, Shanghai People's Publishing House, 1997.

Zhang Jun, Shi Shaohua: Changes in Total factor Productivity of Chinese economy: 1952–1998, *Journal of World Economics*, 2003 (2), 8.

Part IV
Productivity and Economic Growth

Chapter 7
Industrial Reform and Efficiency Change in China: Methods, Data, Literatures and Existing Results

7.1 Introduction

For all its limitations, there is nothing more fascinating for economists than the study of economic growth and productivity changes (mainly called "total factor productivity" or "TFP"). Since economists developed a theoretical framework and accounting techniques for economic growth in the 1950s, the study of productivity has reached a period of sustained prosperity. In the early days, productivity studies were mainly done in the United States and other developed economies, such as Solow (1957), Denison (1969) and Jorgenson and Griliches (1967).[1] Later, the research was shifted to the Soviet economy (see Jun Zhang and Han Xianwang's theoretical review of these research documents).[2] From the1980s, the East Asian economy, which created the so-called "Asian miracle", became the focus of empirical research on productivity and growth accounting and triggered a debate about the sustainability of East Asia's economic growth.[3]

Since the1990s, along with the implementation plan of economic reform in China and the sustained period of its rapid growth, the productivity behind Chinese economic reform and growth once again attracted a large number of economists' interest. In the process of China's rapid economic growth, the industrial sector has received special attention. Unlike the reform of the Chinese agriculture (1978–1984), industrial reform, especially the reform of state-owned sector and non-state sector growth, has always been one of the most important topics for economists to study the efficiency and financial performance of Chinese economy after the reform because

[1] Solow (1957), Denison (1969), Jorgenson and Griliches (1967).

[2] Jun and Xianwang (1996).

[3] To be familiar with the research literatures on East Asian economic growth patterns and their interpretations, see the World Bank's research reports. For details, see: World Bank (1995). In addition, Felipe (1999) provides a clear and beautiful overview of the research literature and its debates on total factor productivity (TFP) changes in East Asia's economic growth. See Felipe (1999).

J. Zhang, *Reform, Transformation and Growth*, Understanding China,
https://doi.org/10.1007/978-981-99-5712-5_7

of its complex and challenging nature. Therefore, in the economics circle, a large number of research resources have been put into the empirical research and policy evaluation of China's industrial reform performance, which eventually provided us with a lot of rich research literatures. Although the literatures in many ways still contain differences in understanding and explanations—some views are even quite different—the differences in methods and conclusions provides us with a new perspective, alternative ideas and rich evidence to better understand the nature and strategies of the Chinese industrial reform and the influence of reform on industrial performance.

It is worth pointing out that the economic research on China's industrial reform has also directly promoted the process of China's economic research and statistical data construction. In the early 1980s, some international research projects on China's industry reform began to focus on the defects of industrial statistics of China, which are amending, converting and constructing a lot of time series data and price index of Chinese industry. Later research projects, based on extensive surveys, began to acquire first-hand data from their sample businesses (ranging from a dozen to thousands of enterprises). It can be said that without these research projects and their results, our confidence in China's industrial statistics and the ability to evaluate the performance of industrial reform will be greatly reduced. Therefore, it should be said that these research documents themselves have constituted an important achievement of China's economic reform.

The study of China's industrial reform should not only overcome the problems of data, but also involve testing of many propositions of economics and techniques of econometrics and their applications in detail. Today, familiarity with these documents itself will be a challenging and frontier work. Therefore, we believe that it is necessary to review and summarize these important research literatures about China's industrial reform in the past 20 years, which not only has an important significance for us to understand China's industrial innovation performance, but also very important for us to better master the analysis ability and empirical technology for studying modern economics and understand the application of economics theory. In this paper, we aim at the research literatures on the change of total factor productivity, because the research in this field reflects the creative work of economists in the two aspects of data and technology.

The structure of this paper is as follows: in the second part, we provide a simple "manual" on the definition and calculation methods of total factor productivity based on the existing literature. Then, in the third part, we give a general introduction to the basic viewpoints and theoretical basis of the existing literature on whether China's industrial reform has improved the efficiency of state-owned enterprises. The fourth part is a relatively technical review and discussion on the differences and the reasons for different conclusions in the existing research literature on the problem of total factor productivity of China's industrial sector. The fifth part deals with the possible sources used by economists to explain the change of total factor productivity, including interpretation and experience studies on technical efficiency, technology progress, scale economy and other issues. The sixth part briefly summarizes and examines the model of efficiency change of township enterprises, and compares them with the overall productivity change model of Chinese economy. The final part is the conclusion of this article.

7.2 Definition and Calculation of Total Factor Productivity (TFP)[4]

In economics, "productivity" refers to the efficiency of turning inputs into output during production. In the past, our productivity index in traditional social economic statistics only had "single factor productivity", such as labor productivity, capital output ratio etc. However, the production process usually requires the simultaneous use of labor and capital as the two elements of production. When we use the capital to replace labor (i.e., increase capital investment and reduce labor input) and produce the same amount of products as before, labor productivity will increase because of reduced labor input, while capital productivity decreases due to the increase in capital investment. In this case, single factor productivity is not a good indicator of productivity change. Therefore, in the literatures of economic research, total factor productivity (TFP) and its changes are often used to measure the level of productivity and productivity change of an enterprise.

Unlike single factor productivity, TFP, or multi-factor productivity (MFP), refers to the ratio of total output to comprehensive factor inputs. The so-called comprehensive factor input is a weighted average of all factors inputs. For example, the quantity of labor and capital invested in a production process is L and K respectively, and its comprehensive factor inputs can be written in the following way (or other forms):

$$X = L^{\alpha} K^{\beta}$$

α and β are normalized labor and capital output elasticity, that is, $\alpha + \beta = 1$. If the output is Y, the total factor productivity obtained in accordance with the above definition shall be:

$$TFP = Y/X = Y/(L^{\alpha} K^{\beta})$$

Calculated by total differential and reorganized, the equation will become:

$$\frac{\mathrm{d}(TFP)}{TFP} = \frac{\mathrm{d}Y}{Y} - \alpha\frac{\mathrm{d}L}{L} - \beta\frac{\mathrm{d}K}{K}$$

We use a, y, l and k to represent the growth rate of TFP, Y, L and K, then we get:

$$a = y - \alpha l - \beta k$$

[4] Here, I used part of Shi Shaohua's earlier work.

According to the definition, αl and βk are the output elasticity of labor and capital, representative of the output growth caused by the increase of labor and capital; therefore, what is reflected in TFP growth is the output growth that cannot be explained by factor input growth. It is usually interpreted as technological progress. Since Solow (1957) has made a pioneering work on the theory of aggregate production function and total factor productivity, we generally call a the "Solow residual". We can also see from $a = y - \alpha l - \beta k = \alpha(y - l) + \beta(y - k)$ that, the change in *TFP* is actually a weighted average of changes in the productivity of each single factor.

So far, the most popular method of measuring total factor productivity change is the Solow residual, which uses $a = y - \alpha l - \beta k$ in the above definition to calculate the growth rate of *TFP*. Because we can obtain directly the growth rate of output, labor input and capital investment through the statistical data, so the key point of this method is to accurately estimate the coefficient value of α and β contributed by labor and capital to output growth. People usually use two methods to get the coefficient, the first method being the econometric one, namely, to estimate the output elasticity of labor and capital through regression of an enterprise's production function and use the output elasticity as the estimated values α and β; The second approach is to use the proportion of labor remuneration and capital compensation in net output as the approximate values of α and β. Next, we will give a brief introduction and discussion of different methods for computing *TFP* based on a large number of existing literatures.

Method (1):

Suppose the production function of an enterprise is a Cobb Douglas production function:

$$Y = AL^{\alpha_L} K^{\alpha_K}$$

If we use logarithm form for this equation, we will get:

$$\text{Ln}\, Y = \text{Ln}\, A + \alpha_L \,\text{Ln}\, L + \alpha_K \,\text{Ln}\, K$$

With output, capital and labor data, we can estimate the labor and capital output elasticity of α_L and α_K by using OLS. It should be pointed out that $\alpha_L + \alpha_K$ is not necessarily equal to 1, although in most cases, economists prefer to assume $\alpha_L + \alpha_K = 1$. The meaning of $\alpha_L + \alpha_K = 1$ is that the scale returns remain unchanged; if $\alpha_L + \alpha_K > 1$, the scale returns increase; conversely, the returns decrease. According to the previous definition of *TFP*, $\alpha + \beta$ must be equal to 1, so we will normalize α_L and α_K to make them as:

$$\alpha = \alpha_L/(\alpha_L + \alpha_K)$$

$$\beta = \alpha_K/(\alpha_L + \alpha_K)$$

Obviously, $\alpha+\beta = 1$. By introducing α and β into the formula of Solow residuals, we can get the growth rate of *TFP*:

$$a = y - \alpha l - \beta k$$

More generally, we can assume that the production function of an enterprise is "transcendental logarithmic function":

$$\begin{aligned}\mathrm{Ln}(Y_t) = \alpha_0 0 + \alpha_L \mathrm{Ln}(L_t) + \alpha_K \mathrm{Ln}(K_t) + 1/2 \cdot \alpha_{LL} \mathrm{Ln}^2(L_t) \\ + 1/2 \cdot \alpha_{KK} \mathrm{Ln}^2(K_t) + \alpha_{LK} \mathrm{Ln}(L_t) \mathrm{Ln}(K_t)\end{aligned}$$

When $\alpha_{LL} = \alpha_{KK} = \alpha_{LK} = 0$, the above formula is reduced to:

$$\mathrm{Ln}(Y_t) = \alpha_0 + \alpha_L \mathrm{Ln}(L_t) + \alpha_K \mathrm{Ln}(K_t)$$

It is obvious that the Cobb Douglas function is a special form when the quadratic term coefficient of the transcendental logarithmic function is 0. Since there are quadratic items in the transcendental logarithmic production function, the output elasticity is not only α_L and α_K, it is also related to the variable values in the expanded formula and the quadratic term coefficients, and therefore is dynamic. The output elasticity of labor and capital defined by the above transcendental logarithmic production function should be:

$$S_{Lt} = \alpha_L + \alpha_{LL} \mathrm{Ln}(L_t) + \alpha_{LK} \mathrm{Ln}(K_t)$$

$$S_{Kt} = \alpha_K + \alpha_{KK} \mathrm{Ln}(K_t) + \alpha_{LK} \mathrm{Ln}(L_t)$$

Dealt with normalization, the estimated value of α and β in the Solow residual formula can be obtained:

$$\alpha_t = S_{Lt}/(S_{Lt} + S_{Kt})$$

$$\beta_t = S_{Kt}/(S_{Lt} + S_{Kt})$$

As a result, the TFP growth rate for phase t is:

$$a_t = y_t - \alpha_t l_t - \beta_t k_t$$

Method (2):

The proportion of labor and capital reward in net output is used as the approximate value of α and β. Suppose that the production function of an enterprise is $Y = AL^{\alpha_L} K^{\alpha_K}$ and this hypothesis can satisfy the fact that the scale returns are constant, i.e., $\alpha_L + \alpha_K = 1$. The marginal outputs of labor and capital are:

$$dY/dL = \alpha_L A L^{1-\alpha_L} K^{\alpha_K} = \alpha_L Y/L$$

$$dY/dK = \alpha_K A L^{\alpha_L} K^{1-\alpha_K} = \alpha_K Y/K$$

Because in the case of producer equilibrium, the price of labor and capital should be equal to its marginal output, that is:

$$P_L = dY/dL = \alpha_L Y/L$$

$$P_K = dY/dK = \alpha_K Y/K$$

The proportion of labor remuneration and capital remuneration in net output is:

$$R_L = P_L L/Y = \alpha_L, R_K = P_K K/Y = \alpha_K$$

That is to say, under the condition that the competitive producer equilibrium can be satisfied, the proportion of capital and labor remunerations in the net output is directly equal to the output elasticity of labor and capital, so we can calculate the growth rate of TFP by approximately using the proportion of labor and capital remunerations in the net output as the estimated value of α and β.

In the first method introduced earlier, the production function itself does not change over time, which is suitable for analyzing cross sectional data. But for the time sequence data, a more reasonable assumption is that with the improvement of TFP, technological progress has also caused changes in the production function. Under the assumption of "Hicks neutral" technological progress, the Cobb Douglas production function considering technological progress is $Y_t = A(t)L_t{}^{\alpha_L} K_t{}^{\alpha_K}$, out of which $A(t)$ represents the level of production technology in stage t; assuming $A(t) = A_0 e^{\alpha_T t}$, then:

$$Y_t = A_0 e^{\alpha_T t} L_t{}^{\alpha_L} K_t{}^{\alpha_k}$$

Calculated by total differential and reorganized, the equation will be:

$$dY_t/Y_t = \alpha_T + \alpha_L dL_t/L_t + \alpha_K dK_t/K_t$$

Or,

$$\alpha_T = y - \alpha_L l - \alpha_K k$$

We have noted that, when $\alpha_L + \alpha_K = 1$, α_T is identical with Solow residuals. As a result, we have obtained another method for estimating the time parameter of TFP growth rate.

Method (3):

Time parameter method. Suppose the production function of an enterprise is a Cobb Douglas function:

$$\mathrm{Ln}(Y_t) = \alpha_0 + \alpha_T t + \alpha_L \mathrm{Ln}(L_t) + \alpha_K \mathrm{Ln}(K_t)$$

or a transcendental logarithmic function:

$$\begin{aligned}\mathrm{Ln}(Y_t) = \alpha_0 + \alpha_T t + \alpha_L \mathrm{Ln}(L_t) + \alpha_K \mathrm{Ln}(K_t) + 1/2 \cdot \alpha_{LL} \mathrm{Ln}^2(L_t) \\ + 1/2 \cdot \alpha_{KK} \mathrm{Ln}^2(K_t) + \alpha_{LK} \mathrm{Ln}(L_t) \mathrm{Ln}(K_t)\end{aligned}$$

We can get the estimated value of α_T by regressing the actual time sequence data, and the estimated value can be regarded as the growth rate of TFP we want to estimate.

In the methods we have mentioned, we can think of Solow residual or the growth of TFP as "technological progress". However, in theory, this needs to satisfy a condition, that is, the enterprise should have 100% technical efficiency. That is, under the given technical conditions and input constraints, the output of the enterprise must be maximized; in other words, the enterprise always produces on the frontier (or boundary) of its possibility of production. However, it is impossible to satisfy this condition, for most enterprises are producing within the frontiers of their production possibilities. In this case, both the absolute change of technology (technological progress) and the change of technical efficiency will affect the TFP. Or, even without any technological progress, the improvement of technical efficiency alone should also lead to a rise in total factor productivity. This leads us to the so-called production frontier approach.[5] Obviously, this approach actually breaks down the sources of change in TFP and is therefore valuable in empirical research. We will now introduce the method of production function of stochastic frontier.

Method (4):

Method of stochastic frontier production function. Suppose the production function of enterprise i is:

$$\mathrm{Ln}\, Y_i(t) = \alpha_0 + \alpha_T t + \alpha_L \mathrm{Ln}\, L_i(t) + \alpha_K \mathrm{Ln}\, K_i(t) + u_i(t)$$

The $u_i(t) \leq 0$, which means enterprise i is inefficient technically; when $u_i(t) = 0$, enterprise i is located in the production possibility frontier. The technical efficiency of enterprise i is defined as:

---

[5] The early literatures on production frontier approach mainly include R. Shephard (1953), Solow (1957), M. J. Farrel (1957) and D. J. Aigner & S. Chu (1968). Among them, Farrel's thesis is recognized as a groundbreaking classic. In empirical research, there are promising frontier approaches, stochastic frontier methods and panel data methods. A review of these literatures can be found in Wu (1996).

$$TE_i(t) = \frac{\text{the actual output of enterprise } i}{\text{the maximum possible output of enterprise } i} = e^{u_i(t)}$$

Because $u_i(t) \leq 0$, the technology efficiency of enterprise i $0 < TE_i(t) \leq 1$. When both sides of the production function are calculated by total differential and reorganized, we get:

$$dY_i(t)/Y_i(t) = \alpha_T + \alpha_L dL_i(t)/L_i(t) + \alpha_K dK_i(t)/K_i(t) + ui\prime(t)$$

Because $u_i\prime(t) = dTE_i(t)/TE_i(t)$, the TFP growth rate of enterprise i is

$$\frac{d(TFP_i(t))}{TFP_i(t)} = \alpha_T + \frac{d(TE_i(t))}{TE_i(t)}$$

Therefore, TFP growth rate = technical progress rate + technical efficiency change rate.

Unlike the Solow residual method, the stochastic frontier production function method breaks down the TFP change into two parts, namely, pure technological progress and relative technical efficiency change. Figure 7.1 illustrates the difference and relationship between TFP growth rate obtained by Solow residual method and stochastic frontier production function method. In the Solow residual method, the firm is assumed to have 100% technical efficiency. Therefore, in the t period, under the input level of X_1, the output level is $Y_1{}^t$; in the $t + 1$ period and under the X_2 input level, the output level is $Y_2{}^{t+1}$. The contribution of technological progress to output is indicated by two vertical distance TC of the production possibility frontier (represented in Fig. 7.1 by dotted lines). The contribution of input growth to output is expressed by ΔX, so we have got:

$$Y_2{}^{t+1} - Y_1{}^t = \left(Y_2{}^{t+1} - Y_1{}^{t+1}\right) + \left(Y_1{}^{t+1} - Y_1{}^t\right) = \Delta X + TC$$

The change in total factor productivity obtained by Solow residual method is:

$$\Delta TFP = \Delta Y - \Delta X = TC$$

However, the technical efficiency of a real enterprise is not 100%, so the actual production curve of enterprises (indicated by solid lines in Fig. 7.1) is below the production possibility frontier, and the vertical distance between the curves of actual production and the production possibility frontier has measured the level of the technical inefficiency of enterprise. In the t period, under the input of X_1, the actual output was Y_1; in the $t + 1$ period, under the input of X_2, the actual output was Y_2. Hence:

$$\begin{aligned} Y_2 - Y_1 &= \left(Y_2{}^{t+1} - Y_1{}^{t+1}\right) + \left(Y_1{}^{t+1} - Y_1{}^t\right) + [\left(Y_1{}^{t+1} - Y_1\right) - \left(Y_2{}^{t+1} - Y_2\right) \\ &= \Delta X + TC + (TI_1 - TI_2) \end{aligned}$$

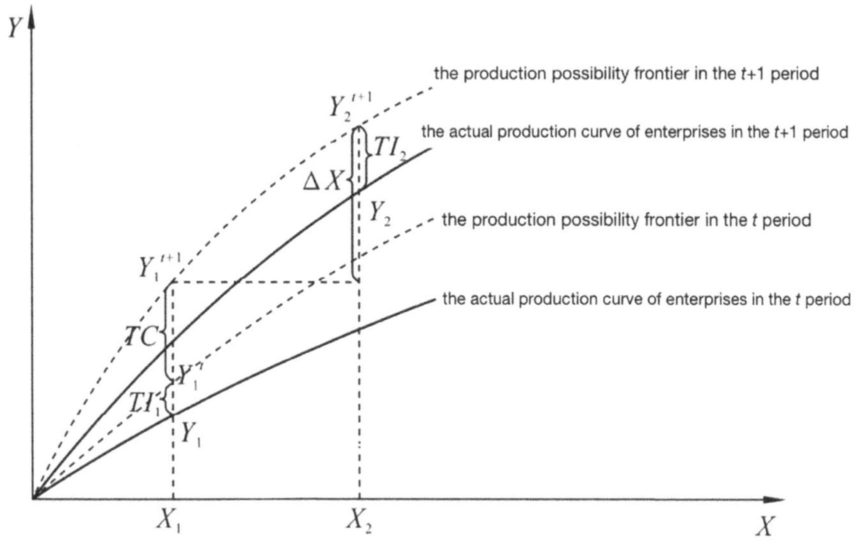

Fig. 7.1 TFP Calculated by Solow residual and Stochastic Frontier production function methods

the change of TFP obtained by the stochastic frontier production function method is:

$$\Delta TFP = TC + (TI_1 - TI_2)$$

That is to say, in the change of TFP, besides technical progress factor, there is also the change of technical efficiency. When technical efficiency is raised, i.e., when TI falls, the growth rate of TFP will be higher than the rate of technological progress.

7.3 Souring Out and Review of Main Literatures[6]

At the beginning of China's economic reform and opening up, the World Bank sent an economists' delegation which made an investigation tour in China for several months. After that, the World Bank published their report.[7] When it comes to China's industrial sector, the report says: "China's industrial productivity growth is not striking." During the years of 1957–1979, the average actual output value of each worker increased by about 3.7%, slightly higher than the average of other low-income and middle-income countries. But the amount of capital occupied by each worker grew faster. Therefore, if labor and capital were calculated together, the TFP, since 1957, seems to have stalled (which means that the output increase was completely due to

[6] This part is a further expansion of our earlier literature review.

[7] World Bank (1982).

the increase of use of factors of production, rather than the increasing efficiency of production factors)."

In 1984, the World Bank carried out another survey of China's economy, and the report published in 1985 again highlighted the view two years before: "The productivity level is disappointing..... In China's state-owned enterprises, TFP had increased in the period of 1952–1957, but in the following years from 1957 to 1982, it has been stagnant and even gone backward."[8]

These are, in fact, the mainstream views of the majority of foreign research in that period on the productivity of China's (state-owned) industrial sector before the reform. Part of this view should be the basic conclusion of empirical research from earlier Western economic circles on the productivity of state-owned enterprises of the Soviet Union, which held that the output growth of state-owned enterprises is mainly due to faster increase of investment, rather than the efficiency improvement or technology progress. A study by Professor Zou Zhizhuang at this time seems to have strengthened the understanding of the mainstream economists in the West. Using "comparable price" as a deflator of input and output prices for China's industrial enterprises commonly used in China, Zou Zhizhuang (1984) estimated the "real" inputs and outputs of the industrial enterprises in China, and then calculated the growth rate of total factor productivity of Chinese industry but found no trend of growth. Therefore, he believed that the increase in China's industrial output is mainly due to the increase of capital assets, not the improvement of technology.[9]

Chinese economists disagreed about these early studies. For example, Shi Qingqi and others (1986) pointed out in the evaluation of the World Bank report that, the fact that capital equipment radio (capital labor ratio) grew faster than productivity growth does not necessarily mean that there is no TFP growth.[10] We know from the simplest theoretical method that TFP growth is equal to the product of labor productivity growth minus output elasticity of capital and growth rate of capital equipment rate. Unless the output elasticity of capital is equal to 1, the TFP should grow. They believe that the output elasticity of capital of China's industry is unlikely close to 1, but between 0.2 and 0.3, which means that only when the growth rate of capital-output ratio is 3–5 times more than the labor productivity growth rate can the TFP growth rate become negative. Shi Qingqi and others estimated that the TFP of China's industrial sector grew by an average of about 1.82% a year over the years of 1964–1982, and its contribution to output growth was 20%. Later, Chen Shizhong and Sang Gengtao (1986) also reached a similar conclusion in another way. They noted that during 1976–1982, the average annual TFP growth of Chinese industrial enterprises was 2.23%, a 23.8% contribution to output growth.[11]

However, earlier studies and disagreements involve data authenticity and differences in the range of estimate of output elasticity of capital. Rather than estimating the production function, they tend to determine the range of values of output elasticity

[8] World Bank (1985).

[9] Zhizhuang (1984).

[10] Qingqi et al. (1986).

[11] Shizhong and Sangtao (1986).

based on experience before using Solow's residual approach to calculate the growth rate of TFP. The flaw was not corrected until 1988. In 1988, Chen Kuan, Jefferson, Rawski, Wang Hongchang and Zheng Yuxin jointly published a paper titled Change of Chinese industrial Productivity: 1953–1985,[12] which is one of the most influential Western documents in the study of efficiency change in China's industrial sectors in the 1980s. In their research, the authors first reviewed previous studies and pointed out and summarized the problems in the data in the earlier studies as follows: ① the data of output and input is inconsistent. Earlier studies often used output data from all state-owned enterprises, but only the input data from independent accounting state-owned enterprises; ② To calculate capital stock based on the original value of fixed assets published in Chinese statistics tends to exaggerate the actual growth rate of the stock of fixed capital which may underestimate the TFP growth rate as an "item of the "residual error"; ③ The capital and labor data in China contain a large number of non-productive components, which, if not excluded, will also underestimate the growth rate of TFP; ④ the obtaining of value for output elasticity of capital is arbitrary. If the output elasticity of capital is underestimated, so will the growth rate of TFP.

They tried to overcome the problems in these data, on the basis of which they sorted out the data of 1953–1985, and regressed the given Cobb Douglas production function and transcendental logarithm production function. But they mainly used the output elasticity of capital estimated by the trans-log production function. They found that, during 1953–1985, the TFP of China's state-owned enterprises grew by about 1.9–2.8% annually. In particular, the growth rates of net output during the periods of 1957–1978 and 1978–1985 were almost the same, but the growth rates of TFP were quite different. During 1957–1978, TFP grew only by 0.4–1.4%, and during 1978–1985 after the economic reform, the growth rate of TFP was up to 4.8–5.9%, which means that the efficiency of state-owned enterprises has been remarkably improved by the Chinese economic reform.

Similar to the conclusion of Chen Kuan's study, Jefferson and others also confirmed that the efficiency of Chinese industry has a significant trend of growth since the reform in another paper published in 1992 titled Growth, Efficiency and Convergence in China's State and Collective Industry.[13] But they used the sample cross-section data of 293 companies in 1984 and 1987 and, in their study, the inputs also include the intermediate products, that is, three factor production function, which uses output as the total output value instead of net output value, is used. The paper found that the efficiency of state-owned enterprises during 1980–1987 was significantly improved with the average annual growth rate of TFP reaching 2.4% and the TFP growth rate of the collective enterprise was even higher, reaching 4.6%. They also relaxed the hypothesis of constant returns to scale, and found that there is a significant scale effect in state-owned and collective enterprises.

It can be said that after the publication of Chen Kuan and Jefferson's papers, the conclusion that China's economic reform has a significant positive effects on the

[12] Chen Kuan et al. (1988).

[13] Jefferson et al. (1992).

improvement of the efficiency of the industrial sector (including state-owned enterprises) has almost been accepted. Of course, the literatures during this period also include papers of Dollar (1990), Groves et al. (1994), Huang and Meng (1995), Wan Guanghua (1995) and Guo Kesha (1993), which all found the calculated TFP of Chinese state-owned enterprises grew significantly in the 1980s after the reform.[14] But in 1994, Hu Yongtai, Sachs and others published a paper challenging this "optimistic" view, which stirred a heated debate in the economic world.[15]

The article by Hu Yongtai and others differs significantly from the conclusion of the above studies. They used 300 large and medium-sized enterprises' data in the period of 1984–1988 and found that the TFP growth rate of state-owned enterprises in that period was zero at most, although they also confirmed the discovery by Jefferson and others that the collective enterprises have a higher TFP growth rate than state-owned enterprises. They argued through their study that Chen Kuan and others had gone too far in eliminating the nonproductive investment in the Chinese industrial sector, so they could not accept their approach of completely eliminating the nonproductive investment. At the same time, Hu Yongtai and others believed that the reason for Jefferson to claim that the state-owned enterprises enjoyed a positive TFP growth rate was mainly because they overestimated the price index of intermediate products. We will discuss the selection of "nonproductive inputs" and price index in part four.

Jefferson and others then responded immediately to Hu Yongtai's criticism. They argue that their research does not overestimate the actual output data of state-owned enterprises and underestimate the actual value of their intermediate inputs; instead, they believe that the output data of township enterprises may have been overestimated. The issue became clear later as China published data in the third national industrial census in 1995 (we will review the problem of overestimation later in conjunction with the data of industry census).

In order to give a clearer picture of the differences in the conclusions of existing research on changes in the total factor productivity of state-owned enterprises, we have summarized the major findings and conclusions collected in Table 7.1. We also noted that in 1997, Sachs and Hu Yongtai wrote in collaboration a 60-page therotical summary titled Understanding the Performance of Chinese Economy. Concerning the content of the reform in the state-owned sector, the summery made a comment on the research literatures about whether the TFP of Chinese state-owned enterprise is growing, which is a typical example of articles of the this kind.[16]

For example, the authors wrote: "The productivity of state-owned enterprises is a highly controversial issue. Some studies suggest it has been improved, while others say there is no improvement at all. However, before commenting on these arguments, it is necessary to note two consistent views: ① the productivity growth of state-owned enterprises is slower than that of non-state-owned enterprises; ② even if there is a

---

[14] Dollar (1990), Groves et al. (1994), Huang and Meng (1995), Wan Guanghua (1995), Guo Kesha (1993).

[15] Woo et al. (1994).

[16] Sachs and Woo (1997).

Table 7.1 Different estimated results of TFP growth rate of China's industrial enterprises

Researcher	Time	Average annual growth rates of TFP (%)	
		State enterprise	Collective enterprise
Zou Zhizhuang (Chinese ed., 1984)	1952–1981	≤0	
World Bank (Chinese ed., 1985)	1952–1982 1952–1957 1957–1978 1978–1982	0.6–1.5 7.5–9.3 −0.5–0.4 −2.0–1.9	
Shi Qingqi et al. (1986)	1964–1982	1.82	
Chen Shizhong and Sang Gengtao (1986)	1970–1982 1970–1976 1976–1982	0.47 −1.26 2.23	
Chen Kuan et al. (1988)	1953–1985 1953–1957 1957–1978 1978–1985	2.6 4.6 1.1 5.9	
Gordon and Li (1989)	1983–1987	4.6	
Dollar (1990)	1978–1992	4.7	
Zhang Junkuo (1991)[a]	1953–1989 1953–1977 1978–1989	0.65 0.01 2.56	
Li Jingwen et al. (1992)[b]	1953–1990 1953–1978 1979–1990	0.37 −0.8 2.532	
Jefferson et al. (1992)	1980–1988 1980–1984 1984–1988	2.40 1.80 3.01	4.63 3.45 5.86
World Bank (Chinese ed.,1992)	1980–1984 1984–1988 1980–1988	1.8 3.0 2.4	3.45 5.86 4.63
Ma Jun and Jin (1992)	1978–1990	1.0	9.1
Jefferson and Singh (1993)[c]	1980–1988	2.5	
Guo Kesha (1993)	1953–1978 1979–1990	0.2 3.6	
Groves et al. (1994)	1980–1989	4.5	
Woo et al. (1994)	1984–1988	≤0	8.8–11.2
Wan Guanghua (1995)	1957–1988 1957–1978 1978–1988	1.8 1.3 2.8	
Jefferson et al. (Chinese ed., 1995)[d]	1980–1992 1980–1984 1984–1988 1988–1992	2.50 2.24 3.68 1.58	3.43 2.80 4.52 2.98

(continued)

Table 7.1 (continued)

Researcher	Time	Average annual growth rates of TFP (%)	
		State enterprise	Collective enterprise
Wang Jun (1996)[e]	1980–1992	2.58	
Zhang Ronggang (1997)[f]	1991–1994	3.84	

[a]Junkuo (1991)
[b]Jingwen et al. (1992)
[c]Jefferson and Singh (1993)
[d]Jefferson and Yuxin (1995)
[e]Jun (1996)
[f]Ronggang (1997)

growth, the improvement of TFP is insignificant." The debate, however, is whether, in the course of China's reform, the growth rate of TFP in state-owned enterprises is actually declining.

The first generation of empirical research generally considered that the reform of state-owned enterprises after 1978 did not bring about the the growth of TFP. This argument became blurred with the subsequent three conclusions. The first conclusion found a "higher" TFP growth rate as in the studies by Jefferson, Rawski, Zheng and (JRZ, 1992), Groves, Hong, McMillan, Naughton (GHMN, 1994); the second conclusion found almost no or deteriorating technical changes as in the studies by Woo, Hai, Jin, Fan (WHJF, 1994). The results of the third conclusion were between the previous two claiming that TFP growth slowed down after 1985.[17]

Recently, Japanese economist O. Keijiro and others made another estimation of the TFP change of Chinese state-owned enterprises since the reform of the China according to the statistical data of the official publications of the *Chinese Statistical Yearbook* and *Statistical Yearbook of Chinese Industrial Economy*.[18] Based on the research results mentioned above, they first estimated the actual output of China's state-owned enterprises by reducing the net industrial output value calculated via price for many years. But in order to obtain the price index needed to reduce the net industrial output value, they calculated the price index with the total industrial output value expressed by the current price and the constant price of the state-owned enterprises. With regard to labor input, they distinguished productive from non-productive workers, and dealt with the number of productive workers in each year by estimating the proportion of productive workers (0.85) based on the composition of state-owned enterprises in 1984 and 1990. In estimating capital input, they used the methods of Chen Kuan and others, but used data from all state-owned industrial

[17] A few years ago, Jefferson and Rawski mentioned that among the 13 empirical studies of total factor productivity of China's state-owned enterprises they had observed, 9 indicated that the efficiency of state-owned enterprise has been significantly improved s after the reform, with an annual 2–4% growth rate of TFP on average. Of the remaining 4 studies, the results of 2 were higher than this growth rate, while the results of the other 2 were lower. See Jefferson and Rawski (1994).

[18] Keijiro et al. (2000).

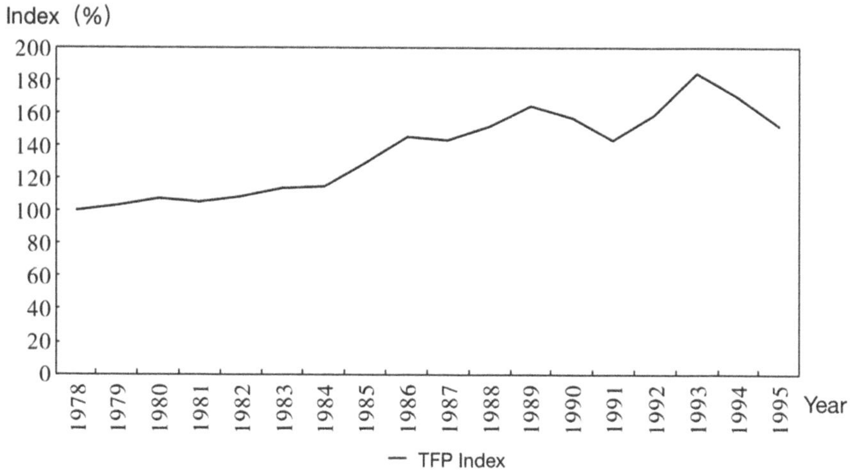

Fig. 7.2 TFP index of China's state-owned enterprises (1978–1995)

enterprises (including non independent accounting). Finally, they also used the capital and labor output elasticities—0.54 and 0.46—estimated by Chen Kuan and others (1988).

Based on these preparations, they calculated and indexed the total factor productivity of state-owned enterprises in the period of 1978–1995, the results of which are shown in Fig. 7.2. According to their calculations, the net industrial output value of state-owned enterprises grew at an average annual rate of 6.3% during 1978–1995, while the average TFP of the same period increased by 2.5%. This means that the reform has had a positive impact on the efficiency of state-owned enterprises. However, based on the index change of TFP, the total factor productivity of state-owned enterprises has been at a standstill since the end of the 1980s, meaning that the reform after the 90 s barely affected the production efficiency of the state-owned enterprises. It is consistent with the conclusion of more detailed studies done by Wu (1995) and Jefferson (Jefferson et al. 1996) a few years ago, which found that the total factor productivity of state-owned enterprises had a trend of decline at the end of the 80s.[19]

In conclusion, despite the debate, much of the research into the total factor productivity changes in Chinese SOEs has contributed significantly to our understanding of the performance of China's industrial reform. Of course, the problem we cannot avoid is that, for the state-owned enterprises in transition, because of the inherent institutional constraints and market deficiencies, the mere TFP change itself does not necessarily lead to the improvement of social welfare. Therefore, the research on TFP still has some limitations in evaluating the effectiveness of the reform. This problem has finally been raised by Bai, Li and Wang (1999) in their paper.[20]

[19] Wu (1995).

[20] Bai et al. (1999).

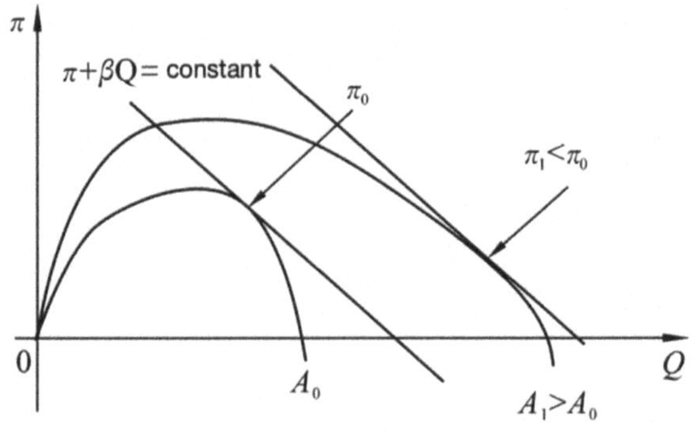

Fig. 7.3 Relationship between TFP and social welfare

In their paper, they argue that the use of TFP growth rate as the "bottom line" in evaluating the performance of state-owned enterprises in reform is questionable. They set up a simple model to show that when an enterprise, due to some reasons, does not want to maximize its profits, high productivity may in fact lead to more serious distorted resources allocation and deterioration of profits and economic efficiency. Therefore, with regard to the performance of state-owned enterprises during the reform period, the mere observation of the results of TFP may lead to misleading information.

They used Fig. 7.3 to illustrate the optimization problem faced by state-owned enterprises: when the managers of state-owned enterprises do not intend to maximize profits, the higher productivity levels will lead to lower profits. π and Q are the profits and outputs of state-owned enterprises respectively. A_0 and A_1 are two different productivity levels, while the inverted U curve represents an alternative relationship between profit and output. The objective function of the SOE manager is assumed to be $U(\pi, Q), = \pi + \beta Q$.

The logic of their views is as follows. The efficiency of an enterprise is determined by both technology and management decisions. The increase in productivity can enable firms to translate inputs into outputs at greater efficiency. The question, however, is how this technological improvement will affect the choice of the firm's output levels. When firms seek maximum profits, their actions will ensure that higher productivity can always improve social welfare levels and lead to greater efficiency. However, when the manager of the enterprise deviates from the goal of maximizing profits, higher productivity will lead to distorted business decision, thus partially or even completely offsetting the efficiency gained from the improved technology. For example, when managers of state-owned enterprises prefer higher output, the higher productivity (e.g., $A_1 > A_0$) will induce managers to stay away from output levels with maximized profits. As a result, the growth of TFP does not automatically mean improvement in social welfare and efficiency.

However, this criticism may not be directed solely at the research literature of Chinese state-owned enterprises, the theoretical questions raised here is universal. Indeed, TFP's study has its limitations; TFP as well as the measure of TFP are always faced with various theoretical challenges. But because of this, it has attracted so much attention and interest of economists.

7.4 Empirical Research Methods and Difference of Data[21]

Why there are controversial viewpoints about the changes of total factor productivity of Chinese state-owned enterprises in the existing literature? The reason both lie in the data selection (such as the use of official data, survey data or regional data, etc.), and the use of different production functions (some use Cobb Douglas production function while others use stochastic frontier production function); another reason is different estimation methods (for example, whether parameter method or non parametric method is used in the calculation of TFP growth rate), all of which result in different conclusions. We will now look at some research documents to show how differences in methods and data lead to inconsistent results.

(1) Estimation methods

In the calculation of total factor productivity, there are generally two estimation methods: parametric method and nonparametric method. Parameter method is mainly applied to the estimation of time sequence data. Specifically, there is a time parameter in the given production function whose coefficient value can be considered as the estimated value of the TFP. For example, if we set a simplest Cobb Douglas production function, $Q = AK^{\alpha}L^{\beta}$. When we need to analyze time sequence data, we have to add time vectors to have it extended to $Q = Ae^{mt}K^{\alpha}L^{\beta}$. Then, the function is to derive from time t, and $q = m + \alpha k + \beta l$, that is, $m = q - \alpha k - \beta l$, is obtained,[22] which is just the growth rate of TFP. Therefore, in many studies, researchers directly estimate the coefficient of the time parameter t as an estimated value of the growth rate of TFP. This is the parameter method.

As far as non time sequence data is concerned, only nonparametric estimation method can be used to estimate the growth rate of TFP. This method is to obtain the estimated value of capital and labor output elasticity by regressing the the production functions, and then use the Solow residual formula to calculate the growth rate of TFP directly. Of course, nonparametric methods can also be applied to time sequence data analysis. Sometimes, parametric methods and non parametric methods can be used together, namely, to estimate the time coefficient and the output elasticity of capital and labor at the same time, and then use these elasticities to calculate the growth rate of TFP according to the non parameter method.

For example, in the previous literature we mentioned, although Chen Kuan (Chen et al. 1988) and Hu Yongtai (Woo et al. 1994) have set more or less similar production function s in their papers, Chen uses a hybrid estimation method of parameters and non parameters to find that during 1978–1985, the growth rate of TFP of state-owned

---

[21] Chen Shiyi provided me with the data I needed to prepare this section.

[22] The small-case letters here mean growth rates.

enterprises were 4.8–5.9%. But the coefficient of t estimated by using the parameter method was only 1.3%, a difference of as much as four times between the two. Thus, as Wan Guanghua (Wan 1995) once pointed out, the use of parameter estimation would lead to a severe underestimation of the TFP growth rate. This is because the coefficient of t captures only the so-called "neutral" part of technological progress, yet in fact, non-neutral technological advances may be the most important component of TFP growth. When the state-owned enterprises have experienced the rising capital-labor ratio since the reform, the output elasticity of capital may decline, which indicates that the technological progress of state-owned enterprises is not neutral. Therefore, in Hu Yongtai (Woo et al. 1994) and Zou Zhizhuang (1984)'s studies, coefficient of t, as the estimated value of the TFP growth rate, obviously underestimated the growth rate of TFP of Chinese state-owned enterprises. In addition, in the parameter method, the growth rate of TFP is simply assumed to be an average value in the whole samples, so if the growth rate of TFP is negative in the first place and turns to positive, then the average value will be close to zero, which could also lead to zero, even negative growth for TFP calculated by the parameter method.

(2) Data Processing

In the case of China, data processing mainly involves the selection and calculation of price index of industrial added value, estimation of the actual capital stock as well as elimination of non-productive inputs, etc. In the existing literature, these problems appear to be more complex and diversified than the methods of estimation.

① Industrial added value (and net output value) and price index. In data processing, the first problem is to obtain the data of industrial added value of time sequence and to deflate the corresponding price index needed by the industrial added value. However, China's official statistics do not have complete data on industrial added value, because only the net industrial output value is available before the adjustment of the statistical system in 1994. Therefore, most studies use industrial net output as output data, but the data of industrial added value after 1994 need to be approximately converted to net industrial output value according to empirical hypothesis as proposed by O. Keijiro and others. If industrial added value is used, then the data of industrial net output value before 1993 should be approximately converted according to hypothesis to obtain the industrial added value data of time sequence.

After getting the data of net industrial output value, the price index problem occurs, because the statistical data in China lacks the net industrial output value and the price index of intermediate products. Most studies can only use the price index of industrial output value as an approximate substitute for the price index of industrial net output value to deflate net output value. The specific method is often to divide the current price of total industrial output value by the constant price of total industrial output value to obtain the implicit price deflator of total industrial output price. The price index of total industrial output value so produced is called "implied" price index. Most studies use the implicit price index to deflate net Industrial output. In Table 7.2, we use the data from the State Bureau of Statistics to provide the calculation method of the implicit price index of industrial output value. But there are also studies using the results of the "ex factory price index of industrial products" survey carried out by the Urban Investigation Team of the State Statistics Bureau since 1984 to deflate the net industrial output such as those done by Jefferson and others. In the fifth column in Table 7.3 we presented the "general ex-factory price index of industrial products compiled by the Urban Investigation Team of the National Bureau of statistics and the constant 1990 general ex-factory price index of industrial products we calculated according to the above data (column 6).

However, to use the price index of the total output value to replace the net output price index is problematic, because the total industrial output value includes the value of intermediate inputs, and the price index (P_g) of the total output value is the weighted average of the net output price index (P_v) and intermediate product price index (P_m), i.e.:

$$P_g = \frac{P_v P_m}{(VA/GV)P_m + (1 - VA/GV)P_v}$$

VA and GV respectively indicate that the added value and total output value are calculated according to the current price. Therefore, only when the changes of total output value, net output and intermediate product price are consistent, can the net output price index be approximately replaced by the price index of the total output value.

However, with the quickening of China's economic market and the price liberalization, in general, the price of intermediate products is slightly faster than the final products, which will cause the total industrial output value of the same time to be smaller than the price index of intermediate products. According to the above formula, the price index of industrial net output value is lower than the price index of industrial output value. In this way, the relationship of the total output value price index, intermediate product price index and net output price index will become: $P_m > P_g > P_v$. In this case, if total industrial output price index price is used to approximately replace net output price index, it will lead to underestimation of net industrial output and overestimation of the value of intermediate products, so that the calculated growth rate of TFP will also be underestimated.

In the argument we mentioned in the last section, the choice of the price index is an important factor that leads to the difference between conclusions. For example, Hu Yongtai (Woo et al. 1994) believed that the reason that Jefferson (Jefferson et al. 1992) concluded that the total factor productivity of state-owned enterprises increased significantly in his studies is due to their choice of the price index of net industrial output value and the price index of intermediate products. The reason for pointing out the flaw in the price index of net industrial output value is that, if one accepts the data used by Jefferson and others, then it can be calculated that the price index of industrial net output value was decreasing in 1980–1988. But Hu Yongtai and others believe that during the period when other prices have risen, the decline in the price index of industrial net output value is contrary to common sense.

Hu Yongtai also criticized Jefferson for using the price index of intermediate products. Like Jefferson, Hu Yongtai also uses the production function of the three

Table 7.2 Calculation of total industrial output value in China and its price index

Year (1)	Total industrial output value of the country (2)	Total industrial output value of state and state holding enterprises (3)	Total industrial output value of collective enterprises (4)	Total industrial output value index of the whole country (5)	Total industrial output value of state and state holding enterprises (6)	Total industrial output value of collective enterprises (7)	Growth rate of total industrial output value calculated by current price of total output value of the year (last year = 100) (8)	Implicit price index of total industrial output value in 8th five-year-plan (last year = 100) (9)	Price index of total industrial output in column 9 converted into 1990 constant price (10)	Total industrial output value of 1990 constant price obtained by (2)/(10) × 1 (billion *yuan*) (11)
1978	4237	3289	948	113.55	114.44	110.58	113.74	100.17	68.99	6141.47
1979	4681	3674	1008	108.81	108.88	108.57	110.48	101.53	70.05	6682.37
1980	5154	3916	1213	109.27	105.61	119.24	110.1	100.76	70.58	7302.35
1981	5400	4037	1329	104.29	102.53	109.01	104.77	100.76	70.58	7302.35
1982	5811	4326	1442	107.82	107.05	109.54	107.61	99.81	70.77	8211.11
1983	6461	4739	1663	111.19	109.39	115.53	111.19	100	70.77	9129.57
1984	7617	5263	2263	116.28	108.92	134.85	117.89	101.39	71.75	10,616.03
1985	9716	6302	3117	121.39	112.94	132.69	127.56	105.08	75.4	12,885.94
1986	11,194	6971	3752	111.67	106.18	117.97	115.21	103.17	77.79	14,390.02
1987	13,813	8250	4782	117.69	111.3	123.24	123.4	104.85	81.56	16,936
1988	18,224	10,351	6587	120.79	112.61	128.16	131.93	109.23	89.09	20,455.72
1989	22,017	12,343	7858	108.54	103.86	110.48	120.81	111.31	99.17	22,201.27
1990	23,924	13,064	8523	107.76	102.96	109.02	108.66	100.84	100	23,924
1991	26,625	14,955	8783	114.77	108.62	118.4	111.29	96.97	96.97	27,456.95
1992	34,599	17,824	12,135	124.7	112.4	133.3	129.95	104.21	101.05	34,239.49
1993	48,402	22,725	16,464	127.3	105.7	135	139.89	109.89	111.05	43,585.77

(continued)

Table 7.2 (continued)

Year (1)	Total industrial output value of the country (2)	Total industrial output value of state and state holding enterprises (3)	Total industrial output value of collective enterprises (4)	Total industrial output value index of the whole country (5)	Total industrial output value of state and state holding enterprises (6)	Total industrial output value of collective enterprises (7)	Growth rate of total industrial output value calculated by current price of total output value of the year (last year = 100) (8)	Implicit price index of total industrial output value in 8th five-year-plan (last year = 100) (9)	Price index of total industrial output in column 9 converted into 1990 constant price (10)	Total industrial output value of 1990 constant price obtained by (2)/(10) × 1 (billion *yuan*) (11)
1994	70,176	26,201	26,472	124.2	106.5	124.9	144.99	116.74	129.64	54,131.44
1995	91,894	31,220	33,623	120.3	108.2	115.2	130.95	108.85	141.11	65,122.25
1996	99,595	36,173	39,232	116.59	105.13	120.88	108.38	92.96	131.17	75,928.18
1997	113,733	35,968	43,347	113.1	101.03	110.21	114.2	100.97	132.45	85,868.63
1998	119,048	33,621	45,730	110.75	100.1	109.1	104.67	94.51	125.18	95,101.45
1999	126,111	35,571	44,607	111.58	108.81	106	105.93	94.94	118.84	106,118.3

Note The total output value listed in columns 2–4 is 100 million *yuan* calculated at current price of year, and the index of total output value listed in columns 5–7 is calculated at comparable price (last year = 100)

Data Sources All data are from *China Statistical Yearbook* (2000); among them, the data of the total output value of 1979, 1981–1984 and 1986–1989 are missing in the volume of year of 2000, so has been filled up by the 2001 volume of *Chinese Industrial Economic Statistical Yearbook*. The results of 8–11th columns are from our calculations, out of which the growth rate in column 8 (previous year = 100) was gained by the previous period of industrial output value being divided by the current price of next period and then multiplied by 100 listed in column 2

Table 7.3 China's fixed asset price index and Ex factory price index of industrial products

Year (1)	Fixed asset price index constructed by Jefferson and others (1990 = 100) (2)	Fixed assets investment price index of *China Statistical Yearbook* (previous year = 100) (3)	Fixed assets price index calculated from the data of *China Statistical Yearbook* (after 1991) and the date of Jefferson and others (before 1989) (1990 = 100) (4)	General index of ex factory price of industrial products (previous year = 100) (5)	General index of ex factory price of industrial products of constant price of 1990 (6)
1978			41.3		55.98
1979	41.3		41.3	101.5	56.82
1980	41.3		41.3	100.5	57.11
1981	43.8		43.8	100.2	57.22
1982	44		44	99.8	57.11
1983	47.6		47.6	99.9	57.05
1984	51		51	101.4	57.85
1985	58.2		58.2	108.7	62.89
1986	66.6		66.6	103.8	65.27
1987	73.9		73.9	107.9	70.43
1988	79.5		79.5	115	81
1989	98.3		98.3	118.6	96.06
1990	100		100	104.1	100
1991	111.9	109.5	109.5	106.2	106.2
1992	125.5	115.3	126.3	106.8	113.42
1993		126.6	159.8	124	140.64
1994		110.4	176.5	119.5	168.07
1995		105.9	186.9	114.9	193.11
1996		104	194.3	102.9	198.71
1997		101.7	197.6	99.7	198.11
1998		99.8	197.3	95.9	189.99
1999		99.6	196.5	97.6	185.43
2000		101.1	198.6	102.8	190.62

Data Source Data in columns 3 and 4 are from Jefferson and others (1996) and *China Statistical Yearbook* (volumes of 1993–2001). Date of column 4 was calculated from columns 2 and 3. Data in column 5 are from *China Statistical Yearbook* (2001), p. 297 (Tables 9–12). Date in column 6 was recalculated by us

factor total output to estimate the coefficients of time t (TFP's growth rate), with the result that if the price index of intermediate products proposed by Jefferson is used, the TFP growth rate is 2.4%, but if the price index of intermediate products of the 300 large and medium-sized enterprises they have chosen is used, the growth rate of TFP is -1.4%. So, Hu Yongtai and others concluded that it is certain that Jefferson has overestimated the price index of intermediate product and underestimates the real value of intermediate products. Therefore, they also overestimated the actual output of state-owned enterprises and the growth rate of total factor productivity calculated based on these data. Jefferson and others (1995) responded to Hu Yongtai's criticism, arguing that, first, in the early stage of reform and opening up, it is possible for the price index of net industrial output to experience a period of decline because, with the price deregulation, it is possible that the price for purchasing raw materials will rise faster than the ex factory price of industrial products. When the price index of intermediate product is higher than the total output price index to a certain extent, there will be a decline in the net output price index. Second, it is true that the intermediate product price index set up through weighted construction according to the cost of raw material market price and the cost of planning price is indeed higher than the price index of total industrial output value used as an approximate alternative, but it does not exceed the result of survey on price index of intermediate inputs conducted by the Urban Investigation Team of the State Bureau of Statistics since 1984. Actually, it is even more conservative than the result. As a result, they argue that there is no excessive deflator in the value of intermediate products to exaggerate the growth rate of TFP in state-owned enterprises.

② Capital stock and capital price index. In the existing literature, estimates of capital stock are often based on the value of fixed assets. It is not appropriate to directly use the data of original value of fixed assets or net worth in China's statistical publications, because these data are obtained from the simple sum of the value of investment goods of different time and different levels of prices, so we have to make necessary corrections and value deflator on these data. China's statistical yearbooks usually calculate the original value of fixed assets and net worth based on the following two formulas:

$$KFO_t = KFO_{t-1} + I_t$$

$$KF_t = KF_{t-1} + I_t - \delta_t KFO_{t-1}$$

KFO and KF respectively represent the original value of fixed assets and net value, I represents investment in fixed assets in accordance with the current prices of the year, δ represents depreciation rate and t is the year.

In general, due to the factors of price changes, especially since the 1980s, the price of investment goods is rising very quickly; therefore, the investment value and the data of original value of fixed asset each yea since the reform are not comparable. If one simply uses the original value of fixed assets to calculate the fixed asset growth rate, he is bound to overstate the actual growth rate. That is one of the reasons why Chen Kuan (Chen et al. 1988) criticized earlier research literature for seriously underestimating the growth rate of TFP in China's state-owned enterprises. So, in later studies, the use of price index of fixed asset to deflate original value or net value to get the actual value of the data is becoming an important job. By the way, in the estimation of the actual net asset value of China's state-owned enterprises, Chen Kuan and others (1988) made the earliest important contributions.

With regard to the price index of fixed asset investment, the *China Statistical Yearbook* did not provide the index every year until 1993, and only the time sequence data of 1991–2000 was offered and none before 1990 was available.[23] Jefferson (Jefferson et al. 1996, p. 175) estimated the price index of China's fixed capital from 1979 to 1992. As the price index of both the State Bureau of Statistics and Jefferson are calculated through the weighted average of building installation deflator and equipment purchase deflator, the price index of fixed asset investment in *China Statistical Yearbook* and the data produced by Jefferson are consistent. In columns 2–4 in Table 7.3, we summarized the China's price index of fixed assets according to the research literatures of the State Bureau of Statistics and Jefferson. The ex factory price index for industrial products is also included in columns 5–6 of Table 7.3.

As we have mentioned, the price index of investment in fixed assets released by the State Bureau of Statistics (similar to the ex factory price index of industrial products we mentioned above) is based on the results of the survey conducted by the Urban Investigation Team of the State Bureau of Statistics. The survey was organized by the Urban Social and Economic Investigation Team and carried out by the urban investigation teams of provinces, autonomous regions, municipalities directly under the central government and counties according to the unified price survey system drawn up by the State Bureau of Statistics. The results, based on the basic raw data collected, were reported to the State Bureau of Statistics. The price survey of fixed assets investment is a non comprehensive investigation, which adopts the method of combining key investigation with typical case investigation. The price involved includes the actual purchase price or settlement price of the entity invested by the fixed asset. The investigation includes the output value of construction enterprises; major building material prices that constitue the construction engineering entities of current years such as steel, wood, cement, local materials (such as brick, tile, cement, sand, stone, etc.), chemical materials (such as paint etc.) and others; the price of labor as labor input (wages) and fee standards for various costs; investment prices of purchase of equipment and various other expenses.[24]

---

[23] See *China's Statistical Yearbook: 1993*, p. 269 (Tables 7–25), 1995, p. 250 (Tables 8–14), 1996, p. 272 (Tables 8–14), 1997, p. 283 (Tables 8–14), 1998, p. 318 (Tables 9–14), 1999, p. 310 (Tables 9–14), 2000, (Tables 9–14). 2001, Tables 9–14).

[24] Moreover, the selection of sample for fixed assets investment price survey adheres the following principles. First, the principle of choosing the survey site of construction installation projects: ① the sample units should have a certain degree of coverage; ② the investment activities should be excellent typical examples; ③ take into account different economic types; ④ the choice of key projects; ⑤ both the various kinds of economic sectors and different categories of projects should be considered. Second, the principle of choosing other expense survey sites: this principle is basically the same as the principle for construction installation projects, but special attention should be paid to those large

① Elimination of non-productive inputs. As everyone knows, Chinese state-owned enterprises have the excessive employment (the so-called redundant personnel) problem, and have to make a large amount of material and human resources investment for non-direct production because they have to bear a lot of social functions and the burden of welfare spending. However, China's statistics do not make a distinction between non productive capital and labor from the total capital and labor. Interestingly, the output data of state-owned enterprises did not take into account workers' and their family's housing, education, health care and other services value, but have these "non direct productive investment" included in input. Therefore, in calculating the growth rate of total factor productivity of state-owned enterprises, the growth rate of TFP will be underestimated if these non productive inputs are not eliminated. However, it is debatable to what extent the elimination should be done.

In present literatures, Chen Kuan and others fully deducted the housing investment for workers and non productive workers from the total fixed assets and the number of employees. In the paper by Jefferson and others (1992), they actually use the "production capital" of the sample enterprises to replace the the total fixed capital. In another paper, Jefferson and others (1995) deducted housing investment and non productive assets in newly added fixed assets; in terms of the labor force, they eliminated 15–16% of the workers of state-owned enterprises and 7–8% of the collective enterprise workers. While estimating the capital and labor inputs of China's state-owned enterprises, O. Keijiro also completely eliminated the housing investment in the fixed asset investment. When eliminating non productive labor, they used data on the composition of workers in state-owned enterprises in 1984 and 1990 to calculate the ratio of workers directly engaged in industrial production. The ratio of productive workers in these two years was 0.857 and 0.854 respectively, which means about 15% of workers were unproductive labor inputs. Hu Yongtai and others (Woo et al. 1994) commented on the research of Chen Kuan and his coauthors, expressing their doubt in the article. They believe that even though these "services" provided by the enterprises are not directly productive, thereby cannot directly increase the output of enterprises, they play an important role in ensuring the production of enterprises. Therefore, even if one wants to get rid of them, one can only do part of it carefully. Hu Yongtai and others found in their regression that if "non-productive" labor and capital" investment is not eliminated, the estimated value of growth rate of TFP is –4%, and is statistically remarkable; if it is eliminated, the growth rate of TFP is −2%, but not statistically significant. Of course, the way they calculated TFP is different. But it's obvious that eliminating problems is really sensitive.

investment projects. Since the other costs are not easy to get, key investigations should be made in the construction and construction units at the same time coupled with typical case surveys (to get information from the management department). Third, price survey method. The combination of corporate statements and visits by investigators should be adopted. Fourth, determination of weight. The weight calculation of price index of investment in fixed assets is the average proportion of construction and installation engineering projects, purchase of equipment and other expenses of past three years.

② Reliability of the statistical data. Although people in general always believe that China's statistics is unreliable, serious researchers have been cautiously optimistic about official statistics. This is because on the one hand China's statistical reporting system and tools are constantly being improved; on the other hand, the statistics of China are not so bad for the purposes of research. In addition to official publication statistics, researchers now have diversified their ways and sources of acquiring data which provide the basis for further empirical research. Regarding the literature of total factor productivity, the quality of data is naturally a sensitive issue. For example, although most of the researchers have basically accepted the conclusion that township enterprises are more efficient than state-owned enterprises, people are still concerned about the data authenticity of non-state-owned enterprises, especially township enterprises. After all, compared with township enterprises, the statistics of state-owned enterprises are more standardized. With the publication of the third national industrial census of 1995 in 1997, the excessive or false reporting of output value of township enterprises has been proved. Thus, in the statistical yearbooks published in 1997, the statistical data published in 1991–1994 have been rectified.

Table 7.4 presents the total industrial output value of Chinese industrial enterprises before and after the corrections were done using 1992 as an example. In the 1993 volume of *China's Industrial Economic Statistics Yearbook*, the total industrial output value is 37,066 *yuan*, which was reduced to 3.4599 trillion *yuan*, down by 7.1% in the *China Statistical Yearbook* published in 1997 according to the results of the third industrial census. However, the output value of state-owned enterprises has not been corrected. In other words, the "exaggeration" of output value mainly comes from the non state-owned enterprises, especially the collective and urban and rural individual enterprises.

As far as present literature is concerned, there is a large number of studies that do not use official statistics, but acquire their first-hand data through questionnaires

Table 7.4 Adjustment of China's total industrial output value (taking 1992 as an example)

	Gross value of industrial output	State-owned enterprises and departments	Non-state-owned enterprises and departments	Therein		
				Collectively-owned	Individual	Other
Before the adjustment	37,066	17,824	19,242	14,101	2507	2634
After the adjustment	34,599	17,824	16,775	12,135	2006	2634
Proportion of over reporting (%)	7.1	0	14.7	16.2	25	0

Source Data prior to adjustment come from the State Bureau of Statistics: *Chinese Industrial Economic Statistical Yearbook* (1993), Beijing, Chinese Statistical Press, 1993; data after being adjusted come from the State Bureau of Statistics: *Chinese Statistical Yearbook* (1997), Beijing, China Statistics Press, 1997

designed by researchers themselves. For example, Jefferson and Xu (1991), Cao (1994), Groves and others (1994) and, most recently, O. Keijiro, who are all using the survey data of specific industries and large and medium sized enterprises.[25] Limited to space, we will not introduce them one by one.

7.5 Explanation of the Changes of TFP

(1) Allocative efficiency and technical efficiency

Most studies endorsing the improvement of TFP in China's state-owned industrial sector after the reform involve the possible factors that led to the improvement of TFP. According to the existing research literature, the factors mentioned include improvement of resource allocation efficiency and technical efficiency, technological progress and existence of effect of scale economy.

With regard to the distinction between allocation efficiency and technical efficiency, people usually use the conceptual definition of Farrell (1957). Farrel's definition is made by using "frontier" or "boundary" production functions: firms that produce on frontiers or boundaries are efficient. We can illustrate it with the help of Fig. 7.4. Given a production function with constant returns of scale, the frontier technology can be illustrated by unit output line $1 = f(K/Y, L/Y)$.[26] It is obvious that both point C and point B are technically efficient, but only point C has allocative efficiency at the same time. Suppose we have observed that the input portfolio of an enterprise is at point A, it is neither technically efficient nor efficient in allocation. In this way, we can use the ratio of OB/OA to measure the level of technical efficiency, while $(1 - OB/OA)$ gives the degree of inefficiency of technology. The size of the enterprise's allocation efficiency can be measured by OD/OB, because the cost of point D and point C are the same, both less than the cost of point B. Finally, OD/OA is the measure index of the total efficiency level, and $(1 - OD/OA)$ is the measurement of the total non efficiency level, which is approximately equal to the sum of allocation inefficiency and technical inefficiency.

Cao (1994) made an empirically research by using this conceptual framework on the efficiency changes of 99 steel and iron enterprises in China in the period of 1980–1988. The standard form he set up for production function, cost and profit function is as follows:

$$Y = \mathrm{f}(X)$$

$$C(X, Y) = \min_X\{WX|\mathrm{f}(X) \geq Y, X \geq 0\}$$

[25] Jefferson and Xu (1991), Cao (1994).

[26] Assuming the production function is $Y = f(K, L)$, Y, K and L are the output, capital and labor respectively. Since the scale returns are assumed to be constant, the two sides of the production function can be multiplied by $1/Y$ changing it into the form of $1 = f(K/Y, L/Y)$.

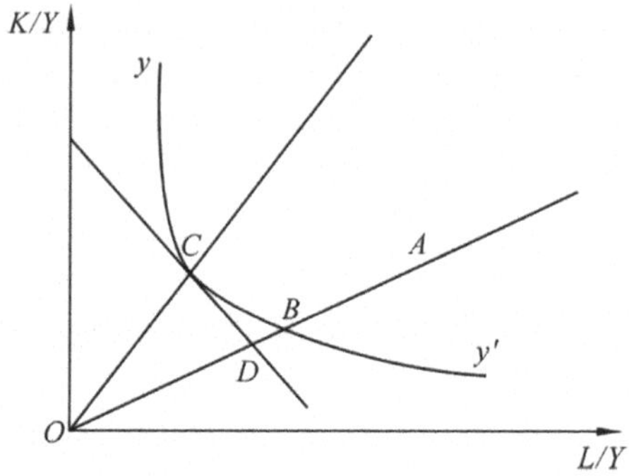

Fig. 7.4 Geometric implications of allocative efficiency and technical efficiency

$$\Pi(P, W) = \max_{Y,X}\{PY - WX|\mathrm{f}(X) \geq Y, X \geq 0, Y \geq 0\}$$

Y is the output vector, X the input vector, W the input price vector, P the output price vector, and C and Π are cost and profit functions respectively. If (Y_0, X_0) is observed in a production unit, then:

$$\text{Technical efficiency: } Y_0 = \mathrm{f}(X_0)$$
$$\text{Technical inefficiency: } Y_0 < \mathrm{f}(X_0)$$

The reason for technical inefficiency is due to the excessive use of inputs by the output given by production. In this case, the cost will be:

$$WX_0 > C(Y_0, W)$$

Profits are not maximized because costs are not minimized:

$$(PY_0 - WX_0) > \Pi(P, W)$$

If factor cost is minimized, we can define accordingly:

$$\text{Allocation efficiency rate: } \mathrm{f}_i(X_0)/\mathrm{f}_j(X_0) = W_i/W_j$$
$$\text{Allocation inefficiency rate: } \mathrm{f}_i(X_0)/\mathrm{f}_j(X_0) \neq W_i/W_j$$

Among them, $\mathrm{f}_i(X_0)$ and $\mathrm{f}_j(X_0)$ are marginal inputs of i and j, while W_i and W_j are the prices of inputs i and j. The reason for inefficient allocation is that the ratio of inputs and their price is asymmetric, which will increase the costs:

$$WX_0 > C(Y_0, W)$$

Profits are not maximized because costs are not minimized:

$$(PY_0 - WX_0) > \Pi(P, W)$$

In order to do a quantitative analysis, Cao (1994) defined the technical efficiency by using the frontier function econometric model developed by Battese and Coelli (1992): the technical efficiency of a given enterprise is defined as the ratio of the average output of this enterprise and the enterprise with the highest efficiency.[27] A model of the sample observations of N enterprises over T periods is defined as follows:

$$y_{it} = \mathrm{f}(x_{it}, \alpha)\exp(V_{it} - U_{it})$$

and

$$U_{it} = \eta_{it} U_i = \{\exp[-\eta(t - T)]\} U_i, t \in \tau(i); i = 1, 2, \ldots, N$$

Technical efficiency $TE_{it} = \exp(-U_{it})$ is defined as:

$$E\big[\exp(-U_{it})|E_i\big] = \left\{\frac{1 - \Phi\big[\eta_{it}\sigma_i^* - (\mu_i^*/\sigma_i^*)\big]}{1 - \Phi(\mu_i^*/\sigma_i^*)}\right\}\exp\left[-\eta_{it}\sigma_i^* + \frac{1}{2}\eta_{it}^2\sigma_i^{*2}\right]$$

Cao's paper also defines allocative efficiency. Considering j kind of input ($j = 1, 2, \ldots, M$) as well as a special input L, allocation efficiency can be defined as:

$$\frac{MP_{ji}}{MP_{Li}} = \frac{W_j}{W_L}\exp(\beta_{jL})_i$$

The $(\beta_{jL})_i$ is the allocation efficiency parameter of investment made by enterprise i between L and j; if $(\beta_{jL})_i = 0$, enterprise i is efficient in allocation; if $\beta \neq 0$, the enterprise has inefficient allocation of resources. Therefore, parameters are meant to measure the degree of inefficiency in allocating resources.

Results gained by Cao are given in Table 7.5. He found by using the stochastic frontier production function estimation method that, if the technical efficiency of enterprises on the boundary is 1, then in 1980, the average technical efficiency level of all enterprises is 0.46, while in 1988 it rose to 0.53, an average annual increase of 1.8% in 8 years. He also found that the technical efficiency of enterprises is directly proportional to the scale of enterprises, and the technical efficiency of large enterprises is higher than that of small and medium-sized enterprises. Therefore, he believes that there is a scale economy in China's steel enterprises. We will discuss this issue later. As can be seen from Table 7.5, the allocative efficiency of the steel enterprises rose in 1980–1985, but declined in 1985–1988. Cao attributed the change model to the imperfect factor market. But he also found that the allocation efficiency of large enterprises is higher than that of small and medium-sized enterprises.

[27] Battese and Coeli (1992).

Table 7.5 Average technical efficiency and allocative efficiency of sample iron and steel enterprises (1980, 1985, 1988)

	1980	1985	1988
All sample enterprises	0.46 (−0.77)	0.49 (−0.60)	0.53 (−0.65)
Large enterprise	0.55 (−0.60)	0.59 (−0.44)	0.62 (−0.44)
Medium sized enterprise	0.47 (−0.80)	0.51 (−0.62)	0.55 (−0.67)
Small enterprise	0.25 (−0.83)	0.29 (−0.64)	0.33 (−0.72)

Note The data in parentheses is the average allocative efficiency

When it comes to allocative efficiency, there are other specialized studies such as those done by Jefferson and Xu (1991, 1994).[28] They believe that whether allocation efficiency of state-owned enterprises has been improved can be proved by observing if the marginal returns of labor, capital and intermediate inputs of enterprises and industrial sectors have a "convergence" trend. In 1991, they sampled 20 large and medium-sized state-owned enterprises in Wuhan and later expanded to 226 enterprises. To observe the degree of convergence of firms'marginal returns, they used the coefficient of variation in marginal returns of factors. The decline of coefficient of variation should reflect the trend of convergence of factor marginal returns among firms. The coefficient of variation is the ratio of standard deviation (SD) and the the average value, or expected value (E):

$$CV_i = SD(MP_{ij})/E(MP_{ij})$$

i is the factor, $j = 1, 2, \ldots, n$ represents the j enterprise; MP_{ij} is the marginal returns of enterprise j and factor i. Because the marginal return of MP_{ij} of the factor can be written as the product of average factor output (Y_j/X_{ij}) and the output elasticity of factors (α_{ij}), and if we assume that the technical conditions of the enterprises are the same, namely the output elasticity of enterprises are the same, the coefficient of variation of marginal return of factors can be approximately substituted by the coefficient of variation of average returns. Jefferson and Xu (1994) have calculated the coefficient of variation of average returns (average output) of 226 large and medium-sized sample enterprises, as shown in Table 7.6.

From Table 7.6, we can see that the coefficients of variation of average output of all factors seem to have experienced a downward trend, which implies an improvement in allocative efficiency.[29] Moreover, the smaller the proportion of planned sales is, the smaller the coefficient of variation, which shows that the influence of marketization on the efficiency of enterprise allocation is obvious. The results of the last column

[28] Jefferson and Xu (1994).

[29] Naughton studied the coefficient of variation in the profitability of China's state-owned enterprises, and also found the trend of average profit margins. For example, his calculations show that during the period of 1985–1989, the coefficient of variation in the profitability of state-owned enterprises in China's 38 industries dropped from 0.77 to 0.44, which means improvement in allocative efficiency. See Naughton (1995).

Table 7.6 Average output and coefficient of variation of nominal TFP of sample enterprises (1980–1989)

	Average output of labor (Y/L)	Average output of capital (Y/K)	Intermediate output intermediate products (Y/M)	Nominal TFP ($NTFP$)
All sample enterprises				
1980	0.86	1.04	0.29	0.32
1985	0.80	0.82	0.26	0.26
1989	0.73	0.64	0.25	0.21
Enterprises (74) with fully planned sales				
1980	0.88	1.00	0.31	0.36
1985	0.83	0.90	0.31	0.33
1989	0.75	0.70	0.29	0.27
Enterprises (105) with partially planned sale				
1980	0.80	1.04	0.21	0.27
1985	0.74	0.69	0.20	0.19
1989	0.66	0.57	0.22	0.15
Enterprises (44) with Fully unplanned sales				
1980	0.83	0.80	0.27	0.22
1985	0.51	0.61	0.21	0.14
1989	0.45	0.49	0.22	0.12

Note The computational formula for *NTFP* isNTFP $= e^{\text{Ln}\,Y-\alpha}K^{\text{Ln}\,K-\alpha}L^{\text{Ln}\,L-\alpha}M^{\text{Ln}\,M}$
Sources G. Jefferson, W. Xu, Assessing Gains in Efficient Production among China's Industrial Enterprises, *Economic Development and Cultural Change*, 1994, 40

show that the coefficient of variation of the total factor productivity of the sample enterprises is also declining, signifying that the efficiency improvement also tends to be same.

Zheng Jinghai, Liu Xiaoxuan and Bigsten (2002) also analyzed the change of total factor productivity of state-owned enterprises in their paper, but they broke down the improvement of total factor productivity into two parts: technical efficiency improvement and technological progress.[30] For this reason, they assume that for $t = 1, \ldots,$ in each period of T, there is a production technology of S^t from $x^t \in R_+^N$ to $y^t \in R_+^M$, and $S^t = \{(x^t, y^t) : x^t \text{ can produce } y^t\}$, and the output distance function

[30] Jinghai et al. (2002).

of period t, or the technical efficiency, is defined as:

$$D_0{}^t\left(x^t, y^t\right) = \inf\left\{\theta : (x^t, y^t/\theta) \in S^t\right\} = \sup\left\{\theta : (x^t, \theta y^t) \in S^t\right\}^{-1}$$

Cross phase distance function is defined as: $D_0{}^t\left(x^{t+1}, y^{t+1}\right) = \inf\left\{\theta : (x^{t+1}, y^{t+1}/\theta) \in S^t\right\}$, then the Malmquist index for the period t is $M^t = D_0{}^t\left(x^{t+1}, y^{t+1}\right)/D_0{}^t\left(x^t, y^t\right)$, the Malmquist index for the period $t+1$ is $M^{t+1} = D_0{}^{t+1}\left(x^{t+1}, y^{t+1}\right)/D_0{}^{t+1}\left(x^t, y^t\right)$. Thus, in order to avoid confusing the benchmarks, they defined an index that measures productivity change based on output; which is the geometric average of the upper two formulas:

$$M_0(x^{t+1}, y^{t+1}, x^t, y^t) = \left\{\left[D_0{}^t\left(x^{t+1}, y^{t+1}\right)/D_0{}^t\left(x^t, y^t\right)\right]\right.$$
$$\left.\left[D_0{}^{t+1}\left(x^{t+1}, y^{t+1}\right)/D_0{}^{t+1}\left(x^t, y^t\right)\right]\right\}^{1/2}$$

They defined the efficiency improvement EFFCH and technological progress TECH as:

$$\text{EFFCH} = D_0{}^{t+1}\left(x^{t+1}, y^{t+1}\right)/D_0\left(x^t, y^t\right)$$

$$\text{TECH} = \left\{\left[D_0{}^t\left(x^{t+1}, y^{t+1}\right)/D_0{}^{t+1}\left(x^{t+1}, y^{t+1}\right)\right]\left[D_0(x, y)/D_0{}^{t+1}\left(x^t, y^t\right)\right]\right\}^{1/2}$$

They collected panel data of 700 state-owned enterprises according to the two surveys conducted by the Chinese Academy of Social Sciences in 1990 and 1996 and provided the data envelopment analysis method and the result of Malmquist index analysis. In terms of technical efficiency, the results showed that after 1990, the technical efficiency of most of industries has been greatly improved; in the aspect of Malmquist index, the estimated results show that in all sectors, productivity is growing. After the productivity was broken down into technical efficiency change and technological progress, they found an interesting phenomenon: in the machinery industry, textile industry, heavy industry and light industry, very few enterprises experienced the improvement of technical efficiency, which means that most of the enterprises depend on technological progress for their productivity growth. Therefore, they concluded that the technical efficiency of these sample companies is generally low, although their productivity growth is remarkable. But this growth is mainly through technical progress rather than by improving the technical efficiency (see Figs. 7.5 and 7.6).

(2) Economies of Scale

If economies of scale exist, they will contribute to the growth of TFP in China's industrial enterprises, especially state-owned enterprises. However, similar to the question of whether TFP has really improved significantly, there is no real consensus in present empirical studies on economies of scale. Some studies have found the existence of economies of scale, while some have not found sufficient evidence of its

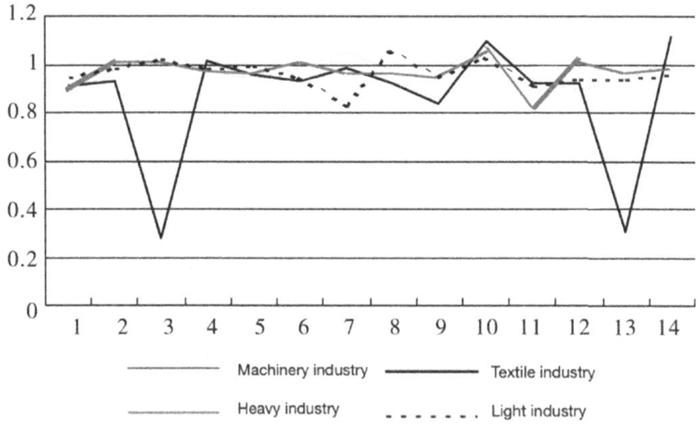

Fig. 7.5 Efficiency change of sample state-owned enterprises (1980–1994). *Note* Zheng Jinghai and others (2002) used the average value, minimum value, maximum value and variance to describe the efficiency change for each industry in their original paper, and only the average value is used here as well as in Fig. 7.5. *Source* Zheng Jinghai, Liu Xiaoxuan, A. Bigsten: Efficiency, Technology Progress and Best Practices of the State-Owned Enterprise during the Period of 1980–1994, *Journal of Economics Quarterly*, 2002 (3)

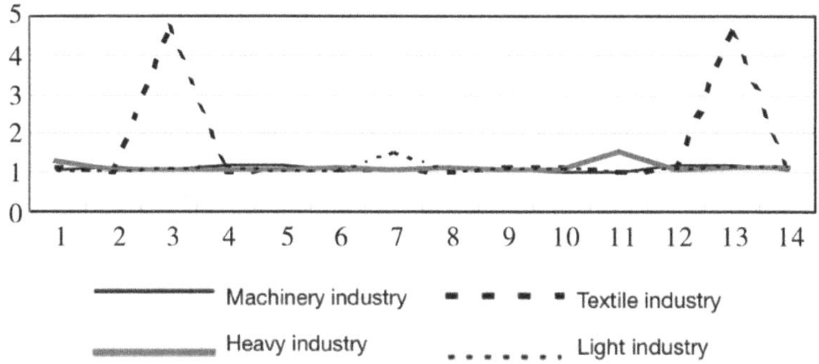

Fig. 7.6 Technological progress of sample state-owned enterprises (1980–1994). *Source* Zheng Jinghai, Liu Xiaoxuan, A. Bigsten: Efficiency, Technology Progress and Best Practices of the State-Owned Enterprise during the Period of 1980–1994, *Journal of Economics Quarterly*, 2002 (3)

existence, and still others have even found diseconomies of scale. The disagreement of these studies concerns the definition of economies of scale, the methods of judgment for empirical research, and the problems of data, which are quite complicated indeed.

The earlier study was conducted by Jefferson (1990) on the Chinese steel and iron industry, which is generally considered to be a sector with potential economies of scale.[31] He found that by fitting the data of Chinese steel and iron industry, we

---

[31] Jefferson (1990).

will know that the output elasticity of capital and the output elasticity of labor were 0.649 and 0.532, which shows the existence of economies of scale in iron and steel industry. He then calculated that, in 1980–1985, out of the growth rate of TFP in the iron and steel industry, about 1/3 came from the contribution of this scale economy.

In 1992, Jefferson, Rawski, Zheng (1992) estimated the output elasticity of capital and labor by using the data of 293 state-owned enterprises, 295 collective enterprises (1984) and 382 (1987) collective enterprise of the period of 1984–1987and the Cobb Douglas production function. They once again found that the hypothesis of unchanging returns to scale does not hold. The scale parameters of state-owned enterprises are 1.071 (1984) and 1.030 (1987), while the parameters of collective enterprise's scale are 1.048 (1984) and 1.020 (1984). However, their results indicate that, although the economy of scale made a contribution to the TFP growth of China's enterprises, the main source of the TFP growth rate came from technological progress (in their paper they broke down the growth rate of TFP into technological advances and changes in the economies of scale).

We have already mentioned before that Cao (1994) found in his study of the iron and steel enterprises in China that, in terms of technical efficiency, the technical efficiency level of medium-sized businesses is close to the average value of the technical efficiency, that of the big companies is higher than the average value and that of small enterprises is lower than the average value. So Cao believed this conclusion shows that there are economies of scale in China's iron and steel enterprises. Zheng Jinghai and others' study (1998) has got a similar conclusion.[32] They found that although in terms of system of ownership, the technical efficiency of state-owned enterprises is lower than that of township and collective enterprises, from the perspective of scale, technical efficiency of large enterprises is higher than small and medium enterprises. In addition, Lo's (1999) research also concluded that the TFP of large enterprises is higher than that of small and medium-sized enterprise.[33]

Keijiro Otsukaand others are skeptical about the existence of economies of scale in Chinese iron and steel industry. They believe that by international standards, the scale of China's large vertical enterprises is too large to have a higher efficiency. They used the questionnaire method to collect the cross section data of Chinese iron and steel enterprise in 1980, 1985, 1991 and 1994 and fitted the cobb–douglas production function, out of which they estimated the effect of economies of scale with the coefficient of the number of workers. The results show that the scale coefficient does not has much difference with zero, so they think that there is no evidence that scale economy exists in iron and steel enterprises. But they (Murakami et al. 1996) found that there is diseconomy of scales in China's machine tool industry in another study.[34]

Looking for a positive relationship between firm size and profitability is also a way of testing the existence of economies of scale. However, interestingly, we can always see in *China Statistical Yearbook* or *Chinese Industrial Economic Statistical*

---

[32] Zheng et al. (1998).

[33] Lo (1999).

[34] Murakami et al. (1996).

Yearbook that the profit margins of "large enterprises" have always been higher than that of small and medium-sized enterprises. Whether this can also prove the existence of the economies of scale is worth further research. We made a detailed research in a separate study on the relationship between the profit margin and the size of manufacturers. We found that the "big, small and medium-sized enterprises" on official statistics yearbook is not a "ranking list" defined according to the assets or the employment scale. So, the higher profit margins of large enterprise defined in such a way do not necessarily reflect the positive effect of scale change on profit margins.

For example, according to the "standards for categorizing large, small and medium-sized industrial enterprises" in the appendix of *Chinese Industrial Economic Statistical Yearbook* (1994), the enterprise's scale of fixed assets or employment is not used as an index of differentiating an enterprise's scale; rather, the scale of vast majority of enterprise is defined according to their "annal producing ability" of products. It is obvious that because, at the 4-digit industry level, the nature or portfolio of the products are quite different, so that at the industry level, companies that are classified as "large" ones are entirely different in their products they manufacture. In machinery sector, for example, "large enterprises" does not cover the largest enterprises in their sectors whose fixed assets have reached a certain scale, but the total sum of enterprises whose production capacity of different products has met a certain indicators. In such aggregate "large enterprises", their actual firm size (asset size) is uneven which will lead to an interesting "aggregate effect". We will take the building materials industry as an example to illustrate this point.

In the industry of building materials, we know from the "large, small and medium-sized industrial enterprise classification standards" that, cement enterprises with an annual capacity of 1.2 million tons and above is classified as large enterprises (large I), those with an annual capacity of 300,000 to 600,000 tons are medium-sized enterprises (medium I); and with respect to "glass fiber enterprises", the standard for classifying large enterprises (large I) are those with an annual production capacity of 80 million tons and above, those with 30 to 50 million tons are "medium (medium I) enterprises". The large (large I) "new type building material enterprises" refer to those with "original value of fixed assets for production" at 120 million *yuan* or more, but other building material enterprises can be classified as "large enterprises" (large I) if they can meet the standard of having 100 million *yuan* or more of "original value of fixed assets for production. Moreover, "large II" enterprises that have also been included in the "large enterprises" are much smaller than "large I" enterprises both in the "annual production capacity and "fixed assets". For example, cement enterprises with an annual production capacity of over 600,000 tons and below 1.2 million tons of cement have been classified as "large II enterprises". Therefore, even in the same industry, the so-called "large enterprises" classified in this way can vary greatly in the size of the real assets or the number of employed workers.

Under these circumstances, once we try to re-rank the so-called "large and medium-sized enterprises" by using the original value of fixed assets as the standard, we will find that there is a lot of "overlapping" in large and medium-sized enterprises in terms of their actual scale. In the scale range with fixed assets from 500 million to 10 billion *yuan*, we found 41 large enterprises, 6 medium-sized enterprises; in the scale range with fixed assets from 100 to 300 million *yuan*, there are 220 large enterprises and 88 medium-sized enterprises; in the scale range of the fixed assets below 100 million *yuan*, there are 1,239 large enterprises and 3,772 medium-sized enterprises.

That is to say, at the sector and the whole industry level, the difference between "large enterprise" and "medium enterprise" is not reflected in asset sizes. It is often the case that within a same sector, a "large enterprise" in an industry (such as watch-making in light industry) is even smaller than a "medium-sized enterprise" or a small enterprise in another segment (such as bicycle manufacturing in light industry) in asset size. So, once the "large enterprises" are added up by institutions of the state, we shall find that the assets of large enterprises are not necessarily bigger than that of medium-sized enterprises, maybe even smaller. In this case, even if the total profits of the "large enterprise" may be much smaller than that of the small and medium-sized enterprise, the calculated rate of profit of the "large enterprises" put together is likely to appear higher than that of the small and medium enterprise because the scale of assets is the denominator for calculating "profit margins".

7.6 Efficiency of Township Enterprises

The study of non-state enterprises, especially the township enterprises, is one of the most important contents in the existing literature on contemporary China's economy.[35] In terms of productivity, no matter how far apart the research literatures on the total factor productivity of state-owned enterprises are, they all show a highly consistent agreement on the efficiency of township enterprises. The fact that efficiency of township enterprises is in general better than that of state-owned enterprises seems to have been proved by most of the empirical studies. For example, the studies done by Byrd and Lin (1990), Weitzman and Xu (1994), Woo and others (1994), Lin Qingsong (1995), Jefferson, Rawski and Zheng (1995), and recently by Keijiro Otsuka.[36]

However, Jefferson and others (1996) pointed out that the total factor productivity of township enterprises is very sensitive to price index, and therefore most likely to result in error because of the inaccuracy of price and other data. As we have mentioned, the price index of total output value of township enterprises may be on the low side. For example, if we use the ratio of total output value of current price and the total output value of constant price of township enterprises as the implicit price index, then we will find that this index decreased after 1989, which is unbelievable as well as not identical with the result that the price index of industrial products rose by

[35] Feng Qu has recently provided a literature review of the theoretical and empirical research on China's township enterprises. See Feng Qu: A Review of Research on Chinese Rural Industry. See Jun (2002).

[36] Byrd and Lin (1990), Weitzman and Xu (1994).

20% during 1989–1992 provided by the survey conducted by the Urban Investigation Team of the State Statistics Bureau.

So, Jefferson and others (1995), in their study on the collective enterprises (mainly township enterprises), chose the ex factory price index of industrial products similar to that of the state-owned enterprises to deflate the total output value of current price of collective enterprises, which is helpful to reduce the "exaggeration" that may exist in the output value of collective enterprises. Their research, however, only covers the period of 1980–1992. During this time, they found that the actual growth rate of the total output value of collective enterprises was no longer 16.1%, but 12.4%. The growth rate of total factor productivity of collective enterprises during 1980–1992 fell by more than half compared with the results they got in 1992, although it was still higher than the growth rate of total factor productivity of state-owned enterprises.

In one of our most recent research projects on industrial reform, we once again estimated the TFP growth rate of township enterprises by extending our study time from Jefferson's 1992 to the year 2000. In our research, first of all, the total output value of township enterprises may have been overestimated, which will lead to exaggeration of the TFP growth rate of township enterprises. Therefore, we, like Jefferson and others (1995), also used the general index of ex factory price of industrial products similar to that of the state-owned enterprises in the absence of suitable deflator for township enterprises (see Table 7.7[37]) to deflate the total output value of present price of township enterprises.[38] Although state-owned and township enterprises are quite different in product structure, quality and market environment which will lead to differences in terms of price changes, we think that we can use the general indext of ex factory price of state industry for township enterprises as a a meaningful approximation because the market is being integrated and the township industry is the main part of township enterprises.[39] It is at least more practical to use this general index than the original implicit price index (i.e., ratio of total output value of present price and total output value of the constant price). Also it has the effect of reducing the actual output growth.

The data of original value of fixed assets of township enterprises in the statistics yearbook is the simple sum of accumulation of the primitive investment, representing the sum of investment goods of different periods and different levels of prices. Since all fixed asset data published in China have not been deflated by fixed price, they cannot provide a reliable basis for estimating the actual growth of fixed assets. Especially since the 1980s, the resulting statistical errors have started to become serious

[37] Out of which, the data of 1979 come from Meng Lian and Wang Xiaolu (2000); the data of 1984–1992 from Jefferson, Rawski and Zheng (1995). In fact, the *Chinese Statistical Yearbook* released in 2001 presents all of these data since the 1980. See Lian and Xiaolu (2000).

[38] The deflator method is from Jefferson, Rawski and Zheng (1995).

[39] For example, according to calculation, the township industry produced 18,812 yuan of added value in 2000, accounting for 69.27% of the 27,156 *yuan* worth of the added value of township enterprises nationwide and rose to 47.3% in the proportion of industrial added value of the whole country. In 2000, the current price industrial output value of township enterprises was 82,456 *yuan*, accounting for 70.99% of the current price total output value of all township enterprises of 116,150 *yuan*.

Table 7.7 Price deflator of the total output value and new fixed capital of township enterprises (1990 = 100)

Year	The total output price deflator P_g	The price deflator P_K of newly added fixed assets	Year	The total output price deflator P_g	the price deflator P_K of newly added fixed assets
1978	55.98	41.3	1990	100.00	100.0
1979	56.82	41.3	1991	106.20	111.9
1980	57.11	41.3	1992	113.42	125.5
1981	57.22	43.8	1993	140.64	158.9
1982	57.11	44.0	1994	168.07	175.4
1983	57.05	47.6	1995	193.11	185.8
1984	57.85	51.0	1996	198.71	193.2
1985	62.89	58.2	1997	198.11	196.5
1986	65.27	66.6	1998	189.99	196.1
1987	70.43	73.9	1999	185.43	195.3
1988	81.00	79.5	2000	190.62	197.5
1989	96.06	98.3			

Source The total output price deflator P_g was calculated according to the ex factory price index of industrial products (previous year = 100) in volumes 9–12 of the *Chinese Statistical Yearbook* (2001); the price deflator P_K of newly added fixed assets was based on the estimated fixed capital price index of 1979–1992 done by by Jefferson and others (1996); the data of 1993 to 2000 is the price indices of investment in fixed assets provided by the price indext section in the volumes of *Chinese Statistical Yearbook* after the 1993, which was also converted into constant prices of 1990

as investment prices have accelerated. So, we use the following methods to calculate the fixed assets of 1978–2000 according to the 1990 constant prices: ① to acquire the newly added fixed assets of each year by the existing statistics; ② to deflate the annual new fixed assets by fixed asset price index (P_K); ③ to add up the annual new fixed assets being deflated. We take the 1990 fixed assets (DOF) of constant price as the capital investment, and assume that before 1978, the price of investment goods is stable. Thus, the original value of fixed assets at the end of 1978 can be used as the initial value for our estimation. The 1990 original value of fixed assets, namely the original value of fixed assets DOF_t after being deflated, can be estimated by the following formula:

$$DOF_t = OF_{78} + \sum_t (OF_t - OF_{t-1})/P_K$$

OF_{78} is the original value of fixed assets at the end of 1978, OF_t, OF_{t-1} are the original value of fixed assets of year t and year $t-1$ respectively. P_K is the fixed

Table 7.8 Adjusted data of the total output value, fixed capital and number employees of township enterprises[41]

Year	Total output value	Fixed capital	No. of employees	Year	Total output value	Fixed capital	No. of employees
1979	971.93	290.62	2867.94	1990	9581.11	3758.69	9315.81
1980	1164.59	407.74	2954.51	1991	10,943.21	4173.34	9436.97
1981	1287.40	519.38	2984.63	1992	15,570.17	4687.75	10,117.1
1982	1481.81	636.32	3041.25	1993	22,411.01	5707.26	11,485.0
1983	1766.64	746.73	3173.77	1994	26,999.46	7140.71	12,181.0
1984	2934.80	893.15	4221.38	1995	35,686.91	8902.28	12,439.0
1985	4380.73	1278.30	6093.57	1996	39,961.75	10,801.93	13,184.5
1986	5489.93	1792.63	7458.09	1997	45,379.33	12,491.70	13,279.0
1987	7025.02	2284.26	8371.16	1998	50,894.26	13,896.38	12,793.5
1988	8663.90	2860.77	9175.32	1999	58,472.74	15,059.27	12,620.5
1989	8746.43	3376.08	9456.12	2000	60,932.75	16,245.39	12,762.0

Note The data before 1984 are the figures of the town and village levels
Source The data of the total output value of current price of township and village enterprises for 1993 and 1996 are not available, so linear interpolation was adopted. Other data are from the relevant volumes of *China's Yearbook of Township Enterprises*, so are the data of fixed capital and number of employees

asset price deflator for year t (see Table 7.7).[40] The average value of the original value of fixed assets after deflator is obtained by the following formula:

The average value of the original value of fixed assets for year $= (DOF_{t-1} + DOF_t)/2$.

In this way, after the above treatment, we have obtained the complete data of total output value, fixed capital and the number of employees of township enterprises in 1979–2000. See Table 7.8.

Then we developed the Cobb Douglas production function (C-D function) and the tran-logarithmic production function to estimate by regression the coefficient of output elasticity of capital and labor in Chinese township enterprises, and used this coefficient to calculate the growth rate of TFP and TFP index (see Appendix). But we find that the regression results of using the constrained C-D function are much better than the unconstrained ones (see Table 7.9). The output elasticity of capital, $\alpha_K = 0.376$, is obtained, which means that when capital increases by 1%,

[40] This paper uses the fixed capital price index of 1979–1992 estimated by Jefferson and others (1996), the data from 1993 to 2000 is the price index of investment in fixed assets provided in volumes of the *Chinese Statistical Yearbook* released after 1993. Since the weighted average calculation of construction and installation deflator and equipment purchase deflator is also used, the data is identical with that of Jefferson.

[41] The units of total output value, fixed capital and number of employment in the table are billion *yuan*, billion *yuan* and million person respectively, and all data were processed by obtaining the approximate values.

Table 7.9 Estimated results of parameter

Coefficient	C-D function	Transcendental function
α_0	−0.471 (−0.910)	−0.568 (−1.338)
α_t	0.089 (3.422)	0.095 (4.483)
α_K	0.376 (1.611)	0.538 (2.714)
$1/2\alpha_{KK}$	n.a	0.121 (3.135)
β	0.132 (1.532)	0.146 (2.055)
$adj.R^2$	0.983	0.988
F	396.252	445.005

output increases by 0.376%, and at the same time the output elasticity of labor, $\alpha_L = 1 - \alpha_K = 0.624$ is also obtained. For the calculation of the TFP growth rate and index of township enterprises, see Table 7.10.[42]

The estimation result of unconstrained tran-logarithmic production function is also not satisfactory. We have also conducted the t test of constant returns to scale: $H_0 : \alpha_K + \alpha_L = 1, \alpha_{KK} = \alpha_{LL} = -\alpha_{KL}.$ We got $t = -0.742$, $|t| < t_{0.025}(14) = 2.145$ by calculation. We cannot refuse the hypothesis that the translog production function of constant returns to scale is the production function suitable for township enterprises. The estimation result we gained through using a constrained translog production function is particularly desirable (see Table 7.9). What with a large and significant quadratic term coefficient, the performance of translog production function, as the aggregate production function of township enterprises, is better than the C-D function.[43] Through estimated $\alpha_K = 0.538, \frac{1}{2}\alpha_{KK} = 0.121$, we got $\alpha_L = 0.462$, $\alpha_{KK} = \alpha_{LL} = 0.242$, $\alpha_{KL} = -0.242$ and calculated the output elasticity of transcendental function. Then we calculated the growth rate and the index of TFP by using the same method as the C-D function. See Table 7.10.

This paper, on the basis of the reliability of large sample statistical test, calculates the output elasticity of each year's variable capital and labor value and TFP by making use of various regression analysis results and the coefficients estimated by transcendental logarithmic production function in order to analyse the trend of changes in TFP of township enterprises and economic growth factors. We have drawn a curve chart of the growth rate and index of total factor productivity of township enterprises estimated by trans-log function (see Fig. 7.7), then conducted accounting of the growth factors according to the fluctuation cycle of TFP growth rate of township enterprises and compared it with the national average level(see Table 7.11).[44]

[42] In the appendix, the growth rate of TFP calculated by Solow's constrained residual value (formular 9) is slightly lower than the unconstrained residual value (formular 8). The gap between the two narrows gradually and is almost equal finally. We have only presented formular (9) here. Even so, the TFP growth rate of township enterprises is still higher than that of the Chinese economy as a whole, the same is true with transcendental function. See: Jun and Shaohua (2003).

[43] But we still use the C-D function and transcendental function in our following regression later on to compare the tested data.

[44] In the growth factor accounting, the figure obtained by trans-log function unconstrained evaluation was used for TFP growth rate of township enterprises in order to make sure that the addition of

Table 7.10 TFP index and growth rate of township enterprises in China

Year	C-D function		Transcendental function			
	TFP gr	TFP ind	TFP gr	TFP ind	S_K	S_L
1979	–	1.000	–	1.000	−0.016	1.016
1980	−0.003	0.997	−0.068	0.932	0.059	0.941
1981	0.022	1.019	−0.013	0.920	0.115	0.886
1982	0.051	1.071	0.013	0.932	0.160	0.840
1983	0.089	1.166	0.066	0.993	0.190	0.810
1984	0.297	1.512	0.317	1.309	0.160	0.840
1985	0.029	1.556	0.029	1.346	0.160	0.840
1986	−0.026	1.516	−0.049	1.280	0.192	0.808
1987	0.088	1.649	0.068	1.367	0.223	0.777
1988	0.063	1.753	0.039	1.421	0.257	0.743
1989	−0.082	1.609	−0.108	1.267	0.289	0.711
1990	0.078	1.735	0.060	1.343	0.318	0.682
1991	0.089	1.889	0.072	1.440	0.342	0.658
1992	0.310	2.474	0.303	1.876	0.352	0.648
1993	0.234	3.054	0.219	2.288	0.369	0.631
1994	0.071	3.270	0.042	2.383	0.407	0.593
1995	0.210	3.957	0.174	2.799	0.456	0.544
1996	0.004	3.973	−0.019	2.746	0.490	0.51
1997	0.074	4.267	0.050	2.883	0.523	0.477
1998	0.104	4.711	0.078	3.108	0.557	0.443
1999	0.129	5.318	0.114	3.462	0.582	0.418
2000	0.005	5.345	−0.006	3.441	0.599	0.401

Note Three decimal places are retained for TFP growth rate and the index and it is same as below

We see that in every fluctuation cycle, the TFP growth rate of township enterprises is higher than that of the national average, and its changing trend has not declined continuously as has the TFP index nationwide since 1992,[45] but is still showing its inherent characteristics: fluctuated up and down, but enjoyed an overall growing trend. Since we deflated the total output value of rural enterprises by the general index of ex factory prices of industrial products, the treatment has resulted in a decrease in the actual output growth and the TFP we have estimated has been significantly reduced. Hence, it is completely reliable that the estimated TFP of township enterprises is higher than that of the national average.

contributing shares of the growth factor will be 100, though not absolutely equal to 100, of course. Moreover, all the other analyses in this paper is based on the TFP obtained by the constrained estimation of transcendental function, and the analysis of the two is consistent.

[45] Jun (2002).

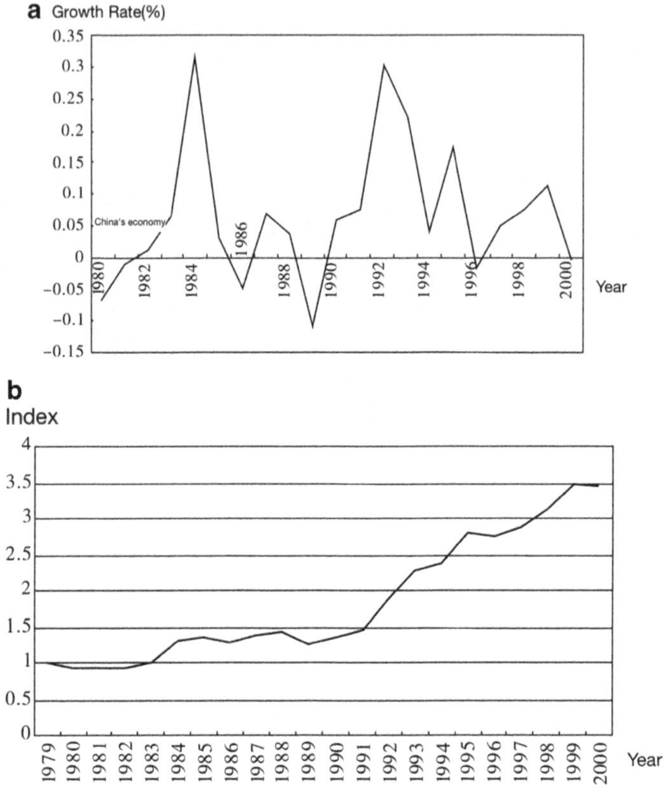

Fig. 7.7 A TFP growth rate of township economy (1980–2000). **b** TFP index of township economy (1979–2000)

Table 7.11 Comparison of accounting results of TFP changes and growth factors between township enterprises and China's economy[46]

	Year	Output Growth	TFP Growth	Factor Growth			
				Capital labor		Labor	
Township Enterprises	1980–2000	0.219 100.00	0.099 45.21	0.202 29.88	[0.065]	0.076 23.29	[0.051]
	1980–1986	0.295 100.00	0.109 36.95	0.280 14.05	[0.041]	0.167 48.14	[0.142]
	1986–1989	0.168 100.00	0.049 29.17	0.235 33.57	[0.056]	0.082 36.90	[0.062]
	1989–1994	0.253 100.00	0.163 64.43	0.162 22.15	[0.056]	0.052 13.44	[0.034]
	1994–1996	0.217 100.00	0.086 39.63	0.230 47.8	[0.104]	0.040 10.14	[0.022]
	1996–2000	0.111 100.00	0.054 48.65	0.107 53.02	[0.059]	−0.008 −3.60	[−0.004
China's Economy	1980–1998	0.099 100.00	0.037 37.37	0.094 47.38	[0.047]	0.028 15.25	[0.014]
	1980–1986	0.104 100.00	0.046 44.23	0.082 39.34	[0.041]	0.032 16.43	[0.016]
	1986–1989	0.089 100.00	0.029 32.58	0.093 52.14	[0.046]	0.026 15.28	[0.013]
	1989–1994	0.106 100.00	0.036 33.96	0.096 45.19	[0.048]	0.040 20.85	[0.020]
	1994–1996	0.100 100.00	0.036 36.00	0.114 56.89	[0.057]	0.012 7.11	[0.006]
	1996–1998	0.083 100.00	0.023 27.71	0.111 66.73	[0.055]	0.008 5.56	[0.004]

Note The corresponding data for China's economy come from Zhang Jun and Shi Shaohua (2003)

7.7 Conclusion

Although the research of total factor productivity (TFP) has its limitations, it has become an important research object of economists as one of the important indicators to understand the mode and structure of economic growth. In theory, the change of total factor productivity may able to identify the effect of system, policy, organization, technology and various other variable changes on the level of labor productivity. Therefore, economists are maintaining an interest in and unremitting efforts of the theory and empirical research of total factor productivity. When we look at the literatures of mainstream economics, whether it is the highly industrialized economies (such as OECD), newly industrialized economies of East Asia, or the so-called emerging market economy (or economy in transition), measuring the

[46] The average growth rate is calculated by using compound interest formula.

levels and patterns of changes of total factor productivity (TFP) is always the main part of contemporary economists in their thinking and understanding of economic growth and development.

China's industrial reform has provided a rich empirical basis for economists to study the different impacts of different forms of enterprise ownerships and the reform policies on the change of productivity. The development of time has made it possible for us to review, comment on, sort out and analyze the valuable research literatures that have been accumulated in the past 10-odd years. We believe that the review and analysis of these literatures are important not only to our understanding of China's industrial reform, but also to the overall understanding of China's economic development model. At the same time, as economic researchers, we are convinced that the existing literature is of positive significance in promoting China's statistical standardization and improving the concept and technology of statistics. Only when we are familiar with the work of these empirical studies can we better explain our empirical observations and be more confident in our observations.

Although economists have a lot of disputes over specific technical details, they have basically reached a consensus on China's industrial reform experience. This consensus can be summarized as follows: economic system reform since the beginning of 1978 in China aimed at the transformation toward a market economy is completely changing the market structure and industrial organization its industrial sector is facing, and constantly creating a manufacturing sector more integrated with the economy of the world. In the process, China's industrial sector has undergone structural and institutional transformations. Although at the beginning of the industrial transition, there has been a marked increase in the productivity of state-owned enterprise sector, new and more competitive industries in the competition has gained rapid growth and expansion opportunities, making the productivity improvement of Chinese industry mainly depend on the growth of non state-owned enterprises and its vitality. The achievements of China's industrial reform, instead of saving the state-owned enterprises, have shrunk its "frontline", resulting in the rise of some non-state, emerging industrial sectors. This is, so far, an important understanding and conclusion we have obtained in the present research literatures.

Appendix: Regression Models and Calculating Formulas for Estimated Growth Rate and Index of TFP of Township Enterprises

Suppose that the aggregate production function of township enterprises of Cobb Douglas type is:

$$Y_t = A_0 \mathrm{e}^{\alpha_T t} K_{t^K}^{\alpha} L_{t^L}^{\alpha} \tag{7.1}$$

Take the logarithm from both sides of the above formula and introduce the dummy variable T_j (j for the special period), we get:

$$\ln Y_t = \ln A_0 + \alpha_T t + \alpha_K \ln K_t + \alpha_L \ln L_t + \sum \beta_j T_j \tag{7.2}$$

When $\alpha_K + \alpha_L = 1$, i.e., the scale return is constant, formula (7.2) can be written as:

$$\ln(Y_t/L_t) = \ln A_0 + \alpha_T t + \alpha_K \ln(K_t/L_t) + \sum \beta_j T_j \tag{7.3}$$

($t = 1, 2, \ldots, 22$, represents the time variable. Sample year: 1979–2000).

Assuming that the transcendental logarithmic production function of the Chinese township enterprises (similarly introducing dummy variables T_j) is:

$$\begin{aligned}\ln Y_t &= \alpha_0 + \alpha_T t + \alpha_K \ln K_t + \alpha_L \ln L_t + \frac{1}{2}\alpha_{KK}(\ln K_t)^2 \\ &\quad + \alpha_{KL} \ln K_t \ln L_t + \frac{1}{2}\alpha_{LL}(\ln L_t)^2 + \sum \beta_j T_j\end{aligned} \tag{7.4}$$

When $\alpha_{KK} = \alpha_{LL} = -\alpha_{KL}$ and scale returns are constant $\alpha_K + \alpha_L = 1$, then formula (7.4) becomes:

$$\ln(Y_t/L_t) = \alpha_0 + \alpha_T t + \alpha_K \ln(K_t/L_t) + \frac{1}{2}\alpha_{KK}[\ln(K_t/L_t)]^2 + \sum \beta_j T_j \tag{7.5}$$

The formula of output elasticity of capital and labor of the transcendental logarithmic production function is:

$$S_{K_t} = \partial \ln Y_t / \partial \ln K_t = \alpha_K + \alpha_{KK} \ln K_t + \alpha_{KL} \ln L_t \tag{7.6}$$

$$S_{L_t} = \partial \ln Y_t / \partial \ln L_t = \alpha_L + \alpha_{LL} \ln L_t + \alpha_{KL} \ln K_t \tag{7.7}$$

And $S_{K_t} + S_{L_t} = 1$.

After estimating the output elasticity coefficient, we use Solow residual method to calculate the growth rate of TFP and its index.

The formula of Solow unconstrained growth rate of TFP is:

$$T\dot{F}P_t = \overset{g}{Y}_t - \alpha_K \overset{g}{K}_t - \alpha_L \overset{g}{L}_t \tag{7.8}$$

$\overset{g}{Y}_t$, $\overset{g}{K}_t$, $\overset{g}{L}_t$ are the growth rate of output, capital and labor, α_K, α_L are the output elasticity of capital and labor (the output elasticity corresponding to transcendental function are S_K, S_L).

The constrained Solow TFP growth rate formula (i.e. the invariant hypothesis of scale return introduced) is:

$$T\dot{F}P_t = \left(Y^g/L\right)_t - \alpha_K\left(K^g/L\right)_t \quad (7.9)$$

$\left(Y^g/L\right)_t$, $\left(K^g/L\right)_t$ is the growth rate of per capita output and capital-labor ratio (the meaning of output elasticity is the same as above).

The TFP index is calculated as follows[47]:

$$TFP_t = TFP_{t-1}(1 + T\dot{F}P_t) \quad (7.10)$$

Author's Notes

With China's implementation of the economic reform plan and the rapid growth of the economy, economists who are concerned about the micro level problems have begun to take a keen interest in the productivity of China's economy. It can be said that the study of productivity is one of the most abundant results in research literatures on China's economy today.

This article was written by me when I was teaching at Kyungpook National Day University of Korea (9–12, 2002), but the literature collection for writing this article can be traced back to 1998. Over the next two years, my students, Chen Shiyi and Shi Shaohua, did a lot of work in sorting out documents and drawing up some fragments of the literature review. But because of my hard work, the research work that I planned to finish in 2000 was not completed. It seems that this article is no longer a review and analysis of existing research literatures, but a research paper based on our own research work.

The value of this paper is that, based on the existing work, we systematically calculated the implicit price index of the total industrial output value in China in 1978–1999 and the price index of constant price in 1990, as well as the total index of the ex factory price of industrial products and the price index of fixed assets in 1978–2000 according to the constant prices of 1990. We also systematically studied the efficiency changes of township enterprises and compared them with those of state-owned enterprises. We hope this article will provide a fundamental and important reference for our future research. This paper was published in the October issue of 2003 of the *Journal of Economics Quarterly* and has been widely cited ever since.

References

C. Bai, D. Li, Y. Wang, Enterprise Productivity and Efficiency: When Is Up Really Down, *Journal of Comparative Economics*, 1999, 24, pp. 265–280.

[47] When calculating the TFP index, the first phase of the sample time series is 1.000.

Battese, G.E., Coeli, T.J., Frontier Production Functions, Technical Efficiency and Panel Data: With Application to Paddy Farmers in India, *Journal of Productivity Analysis*, 1992, 3 (1), pp. 153–169.

W. Byrd, Q. Lin, *China's Rural Industry: Structure, Development and Reform*, Oxford, Oxford University Press, 1990.

Y. Cao, The Impact of Partially Introduced Market Mechanisms on the Efficiency of Chinese Industry: The Case of Iron and Steel Industry, *Economic Systems*, 1994, 18, pp. 335–362.

K. Chen, H. Wang, Y. Zheng, G. Jefferson, T. Rawski, Productivity Change in Chinese Industry: 1953–1985, *Journal of Comparative Economics*, 1988, 12, pp. 570–591.

Chen Shizhong, Geng Sangtao: Comprehensive Productivity Problem in Economic Growth, in Wang Jiye: *Evaluation Theory and Practice for Technological Progress*, Beijing Science and Technology Literature Press, 1986.

E. Denison Why Growth Rates Differ, Brookings Institute, Washington, D.C., 1969.

D. Dollar, Economic Reform and Allocative Efficiency in China's State Owned Industry, *Economic Development and Cultural Change*, 1991, 39, pp. 89–105.

J. Felipe, Total Factor Productivity Growth in East Asia: Acritical Survey, *The Journal of Development Studies*, 1999, 35 (4), pp. 1–41.

Gary Jefferson, Inderjit Singh, *China's State-Owned Industrial Enterprises: How Effective Were the Reforms of the 1980s*, Mimeo, World Bank, 1993.

Gordon Roger, Wei Li, *The Change in Productivity of Chinese State Enterprises, 1983–1987: Initial Results*, Mimeo, University of Michigan, 1989.

T. Groves, Y. Hong, J. McMilan, B. Naughton, Autonomy and Incentives in Chinese State Enterprises, *Quarterly Journal of Economics*, 1994, 109, pp. 183–209.

Guo Kesha: China: *Economic Growth and Structural Change in Reform*. Shanghai SDX Joint Publishing Company, 1993.

Y. Huang, X. Meng, China's Industrial Growth and Efficiency: A Comparison between the State and the TVE Sectors, Australian National University, 1995.

G. Jefferson, China's Iron and Steel Industry: Sources of Enterprise Efficiency and the Impact of Reform, *Journal of Development Economics*, 1990, pp. 329–355.

G. Jefferson, W. Xu, The Impact of Reform on Socialist Enterprises in Transition: Structure, Conduct, and Performance in Chinese Industry, *Journal of Comparative Economics*, 1991, 15, pp. 45–64.

G. Jefferson, T. Rawski, Y. Zheng, Growth, Efficiency, and Convergence in China 's State and Collective Industry, *Economic Development and Cultural Change*, 1992, 40, pp. 239–266.

G. Jefferson, T. Rawski, Enterprise Reform in Chinese Industry, *Journal of Economic Perspectives*, 1994, 8, pp. 47–70.

G. Jefferson, W. Xu, Assessing Gains in Efficient Production among China' s Industrial Enterprises, *Economic Development and Cultural Change*, 1994, 40, pp. 239–266.

Jefferson, Rawski, Zheng Yuxin: Estimation and Reliability Analysis of the Changing Trend of China's Industrial Productivity since the Reform, *Economic Research*, 1995 (12), pp. 10–22.

G. Jefferson, T. Rawski, Y. Zheng, Chinese Industrial Productivity: Trends, Measurement and Recent Development, *Journal of Comparative Economics*, 1996, 23, pp.146–180.

D. Jorgenson, Z. Griliches, The Explanation of Productivity Change, *Review of Economic Studies*, 1967, 34 (3), pp. 249–283.

Li Jingwen, Zheng Youjing, Yang Shuzhuang, Gong Feihong: Analysis of China's Economic Growth, *Chinese Social Social Sciences*, 1992 (1), pp. 15–36.

Lin Qingsong: Analysis of efficiency changes and influencing factors in China's industrial sector since the reform. *Economic Research Journal*, 1995, 30 (10) pp. 27–34.

D. Lo, Reappraising the Performance of China's State Owned Industrial Enterprises: 1980-1996, Cambridge, *Journal of Economics*, 1999, 23, pp. 693–718.

O. Keijiro, Liu Deqiang, Murakami Naoki: *China's Industrial Reform*, Shanghai, SDX Jointing Publishing Company, Shanghai People's Publishing House, 2000.

Meng Lian, Wang Xiaolu: Estimation of Reliability of China's Economic Growth Statistics, in *Economic Research*, 2000 (10).

N. Murakami, D. Liu, K. Otsuka, Market Reform, Division of Labour and Increasing Advantage of Small Scale Enterprises: The Case of Machine Tool Industry in China, *Journal of Comparative Economics*, 1996, 23, pp. 256–277.

B. Naughton, *Growing Out of the Plan: Chinese Economic Reform, 1978-1993*, Cambridge University Press, Cambridge, 1995.

Shi Qingqi, Qin Baoting, Chen Jing: Main Index for Measuring Technological Progress in Economic growth, in Wang Jiye: *Evaluation Theory and Practice for Technological Progress*, Beijing Science and Technology Literature Press, 1986.

J. Sachs, W. Woo, Understanding China's Economic Performance, Working Paper 5935, NBER, Cambridge, MA 02138., 1997.

R. Solow, Technical Change and the Aggregate Production Function, *Review of Economics and Statistics*, 1957, 39, pp. 312–320.

G. Wan, Technical Change in Chinese State Industry: A New Approach, *Journal of Comparative Economics*, 1995, 21, pp. 308–325.

Wang Jun: An Analysis of Economic Performance of State-Owned Enterprises, *Economic Research*, 1996 (8), pp. 37–45.

M. Weitzman, C. Xu, Chinese Township Village Enterprises as Vaguely Defined Cooperatives, *Journal of Comparative Economics*, 1994, 18, pp. 121–145.

World Bank: *China: Development of Socialist Economy*. Beijing, China Finance and Economics Press, 1982.

World Bank: *China: Problems and Solutions for Long-Term Development*. Beijing, China Finance and Economics Press, 1985.

World Bank: *World Development Report 1992: Development and the Environment*. Beijing, Chinese Finance and Economics Press, 1992.

World Bank: *East Asian Miracle: Economic Growth and Public Policy*. Beijing, Chinese Finance and Economics Press, 1995.

W. Woo, W. Hai, Y. Jin, G. Fan, How Successful Has Chinese Enterprise Reform Been, Pitfals in Opposite Biases and Focus, *Journal of Comparative Economics*, 1994, 18, pp. 410–437.

Y. Wu, Productive Growth, Technological Progress, and Technical Efficiency Change in China: A Three Sector Analysis, *Journal of Comparative Economics*, 1995, 21, pp. 207–229.

Y. Wu, *Productive Performance in Chinese Enterprises: An Empirical Study*, New York, MacMilan Press Ltd., 1996.

Zhang Jun, *Transition and Growth*, Shanghai, Shanghai Far East Press, 2002.

Zhang Jun: Growth, Capital Formation and Technological Choice: Explanation of the Factors for Long-Term Decline of Economic Growth in China, *Journal of Economics Quarterly*, 2002, 1 (2), pp. 301–338.

Zhang Jun, Han Xianwang: Growth Mode of the Soviet Union: A Review, *Economic Studies*, 1996 (8).

Zhang Jun, Shi Shaohua: TFP Change of Chinese Economy: 1952–1998, *Collection of World Economy*, 2003 (2).

Zhang Junkuo: A Comprehensive Analysis of Economic Benefits during the 7th "Five-Year-Plan" Period, *Economic Research*, 1991 (4), pp. 8–17.

Zhang Ronggang. An Analysis of Output Growth and Factor Contribution of State-Owned Enterprises, *Economic Research*, 1997 (6), pp. 27–35.

J. Zheng, X. Liu, A. Bigsten, Ownership Structure and Determinants of Technical Efficiency: An Application of Data Envelopment Analysis to Chinese Enterprises (1986–1990), 1998, 26, pp. 465–484.

Zheng Jinghai, Liu Xiaoxuan, A. Bigsten: Efficiency, Technology Progress and Best Practices of the State-Owned Enterprise during the Period of 1980–1994, *Journal of Economics Quarterly*, 2002 (3), pp. 521–540.

Zou Zhizhuang: *Chinese Economy*, Tianjin, Nankai University Press, 1984.

Chapter 8
Decline of China's Investment Efficiency and the Aggregate Characteristics of Capital Formation

8.1 Introduction

Since the 1980s, China has sustained a rapid economic growth for 20 years. This is unique not only among all the transition economies, but also surpassed the growth record of the "four dragons" of East Asia during their period of rapid growth (60s–80s in the past century). However, in the 90s, especially since the late 90s, there has appeared a continued downward trend in the increase rate (see Fig. 8.1). So, whether China can continue to maintain its momentum of rapid economic growth and growth pattern has begun to draw more and more attention from researchers of economics (e.g., Zhang et al. 2002; Rawski 2002; Qin and Song 2002).[1]

Although China is a transitional economy, its economic growth is largely similar to the strategic pattern of the emerging industrialization, and can be defined as "industrialization driven" (Zhang et al. 2002). There used to have more than 70% (now about 63%) of the population in the Chinese countryside, but, like the East Asia's newly industrial economies, China's economic growth does not depend on the agricultural sector (except for the early 1980s), but on the industrial sector, especially the expansion of manufacturing industry. The industrial added value has accounted for about 45% of GDP, but the contribution from the agricultural sector is only 10%, and this share is still declining. That is to say, China's economic growth is, in fact, driven by a manufacturing sector, not an agricultural sector.

Because of the role of the manufacturing sector, another sector, trade, which is also similar to East Asia's economic development, is also of importance in economic growth. Although the East Asian economy shows a different pattern of foreign direct investment from China, there is a great similarity between China and the East Asian economy in terms of export promotion and trade expansion. Today, exports and foreign direct investment is playing an increasingly important role in

[1] Qin and Song (2002).

J. Zhang, *Reform, Transformation and Growth*, Understanding China,
https://doi.org/10.1007/978-981-99-5712-5_8

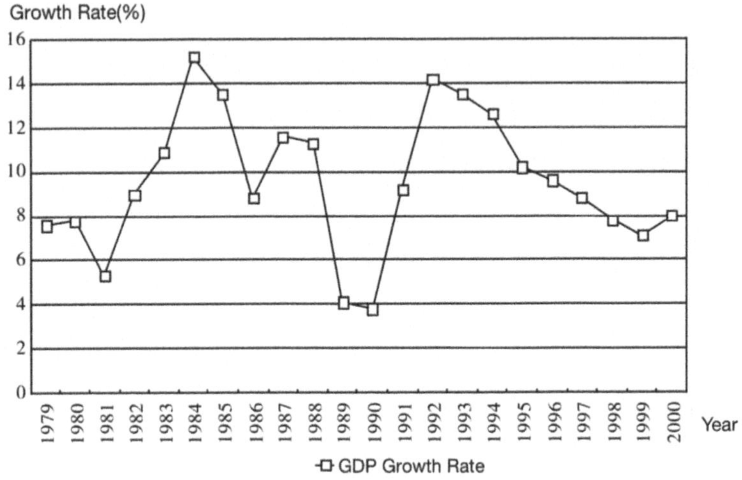

Fig. 8.1 China's GDP growth rate (1979–2000)

China's economic growth.[2] However, the importance of export trade and foreign

---

[2] But in many research literatures, the contribution of trade growth to China's economic growth is often seriously underestimated. The fallacy stems from the "net export" project in the national income accounting equation. "Net exports" is the difference between exports and imports, equal to the balance of trade. In general, this balance accounts for only 1–2% in China's GDP; therefore, if one tries to calculate its contribution to economic growth, not only is the "net export" not worth mentioning, it will actually make the growth rate of GDP decrease in the economic trade deficit. For this reason, most studies agree that trade growth is almost negligible in China's high rate of economic growth. Some studies have even concluded that in the 20 years of economic growth in China, exports are not the main driving force, and that China's economic growth is mainly driven by domestic demand. Especially after the financial crisis in Southeast Asia in 1997, the "introversion" of China's economy has actually become a "consensus". Because the total consumption and investment accounted for 90% of China's GDP, it seems to be a common sense to claim that Chinese economy and its growth are mainly driven by domestic demands. Unfortunately, however, this common sense may lead to a fallacy.

It should not be hard to imagine that consumption, investment, import and export are interrelated. Moreover, the contribution of import and export to other sectors of economy is likely to be greater for a manufacturing economy like China. Theoretically, if we simply calculate the contribution of "net export" to economic growth from the identical GDP equation before we ascertain the impact of export on other items of expenditures that constitute GDP, we will naturally neglect "indirect contribution" of exports to other items of expenditures. Therefore, using the national income identical equation to directly calculate the contribution of net exports to GDP would seriously underestimate the importance of trade to China's economic growth. One of the correct estimation methods is to estimate the impact of export on consumption, investment and import before estimating the contribution of exports to GDP. And that requires economists to do research in a serious way.

We have noticed that this issue has attracted the attention of Chinese economists, and some people have begun to use similar methods to re-estimate the contribution of China's exports to GDP. For example, Lin and Li (2002) first estimated the positive effects of export on consumption, investment and import, then, they estimated the contribution of export growth to GDP growth. They found that, on average, 10% export growth can boost 1% of GDP growth. Lo (1999), on the other

direct investment is tied to the fact that China's economic growth depends mainly on the manufacturing sector. As everyone knows, 80% of Chinese export is material processing and export of manufactured goods, mostly from foreign-funded enterprises in China. In direct investment in China, foreign capital is mostly concentrated in the manufacturing sector.

If the above understanding is correct, then, as an economic system in transformation, the growth mechanism that the Chinese economy depends on does not seem to be particularly different from the earlier East Asian economies—all dependent on rapid industrialization to promote fast economic growth. What needs to be pointed out is that, as a major economy, this similarity to the East Asian economic growth mechanism is manifested in the process of growing regional extremes (i.e., industrialization continues to gather in the eastern and southern coastal regions). In other words, the geographical features of Chinese economy and the "East Asia miracle" in the growth model are different.[3] Therefore, on the whole, a lot of literatures on economic growth and industrialization (for example, Young 1994; Lau and Kim 1992; Kim and Lau 1996) are mainly concerned with East Asian economies, they are also crucial for us to explain the growth mechanism and sustainability of economic growth in China.[4] In theory, the growth model of industrialization is close to the neoclassical growth model.[5] Higher savings rate and rapid capital formation have become the main source of economic growth. However, with the increase of capital density, the marginal productivity of capital will decrease, thus slowing down the speed of economic growth.

For an economy with an excess supply of labor in China, the process of industrialization should be able to last longer. As long as the formation of capital can attract and match more labor, China's economy will remain at a steady state of growth for a long time, and there will be a lot of room for economic growth. However, our experience shows that the capital density of China's economy has risen markedly and rapidly over the past 10 years. This is difficult to understand for an economy with a surplus supply of labor, because the significant increase in capital density

---

hand, studied the contribution of imports to China's economic growth. Although we need more empirical studies to determine how much exports and trade contribute to China's economic growth, the new conclusions seem to be closer to our intuition. For details, see Lin and Li (2002), Lo (1999).

[3] It is worth noting that the geographical difference in Chinese economic growth has become one of the major issues for economists in recent years and there have been a lot of research literature on this issue as well (for example, Wei 1997; Liu et al. 1994; Demurger et al. 2001; Liu et al. 1999). See Wei (1997), Liu et al. (1994), Demurger et al. (2001). Liu et al. (1999).

[4] Young (1994) in his paper titled Lessons from East Asian NICs: A Different View, provided a simple and technical approach for the East Asian economic growth pattern. His conclusion is more straightforward: "The most important feature of the newly industrialized countries in East Asia is not their unusual quick growth of manufacturing industry, but their success in expanding investment in manufacturing and employment, so they enjoy the reputation of "industrialization". Krugman (1994) commented on the growth model of the "East Asia miracle" in nontechnical language in a playful article. Felipe (1999) provided us with a very beautiful literature review on economic growth and efficiency change in East Asia. See A. Young, Lessons from the East Asian NICs: A Different View, NBER working paper, No.4482 1994. Krugman (1994). Felipe (1999).

[5] Lau and Kim (1992), Kim and Lau (1996).

usually occurs when the economic development is close to full employment. And it is a common sense that China's economy has almost unlimited supply of labor resources. It can be seen that there are institutional reasons behind this "deepening of capital" that appeared ahead of time. And according to our understanding, this is a phenomenon that needs to be well explained in the context of investment system of China.

The characteristics of China's investment system and its impact on the efficiency of China's capital formation require special study. However, as we pointed out in another study, Chinese economic capital formation is the result of growth targets of local government and competition in a non integrated economic environment (Zhang et al. 2002). Such an investment system has resulted in the uniformity of the investment structure and the economic sector structure of China's local economy since the reform (Young 2000).[6] The total amount of investment is much higher than the optimal equilibrium value under the integrated market system (Qin and Song 2002). As a result of excessive investment, large amounts of capital have been deposited in areas of excess capacity (resulting in the worsening of profitability) that has led to a sustained and significant downward trend in China's capital productivity over the past the years. Excessive investment also weakens the ability of absorbing labor force by economic growth (Yuan 2002), which restricts the rapid growth of the economy.[7] Although there are a lot of literatures that have revealed the problems of Chinese investment system mentioned above, there is still a lack of systematic empirical investigation in present literature on the changes of investment efficiency and some aggregate features of capital formation (such as the capital formation rate, structures of investment sector and ownerships) since the reform in China. The purpose of this paper is to discuss the changes in the efficiency of China's investment and their relationship with the aggregate characteristics of capital formation. We hope that through such research, we can further reveal the possible inhibitory effects of low investment efficiency on China's economic growth.

This paper consists of the following 5 parts. In addition to the introduction, in the second part, we will examine and discuss the changing patterns of capital productivity, and the third part will be focused on analyzing the rise in capital density. The fourth part will discuss some aggregate characteristics of capital formation. The final part is the basic conclusion and its implications.

[6] Young (2000).

[7] Yuan (2002).

8.2 Efficiency of Investment and the "Incremental Capital-Output Ratio (ICOR)"

We know that the capital, relative to the speed of output growth, is expressed as marginal efficiency of capital or marginal productivity of capital. Thus, a measurement of the change in capital productivity is to observe the growth rate of the "capital-output" ratio. On the basis of a simple breakdown method of growth accounting developed by Solow (1957), under the assumption of constant returns to scale, exogenous technological progress and competitive market, the growth rate of output can be broken down into:

$$g_y = \alpha g_l + (1 - \alpha) g_k + e$$

Among them, g_y, g_l and g_k are output, labor and capital growth rate respectively. α is the output elasticity of labor, and e is the Solow residual, or the growth rate of total factor productivity (TFP). Here, it can reflect or pinpoint changes in technology or dynamic efficiency. Through transformation, we can get the formula of the growth rate of capital-output ratio:

$$g_k - g_y = \alpha(g_k - g_l) - e$$

or

$$g(K/Y) = \alpha g(K/L) - g(\text{TFP})$$

This shows that, in the assumption of neoclassical production theory, the change of capital-output ratio is the result of "net effect" between the change of capital-labor ratio (i.e. per capita capital or "capital equipment ratio") and TFP change rate. If the capital-labor ratio or the density of factors remains the same, then the growth of TFP will be translated into a decline in the capital-output ratio. Since the reciprocal of the capital-output ratio is the productivity of capital, the change in the productivity of capital is equivalent to the improvement in technology or efficiency as long as the density of the factors remains unchanged. However, if the factor density in the process constantly increases, the change of capital-output ratio (thus the productivity of capital changes in the opposite direction) can only depends on the net effect of factor density changes as well as the changes of total factor productivity.

In the existing literature, the marginal efficiency of capital is often measured by incremental capital-output ratio (ICOR) which is an indicator more easily calculated. Because by definition, marginal productivity of capital is the marginal output of capital stock (dY/dK), i.e. the ratio of changes of output increments to capital stock. Since the change in capital stock (dY) equals investment flows (I), the marginal productivity of capital can be expressed in terms of the ratio of GDP increments to investment ($d\text{GDP}/I$) in total amount. Obviously, ICOR is the inverse of the marginal productivity ($d\text{GDP}/I$) of the capital:

$$ICOR = I/\mathrm{d}GDP$$

In theory, the improvement of investment efficiency will tend to synchronize the changes of capital and output, so regardless of the capital-output ratio, or the use of ICOR, their growth rate will become very small, or close to zero. For example, Blanchard and Fisher (1998), when analyzing the changes in the capital-output ratio of the US economy from 1874 to 1984, also noted, "The existing measurement of capital shows that capital and output grow at roughly the same rate, so the $g_y - g_x$ (the difference between the growth rate of capital and the growth rate of output......note by me) is close to zero.... The relative invariance of the output-capital ratio contains a positive Solow surplus value, roughly equal to the labor share multiplied by the growth rate of labor productivity."[8]

Of course, these indicators are often related to the way of economic growth or the strategic choice of economic development. For example, Young (1993) roughly compared the East Asian mode of economic growth with other regions in his paper and found that: "In the period of 1960–1985, every newly emergent industrialized economies have experienced a significant increase of investment in the ratio of GDP. During 1960–1980, the I/GDP ratio in Taiwan increased by 1 time, that in South Korea and Singapore increased by 2 and 3 times respectively.... The rise in this rate is not typical of the world economy, because in other economies, the I/GDP ratio is constant or declining, except for Asia, a region with exceptional performance."

Krueger (1984) also noted in her paper titled Comparative Advantage and Development Policy: 20 Years Later: "The great differences among countries in ICOR showed that under the different trade policies exists either the proportion of factors, or significant difference in efficiency.[9] During the years of 1960–1973, the incremental capital output ratio in South Korea, Singapore and Taiwan of China was between 1.7 and 2.5, which is in sharp contrast with 5.5 and 5.7 in Chile and India (see Balassa 1978). When Brazil changed its trading strategy, its incremental capital output ratio dropped from 3.8 in 1960–1966 to 2.1 in 1966–1973. Although there may be many reasons for the changes in these ratios, the difference in factor proportions and the ability of exporters to employ appropriate factor density to expand production are undoubtedly the most important reasons."

According to this definition, we calculated the incremental capital output ratio of China in 1980–2000 in Table 8.1, and depicted the change format of the 5 year's moving average of ICOR in Fig. 8.2. Figure 8.2 clearly shows that since the reform, the incremental capital output ratio of China, after maintaining over 10 years of constant quality, rose sharply from the beginning of 1994, meaning that the marginal efficiency of investment since 1994 has been deteriorating significantly. This result is consistent with our direct calculation of the capital-output ratio in the same time range (Zhang et al. 2002). Taking into account the high degree of correlation between China's economic growth and investment and comparing with the growth rate curve

[8] Blanchard and Fisher (1998).

[9] Krueger (1984).

Table 8.1 ICOR in China

Year	GDP (BN yuan)	GFCF (BN yuan)	ICOR	ICOR (Moving average for 5 years)
1980	479.6	910.9	1.9	
1981	344.6	961	2.79	
1982	432.3	1230.4	2.85	2.25
1983	639.8	1430.1	2.24	2.16
1984	1236.5	1832.9	1.48	2.1
1985	1793.4	2543.2	1.42	1.96
1986	1237.8	3120.6	2.52	1.83
1987	1760.3	3791.7	2.15	1.98
1988	2965.8	4753.8	1.6	2.25
1989	1980.9	4410.4	2.23	2.11
1990	1638.7	4517	2.76	2
1991	3069.9	5594.5	1.82	2.01
1992	5020.3	8080.1	1.61	1.85
1993	7996.3	13,072.3	1.63	1.64
1994	12,125	17,042.1	1.41	1.76
1995	11,718.7	20,019.3	1.71	2.2
1996	9406.5	22,913.5	2.44	3.33
1997	6578	24,941.1	3.79	4.66
1998	3882.6	28,406.2	7.32	5.21
1999	3722.3	29,854.7	8.02	
2000	7336.1	32,917.7	4.49	

Note ICOR = increments of the whole country's fixed capital investment (GFCF)/GDP, that is, the inverse of the marginal productivity of capital, and the greater the ICOR, the lower the efficiency of investment
Source State Bureau of Statistics: China Statistical Yearbook (2001), Beijing, China Statistics Press, 2001

of China's GDP in Fig. 8.1, it is easy to see that the decline in China's economic growth seems to be due mainly to the rapid deterioration of investment efficiency.

Because ICOR is equal to the product of output elasticity of capital and capital-output ratio (K/Y),[10] the change pattern of ICOR shown in Fig. 8.2 also implies similar changes in the capital-output ratio. We used the framework of the growth accounting (the total factor productivity there is seen as an exogenous independent variable) to look at the causes of the rising capital-output ratio, and attributed the reasons to the combined results of the rise of capital-labor ratio (K/L) and (or) the decline of TFP growth rate (Zhang et al. 2002). Moreover, we do find in our experience

[10] Note: This is because the output elasticity of capital (a) equals the ratio of marginal product of capital ($\mathrm{d}Y/\mathrm{d}K$) to average output (Y/K). The marginal product of capital ($\mathrm{d}Y/\mathrm{d}K$) is equal to the reciprocal of the incremental capital output ratio ($\mathrm{d}Y/\mathrm{d}K = I/\mathrm{d}Y$).

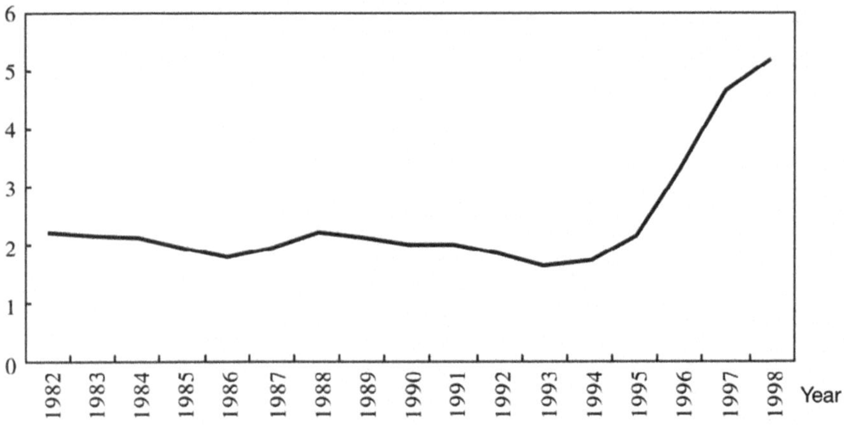

Fig. 8.2 China's ICOR (5 year's moving average)

that the TFP growth rate has continued to decline since 1992 (Zhang and Shi 2003), and the growth rate of capital-labor ratio calculated by industrial sectors also began to rise sharply during 1993–1994 (Zhang et al. 2002).[11]

However, we also noted that there is a nonlinear correlation between TFP change and the change in capital density itself. Now, based on similar arguments of Ohkawa (1984) and Toh and Ng (2002), as well as considering the nonlinear relationship between changes in TFP and capital-labor ratio, we have handled the change of total factor productivity as the "quadratic function" of the change of the capital-labor ratio.[12] According to Toh and Ng (2002), we have defined the total factor productivity, $g(K/L)$, as the following quadratic function of the capital-labor ratio (K/L):

$$g(TFP) = \alpha_0 + \alpha_1 g(K/L) + \alpha_2 \left[g(K/L)\right]^2$$

Parameter α_0 is the variation of total factor productivity $g(TFP)$ that cannot be explained by changes in the capital-labor ratio (K/L), and according to Toh and Ng, we expect α_1 to be positive and α_2 to be negative. This means that when the capital-labor ratio (K/L) rises to a certain critical level, the growth rate of total factor productivity $g(TFP)$ will begin to decline. The critical value of g $g(K/L)$ can be obtained by solving the maximum value of the total factor productivity growth rate $g(TFP)$: the first derivative of $g(TFP)$ to $g(K/L)$ is zero, and we obtain the critical value (X^*) of $g(K/L)$ as:

$$X^* = -\alpha_2/(2 - \alpha_1)$$

[11] Zhang and Shi (2003).

[12] Ohkawa (1984), Toh and Ng (2002).

Table 8.2 Regression of quadratic equation

	α_0	α_1	α_2
Estimated value of coefficient	1.141	0.984	−0.0722
Coefficient standard errors	1.281	0.229	0.025
T statistical quantity	0.891	4.297	−2.86
X^*	6.814		
Y^*	4.494		

Note The quadratic equation is $g(TFP) = \alpha_0 + \alpha_1 g(\frac{K}{L}) + \alpha_2[g(\frac{K}{L})]^2$

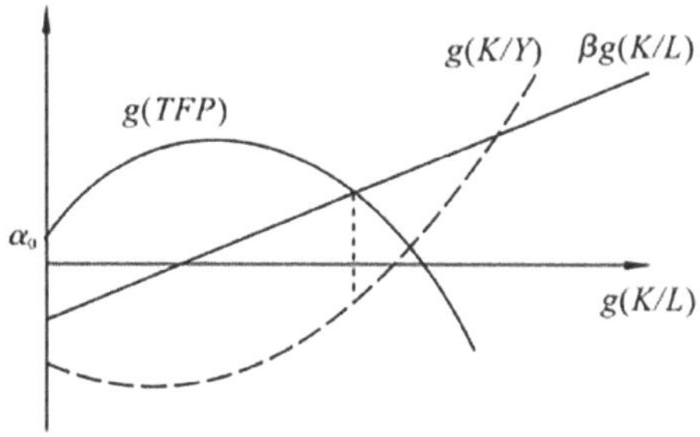

Fig. 8.3 Quadratic function relation between $\mathbf{g}(\boldsymbol{K}/\boldsymbol{L})$ and $\mathbf{g}(\boldsymbol{TFP})$

Then, we can solve the maximum value Y^* of $g(TFP)$.

We obtained the estimated value of parameters α_0 α_1 and α_2 and calculated the critical value (X^*) of $g(K/L)$ and the corresponding maximum value (Y^*) of $g(TFP)$ by using the basic statistical data of 1978–1998 provided by Zhang and Shi (2003), adding three years' data of 1998–2000 and fitting the quadratic function mentioned above. We summarized this fitting result in Table 8.2 and the goodness of fit is quite satisfactory—the parameter value α_2 is negative, the critical value of (X^*) of $g(K/L)$ is 6.814, and the maximum value (Y^*) of $g(TFP)$ is 4.494. We can describe the empirical result of this quadratic function in Fig. 8.3.

As we mentioned earlier, according to the accounting of growth, the growth rate of capital-output ratio $g(K/L)$ can be broken down into:

$$g(K/L) = \beta g(K/L) - g(TFP)$$

β is the output elasticity of labor. And now, because the TFP growth rate, $g(TFP)$, is the quadratic function of the growth rate of capital-labor ratio $g(K/L)$, $g(TFP)$ can be replaced by this quadratic function so as to get the formula of the growth rate of the capital-output ratio of $g(K/L)$ expressed by $g(K/L)$:

$$g(K/L) = -\alpha_0 + (\beta - \alpha_1)g(K/L) - \alpha_2[g(K/L)]^2$$

In order to obtain the positive effect of the change of $g(K/L)$ on $g(K/L)$, let us make the first derivative of $g(K/L)$ to $g(K/L)$ greater than zero so as to obtain:

$$g(K/L) > (\alpha_1 - \beta)/(2|\alpha_2|)$$

For example, according to the empirical results of fitting, we already know parameters α_1 and α_2 are 0.984 and -0.0722 and β is $1 - 0.61 = 0.39$; so, when $g(K/L)$ is more than 4%, the rise of capital-labor ratio (K/L) will lead to the rise of the growth rate of the capital-output ratio $(g(K/L))$. Because the capital output ratio (K/Y) is the product of output elasticity of capital $(1 - \beta)$ and *ICOR*, if the capital-labor ratio $(g(K/L))$ grows too fast, it will in fact cause the rise of *ICOR* or the significant decrease of investment efficiency.

With regard to the "quadratic relation" between the capital density growth rate $(g(K/L))$ and the growth rate of total factor productivity $(g(TFP))$, a possible explanation is that in the early stage of economic development, with the sustained and massive investment in production capacity and infrastructure, capital-labor ratio will accelerate resulting in the deepening of capital. At this stage, the growth of TFP will tend to slow down. With the completion of investment in production facilities and infrastructure, the growth of capital-labor ratio will gradually slow down, thus the growth of TFP will begin to accelerate.[13] However, the period of economic growth in the late stage of China's reform does not seem to have followed this "cycle of development", probably because before the reform and opening up, China had gone through nearly 30 years of planned economy and heavy industrialization development. Based on the growth rate of the capital-labor ratio in China's industrial sector, which is calculated in the third part, the accelerated rise in the capital-labor ratio took place after the 90s rather than in the 80s (Zhang et al. 2002). We will analysis and explain in the following part that the deepening of capital investment since the 90s looks more like an institutional problem rather than the reflection of the cycle of economic development.

8.3 Evidence of Capital Density Changes

In the late period of reform, the capital density of China's economy rose significantly in the late 1980s and since the 1990s. This can be confirmed first by the model of change in the actual labor-capital ratio of the economy as a whole calculated by us as shown in Fig. 8.4. Here is the aggregate data of capital and labor sorted out by Zhang and Shi (2003) for 1978–1998. Concerning the capital stock data, first of all, the data of 1978–1990 are from He (1992)'s research on the estimated stock of assets

[13] For example, Toh and Ng (2002) explained the changing patterns of TFP in Singapore based on this hypothesis. He also mentioned that this view of development cycle was also expressed in a similar way by Ohkawa (1984).

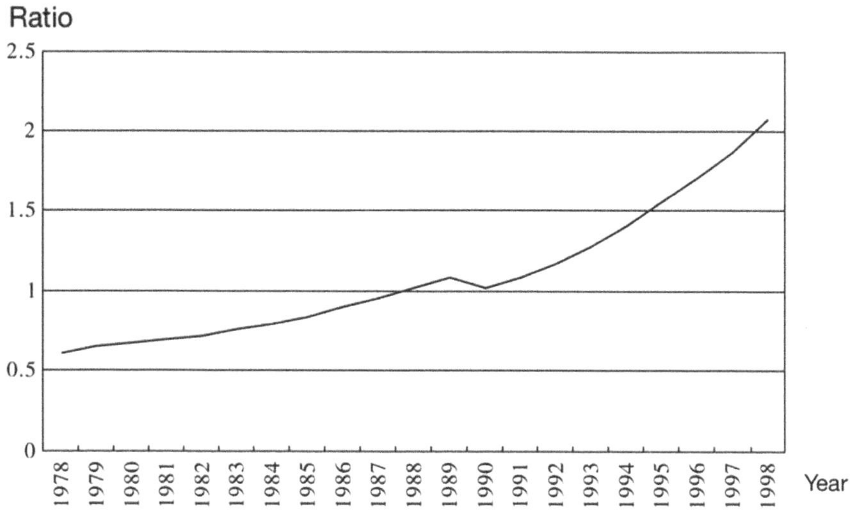

Fig. 8.4 Real capital-labor ratio of China's economy (1978–1998)

in China.[14] In order to maintain consistency, we calculated the yearly capital stock data of 1991–1998 by following his method and according to the country's yearly total investment in fixed assets during 1991–1998. For details of the data, see Zhang and Shi (2003).

In order to further observe the change pattern of capital density, we also calculated the actual capital-labor ratio of the state-owned enterprises and collective enterprises (especially the township enterprises) since the reform. Figure 8.5 depicts the model of changes in the real capital-labor ratio of state-owned enterprises we estimated during the period of 1980–1998. In the calculation of the capital-labor ratio of state-owned enterprises, we did not specifically estimated the proportion of productive and non-productive labor, because our focus was on the changing mode of capital-labor ratio, and the total amount of labor used obviously would strengthen our observation. In addition, as in many studies, we also used fixed net asset value as capital stock. The fixed net asset value is the accumulated amount of the original investment minus the accumulated depreciation. Since all fixed asset data published in China has not been deflated by constant price, we must use the following method to estimate the actual value of the fixed net asset.

We used the following methods to calculate the net value of fixed assets of 1980–1998 (using 1990 constant price): ① by annually added net value of fixed assets obtained through existing statistics; ② using fixed asset price index (P_K) to deflate the annually added net value of fixed assets; ③ add up the annually added fixed assets being deflated. Assuming that the prices of investment goods are stable before 1980, the fixed net asset value at the end of 1980 can be used as the initial value for our estimation. The net value of fixed assets of constant price in 1990, or the net value

[14] He (1992).

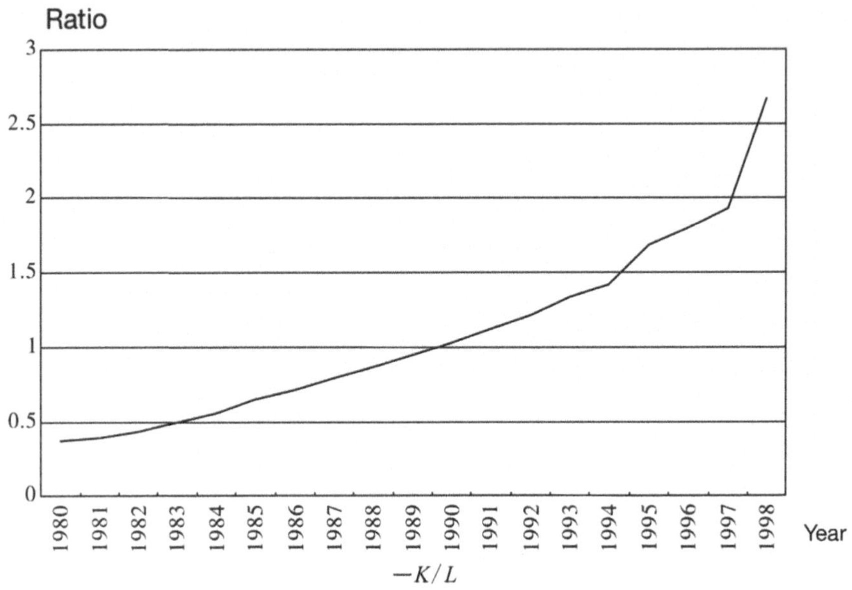

Fig. 8.5 Actual capital-labor ratio of China's state-owned enterprises (1980–1998)

of fixed assets being deflated, DNF_t, can be estimated by the following formula:

$$DNF_t = NF_{80} + \sum_t (NF_t - NF_{t-1})/P_K$$

NF_{80} is the net value of fixed assets at the end of 1980, NF_t, NF_{t-1} are the net value of fixed assets of year t and year $t - 1$. P_K is the fixed asset price deflator for year t. In this paper, the fixed capital price index of 1980–1992 estimated by Jefferson et al. (1996) was used. The data from 1993 to 1998 was the investment price index of fixed assets provided by various volumes of the *Chinese Statistical Yearbook* after 1993, which is consistent with that of Jefferson, for the calculating method of average weight of construction and installation deflator and equipment purchase deflator is used.[15]

In calculating the actual capital-labor ratio of collective enterprises, we used the data about the capital stock and labor force of collective enterprises provided by Lo (1999) in his paper titled Re-Evaluation of the Performance of Chinese State-Owned Enterprises: 1980–1996, but the data was only available until 1986. The data of the capital is also the net value of the fixes assets after depreciation being deducted, and the capital price index is used to deflate the net value of fixed capital in a similar way. Likewise, the capital price index of 1980–1991 was borrowed from Jefferson et al. (1996), while the capital goods price index of 1992–1996 was calculated by

[15] Jefferson et al. (1996).

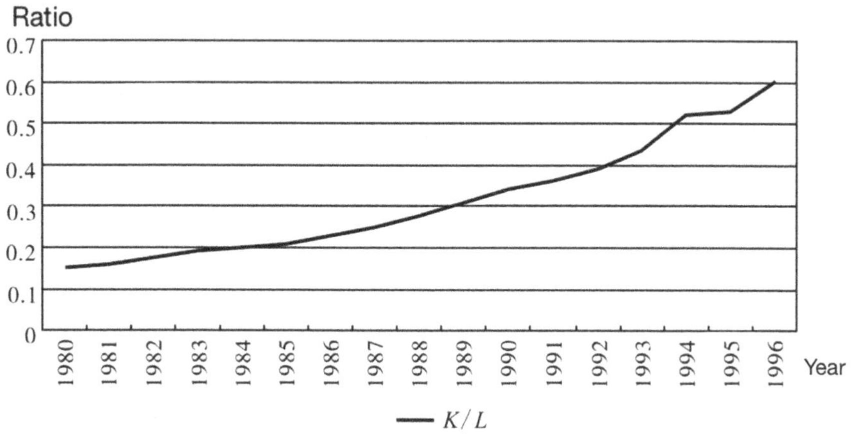

Fig. 8.6 The increasing actual capital-labor ratio of China's collective enterprises (1980–1996)

me on the basis of the stable relationship between the price index of capital and the ex factory price index of industrial output. We have described the results of the calculations in Fig. 8.6. We can see that the growth trend of the capital-labor ratio in the collective industrial sector is still very significant.

In a study of township enterprises, we have also calculated the actual capital-labor ratio of township enterprises and its growth rate (1980–2000)[16] as shown in Fig. 8.7. We found that the capital-labor ratio of township enterprises began to rise steadily in the 90s after experiencing a stable pattern in the 1980s, which is in agreement with the study of Chen (1999).[17] Chen (1999) found that since late 80s (especially the 90s), the development of township enterprises began to show changes and characteristics that economists failed to fully predicted–the path of its technical choice began to deviate and its technology changes did not develop along the path of technology neutrality or saving capital elements as is expected by the traditional theory. Instead, its capital intensity had shown a rising trend. As we have already mentioned, in Chen Jianbo's data, the two-tier enterprises at the town and village levels experienced a significant rise in capital-labor ratio and average asset scale over the period of 1978–1996.

Obviously, since the late 1980s, both the state-owned and collective enterprises have experienced a sustained and significant upward trend in the capital-labor ratio. Moreover, as we Zhang et al. (2002) once pointed out, the existing studies have found that the rapid rise in capital-labor ratio of township enterprises is not primarily due to the fast rising of labor prices faced by township enterprises (Chen 1999; Otsuka et al. 2000), but the result of "over entry" and "over competition".[18] Our

[16] The capital data we use here is the data after the original value of fixed assets has been deflated, which, of course, will only affect the absolute value of capital-labor ratio but not its pattern of changes. See Zhang et al. (2003).

[17] Chen (1999).

[18] Keijiro et al. (2000).

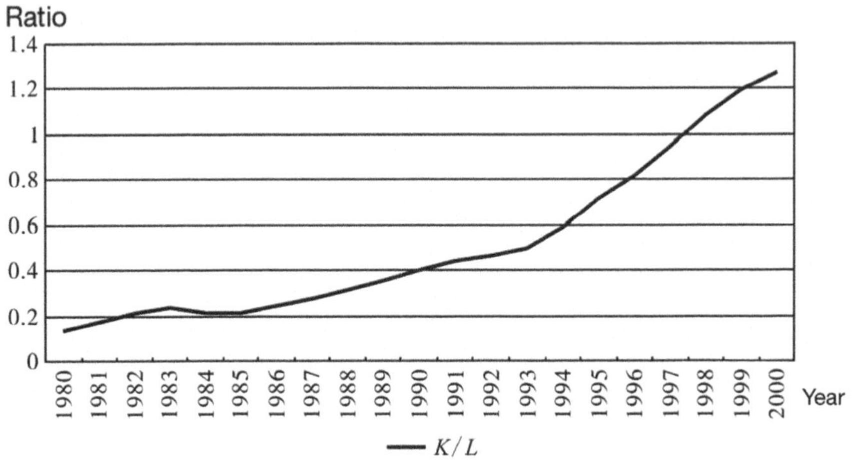

Fig. 8.7 The increasing actual capital-labor ratio of China's rural enterprises (1980–2000)

further explanation is that, because of the specific property system and environment of demand, especially the intervention of local governments, the township enterprises followed the characteristics of "classical competition" in their entry into the industrial sectors, resulting in excessive entry and escalating investment. According to this explanation, the increasing capital density is not the result of the rising or extremely fast rising of the actual price of the labor force, but the excessive investment by the township enterprises.

In short, in the first 10 years of the Chinese economic reform, or the 1980s, the growth rate of China's capital-labor ratio basically experienced a modest decline, while the rising capital density accelerated from the end of the 1980s and the beginning of early 90s. So, in general, the period of 1989–1990 seems to be a turning point in China's economic growth, because before 1989, the change in capital-labor ratio or capital density was not significant in the industrial sector. Moreover, it was only after the 1990s that we saw the growth of the capital-output ratio accelerating (Zhang et al. 2002). In fact, in 1989–2001, the growth rate of China's fixed asset investment was always 4 percentage points higher than the growth rate of GDP. This is clearly a growth mode that cannot be sustained for a long time.[19]

[19] A recent study by Qin and Song (2002) also confirmed the Chinese economic growth in the past 10 years was mainly driven by excessive investment demand, and the rapid growth of capital formation has led to the loss of investment efficiency. They used Chinese provincial investment data of 1989–2000 to calculate the excessive demand for investment and the loss of investment efficiency. Clearly, excessive investment demand and loss of investment efficiency are responsible for the decline of China's economic growth.

8.4 Some of the Aggregate Characteristics of Overinvestment

We have stressed that the changes of capital-labor ratio from basically being stable to rapid increase mostly reflects the fact that there is still an institutional factor of excessive investment in China's economy after the reform. This kind of factor has played an important role in promoting the transformation of the economic sector structure and the ability to increase the total supply rapidly. However, as time goes on, the tendency of excessive investment begins to emerge, and excessive accumulation and inactivity of production capacity are increasingly becoming the restricting factors for sustained and rapid economic growth. Now, we will try to understand the institutional characteristics of overinvestment from several important aspects such as the speed of capital formation, proportion of manufacturing industry and the public investment share.

(1) Rate of Investment

We will begin by examining the changing format of the speed of capital formation. Table 8.3 shows the China's capital formation rate of 1978–2000 calculated according to different ways, or the proportion of investment in GDP. Here, we first calculated the rate of China's investment according to the "investment in fixed assets of the whole society" (that is, investment rate 1).[20] This is a unique statistical way in China. At the same time, we also used GDP calculated by the expenditure method and the composition of total amount of capital formation to calculate the concept of the other two standard rate of investment. Because in the GDP calculated by the expenditure method, the total capital formation includes the formation of fixed capital and the increase in inventories, so we provided the calculation results of the two definitions of the capital formation rate and the formation rate of fixed assets (i.e. investment rate 2 and investment rate 3), and the difference between them is the ratio of stock increase to GDP.

We described the time series of China's fixed assets investment rate 1 and 3 during 1980–2000 in Fig. 8.8. Despite a significant decline in the three-year period in 1989–1991, the overall pattern of investment in fixed assets experienced a continuing upward trend. In particular, in the past 10 years, the average investment rate of fixed assets was as high as 36%. The figure is much higher than the investment rate of two regions in Hong Kong and Taiwan since the 60s, which were 25.4% and 23.7% respectively in 1966–1998 (Toh and Ng 2002), but is almost equal with that in Singapore (since the 60s), South Korea, Thailand and Malaysia (after the 70s).

[20] According to the definition of *Chinese Statistical Yearbook*, The range of total fixed asset investment statistics include: basic construction investment, renovation investment, investment in real estate development, other state-owned fixed assets investment, collective investment in fixed assets (including urban and rural), private housing investment (including industrial and mining areas of cities and rural areas).

Table 8.3 China's capital formation rate since the reform (1978–2000)

Year	GDP	Total fixed asset investment statistics	Investment rate 1	GDP calculated by the expenditure method	Gross capital formation therein	Investment rate 2	Total fixed capital formation therein	Investment rate 3
1978				3605.6	1377.9	38.2	1073.9	29.78
1979	4038.2			4074	1474.2	36.2	1151.2	28.26
1980	4517.8	910.9	20.16	4551.3	1590	34.9	1318	28.96
1981	4862.4	961	19.76	4901.4	1581	32.3	1253	25.56
1982	5294.7	1230.4	23.24	5489.2	1760.2	32.1	1493.2	27.2
1983	5934.5	1430.1	24.1	6076.3	2005	33	1709	28.13
1984	7171	1832.9	25.56	7164.4	2468.6	34.5	2125.6	29.67
1985	8964.4	2543.2	28.37	8792.1	3386	38.5	2641	30.04
1986	10,202.2	3120.6	30.59	10,132.8	3846	38	3098	30.57
1987	11,962.5	3791.7	31.7	11,784.7	4322	36.7	3742	31.75
1988	14,928.3	4753.8	31.84	14,704	5495	37.4	4624	31.45
1989	16,909.2	4410.4	26.08	16,466	6095	37	4339	26.35
1990	18,547.9	4517	24.35	18,319.5	6444	35.2	4732	25.83
1991	21,671.8	5594.5	25.88	21,280.4	7517	35.3	5940	27.91
1992	26,638.1	8080.1	30.33	25,863.7	9636	37.3	8317	32.16
1993	34,634.4	13,072.3	37.74	34,500.7	14,998	43.5	12,980	37.62
1994	46,759.4	17,042.1	36.45	46,690.7	19,260.6	41.3	16,856.3	36.1
1995	58,478.1	20,019.3	34.23	58,510.5	23,877	40.8	20,300.5	34.7
1996	67,884.6	22,913.5	33.75	68,330.4	26,867.2	39.3	23,336.1	34.15
1997	74,462.6	24,941.1	33.49	74,894.2	28,457.6	38	25,154.2	33.59

(continued)

Table 8.3 (continued)

Year	GDP	Total fixed asset investment statistics	Investment rate 1	GDP calculated by the expenditure method	Gross capital formation therein	Investment rate 2	Total fixed capital formation therein	Investment rate 3
1998	78,345.2	28,406.2	36.26	79,003.3	29,545.9	37.4	27,630.8	34.97
1999	82,067.5	29,854.7	36.38	82,673.1	30,701.6	37.1	29,475.5	35.65
2000	89,403.6	32,917.7	36.82	89,112.5	32,255	36.2	32,623.8	36.61

Note Investment rate 1 = total amount of fixed assets investment of the whole society/GDP × 100%. We also gave the GDP calculated by the expenditure method and the gross capital formation therein. The gross capital formation is further divided into fixed capital formation and inventory increase; therefore, we also calculated the corresponding investment rates 2 and 3 according to the total capital formation and total fixed capital formation. The unit of investment is 100 million yuan, and the investment rate unit is %

Source State Bureau of Statistics: *Chinese Statistical Yearbook* (2001), Beijing, China Statistics Press, 2001

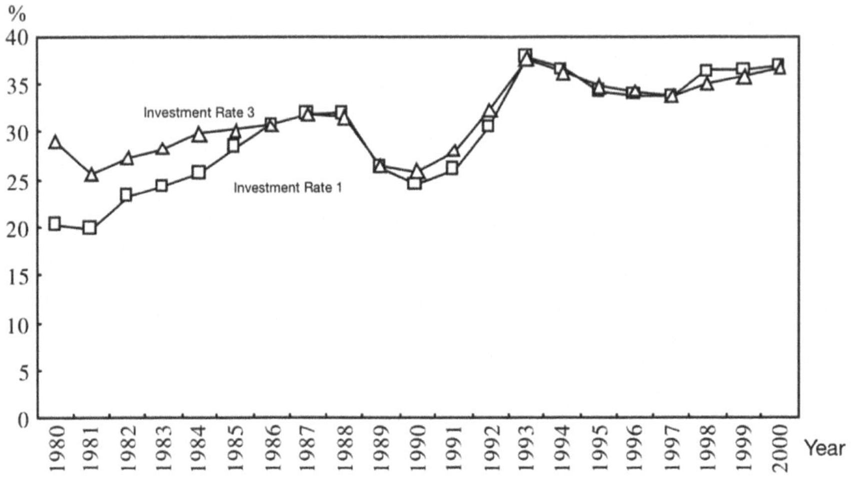

Fig. 8.8 Investment rate in fixed assets in China (1980–2000)

For example, Singapore's average fixed-asset investment rate in the 23 years during 1966–1998 was 35.4%, the highest among the Asian "four dragons".[21]

Next, let's look at the changes in inventory investment. The ratio of increase in inventory to GDP can be obtained by calculating the difference between investment rate 2 and 3 given in Table 8.3. We show the results in Fig. 8.9. By comparing Figs. 8.8 and 8.9, we can see that, while the rate of fixed capital investment continues to rise, the inventory investment rate has declined significantly since 1995. Usually, inventory investment reflects the degree of utilization of existing production capacity. In general, the increase in inventory means the increased utilization of the existing production capacity (capital stock) while the reduced inventory investment is a signal of excessive production capacity or the existing capital stock being laid idle. It is noteworthy that, while the inventory investment has been declining since 1994, fixed capital investment continues to grow. In other words, although the utilization of the existing production capacity is declining, the new production capacity is still being formed and expanded.

So, does such a high fixed asset investment rate in China contain a large proportion of housing investment? In other words, to what extent can the housing construction investment growth explain China's extremely high investment rate? Just as we have mentioned, Toh and Ng (2002), when interpreting the high investment rate of Singapore in the 70s–80s, particularly emphasized the proportion of housing construction investment in Singapore. In their data, in Singapore's high investment rate, especially the investment boom during 1981–1985, housing construction investment in

[21] During 1981–1985, the rate of fixed asset investment in Singapore was as high as 46%, which may be related to the rapid growth of Singapore's infrastructure investment at the time. According to Toh and Ng (2002), more than half of the investment was on residential and factory buildings.

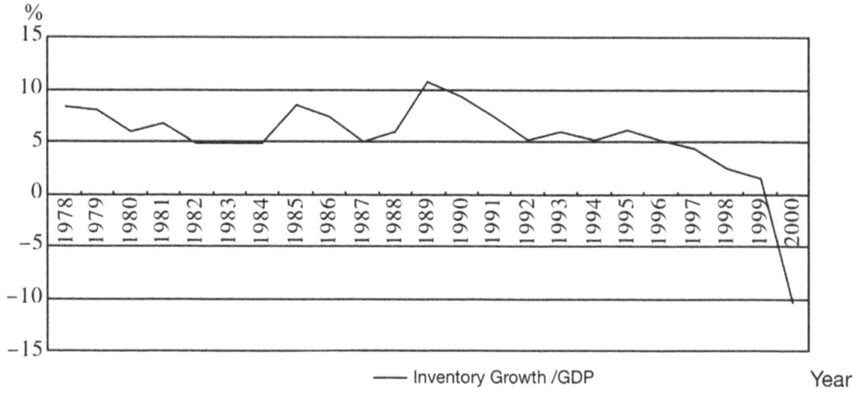

Fig. 8.9 Change in ratio of inventory growth/GDP in China (1978–2000)

fact accounted for quite a large share.[22] Then, in the annual fixed asset investment, what is the proportion of China's housing construction investment?

Because of the lack of direct access to the time series data on housing investment, we have no statistical data of housing construction investment that can be directly quoted. The only way is to calculate indirectly from publications such as *Chinese Statistical Yearbook* and *Chinese Fixed Assets Investment Yearbook*. On the basis of the *Chinese Statistical Yearbook, Chinese Investment Yearbook, Chinese Fixed Assets Investment Statistics Yearbook* and *Chinese Finance Yearbook*, we found that the *Chinese Statistical Yearbook* mainly provides three types of time series data on the basic construction and renovation investment in housing projects, completion area of urban and rural housing construction and the completion area of the residential housing, while the other three yearbooks basically copied the information of the *Chinese Statistical Yearbook*, so necessary calculation must be done by using these data in order to get the housing construction investment data.

In the *Chinese Statistical Yearbook*, the range of total fixed asset investment statistics includes: basic construction investment, renovation investment, investment in real estate development, investment in other state-owned fixed assets and investment in collective fixed assets (including urban and rural), private housing investment (including industrial mining areas in cities and rural areas). Thus, the total investment in housing construction in each of these parts should constitute the total amount of investment in housing construction in the whole society. Specifically, the amount of housing construction investment data of the whole social can be calculated from such a roundabout way: to get the corresponding data of housing construction area of the whole country from the various issues of statistical yearbooks (Table 8.4), and have this housing area multiplied by the housing cost (yuan/per square meter) as seen

22 For example, the author noted that the rate of investment in 1981–1985 rose sharply, half of which was caused by the expansion of investment in construction projects. The boom in the property market and the government housing schemes all raised the rate of fixed capital investment in Singapore (Toh and Ng 2002).

in Table 8.5. Finally, we use the weighted method to calculate the total amount of housing investment data (the investment of housing); the same method can be used to calculate the data of the amount of residential housing investment (the investment of residential housing).

The housing construction area of the whole society can be divided into urban and rural categories, of which the rural category accounts for most of the proportion. The rural category is mainly represented by individual housing (this can be seen from the comparison of columns 3 and 9 in Table 8.4). The housing costs of urban and rural regions are different, but we have known or can obtain the construction costs of per square meter of urban and rural housing (see Table 8.5. We can only get the individual housing cost in urban area, while the data of the average rural cost and rural individual housing cost is almost the same. But it should also be reasonable to replace the average cost of the urban and township housing with the urban individual housing cost), and then use the respective proportions of urban and rural housing in the total housing construction area as the corresponding cost weight. In this way, the average per square meter cost of housing construction area of the whole society can be obtained: housing construction area of the whole society × the average cost of housing construction = investment of housing construction; the investment in residential part (i.e. residential housing investment) contained in housing construction area of the whole society can be calculated according to the same method: the former − the latter = non residential housing investment. Table 8.6 shows the housing investment we have measured in accordance with the above method and the investment in residential and non residential housing it contains.

It is easy to calculate the proportion of housing investment in the proportion of fixed assets investment of the whole society by using the amount of the housing investment provided in Table 8.6 and the total amount of fixed asset investment of the whole society provided in Table 8.3. We found in our calculations that this proportion was higher in the first 10 years of the reform, about 30%, while it has declined since the 1990s until the late 90s when investment in housing only accounted for about 20% of the total fixed asset investment in the whole society. If converted to the proportion of GDP, then, since the 90s, the average housing construction investment accounted for only 6–7 percentage points of the GDP, far less than that in Singapore in 1966–1998 where the housing investment accounted for 14.4% of the proportion of GDP on average.[23] Therefore, different from Singapore, it seems that housing investment is not the main factor of the too rapid capital formation, nor it can explain the sign of "capital deepening" that has constantly been revealed after the mid-90s.

(2) Proportion of Manufacturing Industry

We believe that since the industrial reform in China, the expansion of the manufacturing sector has been the main reason for the growth of fixed asset investment. The important role of the manufacturing sector in the later stage of the reform can

[23] The proportion of investment in housing construction in mainland China is lower than that in Hong Kong, but is close to that in Taiwan. The average proportion in Hong Kong in 1966–1998 was 12.6%, while that in Taiwan was 6.8%. The data of proportion of housing construction investment in GDP in Singapore, Hong Kong and Taiwan Ch are from Toh and Ng (2002).

Table 8.4 China's total housing construction area (1985–2000)

Year	The completed housing construction area of the whole society (Million square meters)		The completed individual housing construction area in rural area (Million square meters)		The proportion of completed rural individual housing construction area in the whole society		The proportion of completed urban housing construction area in the whole society		The completed housing construction area in rural areas (Hundred million square meters) (9)
	Total (1)	Residential Housing (2)	Total (3)	Residential Housing (4)	Total (5) = (3)/(1)	Residential Housing (6) = (4)/(2)	Total (7) = 1-(6)	Residential housing (8) = 1-(6)	
1985	122,084	90,972	78,973	69,542	0.65	0.76	0.35	0.24	7.22
1986	151,184	117,667	103,225	94,468	0.68	0.80	0.32	0.20	9.84
1987	141,963	107,697	96,477	85,524	0.68	0.79	0.32	0.21	8.84
1988	135,943	104,801	89,092	80,799	0.66	0.77	0.34	0.23	8.45
1989	105,749	83,197	71,026	66,134	0.67	0.79	0.33	0.21	6.76
1990	107,793	86,289	71,136	67,812	0.66	0.79	0.34	0.21	6.91
1991	119,107	94,002	79,501	74,193	0.67	0.79	0.33	0.21	7.54
1992	114,800	85,017	65,338	60,442	0.57	0.71	0.43	0.29	6.19
1993	122,021	76,779	56,012	46,129	0.46	0.60	0.54	0.40	4.81
1994	136,550	97,510	65,390	57,646	0.48	0.59	0.52	0.41	6.18
1995	145,600	107,433	73,522	66,230	0.5	0.62	0.52	0.38	6.99
1996	161,988.98	121,932.92	87,277	79,531	0.54	0.65	0.46	0.35	8.28
1997	166,057.13	121,100.96	85,888	77,287	0.52	0.64	0.48	0.36	8.06
1998	170,904.75	127,571.61	83,864	77,031	0.49	0.60	0.51	0.40	7.99

(continued)

Table 8.4 (continued)

Year	The completed housing construction area of the whole society (Million square meters)		The completed individual housing construction area in rural area (Million square meters)		The proportion of completed rural individual housing construction area in the whole society		The proportion of completed urban housing construction area in the whole society		The completed housing construction area in rural areas (Hundred million square meters) (9)
	Total (1)	Residential Housing (2)	Total (3)	Residential Housing (4)	Total (5) = (3)/(1)	Residential Housing (6) = (4)/(2)	Total (7) = 1-(6)	Residential housing (8) = 1-(6)	
1999	187,357.07	139,305.93	83,244	76,758	0.44	0.55	0.56	0.45	8.34
2000	181,974.44	134,528.83	81,270	75,515	0.45	0.56	0.55	0.44	7.97

Source The data in column 1 and column 2 is from the issues of *China Statistical Yearbook* respectively. The data in column 3 and 4 is from *China Statistical Yearbook* (2001). The data in 5–8 column is calculated; The data in column 9 is from *China Statistical Yearbook* (2001)

Table 8.5 Cost of housing construction and cost of individual residential housing construction

Year	Individual housing construction in urban and industrial and mining area		Individual housing construction in rural area					
	The completed housing construction area (Million square meters)		Value of the completed housing (Ten thousand yuan)		Cost of the completed housing (Yuan/square meter)		Cost of the completed housing (Yuan/square meter)	
	Total (1)	Residential housing (2)	Total (3)	Residential Housing (4)	Total (5) = (3)/(1)	Residential housing (6) = (4)/(2)	Total (7)	Residential housing (8)
1985	7081.36	6306.80	567,917	493,872	80.2	78.31	44	45
1986	8115.37	7234.80	745,623	654,192	91.88	90.42	49	41
1987	9120.19	8294.36	1,005,133	899,614	110.21	108.46	63	57
1988	10,526.83	9433.15	1,568,475	1,401,141	149	148.53	83	72
1989	8565.38	7822.55	1,402,278	1,260,234	163.71	161.1	112	97
1990	7180.55	6492.93	1,247,034	1,103,317	173.67	169.93	109	96
1991	7554.40	6808.24	1,403,230	1,250,861	185.75	183.73	115	102
1992	9673.43	8586.22	2,164,663	1,897,651	223.77	221.01	143	112
1993	11,463.44	9812.95	3,385,002	2,804,212	295.29	285.77	181	165
1994	14,098.18	12,268.36	4,513,203	3,870,038	320.13	315.45	201	174
1995	15,194.84	13,333.90	5,523,894	4,770,290	363.54	357.76	233	204
1996	16,556.86	14,518.78	6,552,198	5,629,097	395.74	387.71	258	222
1997	17,570.24	15,165.03	7,041,112	5,938,633	400.74	391.6	280	245
1998	20,781.49	18,227.39	8,485,630	7,272,165	408.33	398.97	286	248
1999	21,830.37	19,246.43	9,175,357	7,818,281	420.3	406.22	229	234
2000	21,763.53	18,929.01	9,529,931	8,120,225	437.89	428.98	242	245

Source The data in 1–4 column is from the issues of *China Statistical Yearbook* respectively. The data in 5–6 column is calculated; The data in 7–8 column is from *China Statistical Yearbook* (2001)

be illustrated by the departmental structure of GDP. It can be seen from the change pattern of proportion of industrial and construction sectors in GDP in 1978–2000 in accordance with our calculation that, although the industrial sector's share in GDP slightly declined in 1980–1992 since the reform due to the success of the reform of agriculture (1978–1985), this share rose again after 1993, showing that the expansion of manufacturing sector was accelerated in the 90s. The share of the construction industry in GDP is constantly on the rise as shown in Figs. 8.10 and 8.11. The share of industry in GDP is more than 40%, which is similar to what South Korea, Singapore and other Asian developing economies in Asia have experienced.

The importance of the industrial sector can also be reflected in the categories of investment spending. In Table 8.7, we broke down the investment in the fixed assets

Table 8.6 Housing construction investment in China (including residential and non-residential housing construction)

Year	The average cost of housing construction in the whole society (yuan/square meter) (1)	The average cost of residential housing construction (yuan/square meter) (2)	Housing construction investment (hundred million yuan)	Residential housing construction investment (hundred million yuan)	Non-residential housing construction investment (hundred million yuan)
1985	56.67	52.99	691.85	482.06	209.79
1986	62.72	50.88	948.23	598.69	349.54
1987	78.11	67.81	1108.87	730.29	378.58
1988	105.44	89.6	1433.38	939.02	494.37
1989	129.06	110.46	1364.8	918.99	445.8
1990	130.99	111.53	1411.98	962.38	449.6
1991	138.35	119.16	1647.85	1120.13	527.72
1992	177.73	143.61	2040.34	1220.93	819.41
1993	242.72	213.31	2961.69	1637.77	1323.92
1994	262.95	231.99	3590.58	2262.13	1328.45
1995	298.27	262.43	4342.81	2819.36	1523.45
1996	321.36	280	5205.68	3414.12	1791.56
1997	337.96	297.78	5612.07	3606.14	2005.92
1998	348.39	308.39	5954.15	3934.18	2019.97
1999	336.13	311.5	6297.63	4339.38	1958.25
2000	349.74	325.95	6364.37	4384.97	1979.41

Note Data in the first column = table 5 (5) × table 4 (7) + Table 5(7) × table 4 (5); data in second column = Table 5 (6) × table 4(8) + Table 5(8) × 4 (6); data in the third column = table6 (1) × Table 2 (1) ÷ 10000; data in fourth columns = table 6 (2) × table 5 (2) ÷ 1000; data in fifth column= table 6(3) – table 6(4)

according to their composition and calculated the corresponding investment rate of each component. As we have seen, in the investment of fixed assets, building installations and the purchase of tools and equipment have always occupied an absolute proportion, which will constantly improve the equipment level of the industrial sector (especially the manufacturing sector). Relatively speaking, construction installation and purchase of equipment of Chinese Hong Kong in the proportion of GDP is the lowest in the East Asian economy, probably because in the economy of Hong Kong, the development of service industry has been faster than other countries and regions of East Asian economy.

There is no doubt that the manufacturing sector has an absolute share in the industrial sector. In Table 8.8, we also calculated the changes in the structure of the sectors of the manufacturing investment in 1981, 1998 and 2000. For the purpose of analysis, we have divided manufacturing industry into 11 broad categories. Our

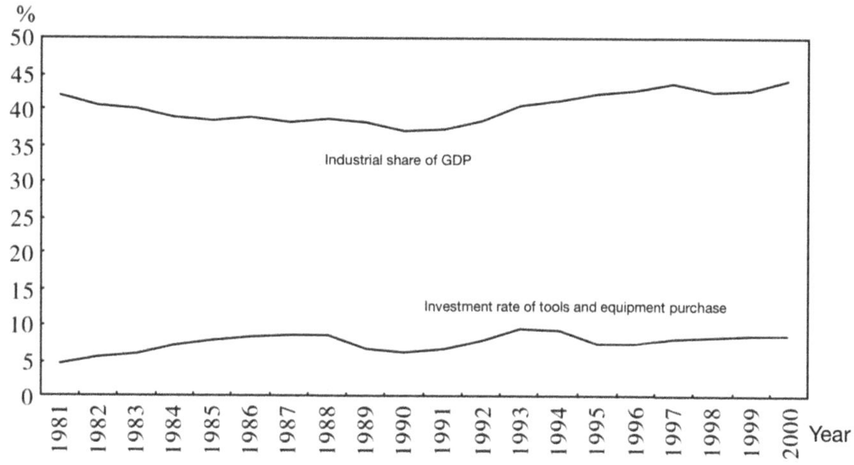

Fig. 8.10 China's industrial share of GDP and equipment investment rate

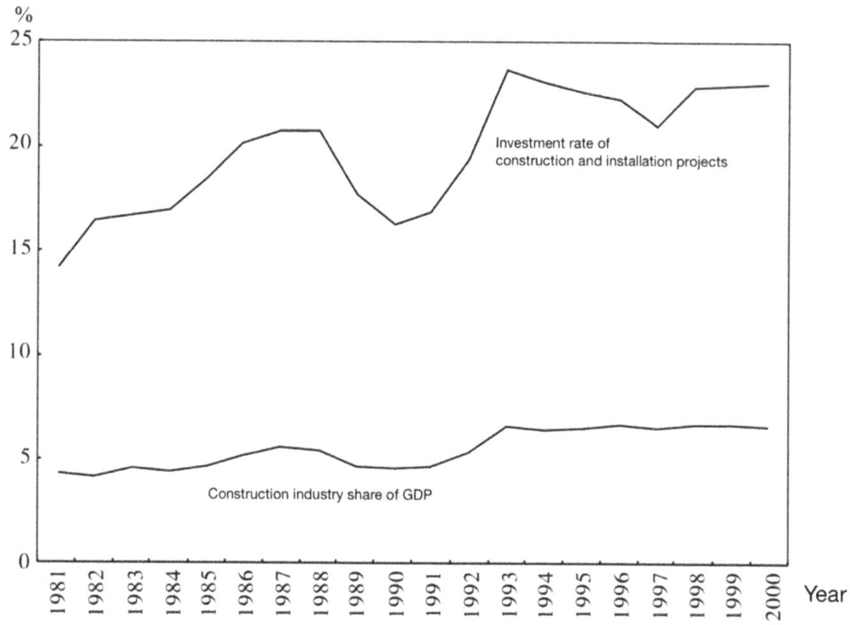

Fig. 8.11 China's construction industry share of GDP and investment rate of construction and installation projects

Table 8.7 Composition of China's fixed assets investment (1981–2000)

Year	Fixed assets investment of the whole society (hundred million yuan)	Composition			Investment rate (%)	Composition		
		Construction and installation investment (hundred million yuan)	The purchase of tools and equipment (hundred million yuan)	Others (hundred million yuan)		Construction and installation investment (%)	The purchase of tools and equipment (%)	Others (%)
1981	961	689.83	223.64	47.54	19.76	14.19	4.60	0.98
1982	1230.4	871.12	291.41	67.87	23.24	16.45	5.50	1.28
1983	1430.1	993.32	358.31	78.43	24.10	16.74	6.04	1.32
1984	1832.9	1217.58	509.23	106.06	25.56	16.98	7.10	1.48
1985	2543.2	1655.46	718.08	169.65	28.37	18.47	8.01	1.89
1986	3120.6	2059.66	851.95	208.99	30.59	20.19	8.35	2.05
1987	3791.7	2475.65	1038.78	277.26	31.70	20.70	8.68	2.32
1988	4753.8	3099.66	1305.37	348.77	31.84	20.76	8.74	2.34
1989	4410.4	2994.59	1115.81	300.00	26.08	17.71	6.60	1.77
1990	4517	3008.72	1165.54	342.74	24.35	16.22	6.28	1.85
1991	5594.5	3647.68	1460.19	486.63	25.88	16.87	6.75	2.25
1992	8080.1	5163.37	2125.14	791.58	30.33	19.38	7.98	2.97
1993	13,072.3	8201.21	3315.92	155,518	37.74	23.68	9.57	4.49
1994	17,042.1	10,786.52	4328.26	1928.08	36.45	23.07	9.26	4.12
1995	20,019.3	13,173.33	4262.46	2583.48	34.23	22.53	7.26	4.42
1996	22,913.5	15,109.29	4925.98	2878.28	33.75	22.26	8.12	4.24
1997	24,941.1	15,614.03	6044.84	3282.25	33.49	20.97	8.33	4.41
1998	28,406.2	17,874.53	6528.53	4003.10	36.26	22.82	8.59	5.11

(continued)

Table 8.7 (continued)

Year	Fixed assets investment of the whole society (hundred million yuan)	Composition			Investment rate (%)	Composition		
		Construction and installation investment (hundred million yuan)	The purchase of tools and equipment (hundred million yuan)	Others (hundred million yuan)		Construction and installation investment (%)	The purchase of tools and equipment (%)	Others (%)
1999	29,854.7	20,536.26	7053.04	4005.74	36.38	22.90	8.71	4.88
2000	32,917.7		7785.62	4595.85	36.82	22.97		5.14
1981–2000			30.35	19.79	7.59	2.97		

Note The average investment rate of 1981–2000 is arithmetic average. *Source* State Bureau of Statistics: *Chinese Statistical Yearbook* (2001), Beijing, China Statistics Press, 2001

results show that since the reform, the proportion of investment of the main manufacturing sections under the planned economic system in the entire manufacturing industry has greatly decreased, including the textile industry, general machinery and equipment manufacturing and the traditional sectors defined as "other manufacturing industries". However, the proportion of investment of the rest of the 9 major categories of manufacturing sector is rising rapidly. The manufacturing industries with the largest increase include: electronic products and equipment, transportation equipment manufacturing, metal smelting and metal products. The investment share of food, beverages and tobacco, rubber and plastic product industries also had a considerable increase. As far as the present structure of investment in manufacturing is concerned, chemical and chemical products, electronic and electrical machinery and basic metal have become sectors in China's manufacturing industry with the highest share of the investment. Apparent, most manufacturing sectors with rapid growth of investment have higher equipment level or capital density.

(3) Share of Public Investment

Under the present statistical items in China, the statistical data of investment in fixed assets is classified in accordance with "economic type", "management channel", "source of funds" and "composition" categories. As everyone knows, if the total data of investment in fixed assets is divided up by "economic type" and "source of funds", there is no doubt that the non state-owned investment (referring to the sum of investment of "individual economy" and "other investment"[24]) and its share in the fixed asset investment of the whole society increase significantly. On the other hand, judging from the source of funds, it is needless to say that the proportion of investment within the national budget falls substantially.[25] However, the investment rate of state-owned and collective economy has not declined significantly.

Table 8.9 shows the changes in the structure of investors in accordance with the nature of ownership or the type of economy. Among them, when calculating the "private investment rate", we have combined the data of the amounts of individual economic investment and other investments. Therefore, the "private investment rate" should reflect the changing trend of the major investment of the non-state sector. It is worth noting that the rate of investment of the state-owned and collective economies has not declined, and basically maintained its share of the investment in fixed assets of the whole society. Only after 1993 did the rate of private investment rise significantly along with the rapid growth of foreign investment, almost 2 times as much as in the 1980s. However, in the investment rate of fixed assets of the whole society, the investment rate of the state-owned economy still accounted for about 61.25% on average in the 21 years from 1980 to 2000, and the investment of the collective

---

[24] "Other investment" refers to economic sectors outside the joint venture economy, share-holding economy, foreign-funded economy, economy invested by China's Hong Kong, Macao and Taiwan regions, as well as state-owned, collective and individual economies.

[25] For example, if broken down according to sources of funding, in 1998, among the total investment in capital construction, the state budget funds accounted for only about 10%; and out of the investment of 451.675 billion *yuan* in renovation projects, the state budget funds only accounted for 6.1 billion *yuan*. See The State Bureau of Statistics (2001).

Table 8.8 Investment structure of China's manufacturing sectors: breakdown data of sectors

		In 2000				In 1998				In 1981	
		Investment in capital construction	Investment in renovation	Total	Composition (%)	Investment in capital construction	Investment in renovation	Total	Composition (%)	Investment in capital construction	Composition (%)
	Manufacturing industry	1175.11	2104.15	3279.26	100.00	1484.08	1797.3	3281.38	100	216.01	100
Electronic and electrical appliances	Electronic machinery and equipment manufacturing	29.19	79.09			34.62	71.37				
	Manufacturing of electronic and communications equipment	214.80	147.52			178.05	76.6				
	Instruments and cultural office machinery manufacturing	9.21	10.55			7.39	8.02				
	Total	253.20	237.16	490.36	14.95	220.06	155.99	376.05	11.46	5.06	2.34
Chemicals and chemical products	Manufacturing of raw chemical materials and chemical products	172.18	274.67			201.91	280.32				
	Medical manufacturing	42.42	91.20			30.22	52.01				

(continued)

Table 8.8 (continued)

		In 2000				In 1998				In 1981	
		Investment in capital construction	Investment in renovation	Total	Composition (%)	Investment in capital construction	Investment in renovation	Total	Composition (%)	Investment in capital construction	Composition (%)
	Chemical fiber manufacturing	11.79	34.94			53.02	20.01				
	Total	226.39	400.81	627.20	19.13	285.15	352.34	637.49	19.43	16.34	7.56
Transportation equipment	Transportation equipment manufacturing	107.56	178.90	286.46	8.74	186.66	150.05	336.71	10.26	2.6	1.2
	General machinery manufacturing	31.18	61.08			27.83	67.45				
	Special equipment manufacturing	29.93	43.10			23.42	47.1				
	Total	61.11	104.17	165.28	5.04	51.25	114.55	165.8	5.05	15.53	7.19
Metal Products	Manufacturing of Metal Products	17.28	29.20	46.48	1.42	19.18	21.62	40.8	1.24	1.2	0.56
Petroleum processing and coking	Manufacturing of petroleum processing and coking	32.79	129.91	162.70	4.96	137.84	105.03	242.87	7.4	8.21	3.8

(continued)

Table 8.8 (continued)

		In 2000				In 1998				In 1981	
		Investment in capital construction	Investment in renovation	Total	Composition (%)	Investment in capital construction	Investment in renovation	Total	Composition (%)	Investment in capital construction	Composition (%)
Rubber and plastic products	Rubber products manufacturing	8.40	20.86			11.61	29.5				
	Plastic products manufacturing	27.70	38.96			17.15	30.97				
	Manufacturing of non-metallic mineral products	61.42	112.18			70.67	103.9				
	Total	97.52	172.00	269.52	8.22	99.43	164.37	263.8	8.04	2.68	1.24
Base metals	Smelting and pressing of ferrous metals	50.85	269.11			155.95	242.99				
	Smelting and pressing of non-ferrous metals	39.76	82.00			24.35	61.3				
	Total	90.61	351.11	441.72	13.47	180.3	304.29	484.59	14.77	21.51	9.96
Food, beverage and tobacco	Food processing	32.43	43.95			33.09	49.93				
	Food manufacturing	37.57	47.75			26.99	28.09				

(continued)

Table 8.8 (continued)

		In 2000				In 1998				In 1981	
		Investment in capital construction	Investment in renovation	Total	Composition (%)	Investment in capital construction	Investment in renovation	Total	Composition (%)	Investment in capital construction	Composition (%)
	Beverage manufacturing	26.27	82.52			25.23	84.14				
	Tobacco processing	18.23	45.24			8.95	69.23				
	Total	114.50	219.47	448.47	13.68	94.26	231.39	325.65	9.92	9.26	4.27
Textile	Textile manufacturing	29.57	107.86			23.13	61.97				
	Clothing and fiber products manufacturing	17.67	17.28			10	12.27				
	Total	47.25	125.14	172.39	5.26	33.13	74.24	107.37	3.27	19.86	9.19
Others	Leather, fur, down feather and its products mamufacturing	12.18	4.54			8.89	4.58				
	Wood processing and bamboo and rattan palm grass products manufacturing	8.22	15.15			9.58	13.96				

(continued)

Table 8.8 (continued)

	In 2000				In 1998				In 1981	
	Investment in capital construction	Investment in renovation	Total	Composition (%)	Investment in capital construction	Investment in renovation	Total	Composition (%)	Investment in capital construction	Composition (%)
Furniture manufacturing	7.15	5.55			8.07	4.05				
Paper making and paper products manufacturing	39.54	79.91			117.02	58.44				
Printing and reproduction of recording media	13.05	22.85			15.47	18.05				
Culture, education and sporting goods manufacturing	2.66	3.66			0.97	2.53				
Others manufacturing	44.11	24.60			16.84	22.64				
Total	126.92	156.27	285.89	8.72	176.84	124.25	301.09	9.18	113.76	52.66

Note The absolute value of the unit is 100 million yuan

Source Date of 1999 is from *Chinese Statistical Yearbook* (1999); the total sum and composition were calculated value of the author; the data of 1984 is based on the capital construction investment data in the *Chinese Statistical Yearbook* (1981)and obtained in accordance with the same classification calculation, but the total amount of the capital construction investment in manufacturing industry of the said year was from *Chinese Investment Yearbook* (2001), and the investment in transformation of manufacturing industry for the said year was 9 billion and 220 million yuan

economy accounted for about 14%. While in private investment, over the past few years, individual investment accounted for an average of 40%. Take 1996, a year with a higher inflow of foreign direct investment (FDI), as an example: foreign investment (including investment from Hong Kong, Macao and Taiwan) accounted for 12% of the total fixed investment, about 274 billion yuan. Even so it accounted for only 40% of the private investment.

Therefore, generally speaking, among the total investment in fixed assets, the proportion of real "private" investment (the sum of foreign investment and individual economic investment) should be no more than 20%, because in 1980–2000, China's total fixed asset investment rate (that is, the proportion of total fixed asset investment of the whole society in GDP) averaged 29.86%, which means that in China, the proportion of public investment (of which the investment of state-owned sector and the investment of collective sector under direct government intervention accounted for a larger proportion) in GDP is still as high as 24%, much higher than the average of Singapore and Taiwan in 1966–1998 (the latter two were 9.1% and 10.6% respectively).[26]

Source State Bureau of Statistics: *Chinese Statistical Yearbook* (2001), Beijing, Chinese Statistics Press, 2001

Therefore, although private investment including foreign direct investment (FDI) has increased significantly, public investment still dominates in China's fixed asset investment. In fact, if there were no such a high public investment rate, it would be difficult for us to explain why in the past 10 years, the efficiency of investment of Chinese economy in general experienced a sharp deterioration despite the significant increase of the proportion of private investment. Therefore, the proportion of such high public investment seems to have basically explained the institutional reasons behind excessive investment. Moreover, it should not be difficult to imagine that even for "private investment", a considerable part of it is still subject to various interventions of the government.

8.5 Preliminary Conclusion and Implications

In this paper, we have studied the efficiency of investment in China and its changing patterns. Similar to the conclusions of our previous researches, we have once again confirmed that the investment efficiency, after 10 years of improvement in the wake of reform, rapidly changed into a declining pattern, which is the main reason for the decline of China's economic growth in recent years. At the same time, the serious non-performing assets in China's financial sector and the decline of employment elasticity of economic growth found in existing research[27] should all be able to

---

[26] According to the data provided by Toh and Ng (2002), the rate of public investment in Hong Kong in the same period was relatively low, only 3.7%.

[27] As everyone knows, the scale of accumulated non-performing assets in the banking sector (currently estimated value is $700 billion by other countries, accounting for about 60% of Chinese GDP. However, the assistant to the governor of the People's Bank of China publicly corrected this

Table 8.9 State, collective and private investment rates (1980–2000)

Year	State economic investment	Collective economic investment	Individual economic investment	Others investment	Private investment	Fixed asset investment rate of the whole society	Composition		
							State economic investment rate	Collective economic investment rate	Private investment rate
1980	745.9	46	119		119	20.16	16.51	1.02	2.63
1981	667.5	115.2	178.3		178.3	19.76	13.73	2.37	3.66
1982	845.3	174.3	210.8		210.8	23.24	15.97	3.29	3.98
1983	952	156.3	321.8		321.8	24.1	16.04	2.63	5.42
1984	1185.2	238.7	409		409	25.56	16.53	3.33	5.7
1985	1680.5	327.5	535.2		535.2	28.37	18.75	3.65	5.97
1986	2079.4	391.8	649.4		649.4	30.59	20.38	3.84	6.37
1987	2448.8	547	795.9		795.9	31.7	20.47	4.57	6.65
1988	3020	711.7	1022.1		1022.1	31.84	20.23	4.77	6.85
1989	2808.2	570	1032.2		1032.2	26.08	16.61	3.37	6.1
1990	2986.3	529.5	1001.2		1001.2	24.35	16.1	2.85	5.4
1991	3713.8	697.8	1182.9		1182.9	25.88	17.18	3.23	5.47
1992	5498.7	1359.4	1222		1222	30.33	20.64	5.1	4.59
1993	7925.9	2317.3	1476.2	1352.9	2829.1	37.74	22.88	6.69	8.17
1994	9615	2758.9	1970.6	2697.6	4668.2	36.45	20.56	5.9	9.98
1995	10,898.2	3289.4	2560.2	3271.5	5831.7	34.23	18.64	5.63	9.97
1996	12,006.2	3651.5	3211.2	4044.6	7255.8	33.75	17.69	5.38	10.69
1997	13,091.7	3850.9	3429.4	4569.1	7998.5	33.49	17.58	5.17	10.74

(continued)

Table 8.9 (continued)

Year	State economic investment	Collective economic investment	Individual economic investment	Others investment	Private investment	Fixed asset investment rate of the whole society	Composition		
							State economic investment rate	Collective economic investment rate	Private investment rate
1998	15,369.3	4192.2	3744.4	5100.3	8844.7	36.26	19.62	5.35	11.29
1999	15,947.8	4338.6	4195.7	5372.7	9568.4	36.38	19.43	5.29	11.66
2000	16,504.4	4801.5	4709.4	6902.5	11,611.9	36.82	18.46	5.37	12.99
1980–2000						29.86	18.29	4.23	7.34
						100%	61.25%	14.17%	24.58

Note The unit of amount of investment is 100 million yuan, and the unit of investment rate is%. This table divides, according to economic types, the investment in fixed assets of the whole society into investment of state-owned economy, collective economy, individual economy and other economies (including economic components outside the state-owned, collective and individual economies of joint venture economy, shareholding economy, foreign invested economy and economy invested by China's Hong Kong, Macao and Taiwan). The "private investment" here is the sum of the individual and other economic investments

offer corresponding explanations from excessive investment and deterioration in investment efficiency.

Generally speaking, from the overall consideration, China, which is different from the economy of East Asia, will experience a long period of surplus labor before reaching the supply shortage of labor, which means that the industrialization will provide Chinese economy with the ability to achieve long-term growth for a long time. However, the sustainability of the growth depends not only on the supply capacity of factors, but also on the ability to effectively allocate the factors. Therefore, from the institutional point of view, in order to achieve sustained and rapid economic growth, what we need is capital instead of more labor force. We also need investment to create more jobs. Therefore, for the medium and long term periods, the choice and efficiency of investment are the most important determinants of sustained economic growth. The function of the financial system can also help to screen the efficient projects for investment and improve the investment efficiency, so, to achieve sustained economic growth, an effective financial system and investment decision-making is more important than the factor itself.

As we all know, since the reform and opening up, the change of China's investment system is mainly manifested in the ways of financing, from the past single government financial financing to the credit and so-called self financing-based diversification. However, in the choice of investment projects and investment decisions, which can largely determine the return on investment, no thorough reform has been undertaken. China's investment system was formed in the planned economy period and since the reform, the administrative decision-making mechanism of investment has been more decentralized, almost entirely built on the basis of the autonomy of local government for growth targets. Capital allocation and the industrialization process are solely rested on a "classical competition" environment of division rather than integration.[28] Not only in the investment decision-making of public infrastructure, but also in almost all stages of the investment decision of "private realms", the preference and influence of the government directly determine the choice of investment projects. The localized investment choices and decisions have typically caused a large number of investments to yield no real gains but lead to repeated constructions. Similar production capacities have been accumulated and laid idle, and buildings are left vacant; all of these consequences have often been exposed in Chinese media and known to all.

estimate claiming that the ratio of non-performing loans in the four major Chinese banks is 28%) is becoming one of the most serious problems facing the financial sector in China. The accumulation of excessive non-performing loans essentially reflects the problems of China's investment decision making system itself. Moreover, in recent years, the capacity of China's economic growth to absorb labor force has been weakened, which has attracted the attention of labor economists. See Liu and Liu (1995) and Yuan Zhigang (2002)'s discussions on this issue. For details, see Liu and Liu (1995).

[28] The so-called "classical competition" is an adjustment process whereby zero profit equilibrium is achieved by free entry and increase of the number of producers. Although this process realizes the static efficiency, there is a lack of sustained, dynamic efficiency improvement mechanism, thus it is not conducive to economic growth.

It is also found in the studies on China's investment decisions that, due to the investment system that has caused excessive investment, the total investment of China not only significantly deviated from the optimal level of market, it also lacks the ability of short-term adjustment. For example, the recent studies done by Sun (1998), Song et al. (2001), Qin and Song (2002) have confirmed that China's short-term total investment is extremely slow in adjusting the imbalance in the amount of long-term investment, causing violent ups and downs and significant loss of investment.[29] Rawski (2002), in his latest comments from the perspective of investment fluctuations (see Table 8.7), more vividly describes the loss of investment efficiency caused by the Chinese system for investment:

> Chinese economy shows a usual pattern of substantial seasonal fluctuations..... Seasonal fluctuations are far more violent than other East Asian economies around it. China's GDP often drops by more than 25% in the first quarter, and jumps by 20% in the last 3 months of the year. Anyone familiar with the planning economy knows that this behavior model does not appear in the market system. For example, back in 1875, figures show that the quarterly fluctuations in the U.S. economy were only around 9% in the GDP. In China, as with the pre-reform planning system, seasonal output swings are mainly caused by fluctuations in investment spending...... In March each year, the National People's Congress approves the annual plan for investment and credits. In April, the government decides the implementation of these decisions. By May, detailed plans began to arrive at the grassroots level. Under this schedule, the loan commitments and project spending proceed slowly in the first two quarters, resulting in a seasonal pattern of investment spending that was almost the same as in the decades prior to reform.

As a transitional economy from the planned system to the market system, the road of China's economic growth in the past 20 years is indeed worthy of further study and summary. In the growth of early stage of the reform, the institutional change of the agricultural sector is an important explanatory variable,[30] while in the past 10 years, the sources of growth and huge foreign direct investment (FDI) inflows are closely related with the boom of trade.[31] But with regard to the allocation of capital, large financial resources of banks were persuaded to loan to investment projects of state-owned sectors with the government (including the central government and local governments at all levels) background or support from the government. These projects are either the basic construction or renovation for large and key enterprises, or for newly built large and medium-sized entities, or for other non-profit projects. The private sector always finds it hard to get financial support. Due to this system pattern that discriminates against the development of private sector, the distribution of capital structure is seriously in favor of government sponsored and state-owned enterprises; with the result that the ability of capital investment to create jobs will not be improved and it is also difficult to reverse the worsening trend of efficiency of investment.

---

[29] Sun (1998), Song et al. (2001).

[30] See Lin (1992).

[31] For the relationship between FDI, trade growth and economic growth in China, see the point of view of Yao and Zhang, Lin and Li (2002).

The decline in growth has reminded us that the private sector has been unduly inhibited by the investment and financial systems which have begun to impede the sustainability of growth. However, since 1998, the mainstream view has defined the problem of China's economy as insufficient aggregate demand, resulting in the adoption of the expansion of fiscal policy. Fiscal expansion was not only unable to prevent the financial resources from tilting towards the state-owned sector, but encouraged the government to spend the increased expenditure it secured through increasing deficit on massive infrastructure and major projects that did not generate significant revenues at the expense of investment efficiency. This short-term increase in spending has also added a heavy burden to the government's finances.[32]

China's growth after the reform seems to have come to a crossroad, because, to judge from the supply capability factors, there will be a long, high growth potential in China, but from the point of view of system distortion, China seems to have been on the road of over-industrialization development which has profoundly exposed the shortcomings of China's ability to effectively deploy key factors of the economy. From the future perspective, encouraging and expanding the private sector of the economy and giving private entrepreneurs full access to financial resources is critically important. Only by the development of private sector can entrepreneurs be able to determine the allocation of capital, which, of course, requires real reform of the existing financial system and the banking sector that match the state sector. The reform of China's investment system and the financial sector has been delayed and lagged behind, yet the critical moment to reform these systems has finally arrived now.

Author's Note

This article, also written during my teaching at Kyungpook National University in South Korea (2002 9–12), has not been published in the journal, but included in my book, *China's Industrial Reform and Economic Growth* (Shanghai DXS Joint Publishing Company and Shanghai People's Publishing House, 2003). The focus of this article is to study the change of the investment efficiency in China and some characteristics of the capital formation related to it including characteristics of investment rate, investment sector's structure and ownership structure. Such an investigation can better help us understand a series of important characteristics of capital formation in China's investment system.

In this article, I calculated incremental capital output ratio (ICOR) of China's economy, which is an important indicator of the efficiency of investment. Typically, ICOR will remain basically stable if investment is efficient or has not undergone the deepening of capital. Our calculations found that ICOR showed this characteristic before 1994, but then it began to rise sharply. This shows that the efficiency of investment has deteriorated significantly during this period. Then I constructed a simple

[32] Since 1998, the government deficit has increased sharply from less than 1% in GDP to about 3%, and increased government spending is almost entirely supported with the government's debt. The net treasury bonds each year (the amount of the treasury bonds issued minus the balance of capital and interest repaid) are almost equal to the fiscal deficit of that year.

model for explaining the rising of ICOR, which takes into account the "quadratic function" relationship between TFP and capital density change. We found the existence of this relationship after using the Chinese data to fit it. Thus, the only variable explaining ICOR is the rate of change in the density of capital (i.e. capital-labor ratio), and the accelerated rise in capital density has been well documented in the empirical data we used. While doing investigation for writing this article, the accelerated rise in capital density has reflected the tendency to over-investment which poses a challenge to the sustainability of long-term growth.

References

Bela Balassa: Exports and Economic Growth: Further Evidence. *Journal of Development Economics*, 1978, 5 (2),181–189.

Olivier Blanchard, Stanley Fisher: *Macroeconomics* (Advanced Coursebook), Liu Shucheng, Shen Lisheng tr. Beijing, Economic Science Press, 1998.

Chen Jianbo: Technical Acquisition and Technical Choices of Township Enterprises in the Evolution of Market Economy, *Economic Research*, 1999 (4), pp. 36–41.

S. Demurger, J. Sachs, W. Woo, S. Bao, G. Chang, A. Melinger, Geography, Economic Policy and Regional Development in China, CID working paper No.77, 2001

J. Felipe, Total Factor Productivity Growth in East Asia: A Critical Survey, *The Journal of Development Studies*, 1999, 35 (4), pp. 1–41.

He Juhuang: Estimation of China's Assets, *Quantitative Economy and Technical Economy Research*, 1992 (8).

G. Jefferson, T. Rawski, Y. Zheng, Chinese Industrial Productivity: Trends, Measurement and Recent Development, *Journal of Comparative Economics*, 1996, 23, pp. 146–180.

J. Kim, L. Lau, The Sources of Asian Pacific Economic Growth, *The Canadian Journal of Economics*, 1996, 29 (4), pp. 448–454.

A. Krueger, Comparative Advantage and Development Policy: 20 Years Later, in M.Syrquin, L.Tayor, L.Westphal, *Economic Structure and Performance*, 1984.

P. Krugman, The Myth of Asia's Miracle, *Foreign Affairs*, 1994, 11/12, pp. 62–78.

L. Lau, J. Kim, The Sources of Growth of the East Asian Newly Industrialized Countries, *Journal of the Japanese and International Economies*, 1992.

Lin Yifu, Li Yongjun: Exports and China's Economic Growth: A Demand Oriented Analysis, Beijing, Chinese Center for Economic Research at Peking University, working paper, 2002

Lin Yifu, Rural Reforms and Agricultural Growth in China, *The American Economic Review*, 1992, 82 (1), pp. 34–51.

A. Liu, S. Yao, Z. Zhang, Economic Growth and Structural Changes in Employment and Investments in China: 1985-1994, *Economic Planning*, 1999, 32, pp. 171–190.

Liu Shucheng, Li Qiang, Xue Tiandong: *Research Regional Economic Development in China*, Beijing, Chinese Statistical Press, 1994.

Liu Xuegong, Liu Jun: Has Chinese Economic Growth Weakened Its Ability to Absorb Labor Force, *Chinese Labor Science*, 1995 (12).

D. Lo, Reappraising the Performance of China's State-Owned Industrial Enterprises:1980–1996, *Cambridge Journal of Economics*, 1999, 23, pp. 693–718

K. Ohkawa, Capital Output Rations and the Issues of Development 'Residuals': Issues of Development Planning, International Development Center of Japan, IDCJ working paper No. 28, 1984.

Otsuka Keijiro, Liu Deqiang, Murakami Naoki: *China's Industrial Reform*, Shanghai, SDX Joint Publishing Company, Shanghai People's Publishing House, 2000.

Thomas G. Rawski: Measuring China's Recent GDP Growth: where Do We Stand. *China Economic Quarterly*, 2002, 11 (1), pp. 143–206.

D. Qin, H. Song, Excess Investment Demand and Efficiency Loss during Reforms: The Case of Provincial-level Fixed-Asset Investment in China, Mimeo, 2002.

Robert M. Solow: Technical Change and the Aggregate Production Function. *Review of Economics and Statistics*, 1957, 39 (3), pp. 312–320.

H. Song, Z. Liu, P. Jiang, Analysing the Determinants of China's Aggregate Investment in the Reform Period, *China Economic Review*, 2001, 12, pp. 227–242.

X. Sun, Estimating Investment Function Based on Co-Integration: the Case of China, *Journal of Comparative Economics*, 1998, 26, pp. 175–191.

The State Bureau of Statistics: *Chinese Statistical Yearbook* (2001), Beijing, China Statistics Press, 2001.

M. Toh, W. Ng, Efficiency of Investment in Asian Economies: Has Singapore Over-Invested? *Journal of Asian Economics*, 2002, 13, pp. 52–71.

Wei Houkai: *Regional Development in China: Economic Growth, Institutional Changes and Regional Differences*, Beijing Economic Management Press, 1997.

Young, Alwyn: Substitution and Complementarity in Endogenous Innovation. *The Quarterly Journal of Economics*, 1993, 108 (3), pp. 775–807.

Young, Alwyn: Lessons from the East Asian NICS: A Contrarian View. *European Economic Review*, 1994, 38 (3–4), pp. 964–973.

A. Young, The Razor' s Edge: Distortions and Incremental Reform in the People' s Republic of China, *Quarterly Journal of Economics*, 2000, 11.

Yuan Zhigang: *China's Employment Report*, Beijing, Economic Science Press, 2002.

Zhang Jun, Shi Shaohua: Change of Total Factor Productivity of Chinese Economy: 1952–1998, *Collection of World Economy*, 2003, 8 (2).

Zhang J, et al. Growth, Capital Formation and Technological Choice: Explanation of Long-Term Factors for Recent Decline of Economic Growth in China. *Economics*, 2002 (01), pp. 87–124.

Zhang Jun, Shi Shaohua, Chen Shiyi: Industrial Reform and Efficiency Change in China: Methods, Data, Literatures and Present Results, *Quarterly Journal of Economics*, 2003, 3 (1).

Chapter 9
Growth, Capital Formation and Technological Choice: Explanation of Long-Term Factors for Recent Decline of Economic Growth in China

9.1 Introduction

With cregard to the transition from a planned economy to market economy, how to realize and sustain the economic growth is of primary importance. In view of this, China's industrial reform since 1984 has undoubtedly achieved unparalleled success in improving its supply capacity and achieving rapid economic growth. The existing literature mainly has two different explanations for the "mechanism" of China's rapid economic growth. One explanation is that China's rapid economic growth has been the result of the "bottom-up" strategy of autonomy since the reform (especially in the 1980s) (Naughton 1995; McKinnon, 1994; Zhang 1997).[1] In their view, the nature of "bottom-up" reform is a learning, continuous improvement and innovation process, the most striking feature of which is the use of contracts to replace government control. Famous examples include the dual track system of price and distribution, production responsibility system and the so-called popular "contract system" and so on.

Different from this interpretation that focuses on institutional changes, another view emphasizes the "development" feature of China's economic growth, arguing that China's economy since the reform is actually an extension of the "mode of development of East Asia". Successful development of the economy of rural industrialization, the inflow of foreign capital, trade oriented policies etc. that have helped the "four tigers" of East Asia to achieve high-speed economic growth factors can also be found in the development of Chinese economy. In this sense, the rapid economic growth in China is not only the result of a series of institutional innovations, but also the result of "convergence" with the newly industrialized economic mode of Eastern Asia (Sachs and Woo 1994; Yifu et al. 1994).[2] There is no doubt that these different explanations are very important theoretical literatures for us to understand

[1] Naughton (1995), McKinnon (1994), Zhang (1997).

[2] Sachs and Woo (1994), Lin et al. (1994).

J. Zhang, *Reform, Transformation and Growth*, Understanding China,
https://doi.org/10.1007/978-981-99-5712-5_9

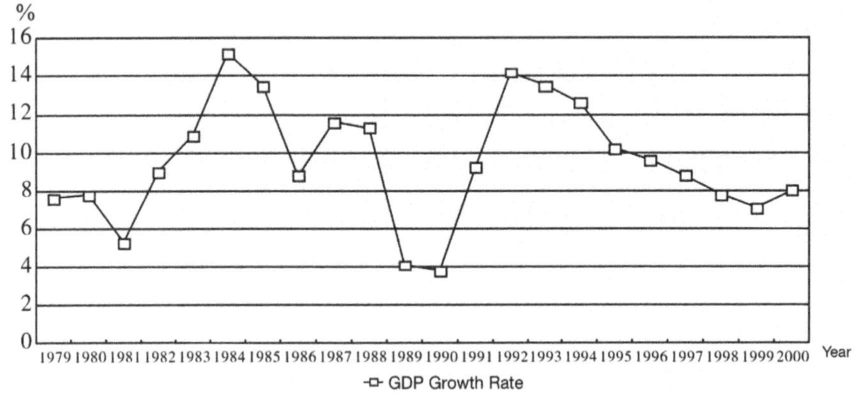

Fig. 9.1 China's GDP growth rate (1979–2000)

the different manifestations of the former planned economies (especially that of China and Soviet Union) in the early stage of the transition and are highly complementary when we face Chinese economy.

But all of the existing theories just explained "why growth occurred", but are not the answers to the question "why growth is declining". A further discussion of the former question has been left to the study of transition economics, and the latter is drawing more attention from economists. Experience over the past years has shown that it seems more and more difficult for China's economy to continue to maintain a rapid growth. In particular, there has been a significant and sustained downward trend of Chinese economic growth since 1994 and1995, although the scale of growth decline is worth further estimating.[3] However, as shown in Fig. 9.1, at least in the 1980s, what we saw was a high cyclical fluctuation of economic growth, but this fluctuation pattern changed significantly after the 90s.

Based on official growth rate data, we have found by calculation that since 1995, not only the average growth rate has declined, but the coefficient of variation has declined more significantly. During 1979–1994, the coefficient of variation for growth was 0.36, while in 1995–2000 it dropped to 0.13. This suggests that the high volatility of the economy may have been superseded by a downward trend in growth rates. Based on this observation, we have reason to suspect that behind the "short-term" economic instability, the decline in economic growth since 1995 is

[3] This article does not intend to discuss the statistical problems of China's economic growth rate. Interested readers can refer to the existing research literature. Rawski, for example, has done a series of studies on recent declines in economic growth (www.pitt.edu/~tgrawski/). He even reexamined China's GDP growth rate in 1997 and 1998, adjusting the growth rate of the official data below 5.7% (Gary et al. 2000, Rawski 2001). In addition, in recent years there have been many research articles published on the reliability of China's official GDP growth rate data since the reform. For example, some economists found that in 1978–1991, the average growth rate of GDP of China was overvalued by 1 percentage points, while in 1992–1997, it was overvalued by 2.5 percentage points (Meng and Xiaolu 2000).

likely to have reflected the restriction (i.e. at technical level) of certain "long-term" factors.

If this observation is correct, that is to say, some long-term factors have restricted the sustainable economic growth of China in the middle of the 1990s, then, the macro economic theory that aims at explaining the economic stability (or instability) will do little to help us explain the sustainability of growth. There is no doubt that China's economy has not suffered a recession, although the growth rate has shown a downward trend. Similarly, at the macro level, aggregate demand has not declined, and only the growth rate of demand has changed. Therefore, the macro theory (especially the concept of "aggregate demand") has a limited capacity to explain the downward trend of China's economic growth in recent years. Not only that, the "aggregate demand" changes, especially the decline of investment demand growth rate in recent years that many economists are concerned about, is actually the result rather than the reason for economic growth decline.

In economics, investment is both a short-term concept (a demand concept) and a long term concept (supply concept). As a short-term concept, investment is a demand factor, and an important component of the total social demand. The growth of investment as a demand has a short-term impact on the stability of the economy (growth). The discussion of economic stability belongs to the field of macroeconomics. And economic growth is a long-term concept. Here, investment in a long-term sense has different meanings. The growth of investment can expand the production capacity in the long run and impact the sustainability of economic growth. However, the role of investment in influencing long-term economic growth actually depends on the "efficiency" of investment and the progress and nature of investment-driven technology. Based on this conceptual classification, especially the observed changing patterns of the growth trajectory of Chinese economy shown since 1994 and 1995, it seems that we have reason to believe that the model of economic growth in China has shown a long-term (i.e. sustained growth) restricting factors; therefore, it is necessary to look at the trajectory change of the Chinese economic growth from a long-term perspective (or growth economics). This means that we must make an empirical analysis and discussion on the types of China's economic growth.

In order to observe and investigate the long-term factors of changes of Chinese economic growth since the reform, we calculated the change pattern of real capital-output ratio in China since the reform in this paper. We found that there is a clear diffused change pattern between the growth rate of capital-output ratio and the economic growth rate. Through further analysis, we found that an important message from this diffused model is that, in China, the formation of capital is largely insensitive to changes in economic growth. This not only demonstrates that the influence of the government is still playing a very important role in capital formation, but also that the acceleration of capital deepening may be the main reason for the continued decline of China's economic growth since the mid-90s.

We then developed a simple theory to illustrate the main reason for the change of the capital-output ratio and confirmed the rationality of our interpretation empirically. It also helps us realize that selection deviation of technology is the main reason for the slowdown in the economic growth rate, because it has accelerated the process of capital deepening, causing a quick decreasing trend in the marginal return of capital. Our findings actually mean that the continued deceleration of China's economic growth since the middle of the 90s may be the result of typical "epitaxial" growth rather than the short-term fluctuations in demand. Short term demand fluctuation (the change in demand growth rate) should be primarily understood as the result of economic slowdown rather than its cause.

We know that the path of change in the capital-labor ratio in an economy is the result of the manufacturer's choice of production technology (investment). In a "standard market system", given the price of the factor and the perfectly competitive market structure, the manufacturers' choice of technology is to seek the "solution" of minimized cost: ratio factor depends on the factor parity. However, for a transitional economy, the formation of its market structure depends to a large extent on the entry-competition mode between its existing production sector and the emerging sector. Concretely speaking, because the state-owned sector has a higher capital-labor ratio, rapid growth of economy seems to occur only when the new sector enters the industrial sectors where relatively small capital is required. But the entrants to China's emerging sectors are not real private enterprises, but collective enterprises (especially township enterprise) established or supported by the local governments.

Moreover, different from the process of industrialization and the economy of East Asia, the entry of township enterprises haven't led to division of labor and cooperation with the existing large enterprises and gradually set up an effective industrial organization structure.[4] On the contrary, although the collective sector quickly entered into the labor intensive and simple manufacturing sector that the state enterprises are seldom involved, it also soon moved at the same time into the industrial sector that the state-owned enterprises are actively involved. Needless to say, the entry of non-state-owned enterprises quickly evolved into a direct competition between "state-owned enterprises" and "collective enterprises" or governments at various levels. This competitive pattern has produced a series of results that have already been confirmed by the existing economic research including the market segmentation and a continued converging structure emerging among the manufacturing sectors in different regions since the reform (Young 2000); errors in technology selection by township enterprises and excessive growth of the scale (Chen 1999); continued worsening of industrial sector's investment yields or profitability over the past 10 years, the decline of utilization of a large number of products, and continued increase of the proportion of the loss-making enterprises (Zhang 1998; Lo 1999).[5]

The structure of this paper is organized as follows: in the second part, we observed from experience the clear, diffused patterns between the economic growth and capital-output ratio changes of China since the reform, and, by using the traditional growth accounting approach, explained this relationship. The third part examined the changing track of TFP in China's economy since the reform. In the fourth part we

---

[4] For the process of industrialization in East Asia and the comparative analysis of rural enterprises, see the fourth part of this paper.

[5] Young (2000), 4; Chen (1999), Zhang (1999), Zhang (2001), Lo (1999).

observed and explained the capital deepening process of the industrial sector (especially the township enterprise sector), and analyzed the structure of the industrial organization in the transitional period and the entry-competition mode in the fifth part. In the sixth part we statistically tested the negative effects of the increase of capital density on the return on investment in the industrial sector. The last part is the conclusion of this paper.

9.2 Empirical Observation and Theoretical Construction

The main purpose of this paper is to find out whether the long term factors that influence the growth of China's economy are clearly visible. To observe such long-term factors, we can start by choosing the gross index of the capital-output ratio according to the analytical paradigm of (neoclassical) growth economics. We have calculated the actual capital-output ratio and its growth rate in China during 1979–1998 (see Figs. 9.2 and 9.3). As indicated in Fig. 9.3, we found that, before 1994 and 1995, the reform has brought about a significant change in the closed development model in the original planned economy, inhibited the speed of excessive capital accumulation, utilized the cheap labor resources by capital growth, thus achieving a rapid economic growth. During this period, the capital-output ratio not only did not rise, but declined slightly (the average growth rate of 1979–1994 was −0.89%). But after 1994, the capital-output ratio did rise significantly and steadily (for instance, the capital-output ratio of 1995–1998 averaged 1.92% per year).[6] As a result, the capital-output ratio has risen further significantly.

In order to explain the changing trend of Chinese economic growth since 1978 as a whole, we first used the GDP growth rate of 1978–1998 to make a regression observation of the growth rate of the actual capital output-ratio in the same period. Figure 9.4 shows the "scattered" distribution between the two, clearly demonstrating the negative correlation between the rate of economic growth and the capital-output ratio. The linear trend equation we estimated is:

$$
\begin{aligned}
&y\ (economic\ growth\ rate) = \\
&9.4016 - 100.73x\ (growth\ rate\ of\ capital - output\ ratio)
\end{aligned}
$$

$$
(R^2 = 0.7715)
$$

This simple empirical observation shows that the change in the capital-output ratio is opposite to the direction in which the economic growth rate changes. This diffused model can be shown more clearly by comparing Figs. 9.1 and 9.3: during the period of accelerated economic growth, changes in the capital-output ratio are

[6] It should be noted that, according to information provided by Easterly and Fischer (1994), due to the long-term results of epitaxial growth, the capital-output ratio during 1950–1987 before the disintegration of the Soviet Union had an annual increase of about 2.5%.

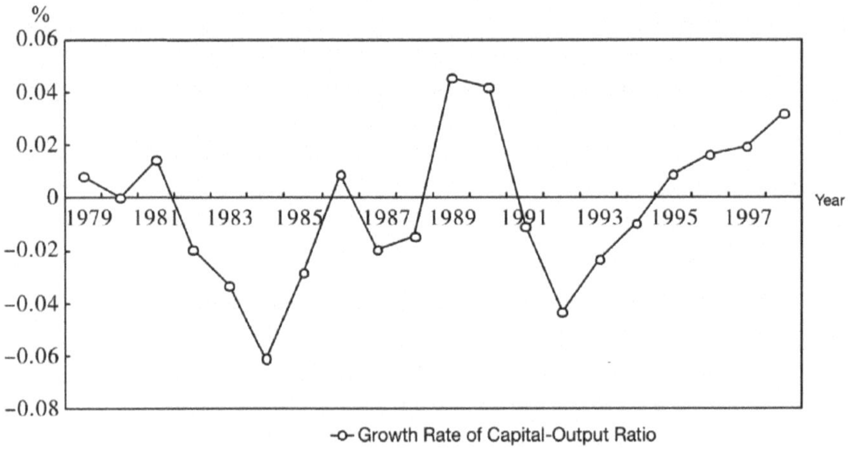

Fig. 9.2 Growth rate of China's capital-output ratio (1979–1998)

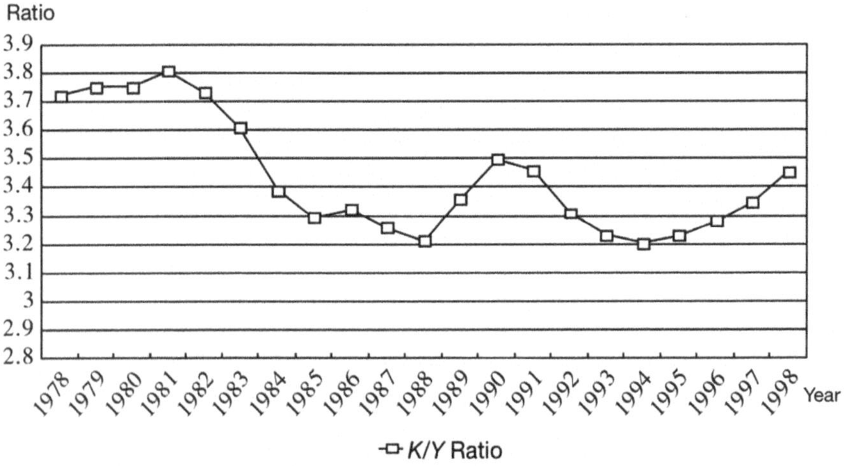

Fig. 9.3 China's actual capital-output ratio (1978–1998)

showing a trend of decreased speed; and in the period of accelerated growth of the capital-output ratio, economic growth is on the downward trend. It seems that we need to theoretically explain the interesting change pattern of capital formation and economic growth rate.

Before giving a theoretical explanation of this changing model, let us first examine the implications of the changing model between the capital-output ratio and the rate of economic growth for the speed of capital formation. To this end, let us return to the "capital-output ratio" growth rate. We used the following growth rate definition when we calculated the growth rate of "capital-output ratio" by using the Chinese

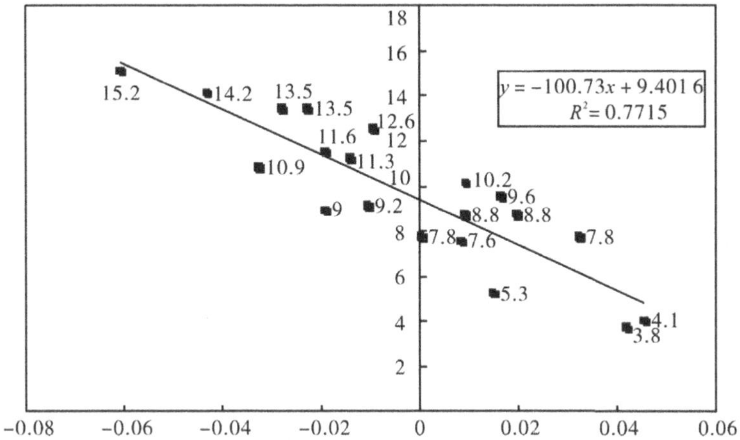

Fig. 9.4 Changes in China's economic growth rate and capital-output ratio (1979–1998)

economic data of 1978–1998:

$$\left(\frac{\hat{Y}}{y}\right)_t = \frac{K_t/Y_t - K_{t-1}/Y_{t-1}}{K_{t-1}/Y_{t-1}} = \frac{K_t/K_{t-1}}{Y_t/Y_{t-1}} - 1$$

$$= \frac{(K_t - K_{t-1}/K_{t-1}) + 1}{(Y_t - Y_{t-1}/Y_{t-1}) + 1} - 1 = \frac{\hat{K}_t - \hat{Y}_t}{\hat{Y}_t + 1}$$

K and Y represent the capital stock and output level respectively. Subscript t indicates current time, and $t - 1$ indicates prophase. The symbol "∧"represents "growth rate". The above calculation formula can help us explore the meaning of the empirical equation between the economic growth rate and the growth rate of capital-output ratio we estimated for the speed of capital formation. First of all, according to the estimation equation, we know that if $\widehat{Y}$ rises, then $(\widehat{K/Y})$ drops. According to the growth rate formula of the capital-output ratio we defined, when $\widehat{Y}$ intends to drop while ascending $(\widehat{K} - \widehat{Y}/\widehat{Y} + 1)$, at least $\widehat{K}$ should not have any pressure to rise, i.e. $\widehat{K}$ can either drop or remain unchanged. Secondly, according to the estimation equation again, we know that when $\widehat{Y}$ drops $(\widehat{K/Y})$ will rise. And according to the definition of the capital-output growth rate given above, if $\widehat{Y}$ intends to rise at the time of dropping $(\widehat{K} - \widehat{Y}/\widehat{Y} + 1)$, at least $\widehat{K}$ should have no downward pressure. In other words, $\widehat{K}$ can either rise or remain unchanged.

These simple discussions have important implications for China's economic growth. Because the change in the capital stock is the result of investment, it is clear that the equation we estimated for the rate of economic growth and the growth rate of capital-output ratio obviously has theoretical significance. Roughly speaking, compared with the changes in economic growth rates, changes in the capital stock seem to be basically stable. That is to say, the speed of capital formation is relatively insensitive to GDP growth rate: when economic growth accelerates, capital formation speed does not accelerate correspondingly, resulting in the decline of the ratio of capital-output; and when the economic growth is in decline, the capital formation does not slow down, resulting in the rise of the ratio of capital-output. This is also the basic reason why capital-output ratio can still be observed as growing while the economic growth rate continues to decline.

So, why can we observe this time changing mode of capital formation in China's post-reform period? In order to explain this pattern, we need to seek the "production theory" behind the total index changes of the capital-output ratio, because the changes of capital-output ratio in theory should reflect the changes of the "mode of production" in the economy from the micro perspective. To this end, let us turn to Solow (1960, 1962) and Dension (1967), who later developed the so-called "growth accounting" framework, to help explain the micro foundation of capital-output ratio changes.[7] Firstly, a production function of the Khub-Douglas structure of constant returns to scale is given:

$$Y = AK^{\partial}L^{1-\partial} \tag{9.1}$$

Y, K, L respectively represent output, capital stock and labor, while ∂ is the output elasticity of capital. In addition, it is assumed that technological progress is neutral and the rate of change is constant. We can easily derive the growth equation of per capita output (K/L) from (9.1). For example, we can get the total output function of "per capita" by dividing the two sides of formula (9.1) by L:

$$Y/L = A(K/L)^{\partial} \tag{9.2}$$

To infer the technical factors behind the changes in the capital-output ratio, let us first look at the capital output ratio (K/Y). We know that the capital-output ratio (K/Y) can actually be written as the "capital-labor ratio" (K/L) and the "per capita output" (Y/L) quotient, that is:

$$K/Y = (K/L)/(Y/L) \tag{9.3}$$

By bringing this expression (9.3) in the definition of capital-output above, we have obtained the capital-output ratio expressed by the capital-labor ratio:

$$K/Y = 1/A(K/L)^{1-\partial} \tag{9.4}$$

Now obtain the natural logarithm from both sides of formula (9.4), and convert the logarithmic expression into "growth rate" form (we still use symbol "$\wedge$" to represent the growth rate and define the growth rate A as the growth rate of "total factor productivity" (TFP)), and we will get a simple accounting equation about "capital-output ratio":

[7] Solow (1962), Dension (1967).

$$\frac{\widehat{K}}{y} = (1-\alpha)\frac{\widehat{K}}{l} - \widehat{tfp} \quad (9.5)$$

In the assumption of neoclassical production theory, formula (9.5) clearly shows that the capital-output ratio change is the difference between the contribution of changes of the capital-labor ratio (i.e. per capita capital or "capital equipment ratio") and the rate of change of total factor productivity (TFP). So, in terms of China's economic growth we are concerned with, we obviously need to focus on the time pattern of the changes of the capital-labor ratio and the total factor productivity (TFP) since the reform.

According to the above expression (9.5), we can now give a basic explanation of the slowness of the formation of capital relative to economic growth. Assuming that investment constantly grows which can effectively throw more labor inputs into the production process so that capital-labor ratio has no upward pressure at all, at this time, according to formula (9.5), unless TFP is deteriorating, the capital-output ratio will not rise along with the economic growth, because the increase of capital has been matched by growth of labor. Under such conditions, we may observe that the significant rise in the capital-output ratio is not accompanied by the rapid growth of the economy, even if this growth is largely dependent on the growth of factor inputs. For an economy with a scarce capital but rich in labor, this means that, as long as the technical efficiency (TFP) is being continuously improved, and the choice of technology does not deviate towards the path where labor is being substituted by capital, sustained economic growth will be maintained.

The opposite path is the deviation of technology choice that results in labor being constantly substituted by capital. In this case, the growth of investment will lead to an increase in the capital-labor ratio, and an accelerating trend of the so-called "capital deepening" process. As a result, as the growth of capital continues to increase faster than labor, the marginal return of capital tends to decrease, which eventually leads to a decline in the rate of economic growth. In the existing literature, this is exactly what the "extension hypothesis" of growth aims at: once the excessive "capital deepening" occurs, or the capital density in the economy continues to rise, the economic growth rate will be decreased because of the diminishing marginal return on investment, or the economy will even eventually fall in recession. We suspect that it is because of this reason that we have observed an upward trend in the capital-output ratio despite the fact that China's economic growth is slowing down. In fact, according to our explanation above, the causality behind this empirical observation is that excessive capital accumulation has led to a sustained decline in the marginal rate of return of capital and a slowdown in economic growth.

As we all know, in the existing literature on economic growth, a popular theory on the "Soviet style" growth deterioration has been the so-called "extension hypothesis". The basic proposition of this hypothesis is that the rapid economic growth mainly depends on the accumulation of capital, but once the capital continues to grow faster than the growth of output, the capital marginal return rate tends to decline and eventually leads to the decline in aggregate output growth and economic recession. In theory, as long as there is always labor that can match capital, even if technological progress is not significant, the capital-output ratio is not likely to rise too early and fast, and investment growth will still promote total economic growth. Under this condition, the growth driven by factor input should last much longer. This in turn reminds us that, in addition to the factors of technological progress (technical efficiency), the fast growth of the capital-output ratio is certainly the direct result of capital growing faster than labor. Based on this fact, the situation in China is likely to be that in the production sector, the capital-labor ratio began to rise rapidly in the 1990s.

In the existing literature, the "extension hypothesis" is a good explanation of the growth trajectory of the Soviet Union. For a long time, many economists noted that although the Soviet Union achieved a higher economic growth rate than the average level of the world in the 1950s, the "good times don't last long". Its economy deteriorated rapidly after the 60s, and its growth rate continued to decline, which eventually turned into a severe recession.[8] Also based on the new classical theory of production function, the "business accounting", which was targeted at economic growth in East Asia in the past 10 years, also found that the rapid growth of "East Asian" economy (mainly refers to the newly industrialized economy in the 50–80s) also has the remarkable characteristics of "extension". That is to say, the results of the accounting on growth from the "new classical" point view show that economic growth is mainly based on the continuous growth of investment while the technological progress is very slow. In this region, the contribution of technological progress to the rapid growth of the economy has not been even found in some economies, such as Singapore (Young 1992, 1994; Kim and Lau 1994).[9] Of course, people may raise the question–why the "East Asian" "extension" growth has created the "East Asian miracle"? Why the growth there can last longer?

In this paper, we do not intend to further examine the findings and explanations of the existing literature on the source of economic growth in East Asia. We are even willing to accept the conclusion of the accounting for "East Asian" growth for the time being in the neoclassical sense. Regarding these problems, our initial response is that the so-called longer period of sustained growth of the "extension" of "East Asia" is mainly because they can actually make full use of cheap labor in a very long time. As long as the workforce continues to be mobilized, rapid growth can depend on growth in investment. Although some accounting of the "East Asia" growth found that the growth record of TFP of "East Asia" is not satisfactory (this point was taken by Krugman to make a comparison with the Soviet Union), careful analysis has indeed confirmed that, in the period of rapid growth, the rate of return on investment in "East Asia" has been relatively high, and the decline in rate of return is not sharp but slow (Radelet and Sachs 1997).[10] This suggests that, in the growth

[8] Zhang and Han (1996) provided a literature review of the empirical research on the mode of economic growth in the Soviet Union. See Zhang and Han (1996).

[9] (1992).

[10] Radelet and Sachs (1997).

of East Asia's economy, (we suspect) that the ratio of capital to labor probably did not actually rise sharply as in the Soviet Union.

Therefore, in terms of growth model, the growth of the "East Asia miracle" period should be very different from that of the Soviet Union after the 1960s. In the Soviet Union, due to the entirely different nature of investment decisions, there was a significant difference between the yields of the Soviet Union's planned investment and the market oriented investment in East Asia's economy. Not only did the Soviet TFP at the end of the 50s deteriorate and turn negative growth, but its investment rate of return after the 50s declined sharply in the 60s and 70s until it dropped to zero (Easterly and Fischer 1994). This kind of result was not found in East Asia.

9.3 Change of TFP

In order to explain the changing mode of capital-output ratio of the Chinese economy, we will first, after the discussion of the theoretical framework, observe the changes of technical efficiency or "total factor productivity" (TFP) of production department, especially the changing trend after the 1990s. It should be said that the overall observation on technical efficiency is not very difficult, because the existing literature has provided the results of a large number of empirical studies on the changes in technical efficiency of Chinese industrial sectors (especially the state-owned industrial sector)since the 1980s (e.g. Chen et al. (1988); Jefferson et al. (1992, 1996).[11] Although there is no lack of criticism and controversy about the established empirical estimates in these literatures (the arguments are related to the source and the reliability of data and the theories used and the methods and techniques for dealing with data), these research achievements have greatly improved our knowledge of technological progress or changing trends of technological efficiency in China's economic growth: we have known more, not less.

However, although the existing researches are very valuable in explaining texts, it is necessary to make a general research on the change of TFP in the whole economy by using the available data considering that most existing research was mainly done according to different ownerships. In order to maintain consistency with existing literature, we still use neoclassical theories and techniques. At the same time, in order to better observe the changing trend of China's economic technological efficiency, we hope to extend the observation period to 1952–1998. Like many studies, we assume that the aggregate production function of China's economy is:

---

[11] To know more about the main literature on the empirical study of the changes in the total factor productivity of China's industrial sector since the reform, refer to the literature review provided by Zhang and Shi (2000). Moreover, among the recently published books, O Keijiro, Liu Deqiang and Murakami Naoki made an empirical study on the efficiency changes of state-owned and township enterprises and a comparison of the relative efficiency. In fact, in the second chapter of their work they also provided an overview of relevant literature. See Zhang and Shi (2003), Keijiro et al. (2000), Chen et al. (1988), Jefferson et al. (1992, 1996).

$$Y_t = A_0 + e^{\alpha_T t} + K_t^{\alpha_K} + L_t^{\alpha_L} \tag{9.6}$$

α_K and α_L represent the elasticity of output of capital and labor respectively. Take the natural logarithm from both sides of (9.6), we get:

$$\ln Y_t = \ln A_0 + \alpha_T t + \alpha_K \ln K_t + \alpha_L \ln L_t \tag{9.7}$$

When $\alpha_K + \alpha_L = 1$, i.e., the scale returns are constant, (9.7) is:

$$\ln(Y_t/L_t) = \ln A_0 + \alpha_T t + \alpha_K \ln(K_t/L_t) \tag{9.8}$$

In order to control the influence of some of the main exogenous variables in different periods (such as the "Cultural Revolution" or the start of the economic reform policy of China after 1978) of China's economic growth, we decided to use the "dummy variable" D_i to represent the i (th) dummy variable, so that models (9.7) and (9.8) are respectively changed into:

$$\ln Y_t = \ln A_0 + \alpha_T t + \alpha_K \ln K_t + \alpha_L \ln L_t + \sum \beta_i D_i \tag{9.9}$$

$$\ln(Y_t/L_t) = \ln A_0 + \alpha_T t + \alpha_K \ln(K_t/L_t) + \sum \beta_i D_i \tag{9.10}$$

By regression fitting the Eqs. (9.9) and (9.10), we can estimate α_K and α_L, the output elasticity of capital and labor. After regularization, we can obtain:

$$\alpha_K^* = \alpha_K/(\alpha_K + \alpha_L)$$

$$\alpha_L^* = \alpha_L/(\alpha_K + \alpha_L)$$

Now we can define total factor productivity or TFP as:

$$\text{TFP}_t = \frac{Y_t}{K_t^{\alpha_K^*} L_t^{\alpha_L^*}}$$

By this definition, the TFP growth rate for the year t shall be:

$$\text{TFP}_t = \frac{\text{TFP}_t}{\text{TFP}_{t-i}} - 1$$

And the TFP growth rate for the year $t_1 - t_2$ is:

$$\text{TFP}_{t_1-t_2} = \sqrt[t_2-t_1]{\text{TFP}_{t_2}/\text{TFP}_{t_1}} - 1$$

In order to compute the TFP and its growth rate, we included the time series data of the total output, capital and labor inputs of the Chinese economy from 1952–1998 in the "Data Appendix" at the end of this article. The Data Appendix also gives a detailed description of the data source, which we will not repeat here. There, we used gross domestic product (GDP) as an indicator of total output, the basic data of which was from the issues of *Chinese Statistical Yearbook* over the years and deflated by the constant prices of 1990. As for the labor input data, according to the general routine practice, we used the number of social workers of each year as indicators of labor input over the years. The capital investment, as the capital stock that directly or indirectly constitutes the production capacity, not only includes direct production and various fixed assets and current assets that provide a variety of material products and services, but also includes the various services and welfare facility capital that provides service for life such as housing, etc.

In general, the most commonly used methods to estimate the capital stock computed according to the comparable price are: ① calculate the social capital stock of a base period of calculation through census or according to certain presumed estimation; ② obtain each year's investment figures of industry sectors, and convert each year's investment amount calculated at each year's price into investment amount calculated by comparable prices; ③ calculate the annual scrap value of capital and make a summary according to the composition of various types of assets invested each year, and on the basis of the average age of various types of assets estimated by special investigation (that is, from the time of putting into use to completely declared worthless); ④ the total value of scrap is deducted from the amount of investment each year and obtain the actual incremental capital of each year; ⑤ calculate the capital stock figures of each year according to the principle of last year's capital stock plus this year's capital increment being equal to this year's capital stock. By the way, for the capital data of 1952–1990, we chose to use the estimated value of the price adjusted capital stock provided by He (1992), and the capital data of 1991–1998 was also estimated according to his method.[12]

We performed a regression of three different least squares (OLS) for the above data. In the first regression, the regression equation we used is:

$$\ln Y_t = \ln A_0 + \alpha_T t + \alpha_K \ln K_t + \alpha_L \ln L_t + \beta_1 D_1 + \beta_2 D_2 + \beta_3 D_3 + \beta_4 D_4 + \varepsilon_t$$

The four dummy variables, D_1, D_2, D_3, D_4 respectively represent the four special periods. D_1 stands for the years of 1961–1964 when the output was obviously very low because of the so-called "three year's natural disaster" and the Soviet Union's withdrawal of aid to China; D_2 stands for 1967–1969 which were the beginning years of the "Cultural Revolution". The economic reform policies introduced after 1978 were divided into two stages, represented by D_3 and D_4 respectively. The reason for the division is because it was mainly agricultural reform before 1984, and the industrial reform did not actually start until after 1984.

From the regression results, as we have expected, both the "three years of natural disasters" and the "Cultural Revolution" had a negative impact on the Chinese economy while the economic reform plan had a significant positive impact on the

[12] He (1992).

Chinese economic growth. However, we noted that the coefficient of time variable t is negative, indicating that the technical level of production has declined over time. However, considering the fact that we used many virtual time variables in the regression process, technological progress or technical efficiency improvements may have been reflected in the coefficients of the dummy variables. Moreover, the biggest problem of the first regression is that the output elasticity of capital and labor is difficult to understand ($\alpha_K = 0.584$, $\alpha_L = 1.806$), and has a particularly high level. Through further examinations, we found that the reason may be that there is multi collinearity between capital and labor. To avoid this problem, we assume that $\alpha_K + \alpha_L = 1$, i.e., the production scale returns remain unchanged. In this way, the regression equation correspondingly becomes:

$$\ln(Y_t/L_t) = \ln A_0 + \alpha_T t + \alpha_K \ln(K_t/L_t) + \beta_1 D_1 + \beta_2 D_2 + \beta_3 D_3 + \beta_4 D_4 + \varepsilon_t$$

As far as the result of the second regression is concerned, the coefficient and significance level of time variable t are not high. Therefore, we decided to remove t in the explanatory variable and make the third regression. The indicators of the data of the third regressions are quite good, so we used the third regression result as the final result here. The regression results are summarized in the "Data Appendix" of this article. Our estimated capital-output elasticity is $\alpha_K = 0.499$, and the output elasticity of labor is $\alpha_L = 1 - \alpha_K = 0.501$. Therefore by definition, the total factor productivity or TFP of year t is:

$$\text{TFP}_t = \frac{Y_t}{K_t^{0.499} L_t^{0.501}}$$

The growth rate of TFP of the year t is:

$$\text{TFP}_t = \frac{\text{TFP}_t}{\text{TFP}_{t-1}} - 1$$

According to this formula and letting the TFP index in 1952 be 100, we calculated the TFP index and its growth rate in 1952–1998 (the results are in the Data Appendix of this article). We have visually depicted this calculation in Fig. 9.5. We found that the average growth rate of TFP of 1953–1998 was about 1.07%, and, as we have expected, the average TFP growth rate during 1953–1978 before the reform was about 0.4%, so, the contribution of TFP growth to output growth was only about 6.8%; while the average TFP growth rate during 1979–1998 after the reform rose to about 2.81% TFP, and the contribution of TFP growth to output growth was also up to about 31%,[13] indicating that economic reform has a significant and positive effect

[13] It should be pointed out that our estimation results are strikingly similar to those of Li and others (1992). See Li et al. (1992).

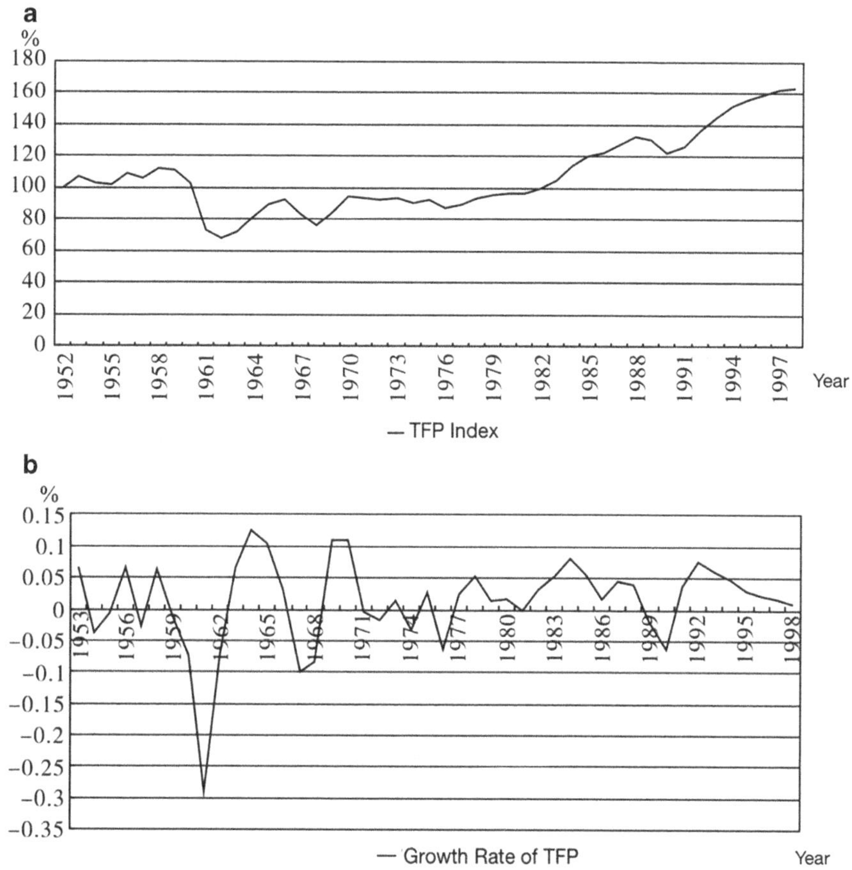

Fig. 9.5 **a** China's economic TFP index (1952–1998). **b** Growth rate of TFP of Chinese economy (1953–1998)

on the improvement of production efficiency.[14] However, the growth rate of TFP has been decreasing since 1992. As shown in Fig. 9.5, while overall factor productivity is still growing slowly, its growth rate has been declining steadily since 1992.

Our results reminded us of the estimated result obtained by Keijiro et al. (2000) that the TFP growth of state sector slowed down after the 1990s. At the same time, our results are also fairly consistent with the estimate produced by Jefferson and Zheng (1995) that there was a downward trend for the TFP growth rate in state-owned and collective industrial sectors during 1988–1992.[15] They offered such a comment on the meaning of their estimated results: "We should pay enough attention to the deep

[14] We also noted that in 1977–1988, the average TFP growth rate was about 4.1%, and the contribution of TFP growth to output growth was about 41.9%. That was the golden period of the growth of TFP in Chinese economy. In 12 years, TFP maintained a positive growth.

[15] Jefferson and Zheng (1995).

reason of the slowing growth trend of industrial productivity in China. Does this trend mean that China, after the release of the reform potential, will be eventually like what the emerging countries and regions in East Asia have experienced embarking on the road of epitaxial growth? What is its intrinsic inevitability? This is a problem worthy of study."

Therefore, we have reason to believe that the continued decline of the growth rate of the total factor productivity (TFP) of production sector after the1990s seems to bear some responsibility for the acceleration of the deepening of capital in Chinese economy in this period. We do not intend to discuss in detail the main factors leading to a sustained decline in TFP growth rate since the 90s, but in a nutshell, the decline in TFP growth can be explained mainly by a number of factors. First, as we will mention in the fifth part of this article, the scale effect is not very significant in China's industrial organizations. In some cases, firms with large investment size also have diseconomies of scale (Murakami et al. 1994, 1996).[16] Second, after the 90s, particularly during 1992–1994, a lot of inefficient investment were encouraged by financial policies, so a large amount of credits was actually allocated to projects that were improperly selected, the consequences of which affected the improvement of TFP. Third, the downward trend of TFP also reflects the problems of internal mechanisms and governance of enterprises (especially state-owned and collective enterprises). The reform of state-owned enterprise's system after the 90s encountered many difficulties. The bankruptcy and reorganization of enterprises have not really accelerated with the intensification of market competition, and the cases of "survival of the fittest" are rare, far from becoming a normal business practice. All these have helped us explain the decline in TFP growth rate since the 90s.

9.4 Capital-Labor Ratio

By using the data provided in the Data Appendix of this article, we can easily observe the changing trajectory of the capital-labor ratio of Chinese economy since the reform, which reflects the process and speed of capital deepening at the technical level. In order to make a further explanation, in this part, we will focus our analysis on the manufacturing sector, because the growth in the industrial sector is a major contribution to Chinese economic growth–the industrial added value (industrial GDP) accounts for 70% of GDP.[17] Therefore, observing the growth mechanism of the industrial sector is of typical significance for understanding the decline of

[16] Murakami et al. (1995, 1995).

[17] In 1999, for example, GDP grew by 7.1%, of which 4.3 percentage points were contributed by industrial growth (Macroeconomic Research Team of the Institute of Economics of the Chinese Academy of Social Sciences, 2000). Therefore, to observe and explain the growth of GDP, we can focus mainly on the growth of industrial added value.

China's economic growth rate since the mid-90s. Specifically, we will mainly investigate the changes of capital-labor ratio and the scale of enterprises of state-owned and township enterprises since the reform.

1. Growth of the Capital-Labor Ratio

In order to observe the capital-labor ratio changes of Chinese industrial sectors of different ownerships, in Table 9.1 we calculated and provided the capital labor ratio and its growth rate of the state sector, collective sector as well as large and medium-sized enterprises during 1981–1996 by using the official data we obtained. In the calculation of the capital-labor ratio, we used the official nominal value capital data and the actual value capital data adjusted by the fixed asset price index respectively.[18] Obviously, in the years of 1981–1996, especially since the late 1980s, both the state-owned enterprises and the collective enterprises have experienced a sustained and significant upward trend in the capital-labor ratio. However, it is worth noting that the capital-labor ratio of collective enterprise sector has been rising faster than that of the state-owned sector, whether it is calculated according to nominal value or actual value. This shows that the collective enterprise sector has experienced a very rapid capital deepening process since the late 1980s. Taking into account the fact that the collective sector mainly comprises the "township enterprises", the implication of this result is extremely clear– the capital-labor ratio of township enterprises in rapidly on the rise.

Our observations are consistent with a number of existing studies. For example, Chen (1999) also found in his study that since the late 1980s (especially in the 90 s), the development of township enterprises began to show changes and characteristics that economists totally failed to expect. They committed errors in selecting technologies and their technological change has not been developed along the path of technical neutrality or capital saving as expected by orthodox theory. On the other hand, their capital density has shown a rising trend. As shown in Table 9.2, the two-tier enterprises at the town and village levels experienced a significant rise in capital-labor ratio and average asset size over the years of 1978–1996.[19] The capital-output ratio of township enterprises is rising because of the increase of capital density. Almost since then, township enterprises have experienced a similar expansion model and financial performance as the state sector Zhang (2000).[20] From the perspective of the orthodox theory of development economics, if all other things remain unchanged, the efficiency of township enterprises and development prospects depend, to a large extent, on their ways of selecting technology and the consistency of changes of the factor structure of China. And the surplus labor force that has existed for a long time is apparently the most important characteristic that decides factor structure of

[18] For the account and sources of these price index as well as data, see "Data Appendix" of this article.

[19] Table 9.3 is quoted from Chen (1999). But it needs to be reminded that since the author did not mention the source of the data and how the data was processed in his paper, his data may be the nominal value not adjusted by price. Of course, based on our calculations in Table 9.1, we know that the use of nominal values does not actually affect the validity of his basic conclusions.

[20] Zhang (2000).

Table 9.1 Growth rate of capital-labor ratio in China's industrial sector (1981–1996)

	Nominal value			Actual value		
	State-owned enterprises	Collective enterprise	Large and medium-sized enterprises	State-owned enterprises	Collective enterprise	Large and medium-sized enterprises
1981	0.8	12.62	−0.01	1.74	5.27	0.33
1982	3.61	6.07	2.62	2.28	9.56	1.67
1983	6.23	10.64	13.45	5.03	10.10	12.6
1984	4.41	7.62	8.07	3.76	4.15	6.99
1985	13.75	14.81	4.74	5.48	4.97	0.78
1986	8.23	12.77	8.34	6.37	7.82	3.34
1987	11.54	15.52	10.25	5.47	8.85	3.76
1988	12.14	18.02	12.06	6.55	11.41	5.58
1989	13.91	19.02	13.52	6.51	12.52	4.38
1990	13.23	14.21	11.78	6.73	10.24	4.50
1991	14.62	12.70	13.80	6.01	6.32	4.08
1992	13.84	15.16	13.04	6.83	7.23	3.10
1993	9.01	20.04	2.22	7.39	11.78	1.25
1994	21.37	31.05	27.56	13.50	19.29	13.21
1995	31.66	8.20	22.89	16.91	21.26	10.83
1996	30.88	23.09	23.65	15.50	13.29	10.45
Average growth rate(1981–1996)	13.08	15.10	11.75	7.25	9.06	5.39
Average growth rate (1988–1996)	17.85	17.94	15.61	9.55	10.47	6.37

Note The unit in this table is %. Only two decimal places are retained in calculation and no rounding was done

Data sources From the Data Appendix at the end of this article

Chinese economy. This means whether the township enterprises will be able to maintain their relative efficiency and dominate China's manufacturing economy depends on its ability to rationally choose what is known as "appropriate technology". Therefore, the rapid growth of the capital-labor ratio shown in the township enterprise sector will affect the long-term development of China's economy and the process of rural industrialization.

The existing research literature has indicated the township enterprise sector is considered to be the most "dynamic" sector in the Chinese economy since the reform. A great deal of observations and researches show that township enterprises have entered and dominated the "labor-intensive" industrial sectors because they have an easy access to the rural surplus labor force. This hypothesis has been further confirmed by extensive empirical studies. For example, since the reform, township enterprises have been proved to have achieved higher "total factor productivity" than that of the state-owned sector which means that the township enterprises have higher

Table 9.2 Change Trajectory of Average Asset Size and Capital-Labor Ratio of Rural Enterprises at Township and Village Levels in China (1978–1996)

Year	Total assets (ten thousand *yuan*)	Labor (ten thousand)	Number of enterprises (ten thousand)	average asset size	Capital-labor ratio
1978	276.8	2826.5	152.4	1.82	0.10
1979	358.8	2909.3	148	2.42	0.12
1980	443.2	2999.7	142.4	3.11	0.15
1981	505.01	2969.6	133.7	3.78	0.17
1982	572.88	3112.9	136.2	4.21	0.18
1983	635.48	3234.6	134.6	4.72	0.20
1984	844.36	3848.1	165	5.12	0.22
1985	1179.89	4152.1	156.9	7.52	0.28
1986	1512.97	4391.52	151.74	9.97	0.34
1987	2094.41	4718.23	158.28	13.23	0.44
1988	2775.06	4893.93	159	17.45	0.57
1989	3376.28	4720.1	153.5	22	0.72
1990	4227	4592	146	28.95	0.92
1991	4118	4769	144	18.6	0.86
1992	6841	5176	153	44.7	1.32
1993	10,103	5768	168	60.14	1.75
1994	15,046	5899	164.1	91.69	2.55
1995	19,887	6060	162	122.76	3.28
1996	23,337	5628	155	150.56	4.15

Source Chen Jianbo: Technological Acquisition and Technological Choice of Township Enterprises in the Evolution of Market Economy, *Economic Research*, 1999 (4)

production efficiency than state-owned enterprises (Otsuka et al. 1998).[21] There is no doubt that the rapid rise and expansion of rural enterprises represented by township enterprises is one of the most important achievements since China's economic reform. After 20 years of development, the added value of township enterprises has accounted for 49% of China's industrial added value (*Xinhua Daily News*, July 8, 2000), while their contribution to the GDP growth rate has reached 30%. In China's "non -state sector", township enterprises have become the largest manufacturing sector. Needless to say, the township enterprise sector is playing an important role in the adjustment of China's industrial structure and the process of rural industrialization.

But for economists, the extraordinary expansion model of the township enterprise sector over the past 20 years may have left us with more questions, not solutions. In the early days, economists were trying to understand the engine of growth, efficiency and source of efficiency of the rapid growth of township enterprises. While in the middle stage, economists paid special attention to the prospect of township

[21] Otsuka (1998).

Table 9.3 Average scale of rural enterprises in Japan, Taiwan and Chinese Mainland. (Measured by the Number of Employed Persons)

Regional	1971/1976	1981	1991
Japan*			
All manufacturing industry	17.8	15.1	16.6
Food and drink	12.8	14.3	16.4
Textile	11.0	7.9	8.0
Clothing	12.9	11.7	12.3
Basic metal products	70.2	47.1	41.9
Metal Fiber	12.3	9.6	10.7
Engineering	24.9	17.2	17.0
Taiwan, China***			
All manufacturing industry	20.1	18.1	16.6
Food and drink	8.2	9.4	11.2
Textile	55.7	37.2	23.6
Clothing	54.9	45.9	26.4
Basic metal products	34.0	25.2	21.6
Metal Fiber	9.4	7.5	8.2
Engineering	11.9	10.0	10.7
Mainland China			
All Manufacturing Industry	–	30.6	43.9
Food and Drink	–	8.3	9.7
Textile	–	82.2	108.1
Clothing	–	51.5	69.6
Basic metal products	–	60.2	71.2
Metal fiber	–	36.5	42.5
Engineering	–	40.8	48.5
Jiangsu, China***		87.8	–
Wuxi, Jiangsu***		119.4	–

Note * Japan's data is for the entire manufacturing industry rather than the rural enterprises only; ** refers to 1976 data in Taiwan; *** refers to the data of township and village enterprises in 1984 calculated in accordance with the weighted average of output value proportion of the two types of enterprises provided by Byrd and Zhu (1990).[22]
Source The original data is from the relevant volumes of the *Chinese Statistical Yearbook, Chinese Industrial Economc Statistics Yearbook* and field investigations. The data on Jiangsu and Wuxi were calculated by the author of this articale based on the data provided by Byrd and Zhu (1990). Other data are from Otsuka (1998, pp.457–458).[23]

enterprises. Whether the township enterprises will take the place of the state-owned enterprises and dominate the Chinese economy has become a very important issue. In a comparative sense, do China's township enterprises represent a new mode of

22 Byrd and Zhu (1990).

23 Ostuka (1996).

rural industrialization? Or are they also the replica of small rural enterprises among the East Asian economy? All these have become important factors of understanding and interpreting the long-term economic development in China. In the past 5 years, although the transformation (privatization) of the structure of property rights of township enterprises in many areas has attracted the interest of economists, it is still not clear at present what kind of impact the reform will produce on the future of technology choice and mode of development of township enterprises. So it is worth further observation. There is no doubt that this is an important issue and we encourage economists to think about it and its implications for China's economic development.

In addition to the state-owned and the collective sectors, we also calculated the growth rate of capital-labor ratio in large and medium-sized enterprises in Table 9.1. The results show that the growth rate of capital-labor ratio in large and medium-sized enterprises is obviously lower than that of state-owned and collective enterprises. One reason for this result is that, in the early years of reform, large and medium enterprises already had a fairly high capital-labor ratio, and always maintained a gap in capital-labor ratio with small businesses. For example, in our calculations, in 1980, the capital-labor ratio of large and medium-sized enterprises was almost 7 times that of the collective sector. As is known to all, due to the planned economy system and the long-term implementation of priority development strategy for heavy industry, in most industrial sectors, state-owned enterprises are not only large in scale, but also equipped with capital intensive technology.

For example, we calculated the distribution of large enterprises in the manufacturing sector in China based on the data of large enterprises defined as having original value of fixed assets of more than 100 million *yuan* in 1991. Judging from the organizational structure of the given sectors, in sectors such as oil and oil processing, timber harvesting, tobacco processing, chemical fiber, ferrous and non-ferrous metal smelting and electric heating, large enterprises occupy a significant proportion. Among the oil mining and tobacco processing sectors, the proportion of large enterprises accounted for 51.4% and 15.2% respectively. On the other hand, according to the proportion of enterprises of one industrial sector in all the large enterprises, large enterprises are mainly found in machinery, textile, chemical, building materials, coal, ferrous and non-ferrous metal smelting equipment, transportation and other sectors. This means that although small and medium-sized enterprises accounted for the absolute proportion in sectors such as textiles and machinery, the absolute number of large enterprises is very large, accounting for 122 and 186 respectively.[24] Under the planned economic system, the state-owned enterprises (especially large enterprises) tended to evolve into a typical vertical and integrated organizational structure.[25] It

[24] If the definition of large enterprises was changed from the original value of fixed assets of 100 million *yuan* to 50 million *yuan*, the number of large enterprises in the textile and machinery industries would have soared to 471 and 491. See State Bureau of Statistics: *Chinese Industrial Economic Statistical Yearbook* (1992), Beijing, China Statistics Press, 1992.

[25] In China, this vertical and integrated structure is commonly known as "all-embracing regardless big or small". Of course, this kind of vertically integrated structure is still typical of state-owned large enterprises. We have carried out a thorough analysis of the logic of this structure of the state-owned enterprises under the planned economy system. See Jun Zhang: Information Costs, Limited

is often the case that large state-owned enterprises not only produce final products, but also spare parts and intermediate products, so their scale is relatively large with intensive capital.

However, as the capital deepening of the collective sector developed very fast, the capital-labor ratio of the collective sector rose to about 1/4 of that of the medium and large enterprises by 1996. Of course, the capital-labor ratio of large and medium-sized enterprises is still increasing, otherwise, according to the present growth model, the collective enterprise sector would soon catch up with the large and medium-sized enterprises in terms of the capital-labor ratio. Based on this observation, we are more convinced that the sustained productivity growth of collective enterprise sector seems to be the result of the fast deepening of capital to a large extent, although we do not deny that the township enterprises may be more efficient than some state-owned enterprises.[26] By using official data which was processed according to industrial output value index, we show in Fig. 9.6 the labor productivity curve of China's industrial enterprises in the 1980–1996 calculated by the actual industrial net output value.[27] This labor productivity growth curve calculated on the basis of ownerships shows that although the labor productivity of collective enterprise sector in the 80 s was lower than that of the state-owned enterprises, it surpassed the state-owned enterprise sector in this regard starting from the beginning of 1992. The partial explanation for this observation is often that the collective enterprise sector has a significant comparative advantage in the labor intensive sector. However, even if we believe that the TFP of collective enterprises (mainly township enterprises) have a significantly higher growth in the post-reform period, it seems that we also cannot ignore and dismiss the "contribution" of rapid increase of capital-labor ratio to the productivity growth. At least from Fig. 9.6, we can see that the differences in labor productivity and its changing pattern among the state-owned, collective sectors and large and medium-sized enterprises are very consistent with the difference in the growth rate of capital-labor ratio (equipment level) among them shown in Table 9.1.

(B) Scale Growth of Township Enterprises

The observation of scale changes in Chinese township enterprises provides us with another important perspective to explain the deepening of capital. For many economists, the large-scale rise of township enterprises in China in the late 1970s seems to be another evidence of the economic development model in East Asia. Indeed, by using the experience of rural industrialization in East Asia as the background to examine China's rural enterprises, we will find many similar features at the "sector" level. For example, in the early 80 s, many township enterprises came

---

Reason and Planned Simplification: An Analysis of the Structure of Chinese Planned Economy, *Economic Development Research*, 1992 (2).

[26] We know that, according to the new classical theory of the production function and by using the framework of section two, we can conclude that the growth rate of labor productivity can be broken down into growth rate of capital-labor ratio and weighted sum of TFP growth rate.

[27] In calculating the actual labor productivity, we used the industrial net output value index provided by Lo (1999). See Data Appendix of this article.

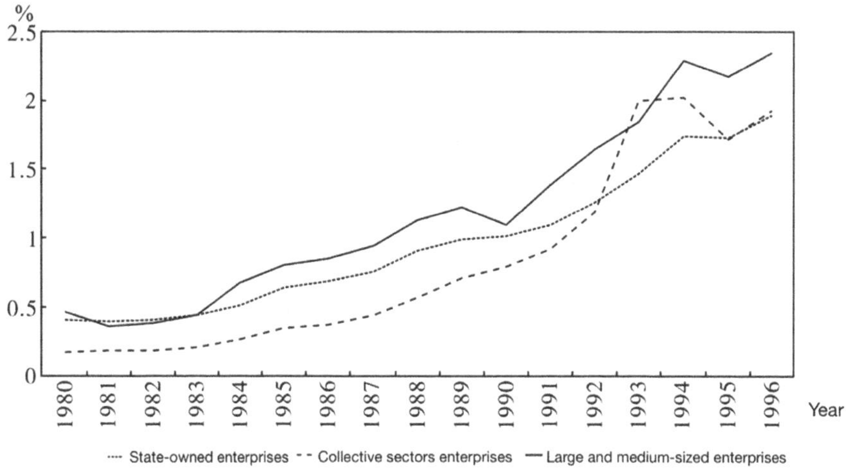

Fig. 9.6 Changing trajectory of the actual labor productivity of China's industrial enterprises (1980–1996)

into being through cooperation and subcontracting with the state-owned enterprises nearby.[28] In addition, since the 80 s, township enterprises have undoubtedly entered and dominated the labor intensive production sectors, and absorbed a large number of surplus labor in rural areas, all of which have similar features with the process of the development and the industrialization of rural areas of East Asian economy. It should be said that these traits were most remarkable by the end of the 80 s. But on the enterprise level, we find that there is a great difference between the township enterprises in China and the typical rural enterprises in East Asia. The most striking difference is that the average size of China's township enterprises is much larger than that of rural enterprises in Japan and China's Taiwan region.

Table 9.3 shows the comparision of the average number of employees of rural enterprises in mainland China, Japan and Chinese Taiwan area (using the average number of workers of the enterprises as an indicator of the enterprise scale). We find that the rural enterprises in Japan and Taiwan are relatively similar in scale, with an average enterprise size of less than 20 persons, much smaller than that of mainland China. According to the data in Table 9.3, in the textile industry, the average size of China's township enterprises is about 14 times larger than those in Japan. Table 9.3 also shows that the scale of enterprises in textile and garment industries in Japan is even smaller than that in Taiwan, suggesting that the speicalizationl level of Japan's small enterprises is higher than that in Taiwan (Otsuka 1998). Maybe it is because that in Japan, the vast majority of small and medium-sized enterprises are relying on large enterprises and trading companies to survive under the subcontracting relationship

[28] For example, the World Bank's survey (Byrd 1992) and Chen (1999) provided many typical cases about the rise of township enterprises. As they pointed out, in the early days, township enterprises were even established through informal channels such as "personal relations" with state-owned enterprises. See Byrd (1992).

(Patrick and Rohlen 1987).[29] Finally, we further find from Table 9.3 that the average size of rural manufacturing enterprises in China's Taiwan region is becoming smaller, while the average scale of rural enterprises in mainland China is increasing.

Indeed, China's township enterprises are much larger in scale than the rural enterprises in Japan and China's Taiwan region. Moreover, if the average asset size of enterprises is used as a measure of enterprise scale, the two-tiered rural enterprises in the late 80s actually experienced a very significant scale expansion. During 1980–1985, the average asset size of the rural two-levled enterprises was about 40 thousand *yuan*, which rose to about 200 thousand *yuan* in 1986–1992 and was as high as 940 thousand *yuan* in 1992–1996.[30] In Jiangsu province with relatively developed township enterprises, even in the middle of 80s, the average scale of township enterprises there was almost two times that of the national average, while the township enterprises in Wuxi, Jiangsu were almost five times larger than the national average (Byrd and Zhu 1990). Of course, at the village level or in some economically backward areas, the scale of township enterprises is smaller. However, even the enterprises at the village level, the average size of enterprises in textile and machine tools industries (59 and 34 persons respectively in 1985) is also greater than similar enterprises in Japan and Chinese Taiwan. In fact, in the textile industry, if measured according to the number of employees by enterprises, the average size of China's village textile enterprises (59 persons) is about 7–8 times as large as that in Japan. A survey of 200 large township enterprises carried out in the middle of the 80s shows that the average industrial output of the sampled enterprises is 4 million *yuan*, the average profit is 560 thousand *yuan*, the fixed asset is 1.2 million *yuan*, and the number of employees is up to 370.[31]

However, although the scale of Chinese township enterprises is too large compared with the East Asian economic development and rural industrialization experience, interestingly, it is often denounced as "too small" to produce any effect of scale economy by Chinese government departments or some economists. In the process of economic development in East Asia, one of the most important experiences widely accepted is the relative success of rural industrialization. Contrary to the widely held point of view, during the process of rural industrialization in East Asia, a large number of dispersed small and medium-sized enterprises played a very important role. Especially in the early stage of economic development of Japan and Taiwan area, small rural enterprises made important contribution to the export of labor-intensive products by successfully motilizing the surplus rural labor force and the relatively low price of labor (Ranis 1995; Chinn 1979).[32] In the development of theory, deeming the full use of and bringing into play the comparative advantages of the cheap labor force in the rural areas as a successful strategy for the realization of rural industrialization

[29] Patrick and Rohlen 1987.

[30] This data was calculated from the basic data provided in Table 9.1 (1999) by Chen Jianbo.

[31] According to the data in 1999, there were more than 68, 000 township enterprises with sales income of more than 5 million yuan, among which are more than 8,000 large and medium-sized township enterprises (*Xinhua Daily Telegraph*, July 8, 2000).

[32] Ranis (1995, Chinn 1979).

in East Asian economy has almost become the consensus among economists (Mead 1984).[33]

Obviously, the scale of township enterprises in China has not been truly understood. Generally speaking, the main reason given by those who think of the scale of township enterprises as being small is that, the development of township enterprises is partially restricted by the capital market, so that the lack of adequate capital and newer technology have limited the expansion of the scale of township enterprises. The implication of this hypothesis is that the scale of township enterprises will be further expanded with the improvement of the capital market. In the process of rural industrialization in East Asia, the same problem was often raised as well: has the rural enterprise scale being constrained by the flaws of the financial market? While another view is that, the reason that the rural enterprises in East Asia are so small is not because of the defects in the financial market, but is the result of highly developed relationship between the division of labor (between urban and rural or large enterprises and small businesses) and specialized market. Among them, the "subcontracting system" between rural enterprises and urban large enterprises is regarded as the typical mechanism of this specialized relationship (Hayami 1998).[34]

In fact, dispersed and small enterprises can indeed survive in the modern economic development process and contribute to economic growth. Traditionally, rural industry was often considered a household handicraft business, using primitive technology to produce goods for local consumption.[35] Therefore, this kind of manual production cannot contribute to the development of modern economy. However, as some scholars have stressed, the traditional family industry, as long as it can be combined with the modern mode of production, may have the potential to promote economic growth (Ranis and Stewart, 1993).[36] This is the key to understanding the successful experience of rural industrialization in East Asia. A large number of studies have pointed out that the introduction and development of "subcontract" system is the most typical channel to transform rural industry into the modern mode of production in East Asia. With the help of this system, small rurual businesses and large industries in cities have established an industrial organization structure of effective division of labor and specialization which overcame the constraints of shortage of capital, technology and sales system in rural areas (Watanabe 1979; Mead 1984; Hayami 1998).[37]

Based on this explanation, the small scale of rural enterprises is by no means a source of inefficiency; rather, it has the potential of efficiency and economic growth, which has become the important implication of "East Asian mode" of economic development and rural industrialization. It seems that, viewed within this framework of theory, the difference between the scale of China's township enterprises and East

---

[33] Mead (1984).

[34] Hayami (1998).

[35] In the literature of development economics, this simple and traditional product of rural industrial production is called "Z- goods".

[36] Ranis and Stewart 1993.

[37] Watanabe (1979).

Asian experiences can be explained by the different degrees of specialization. As O Keijiro explains: "Why are Chinese rural enterprises so big? Unlike the huge, vertically integrated state-owned enterprises set up under the socialist system, the township enterprises are relatively young and free to engage in market transactions. In our analysis, one of the most reasonable explanations for the large size of the firm is the low efficiency of market transactions and the weak coordination between firms." Indeed, the flaws of financial markets are clearly present in the developing economy. But, it is precisely because of the defects in the formal financial market that the informal financial market (private finance) has been developed. And with regard to the East Asian experience, the development of rural enterprises mainly depended on the development of informal finance. In fact, "subcontracting" should also be interpreted as a financial system that responds to financial market deficiencies. In any case, perhaps the most important consequence of incomplete financial market is that rural enterprises have chosen to use less capital technology, but to produce large quantities of highly labor-intensive products. In other words, the discussion about the scale change of rural enterprises should be related to the choice of technology and the density of factors.

Therefore, if the change (increase) of the size of the firm does not change the density of factors (increasing the capital-labor ratio), then it seems that we should not criticize the expansion of the scale of the enterprise. Moreover, it seems that only under such circusmtances can the scale effect (economies of scale) be truly a source to improve productivity. Some econometric studies have found that in the labor intensive sector, market (demand) expansion often contributes to the improvement of total factor productivity of enterprises but will not significantly change the density of factor. This efficiency improvement is often typically achieved by economies of scale (Dollar and Sokoloff 1990).[38] On the contrary, if the growth of enterprise scale is accompanied by the increase of capital density, then what we should pay attention to is not whether the scale of enterprise is appropriate or not, but whether the technical choice of the enterprise is reasonable or not.[39] Therefore, the explanation of the scale of township enterprises in China should, of course, be associated with the significant increase in the density of factors experienced by township enterprises. In addition, we also do not deny that the low division of labor and specialization degree in the market may be another cause of relatively large scale of township enterprises in China. Even so, we still need to answer the question: What are the factors that have caused such a low professional level? Why those institutional factors that can constantly improve the professional level cannot be maintained in the process of rural industrialization (such as "subcontracting" system)? This obviously requires us to seek explanation from the formation process of market structure and industrial organization.

---

[38] Dollar and Sokoloff (1990).

[39] Zhang (2001) made theoretical discussions and empirical tests on the scale of China's industries and economies of scale. We find that the higher profitability shown by China's big business sector does not seem to be the result of economies of scale, but is more likely to be a "sector effect". Because the most skilled labor force and engineering personnel in China's economy are concentrated in those sectors, they have higher skills in learning and mastering technoglies than those of small and medium-sized enterprises.

9.5 Classical Competition and Overinvestment

In this section, we hope to offer an explanation for the rapidly rising capital-labor ratio in the township sector. We believe that the main determinants of capital deepening in township enterprises also provides, to a great extent, an interpretation of the mode of change in the capital-labor ratio for the entire industrial sector (including state-owned enterprises). First of all, we should point out that the rapid rise in capital-labor ratio of township enterprises is not because of the fast rising prices of labor faced by township enterprises. In fact, some research found that the average annual growth rate of total wages of township enterprises in 1978–1984 was 18.43%, and in 1985–1990, it was 15%. Over the same periods, the average annual growth rate of per capita wage of township enterprises were 4.27% and 12.52% respectively. And if the price growth factor is deducted, the latter's growth rate is actually declining (Chen 1999).

Moreover, whether the actual wage level of township enterprises has been experiencing rapid growth can be answered by examining whether the rural labor force has normal flow among the regions. We have noted that Keijiro and others (2000) did a formal statistical fitting of the wage decision function of township enterprises based on the sample data in 1990 and 1995 of township enterprises in the suburbs of Shanghai, Ji'ning, Shenyang and Dalian. In theory, the key to examining the real wage growth trend of township enterprises is to observe the labor force flow pattern across regions, because if the areas with more developed township enterprises tend to adopt the exclusion or discrimination policy against labor force from other regions, it will lead to rapid growth of the wage level of township enterprises. Therefore, they put forward a different hypothesis, arguing that the fierce competition will make it hard for township enterprises that discriminate against migrant workers to survive, so, as long as labor force can flow between regions, the wages of township enterprises are unlikely to grow very fast. They found that the per capita fixed assets has a significant positive impact on the ratio of immigrant labor force, which means that the labor mobility has significantly reduced the potential regional wage gap caused by different levels of development of township enterprises.

If the wage level of the rural labor force does not show rapid growth, then the rising capital-labor ratio of township enterprises is not a rational reaction to the price of labor force, but a problem that needs to be explained from the angle of industrial organization/market structure. To this end, we have developed a simple "excessive entry" conceptual framework to explain the structural characteriscs of industrial organization in transition (Hallagan and Zhang 1998; Zhang and Halagan 1998).[40] Our model implies that, because of the specific property system and demand environment, especially the local government's intervention, township enterprises followed the characteristics of "classical" competition in their foray into the industrial sector, resulting in excessive entry and escalating investment. According to this explanation, the increasing capital density is not the result of the rising or too rapid rising of the actual price of the labor force, but the product of overinvestment and over-entry of the township enterprises.

[40] Hallagan and Zhang (1998), Zhang and Halagan (1998).

In our view, the entry mode of township enterprises determines the form of their capital formation. And the excessive entry of township enterprises is not, as is generally believed, caused by the imcompleteness of credit market, but because the credit market is subject to the interference of government. But in other emerging market economies, because of the incomplete capital market, the entry of new sectors is not only very slow, but also leads to small scale of enterprises. In the process of rural industrialization in East Asia, the rural enterprises, also because of incomplete capital market, are not only small, but they typically chose to set up a "subcontracting" relationship with urban industries in response to the shortage of capital. Under these circumstances, the development of small rural enterprises continues to absorb the surplus labor force and promote the process of industrialization. By contrast, China's township enterprises have "prematurely" embarked on the path of selecting capital intensive technology, and their absorptive capacity for the surplus labor force has been declining.

When we review the history, we find that in the early stage of China's rural industrial development (during the 50–70s of last centuary), the path of development and choice of technology of township enterprises (then known as the "enterprises of communes and production teams") was obviously characterised by the rural industrialization of "East Asia". For example, Chen (1999) offered such a description of the way of early development and acquisition of technology by China's township enterprises: "When the development of rural industry took place in the 50s, there was almost no modern industrial technology in the Chinese countryside except the traditional handicraft industry. In the middle and late 60s, with the promotion of agricultural mechanization, some farm machinery repair enterprises were established in some areas, thus mechanical processing technology gradually came into being in rural enterprises. In the 70s, in response to the call of the central government to actively promote agricultural mechanization, a number of simple machine tools began to appear in the agricultural machinery repairing enterprises in rural regions. At this stage, the prototype of township machinery industry based on agricultural machinery and tools was formed. At the same time, in order to meet the needs of agricultural production and farmers' life, some areas with favorable conditions began to use a number of small equipment and technologies, while those rural areas that were close to the city and engaged in supporting production for big urban industrial products received technical guidance of the technical personnel of the industrial cities and pieces of equipment through a way similar to "subcontracting".

Even in the late 1970s to the mid-80s, the technological sources of township enterprises mainly depended on the informal access to state-owned enterprises. The equipment discarded by state-owned enterprises as well as engineering and technical personnel from state-owned enterprises became an important source of technology for township enterprises. Therefore, the township enterprises actually chose the production of highly intensive labor products. Typically, township enterprises are different from state-owned enterprises in that they tend not to produce many products, but rather a single product, and most products are subcontracted from the state-owned enterprises in cities (Naughton 1995; Tao Youzhi, 1988).[41] However, this subcontracting relationship failed to evolve into a stable division of labor and contractual relations of cooperation. Moreover, in some areas with developed township enterprises, township enterprises are highly motivated to try to lessen or get rid of their dependence on state-owned enterprises. According to the survey of Jiangsu Academy of Social Sciences, in the total industrial output value of township enterprises in Wuxi, the proportion of subcontracting from urban state-owned enterprises exceeded 70% in 1981, but down to 21% in 1985.[42]

In fact, in the middle and late 1980s, although the government adopted the policy of encouraging township and state-owned enterprises to widely establish the so-called "horizontal co-operation", the effort did not receive a positive response from township enterprises, finally ending up in failure.[43] However, if there is not a stable contractual relationship of division of labor and cooperation with the state-owned sector, the entry of the township enterprises would become a competitor of the state-owned enterprises. We believe that understanding the entry-competition relationship between township and state-owned enterprises is very important for explaining the rapid capital deepening of township enterprises. It is not the purpose of this paper to provide any theoretical explanation for the competition mode between the state-owned and township enterprises; on the contrary, we hope to provide some empirical description of the competition to help illustrate the basic reason of rapid increase of the capital-labor ratio of township enterprises.

In order to describe this mode of competition, we must first point out that the large-scale entry of township enterprises cannot be explained simply and separately by the "comparative advantages" of township enterprises compared with those of state-owned enterprises. Because many distortions under the planned economic system still existed at the beginning of the 80 s, the entry of township enterprises may be due to their so-called "comparative advantage" compared with the state-owned enterprises, or may be a rational response to the economic distortions in the factor and product market. As a matter of fact, the entry of township enterprises was helpful to rectify the overly heavy industrial structure and product structure in some areas where the demands had not been satisfied by the state-owned sector. In the labour intensive production areas, township enterprises did bring into full play their comparative advantage in making use of cheap labour.

[41] Tao Youzhi: *Mode of Southern Jiangsu and Way to Wealth*, Shanghai, Shanghai Academy of Social Sciences Press, 1988.

[42] This figure was indirectly obtained from the World Bank's research publications. See Byrd and Lin (1990).

[43] The Fudan University's Economic Research Centerconducted a large survey on the "horizontal cooperation" between the state-owned enterprises in Shanghai and township enterprises in other parts of the country in 1987, which provided us with substantial information. This information is worth careful analysis because it can help us understand the complex motivations and ways of cooperation between township and state-owned enterprises. See the report of the survey: Enterprise Reform and the Development of A New Road: A Collection of Investigation Reports of Horizontal Cooperation of Industrial Enterprises in Shanghai.

On other occasions, such as textile industry, the entry of township enterprises was more likely to be attracted by the distorted, high profit environment, and their entry actually did take away the output and profits from the state-owned enterprises. A study report published by the World Bank on China's enterprise reform (Byrd 1992) provided us with some background information of the structural features of China's industrial organizations in the 1980s. For example, China's textile industry typically exhibits a pattern of coexistence of multiple ownerships and enterprises of different sizes. Although there was a large number of state-owned large enterprises, up to early 80 s, among the 17,100 textile enterprises, 2/3 enterprises were small local enterprises, and only 1/3 belonged to the Ministry of Textile Industry and the textile industry bureau of local government. Among these, there were 3,261 state-owned enterprises, 2,314 urban collective enterprises, 66 joint ventures between state-owned and collective enterprises or with Chinese enterprises in Hong Kong (Sabin 1987).[44] But under these circumstances, it seems uncertain that the entry of township enterprises has improved the efficiency of the economy in general.[45] In fact, because of excessive entry and competition, the profitability of this sector has actually deteriorated. Naughton (1995) once analyzed the situation of township enterprises entering the textile industry. He found that because of the excessive use of labor by township enterprises, their production was no more efficient than that of state-owned enterprises. Therefore, he also tended to think that, in some manufacturing sectors, the entry and growth of township enterprises may actually have worsened the level of social welfare.

In the first case, although the township enterprises gave play to their comparative advantage, the fierce rival between township enterprises plus the fact that township enterprises are the properties of the community often endowed this competition with a typical "new classical adjustment" feature: a new market opportunity will quickly induce plenty of imitators to enter, with the result that the price and profit margins decline until the market is saturated, profits come to zero and equilibrium appeares (Byrd and Zhu 1990). Even though this kind of competition will lead to one-time improvement of efficiency, the resulting industrial organization formed no doubt lacks a sustained and dynamic improvement mechanism (such as innovation, restructuring, stable business relationship and reputation etc.). In terms of direct competition with state-owned enterprises, as the state-owned enterprises, especially

[44] With regard to sub-sectors, in 1990, the number of township enterprises entering the ferrous and non-ferrous metal smelting and rolling processing industries were 5,648 and 3,839; the number entering transportation equipment manufacturing industry and electronic and communication equipment manufacturing industry were 7,603 and 3,506. In the iron and steel industry dominated by the state-owned enterprises with the scale of increasing returns, township enterprises also occupy a considerable proportion. These township enterprises mainly produce the final products (steel products). The *Chinese Statistical Yearbook* (1995) shows that in 1994, the number of township enterprises producing steel reached 17,455, providing 26% of the total output value of iron and steel industry. Sabin (1987).

[45] Hallagan and Zhang (1996) developed a theoretical model of "excessive entry" for welfare analysis by which they discussed the welfare consequences of excessive entry. Recently, Young(2000), in his statistical analysis on the similarity of regional production structure in China, also seems to support this view.

large and medium-sized enterprises, have relatively high level of capital equipment, township enterprises are bound to be faced with the problem of how to overcome the higher market barriers. This means that the direct competition between township and state-owned enterprises is, in fact, a process in which township enterprises continuously try to narrow (and surpass) the level of equipment (i.e. capital-labor ratio) of the state-owned enterprises. This can be partly proved by the average size of the fixed assets of the new projects and the growth rate of the total investment of each project. In 1986, the average investment scale of fixed assets of new projects in rural enterprises was 175,100 *yuan*, and the average investment scale of each project was 172,100 *yuan*, while in 1992, the numbers were 428,300 *yuan* and 261,900 *yuan*, up 144.6% and 51.65% respectively compared with 1986.

The rapid deepening of capital achieved by ownship enterprises is naturally attributed to the support of local governments in credit. In the existing literature, the relationship between the local government and township enterprises has often been interpreted as a source of efficiency of township enterprises (Weitzman and Xu 1996; Nee 1992). This is mainly because it was found that the local government's intervention has reduced the high transaction cost for township enterprises to enter the market.[46] But what has been ignored is that the local government's intervention interfered the credit market and helped township enterprises to have a certain expectation, which led to widespread excessive entry and investment (excess production capacity). In the face of excessive entry, local government and township enterprises tend to further improve the level of equipment as a competitive strategy, because the intervention in the credit market by the local government has made acquisition of capital much easier than the organizational restructuring of existing production capacity. Therefore, it can be said that the overall involvement of local governments is not only the reason for the rapid expansion of township enterprises, but has also imposed constraints at the technical level on the sustained growth of township enterprises.

9.6 Time Pattern of Yield Change

The continued decline in the profitability of China's industrial sector since the reform is a well known fact. In Table 9.4, we used official data to give a time pattern of changes in profit margins of China's different industrial sectors over the years of 1985–1997. It is easy to see that the profitability of all industries has declined significantly. However, the problem is that although the decline of industrial sector's profit margins in the 80 s could be regarded as "normal fall" in the post-reform period, the continued deterioration since the 90 s apparently can no longer be explained as the "normal fall". We have further observed that the loss proportion and loss amount of China's industrial enterprises did not increase sharply and continuously until after 1989/1990 (Zhang 1998). In Fig. 9.7 we have shown the time trajectory of the losses

[46] Weitzman and Xu (1996), Nee (1992).

change of state-owned sector.[47] In order to highlight the rapid growth characteristics of losses after 1988/1989, we used the profits of the state-owned sector to subtract losses and regarded the "surplus" as the observation curve. It is easy to see that this "surplus" dropped rapidly after 1988/1989, and became negative ever since 1995. All of these observations seem to indicate that there is an obvious time pattern in the deterioration of the return on investment.

The key to explaining this time pattern clearly does not lie in the power of competition itself. In theory, competition pressure can improve corporate profitability rather than causing it to deteriorate. However, the positive effect of competition on profitability improvement can only exist in a mature "market structure" (Hallagan and Zhang 1998), and, for an economy in transition, a highly decentralized market and excessive intervention of local government (including the direct intervention in credits) can easily lead to the formation of an industrial organizational structure of "excessive entry". The basic hypothesis we want to develop is that, from a deeper perspective, the continued deterioration of profit rate of the manufacturing sector has resulted in serious low efficiency reflected in excessive competition, excessive investment and cumulative production capacity being left idle since the 90 s. In other words, the mode of continued and significant deterioration of profit margins of Chinese industrial sector is mainly the result of excessive entry and investment. Therefore, all of these results should help explain the continuing deterioration in the return on investment.

To find the empirical evidence to support our hypothesis statistically, we need to make some simple inferences. We focus here on two testable propositions: first, the rise in the capital-labor ratio in China's industrial sector will have a significant negative impact on sector profitability. A basic basis for this proposition is that excessive competition will lead to a rapid rise in the capital-labor ratio in China's industrial sector, thus speeding up the process of capital deepening. The statistical tests for this proposition can be carried out by estimating the sector's profit margin function to be explained. If we can find statistically that the rise in the capital-labor ratio has a significant negative impact on sector profitability, we can see the results as empirical support for our hypothesis. The second testable proposition is that the accumulation and inactivity of China's industrial production capacity generally have limited the improvement of the profitability of industrial enterprises. The basic theory of this proposition is that the idle production capacity is the result of overinvestment and excessive competition, and the continued growth of loss-making enterprises has led to the "erosion" and deterioration of the profit margin of Chinese industrial sector (Zhang 2001).

In Table 9.5 we reported and summarizzed the estimation results of the profit rate function of state-owned and township enterprises as well as all the industrial sectors.[48] The estimation results of state-owned and township enterprise sectors (1) and (2) were from Keijiro et al. (2000), and the estimation results of profit rate

[47] In fact, time mode of the entire industrial sector is similar to that of the state-owned sector losses, see Zhang (1998).

[48] Data comes from the Data Appendix of this article.

Table 9.4 Changes in profit margins of China's industrial sectors during the late period of reform (1985–1997). Unit: %

Year	All the industrial sectors	State-owned sectors	Collective sectors	Other sectors	Heavy industry	Light industry	Large-sized enterprises	Medium-sized enterprises	Small-sized enterprises
1985	23.76	23.53	24.57	28.21	20.29	31.84			
1986	20.43	20.65	19.36	23.29	17.23	27.46	22.25	22.41	17.76
1987	19.95	20.3	18.19	24.92	17.03	25.96	22.6	20.78	17.03
1988	20.53	20.63	19.76	24.66	17.25	26.91	22.12	21.55	18.5
1989	16.79	17.18	15.43	16.21	14.36	21.3	18.3	17.65	14.78
1990	12.2	12.43	11.48	11.31	9.95	16.35	14.18	12.17	9.99
1991	11.88	11.81	11.89	12.85	10.17	14.95	13.72	11.25	10.03
1992	9.89	9.71	10.06	11.08	9.5	10.51	11.15	9.64	8.59
1993	10.33	9.7	10.94	11.6	10.55	9.94	11.88	9.42	8.97
1994	10.21	9.8	10.71	12	9.84	10.87	12.6	7.9	8.28
1995	8.01	7.2	7.24	15.41			10.57	6.19	6.22
1996	7.11	6.54	8.14	9.96	6.62	8.02	8.98	4.78	5.64
1997	6.92	6.27	8.27	8.29	6.26	8.14	8.51	4.63	5.71

Note The profit margin in in table is the rate of profits and taxes on fund. Until 1985, there was no official statistical data on the profitability of non state-owned enterprises (various ownerships) in China

Data source The 1985–1992 data are from the *Chinese Industrial Economic Statistical Yearbook*(1993); the state sector data of 1993–1997 are from the *Chinese Industrial Economic Statistical Yearbook* (1998); the total data of the country are from the *Chinese Statistical Yearbook* (1994–1998); other data are from the *Chinese Statistical Yearbook*, among which, the rate of profit of other sectors refers to the arithmetic average of profit rate of private, joint-stock, shareholding, foreign-funded, Chinese, Hong Kong and Taiwan investment enterprises

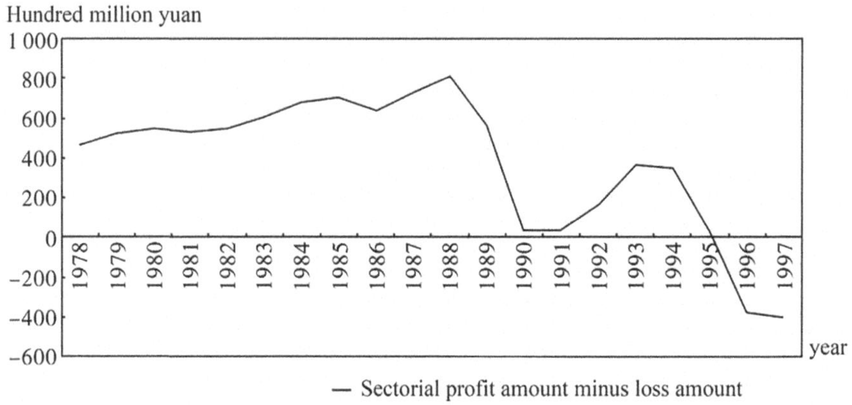

Fig. 9.7 Fluctuaion curve of profit "surplus" of China's state-owned sector (1978–1997)

(5) of all industrial sector (sample) were from another study of me (Liang, Zhang, Murakami, 2000). In the estimation of sector's profit rate function, the explanatory variables that were mainly considered are the capital-labor ratio, scale of investment and thte share of entry of township enterprises. According to our explanation of the nature of the decline in economic growth in China, we expect to find in statistics: ① the rise of the capital-labor ratio has a remarkable negative effect on the profit rate of sectors; ② continued entry of township enterprises took away the profits of state-owned enterprises, causing the profit rate of the enterprise to deteriorate; ③ the scale of investment of enterprises has no significant "scale effect" on the profit margin". For the state-owned and the township enterprise sectors, the profit rate estimation function used for regression is:

$$\Pi_{it} = \alpha_{it} + \sum \alpha_{ij} D_{ij} + \beta_1 (K/L)_{it} + \beta_2 (K)_{it} + \gamma (X)_{it} + \varepsilon_{it} \tag{9.11}$$

Π_{it} is the profit margin, D is the characteristics of the industrial sector, K/L is capital-labor ratio, K is investment scale of enterprise, X represents the share of entry of township enterprises, ε is the error term, if it is assumed to conform to normal distribution. Statistical tests used the "panel data" (i.e. $t = 6$, $i = 39$) of 39 industrial sectors over 1987–1992 with 234 samples. (3) and (4) in the table use the share of township enterprises with the lag of one year, thus the data samples decreased to 195. In addition, the following form is used for the mixed profit margin estimation function of entire industrial samples:

$$\begin{aligned} \Pi_{ij} = {} & b_i + b_1 \ln(K/L_{ij}) + b_2 \ln(K_{ij}) + b_3 ENG_{ij} + b_4 EXP_{ij} \\ & + b_5 WEL_{ij} + b_6 SDY + b_7 TDY + u \end{aligned} \tag{9.12}$$

Π_{ij} is the profit rate (%) for i (th) 4-digit industry and j (th) type of ownership, K/L_{ij} is the capital-labor ratio, K_{ij} is the scale of investment in fixed assets, ENG_{ij} is

Table 9.5 Fixed effect estimation of profit margin functions of Chinese industry

	State-owned enterprises (1)	Township enterprises (2)	State-owned enterprises (3)	Township enterprises (4)	The whole industry
Data in 1987–1955:					
Share of township enterprises (that very year)	−0.41** (−4.59)	0.19* (1.94)	–	–	–
Share of township enterprises (last year)	–	–	−0.22* (−2.27)	0.17 (1.45)	–
Capital–labor ratio (State-owned enterprises)	−0.19** (−3.55)	–	− 0.02 (−0.28)		–
Capital–labor ratio (Township enterprises)	–	−0.58* (−2.25)	–	−0.93** (−3.55)	–
Enterprise scale (State-owned enterprises)	0.15 (0.83)	–	0.16 (0.74)		–
Enterprise scale (State-owned enterprises)	–	30.83* (2.13)	–	38.13** (2.74)	–
Census data in 1995:					
Ln (capital–labor ratio)	–	–	–	–	−0.013** (2.73)
Ln (Capital deposit)	–	–	–	–	0.007* (2.57)

Note The numbers in parentheses is t statistical quantity. * is 5% significant level while ** is 1% significant level

Source The regression results of 1987-1992 are from Keijiro et al. (2000); the results of the regression of 1995 census data are from Liang et al. (2000)[49]

the proportion (%) of engineers in industrial sectors, EXP_{ij} is the proportion of exports (%), WEL_{ij} is the welfare payment proportion (%). SDY is the dummy variable of state-owned enterprise, and TDY is the dummy variable of township enterprise. a is the constant of the regression equation, $a_k (k = 1, \ldots, 9)$ is the coefficient, e is

[49] Liang et al. (2000).

the error term. b_i is a constant related to the i (th) 4-digit industry, which remains unchanged among firms of different ownership types, but varies among different 4-digit industries.$b_h = (h = 1, \ldots, 7)$ is the coefficient, and u is the error term. It is important to point out that in estimating the profit margin function of all industries, we used the "cross section" sample data (sample number 1266[50]) provided by the third National Industrial Census (1995). In fact, if we can find a statistically significant negative correlation between the profit rate and capital-labor ratios of sectors in the cross section, then this empirical result may after all be regarded as a significant empirical support for our theoretical hypothesis.

In order to highlight the estimated results we expected, only the coefficients of the variables that are related to our problems are given selectively in Table 9.5. According to the regression results (1) and (2), we found that the rise of capital-labor ratio and increase in the share of township enterprises have a significant negative impact on the state-owned sector's profit margins (their coefficient is negative and their absolute value of t statistical quantity is very high). Considering that (1) and (2) are the estimated results obtained by using "panel data" of 1987–1992, we have reason to believe that decline in profit margins of the state-owned sector in this period of time can be explained by the rise of capital-labor ratio and the entry of township enterprises. Furthermore, according to (2), the rise of capital-labor ratio of township enterprises also reduced the profitability of township enterprises. In order to avoid the problem of simultaneous equation bias, (3) and (4) are the regression results gotten from the share of the township enterprises with a lag of one year, but their results are basically do not differ much from that of (1) and (2). Moreover, as far as the township enterprises are concerned, the conspicousness of the capital - labor ratio and investment scale of enterprises have been significantly improved.

The fifth column (5) in Table 9.5 is the regression result of the profit function (2) by using the cross-sectional data provided by the third industrial census. Here we left out discussions of the regression results of other variables, giving only the estimated values of the coefficient of capital-labor ratio and scale of fixed asset. As we have expected, the rising capital-labor ratio has a significant negative impact on the industrial sector's profits, so does the scale of investment in fixed assets that has barely produced any positive effects on the profit rate, for 1% added value of capital stock only increased the rate of profit by 0.007%. This result is essentially the same as the results of (1) and (3). However, we noted that in results (2) and (4), the scale coefficient of township enterprises is positive and very large, which seems puzzling.[51] A possible explanation is that the regression used very simple equations that contained only a small number of explanatory variables, so the data is rather crude. Another possibility is that, although the average size of township enterprises

[50] Strictly speaking, almost all explanatory variables in our model are not exogenous variables, but endogenous ones. However, it is difficult to construct simultaneous models because of the lack of proper variable definitions. We can only assume that these variables are predetermined and/or determined by institutions.

[51] Another possibility is that, because the capital stock is the nominal value, therefore, the estimated value of coefficient of the scale of township enterprise is positive, which, to a certain extent, also reflects the fact that the newer and more expensive machines have a higher quality.

Table 9.6 Constituent shares of China's GDP and their contribution (1995–1999)

Year	1995	1996	1997	1998	1999
Final consumption	58.1 (6.2)	59.2 (6.3)	58.8 (4.4)	58.7 (5.4)	60.3 (6.8)
Capital formation	34.2 (2.9)	33.6 (2.9)	33.8 (2.8)	37.4 (2.1)	37.0 (2.0)
Increased of inventories	6.0 (1.0)	5.1 (−0.06)	3.8 (−0.8)	2.4 (−2.6)	1.2 (−1.9)
Net exports	1.7 (0.4)	2.1 (0.45)	3.6 (1.5)	3.9 (0.3)	2.7 (−1.7)
GDP	100 (10.5)	100 (9.6)	100 (8.8)	100 (7.8)	100 (7.1)

Note The unit in this table is %. The data in parentheses in the line of GDP is the growth rate of GDP. The data in the remaining brackets are the contribution of constituent shares to the GDP growth rate. Our method of calculating "contribution" is: first, calculate each year's marginal value of each constituent item to GDP, and then multiply the yearly growth rate of GDP respectivley. All data were processed by obtaining approximate value
Source State Bureau of Statistics: *Chinese Statistical Yearbook* (2000), pp. 5–66, Beijing, China Statistics Press, 2000

is very larger, large township enterprises have more advantages than small township enterprises in the acquisition of capital, owing to the high incompleteness of the capital market.

Before discussing the effect of idle production capacity on the profitability of industrial sector, it is necessary for us to briefly discuss the changing features of capital formation in recent years in China, because the cumulative idle production capacity is the product of the continued expansion of capital formation. We have found statistically that since the 1990s, not only has the annual capital formation rate been maintained between 35 and 40% of the GDP, but its average annual growth rate is significantly higher than GDP.[52] Notably after the 90 s, though, in the growth of capital formation, the proportion of the increase in inventories (i.e., investment in inventories) has exhibited a downward trend. In Table 9.6, we present the composition of China's GDP in 1995–1999 and the contribution of each component to the GDP growth rate. We noted that, in China's total GDP, the proportion of inventory investment, relatively speaking, was not only very small, but more importantly, continued to decline in GDP. For example, during 1995–1999, the proportions of inventory investment in GDP were 6%, 5.1%, 3.8%, 2.4% and 1.2% respectively. However, the question is, while most economists believe the aggregate demand has been rather inadequate over the years, why haven't they observed the trend of faster growth of inventories?

The reason behind this statistical number, or the trend that inventories have not shown a faster growth since the 1990s is largely because the fixed asset investment is growing faster. This is also the reason we often see in statistics that the sale rate of capital goods has almost always maintained at the 100% level. In other words, the capital goods produced by the industrial sector have hardly become the increase

[52] So, there is obviously a lack of empirial basis to attribute the continued decline of the Chinese economic growth rate in recent years to the decrease of total demand (among which consumption demand and investment demand accounted for more than 90%). Also, there is confusion of concept in theory.

in inventories, but have been bought by investors to create new production capacity. Because of this, the faster growth of fixed asset investment is bound to continue to be accumulated into idle production capacity. This includes low operating rate of enterprises, low investment in introducing equipment, high vacancy rates of buildings and so on. It is almost certain that the rapid accumulation of idle production capacity has rapidly become the most serious institutional problem facing China's industrial growth since the 90 s. Moreover, the utilization rate data of production capacity of 112 kinds of industrial products obtained during the 1995 third national industrial census revealed the situation of the excess production capacity accumulated by overinvestment in the past in the industrial economy.

Because of the defect and restriction of production capacity data, it is difficult to make a systematic statistical test on the correlation between the loss-making model of China's industrial sector and excess production capacity. However, as a simple and partial analysis, we can refer to the research conclusion of Lo (2000). In the publications of the third national industrial census conducted in 1995, Lo classified the utilization rate of the production capacity of 53 products out of 112 kinds of industrial products and placed them in the industry classification data of loss-making sectors, thus making possible the relevant analysis of single variable. He used three measuring indicators of the degree of industry losses. They are loss ratio, loss rate (1) and loss rate (2), among which, the loss ratio is the number of loss-making enterprises and the number of all industrial enterprises, loss rate (1) is the ratio of amount of losses and net value of fixed assets, and loss rate (2) is the ratio of amount of losses and net industrial output. He then used the utilization rate of production capacity of given industries as an explanatory variable and regressed the correlation between the utilization rate of production capacity and the three los-making indicators. The regression result is shown in Table 9.7. Obviously, for the three loss indicators, the coefficients of productivity utilization rate are negative and statistically significant. This means that the three loss indicators have been largely explained by excess production capacity levels.

9.7 Conclusion

Although China's economy maintained the highest average growth rate in the world in the past 20 years, its economic growth trajectory seems to have deviated from the characteristic periods of fluctuation in the 80 s and has been declining since the mid 1990s. Some economists reassessed the growth rate and argued that after 1997/1998, the economy's real growth rate is much lower than the official figures. In fact, if we simply look backe at 1992–1994, the period of rapid growth, we can observe clearly the mode of continued decline of economic growth rate after that period, while before 1995, economic growth was volently fluctuating. Such an empirical observation is the reason for us to shift our attention to the technological (long-term) problem of China's economic growth.

Table 9.7 Change of loss and change of utilization rate of production capacity: regression analysis (1995)

	Variable being Explained		
	Proportion of loss making enterprises	Loss rate (1)	Loss rate (2)
Explanatory variable			
Constant	38.496 (10.523)**	10.192 (8.406)**	16.729 (5.369)***
Utilization ratio of production capacity	−0.166 (−2.950)**	−0.087 (−4.661)**	−0.112 (−2.342)*
Adjusted R^2	0.129	0.285	0.0794
Observation value	53	53	53

Note Loss rate (1) = amount of loss/fixed assets net value; loss rate (2) = amount of loss/ net industrial output value. The numbers in parentheses are t statistical quantity. * and ** were 5% and 1% significant level respectively

As we have noted, we do not deny that the growth of inputs of factors is the main source of economic growth of China, but the problem is, for an economy with so abundant a labor supply, why its economic growth has encountered so many difficulties so soon? We have found in this article that from the technical perspective, the answer to this question lies in the fact that capital-labor ratio has risen much too quickly, so that the rate of return on investment has suffered a sustained and significant deterioration trend after the 90 s. Although since the reform, enterprise's technical efficiency or production efficiency (TFP) has been improved significantly, the investment efficiency is on serious decline after the 90 s, and the industrial sector's profitability and growing losses have dramatically deteriated after the 90 s as well (Zhang 2001). So, logically, the continued decline of China's growth rate since the mid-90s should be the consequence of excessive speed of capital deepening and investment income decline, instead of being interpreted as the problem of insufficient aggregate demand in the short term. Moreover, according to our explanatory logic, the decline in aggregate demand since 1995 is only the result of the decline in economic growth, not the reason for the decline in economic growth.

It is found in this article that after the growth of China's economy in the 1980s and the supernormal growth in 1992–1994, a series of inefficiencies in the formation of capital have begun to show up. The main reason for the result is the mixed transition system known as over investment and over competition. Due to excessive investment and competition, the choice of technology by enterprises showed a deviation of the substitution of capital for labor, thus the technological path gradually deviated from the natural structure of factors, and the capital-labor ratio continued to rise that led to the speeding up of the process of capital deepening, resulting in continued and significant deterioration of investment yields. On this issue, our explanation and the serious evaluation on China's economic reform made by recently are consistent logically. In his recent studies, (2000) confirmed from the statistics that a convergence structure gradually appeared in the Chinese industrial sector since the reform among regions, with the result that the duplication of production capacity and interregional competition have posed a serious threat to the production capacity of the Chinese industrial sector's profitability, resulting in regional production patterns deviating more and more from their comparative advantage. He found that this deviation even worsened after the 90s.

Our research revealed an important institutional distortion in our economic growth, which has led to excessive investment and excessive inter-regional competition. In a typical centralized planning economy, the prices of factors were seriously distorted to subsidize industrialization and urbanization by "creating" many artificial industrial rents. In transition economies, the planned control of essential factors (mainly resources and capital) has been relaxed and replaced by the control of local government. Similarly, local governments, encouraged to seek rents, are competing to develop profitable manufacturing industry. The formation of capital continues to increase the ratio of capital to labor. In terms of financing, although the investment system since the reform has undergone great changes, this change has not been accompanied by the rapid development of the real capital (ownership) market. The reform of the investment system has turned financial funds into credit funds, and investment by centralized decision was replaced by decentralized decision-making. However, because no effective capital ownership system has been set up, capital has not really become a scarce factor, so the use of the credit funds is still largely subject to government intervention. Under such a financial system, the excessive use of funds is quite common, which can be seen from the generally high debt ratio of Chinese industrial enterprises (including state-owned and township enterprises).

There is no doubt that the continued deterioration of the profitability of the industrial sector, as well as the capital formation system and financial system that seriously threaten the yield of investment, will be the severe constraints on the rapid growth of China's economy in the future. Their existence and the roles they play will also make China to pay a higher and higher price for maintainng its rapid economic growth, because under the current system, a large number of inefficient capital, once formed, will further strengthen the inefficient allocation of financial resources. And in the short term, to encourage investment may even further strengthen the formation of long-term factors. All these problems will continue to have a negative impact on the sustained growth.

9.8 Data Appendix

The original data for this article are mainly derived from two existing studies. They are the empirical study of Zhang and Shi (2000), and the study of Lo (1999). The study of Jun Zhang and Shi Shaohua mainly depends on the statistical data of aggregate output, capital and labor of Chinese economy during 1952–1998. Among them, the aggregate data of output and the number of workers were taken from various volumns of *Chinese Statistical Yearbook* over the years, and the output (GDP, unit is of 100 million *yuan*) was converted in accordance with the constant price of 1990. The data of capital of 1952–1990 were taken from the estimation study of He (1992) on the scale of China's asset stock. We also calculated the yearly capital stock for the period of 1992–1998 by following his method and according to annual investment in fixed assets of the whole country during 1992–1998 (Table 9.8).

In calculating the capital-labor ratio classified by the system ownerships, we calculated the nominal value and actual value of the ratio respectively. In calculating the actual value, we used the data provided by Lo (1999) in his paper titled Re-Evaluation of the Performance of China's State-Owned Industrial Enterprises: 1980–1996. In this aggregate data, the capital stock and labor force were subdivided according to the state sector, the collective sector and large and medium-sized sector. Among them, the data of capital have been deflated according to the price index of capital. The capital price index of 1980–1991 were from Jefferson et al. (1996)'s research, and 1992–1998 capital price index was calculated by me based on the stable relationship between the capital price index and the ex factory price index of industrial output. The method converting nominal value to the actual value is as follows: first, $\Delta K_t = K_t - K_{t-1}$; second, $\Delta K\prime_t = \Delta K_t / P_k$; third, $K\prime_t = K\prime_{t-1} + \Delta K\prime_t$ out of which K is nominal value, $K\prime$ is actual value and P_k is capital price index (Table 9.9).

Table 9.8 Capital-output ratio of China's economy (1978–1998)

Year	K	Y	K/Y ratio	K/Y growth rate
1978	24,501	6584.4	3.721068	
1979	26,574	7083.1	3.751747	0.008245
1980	28,654	7637.6	3.751702	$-1.2\ \mathrm{E}^{-05}$
1981	30,596	8038.5	3.806183	0.014522
1982	32,717	8766.2	3.732176	−0.01944
1983	35,076	9718.8	3.609088	−0.03298
1984	37,936	11,192.4	3.389443	−0.06086
1985	41,828	12,699.6	3.293647	−0.02826
1986	45,937	13,824	3.322989	0.008909
1987	50,254	15,424.7	3.258021	−0.01955
1988	55,119	17,165.1	3.211109	−0.0144
1989	59,955	17,862.1	3.356548	0.045293
1990	64,850	18,547.9	3.496353	0.041651
1991	70,045	20,253.2	3.458466	−0.01084
1992	76,553	23,137.1	3.308669	−0.04331
1993	84,872	26,258.1	3.232222	−0.02311
1994	94,695	29,583.1	3.200983	−0.00966
1995	105,590	32,690.9	3.229951	0.00905
1996	117,585	35,825	3.282205	0.016178
1997	130,420	38,978.9	3.345913	0.01941
1998	145,089	42,019.3	3.452913	0.031979

Table 9.9 Capital-labor ratio of China's industry (1980–1996)

Year	Capital (the nominal value, unit is of 100 million yuan)			Capital (the actual value, unit is of 100 million *yuan)*			Labor force (ten thousand)			The nominal capital-labor ratio			The actual capital-labor ratio		
	SOE	COE	LME	SOE	COE	LME	SOE	COE	LME	SOE	COE	LME	SOE	COE	LME
1980	2567	268	1946	2473	256	1873	3179	1688	1854	0.807487	0.158768	1.049622	0.777918	0.151659	1.010248
1981	2709	336	2081	2634	300	2010	3328	1879	1983	0.814002	0.178819	1.04942	0.791466	0.159659	1.013616
1982	2914	386	2252	2797	356	2155	3455	2035	2091	0.843415	0.189681	1.076997	0.809551	0.174939	1.030607
1983	3161	438	2461	3000	402	2326	3528	2087	2014	0.895975	0.209871	1.221946	0.85034	0.192621	1.154916
1984	3396	510	2673	3203	453	2501	3630	2258	2024	0.935537	0.225864	1.320652	0.822369	0.20062	1.235672
1985	4026	660	3004	3521	536	2705	3783	2545	2172	1.064235	0.259332	1.383057	0.930743	0.210609	1.245396
1986	4544	823	3445	3906	639	2959	3945	2814	2299	1.151838	0.292466	1.498478	0.990114	0.227079	1.287081
1987	5242	1017	4033	4261	744	3260	4080	3010	2441	1.284804	0.337874	1.652192	1.044363	0.247176	1.335518
1988	6040	1241	4736	4665	857	3607	4192	3112	2558	1.44084	0.398779	1.851446	1.112834	0.275386	1.410086
1989	7033	1478	5700	5079	965	3992	4285	3114	2712	1.641307	0.474631	2.10177	1.185298	0.309891	1.471976
1990	8088	1674	6731	5506	1055	4407	4352	3088	2865	1.848456	0.542098	2.349389	1.265165	0.341645	1.53822
1991	9507	1919	8155	5986	1141	4883	4463	3141	3050	2.130181	0.610952	2.67377	1.34125	0.36326	1.600984
1992	10,983	2236	9968	6490	1238	5444	4529	3178	3298	2.425039	0.703587	3.022438	1.432987	0.389553	1.650697
1993	11,881	2729	10,990	6916	1407	5945	4494	3231	3557	2.643747	0.84463	3.089682	1.538941	0.435469	1.671352
1994	13,673	3520	14,217	7443	1652	6825	4261	3180	3607	3.208871	1.106918	3.941503	1.746773	0.519497	1.892154
1995	17,474	4294	18,848	8447	1902	8160	4136	3585	3891	4.224855	1.197768	4.843999	2.042311	0.530544	2.097147
1996	22,141	5075	23,888	9445	2069	9238	4004	3442	3988	5.52972	1.474433	5.98997	2.358891	0.601104	2.316449

Note SOE is state-owned enterprise; COE is collective enterprise; and LME is a large and medium enterprise

Author's Note

This paper was written during my visit to the Harvard University's Yenching Institute from September 2000 to September 2001, which was later published in the first issue of *China Economic Quarterly* in 2002 run by the Chinese Economic Research Center of Peking University. Before its publication, however, I had revised this article from different perspectives, resulting in two more concise versions. The first version is titled Understanding Chinese Capital Formation and Economic Growth which was published in the first issue of *World Economy Papers* in 2002. The second version is called Capital Formation, Industrialization and Economic Growth: Transition Characteristics in China. The latter was actually prepared for and read at the International Conference on economic transition and institutional change held in Hangzhou in April 2002. In June of that year, at the international conference sponsored by Wuhan University on the theme Development Economics and China's Economic Development, I read this paper again. At the same time, the latter version of the paper was published on the 6th issue of *Economic Research Journal* in 2002 after being revised.

In this article I give an explanation of the decline of China's economic growth based on the productivity rate of capital or the efficiency of investment. This explanation is based on the conceptual framework of Solow's economics of growth. In this framework, excessive growth of capital will lead to a downward trend in output growth. In China, depite a surplus supply of labor, there is always an excessive demand for capital rather than labor, thus making the technical path of Chinese economic growth gradually deviate from the the best way of using less capital and more labor. In aggregate terms, such a technical bias has led to a sustained and significant rise in the capital-output ratio over the past 10 years. So, I measured the Chinese economic capital-output ratio since the reform in this article, did an empirical analysis of its changing mode, and further studied the time mode of changes of total factor productivity (TFP) and capital density (capital-labor ratio) within the framework of breaking down the capital-output ratio. The paper was widely cited after its publication.

References

W. Byrd, *Chinese Industrial Firms under Reform*, Oxford, Oxford University Press, 1992

W. Byrd, Q. Lin, *China's Rural Industry: Structure, Development and Reform*, Oxford, Oxford University Press, 1990.

W. Byrd, N. Zhu, Market Interactions and Industrial Structure, in: W. Byrd, Q. Lin, China's Rural *Industry: Structure, Development and Reform*, Oxford, Oxford University Press, 1990.

K. Chen, H. Wang, Y. Zheng, G. Jefferson, T. Rawski, Productivity Change in Chinese Industry:1953-1985, *Journal of Comparative Economics*, 1988, 12, pp.570-591

Chen Jianbo: Acquisition and Choices of Technology by Township Enterprises in the Evolution of the Market Economy, *Economy Research*, 1999 (4)

D. Chinn, Rural Poverty and the Structure of Farm Household Income in Developing Countries: Evidence fromT aiwan, *Economic Development and Cultural Change*, 1979, 27 (2), pp.283-301.

Dension, Why Growth Rates Differ, Brookings Institute, Washington, D.C, 1967.

D.Dolar, K.Sokoloff, Patterns of Productivity Growth in South Korean Manufacturing Industries: 1963-1979, *Journal of Development Economics*, 1990, 33, pp.309-327.

Easterly, William, Stanley Fischer: The Soviet Economic Decline: Historical and Republican Data. Working Paper No.4735 (1994).

Jefferson, Gary H., Rawski, Thomas G., Wang, Li, and Zheng, Yuxin: Ownership, Productivity Change, and Financial Performance in Chinese Industry, *Journal of Comparative Economics*, 2000 (28), 786–813.

W. Hallagan, J. Zhang: Reform Starting Points and Reform Paths: A Feasible Simulation,E conomic Studies, 1996 (1).

W. Halagan, J. Zhang, Excessive Entry in Transitional Economices, manuscript, 1998

Y. Hayami, Toward an Alternative Paradigm of Economic Development: An Introduction, in: Y. Hayami, *Toward the Rural-Based Development of Commerce and Industry: Selected Experiences from East Asia*, The World Bank, Washington D.C., 1998.

He Juhuang: Assets Estimation in China, *Quantitative Economics and Technical Economy Research*, 1992 (8).

G. Jefferson, T. Rawski, Y. Zheng, Growth, Efficiency, and Convergence in China's State and Collective Industry, Economic Development and Cultural Change, 1992, 40, pp.239-266.

G. Jefferson, T. Rawski, Y. Zheng, Chinese Industrial Productivity: Trends, Measurement and Recent Development, *Journal of Comparative Economics*, 1996, 23, pp.146-180.

Jefferson, Rawski, Zheng Yuxin: Estimation and Reliability Analysis of the Changing Trend in Chinese Industrial Productivity since the Reform, *Economic Research*, 1995 (12), 10–22.

Zhang Jun: *Dual Track Economics: Economic Reform in China 1978-1992*, Shanghai SDX Joint Publishing Company, Shanghai People's Publishing House, 1997

Zhang Jun: Information Costs, Limited Reason and Planned Simplification: An Analysis of the Structure of Chinese Planned Economy, *Economic Development Research*, 1992 (2).

O Keijiro, Liu Deqiang, Murakami Naoki: *Chinese Industrial Reform*, Shanghai, Shanghai SDX Joint Publishing Company, Shanghai People's Publishing House, 2000

Kim, Jong-il, Lawrence J. Lau: The Sources of Economic Growth of the East Asian Newly Industrialized Countries. *Journal of The Japanese and International Economies*, 8 (1994), pp. 235–271.

See Li Jingwen, Zheng Youjing, Yang Shuzhuang, Gong Feihong: An Analysis of Chinese Economic Growth, *Chinese Social Sciences*, 1992 (1).

Wang Lian, Wang Xiaolu: Estimation of the Reliability of Statistical Data of China's Economic Growth, *Economic Research*, 2000 (10).

J. Liang, J. Zhang, N. Murakami, The Determinates of Profitability in China's Manufacturing Industry: Evidence from the Census Data, working paper, *Faculty of Economics*, Tokyo, 2000.

Yifu Lin, Cai Fang, Li Zhou: *Chinese Miracle: Developmental Strategy and Economic Reform*, Shanghai, Shanghai SDX Joint Publishing Company, 1994.

D. Lo, Reappraising the Performance of China's State-Owned Industrial Enterprises:1980-1996, *Cambridge Journal of Economics*, 1999, 23, pp.693-718.

Lo, Dic, Y-S Cheng: Explaining the financial performance of Chinese industrial enterprises. *Economic Research Journal*, 2000 (7), pp. 39–47.

R. McKinnon, Gradual versus Rapid Liberalization in Socialist Economies: the Problem of Macroeconomic Control, in The World Bank: Proceedings of the World Bank Annual Conference on Development Economics, 1994

D. Mead, Of Contracts and Subcontracts: Small, Firms in Vertically Disintegrated Production/ Distribution Systems in LDCs, *World Development*, 1984, 12 (11), pp.1095-1106.

Meng Lian, Wang Xiaolu: An Estimation of the Reliability of Statistic Data on China's Economic Growth, *Economic Research*, 2000 (10).

N. Murakami, D. Liu, K. Otsuka, Technical and Allocative Efficiency among Socialist Enterprises: The Case of the Garment Industry in China, *Journal of Comparative Economics*, 1994, 19, pp.410-433

N. Murakami, D. Liu, K. Otsuka, Market Reform, Division of Labor and Increasing Advantage of Small Scale Enterprises: The Case of Machine Tool Industry in China, *Journal of Comparative Economics*, 1996, 23, pp.256-277

B. Naughton, *Growing Out of the Plan: Chinese Economic Reform*, Cambridge, Cambridge University Press, 1995

V. Nee, Organizational Dynamics of Market Transition: Hybrid Form, Property Rights, and Mixed Economy in China, *Administrative Science Quarterly*, 1992, 37 (1)

K. Ostuka, Rural Industrialization in East Asia, paper presented at the International Conference on the Institutional Foundation of Economic Development in East Asia, Tokyo, 1996.

K. Otsuka, Rural Industrialization in East Asia, paper presented at the International Conference on the Institutional Foundation of Economic Developmentin East Asia, Tokyo,1998.

Otsuka, Keijiro, Abhijit Banerjee: Rural Industrialization in East Asia. (1998).

H. Patrick, T. Rohlen, Small Scale Family Enterprises, in: K. Yammamura, Y.Yasuba, *The Political Economy in Japan*, Stanford, Stanford University Press, 1987.

S. Radelet, J. Sachs, Asia's Reemergence, *Foreign, Affairs*, 1997, 11/12, pp.44-59

G. Ranis, Another Look at the East Asian Miracle, *World Bank Economic Review*, 1995, 9 (3), pp.509-534.

G. Ranis, F. Stewart, Rural Nonargicultural Activities in Development: Theory and Application, *Journal of Development Economics*, 1993, 40 (1), pp.75-101.

L.Sabin, The Qinghe WoolenTextile Mill, in: W. Byrd, *Chinese Industrial Firms under Reform*, Oxford, Oxford UniversityPress, 1992.

J. Sachs, W. Woo, Structural Factors in Economic Reforms of China, Eastern Europe and the Former Soviet Union, *Economic Policy*, 1994, 4.

P.A. Samuelson, R. M. Solow: Analytical Aspects of Anti-Inflation Policy, *American Economic Review*, 1960, 50 (2), pp. 177–194.

R. Solow, Technical Progress, Capital Formation and Economic Growth, *American Economic Review*, 1962, 52, pp.76–86.E

State Bureau of Statistics: *Chinese Industrial Economic Statistical Yearbook* (1992), Beijing, China Statistics Press, 1992.

Thomas G. Rawski: What is happening to China's GDP statistics? *China Economic Review*, 2001, 12 pp. 347–354.

S. Watanabe, Entrepreneurshuip in Small Enterprises in Japane' s Manufacturing, *International Labor Review*, 1979102 (6), pp.531–576.

M. Weitzman, C. Xu, Chinese Township-Village Enterprises as Vaguely Defined Cooperatives, *Journal of Comparative Economics*, 1996, 18, pp.121–145.

A. Young, *A Tale of Two Cities: Accumulation and Technical Change*, in Hong Kong and Singapore, Cambridge, MIT Press, 1992.

Young, Alwyn: Lessons from the East Asian NICS: A Contrarian View. *European Economic Review*, 1994, 38 (3–4), pp. 964–973.

A. Young, The Razor's Edge: Distortions and Incremental Reform in the People's Republic of China, *Quarterly Journal of Economics*, 2000, 4

Tao Youzhi: *Mode of Southern Jiangsu and Way to Wealth*, Shanghai, Shanghai Academy of Social Sciences Press, 1988.

J. Zhang, Market Size, Scale Economies, and the Pattern of Loss Making in China's Industry: 1978-1997, *East Asian Review*, 2000, 3 (3), pp.1–27.

Zhang Jun, Halagan: Excessive Entry in Transition Economy: An Economic Analysis of the Duplication of Construction, *Journal of Fudan University* (1), 1998.

Zhang Jun, Han Xianwang: The Soviet Union's Mode of Growth: A Review, *Economy Research*, 1996 (8).

Zhang Jun, Shi Shaohua: Total Factor Productivity Change in Chinese Economy: 1952–1998, *World Economy Forum*, 2000 (2).

Zhang Jun: Demand, Scale Effect and the Loss Model of Chinese State-Owned Industry, *Economic Research*, 1998 (8).

Zhang Jun: Demand, Scale Effect and the Chinese State-Owned Industrial Loss Model, Economic Research, 1999 (8).
Zhang Jun: Changing Mode of Profit Rate of Chinese State-Owned Industrial Sector, 1980–1998, *Economic Research*, 2001 (3).

Part V
New Political Economics

Chapter 10
Decentralization and Growth: The Story of China

10.1 Introduction

Many economists have predicted that the transformation and rapid growth of China's economy over the past 30 years will have a profound impact on the development of economics. It is undeniable that over the years, modern economics has had an extraordinary impact on the transformation and growth of China's economy, and helped us understand many of the stories that have taken place in China over the past 30 years. But at the same time, China's economic transformation and growth experience are also affecting and promoting the development of economics. This is by no means a game of words. Werner Heisenberg, a famous German physicist, once said that it's the theory that determines what we can really see. The implication of this sentence is profound, not just for quantum physics. For economists, when they look at China's experience, they may often not find good experience before creating a theory, but it is easy for them to find good experience with theories. In fact, there are many ready-made theories and knowledge systems in the minds of economists, which determine, to a great extent, what economists can see in China's economic transition.

A good piece of evidence is the theory about "fiscal federalism" and the formation of Chinese empirical observation. Over the past 10 years, economists have shown a strong interest in China's intergovernmental fiscal relations and fiscal decentralization, and the research literature has increased rapidly. And behind these research documents, one can actually find very rich research literature about federalism. This may provide another footnote to Heisenberg's statement mentioned above.

Federalism is a very important constitutional system in the political system which divides the rights and obligations between the governments at higher and lower levels, and establishes the political order. Of course, as a result of historical and political traditions, though countries with a federal system are numerous in the world, they differ widely in their patterns. Even with countries belonging to the Commonwealth, the federal systems of Canada and Australia are at least a far cry from each other

J. Zhang, *Reform, Transformation and Growth*, Understanding China,
https://doi.org/10.1007/978-981-99-5712-5_10

in the fiscal sense. Because the institutional differences are always there, at least in the last half century, political scientists and economists have never been less interested in the study of fiscal federalism. These studies not only have provided a perspective for economists to observe Chinese experience after the reform, but more importantly, they wanted to find something they may not have been familiar with in their observation and study of Chinese experience in economic transition and growth.

China is not a federal state. But soon after the implementation of a mode of centralized planned economy in the 1950s, the argument of central and local powers around the plan management and financial revenue and expenditure management system has been the focus of policy and theories, resulting in repeated divisions, adjustments and compromise of powers between the central and local governments. It also led to the publication of the famous On the Ten Major Relationships written by Mao Zedong in 1956.

This phenomenon in China, however, is not typical and rarely seen in the mode of centrally planned economy. The Soviet model of centralized planning had always been based on the vertical planned control of producers by the central specialized departments, and the local government had no independent authority in finance. But China's planned economic model was branded as a "decentralized" from the very beginning. Even though the central authorities have made many attempts to restore its centralized power, the power of local governments has never been weakened. Every effort of centralization was short-lived, unsuccessful, and ended with a transition to a greater degree of separation of powers. Professor Wang Shaoguang, who is also a political scientist, once said that Mao Zedong himself did not like the Soviet centralized planning model from the bottom of his heart. He had been trying to smash the Soviet-style model and enforce the governance system of the "nominal monarch republic" economically.[1]

In short, as a result of the long period of evolution of the decentralized system of planning management and finance to the local government, especially through the "Cultural Revolution" and the large-scale decentralization drive in 1970,[2] China acquired a very different initial condition from the standard Soviet planned economy after it decided to implement the strategy of transformation of economic liberalization in 1978. This phenomenon later became an important empirical observation by some economists to explain the success of China's economic transformation.

[1] Wang Shaoguang (1997).

[2] The massive separation of powers in 1970 was also caused by strategic reason or reason of military preparation. Mao Zedong believed at that time that a new world war was about to break out, so this division of power had a more clear purpose for war preparation. To achieve this end, the whole country was divided into 10 cooperation zones, and the central committee of the Party called on the cooperation areas (including some provinces and municipalities) to set up their own industrial system to prepare for the war.

10.2 How Important is Decentralization?

On March 2–3, 2007, Macao University held an international conference on the theme of China's Economic Growth: Causes and Prospects, focusing on China's economic growth.[3] Professor Douglas North was invited to attend the meeting and delivered an important speech. In his speech he gave a clear account of the evolution of the history and institutions of Britain and Western Europe, and, as always, emphasized the importance of the institutions in economic growth. This is an important theory of the "new economic history", which holds that it is the "good system" that has led to economic growth rather than the opposite. Indeed, this theory can explain many important historical phenomena.

The "good system" Professor North mentioned probably always refers to that developed in Anglo-American countries, such as the clear definition and protection of private property, effective capital market, independent judicial procedure and efficient law enforcement, etc. It is obvious that China has not really set up such a system, nor does it have a system that can be compared with it. Therefore, the predictions made by Professor North's theory do not tally with China's experience. But most economists don't think his theory is wrong. "System is the most important" has been a widely accepted concept.

But economic growth is a complex phenomenon driven by many factors and it relies on many unknown conditions. For the last 20 years, economists have used their extraordinary wisdom and energy to try to figure out why some economies have developed while others have not.[4] Even if the system is the most important, there may be diversified forms of system. Indeed, there is a difference between the experience we see in the British and American countries and the phenomena we see in China (including many other economic experiences). Although many systems differ greatly in form, they may perform similar functions that can be substituted for one another. As for why they are different, it is another question that needs to be studied and answered.

Along this line of thought, to unlock the mystery of China's economic growth, we need to answer what the alternative institutions are. What's interesting is that at the meeting at the University of Macao, Professor Xu Chenggang of the London School of Economics also made a report in which he repeated a theory he proposed in the past 10 years with Qian Yingyi that emphasizes the importance of fiscal decentralization in explaining the economic growth in China after the reform. As for China's growth, Xu Chenggang's explanation is that it is not due to the system that North talks about, for they are not readily available in China. The system that drives growth is, in fact,

---

[3] The economists invited to be guest speakers included two Nobel prize winners in economics, Professor Douglas North (Washington University) and Professor James Mirrlees (Cambridge University). There were also Professor Xu Chenggang of the London School of Economics, Professor John Wong of National University of Singapore and Jun Zhang.

[4] Jones (1998), Shirk (1993). He gave a wonderful introduction to the theoretical and empirical research on the economic growth. Jones (2002).

regional decentralization. This dates back to a theoretical study he had done before 1993.

In 1993, he and Qian Yingyi published a lengthy article entitled Why China's Economic Reforms Differ: the M-Form Hierarchy and Entry/Expansion of the Non-State Sector in the journal of *Economics of Transition*.[5] The early version of this paper was first printed as a working paper at the London School of Economics' Suntory Toyota Research Center (STICFRD) which led them to begin a study of fiscal federalism for ten years. In the paper published in 1993, they made a preliminary observation that Chinese economy was different in the sense of organization before the reform from that of the Soviet Union, and they think this different organization structure affected the way of reform and economic growth later on. In the Soviet Union, the planned economy management was vertical and longitudinal, whereas there were multi-level and multi area management levels within the Chinese planning system, constituting what the study of industrial organization calls a U- and M-type structure. In China, the structure is customarily referred to as "vertical lines of leadership" (central ministries and commissions) and "horizontal lines of leadership" (local governments at all levels).

Obviously, in their early observations, they noticed the unusual role of Chinese local governments in their relation to the central government. Then they further theorized their observation of the empirical phenomenon based on China. So in 2000, Xu jointly published a paper titled Incentive, Information and Organization Form with Eric Maskin and Qian Yingyi.[6] In a sense, this theoretical article elevated the economic significance of Chinese experience, although some of the more fundamental problems were still left unsolved by the theory. For example, it cannot answer this question: why the local competition driven by decentralization is bound to race to the top rather than race to the bottom? However, the thinking of decentralization has been further developed in theory, leading to the subsequent conceptual framework of "fiscal federalism with Chinese characteristics". This has pushed forward the study of fiscal federalism that has long existed in economics and the public finance literatures, and adjusted its direction.

In the economic literature, the study of fiscal federalism has been done for at least half a century. It is generally believed that A Pure Theory of Local Expenditure, published by Charles Tiebout in 1957 in the *Journal of Political Economy* in University of Chicago, is a turning point.[7] Before this, the doctrine of public finance, if any, was either about the theory of national finance or the theory of "centralization". After the publication of this classic essay, the importance of decentralization began to draw the attention of economists. Subsequently, economists such as Richard Musgrave (1959),[8] especially Wallace Oates (1969, 1972, 1985, 1999), further developed the idea of decentralization,[9] and formed the early literature of fiscal federalism

[5] Xu and Qian (1993).

[6] Xu et al. (2000).

[7] Tiebout (1957).

[8] Musgrave (1959).

[9] Oates (1972, 1969, 1985, 1999).

which can be regarded as the first generation of fiscal decentralization theory. In June 2006, the 50th anniversary of the publication by Charles Tiebout of his classic paper in1956, The Lincoln Institute of Land Policy published a commemorative collection of papers on public economics edited by William Fischel entitled *The Tiebout Model at Fifty: Essays in Public Economics in Honor of Wallace Oates*. Written on the cover are the words: "In recognition of the contribution of Oates Wallace".[10]

Simply put, Charles Tiebout's theory of decentralization is as follows. In the supply of public goods, decentralization of power to local government can solve the problem of inadequate information that the central government is facing, because, as long as residents can move freely between different places, their own true preferences are actually shown by the mechanism of "voting with their feet". Moreover, because the local government's revenue and the number of "escaped" residents are inversely proportional, competition among local governments will inevitably occur, and this mechanism–similar to the competitive market–can affect the public expenditure model of local government. This important concept was later developed by many economists, and gradually became the basic theoretical framework of fiscal federalism between the central government and the local authorities.

However, the early generation of fiscal federalism was mainly confined to the category of public finance without involving the incentive mode of local government, although it had also touched upon the relationship between decentralization and economic growth. It was not until the early 1990s that the idea of early fiscal federalism was carried forward with the experience of economic transition countries like China and Russia being paid attention to. At this time, Xu Chenggang, Qian Yingyi, Gerard Roland and political scientist Barry Weingast began to link the ideas of fiscal decentralization with the incentive of local government, economic restructuring and economic growth. Largely influenced by Chinese and Russia's economic transformation experience, they are different in their research methods and perspectives from the early theory of public finance, thus they introduced the public economics into a more exciting field, constituting what can be called today the basic documents of the second generation of fiscal decentralization and fiscal federalism.[11]

The contribution of these studies is that they developed the early decentralization theory, which especially broke free from the limitation of supply of public goods and linked up the fiscal decentralization with the incentives of local government and local competition as well as developed a conceptual framework to explain the economic transformation. In this framework, they emphasized that the decentralization has created the condition for local competition, which they obviously deemed to be "race to the top". In general, the competitive advantages of decentralization are as follows: ① has promoted and maintained the development of the irreversible market mechanism (i.e. market preserving); ② has promoted development of township enterprises (TVFs); ③ has promoted urbanization and construction of infrastructure; ④ has promoted reform experiments and imitation; ⑤ has promoted the inflow of foreign direct investment (FDIs).

---

[10] Fischel (2006).

[11] Oates (2005).

There is no doubt that their theory of decentralization relies on the empirical foundations of economic transition in China and Russia, which is very important, of course. But because of this, the economic theory of fiscal decentralization needs to be linked to politics in order to become more complete. If the fiscal decentralization has made the local governments in China play a "helping hand" mentioned above, the decentralization in Russia, on the other hand, has made the local governments captured by interest groups and become the "grabbing hand".[12] Therefore, it is necessary to emphasize the Chinese characteristics of fiscal decentralization.

Then, what are the Chinese characteristics of decentralization? With regard to the incentive by the local government to promote growth, even though the financial system, along with the administrative decentralization between central and local governments has always been changing since the 1980s, why the incentive for local officials to promote economic growth has not changed at all? This question was raised by Professor Zhou Lian of Peking University in his research.[13] He believes that although the administrative and fiscal decentralizations do constitute an important source of incentives for local governments, but whether they have constituted the most basic and long-term source of internal incentive for the Chinese local governments is worth further study and discussion. Since China is not really a federal state, according to the present system, the decentralization of power between the central and local authorities can only be delegated under the nature of administrative management, and the devolution of powers can be withdrawn at any time. In fact, since the reform of decentralization, the division of administrative authority between the central and local authorities has always been in the process of adjustments and change. But why does the growth incentive for local governments almost remain unchanged?

This problem can be answered by a simple model given by Blanchard and Shleifer.[14] They compared the differences of fiscal decentralization and local government behavior between China and Russia. According to their observations, unlike Russia, the Chinese fiscal decentralization "race to the top" mainly because at the time when the fiscal decentralization is being carried out, the central government of China still maintains the political centralization and the power of rewarding and punishing local officials. In short, the central government can have "carrot" and "big stick" to encourage local governments to promote rather than hinder economic growth. Let us assume that the sharing ratio (carrot) of local government's revenue is a, which is determined by the central authorities; then, assuming that the retention (or promotion) probability of the local officials in choosing to promote economic growth is p_y; the probability of hindering economic growth yet still remaining in office is p_x, and demand that $p = p_y/p_x$. If a local official is appointed by the central authorities instead of elected locally, then p will be large. Let us make y the financial growth as a result of economic growth, b is the private gain (such as bribery or votes for interest groups) of local officials for blocking the economic growth. For local government officials, the condition for choosing a strategy for economic growth is:

---

[12] Shleifer (1997), Treisman (1999).

[13] Zhou Li'an (2007).

[14] Blanchard and Shleifer (2000).

$$pay > b$$

This simple train of thought can sum up the fiscal federalism with Chinese characteristics as the combination of fiscal decentralization and political centralization. Blanchard and Shleifer (2000) were more straightforward in saying: "The key to getting economic gains of decentralization from the federal system is to rely on some form of political centralization, without which the incentives for adopting localism policy by local government will be strong and it would be difficult to overcome this tendency by relying solely on economic or financial arrangements."[15]

Of course, even so, the theory of decentralization with Chinese characteristics also faces some challenges. First, the core of this theory is that decentralization leads to local competition which protects the market and promotes economic growth. A natural question is, of course, is this "race to the top" competition inevitable? What we may need to ask is, what are the conditions for this competition? And in what circumstances may decentralization lead to "race to the bottom"? The problem is that "race to the top" and "race to the bottom" seem to have occurred at the same time in China, though in the early stage of economic transformation, the benefits from decentralization was much greater. But in the late stages of economic transition and economic growth, the external cost of decentralization increased faster. Market segmentation, local protectionism, duplication of construction, excessive investment and competition, failure in macro-control, judicial injustice, expansion of regional gap, destruction of environment, "crony capitalism" and the neglect of basic education and health care expenditure have all been used to describe the "race to the bottom" phenomenon in transformation and growth. At present, there is an internal contradiction in the incentive model of managing China's local government officials and the cultivation of an effective market system. In other words, there is a serious conflict between this kind of incentive mode and the "multi-task" functions of government needed for a good market economy, with the result that the administrative and fiscal decentralization may not ensure a lasting and reasonable incentive for maintaining the market.

Wang Yongqin and others (2007), in an article entitled China's Great Power Development Model: Pros and Cons of Decentralized Reform, offered four reasons to explain why it is impossible for the incentive model of China's local government to coordinate with the functions of the government that the market economy needs.[16] They argue that incentives in political organizations are very different from those in economic organizations.

Firstly, the preferences of the clients of political organizations are often different, while the preferences of shareholders in enterprise organizations are basically the same, that is, to maximize returns. In political organizations, each interest group has

---

[15] They said in the article that this idea, in fact, was expressed by political scientist William Riker as early as 40 years ago, and that the federal system cannot operate effectively and continuously unless it is accompanied by political centralization.

[16] Yongqin et al. (2007).

its own preferences and interests, so it is difficult to define an indicator to measure the performance either for the task itself or for the client.

Second, another thing that is related with the nature of client preferences is that political organizations generally have multitasks, which is different from firms that mainly seek to maximize profits. In addition to efficiency and economic growth, political organizations also need to pursue social justice, equality of income, environmental protection, public service quality and other objectives. So, in theory, because of the multi tasks in a political organization, it is difficult to pursue various goals based on a strong, single dimensional (task) incentive similar to the wage piece approach in enterprises, and it is very easy to undermine other social goals if the evaluation is based on the goal of growth only.

Third, it is difficult to find a standard that can be referenced for the performance of the political organizations as in the case of enterprises. Although some comparisons can be made among local governments in China, the great regional difference makes this mutual reference very limited. In other words, a political organization is a monopoly, so it is difficult to find a sufficient information index to compare it with its counterparts.

Fourth, political organizations, different from economic organizations, tend to adopt relative performance evaluation rather than absolute performance evaluation in the design of incentive mechanism. In China, a mechanism that has been evolved is the relative GDP growth rate as the only information for evaluation. But the relative performance evaluation is likely to cause vicious competition among agents. Among them, the most typical is the local protectionism in various forms, which will cause regional segmentation and the "vassal economy", hindering the integration of China's domestic market process. The profound influence on the allocation of resources is that this market segmentation will limit the scope of the product, service (even idea) market, which will in turn restrict the scope of division of labor and specialization. The result is disadvantageous to the long-term progress of technology and change of system which will eventually harm the long-term economic development and international competitiveness of China.

These problems are a kind reminder for us. With the existing political organization and political centralized system unchanged, the decentralization is not only beneficial, but also comes at a cost. This seems to be a trade-off and no solutions can be found to redress this problem within the context of fiscal decentralization.

10.3 Politics of Decentralization

It is said that in economic research, China is too big to be dealt with as a single economy. Indeed, China today is a big country. In land area, China is100 times bigger than South Korea, and in terms of population, it is 30 times larger than that of South Korea. The governance of such a vast country with a large population and size is a huge challenge in the world. If we imagine China's economy as a huge airbus A380, the question that really merits our pondering is what power can drive it off the runway and make it take off economically. Chinese people have been thinking and exploring this problem for at least 150 years.

In the eyes of political scientists and administrators, the relationship between centralization and decentralization occupies an extremely important position in the Chinese history of state governance. Zhang Minggeng and Zhang Mingju (1996) wrote a book entitled *Historical Administrative Divisions of China: 221 BC–AD 1991*, in which they reviewed the long history of the regional administrative divisions in China and the evolution of the relationship between central and local governments.[17] In 2000, Mr. Xin Xiangyang published *A Century's Game: 100 Years' Relations between China's Central and Local Governments*.[18] This book also wonderfully and vividly reviews the major adjustments and events that have happened in the relationship between China's central and local governments throughout the twentieth century.

According to Zhang Minggeng and Zhang Mingju (1996), the regional administrative divisions in the history of China did not really begin until after Qin Shihuang, the first emperor of China, unified the six states. After the State of Qin unified China in 221 BC, it completely abolished the feudal system and implemented a centralized system under which were established many prefectures and counties in local regions. This system was then promoted across the whole country. Local governments were established under this political system of prefectures and counties and local officials were appointed by the central government to assist the central authorities in administrative work. Since the Qin Dynasty, the system was imitated and, despite the alternation of dynasties, the local administrative divisions were kept either at two levels, or sometimes five levels. Although there were changes in the local administrative levels in each era, each dynasty shared a common goal—to strengthen the central rule and leadership over the country.

The adjustment of administrative divisions after 1949 seemed to only involve the allocation of administrative power, but, because it was badly needed to establish a centralized planned economy in the middle of 1950s, the distribution of administrative authority between the central and local governments within the administrative division structure became the real contradiction under the system of planned economy, for the planned economy system is essentially a decision-making system of centralization. Such a centralized planning management came into being around the middle and late 1950s.

Originally, in the 1940s before the Chinese Communist Party won the revolutionary victory in 1949, Mao Zedong harbored an important thought. He had always believed—as shown in On New Democracy he wrote in January 1940 and On A Coalition Government published in April 1945—that the new democratic economy in China was to develop vigorously the economy of "capitalism" in the new democratic regime. And he reckoned that it would take China 10–15 years before considering

[17] Zhang Minggeng, Zhang Mingju (1996).

[18] Xin Xiangyang (2000).

the transition to socialism.[19] But by the time the land reform was completed in 1952, he changed his mind substantially. In 1953, he formally put forward the "general guideline of the transition period", according to which, the time of the transition was actually shortened for 3 years. To achieve this target, the important task was to speed up the reform of capitalism and the nationalization of the ownership system. And that was the beginning of the establishment of China's centrally planned economic system.

In fact, at the beginning of the establishment of China's centralized planned economy, the issue of centralization and decentralization had become the focus of controversy. Professor Wu Jinglian believes that this is actually the first proposed reform of China's economic system since the founding of new China.[20] He mentioned in his *Economic Reform in Contemporary China* (2003) that because that was the liberal period when Mao Zedong advocated "let a hundred flowers bloom, and a hundred schools of thought contend", in 1956, economists Sun Yefang[21] and Gu Zhun[22] offered their sharp criticism of the centralization mode for the centrally planned economy, both pointing out the important idea that socialist economy could not run counter to the laws of the market. Although the ideas of the two were severely criticized after 1958, at least during 1956–1958, leaders of central authority were aware of and responded to the shortcomings of the centralized mode.

According to Mr. Bo Yibo's memoir,[23] in order to prepare for the Eighth National Congress of the Communist Party of China, Mao Zedong heard work reports from 34 leaders of central ministries and provinces and municipalities from February to May in 1956. These reports involved many aspects, including the relationship between the central and the local authorities. After that, the political bureau of the central committee discussed these issues many times and summed them up in ten aspects. So, at the end of April to early May1956, Mao Zedong elaborated the ten aspects of the problems at the enlarged meeting of the political bureau and the summit conference of the State Council. After the death of Mao Zedong in September 1976, Mao Zedong's speech script, On the Ten Major Relations, was edited by Hu Qiaomu and was officially included in the fifth volume of the *Selected Works of Mao Zedong*. This is the way Mao Zedong's famous article On the Ten Major Relations was written. In the treatise, the "relationship between central and local governments" is in listed as the fifth relation.

Mao Zedong's speech, On the Ten Major Relations, made in April and May in 1956, directly determined the decision of the Eighth National Congress of the Communist Party of China on the reform of the economic management system. Thus, the decentralization of power was initiated for the first time in 1958 which mainly included: ① decentralization of planning power to the local government. The planned

---

[19] For the full text of these two classic documents, see *Selected Works of Mao Zedong*, Vol. 2, pp. 662–771, and Vol. 3, pp. 1056–1060.

[20] Wu Jinglian (2003).

[21] Sun Yefang (1984).

[22] Gu Zhun (1994).

[23] Bo Yibo (1991).

management system from central to local levels has been changed to a planned management system combining specialized departments and regions. ② transfer the management power over most of the state-owned enterprises to the local governments (including neighborhood committees and the people's communes); ③ delegate to the local governments the power of material distribution and labor management; ④ delegate to local governments the power of finance and tax collecting to increase the revenues of the local governments; ⑤ transfer the approval power of investment and credit to local governments.

The details of fiscal decentralization between central and local authorities will be discussed later. However, due to the fact that the guiding ideology of devolution of powers to local governments in1958 was to cooperate with the "great leap forward" movement initiated by Mao Zedong's, plus the compulsory promotion of the collective farming system and the "people's communes",[24] economic chaos ensued followed by an unprecedented famine during 1959–1961, resulting in the loss of tens of millions of lives.[25]

In the face of the serious consequences of the "great leap forward", the central government had to adjust its policy and recalled its delegated power starting from 1961. One of the most famous events was the enlarged work conference held in January 1962 which was attended by officials of the central bureaus, provinces, cities, prefectures and counties. The event was also called the "seven thousand people conference". Mao Zedong acknowledged his mistake at the meeting and was willing to take responsibility. At the same time, the central financial and economic leading group headed by Chen Yun was restored to be responsible for economic readjustment and recovery. At the meeting, it was decided to again strengthen the centralism and coordinate all the activities of the nation as a whole. Most of the original power decentralized to local regions was taken back, and the centralized leadership of the central authority on financing, financial and statistical practice was strengthened.

By 1963, China's economy was partially recovered. However, according to political scientist Wang Shaoguang, the taking back of power was merely an expedient to escape from the temporary difficulties for Mao Zedong—he was determined to break free from the centralized planning system of Soviet style again as soon as the

[24] Wu Jinglian noted in the Fifty Years of Economy of the Republic of China: "In this round of reform, a movement happened in rural areas that was developed in the opposite direction from the state industrial and commercial system: for the latter, it was the devolution of power and revenue, for the former, the original agricultural cooperatives comprising 15 to 20 households were merged into "huge communes", and in the summer and autumn in1958, people's communes, characterized by large scale and public ownership were set up. Under the condition that the general framework of the command economy plus administrative coordination remains unchanged, the administrative socialist system with decentralized administration and the people's commune in the countryside constituted the organizational foundation of the "great leap forward." This was an important cause of the confusion in China's economic life in 1958.".

[25] The number of deaths caused by the famine does not have an agreed figure, and scholars have different estimates in their studies. The figure is between 15 and 35 million. The Chinese government has so far failed to publish any data on the number of deaths in the three-year famine. Speculation and estimates by scholars are mostly based on the national census data in 1953, 1964 and 1982 aided by the "1/1000 Fertility Survey of 1982 and other data.

economy improved. In March 1966, Mao Zedong put forward the slogan of "nominal monarch of the republic" at a political bureau meeting held in Hangzhou. In his view, the central government should only be a "symbolic monarch", the economic power should be dispersed to various regions. He criticized the central authorities for having gone too far in taking back power and indicated that all the powers that had been taken back should be returned to the local authorities, or, in his words, "drive away all the people and horses".[26] Then, the "Cultural Revolution" broke out and the situation of decentralization lasted until the death of Mao Zedong and the end of the "Cultural Revolution" in1976.[27]

Political scientist Wang Shaoguang noted in the *Bottom Line of Decentralization* that Mao Zedong's idea of decentralization not only aroused the awareness of self interest of local government, but also expanded the financial resources of the local government. Self consciousness coupled with independent resources of finance might make local governments be at odds with the leadership of the central authority. The political legacy left by Mao Zedong includes both a totalitarian regime and a political and economic system full of flaws.

In fact, from 1951 to 1978 before the economic reform, frequent changes took place in the fiscal relations between the central and local authorities in China, fully reflecting the impossibility of finding a balance between centralization and decentralization within the centralized planning system. Professor Huang Xiaoguang of Soochow University made a detailed review of the changes in the fiscal relations between central and local governments during the planned economy.[28] On the basis of the information he provided, I would like to explain this fiscal relations as follows.

During 1951–1957, the system of dividing revenue and expenditure and grading management was implemented. In 1950, the State Council issued On the Resolution of Unified Management of the 1950 Annual Fiscal Revenue and Expenditure and decided to implement the financial system of centralized management and unified control over revenue and expenditure. The Decision stipulated that local revenues shall be turned over to the central authorities, and local expenditures shall be allocated by the central government, Thus, the connection between the revenue and expenditure in local government no longer existed.

A year later, in March1951, the State Council promulgated a document entitled the Decision on the Division of Fiscal Revenue and Expenditure System in 1951, which revised the decision of 1950 and established the system of dividing revenue and expenditure between the central government and local authorities and hierarchical management. Revenue was divided into the central budget revenue, local budget revenue and shared revenue between central and local authorities. The ratio of shared revenue would be determined on a yearly basis. The scope of expenditure was also defined for the central and local authorities.

---

[26] Wang Shaoguang (1997).

[27] Wang Shaoguang made a political analysis of the separation of powers and economic confusion during the "Cultural Revolution". Wu Jinglian also analyzed the process of administrative decentralization from the perspective of economics. See Wu Jinglian (2003).

[28] Huang Xiaoguang (2001).

In 1953, China initiated its first "Five-Year-Plan" (1953–1957). In order to meet the needs of economic construction in this period, not only was the administrative divisions adjusted, but the decision on the division of revenue and expenditure made in 1951 was also adhered to and a central provincial- and county-level financial system was implemented. It was also decided that the local governments were allowed to keep their "surplus revenues and saved expenditures".

After Mao Zedong published On the Ten Major Relations in 1956, which he stressed the importance of giving full play to the local initiative, the central government decided to transfer the planning management control over enterprises to the local government on a large scale. The State Council promulgated Decision on the Improvement of the Financial Management System in November 1957, stipulating the implementation of the system of "expenditure is determined by revenue for five years" starting from 1958. But because of the economic chaos caused by the "great leap forward" movement, the system was only executed less than a year. In September 1958 the State Council decided to use "sharing the total amount which will be determined on a yearly basis" to replace the original provision of "expenditure is determined by revenue for five years".

From 1959 to 1971, the central and local fiscal system was basically modified in this framework. Meanwhile, because of the great famine, the central government once again implemented a centralized management system in 1961 to recover and adjust the economy, which was again quickly shifted to an expansion of fiscal and administrative power for the local governments. Owing to the outbreak of the "Cultural Revolution" and of economic chaos, the decision to implement the separation of revenue and expenditure made by the central committee in 1968 was not implemented.

Around 1970, the central government decided to devolve most of the enterprises to local governments. To this end, from 1971, that is, starting from the 4th five-year-plan, the central government decided to implement the "all-round contract" system for fiscal revenue and expenditure with the local authorities. The specific approach is "predetermine the amount of revenue and expenditure, guarantee the fulfillment and payment of the assigned task (or through deficiency payment), retain the surplus and worked out the contract on a yearly basis". The system expanded the scope of budget of the local governments and, in theory, could increase the disposable income and improve the incentives of local governments.

However, it was soon found out in the implementation that the amount of the local surplus was far from being even. More importantly, because the "Cultural Revolution" had caused a lot of political and economic turmoil, it was difficult for most local regions to balance their budgetary revenue and expenditures, so surplus revenue became an empty talk. Therefore, during 1974–1975, the central government corrected the "all-round contract" system, adjusting it into "income can be retained according to fixed ratio, proportion of shared surplus will be decided once more, and expenses will be completed according to target". This rule obviously cut off the link between the local revenue and expenditure, and therefore was difficult to motivate the local authorities.

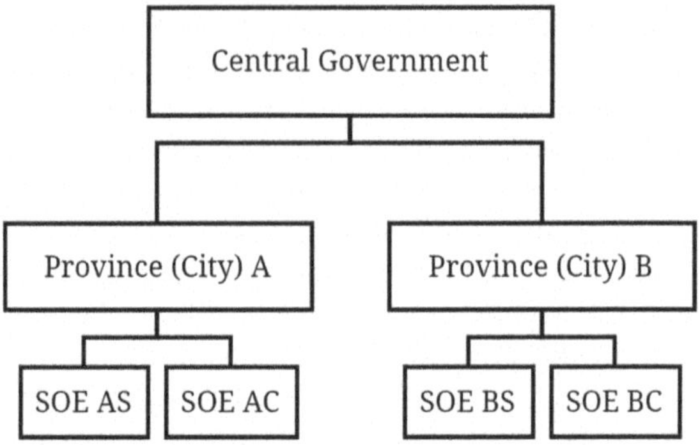

Fig. 10.1 Decentralized authoritarianism. *Source* Adapted from a speech by Xu Chenggang at a conference held at University of Macao

As a result, in 1976, the central government made readjustment and renewed the previous rule, namely, to "link up revenue with expenditure and share the total amount". At the same time, a pilot reform of the financial management system was launched in Jiangsu province in 1977 to test the "fixed proportion contract system". In accordance with the pilot system, the Jiangsu provincial government could determine the proportion paid to the central government and retained by itself according to the proportion of its budgetary expenditures in the budgetary revenues in recent years. Once determined, the proportion shall remain unchanged for four years. After the proportion was determined, the local budgetary expenditure would be derived from the income left for the local areas—the more income, the more expenditures and vice versa. So it was the local government's duty to strike a balance. In 1978, the central government selected 10 provinces and municipalities to carry out the pilot project of "linking revenue to expenditure and sharing the surplus income", giving local governments incentives for increasing their budgetary revenues.

One of the important results of all these reforms is to change the previous fiscal system of "combine central and local leadership with central ministries playing the main role" into one of "combine the central and local leadership with emphasis on the latter". It can be said that in the 20-odd years from 1957 to1978, the central planning and centralized financial systems in China were constantly modified and collapsed. The damage caused by political events such as the "great leap forward and "Cultural Revolution" to the Chinese economic system was more like what economist Xiong Bide called "creative destruction", because it destroyed the centrally planned economy mode of Soviet style, gradually making it evolve into the decentralized authoritarianism shown in Fig. 10.1. And this became the "political logic" of subsequent China's economic reform.[29]

[29] Political scientist Susan Shirk (1993) made a theoretical analysis of the political logic of China's economic reform.

10.4 Fiscal Decentralization After 1978

Since 1980, the fiscal relations between the central and local governments have followed an "all-round-contract" system. The word "all-round contract" is commonly used to refer to a simple form of contract by Chinese. What is interesting is that in the past 30 years, China's economic reforms have basically been promoted by way of "all-round contracting" at the micro level. The ownership of private property is an ideological "out-of bounds area" in China's economic reform, but in practical terms, "all-round contract" is very easy to be accepted by reformers, because the government still has the ownership in this kind of contract. In economics terms, the "all-round contract" is probably a sort of "fixed rental contract".

So, after entering the period of economic reform, the financial relationship between the central and local governments began to be characterized by the signing of fiscal "contracting between central and local leaderships, forming an agreement relationship of apportioning revenue and expenditure between central and local authorities while holding the latter responsible for their own balanced finances at each level. The system is also often called "each administrative level having its own source of revenue and expenditure". But in the meantime, because of the implementation of the state-owned enterprise reform policy, some adjustments were also made accordingly for the central and local fiscal system.

In 1982, the State Council issued the Interim Provisions on the Implementation of the Financial System of Apportioning Revenues and Expenditures between Central and Local Authorities while Holding the Latter Responsible for Their Own Finances at Each Level. According to the provision, except the three municipalities directly under the central government, all localities were required to implement various forms of fiscal responsibility system, or the so-called "each administrative level having its own source of revenue and expenditure". The main content of this provision was to classify the financial income into fixed income, shared income and adjustment income. The fiscal expenditure was allocated in accordance with the administrative affiliation of enterprises and government institutions. For a local government, the more its fiscal revenue is, the more expenditure it will spend and vice versa. It is responsible for its own fiscal balance.

However, as the level of economic development in different regions and the initial financial conditions were different, in the actual implementation process, the regional contracting scheme was different. According to Professor Zhong Xiaomin's summary and analysis, between 1980 and 1985, about four types of schemes were implemented in different regions.

The first type was the standard "apportioning revenues and expenditures between central and local authorities while holding the latter responsible for their own finances at each level". This system was implemented in 15 provinces including Sichuan. The 15 provinces, based on the estimated amount of revenue and expenditure in 1979, should turn over the surplus revenue to the higher authorities at the prescribed ratio, and if their revenue was less than expenditure, the deficiency should be made up by the central government at a certain percentage from the industrial and commercial tax. The central government promised that this scheme would remain unchanged for five years and that it was the obligation of the local government to keep its financial balance.

The second type is a special financial system of local budget. This scheme was implemented mainly in the five autonomous regions of minority nationalities including Xinjiang and several provinces with the status of autonomous regions. According to this scheme, In addition to enjoying the preferential treatment, these areas were also required to apportion the scope of revenue and expenditure with reference to the first category of scheme, determine the amount of subsidy coming from the central government, which was guaranteed an increase of 5% per year and remains unchanged for five years. All growth of local revenue would be kept by the local region.

The third category was designed for the two provinces of Guangdong and Fujian. What was implemented there was "apportion revenues and expenditures, turn over fixed ratio or receive fixed subsidy". This particular policy was designed to aid in the opening up and construction of special economic zones.

The fourth category was the pilot scheme we mentioned earlier in Jiangsu. After 1980, Jiangsu continued to follow the pilot measures, namely, the system of "all-round contract of fixed proportion". But in fact, after 1981, the first kind of contract system mentioned above was also implemented in Jiangsu.

After the central authority decided to implement the basic system of fiscal contract in 1980, the policy maker's original idea was to take the system of "each administrative level having its own source of revenue and expenditure" as a transitional system for 5 years only. According to the reform design of that time, the plan of dividing the fiscal revenue between central and local authorities in accordance with tax categories was to be implemented later. In 1986, the State Council, while designing the reform scheme of "price, tax, finance, funds and trade", was preparing to replace the practice of "each administrative level having its own source of revenue and expenditure" with the tax sharing system.[30] Later, after the abortion of this supporting reform scheme, the State Council decided to continue the system of financial contract by promoting it to a wider area in 1988.

In 1988, the financial contract system was basically a continuation of the system in 1980, but, as the emerging "cities specifically designated in the state plan" were also included in the scope of the financial contract, the contract system now covered 37 provinces, autonomous regions and cities specifically designated in the state plan. As shown in Table 10.1, there are six categories under the financial contract.[31]

(1) Revenue increase contract. Determine the increase rate of income (year on year) of local government and its portion to be retained and turned over to the higher authorities based on the final accounting of revenue and expenditure in 1978 and the revenue growth in recent years. The revenue within the rate of increase shall be shared between the central and local government according to the prescribed

---

[30] Wu Jinglian (2003).

[31] Zhong Xiaomin (1998). I consulted here documents provided by Zhong Xiaomin (1998), Huang Xiaoguang (2001) and Wu Jinglian (2003).

Table 10.1 Sharing contract types of financial revenue between central and local authorities in 1988–1993

	Revenue increase contract		Sharing the total amount	Sharing total amount and growth		Contract of increasing the turned over portion		Turn over by quota (Hundred million yuan)	Quota subsidy (Hundred million yuan)
	Increase ratio stipulated in the contract (%)	The ratio of the local retained portion (%)		The ratio of the total share amount (%)	The ratio of the growth share amount (%)	The turned over portion (Hundred million yuan)	Contract of increasing ratio (%)		
Beijing	4	50							
Hebei	4.5	70							
Liaoning	3.5	58.3							
Shenyang	4	30.3							
Jiangsu	5	41							
Zhejiang	6.5	61.5							
Ningbo	5.3	27.9							
Henan	5	80							
Chongqing	4	33.5							
Haerbin	5	45							
Tianjin			46.5						
Shanxi			87.6						
Anhui			77.5						
Dalian				27.7	27.3				

(continued)

Table 10.1 (continued)

	Revenue increase contract		Sharing the total amount	Sharing total amount and growth		Contract of increasing the turned over portion		Turn over by quota (Hundred million yuan)	Quota subsidy (Hundred million yuan)
Qingdao				16	34				
Wuhan				17	25				
Guangdong						14.1	9		
Hunan						8	7		
Shanghai								105	
Heilongjiang								2.9	
Shandong								3	
Jilin									1.1
Jiangxi									0.5
Shaanxi									1.2
Gansu									1.3
Fujian									0.5
Inner Mongolia									18.4
Guangxi									6.1
Tibet									9
Ningxia									5.3

(continued)

Table 10.1 (continued)

	Revenue increase contract		Sharing the total amount	Sharing total amount and growth		Contract of increasing the turned over portion		Turn over by quota (Hundred million yuan)	Quota subsidy (Hundred million yuan)
Xinjiang									15.3
Guizhou									7.4
Yunnan									6.7
Qinghai									6.6
Hainan									1.4

Note Guangdong in this table includes city of Guangzhou and Shaanxi includes city of Xi'an. After the separation of Wuhan and Chongqing from Hubei and Sichuan, the latter two provinces started to receive net subsidies from rather than turned over net tax to the central authorities. Their balance of payments was made up by the revenues paid to them by Wuhan and Chongqing as the subsidies granted by the central government. The percentages of revenues Wuhan and Chongqing turned over to their respective provinces were 4.6% and 10.7% respectively

Source Budget Management Department of the Ministry of Finance and Financial Affairs Bureau of IFM: *Intergovernmental Fiscal Relations in China*, pp. 26–27, Beijing, Chinese Economic Press, 1993; Zhong Xiaomin: *Payment Theory of Intergovernmental Fiscal Transfer*, Shanghai, Lixin Accounting Press, 1998

proportion to be retained and turned over; the portion beyond the increase rate shall be kept by the local government. If the rate of increase cannot be reached, the local government should solve it by itself. It can be seen from Table 10.1 that this system was implemented in 10 provinces and cities including Beijing, Hebei, Liaoning.

(2) Sharing the total amount. Decide the base amount of revenue and expenditure according to the financial situation of the previous two years, and determine the proportion to be retained and turned over based on the ratio of expenditure to the total revenue of local government. The scheme was implemented in Tianjin, Shanxi and Anhui.

(3) Sharing total amount and growth. This method was to share the portion of increased revenue between the central and local authorities on top of "total amount sharing". This system was implemented in Dalian, Qingdao and Wuhan, all cities specifically designated in the state plan.

(4) Contract of increasing the turned over portion. Based on the revenue turned over to the central government in 1987, increase the portion to be turned over every year according to a certain proportion. The system was adopted in Guangdong (including Guangzhou) and Hunan.

(5) Turn over by quota. In accordance with the original approved basis, determine the fixed amount to be turned over on the portion of income exceeding expenditure. This plan was implemented in Shanghai, Heilongjiang and Shandong.

(6) Quota subsidy. In accordance with the originally approved basis, offer quota subsidy on the portion of expenditure exceeding revenue. The plan was implemented in 15 provinces and cities including Jilin and Jiangxi.

As a variant of a fixed lease contract, a wide variety of financial contracting systems changed the incentives for local government at least on the margins and should significantly boost the local government efforts to increase revenues. This issue will be discussed in detail in the next section in conjunction with a number of economic studies. However, this fiscal decentralization also produced many negative results. The most obvious one may be the uneven "treatment" among regions. The most prominent cases are Guangdong and Shanghai. For example, in the middle of 1980s, Shanghai paid 12 billion *yuan* to the central government every year, while Guangdong still turned over only about 10 billion *yuan* even after its rapid economic development. In addition, economists also believe that the financial contracting system also caused blockade among local economies, hindering the integration of the market. But more importantly, the implementation of the financial contract in a large area has gradually changed the growth pattern and the relative position of the central government's financial budget, which were reflected in the trend that its budget revenue growth began to lag behind the GDP growth, and its finance declined as well as shown in Fig. 10.2.

Professor Wang Shaoguang, in his *Bottom Line of Decentralization*, offers an interesting explanation of the reason of the decline of the proportion of the total government budget revenue in GDP caused by fiscal decentralization. He believes that

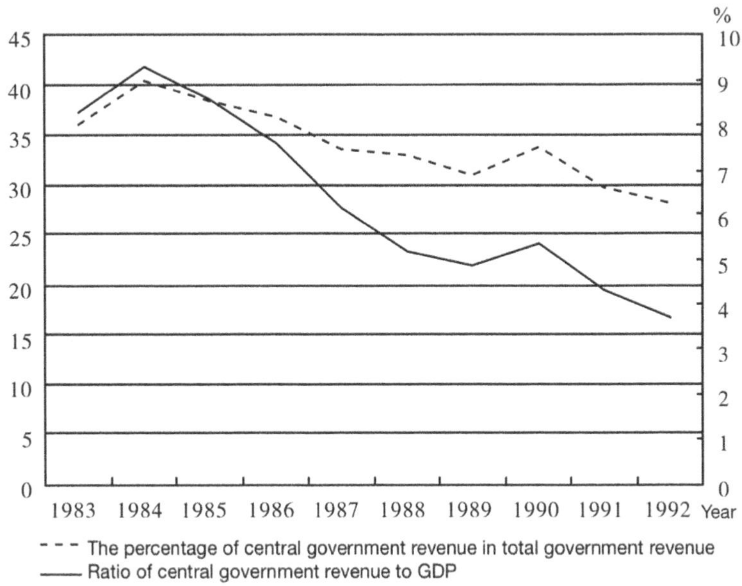

Fig. 10.2 Relative decline of the fiscal capacity of central government. *Source* State Bureau of Statistics: *Chinese Statistical Yearbook* (1995), Beijing, China Statistics Press, 1995

China's financial contract system was originally intended to mobilize the enthusiasm of local governments, and stimulate them to increase taxation, so that the central and local governments can benefit from the tax increase. However, the result was not as it had been expected. Not only did the financial tension cause conflicts between the central and local governments, but the financial strain also appeared during the period of China's sustained economic growth which was a paradox. In his words, the root of the paradox is that the design of the Chinese financial system has allowed the central and local governments to have too much discretion, which provided convenient ways for the prevalence of opportunist behavior. The central and local governments both expected to benefit from opportunistic practices, only ending up in seeing their financial revenue decline (relative to GDP), because both of them are in a typical prisoner's dilemma: "if the local government spares no effort to increase taxation, they have reason to worry that the central authority will demand a higher proportion of tax from them in the next round of negotiations. All local governments know that the contract they have reached with the central government will be negotiated again in a few years, while the central government would get the bad reputation of "whipping the ox that works fast": the base amount may be reduced for provinces with the rapid growth of fiscal revenue, but their proportion of paid taxes may be increased. Preempting the opportunism of the central government, the local governments responded with their own opportunism—holding back a trick or two in their effort to levy taxes."[32]

[32] Wang Shaoguang (1997).

Indeed, many scholars have pointed out that the frequent adjustments of the financial system since the 1980s have compromised the stability of the fiscal allocation relation between central and local governments. For example, economist Huang Peihua, an expertise on the relationship between the central and local governments (1992, 2005)[33] also noted that, the central authority, in order to expand its share in the total revenue, took a variety of measures to frequently "transfer" funds from the local finance. The examples she cited include: from 1981 onwards, the state issued government bonds each year by borrowing money from the local governments; since1983, taxes were collected on key construction funds for energy and transportation, and backbone enterprises were regained by the central government; in 1987, power construction bonds were issued; in 1988, the provision for increased quota subsidy to minority nationalities was cancelled. In addition, the central government also introduced what were jokingly called "central government stands treat, but local governments pay the bill" measures to increase income and reduce expenditures, resulting in the financial contract system becoming very unstable and local enthusiasm being dampened. Faced with this situation, local governments have also developed a series of tactical measures to deal with the central government. According to Yan Bin (1991),[34] the practice of "transferring funds" by the central government and "doing one thing under the cover of another" by local governments significantly put the two sides on the alert.

Zhang Yanlong (2006) noted in his article titled Evolution of Relation between Fiscal Decentralization and Governments below the Provincial Levels that,[35] some of the wording in the related documents of the policy of central authority can clearly reveal the huge friction between central and local authorities in their fiscal relation during that period. For example, at the end of the many documents issued by the State Council in 1988, such sentences were often repeated: "... Leading comrades of the people's governments at all levels should strictly follow the country's principles and policies to develop their economy and manage their finances. They should bear the overall situation In mind and understand the difficulties of the central government so as to correctly handle the interest relation between the central and local authorities". "To strictly enforce the fiscal and financial systems and strengthen the audit supervision. After the fiscal responsibility contact has been introduced, each region should conscientiously implement the provisions of fiscal and financial systems of the state. Taxes shall be turned over on time and in full amount without in violation of the tax authority or taking the liberty to reduce or exempt taxes; it is not allowed to "transfer budgetary revenue to extra budgetary revenue, or own "small exchequer". "All expenses should be paid strictly in accordance with the relevant regulations of the state without in violation of the financial system and accounting system; all income and payments shall be reported according to regulations truthfully without presenting false accounts. Any violation of financial discipline or practice of fraud shall be subject to careful scrutiny of the audit departments or be given disciplinary

[33] Wong (1992, 2005).

[34] Yan Bin (1991).

[35] Zhang Yanlong (2006).

sanctions if the problem is serious.", "It is required to strengthen the guidance of the financial work, actively support the financial departments to fulfill their duties and seriously implement financial discipline. The people's governments at all levels should take the lead in the implementation of the national financial system without acting on their own or beyond their power to undermine the overall situation. Nor shall they instigate, be it in overt or covert ways, the financial department to deal with financial matters in violation of the state regulations."

The above theory of unwilling to pay taxes can help us explain why the growth of budgetary revenues tends to decline in the fiscal contracting system. However, it would be a mistake if we believe the local government has not got more income from the local economic growth; otherwise we cannot explain what has provided strong positive incentives for the local economic growth. Just as the documents of the State Council warned, the practice of "transfer budgetary revenue to extra or non-budgetary revenue, or own "small exchequer" has become an important source of income for the local governments. This very complex problem has led us to a very unique Chinese phenomenon, namely, the existence and growth of local non-budget income.

Non-budgetary income is not the product of fiscal decentralization reform, but had already existed in the planned economy period though in small scale. It was not until after the central and local fiscal decentralization was introduced in the 1980s did non-budgetary revenues evolve into a huge source of local income. There was no fixed pattern for the composition and sources of non-budgetary income, but they were all revenues outside the budget management earned and spent by the local governments. This income generally includes non-budgetary funds managed by the local financial departments (such as tax add-ons and funds, operating income of government-affiliated institutions, fees collected from business), non-budgetary funds managed by the administrative institutions (such as tax add-ons and funds of local government, fees collected from administrative institutions), non-budgetary funds of state-owned enterprises (such as income from depreciation, portions of profits and taxes), and the social security funds managed by local government. According to the calculation of the State Bureau of Statistics, due to the growth of non-budgetary funds, by 1992, the total amount of non-budgetary funds reached 385,5 billion *yuan*, accounting for 97.7% of the budget revenue in that year.[36]

However, in 1994, the central government decided to replace the fiscal contract system that had been implemented for years with the "system of tax distribution", and one of the main reasons for this was the worry of the central government about the continued decline of the proportion of fiscal budget revenue in the total budget revenue or in GDP. This concern had something to do with the discussions in academia in that period, and was due to the fact that the rhetoric of what some political scientists called "new authoritarianism" and "state capability" gained the upper hand.

During 1988–1989, there was a heated debate about "new authoritarianism" in the political and ideological circles of China. Scholars who advocated new authoritarianism (such as Wu Jiaxiang, Xiao Gongqin, Zhang Bingjiu) argued that Chinese

[36] Huang Xiaoguang (2001), pp. 225–228.

political democracy should be based on a full market economy, and that the market economy can only be advanced in China under centralized power; therefore, China needs the government's authority and a centralized system. They based their theory on the political theory of Professor Samuel Huntington of Harvard University, and the experience of South Korea and other countries or regions that, after the "World War II", achieved economic take-off by the elite rule before realizing the political democracy.

This view was immediately attacked and criticized by scholars of political culture represented by Huang Wansheng, Rong Jian and Yu Haocheng. They argued that the financial difficulties, inflation and other problems that occurred in the Chinese economic reform were the negative consequences of highly centralized political and economic systems, so China must promote the reform of political democracy system, and push the market-oriented economic reform movement with a democratic political system. Many young scholars were also involved in the debate in the hope of searching for a road of China's political modernization. After 1989, the debate gradually disappeared. The discussion of "new authoritarianism" had an important influence on the central policy makers who started to look at fiscal decentralization and the decline of financial resources of central government in a new way.

In November 1993, the Third Plenary Session of 14th National Congress of the Communist Party of China adopted the Resolution on the Establishment of the System of Socialist Market Economy, which clearly put forward an overall reform strategy, including establishing a new relation among the governments in fiscal revenue in 1994, i.e. to change the original fiscal contract system into a reasonably apportioned system of tax distribution between the central and local governments (including provincial and county governments). The tax sharing scheme had been prepared and studied for many years before 1986, but was subsequently shelved. In 1992, a piloting project of the tax distribution system was resumed. In December 15, 1993, the State Council promulgated the Decision on the Implementation of the Financial Management System of Tax Distribution, which explained in detail the scheme of the tax sharing system.

The main contents of this system are: ① the central and local authorities clearly defined their respective powers and scope of fiscal expenditures; ② the central and local authorities clearly defined the scope of their revenues, including the central tax, local tax and the shared tax between central and local governments; ③ the establishment of the transferred payment system from the central government to local regions, namely tax rebates and special subsidies to help achieve the regional balance. Moreover, the non-budgetary funds were sorted out and a large number of government fees and charges were cancelled or reduced; an indirect tax system with value-added tax as the main body was implemented, and the personal income tax unified.

The budgetary revenues shared by central and local governments mainly came from value-added tax and resource tax. The value added tax shared by the central government was 75% and that shared by local governments was 25%. Resource tax was divided into different varieties–land resources tax would be taken as the local income, and marine oil resource tax as the revenue of the central authority. The stamp duty on securities transactions would be split up on a fifty to fifty ratio between the central and local areas in 1994, but were changed to central government sharing 97% in 2002.

Figure 10.3 depicts the changes of the ratio of the budgetary revenues and expenditures of the central government to the total revenues and expenditures of the budget before and after the reform of the tax sharing system. The proportion of central government's revenue in the total fiscal revenue decreased from 40.5% to 22% during 1984 to 1993, but the ratio was reversed and increased significantly after the implementation of the tax sharing system. In 2003, the central government's revenue accounted for 54.6% of the total revenue while the local revenues fell from around 70% before 1994 to about 50% after 1994.

Whether Fig. 10.3 has revealed the problem of the design of tax distribution system is controversial. Some financial experts believed that a substantial portion of central revenue was actually returned to the local governments. Therefore, the central budget revenue was not as high as that shown in Fig. 10.3. But most economists argued that, even the transfer payment was taken into account, the 1994 financial system reform,

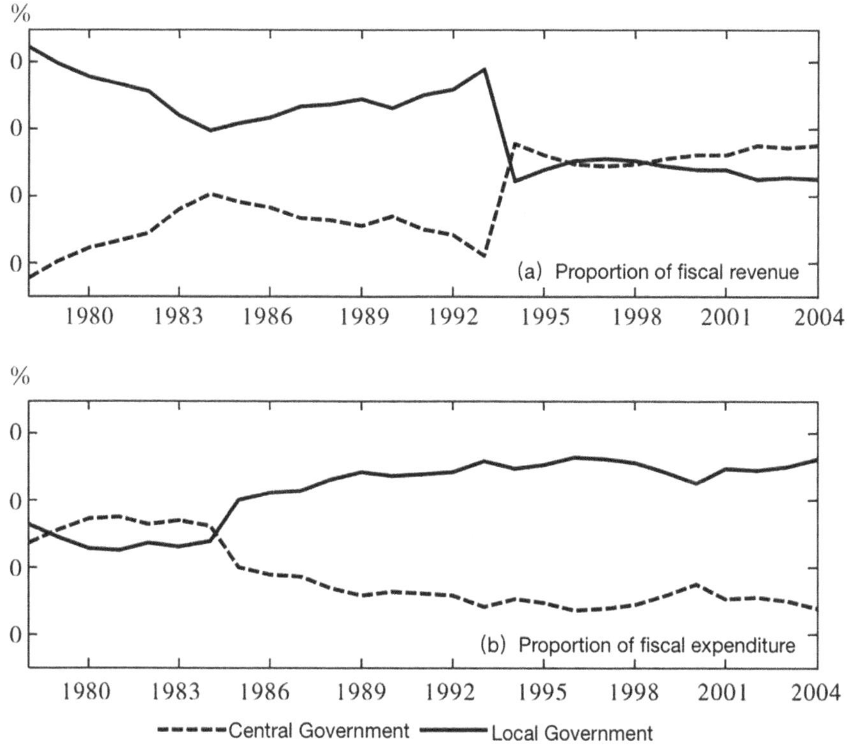

Fig. 10.3 Relative changes of budget revenues and expenditures of central government (impact of the 1994 tax distribution system). *Source* Chen Shiy, Zhang Jun: *A Study on the Efficiency of Fiscal Expenditure of China's Local Government: 1978–2005*, Chinese Social Sciences, 2008 (4)

on the whole, only dealt with the revenue of financial system, while still keeping the expenditure responsibility system with a strong feature of the planned economy before the reform unchanged, that is to say, to let the local governments play the role of the expenditure agent of the central government. Therefore, it was true that the reform of the tax sharing system in 1994 greatly increased the proportion of local government spending relative to the central government. We can see from Fig. 10.3 that the proportion of local fiscal expenditure in the past 20 years has not changed much, basically more than 60%. In fact, in 2002, local governments' revenues accounted for about 45% of the total budget revenue, but 70% of the total budget expenditure was undertaken by the local governments. Even if the return income from the central leadership is taken into account, it is not enough to achieve a balance of payments. More importantly, the reform of the financial system did not provide more choices for local government to increase their financing; after the reform of the tax distribution system in 1994, the connection between income and expenditure was cut off at local government level, thus increased the burden of local governments, especially those in backward areas.

Many subsequent studies have found that even if there are tax rebates and special subsidies from the central government, the implementation of the system of tax distribution does not seem to be able to play a greater role in balancing the regional income gap. In 1994, in order to promote the tax distribution system and win the support of the rich provinces, the central government adopted a concession policy to ensure that the local income would not be less than the 1993 income base. If the central government's income gained from the exclusive tax and sharing tax exceeds its income before the tax reform in 1993, it will return the surplus part to the local governments to ensure that the actual income of local governments would not be less than the region's level of 1993 in the wake of the implementation of the tax sharing system. For the income exceeding the base amount of 1993, the central and local governments would split it on a 7 to 3 proportion. As a result of the strategic motivation of local government to make their "base amount" bigger in 1993, the income return burden for the central government was so great that it directly affected its financial capacity to balance the regional income gap.

Also, as Huang Peihua pointed out,[37] the main part of the sharing tax between the central and local governments and tax return is value-added tax, which mainly comes from the manufacturing and service industries. As a result, the tax distribution system and the transfer payment by the central government mainly based on the tax return is actually a financial system that has widened the gap of local fiscal capacity and is more advantageous to the rich and developed areas. In Table 10.2, we can see roughly that the gap between the rich and poor provinces is widening in economic development and fiscal balance before and after the reform of the tax sharing system.

---

[37] Huang Peihua (2005).

Table 10.2 Financial and economic shares of rich and poor provinces

	1990	1998
5 richest provinces		
Percentage of GDP (%)	22.80	25.10
Percentage of population (%)	12.70	12.20
Percentage of tax revenue (%)	26.00	23.00
Percentage of government spending (%)	19.80	18.50
5 poorest provinces		
Percentage of GDP (%)	12.70	11.70
Percentage of population (%)	18.90	18.70
Percentage of tax revenue (%)	12.30	9.80
Percentage of government spending (%)	14.00	8.60

Note * The richest provinces: Shanghai, Beijing, Tianjin, Guangdong and Zhejiang. ** The poorest provinces: Guizhou, Gansu, Shaanxi, Jiangxi and Henan. Because of the data reasons, Tibet and Hainan are not included

Source Huang Peihua: Can China Change Its Mode of Economic Development in the 21st Century? *Comparison*, 2005 (18)

10.5 Empirical Study of Decentralization and Growth

Recently, I worked with Zhou Lian, a professor at the Peking University, to edit a collection of essays and named it *Compete for Growth: the Political Economy of China's Growth*. The purpose of our editing this work is to summarize and reflect the achievements of Chinese economists on fiscal decentralization and growth over the years. I think this is an important part of the literature on economics of transition. Next, I will review and discuss the empirical literature on the decentralization and growth of China written by economists in the past 10 years based on the content of this collection.

There is no doubt that China has become a highly decentralized country since the fiscal decentralization system was introduced in1985. Even though the tax sharing system initiated in 1994 made the revenue of the central authority more concentrated, it did not change the structure that economic development and investment activities were undertaken by local governments. If it is measured by the relative proportion of local government spending, China may be the most decentralized country in the world today.

The data in *World Development Report in1997: Governments in the Changing World* showed that,[38] in developed countries, the fiscal expenditure of provincial (state) government accounted for only 30% on average in the total expenditures of governments at all levels. Even in most decentralized countries like Canada and Japan, it only accounted for 60%. In the 1990s, the average proportion of provincial spending in developing countries, the transition economies and the United States

[38] World Bank (1997).

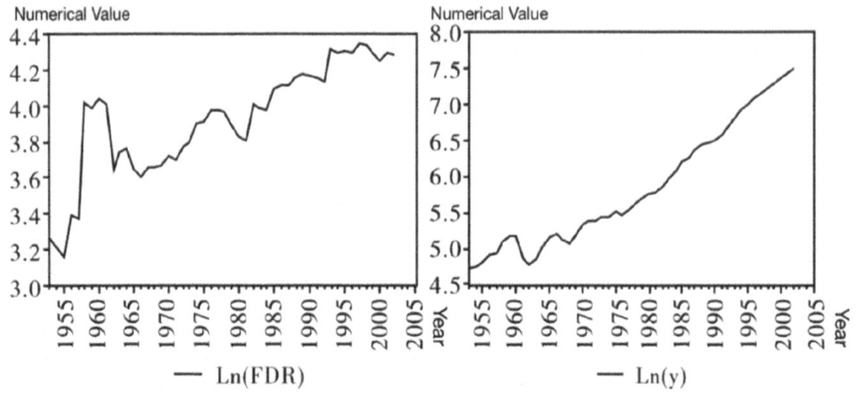

Fig. 10.4 Fiscal decentralization and economic growth in China (1955–2005, numerical value). *Source* Zhou Wenxing, Zhang Zheng: Impact of Fiscal Decentralization on Economic Growth after the Founding of the China: A Hypothesis and Test, *Institutional Economics Research*, 2006 (1)

were 14%, 26% and less than 50% respectively. We can see from Fig. 10.3, however, China's provincial fiscal expenditure has maintained nearly 70% of the nation's fiscal expenditure for more than ten years.[39] Therefore, a high degree of decentralization has become an important characteristic of China's economic growth after the reform.

Empirically, dealing with the relationship between fiscal decentralization and economic growth is a complex task. Let's take a look at Fig. 10.4 first. The diagram on the left shows the decentralization measured by the proportion of provincial government spending in the nation's fiscal expenditure. The diagram on the right gives the actual growth rate of GDP, both of which were processed by logarithms and were tested by unit root tests and are first order, single time series data.[40] The overall trend seems to be that the two have a positive correlation. But the detailed quantitative tests we will mention below will tell us a different "story".

In the economics literature, the classic theory of Charles Tiebout put forward in 1956, and the theory that decentralization will boost growth proposed in the book *Fiscal Federalism* written by Wallace Oates in 1972 have been challenged constantly. For example, Professor Bardhan (2002) once noted[41] that in Tiebout's theory, the full freedom of movement of the factors (especially the residents/voters) and the government's responsibility for the voters are the two most important assumptions. But these two assumptions are too harsh for the underdeveloped economy and are less easily satisfied. As far as China's experience is concerned, the flow of essential factors is indeed accelerating after the reform and opening up, but the great different regional conditions make it difficult to support the hypothesis of factor flow. On the other hand, the particularity of China's political system and officials' governance make the relationship between the government and the local people subtle and complicated. It

[39] Huang Peihua's article was consulted for this data.

[40] Zhou Wenxing and Zhang Zheng (2006).

[41] Bardhan (2002).

seems that China's local governments are more responsible to the central government, but they are also responsible for people under their jurisdiction due to the constraints of the ruling concept (legitimacy) of the central authority and the mode of governance by officials. The changes of governance by officials and political system in China during the 30 years of reform will be discussed in another paper.

The observation and research of empirical phenomena is also very complicated. Technically, factors that affect economic growth are complex and difficult to identify and the method of accurately measuring the degree of decentralization is not easy to obtain, nor is it often unreliable. Growth and decentralization is bound to interact with each other, and it is not easy to find the right instrumental variables to identify the causal relationship therein. Wallace Oates made a detailed discussion and explanation of these issues in his 1993 paper entitled Fiscal Decentralization and Economic Development. Therefore, it is no easy task to find out whether China's fiscal decentralization has positively affected economic growth.

For example, in 1998, Zhang Tao and Zou Hengfu published an article Fiscal Decentralization, Public Spending and China's Economic Growth in the *Journal of Public Economics*,[42] the first paper published in the English world to test the relationship between fiscal decentralization and growth by using the Chinese data system.[43] They used the provincial data of 1978–1992 to test the relationship between fiscal decentralization and economic growth, and found that the theory that fiscal decentralization is conducive to economic growth has not been confirmed by Chinese experience. Their explanation is that after the fiscal decentralization, investment by the central government in infrastructure with strong externalities has been reduced.

In 2000, however, Yifu Lin and Liu Zhiqiang published a paper entitled Fiscal Decentralization and Economic Growth in China, which proved that China's fiscal decentralization has improved economic efficiency and promoted economic growth.[44] They used panel data from 28 provinces and cities in 1970–1993.

The two studies' explanatory variables are per-capita GDP growth rate which were both regression estimated by using Barro Mankiw's growth experience equation. Moreover, these studies are not substantially different in any way other than the method of measuring decentralization and the sources data. Zhang Tao and Zou Hengfu measured the degree of fiscal decentralization by using the traditional indicator of the proportion of local spending relative to the central budget.[45] This method is often criticized for reasons such as whether the transfer payments should be calculated or not. It is also controversial whether spending is more appropriate

[42] Zhang Tao and Zou Hengfu (1998).

[43] Of course, even before 1998, it was not uncommon to discuss qualitatively the relationship between fiscal decentralization and growth in China. In addition, before Zhang Tao and Zou Hengfu's article was published in 1996, it was originally printed in the World Bank.

[44] Lin and Liu (2000), 49 (1), pp. 1–21; Lin and Liu (2000).

[45] Their selected indicators include the ratio of per capita provincial fiscal expenditure to the fiscal expenditure of central government, the ratio of per capita provincial budget expenditure to the budget expenditure of central government, and the ratio of per capita provincial non-budget expenditure to the non-budget expenditure of the central government.

than income to measure fiscal decentralization. But given China's specific situation, spending is more appropriate than income. The real problem is that they used budgetary expenditure to measure the expenditure of decentralization, and given the fact that China's non-budgetary funds are inflated, they must have underestimated the degree of decentralization to the local regions.

In the study of Yifu Lin and Liu Zhiqiang, they argued that fiscal decentralization should be regarded as starting in 1985. They further confirmed that there were 4 types of fiscal decentralization arrangements between central and local authorities in 1985–1987, and 5 arrangements during1988–1993. They used the increased amount of fiscal income retained by the provincial government as the "marginal sharing rate" of the budget income of provincial government and used this indictor to measure the fiscal decentralization. If a province can keep a share of their revenue, the measured degree of fiscal decentralization is equal to the retained share. They found that 14 provinces in 1985–1987 and 5 provinces in 1988–1993 can be classified as belonging to this category. The other types of fiscal arrangements, by definition, all mean a marginal sharing rate of 100%. By this definition, the provinces that receive financial subsidies also mean a marginal rate of 100%. Before 1985, the level of fiscal decentralization in all provinces was 0. As an example, Table 10.3 shows the calculation of marginal sharing rates in some provinces.

It is very likely to regard provinces with different economic development levels and different periods as having the same degree of decentralization by the decentralization indicator measured by Lin Yifu and Liu Zhiqiang in this way. This is a big problem. Thus, in general, these early studies resulted in greater divergence of results due to data constraints and differences in measurement. At the same time, the

Table 10.3 Marginal sharing rates in some provinces

Province	1985–1987		1988–1993	
	The scheme of decentralization	The degree of decentralization	The scheme of decentralization	The degree of decentralization
Beijing	a	49.55	b	100.00
Shanghai	a	23.54	c	100.00
Hebei	a	69.00	b	100.00
Shanxi	a	97.50	a	87.55
Heilongjiang	c	100.00	c	100.00
Jiangsu	a	40.00	b	100.00
Sichuan	a	100.00	a	100.00
Gansu	e	100.00	e	100.00

Note a: A share paid to local income; b: A share paid to the local income in the base year. In the following few years, the total amount paid will increase according to the ratio that has been negotiated; c: A fixed amount of revenue turned over to the central government; f: Receive a fixed amount of subsidies from the central government

Source Revised according to related data provided by Yifu Lin, Liu Zhiqiang in: Fiscal Decentralization and Economic Growth in China, *Journal of Peking University*, 2000 (4)

above two studies did not cover the empirical data after the implementation of the tax sharing system in 1994.

In 2006, Zhang Yan and Gong Liutang published an article titled Reform of the Tax Distribution System, Fiscal Decentralization and Economic Growth in China,[46] which improved the method of measurement of decentralization, obtained more complete data (including the data of 28 provinces and cities in1986–2002) and reexamined the relationship between fiscal decentralization and the growth in China. Although the estimation methods used by them are not different from those mentioned above, they took into account the transfer payments and non-budgetary funds when measuring the degree of decentralization, and defined four types of decentralization. In addition to measuring the degree of decentralization through the traditional way of using the proportion of the local government's budgetary fiscal revenue (expense) in the budgetary fiscal revenue (expenditure) of the central government, they used two other definitions that do not include transfer payments yet include non-budgetary revenue and expenditure. But they found that the estimated results were the same. Since they took into account the tax distribution system in 1994 and covered the data of 1994, their estimates show that there is an obvious time difference between fiscal decentralization and growth in China—it was significantly positive in the period of 1994–2002, while in the period of 1986–1993 it was negative. Therefore, they believe that the tax sharing system has improved the impact of fiscal decentralization on economic growth.

But the econometric tests they conducted for different regions partly provided the reasons for the above conclusions. They found that the impact of fiscal decentralization on economic growth was significantly positive in 14 developed areas with per capita GDP higher than 6,000 *yuan* while the impact was not significant and different from 0 in 14 underdeveloped areas. Therefore, in their view, the impact of fiscal decentralization on growth also has a trans-regional effect.

There is no doubt that such studies are always useful. However, because the relationship between economic growth and decentralization is complex, and they influence each other, how to deal with the problem of endogeneity in empirical research is always a severe challenge for researchers. People can say, of course, that before a better instrumental variable (IV) has been found to address endogeneity, one is justified to treat these findings cautiously. But in any case, the impact of fiscal decentralization on the expenditure behavior of local governments cannot be underestimated. The problem is that this effect may affect economic growth in different regions in different ways.

It is not difficult to explain whether the fiscal incentives of local governments after the fiscal decentralization have been strengthened. Logically, if decentralization causes local governments' spending more and more subject to local fiscal revenue, then in general, the local governments will have greater incentive in investment and economic growth as well as to expand the tax base. So, a simple technique is to do a regression of the local fiscal revenue by its fiscal expenditure and see how much the correlation coefficient will be. This method has been mentioned in a research

[46] Zhang Yan and Gong Liutang (2005).

paper on Russian decentralization published by Ekaterina Zhuravskaya in 2000.[47] She used data from 35 Russian cities to examine the impact of changes in the city's own income on its own spending. The correlation coefficient was found to be – 0.9. In other words, if the local government's own income increased by 1 dollar, the share of local revenue fell by 9 cents, and the local revenue increased by only 1 cents. So she believed that Russia's fiscal decentralization did not provide enough financial incentives for the region. Nor did the local governments have any incentive to develop local economies. Later, in a paper published in 2005, Hehui Jin and others also made a regression analysis by using the provincial panel data of China of 1982–1992,[48] and found that the fiscal situation of China's local governments was very significant. What's interesting is that their thesis' title is Fiscal Federalism, Chinese Style, apparently in response to the title of Fiscal Federalism, Russian Style used by Zhuravskaya.

In May 2007, doctoral student Fu Yong supervised by me also did a test of such a fiscal incentive in his doctoral dissertation Chinese-Style Decentralization, Local Finance Mode and the Supply of Public Goods: A Theoretical and Empirical Research. He extanded the data to 1970–2004 and took into consideration the transfer payment and the tax distribution system. Like Zhuravskaya's research, he also controlled the size of the population and added time dummy variables to control macro volatility. The result is that during 1970–1979, the expenditure coefficient to income was 0.16, indicating that the two were basically not related. Yet in 1980–1993, the coefficient became 0.85–0.91. In the period of 1994–2004 after the tax sharing system, the coefficient was 0.95–1.08, depending on whether it was the fixed effect or the random effect. Xiaobo Zhang (2006) made a similar regression analysis by using the fiscal data of 1,860 counties from 1993 to 2000 and got a very close result[49]: the coefficient was 0.815 in 1993 and 1.144 in 2000.

We will naturally ask such a question: faced with such a strong fiscal stimulus after the decentralization, did the local government promoted or hindered the local economic growth? Hehui Jin and others used data before the reform of tax distribution system in their research. They found that the financial incentive to the local government did promote economic growth. However, Chen Kang, Arye L. Hillman and Gu Qingyang insisted in their paper that the tax distribution system in 1994 strengthened the centralization of the budgetary fiscal revenue of the central authority, thus changed the behavior of the local government–from the "helping hand" back to the "grabbing hand".[50]

However, the logic of Chen Kang, Arye L. Hillman and Gu Qingyang seems to be problematic. In a simple model they gave, the sharing proportion was determined by the central government, and the greater the share of the central authority, the more likely the local government was to choose non-budgetary income to respond. After the central government centralized its power, the best strategy for a local government was

---

47 Zhuravskaya (2000).

48 Jin et al. (2005).

49 Zhang (2006).

50 Kang et al. (2002).

to increase its own interests by choosing non-budgetary revenues. But they argued that the expansion of non-budgetary revenues represents a shift of local governments from a "helping hand" to a "grabbing hand". Their thesis did not confirm whether the non-budgetary revenue growth after the tax distribution system has promoted the growth, but they believed that this change will further foster corruption and reduce investment, which are not conducive to economic growth.

Their reasoning is subject to empirical tests. But the empirical observation seems to be that, for local governments, an increase in non-budget income is likely to encourage them to focus on economic growth. For example, since 1994, the local infrastructure investment activities in fact have speeded up, the investment environment has been improved more significantly, and foreign direct investment (FDI) also speeded up its pace of flowing into China after 1994. However, the question is, whether the changes in the local government's fiscal behavior in the wake of the tax sharing system has promoted or hindered economic growth still depends on the initial conditions of regions.

Take infrastructure investment as an example. We did a research on China's infrastructure[51] and found that the proportion of infrastructure financing within the state budget funds decreased rapidly from 32.6% in 1987 to around 10% in mid-1990s; the proportion of domestic bank loans in recent years have been lingering between 23 to 25%, so independent investment has become the backbone of infrastructure construction in China. This means that the investment in infrastructure construction has shifted to the stage of non-budgetary investment by local government in mid-1990s. Prior to 1994, the investment proportion by central government in infrastructure projects was above 50%, but decreased to 32.5% in 1999. As a result, the gap between infrastructure investment in the eastern and western regions has become very obvious. In Xinjiang, Gansu and other underdeveloped provinces (regions), the proportion of projects by central government is generally higher than the national level, and it even reached 55.9% in Xinjiang in 1998 while in Hainan and other economically developed coastal areas, the project proportion by central government is less than 15%, which entirely relies on independent financing. It is therefore expected that infrastructure investment funds will be skewed towards the coastal areas.

The effect of decentralization and tax sharing on the structure of local fiscal expenditure is not limited to investment in infrastructure. Fu Yong (2007) also examined the influence of fiscal decentralization on the structure of local fiscal expenditure after the tax sharing system in his doctoral dissertation. He used the panel data of 29 provinces during 1994–2004 to estimate how the proportion of basic construction expenditure and expenditures of science, education, public health and culture in fiscal expenditure was influenced by decentralization and local competitions. He used the proportion of per capita provincial fiscal expenditure in the per capita fiscal expenditure of the central government to measure decentralization, and used the actual tax rate of foreign investment enterprises in various regions to divide the mean value as a measurement of the degree of competition. He found after controlling other factors that, in 1994–2004, the effect of fiscal decentralization on the proportion of capital

[51] Jun et al. (2007).

construction expenditure in eastern and western regions was significantly positive, but the impact on the expenditures proportion of science, education, public health and culture was significantly negative. Nor was the effect significant on the central region. He then had the data extended to 1986–2004 and did a regression analysis. He found that before the tax sharing system was introduced in 1994, the effect of fiscal decentralization on basic construction expenditure was not significant, and the impact on the expenditure proportion of science, education, public health and culture was significantly negative.

The findings help to show that, after the tax sharing system was introduced, the fiscal constraints on local governments are more obvious, which seem to lead to the growth-oriented fiscal expenditure structure.[52] Certainly, we have discussed that owing to the difference of regions in economic development level and conditions, the influence of tax sharing system on investment and growth is also different, which will help further widen the gap between regions. Xiaobo Zhang (2006) found that the Gink coefficient of the proportion of productive expenditure in county government expenditure increased from 33.04 in 1993 to 41.61 in 2000, an increase of 26% according to the financial data of 1,860 counties he calculated. He also discovered by regression that the regions with greater spending on agriculture were slow in economic growth. The logic behind this may be that if the industrial foundation was weak in a region, it is easier to collect taxes which can help local governments use the financial resources to improve investment environment and promote economic growth. But in a place with greater spending on agriculture, local businesses will inevitably bear greater tax burden which will worsen the investment climate and is unfavorable to growth. The uneven development of the place will be intensified as well.

We need more empirical research on these issues, of course. The long history of evolution has led to striking differences in the initial conditions of different regions in China, so it is difficult to regard the Chinese economy as a single entity. Therefore, it is more meaningful to regard the regions differently in empirical research. To undertake case tracking and experimental studies of a region are sometimes useful for clarifying some complex empirical phenomena.

A good example is EricThun–his study of the rising model of China's auto industry.[53] After the fiscal decentralization and opening up, the growth of automobile industry in Shanghai, Beijing, Guangzhou, Wuhan and Changchun showed very different patterns. EricThun found that the system and characteristics of Shanghai model is a centralized bureaucratic system with hierarchical relationship of enterprises which is more like that in Japan; the model in Beijing and Guangzhou is a decentralized bureaucratic system with market-oriented corporate relationship; and the model in Changchun and Wuhan is a decentralized bureaucratic system plus a hierarchical relationship of enterprises. More in-depth case studies are required to see more clearly these institutional differences, as well as their impact on the growth

[52] Zhang Henglong and Chen Xian also obtained the similar conclusion in their research. See Zhang Henglong, Chen Xian (2006).

[53] Thun (2006).

and competitiveness of the automotive industry. Eric spent 7 years investigating in these 5 cities and wrote the book, which is well received.

In addition, in some cases, persistent regional differences in conditions, social environment, policy and institutions can also provide us with a good natural experimental field for our economic research. For example, for the evaluation study of the effect on education, poverty, income distribution and public policy, this kind of natural experiment is a rare opportunity, for careful observation often brings extraordinary joy.

10.6 Conclusion

In this paper, I reviewed and summarized the development and empirical study results of the so-called second generation of fiscal decentralization theory on the basis of the institutional evolution in the relationship between central and local governments in China, especially on the important experience after the fiscal decentralization in 1978. Therefore, it is a story of China in transformation and growth told from one point of view.

For 20 years, in order to explain China's economic transition and growth, and better understand the growth differences in transitional countries, economists have developed many theories. Among them, the early theory of decentralization developed by a classic article of Charles Tiebout (1956) was carried forward. A new generation of fiscal decentralization theory (or fiscal federalism) collected components of economics and political science of the past 10 years and is no longer confined to the early stage of the public finance and the supply of public goods, but has turned its vision to the difference of incentive and behavior of local officials in maintaining market, promoting competition and economic growth. An important contribution of these literatures is that they established a "race to the top" conceptual framework by linking up growth with the incentive of fiscal decentralization. The framework is useful to answer the question why China's transformation has contributed to economic growth; it also helps us better understand the performance differences of other transition economies.

However, the theory of decentralization based on China's experience faces a challenge. Essentially, the theory is a "single-task" organizational model. The experience of China tells us that in the early days of transition, when economic growth was seen as the most important goal by the public, it could be tolerated to simplify the local government as a "single-task" organization. Under these conditions, "fiscal federalism with Chinese characteristics" is indeed a very important empirical observation, and its relationship with economic growth is easy to identify. However, with the economic transformation and development, the "multi-task" nature of local governments has become increasingly prominent, so the cost of decentralization will be re-evaluated and began to increase. The expansion of regional gap caused by decentralization, the deterioration of the environment, the ill-use of land, local protectionism and failure of macro coordination will begin to check economic growth.

Therefore, as a theory, we need not only a conceptual framework to explain why Chinese transformation has been accompanied with the economic growth, we also need to place the benefits and costs of decentralization into a "multi-task" theory of decentralization to answer under what conditions the competition of decentralization may break through the bottom line. Of course, it is not very difficult to improve this theory, but it will allow us to see that in China, given the political constraints, growth and decentralization seem to be more and more a "trade-off". In other words, in the framework of authoritarian decentralization, it seems to be difficult for us to find the best answer.

Author's Note

In the past 10 years, in order to explain China's economic transition and growth, and better understand the growth differences in transitional countries, the early theory of decentralization developed by a classic article of Charles Tiebout (1956) was carried forward. A new generation of fiscal decentralization theory (or fiscal federalism) collected components of economics and political science and is no longer confined to the fields of public finance and the supply of public goods, but has turned its vision to the incentive and behavior of local officials in maintaining market, promoting competition and economic growth. In this paper, I reviewed and discussed the development and empirical study results of the second generation of fiscal decentralization theory on the basis of the institutional evolution in the relationship between central and local governments in China, especially on the important experience after the fiscal decentralization in 1978. Therefore, it is a story of China in transformation and growth told from one point of view.

This paper was written during my visit to Queen's University in Canada in the summer of 2007. The wring of this article was purely accidental. I was writing my new book, *A Reform Not Known to the Public*, in which there was a chapter on fiscal decentralization in China. In the course of gathering and reading documents, a clear framework quickly took shape before my eyes, so I decided to write an article and submitted it to the *China Economics Quarterly*. Finally, this article was published in the 1st issue, 7th volume of that journal in October 2007.

References

Bardhan, Pranab, Decentralization of Government and Growth, *Journal of Economic Perspectives*, 2002, 16 (4), pp. 185–205.

Blanchard, Oliver, Shleifer, Andrei, Federalism with and without Political Centralization: China versus Russia, MIT Working Paper 00-15 2000.

Bo Yibo: *Review of a Number of Important Decisions and Events*. Beijing, Central Party School Press, 1991.

Charles Jones: *Introduction to Economic Growth*, Shu Yuan, et al., tr. Beijing, Peking University Press, 2002.

Chen Kang, Arye L. Hilman, Gu Qingyang: Fiscal Centralization and Change of Local Government's Behavior—from Helping Hand to Grabbing Hand, *China Economics Quarterly*, 2002 (2).

Fischel, Wiliam A., *The Tiebout Model at Fifty: Essays in Public Economics in Honor of Wallace Oates*, Cambridge, Lincoln Institute of Land Policy, 2006.

Gu Zhun: *Selected Works of Gu Zhun*, Guiyang, Guizhou People's Press, 1994.

Huang Peihua: Can China Change Its Mode of Economic Development in the 21st Century? *Comparison*, 2005 (18).

Huang Xiaoguang: *Regional Distribution Pattern and Effect of Fiscal Funds*. Suzhou, Soochow University Press, 2001.

Jin, Hehui, Qian, Yingyi, Weingast, Barry, Regional Decentralization and Fiscal Incentives: Federalism, Chinese Style, *Journal of Public Economics*, 2005, 89, pp. 1719–1742.

Jones, Charles, *Introduction to Economic Growth*, W.W. Norton & Company, Inc., 1998.

Lin, Justin Yifu, Liu, Zhiqiang, Fiscal Decentralization and Economic Growth in China, *Economic Development and Cultural Change*, 2000, 49 (1), pp. 1–21

Oates, Walace, The Effects of Property Taxes and Local Public Spending on Property Values: An Empirical Study of Tax Capitalization and the Tiebout Hypothesis, *Journal of Political Economy*, 1969, 77 (8), pp.957-971.

Oates, Walace, *Fiscal Federalism*, New York, Harcourt Brace Jovanovic, 1972.

Oates, Walace, Searching for Leviathan: An Empirical Study, *American Economic Review*, 1985, 75, pp. 748–757.

Oates, Walace, An Essay on Fiscal Federalism, *Journal of Economic Literature*, 1999, 37 pp. 1120–1149.

Oates, Walace, Toward a Second-Generation Theory of Fiscal Federalism, *International Tax and Public Finance*, 2005, 12, pp. 349–373.

R. Musgrave, *The Theory of Public Finance*, New York, McGraw-Hill, 1959.

Shirk, Susan, *The Political Logic of Economic Reform in China*, Berkeley, University of California Press 1993.

Shleifer, Andrei, Schumpeter Lecture: Government in Transition, *European Economic Review*, 1997, 41, PP, 385–410.

Sun Yefang, *Selected Works of Sun Yefang*, Taiyuan, Shanxi People's Publishing House, 1984.

Thun, Eric, *Changing Lanes in China: Foreign Direct Investment, Local Governments and Auto Sector Development*, Cambridge, Cambridge University Press, 2006.

Tiebout, Charles, A Pure Theory of Local Expenditure, *Journal of Political Economy*, 1957, 64, pp. 416–424.

Treisman, Daniel, *After the Deluge*, University of Michigan Press, Ann Arbor, 1999.

Wang Shaoguang: *The Bottom Line of Decentralization*, Beijing, Chinese Planning Press, 1997.

Wang Yongqin, Zhang Yan, Zhang Yuan, Chen Zhao, Lu Ming: China's Great Power Development Mode: Pros and Cons of Decentralization Reform, *Economic Research*, 2007 (1).

Wong, Christine, Fiscal Reform and Local Industrialization: The Problematic Sequencing of Reform in Post-Mao China, *Modern China*, 1992, 18.

Wong, Christine, Can China Change Development Paradigm for the 21st Century, Fiscal Policy Options for Hu Jintao and Wen Jiabao after Two Decades of Muddling Through, Paper for Stiftung Wissenschaft and Politic, 2005.

World Bank: *World Development Report in1997: Governments in the Changing World*. Beijing, China Finance and Economics Press, 1997.

Wu Jinglian: *Economic Reform in Contemporary China*, Shanghai, Shanghai Far East Press, 2003.

Xin Xiangyang: *A Century's Game: 100 Years' Relations between China's Central and Local Governments*, Ji'nan, Shandong People's Publishing House, 2000.

Xu, Chenggang, Maskin, Eric, Qian, Yingyi, Incentives, Information and Organizational Form, *Review of Economic Studies*, 2000, 67 (2), pp. 359–378.

Xu, Chenggang, Qian, Yingyi, Why China's Economic Reforms Differ: The M-Form Hierarchy and Entry/Expansion of the Non-State Sector, *Economics of Transition*, 1993, 1 (2), pp. 135–170.

Yan Bin: Key to Correctly Handling the Fiscal Relationship between the Central and Local Governments: Gradual Implementation of the Tax Distribution System, *Finance and Economics Research*, 1991 (4).

Yifu Lin, Liu Zhiqiang: Fiscal Decentralization and Economic Growth in China, *Journal of Peking University*, 2000 (4).

Zhang Henglong, Chen Xian: Influence of Fiscal Competition on the Local Public Expenditure Structure, *Comparison of Economic and Social Systems*, 2006 (6).

Zhang Jun, Gao Yuan, Fu Yong, Zhang Hong: Why have China had Good Infrastructure, *Economy Research*, 2007 (3).

Zhang Minggeng, Zhang Mingju: *Historical Administrative Divisions of China: 221 BC–AD1991*, Beijing, Overseas Chinese Publishing House, 1996.

Zhang Tao, Zou Hengfu, Fiscal Decentralization, Public Spending, and Economic Growth in China, *Journal of Public Economics*, 1998, 67, pp. 221–240.

Zhang Yan, Gong Liutang: Reform of the Tax Distribution System, Fiscal Decentralization and Economic Growth in China, *China Economics Quarterly*, 2005 (5).

Zhang Yanlong: Evolution of the Relationship between Fiscal Decentralization and Governments below Provincial Levels. *Sociological Studies*, 2006 (3).

Zhang, Xiaobo, Fiscal Decentralization and Political Centralization: Implications for Regional Inequality, 2006.

Zhong Xiaomin: *The Theory of Payments of Intergovernmental Fiscal Transfer*. Shanghai, Lixin Accounting Press, 1998.

Zhou Li'an: Governance of Chinese Local Officials: A Study of the Model of Political Tournaments, *Economic Research*, 2007 (7).

Zhou Wenxing, Zhang Zheng: Impact of Fiscal Decentralization on Economic Growth after the Founding of the China: A Hypothesis and Test, *Institutional Economics Research*, 2006 (1).

Zhuravskaya, Ekaterina, Incentives to Provide Local Public Goods: Fiscal Federalism, Russian Style, *Journal of Public Economics*, 2000, 76, pp. 337–368.

Chapter 11
Why Have China Had a Good Infrastructure: Decentralization Competition, Governance and Infrastructure Investment Decisions

11.1 Introduction

For those who have been in China 30 years ago and revisited China during the past 10 years, the changes in the level of infrastructure in China indeed have made them stunned. Yes, China's infrastructure and urban landscape (especially in the coastal areas) are changing rapidly. Even 15 years ago, no one would have dared to expect the infrastructure in China to reach its present level and update speed. Back in the 1980s, even those Chinese living in cities had also to endure great inconvenience in communication, use of energy, public transport and travel. Today, the number of people traveling on the highway by bus every day can be as many as millions, not to mention the welfare brought about by the changes in the urban infrastructure for the Chinese people.

As a stock of public capital, a good physical infrastructure plays an important and fundamental role in the economic growth and development of a country. At the same time, the continued improvement of infrastructure level is also an important part of China's economic growth. But in the literature on evaluation of China's economic growth, many scholars seem to still belittle "hardware" in favor of the importance of "software". This is particularly evident in the discussions on the "double sticks" between China and India. Although China is far superior to India in infrastructure, it is an undeniable fact that most articles still attach more importance to the "institutional asset" of India. We believe that in the discussion and comparison of different economic growth performances, it is not appropriate to evaluate the "hardware" and "software" separately. The serious lag of infrastructure in India does not mean that India can quickly catch up with China's level, and the improvement of infrastructure is by no means an isolated matter, nor is it simple.

The construction of infrastructure is the improvement of material conditions including highway, rails, airport, communication cables, bus or railway stations and urban public utilities, but it is also far beyond these objects. The difference of these

J. Zhang, *Reform, Transformation and Growth*, Understanding China,
https://doi.org/10.1007/978-981-99-5712-5_11

infrastructures reflects the differences of political governance and government capabilities. There is no doubt that a government system without any accomplishments cannot create these "hard" things. It is found in a large number of research papers in economics that a country's infrastructure level is the typical manifestation of the levels of its government's governance, political management and the efficiency of decentralization. High quality infrastructure has been included in indicators that measure government quality or governance.

In transitional economies, due to the differences in political attributes and transformation of government's governance, the governments in the transitional economy show significant differences. The combination of fiscal decentralization and different modes of political management has also produced different performances of economic growth and development. As observed by many researches, the differences in Russia, India and China in the economic performance after the 1990s is not caused by the different effects of fiscal decentralization, but by the difference in government management.[1] These factors have provided us with an institutional background to seek differences in incentives for infrastructure investment.

At first glance, investing in infrastructure is typically a "supporting hand" action on the part of government. But does this mean that the local governments in China know how to promote public interests? Or is the Chinese political management mode more conducive to the improvement of infrastructure? We must consider the incentives faced by government officials before we are able to answer these questions. This means that we need to carry out economic analysis.

Our observation is that, compared with the unsuccessful business models of research and development (R&D), China has evolved a successful model in improving infrastructure. Since the middle of the1980s, the improvement of China's urban construction and infrastructure has been made by local governments. In theory, the infrastructure has a long investment cycle, low private returns, and fast depreciation, so adequate investment cannot be guaranteed by market forces. In view of this, simply relying on market mechanisms should not be able to solve the serious shortage and underinvestment of China's infrastructure if no substantial returns and commitments are ensured in infrastructure investment. Then, what is the considerable return or commitment the government can give to market investors to invest in infrastructure? Because the government has the land ownership and a complicated and universal control over the land, the returns provided by the government to the market investors certainly should include the business franchise for infrastructure construction, the land transfer under agreement, real estate development and entry permit into local market. In China, deregulation and change of government control are often the result of a mutually beneficial exchange with the market.

The question is, why do Chinese local governments become so "market savvy" in improving infrastructure? On this issue, we often have opposite assumptions about the government. But in theory, economists generally do not assume that a "helping hand" government can be seen everywhere, but is more likely to interpret the government's "public welfare" behavior as the result of profit seeking behavior by officials.

[1] Blanchard and Shleifer (2000).

What matters is not the nature of the government, but what incentives the officials will have. The theory for economists to look at and explain these phenomena is still based on the economic logic of "personal choice". This means that we need to link the efforts of the government that continues to improve the infrastructure with the choice of officials under restraints. Such a combination is the key to uncovering why China has a good infrastructure.

In this article, we will argue that China's outstanding achievements in investment and infrastructure upgrading can be explained by the Chinese fiscal decentralization model and the successful transformation of the government. The success of this decentralization model lies in the fact that the central government has replaced the political preaching to the local governments with "yardstick competition". The top-down political management of the central government is based on the measurable yardstick of local economic development (referred to as "achievements"). Under this intergovernmental political governance mode, not only can local infrastructure improvements "attract investment from overseas" so as to achieve faster economic growth, but it is easier to measure the "achievements" which can best meet the needs of local officials with significantly improved infrastructure.

In the past ten years, most economists have neglected the transformation of the government's own governance in the study of transition economy. In fact, in order to realize the change of governance towards a market-supporting mode so as to support and make use of market function, the professionalism and technicalization of government bureaucrats as well as the transformation of government functions and the renewal of government human capital are the important strategies. In 1996, American economists Shleifer and Vishny noticed the importance of government transformation in the economic transition because they had witnessed the economic transformation process in Russia and Eastern Europe. In the article, Government in Transition, they stressed that "Whether with regard to economy or politics, how to update human capital may be the central issue of the transition."[2] We believe that China has also gone ahead of Russia in these respects. At the local level, the successful transition of the government model toward the "developmental" government can help stimulate government officials' motive to invest in infrastructure, because it is conducive to the officials' political career.

This paper is organized as follows: in the second part we will give a definition and classification of the concept of infrastructure and make a summary and comment on the economics literature on infrastructure; the third part is a comprehensive discussion on the reform of fiscal decentralization, political management and governance transformation in China, in order to provide an institutional background for understanding the motive and incentive model of the local government's investment in infrastructure. In the fourth part, we will describe the situation of the growth of financing for China's capital construction and infrastructure investment since the reform and opening up, and the different models of infrastructure stock between the eastern and western regions. The fifth part constructs a regression model about the

[2] Shleifer and Vishiny (2004).

investment decision of infrastructure, and makes a statistical test with the panel data of 29 provinces (cities) in China in 1988–2001. The sixth part is the conclusion.

11.2 Concept, Definition and Research Literature Review of Infrastructure

(1) Definition Scope of Infrastructure

At the end of the 1980s, the World Bank organized a series of research on infrastructure, and released its findings in 1995—*World Development Report of 1994: Provide Infrastructure for Development*. This report focuses on economic infrastructure, which is defined as the permanent engineering structures, equipment, facilities and the services they provide for the residents and for economic production. These infrastructures include utilities (electric power, gas pipeline, telecommunications, water supply, environmental sanitation facilities and sewage system, collecting and processing system for solid waste), public works (dams, irrigation works and roads) and other transportation sectors (railway, urban transportation, harbor, water transportation and airport). The report concluded that, although infrastructure (or what economists call social capital management) has not been defined very clearly, it always has two clear characteristics: technical characteristics (such as economies of scale) and economic characteristics (such as diffusion of users to non-users).[3]

On the basis of the definition of the World Bank, Prud'homme (2004) divides infrastructure into 8 broad categories according to different types of services provided by infrastructure (see Table 11.1).[4] If the definition of economic infrastructure defined by the World Bank in its1994 report is the principle, then Prud'Homme (2004) makes a refined judgment whether an activity belongs to an economic infrastructure. In this paper, we will refer to the definition of the World Bank and Prud'Homme (2004) and select the appropriate indicators by combining the available data to measure the level and development of China's infrastructure.

Specifically, we mainly selected four indicators: first, transport infrastructure; second, energy infrastructure; third, telecommunication infrastructure; and fourth, urban infrastructure. The first three indicators are categorized by their functions, and the last index is special, specifically referring to city infrastructure system, the main reason of which is: first, the index is reported as a separate item in the statistical yearbook and its data can be obtained accurately; second, each sub-index contained in this item is included in the definition of the World Bank; third, in the discussion of relationship between infrastructure investment and foreign direct investment (FDI), city infrastructure needs special attention, because most foreign investors would invest in Chinese cities.

[3] World Bank (1995).

[4] Prud'hommer, Infrastructure and Development, Paper prepared for The ABCDE (Annual Bank Conference on Development Economics), 2004-03-05.

Table 11.1 Infrastructure defined by the World Bank in terms of the type of service offered

Services	Infrastructure
Transportation	Roads, bridges, railways, tunnels, ports, etc.
Water supply	Dams, reservoirs, water pipes, etc.
Water treatment	Sewer pipes, sewage treatment plants, etc.
Irrigation	Dams, canals, etc.
Garbage disposal	Garbage bins, garbage incinerators, etc.
Heating	Central heating equipment, heating pipes, etc.
Telecommunication service	Automatic switch, cables, etc.
Energy	Power plants, power lines, gas pipelines, etc.

Source Prud'hommer, Infrastructure and Development, Paper prepared for the ABCDF (Annual Bank Conference on Development Economics), 2004-03-05

Traffic or transport infrastructure is composed of three indicators, namely railway mileage, inland waterway mileage and highway mileage. The graded highway refers to the total mileage of highway, grade-1 highway and grade-2 highway. Energy infrastructure consists of two indicators: electricity consumption and energy consumption. More data of communication infrastructure can be obtained in the statistical yearbook covering three aspects of postal service, telecommunications and Internet. Among them, the postal infrastructure is measured by the number of post offices and the total length of postal route; telecommunication infrastructure is measured by long-distance telephones, wireless paging users, mobile phone users, long-distance automatic exchange capacity, switchboard capacity of the local telephone office, mobile telephone exchange capacity and length of long-distance optical cable line; and the Internet infrastructure includes the number of Internet users and the length of long-distance microwave line. The index of city infrastructure includes: city water consumption rate, city gas penetration rate, number of public transportation vehicles used per million people, per capita road area, per capita public green land area, and number of public toilets per million people. Clearly, these indicators have been also included in the definition of the World Bank. In the fifth part, we will deal with the stock index of these infrastructures so as to better depict the changing trend of infrastructure construction and the unbalanced development mode among different regions.

In addition to looking at the changes in the stock levels of infrastructure, we will also examine the flow variation and determinants of infrastructure in this paper. We want to use capital formation of infrastructure or the government investment in infrastructure to reflect the flow rate changes on infrastructure. However, the existing statistical data sources cannot provide us with a corresponding investment data in accordance with the composition of the stock. Fortunately, we can get the concept of the following three categories of capital formation in *Chinese Statistical Yearbook*: ① production and supply industries for electricity, gas and water; ② transportation, storage and telecommunications industry; ③ water conservancy, environment and the management of public facilities. As these three types of investment indicators cover the concept of infrastructure we have defined earlier to a considerable extent, it is not unreasonable to use them to measure the flow indicator of infrastructure investment. In this article, we will discuss the factors that affect the incentives for local government to improve infrastructure investment.

(2) Research Literature on Infrastructure Investment Decisions

The mainstream Western economic literature only dealt with the study of infrastructure 20 years ago. Although Arrow and Kurz (1970),[5] in a classic article entitled Public Investment, the Rate of Return and Optimal Fiscal Policy, first included the public capital stock[6] into the total quantity production function,[7] it did not attract much attention for some time due to the uncertainty of the equilibrium in the model, so the theoretical development halted for that matter. The real enthusiasm of economists for infrastructure began in the late 1980s. The excellent empirical work done by Aschauer (1989a, b, c, 1995) demonstrates the extreme importance of infrastructure investment to economic development.[8] Although this importance was later proved to be highly overrated, the literature on measuring output elasticity of infrastructure did increase after him.

However, the research based on Chinese experience is still very rare though Démurger (2001) is one of the exceptions.[9] He attempts, in this article, to find the significant explanatory power of infrastructure to China's growing regional disparity in the framework of Barro.[10] The author believes that infrastructure includes two aspects of transportation and communication. The empirical results show that transportation and communication have a significant impact on regional economic growth. Through further analysis of the growth rate, Démurger found that infrastructure (especially transportation) has explained a large part of the success of northeastern region and backwardness of the central and western regions, and that the impact of infrastructure on regional disparities seems to be strengthening.

In addition to the above paper, we have noticed a recent literature that examines the impact of infrastructure on the development of China's rural economy.[11] By using

---

[5] Arrow and Kurz (1970).

[6] In concept, public capital is relative to private capital, mainly referring to the capital formed by government investment, both of which constitute the total capital stock. Obviously, the most important component of public capital (especially productive public capital) is infrastructure, and some studies regard the two as equal. Therefore, a considerable part of our literature review is directed at public capital. As we can see from the latter part of the article, in order to estimate the return on infrastructure and the elasticity of output, many studies, when setting the production function, deducted the infrastructure stock from the total capital stock in order to obtain the private capital stock.

[7] Of course, we can also interpret the mainstream economics studies as a revival of the literature on development economics (Murphy, Shleifer, Vishny, 1989; Justman, 1996).

[8] Aschauer (1989a, b, c, 1995).

[9] Démurger (2001).

[10] Barro (1991).

[11] Fan and Zhang (2004).

newly acquired agricultural census data and other official data, Fan and Zhang estimated the production function of agricultural and non-agricultural sectors in rural China and figured out the source of productivity differences among regions, especially estimating the extent of explanatory power of infrastructure over the difference of regional production efficiency. As far as the general agricultural sector is concerned, infrastructure has explained more than 40% of the regional difference in labor productivity, although for the western region, it was only 10%. This discovery differs greatly from that of Démurger (2001), and the abnormal interpretation of infrastructure of the central region and the large residual term indicate that this estimate is far from being perfect.

In addition, Fan Jiuli, Bai Baoli (2004a, b)[12] and Fan Jiuli, Bai Baoli and Pan Liang (2004c)[13] have carried out a series of tests related to infrastructure and economic growth by using the national total data and area data. The infrastructure they used include the following 5 sectors or industries: production and supply industry of power, gas and water; transport, storage and communications; geological prospecting and water conservancy management; municipal utilities (not including gas, water supply and production, which is included in electric power industry); state organs, political party organs and social organizations. Eleven areas of agricultural, forest, animal husbandry, fishery, mining industry and manufacturing industry were defined as the non-infrastructure sectors.

Although research has shown that infrastructure investment is of continuing importance to economic development, its investment has not reached optimal levels in most less developed countries. Randolph, Bogetic, and Hefley (1996),[14] in a 84-page working paper, investigated various factors affecting infrastructure investment decisions by using panel data and time series data of the years of 1980–1986 covering 27 backward and middle-income countries. Their explanatory variable is the government's spending on per capita transportation and communications (calculated in dollars of 1980), involving a large number of explanatory variables that determined the investment in infrastructure by government. Variables describing economic characteristics include: ① The stock of existing infrastructure. They used two stock index; the first is the ratio of total mileage of highway and railway to the per capita GDP (dollar value of 1980); the second index is the total capital stock (including private capital) estimated by the perpetual inventory method. ② Population density. Low population density requires more investment in transportation and communications. However, when the density is not high, inputs such as sewers and medical facilities may not be needed, thereby saving infrastructure investment. Finally, economies of scale make countries with greater population density have a higher level of optimal infrastructure. ③ Urbanization level. If the scale of the supply of infrastructure is significant, then the higher the level of urbanization, the lower the per capita infrastructure. But there may be the opposite effect–infrastructure investment may rise as

[12] Fan Jiuli, Bai Baol (2004a, b).

[13] Fan Jiuli, Bai Baoli, Pan Quan (2004c).

[14] Randolph and Bogetic (1996).

urbanization increases. Moreover, given the prevailing urban tendency, high urbanization will increase per capita expenditure on infrastructure. ④ Urban and rural structure. Differences between urban and rural areas promote mobility of the population between cities and countryside which will increase the government's spending on urban infrastructure. Moreover, the government will curb the outflow of rural population by increasing infrastructure investment to increase agricultural productivity in order to limit the rapid population transfer to the cities. All this means that the greater the gap between urban and rural areas, the higher the level of infrastructure spending should be. The author demonstrated the dynamic conversion of the structure of urban and rural areas by using three indicators: urban and rural population flow rate (i.e. the city population growth rate minus the total population growth rate), per capita agricultural GDP, and the proportion of agriculture to GDP. ⑤ Labor participation rate. The variable is represented by the population of the workforce divided by the total population. Public infrastructure spending will affect corporations' demand for labor and effective labor wages of per unit. The relationship between labor participation rate and public infrastructure expenditure depends on whether the relation between labor and infrastructure investment is complementary or substitutional.

Other indicators that reflect the economic structure include: ① Economic development stage which is represented by actual per capita GDP or actual income. Infrastructure is usually a normal product, and economic growth will increase the returns on infrastructure investment, and is positively related to infrastructure spending. ② Domestic fiscal balance. ③ Balance of international accounts. ④ Scale of the external sector, which is measured by the proportion of imports and exports to the GDP. In some developing countries, tariffs are an important source of fiscal revenue for the government. Therefore, the large external sector means that the government has the ability to provide more infrastructures. In addition, infrastructure can enhance a nation's competitiveness and thus expand exports. In this way, the external sector should have a positive relationship with infrastructure spending. ⑤ Conditions of trade. ⑥ Scale of government debt. ⑦ Institutions, which are measured by the extent of participation of citizens in politics and the freedom of citizens to express their views. But their relationship with infrastructure spending is not clear. On the one hand, a perfect system reduces the transaction costs, thus increasing the possibility of private provision of infrastructure; on the other hand, the improvement of the system promotes the development of private economy, thus increasing the demand for infrastructure. In view of the World Bank's policy, the authors also examined the indicators of government goals, namely, the impact of poverty reduction efforts. The government's policy on poverty reduction will increase infrastructure spending, but if it is done by way of public health, education or social security, the infrastructure spending could also be reduced.

They concluded that per capita spending on infrastructure is the most sensitive to stages of economic development, level of urbanization and labor participation rate. Infrastructure expenditure is positively related to the per capita GDP measurement of economic development. The scale of external sector, urban and rural structures and infrastructure stock level are all important determinants for per capita spending on infrastructure. The bigger the external sector, the greater the per capita expenditure on infrastructure. The structure of urban and rural areas reflects the level of population mobility, which has increased the per capita infrastructure level. The greater the infrastructure stock, the higher the per capita infrastructure expenditure. Higher population density is associated with lower infrastructure spending. The more perfect the system is, the more the central government's spending on infrastructure will be. But when infrastructure level is low, infrastructure spending will decline as the system improves. The budget deficit does not affect the central government's infrastructure spending, but it has a positive relationship with budget spending. Central government's spending on infrastructure is significantly associated with more export-oriented economies, but is not significantly associated with the magnitude of export-oriented economy. Finally, the central government's efforts to combat poverty affect its scale of infrastructure spending.

In a broader sense, the difference in infrastructure investment among countries is not only affected by the stages of economic development and development characteristics, it also reflects the quality factors of government and policy. The study of political scientists and economists since North and Thomas (1973)[15] has found that the government's accomplishments and commitment are the key factors for a country to experience long-term capital formation. It is from this point of view that Henisz (2002)[16] used the 200-year data of more than 100 countries to study the decisions to invest in infrastructure. The key infrastructure refers to the number of telephones installed and the megawatts of power generation. The political constraints mentioned in the article refer to the possibility of policy change, that is to say, any preference change of a branch of government can change its policy to a large extent, which can be represented by the number of government departments that have the veto rights. The results show that the political environment is an important determinant of the key infrastructure investment differences among countries. This means that the political environment is important not only in modern times, but also in the nineteenth century. The regression results showed that adding the institutional environment into the regression model significantly improved the ability of the model to explain the following facts: why did some countries invest in infrastructure earlier than other countries? Why will infrastructure investment continue to grow?

There is also a set of documents relating to infrastructure investment decisions in developing countries. For example, some studies have found that sometimes it seems the government will do something in good faith—actively and honestly helping the private sector increase its productivity and enter the international market. Singapore, South Korea and Taiwan are examples of this kind. This kind of government is referred to in the literature as "developmental states". Evans (1992) found that the professionalization of the state bureaucracy was a necessary condition for a government to become a "developmental government".[17] Evans has developed some

[15] North and Thomas (1973).

[16] Henisz (2002).

[17] Evans (1992).

practical indicators: the ratio of public servants' examination; passing rate of applicants and the average tenure rate of officials. The professionalization of officials may have two aspects of influence. One is that it inhibits the government's negative impact on economic development (limiting rent-seeking activities). Second, the extension of the government's tenure and professionalism can improve the government's incentives to promote infrastructure, as it helps career building. Some scholars have empirically tested the first aspect, while Rauch (1995)[18] has mainly studied the latter aspect. Specifically, he studied the proportion of spending on roads and water supplies—projects that will bring longer period of benefits—in government spending in the first twenty years of the twentieth century of the United states.

In a simple urban growth model constructed by the author, economic growth only depends on the decision-making of the city government. Investing in new infrastructure can attract private investment in the trade sector and labor migration and employment, thereby boosting urban development. Assuming interest rates and wages remain unchanged, city officials can benefit from the inputs and outputs of urban production. The benefits from inputs are assignments of jobs and kickbacks while the benefits from output are the satisfaction of voters and the promotion of prestige and power. Assuming that the government's current revenues come entirely from the fees charged by existing public services, the problem that needs to study is, between the spending that can bring immediate benefits (police, fire prevention) and investment in infrastructure, how will the government allocate their income?

The three major changes in the so-called "progressive era" in the United States were, first, the emergence of the civil service. City officials must pass the exam, which is the core of official professionalism. The second is the appointed government (1901), usually comprising five people who took place of the mayor, the City Council and other elected officials and each had the administrative and legislative powers. The third kind of reform was the emergence of government of city administrators (1908). Under this system, the city manager was appointed and responsible to the City Council, monopolizing the overall power over the whole city. Clearly, there is a big difference between the government of the civil service and the latter two categories of government. In Rauch's view, the "age of progress" provided a natural test ground for the three systems to keep pace with each other.

The infrastructure variable in the paper is the proportion of expenditure on roads, drinking water and sewer to the total expenditure. The regression results of urban fixed effect model after time dummy variables have been added show that in a city with the civil service system, the infrastructure investment proportion was higher than that of the city that did not have the civil service system. The reform resulted in the increase of the proportion of infrastructure investment and the steady economic growth rate of the city. The result of the latter two modes of governance was just the opposite, which shows that the longer the tenure of a government, the more likely it is to put a larger proportion of government resources into projects such as infrastructure.

---

[18] Rauch (1995).

In short, compared with the traditional economics research literature on infrastructure such as its output elasticity, whether it is in short supply and its causal relation with economic growth, the research on the determinants of infrastructure is more important and significant. Even if infrastructure investment is endogenous in economic growth, the important task for economists is to explain how this "endogenous" process takes place. The interdisciplinary research literature of economics and political science is paying more and more attention to this "endogenous" process. Writers of these documents are convinced that the explanation of infrastructure investment decisions (including the laying out of a more general economic policy) should be sought from government officials who try to maximize their objective function. This needs to deem the formulation of policy to be an endogenous rather than a control variable. In fact, the problems faced by economists are not what should be done, but what the officials are actually doing and why.

11.3 Fiscal Decentralization, Political Management and the Incentives Faced by Local Government in China

Since the reform and opening-up to the outside world, especially since the 1990s, China's infrastructure has undergone tremendous changes. Transportation, communications, energy supply and city infrastructure are changing rapidly. The continuous improvement of the infrastructure level itself is an important part of China's economic development and a very important measure of growth. In traffic, for example, 15 years ago, no one would have dared to think of the level and updating pace of today's infrastructure. In the 80s, or even early 90s, Chinese had to rely on the decrepit trains to travel, and it was a big headache to get a train ticket. But the fundamental difference today is that the number of people traveling on the highway in buses every day can be as many as millions.

In order to better explain the reasons for the improvement of China's infrastructure, we need to study the determinants of infrastructure investment. From the above review of the existing literature we can see that infrastructure investment decision is linked to the government and the political process, probably because of the nature of the infrastructure—the investment decisions usually are made by the government and connected with the public finance. Therefore, it is necessary to study the institutional incentive for such decision-making and the model of governance before studying the decisions of infrastructure investment. In a word, the clue of explanation should be found from the angle of political economy. In this section, we will discuss the institutional environment and governance model that affect infrastructure investment decisions.

However, it must be pointed out that there is a significant difference between the political economy and the existing literature on the investment decisions of China's infrastructure compared with the study of European and American countries. In

Western developed countries, because the political and financial decentralization systems are highly mature and stable, the empirical research is more focused on how the allocation of public financial resources to the field of infrastructure is influenced by voters or various parties. This is evident in the literature review of the existing empirical studies of the West described above. However, our research is to examine a particular transition economy, which has undergone the process of economic and fiscal decentralization, but politically it is still highly centralized. What is different from the existing literature is that, in local regions, investment decisions in infrastructure seem to be more associated with achieving economic growth rather than redistribution. Therefore, in order to discuss the determinants of infrastructure investment, we must start with the observation and interpretation of the incentives for local governments and their behavior under the fiscal decentralization system.

First, let us describe how the fiscal decentralization has changed the investment decision environment since the early 1980s in the context of the relationship between the central government and local government. The reform and evolution of China's intergovernmental fiscal system can be roughly described in two stages.[19] In the first stage (1978–1993), the administrative decentralization (all-round fiscal contract system) replaced the centralized, unified revenue and expenditure system prior to 1978. After 1994, a tax sharing system between the central and local government was implemented. It is worth noting that, after the tax sharing system, the proportion of income of the central government increased from 22% in 1993 to 55.7% in 1994, while the proportion of local fiscal expenditure during the reform periods of fiscal contract and tax sharing system was in a steady upward state, rising to 45% in 1981 and as high as 72.3% in 2004. In this sense, China's local governments gained an ever increasing control power over their finances.[20]

In the existing economic literature, although theories and evidences differ as to whether fiscal decentralization to local government had a positive or negative impact on economic growth, in general, Tiebout's (1956)[21] "public expenditure theory" and Oates' (1972)[22] "fiscal federalism theory" have won more recognition, becoming the basic literature of economic research on fiscal decentralization. Tiebout (1956) and Oates (1972) emphasized the positive influence of intergovernmental competition and local government's superiority in accessing information on improving the supply of public goods and the efficiency of economy. In the past 10 years, among the studies of "transition economy", the idea of fiscal federalism has been paid more attention to, and spawned many theories and empirical studies. These studies all emphasized the positive impact of fiscal decentralization on maintaining market reforms and improving efficiency.[23]

[19] Hu Shudong (2001). He made a systematic record and analysis of the changes in the intergovernmental financial system and the central-local relations since the 1950s.

[20] Cheng Shiyi, Zhang Jun (2008).

[21] Tiebout (1956).

[22] Oates (1972).

[23] Qian and Weingast (1997), Qian and Roland (1998), Cao et al. (1999).

These documents are naturally highly relevant to the study of the determinants of infrastructure investment in this paper. It is argued in theory in these models of fiscal decentralization or fiscal federalism targeted at the transition economies that, the central government transferred more power to local governments, resulting in a regional decentralized system similar to federalism. The local governments started to engage in fierce competition with each other in order to attract private capital (including foreign capital) to develop the local economy which will improve the costs of the use of funds and contribute to the hardening of budget constraint, thus having a positive effect on economic growth. In empirical research, the empirical study of Lin and Liu (2000) supports the conclusion that fiscal decentralization is beneficial to economic growth.[24] Zhang Jun and Jin Yu (2005), through their study of provincial panel data, concluded that in the decentralized fiscal system, the local government's fiscal expenditure has significantly caused the increase of the growth rate of TFP.[25] Chen Shiyi and Zhang Jun (2006) further found that fiscal decentralization (especially the tax distribution system) also significantly improved the efficiency of the local government's fiscal expenditure.[26]

However, some empirical studies on the economic transition in Russia have found that the system of fiscal federalism did not produce economic performance similar to that of China.[27] Zhuravskaya (2000) analyzed and compared the fiscal decentralization and the relationship between central and local governments in China and Russia. He finds that in China, there is a positive correlation between the local government's independence in the financial power and the efficiency and incentive of the local government to provide public goods. Under the fiscal decentralization system in Russia, the fiscal incentives for local government is extremely weak on average, because when the local government's income increases, the government at a higher level will cut the transfer payments and reduce the revenue sharing proportion of the local government. Therefore, the local government in Russia did not really get an independent financial status. By contrast, in China, the proportion of revenue shared by local governments is much higher than that in Russia, and the local government is more financially independent. Thus, in Russia, the fiscal federalism actually has limited the establishment of private businesses and suppressed the incentive for local governments to effectively supply public goods. Fiscal decentralization has in part become a market-hampering federalism. Although the public goods in the article

[24] Lin and Liu (2000).

[25] Zhang Jun, Jin Yu (2005).

[26] Of course, there are also some economists who do not support the conclusion of fiscal federalism. For example, Young (2000) and Poncet (2002) argued in their empirical research that China's fiscal decentralization in fact led to the continuous market segmentation, which, in general, is not conducive to the formation of a unified domestic market and improvement of growth efficiency. Chen Kang and others (2002) believe that China's fiscal decentralization (especially the tax sharing system in 1994) has turned the local government from a "helping hand" to a "predatory hand". Ping Xinqiao and Bai Jie (2006) found in their study that the non-budget income in China has expanded the scale of local governments, but the growth of non-budget expenditure has led to the deterioration of the efficiency of capital allocation.

[27] Shleifer (1997), Zhuravskaya (2000).

refer to public health and education (measured respectively by the infant mortality rate and the proportion of students going to school at night), not to infrastructure, the paper clearly reveals that the fiscal arrangement between the governments will exert an important influence on the way the local government provides public goods.

Shleifer (1997)[28] also compared the process of economic transformation of Russia and Poland in earlier studies. His research also noted the importance of fiscal relations and political incentives between the upper and lower levels of government in explaining the transition and growth. He found that the contrasts in economic performance between Russia and Poland were largely determined by differences in government governance (or government performance). In Russia, no economic and political incentives were developed between higher and lower governments to promote the transformation of local government's behavior, thus the "predatory nature" of local governments that impeded local economic development remained unchanged. Moreover, in discussing the incentive problems of local officials, Shleifer believes that one of the important differences between Russia and Poland is that Poland systematically implemented the electoral system, especially the election of local officials, whereas in Russia, the constraints and incentives of election were rather weak.

However, Shleifer's emphasis (1997) on the constraints and incentives for local officials brought about by the electoral system was not helpful in explaining the difference of local governments between China and Russia. It is true that whether local government officials are appointed or elected locally will have different constraints and incentives on their behaviors. The reality is that the officials of the local governments in China are appointed by higher authorities rather than elected at the grassroots level. This is determined by China's political system which has not undergone any changes even after decentralization in economic and fiscal decision-making to lower levels of government was implemented. In contrast to fiscal decentralization, the system is highly centralized politically and the Party central committee has the absolute political authority in appointing local officials. Therefore, when comparing the behavior and performance of government officials in Russia and China, it is obvious that political centralism should be taken into consideration. In fact, Blanchard and Shleifer (2000) soon realized this problem. They argued that whether the central government maintains political centralization is important to explain why Russia's fiscal decentralization has led to looting by local governments. They believed that since the Chinese central government (Party) has the absolute authority and the power to appoint local officials, it has the ability to reward and punish the behavior of local government officials; while the dysfunctional democracy in Russia not only makes it impossible for the central government to implement its goals, but it also lacks the ability to affect the action of local governments.

Similarly, India's fiscal decentralization and the local government's actions are also in sharp contrast to China. Famous Indian economist Pranab Bardhan wrote in a recent article that both China and India have experienced a considerable degree of decentralization, but the nature of the separation of powers experienced by the

[28] This paper was included in Shleifer and Vishiny: *Grabbing Hand*, tr. by Zhao Hongjun, Beijing, CITIC Publishing House, Chapter 11, 2004.

two countries is very different.[29] In India, decentralization has been adopted in the form of local elections, but so far, the real authority and tax revenues delegated to local governments are negligible. The real role of elected officials in most rural and district areas is to snatch the benefits of projects funded by higher authorities (such as employment or credit projects). In many states, resources that are significant to the poor are transferred to non targeted groups through collusion between officials and local forces. In China, on the other hand, local party and government departments have actual authority and share local revenues, thereby driving local officials to play a leading role in local economic development. Unlike China, the local economic development has not been on the agenda of the local government in India.

In China, as the local officials are appointed rather than locally elected, they must obey the authority of the central government and keep their goals in line with the latter even as they reap the benefits of the fiscal decentralization. When the central government has established faster economic development goals, the bottom-up economic growth is not only in line with the interests of local government under the fiscal decentralization system, but in fact it has become the effective evaluation index of higher government to reward or punish local government officials. What is known as "achievement outlook" is very popular among China's local government officials, for it reflects the perfect compatibility between political incentives faced by local officials and incentives for local economic growth.[30]

Compared with the early literatures on China's economic growth which are more focused on the input factors in growth, some literatures in recent years have paid more and more attention to the importance of "effective incentives for the government". Professor Perkins of Harvard University offered a good comment in this respect.[31] He discussed China in depth in his article Economic Growth in China from the Historical and International Perspectives. However, he believes that one cannot understand the achievement of growth in China only from a transnational perspective by discussing how the savings, investment, input factors and geographical conditions are favorable to the economic growth in China. He wrote at the end of the article: "Transnational comparisons only give us a very broad description of why China has accelerated growth since 1978. Based on these comparative analyses, the basic conclusion is that China has done what other economically successful countries have done before. However, to really understand why China is doing so well, we must study more deeply the concrete policies adopted by China and the concrete results achieved by these policies. Most of these achievements come from experiences unique to China, not just the replication of other countries." In our view, China's unique experience is the effective incentives for local governments made possible by its unique decentralization and political management mode. For economists, "do a good job of stimulating

---

[29] Bardhan (2006).

[30] Li and Li (2005). They made an excellent empirical research on how the "achievements" of the local Chinese officials would influence the probability of their promotion.

[31] Perkins (2005).

the government" is an important issue in the economics literature on public sector.[32] Unlike the faith and the transformation strategy of "set the right price" advocated by "post-Washington consensus", the fiscal decentralization of Chinese style has undoubtedly well handled the issue of incentives for local government in terms of the economic growth target.

Specifically, the incentives for local governments have been changed from two reasons. First, the mode combining the multi-layered fiscal decentralization and a single political centralization has changed the governance of "multi-task targets" in the public sector into a simple "yardstick competition" mechanism[33] among local governments. This mechanism, through a top-down rather than bottom-up highly decentralized structure, has created a development consensus and strong incentives of "competing for growth" among governments. China's economic growth is the product of this mechanism. As for the local government, the important strategy of yardstick competition is to attract investment for the local economy, especially to attract foreign direct investment (FDI). This has eventually led to the competitive incentives for improving local infrastructure.

Second, China's top-down political management model has transformed the local government into a "developmental style" government model. One of the most important content is to have reformed the structure and management of public sector, improved the professional level of government, accelerated the renewal of human capital of government, and adhered to the vertical centralized political system and official appointment system. We have mentioned earlier that if the unique centralized political management system and the power of appointing local officials by the central government are absent, fiscal decentralization cannot guarantee that local governments have sufficient incentive to promote economic development and support market transformation. The advantage of Chinese political management mode is to have effectively created the "achievement outlook" for local government officials and their goals of career promotion. And without the large-scale renewal of government officials and the change of the public sector to a professional bureaucratic structure, the transformation of government in the process of market transformation is also unimaginable.

In the relevant literature, the traditional view is that competition between governments at the same level is often an important reason that decentralization can improve government governance. But Treisman (2000) challenges the conclusion that fiscal

[32] Unlike the private sector, the public sector is characterized by multi objectives and multi tasks, difficulty in performance measurement and the different natures of agents. As a result, the research on the incentive mechanism of government departments has become a very active topic for economists in the past 20 years. Wang Yongqin and Ding Juhong (2006) provided a good literature review of the incentive mechanism for the public sector.

[33] In the literature of industrial organizations, the so-called "yardstick competition" means that the competition policy of an enterprise is chosen by observing the performance of other enterprises. In the field of politics or public sector, the meaning of yardstick competition is that when the higher authority can use the performance of other local governments to assess and evaluate a local government, local governments will engage in a mutual imitation competition among themselves. For relevant literature, refer to Besley and Case (1995).

decentralization can effectively regulate government behavior.[34] He holds that decentralization may cause the following negative impacts on the level of government governance. Among big countries implementing the separation of powers, it is difficult for the central government to supervise the lower level governments, which are more likely to be affected by interests groups and engage in conspiracy; vertical competition among governments at different levels will lead to a lack of authority, the governments would compete for levying tax and extracting rent, and shirk the responsibility of providing public services. In this sense, without a vertical political control and the reform and transformation of the government system itself, the evolution of the fiscal decentralization system in China cannot guarantee "do a good job of incentives".

In fact, economists have always focused on the reform and transformation of the economic sector in their study of transitional economy, and ignored the governance transformation of the public sector or the government itself. In order to achieve the transformation of the government to a market-supporting (government transformation) one so as to support and utilize the role of the market, an effective public sector and updating government human capital are crucial. In 1996, it was because of their personal observations of the economic transition process in Russia and Eastern Europe that Shleifer and Vishny took note of the importance of the government transformation in the economic transition. In the article entitled Government in Transition, they found that the biggest difference between Russia and Poland in economic transition and growth was in the efficiency of the public sector and the incentives for local officials. They stressed "Regardless of economics or politics, how to replenish outdated human capital may be central to the transition."[35]

As China accelerated its replenishment rate of Party and government officials (both in central and local governments) since the reform and opening, it has smoothly realized the transformation of local government and the change to a professional structure of technological bureaucrats.[36] This is an important institutional reason why local governments in China are doing better in terms of "market friendliness" and encouragement of economic growth than in India and Russia.[37] The transformation of the Chinese government, in a sense, corresponds to the definition of the professionalism bureaucracy and so-called "developmental government" in the economic literature. Professionalism of bureaucrats and transformation of administrative functions are important parts of the transformation of government's governance. When

---

[34] Treisman (2000).

[35] Shleifer and Vishiny (2004).

[36] In China, to overcome the shackles of "left" ideology and get rid of the influence of the old system as soon as possible are important contents of the ideological emancipation movement and the reform of the cadre system promoted by Mr. Deng Xiaoping. He put forward the political management goal and strategic project to quickly foster younger cadres with professional knowledge. In the Chinese literature, Chen Dongqi (2000) summed up the experience of the reform of the Chinese government system and the improvement of the government administrative efficiency since the reform.

[37] Bardhan (2006) also made a comparative analysis of the political systems and rule of government in China and India in recent papers.

we discussed the relevant literature in the third part, we mentioned that the professionalism of the state bureaucracy is a necessary condition for the government to become a "developmental government" because it has a positive impact on governance and efficiency in two ways. One is that it helps curb rent-seeking by government officials. Second, professionalism of officials can also improve the incentives for government to provide infrastructure and other public goods, as it helps boost the career path of officials. Obviously, in China, thanks to the acceleration of updating of government officials, the professionalism and administrative governance level of local government have been improved rapidly.

In short, motivated both by fiscal decentralization and vertical political centralization, China's local governments are driven more by economic growth than by redistribution of income.[38] Because of this reason, the expenditure of local government is often beneficial to rather than hindering economic growth.[39] In fact, some studies, when comparing the experiences of East Asia's economy and Latin American economic development, have found that the political governance model in Asia has led to a positive impact of government spending on economic growth, while this effect is often negative in other economies.[40] This means that the combination of China's politically centralized management model with the fiscal decentralization system since the middle of 1980s not only prompted a typical "yardstick competition" among local governments, but also promoted the transformation of the government system into a government of development. This paper argues that this is an important clue to understand the sustainability and remarkable improvement of the infrastructure level in China in the past 20 years.

11.4 Overall Change and Regional Differences of China's Physical Infrastructure Level Since Reform and Opening-Up

As shown in Fig. 11.1, since the reform and opening up, especially since the1990s, the regional infrastructure investment China has being developing very rapidly which is one of the important reasons for the rapid economic growth. However, so far, the literature describing and measuring the infrastructure development in various regions of China is very rare. Of course, regarding the level of the infrastructure stock, the fact that we cannot simply add up the units and dimensions of the compositions of infrastructure may have prevented such a work. In the few empirical studies we mentioned earlier, researchers usually use a few or single index such as highway and

[38] Haggard (1990). It is found in study that different from democratic government, politically centralized governments often do not face the pressure of interest group or redistribution.

[39] Zhang Jun (2006). Based on the econometric analysis of panel data of 29 provinces and cities in China during the years of 1987–2001, it is found that, after controlling other factors, the growth of the proportion of government expenditure has a positive impact on TFP growth.

[40] Przeworski and Limongi (1993).

railway mileage to represent the infrastructure stock level, despite the fact that they cannot fully reflect the actual effect of infrastructure on economic growth and other investment returns, thus having the defects of underestimating the contribution of infrastructure. In this paper, we will first examine the changing patterns of infrastructure from the point of view of investment flows, and then we will try to use principal component analysis (PCA) in describing regional differences in infrastructure levels.

As we all know, in the 20 years before the reform and opening up, the Chinese government favored and advanced the economic development strategy of heavy industry and, from the end of the1960s, emphasized the self-sufficiency of provinces. This had a huge impact on China's infrastructure investment, especially in transportation. In order to cope with heavy industrialization, railways were given priority. The railways expanded from 22,900 km in 1952 to 48,600 km in 1978, more than

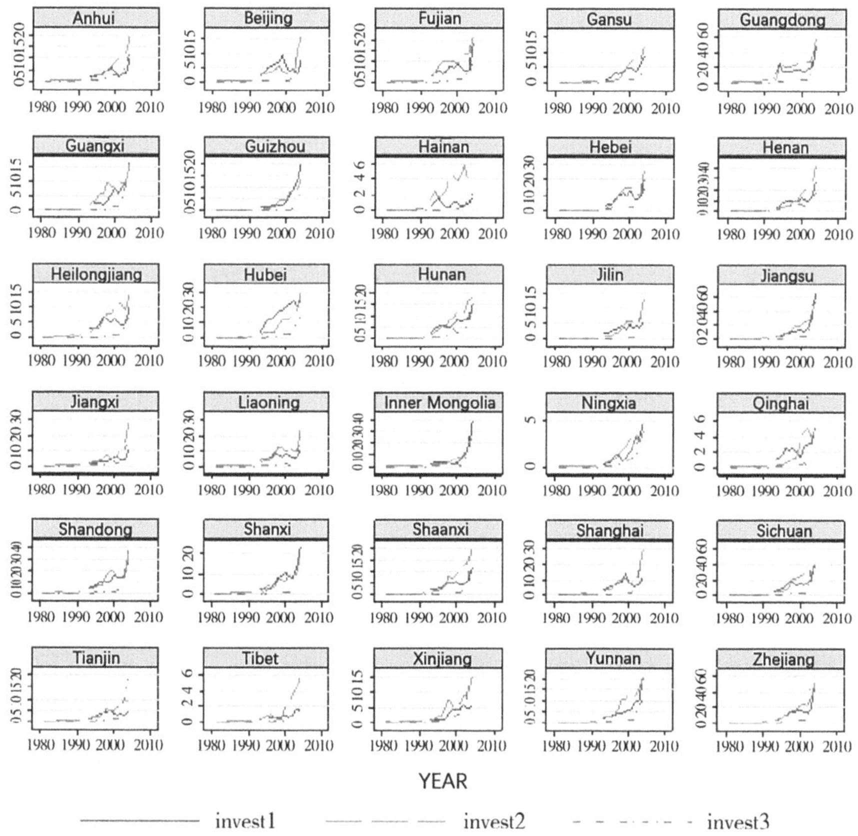

Fig. 11.1 Infrastructure investment changes in China's provinces in 1981–2004 (unit: 1 billion *yuan*). *Note* ① invest 1 refers to investment in the production and supply industry for electricity, gas and water; invest 2 refers to investment in transportation, warehousing and postal industry; invest 3 refers to investment in water conservancy, environment, and management of public facilities. ② Data from Chongqing after 1997 are incorporated into Sichuan province

doubled. Even so, China's transportation infrastructure at that stage was still very backward, while other infrastructure investment was seriously inadequate. Starting from the reform of economic and financial decentralization in the 1980s, investment in energy and infrastructure was obviously improved in China, although in the 80s, transportation and telecommunications investment only accounted for 10% in fixed assets investment, while the energy sector accounted for about 20%.[41] Under the circumstances, traffic shortage and urban congestion were becoming more and more serious. However, in the middle of 90s, after the reform of the "tax sharing system" between central and local governments, infrastructure investment seemed to have entered a period of prosperity, and the gap between regions began to expand significantly.

First of all, with the fiscal decentralization and the transformation of China's economic system, the model of infrastructure investment has undergone dramatic changes. What is more remarkable is that each region has revealed obvious regional disparities in the course of this change, and the difference in the infrastructure investment and financing models will inevitably affect the level of infrastructure investment. Under the planned economic system, the construction of infrastructure followed a unified investment and financing system of the central government, and the projects invested by the central government occupied an absolute position. With the establishment of the fiscal decentralization system, local governments have gradually acquired the investment decision-making power for local infrastructure and local projects are growing in large numbers. As shown in Fig. 11.2, after more than ten years of evolution, the proportion of central and local projects in infrastructure investment has changed markedly.

Wei Xinya (2002) gave a general description of regional differences in China's infrastructure investment.[42] The proportion of the central projects were above 50% before 1991, but accounted for only 32.5% in 1999, showing that China's investment in infrastructure construction has shifted to the stage of local investment. However, the extent of change in the eastern and western regions was markedly different. In Xinjiang, Gansu and other underdeveloped provinces (regions), the proportion of projects of the central government was generally higher than the national level, with those in Xinjiang even reaching 55.9% in 1998 while in Hainan and other economically developed coastal areas, the central projects accounted for less than 15%. This difference means that after the central and local authorities had clearly divided their administrative powers and financial rights, the enthusiasm for local infrastructure construction in China's developed areas has been fully mobilized.

Secondly, significant changes and regional differences in the way of infrastructure financing also took place. In addition to the state budget funds, domestic loans, foreign investment, self financing began to play an important role in the construction of infrastructure. However, the proportion of different sources of funds in total investment varied greatly in different areas. The state budget funds have dropped from 32.6% in 1987 to about 10% today; the proportion of foreign capital decreased from

[41] Demurger (2001).

[42] Wei Xinya (2002).

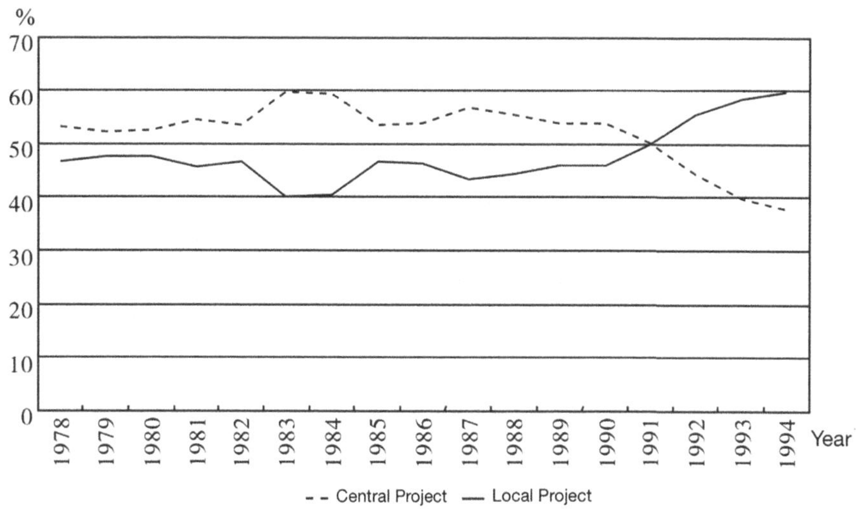

Fig. 11.2 Changes in the proportion of central and local projects in China's capital construction investment since the reform

10.3% in 1987 to 9% in 1999, demonstrating a trend of downturn; domestic loans are affected by the banking system reform; so their proportion has been hovering between 23% and 25% in recent years; by contrast, self fundraising and other funds have constituted the major part of investments in recent years. As the independent and other investments have become the backbone of funding sources of Chinese infrastructure and the state budget funds, domestic loans, foreign investment only a supplementary source of infrastructure investment, it is no wonder that the eastern region has again taken the lead in infrastructure investment. Finally, as the result of the significant changes in infrastructure investment and financing patterns and regional differences over the past 10 years, the stock levels of infrastructure accumulated by past investments are becoming more and more different among regions.

In the existing literature, Li Boxi and Liu Deshun (1995) are among earlier scholars who measured and studied the differences of infrastructure stock levels in various areas.[43] And as far as we know, this is also the only literature to investigate the stock of infrastructure in a meticulous way in China so far. The infrastructure discussed in the paper includes transportation, telecommunications, energy supply, environmental protection equipment, education facilities, healthcare and social welfare facilities. Owing to the absence of data, though, urban water supply and drainage as well as cultural and recreational facilities were not dealt with.

The selected stock index is very rich, and they are as follows. Transport: railway, highway, waterway and shipping. The index of railway is measured by railway mileage; highway is measured by the mileage of highway and the number of civilian vehicles; waterway is measured with mileage of channels, number of motor ships

[43] Li Boxi, Liu Deshun (1995).

and number of port berths; shipping is measured with number of workers. Posts and telecommunications: mail, telephone, telegraph, telex etc. The raw data selected are, number of post offices, number of mail-delivering tools, number of carrier telegraphs, number of telephones, number of fax machines. Energy supply: The data selected are the electricity consumption of industrial sector and energy consumption of industrial sector. Environmental protection: the data selected include number of personnel of environmental protection system, rate of comprehensive utilization of the industrial solid waste, proportion of fuel combustion and exhaust emissions being treated, waste water treatment and reuse, total investment in wastewater treatment. School education: the percentage of population in higher education, number of college students, number of students in technical secondary schools, number of primary and secondary school enrollment, and number of colleges and universities. Healthcare: number of health institutions, number of beds and medical technical personnel. Social welfare: including number of elderly service facilities, number of service facilities for disabled persons, and number of rural social security funds.

In order to add up the information of these indicators for regional comparative studies, they calculated from small to large categories. For example, after calculating the level of railway infrastructure stock in China's 30 provinces, cities and autonomous regions, they further calculated the comprehensive level index of transportation facilities with the comprehensive stock level of highway, water transport and aviation facilities. And, after calculating the measurement indicators of all 7 types of infrastructure, they then calculated the measurement indicators of the comprehensive level of overall infrastructure according to certain formula. Based on this method, they calculated the level of infrastructure in China's 30 provinces, cities and autonomous regions and standardized their results with 100 provinces having the maximum numerical value and the numerical values of other regions are calculated according to proportion.

Among the above 7 categories of infrastructure, transportation, telecommunications and energy supply are called economic public infrastructure by the author, and their index is called economic indicators; while the other 4 types of infrastructure (environmental protection facilities, healthcare, education, social welfare) were defined as social public infrastructure and their index is called social indicators; when the 7 categories of infrastructure are considered as a whole, the index is called comprehensive index. The calculation method of economic indicators is to take the geometric mean from index of transportation, post and telecommunications and energy supply; the calculation method of social indicators is to take geometric mean from the index of environmental facilities, healthcare, culture and education and social welfare; the calculation method of comprehensive index is to take the geometric mean from the index of the above 7 types of infrastructure.

Their research results show that, although there are regional differences in infrastructure, there is a huge difference in infrastructure stock among regions in China as a whole, and the eastern region has obvious advantages. Among them, the largest regional difference in infrastructure is in telecommunications, transportation and education. Their mean values are respectively 20.98, 23.78 and 25.10, and their ratios of maximum value to minimum value are 16.26, 15.13 and 7.63 respectively.

In addition, when the economic indicators and social indicators are compared, in almost all of the provinces, cities and autonomous regions, the indicator in the latter is greater than the former (except Beijing). The mean values of the two indicators are 27.15 and 48.82 and their deviation coefficients are 0.80 and 0.40 respectively.

This shows that the regional difference of economic infrastructure (transportation, communications and energy) is much greater than social infrastructure (environmental protection, education, public health, welfare, etc.)

But their paper, which measures the stock of regional infrastructure, has at least two major technical problems. First, the selection of indicators is too casual and disorderly, lacking a strict selection definition and standard; second, the processing of index is too simple without a distinction of weight for each index with the result that the final comprehensive index may not best reflect the information of the raw data. We will overcome these shortcomings in this article in order to better measure the infrastructure stock levels as well as patterns of regional differences.

First of all, we use the narrow definition of infrastructure, the "economic infrastructure" defined by the World Bank, to measure the stock levels of physical infrastructure. Stock is a static index, mainly measuring the existing level of infrastructure in the country or regions each year which actually reflects the infrastructure investment conditions in the past. Taking into account the availability of data, we selected four major indicators in this paper: traffic infrastructure, energy infrastructure, telecommunication infrastructure, and urban infrastructure. The first three indicators are categorized by their functions, and the last index is special, specifically referring to city infrastructure system mainly because: first, this index is reported as a separate item in the *Chinese Statistical Yearbook*, and one can get accurate data about it; second, each sub-index contained in the item is included in the definition of the World Bank. Specific explanations of the indicators are as follows: ① transportation infrastructure: railway operating mileage (km), inland waterway mileage (km), graded road (km), started from 1985; ② energy infrastructure: electricity consumption (billion kilowatt hours), energy consumption (million tons of standard coal), started from 1985; ③ communication infrastructure: post office, total length of routes (km), long-distance telephone (million times), started from 1985; wireless paging subscribers (million households), mobile phone users (million households), number of Internet users (million persons), long-distance automatic switchboard capacity (terminal), switchboard capacity of local telephone bureau (one million), started from 1998; switchboard capacity of mobile telephone (one million), started from 2001; the length of long distance optical cable lines (km), the length of long distance microwave lines (km), started from 1995; ④ city infrastructure: city water consumption rate (%), city gas penetration rate (%), number of public transport vehicles per 10,000 people, per capita road area (sq. m.), per capita public green space (sq. m.), number of public toilets (seat) per 10,000 persons, started from 1985. All the data came from *Chinese Statistical Yearbook* and *Chinese Energy Statistics Yearbook*, and the data of energy consumption and electricity consumption in 1993 were the average value of 1990 and 1995.

There are different units to measure the infrastructure stock, which we can't simply add up, but we also want a comprehensive index to look at the overall changing pattern. So, in this section, we have two ways to observe the changing patterns of infrastructure levels. First of all, in order to obtain the changing trend of the national level of infrastructure, a representative indicator was chosen from the four indicators we have selected in this paper, and then obtain the total index by way of adding up the same index of each province (city) on a yearly basis. Finally, we convert the index into an exponential series.

Specifically, we selected a representative indicator from traffic, energy, telecommunications and public facilities in the city. They are highway mileage (10,000 km), total energy consumption (million tons of standard coal), total length of postal routes (km) and the per capita area of paved roads (square meters). In order to observe the trend over time, we converted the added data of traffic, energy and city public facilities into index of the base period of 1981, but the base period for post and telecommunications was 1985. Although the data of a few years are missing, it does not significantly affect our observation of the overall trend of change. Moreover, in the treatment of the index of per capita paved road area (square meters), the statistical specifications before and after 2002 changed. For instance, the data of 2000 was 9.1 square meters in the *Chinese Statistical Yearbook* (2001), but was 6.1 square meters in the *Chinese Statistical Yearbook* (2003). As a result, we adjusted the data of 2002 (7.9 square meters) and 2003 (9.3 square meters) forward to 11.8 square meters and 13.9 square meters in accordance with the ratio of data in 2000 (9.1/6.1) to ensure the consistancy of data. We have described the results in Fig. 11.3.

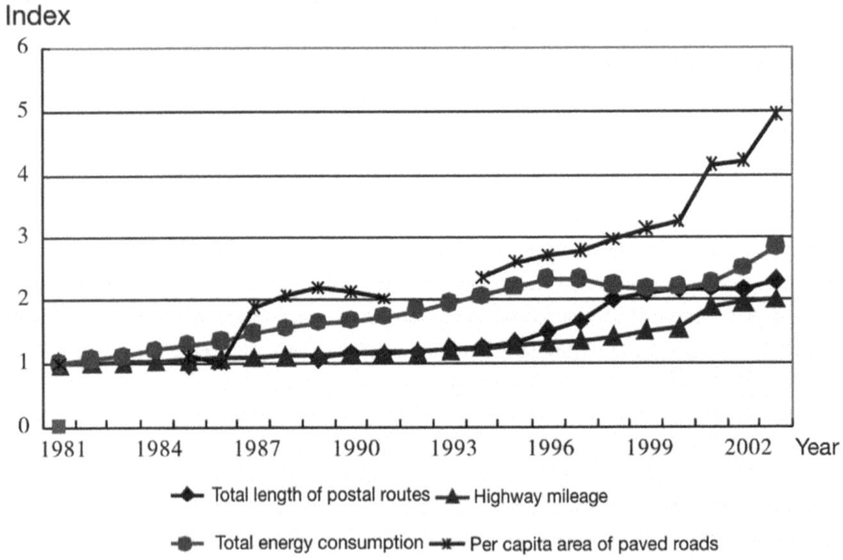

Fig. 11.3 Changing patterns of China's infrastructure level (index, 1981–2003). *Source* Calculated according to the raw data of *Chinese Statistical Yearbook* and *Chinese Energy Statistics Yearbook* of relevant years

Secondly, in order to observe the changing difference in the level of infrastructure stock among regions, we need to add up all the index information of the infrastructure defined in this paper to measure the stock value of the infrastructure. But because these indicators have different units, we can't simply add them up. So we have adopted the "principal component analysis" (PCA) to overcome this problem. First, we consider various indicators of $X_1, \ldots, X_P$ linear combination F is a comprehensive index that can reflect the general situation, but there are infinite groups of linear combinations, and if we make the variance $\mathrm{Var}(F)$ of this combination the largest, the linear combination F will contain the most information of variable $X_1, \ldots, X_P$. For the infrastructure stock, it is to find a linear combination that can best reflect its overall pattern. We mark the F obtained in this way as F_1, and then we look for F_2, F_1 has no connection with F_2 and so on until we find a set of composite variables F_1, $F_2, \ldots, F_m$, the cumulative percentage of all its characteristic values $\lambda_1, \ldots, \lambda_m$ (from large to small) in the proportion of the sum $\sum_{i=1}^{p} \lambda_i$ of all characteristic values is greater than or equal to 95%. Because the ratio of characteristic value to the sum of all characteristic values represents the extent to which the overall index is interpreted, if the cumulative percentage is greater or equal to 95%, it indicates this set of composite variables $F_1, F_2, \ldots, F_m$, basically contains all the information of the original variable. We call F_1 the first principal component, F_2 the second principal component, ... F_m the m(th) principal component.[44] After the corresponding characteristic values is weighted, we obtained $E = \sum_{i=1}^{m} \lambda_i F_i$, the original value of the principal component of the infrastructure stock. With the rapid development of the telecommunications industry in China, we gradually included, starting from 1995, index that can reflect the mobile communication and network infrastructure so that the principal component analysis in different years also contains different characteristic value vectors and comprehensive variables, the results of which cannot be compared directly. Many literatures at present did cross-period comparison[45] by using scoring method, such as those written by Lu Minghong (2002),[46] and Yang Yongheng (2005).[47] But here we add the original values of each province, taking it as the original value of the national infrastructure stock, and then calculate the proportion of the original value of each province to the original value of the whole country. We call it the weighting method. The reason we are using the method is that the scoring method cannot reflect the multi period changes of infrastructure stock of highest provinces, because the scoring value of each year is 100 under the scoring method, whereas the weighting method can reflect multi-period changes. In addition, weighting method also has

---

44 The mathematical procedure is: $X = (x_1, \ldots, x_p)$, set $F = a_1x_1 + \cdots + a_px_p = a'X$, find the coefficient $a(aa' = 1)$, maximize $\mathrm{var}(F)$, that is, $\mathrm{var}(F) = \mathrm{var}(a'X) = a'\mathrm{var}(X) = a'\Sigma a$ is the largest. Set the characteristics root of Σ as $\lambda_1 \geq \lambda_2 \geq \cdots \geq \lambda_p > 0$, the corresponding orthonormal basis is $u_1, u_2, \ldots, u_p$. Then $\mathrm{var}(F) = \lambda_1$, $a = u_1$, mark $F_1 = u'_1x$, F_2 has nothing to do with F_1, $F_2 = u'_2x$, and the rest can be deduced in this way.

45 The principle of the scoring method is that the original maximum value of each year is determined to be 100 points, the minimum is 0 point, and other points are calculated according (original score-the minimum vale) × 100/(maximum value − minimum value).

46 Lu Minghong (2002).

47 Yang Yongheng (2005).

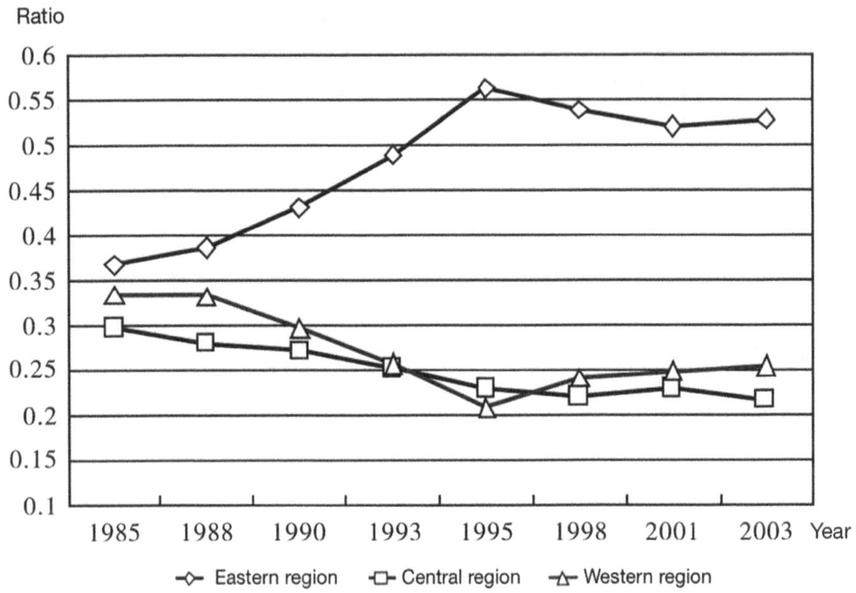

Fig. 11.4 Regional differences in China's infrastructure stock levels since the reform. *Source* Author's calculation data

almost the same inter-provincial comparison as the scoring method.[48] In Fig. 11.4, we calculated the results of the principal components analysis for 1985, 1988, 1990, 1993, 1995, 1998, 2001, 2003, and compared the east, central and west regions.

As can be seen from Fig. 11.4, the infrastructure stock in eastern region showed an upward trend till the mid-1990s when it hovered at high levels, while the proportion of infrastructure stock in western region prior to the middle of the 1990s kept declining before it increased slightly later on. The basic trend of the share of the central region was moderate but continued to decline. Now, let's analyze the changes in specific provinces. As shown in Table 11.2, from 1988 to 2003, the provinces with their proportion of infrastructure stock level increased in the country are ranked as follows by increased size: Beijing, Guangdong, Tianjin, Zhejiang, Fujian, Hainan, Liaoning, Shanghai, and regions in the west: Ningxia, Qinghai and Xinjiang. The proportions of Jiangsu and Shandong in the east remained almost unchanged (although during the period from 1988 to 1998, their proportions increased to a certain extent).

The ranking of the provinces' infrastructure stocks in the country can help us see more clearly their patterns of change. We found that in 1988, provinces

[48] Weighting method also has a drawback. If the original value is negative, the weighting method is not applicable. If the scoring method is used, the relative value between the two provinces is (original score is $i-$ minimum value)/(original sore j − minimum value). If the weighting rule is used, then the original score i/original score j. In general, the smaller the minimum value/original value i or j is, the more likely that the results of the two methods tend to converge. In our data, Ningxia was the province with the minimum original value, for the original values of almost all provinces are more than 5 times higher than Ningxia's.

Table 11.2 Ratio of infrastructure stock of Chinese provinces to the national level and their rankings (PCA method)

Province	1988		1993		1998		2003	
	Ratio %	Ranking	Ratio %	Ranking	Ratio %	Ranking	Ratio %	Ranking
Beijing	1.42	25	2.26	23	2.87	16	4.73	6
Tianjin	1.04	26	1.09	27	1.50	24	1.39	26
Hebei	3.57	12	3.75	12	3.31	12	2.78	17
Shanxi	2.92	20	2.49	20	2.45	21	2.31	21
Inner Mongolia	3.46	14	2.62	19	2.12	23	1.91	23
Liaoning	3.31	18	4.75	6	5.18	5	3.94	7
Jilin	2.70	22	2.40	21	2.67	18	1.83	24
Heilongjiang	3.67	9	3.84	10	3.07	14	2.81	16
Shanghai	3.45	16	3.81	11	3.67	10	3.55	10
Jiangsu	5.86	2	6.41	3	6.19	4	5.81	3
Zhejiang	3.58	11	4.36	7	4.92	6	5.24	4
Anhui	3.57	12	3.19	15	2.52	19	3.51	11
Fujian	2.72	21	3.74	13	4.29	7	3.71	8
Jiangxi	3.45	16	2.74	18	2.49	20	2.95	14
Shandong	5.08	5	5.73	4	6.26	3	4.89	5
Henan	3.72	8	3.95	9	3.91	8	3.59	9
Hubei	4.98	6	4.34	8	3.48	11	3.05	13
Hunan	5.83	3	4.84	5	3.90	9	3.49	12
Guagndong	5.13	4	8.93	1	12.16	1	14.12	1
Guangxi	3.46	14	2.77	17	2.90	15	2.73	18
Hainan	0.71	27	1.66	26	1.07	27	0.85	27
Sichuan	9.60	1	6.90	2	6.53	2	7.47	2
Guizhou	2.45	23	1.81	25	1.45	25	2.08	22
Yunnan	4.51	7	3.48	14	3.27	13	2.91	15
Shaanxi	3.62	10	3.03	16	2.35	22	2.73	19
Gansu	2.95	19	2.39	22	1.40	26	1.68	25
Qinghai	0.66	28	0.50	28	0.65	28	0.73	28
Ningxia	0.39	29	0.35	29	0.60	29	0.54	29
Xinjiang	2.19	24	1.87	24	2.83	17	2.68	20

Source Author's calculation data

with large population and area took up the first positions with Sichuan province ranked first.[49] Advanced rankings also included provinces at boarder areas (such as Yunnan, Heilongjiang). At the beginning of the 1990s, the infrastructure of the coastal provinces grew faster, and Guangdong soon became the province with the largest proportion. The ranking of provinces and cities gradually took shape after the beginning of the 1990s.

According to rankings and specific proportion values shown in Table 11.2, we classified the changing patterns of infrastructure in China's provinces into the following groups: ① Rising group, such as Beijing, Liaoning, Shanghai, Zhejiang, Fujian, Guangdong, Tianjin, all of which are along the coast. Since the beginning of the 1990s, local governments have been making great efforts to improve infrastructure because of the opening-up policy, which made these places surpass many of the provinces with advance rankings. ② Declining group, such as Hebei, Shanxi, Inner Mongolia, Jilin, Heilongjiang, Hubei, Hunan, Yunnan, Hainan, most of which are central and northeastern provinces. Perhaps the local governments in these areas lacked the motivation and incentives to improve infrastructure as their counterparts in the east. This is only a speculation and we need further study in other papers. After the housing bubble and investment boom subsided in the middle of the 1990s, the development of infrastructure in Hainan lagged behind other coastal provinces. ③ Stable group. The proportion and ranking of this group basically have not changed much. The group comprises Jiangsu, Henan, Guangxi and Ningxia. ④ Declining before rising group which includes Anhui, Jiangxi, Sichuan, Guizhou, Shaanxi, Gansu, Xinjiang and Qinghai. We can see that infrastructure in most of the western provinces decreased before picking up the momentum. The direct reason is the "western development strategy" put forward by the central government in 1998, and the more favorable funding terms for investment in infrastructure in the western region, which accelerated the infrastructure investment and significantly improved the level of local infrastructure.

11.5 Yardstick Competition, Government Administration and Infrastructure Investment Decision

(1) Theoretical Basis for Interpretation

From the basic description of the changes in the level of China's infrastructure provided in the previous section, we can find that first, the level of China's infrastructure construction has undergone significant and accelerated growth after the reform and opening up. Second, there are significant differences in the proportion of infrastructure stock levels in the eastern, central and western regions. This reflects the impact of the main factors of infrastructure investment on different regions at different

[49] Chongqing was designated as a municipality directly under the central government in1997, but before that year, the stock of Sichuan included that of Chongqing. In order to make the data consistent and easier to compare, we incorporated Chongqing in Sichuan province after 1997.

times. As can be seen from Table 11.2, the growth of infrastructure has accelerated in most of the eastern provinces and cities since the 1990s, and their relative rankings have risen rapidly. Of course, even the provinces with relatively stable or declining rankings are constantly improving the level of their absolute infrastructure.

No doubt, to better understand the infrastructure growth and changing mode in China, we must consider the change of intergovernmental management system as well as the change of the incentive constraints the local government officials faced and their changed behavior model in the past 20 years. The fourth part of this paper provided us with a basic institutional framework to better understand the changes in this incentive system. We pointed out in that part that, in order to effectively motivate the local government investment behavior and promote "yardstick competition", China accelerated fiscal decentralization and improvement process of the governance of local governments while still retaining the highly centralized political management system. Therefore, it can be said that the incentive for local governments to continuously improve local infrastructure and urban construction since the fiscal decentralization has been motivated by the unique decentralized system of "compete for growth". Based on the existing relevant literature and the basic analysis of the reform characteristics of decentralization we discussed in the fourth part, we will highlight in this paper three key explanatory variables that have affected the infrastructure investment:

① The main way for local governments to carry out "yardstick competition" is to open up and attract foreign direct investment (FDI), and providing and improving local infrastructure is a competitive means for local governments to attract investment. Existing research literature has found that reduction and exemption of tax by acting beyond one's power and provision of good infrastructure to attract investment (mainly FDI) is the main competitive strategy among local governments.[50] The recent empirical research on local government expenditure under the fiscal decentralization system done by Zhang Yan and Fu Yong (2006) also found that, due to the local governments' competition for economic growth, too much of the budget has been spent on the basic construction projects stead of on education, public health and other social services.

In this article, we used the local actual FDI to indirectly measure the extent of the Intergovernmental "yard competition". This is because the yardstick competition of local governments is embodied in the dominant strategy of attracting foreign investment. Of course, tax collection is also a competitive tool for local governments to attract foreign direct investment. Some of the research described the effort of local governments' competition through their competition in levying taxes, because reduction and exemption of tax by acting beyond one's power and provision of good infrastructure to attract investment (mainly FDI) is the main competitive strategy among local governments.[51] The relative tax rate of foreign investment enterprises in each region is used as the proxy variable of competition. As we all know, foreign-invested enterprises have been long enjoying treatment that are far more favorable

[50] Zhang Yan, Xia Jijun (2006).

[51] Zhang Yan, Xia Jijun (2006).

than their Chinese counterparts, and the actual tax rate they paid was quite different from their nominal tax rate. But because of the incomplete data,[52] we mainly used the FDI absorbed by each province as the proxy variable to measure the local competition.

② Governance transition of the government. A "Good government" provides good social and market order, which is conducive to the development of local private and foreign-funded enterprises and the growth of economy. These enterprises will increase their demand for infrastructure and other public goods, and a "good government" will make a sensitive response to this demand. In the existing literature, the measurement of the level of government's governance usually uses the supply level of infrastructure and other public services, as well as the management of corruption (such as anti-corruption) as an indicator of the quality of governance. This is by no means coincidental. The level of government's governance or the quality of the government will naturally affect the structure of public expenditure and the efficiency of providing public goods.

We recognized that indicators of government's governance or government quality are very complex. In the existing research literature, PLSV[53] (1999) was among the earlier economists who measured the governance of government.[54] But in transnational researches, a complex indicator system is used in most of the measurements of the level of governance by government. For example, PLSV developed five sets of indicators. A research group under the leadership of Daniel Kauffman, director of the international project of The World Bank Institute (WBI), released a global governance report where they used hundreds of variables in the measurement of government administration. These measures include the quality of public goods and the level of infrastructure provided by the government. This is typically the way of using the result of governance to measure the government's actions. Such a measure serves specific research purposes. It is based on the assumption that the so-called "good government" is more honest, not the hostage of private sector and can provide better public services and infrastructure and overcome the bureaucracy or is highly efficient. We can certainly use a lot of "good" indicators to measure a "good government". One potential problem with doing so is that there may be a causal relationship among the indicators that have been chosen to measure the level of governance. For example, whether a government is more willing to invest in infrastructure may be influenced by whether government officials have clearer career goals (or an achievement objective), or influenced by opportunities for corruption and whether the government has a greater resolution or commitment against corruption. Therefore, our concern is that if a government is more efficient in governance than another one, or more honest, does that mean the former is more likely to invest in infrastructure than the latter? At least for infrastructure investment, the answer to the first question may be yes, but the

---

[52] We have noted that in the existing literature, Zhang Yan and Fu Yong (2006) only used this data after 1994. In fact, the *Chinese Tax Yearbook* which provided the raw data did not record these data until 1992. Therefore, we cannot obtain the provincial data on the actual tax paid by foreign-invested enterprises after 1988.

[53] It refers to four economists who jointly published a number of important papers: R. LaPorta, F. Lopez-de-Silanes, Andrei Shleifer, and R. Vishny.

[54] LaPorta et al. (1999).

answer to the next question is not sure. This involves the question of how corruption opportunities of officials can affect investment in infrastructure. We tried to separate the two effects. On the one hand, the improvement of government efficiency should promote infrastructure investment; on the other hand, the strengthening of anti-corruption efforts will curb some infrastructure investment that may offer more opportunities for corruption. Of course, the improvement of government governance can also play a role in anti-corruption effort to some extent, but this is called multi-collinearity in measurement equation which requires us to consider and control in measurement.

③ Opportunities for corrupt officials. In our previous review of the existing research literature, we noted that experience has shown that the opportunities for "corruption" or "eliciting rents" by government officials vary in the public goods provided by the government. Compared with investment in public sectors such as human capital (basic education, public health) or other public services, investments in physical infrastructure and city construction are more likely to create rent-seeking opportunities for potential bidders and give government officials the chance of corruption. It is worth pointing out that official corruption or bribery by government officials is not necessarily contrary to the government's actions. We cannot rule out the possibility that local governments may consider the possibility of bribery when considering public spending. Obviously, compared with education, medical care and other expenses, the investment in infrastructure by government is more likely to generate additional personal benefits. As a result, government spending decisions on infrastructure tend to be more linked to the frequency of corruption. Mauro (1998) also found in his empirical study of other countries that, corruption has a significant negative impact on the proportion of government spending on education.[55] He found that, due to the fact that acquisition of bribes varies in difficulty from different expenditures, proportion of public expenditure on education can be significantly reduced, for unlike other areas, it is not easy to get ill-gotten gains from education expenditure. At the same time, Mauro also found that the higher the level of corruption, the greater the proportion of government spending on infrastructure investment such as transportation.

Tanzi and Davoodi (1997) also argue that economists generally support the government in public investment to promote economic growth, while government officials may have different purposes.[56] In fact, serious corruption is often associated with investments in large projects. Government officials have high enthusiasm for infrastructure investments that are easy to identify such as new roads, bridges, ports, and are inclined to expand scale of these projects as well as increase their complexity. However, they are not willing to make reasonable investment in the operation and maintenance of facilities constructed earlier, because the resulting achievement is not very remarkable. Using the indicators of corruption provided by Mauro, Tanzi and Davoodi found in their studies that the higher the level of corruption, the greater the

[55] Mauro (1998).

[56] Tanzi and Davoodi (1997).

scale of government public investment, but the smaller the spending on quality, operations and maintenance of infrastructure. The study powerfully reveals the distortions that corruption causes in infrastructure investment.

(2) Econometric Model, Variable Description and Results Report

The key purpose of econometric model to test the impact of local government competition (to attract foreign direct investment (FDI)), improvement of governance of the local government (such as improving the professional level of governments and their ability to curb corruption) and the corruption opportunity for officials on infrastructure investment. As Rauch (1995) points out, the investment in infrastructure has significant long-term characteristics, and its cycle has at least two parts–the planned preparation period and the construction period, both of which usually exceeds one year. The sustainability of the investment makes it difficult for the government to start new projects before the completion of the old ones. The measurement method to deal with this sustainability is to add the lag term of infrastructure investment as an explanatory variable in the equation. In view of this characteristic and consulting the standard model of Rauch, we set the basic equations of measurement as follows:

$$y_{i,t} - y_{i,t-1} = \alpha_0 y_{i,t-1} + \beta' X_{i,t} + \eta_i + \varepsilon_{i,t} \tag{11.1}$$

y is the numerical value of the per capita actual infrastructure investment, subtract the numerical values of the two periods, and the left side of the equation represents the growth rate of the per capita actual infrastructure investment. X stands for all the other explanatory variables except the y hysteresis, η is the effect of difference of provinces, and ε is the error term. Subscript i and t represent provinces and time. Make a difference of (11.1) formula to eliminate the effect of provincial difference, we will have:

$$\begin{aligned}\left(y_{i,t} - y_{i,t-1}\right) - \left(y_{i,t-1} - y_{i,t-2}\right) = \alpha_0\left(y_{i,t-1} - y_{i,t-2}\right) + \beta\prime(X_{i,t} - X_{i,t-1}) \\ + (\varepsilon_{i,t} - \varepsilon_{i,t-1})\end{aligned} \tag{11.2}$$

In Eq. (11.2), we need to control the endogeneity problem inherent in the hysteretic per capita infrastructure investment variables. The results of fixed effects estimate and random effect estimate at this time will be biased, because the hysteretic explanatory variable $\left(y_{i,t-1} - y_{i,t-2}\right)$ and the error item $(\varepsilon_{i,t} - \varepsilon_{i,t-1})$ are related. In addition, explanatory variables such as foreign direct investment (FDI) that we are concerned with may also be endogenous, which need to be dealt with by using instrumental variables. Based on the consideration of these problems, we adopted the GMM method in this paper, which can overcome the above problems better. In this paper, we used two GMM panel estimation, namely, differential GMM estimation and systematic GMM estimation, which all use the observation value of lag phase of the explanatory variables as the instrumental variables.

Differential GMM estimation was proposed by Arellano and Bond (1991),[57] which is widely used in the study of economic growth, such as Fasterly (1997).[58] It first make a difference on the regression equation, namely, our Eq. (11.2), to eliminate the error of missing variables caused by unobserved provincial difference effect, and then conduct tool substitution for the variable on the right end (the difference values of the original regression type) to eliminate the potential inconsistent parameters caused by simultaneous bias. However, it may not be very effective to use the level variable of lag phase as the instrumental variable of differential variable (if they are of little relevance or the differential variable value is close to 0); it can lead to weak instrumental variable that will result in error of limited samples, inaccurate coefficient, or even affecting the gradation. Bond (2002) demonstrated by using Monte Carlo simulations that, in small and medium samples, the weak nature of the instrumental variables brought about by differential GMM estimation may yield biased coefficients.[59] Therefore, we also used the systematic GMM estimation. According to Arellano and Bover (1995),[60] and Blundell and Bond (1998),[61] using systematic GMM estimation can enhance the effectiveness of instrumental variables in differential estimation and, by increasing the regression equation of original level value, namely Eq. (11.1), to make up for the defect of using only the regression differential equation and solve the problem of weak instrumental variable.

The effectiveness and consistency of the systematic GMM have been greatly improved compared with the differential GMM estimation, so we believe that the estimation results of the systematic GMM should be the best. In addition, Bond (2002) holds that the consistency of the GMM estimates depends on the validity of the tool variables, and that two identification tests are necessary. First is the Sargan over-recognition test, which tests the validity of the instrumental variable; the second is the difference error term correlation test which tests whether the first order sequence is related, and the second order sequence is uncorrelated.

The data from the econometric model are panel data, most of which are from the China Economic Research Center, Fudan University. Our data cover 29 provinces in China (except Tibet and the city of Chongqing) during the years of 1988–2001. Our explained variable is the per capita growth rate of infrastructure investment. The indicators selected for infrastructure investment are electricity, gas and water production and supply industry; transportation, warehousing and postal industry; basic construction investment in water conservancy, environment and management of public facilities. The statistical indicators of water conservancy, environment and management of public facilities before 2002 were geological exploration and management of

---

[57] Arelano and Bond (1991).

[58] Fasterly and Levine (1997).

[59] Bond (2002). In his article, he made a Monte Carlo simulation of three observation numbers—100, 250, 500. Results show that the observation values of 100 and 250 will lead to bias under differential GMM, but the number of observations in our sample was 281 under the differential GMM, and 341 under systematic GMM.

[60] Arelano and Bover (1995).

[61] Blundel and Bond (1998).

water conservancy. The infrastructures provided by Prud′homme (2004) based on the service types they offer include transportation, water supply, water treatment, irrigation, garbage disposal, heating, telecommunications and energy, which can be covered by the three infrastructure investment index we have selected. The data are from the *Chinese Statistical Yearbook, Chinese Industrial Economic Statistical Yearbook* and have been deflated by the price index of investment in fixed assets in various regions. Since only the index after 1991 is available in the statistical yearbook, we used the price index of the fixed assets investment of the provinces calculated by Jun Zhang and others (2004).[62]

Based on our discussion in this article, we selected the following major explanatory variables that appeared in X: initial value of per capita infrastructure investment period (loginfinvpc_1), per capita foreign direct investment (logrfdipc), level of governance (represented by the average administrative expenses of staff logdmexpp), official corruption index (anticorrpp) and per capita urban and rural savings deposits (lo-glocalsavpc) and real per capita GDP (logrgdppc). log means logarithmic processing has been carried out, pc means per capita treatment. Among them, the key explanatory variables include: ① per capita foreign direct investment; ② governance level of local government; ③ opportunity of official corruption.

Regarding the per capita foreign direct investment, we first converted the average exchange rate (mean price) of the RMB of each year against the US dollar and then used the US GDP deflator as the price index. Similar treatment methods was also used by Wei Houkai (2002).[63] As mentioned above, attracting foreign direct investment (FDI) is the dominant strategy of competition for local governments. The important incentive for local governments to improve their infrastructure is to better attract foreign investment and the inflow of foreign investment has also created more demand for local infrastructure. The two-way impact of FDI and infrastructure has been described in many studies and is an important factor in infrastructure investment. In Fig. 11.5, through the simple statistical analysis based on the panel data of 29 provinces (not including Chongqing and Tibet) of 1988–2001, we found that there is a remarkable positive relationship between the real per capita FDI level (logrfdipc) and the per capita infrastructure investment (loginfinvpc) of a region.

We need to make some notes about the level of governance of local governments and the opportunities for corrupt officials. Because of the constraints of available data, we have to make some compromise on the choice of these two variables. In this case, we selected administrative expenses of local government from the existing statistical data and have them divided by the number of public officials to measure the local governance level, because we think that the growth of administrative expenditure largely reflects the development of government agencies and departments and the improvement of governance ability. Indeed, as shown in Fig. 11.6, we found that, based on the panel data of 29 provinces during 1988–2001, there is a highly positive correlation between the average administrative expenses of officials (logdmexpp) and the real per capita infrastructure investment (loginfinvpc).

[62] Zhang Jun, Wu Guiying, Zhang Jipeng (2004).

[63] Wei Houkai (2002).

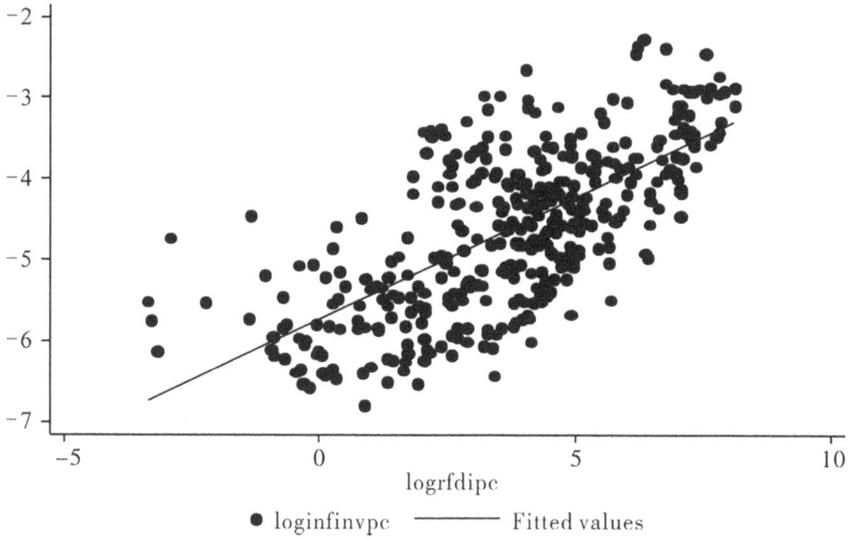

Fig. 11.5 Correlation between actual per capita infrastructure investment and the actual per capita FDI (logarithm, panel data of 29 provinces)

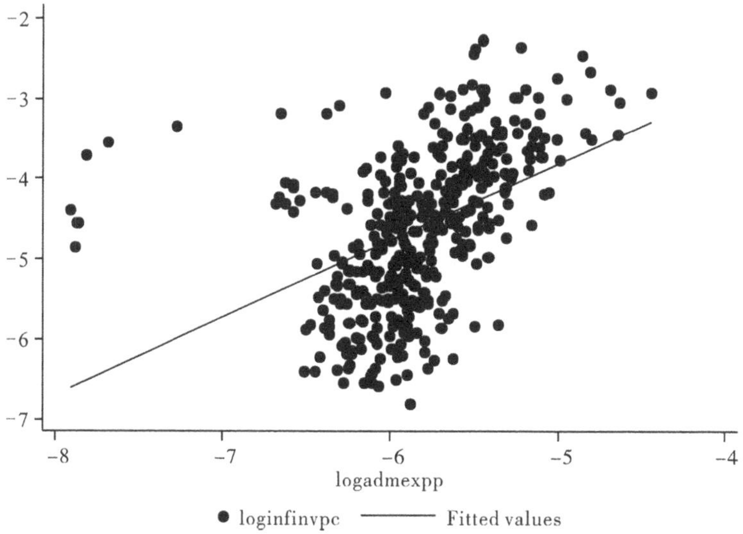

Fig. 11.6 Correlation between actual per capita infrastructure investment and per capita administrative expenditure of public servants (logarithm, panel date of 29 provinces)

In addition, because of the availability of data, it is difficult for us to obtain data on the quantity or proportion of corruption by local officials. Although IT has provided "clean index" to measure the situation of China, so far there has been no systematic research and measurement in the literature aimed at the level of local governance, nor any likelihood for synthetic panel data. However, we are lucky enough to have found some sequential data of the number of corruption and bribery cases of local government officials.

Specifically, we measured the level of government's governance by administrative expenses of public servants. But the administrative costs do not include the judicial, public security and procuratorial expenditures, because the impact of expenditure of these organs on infrastructure investment is not easy to determine. On the one hand, it is closely related to anti-corruption, thus having an inhibiting effect; on the other hand, it has a positive effect on the government to improve the governance. Excluding this expenditure in measurement also helps to reduce the multicollinearity problem. So it is reasonable for us to exclude the expenditure of public security organs, procuratorial organs and people's courts from the administrative expenses. The data come from *A Collection of Statistical Data for New China in Fifty Years* and *the Yearbook of Chinese Finance*.[64] The number of public servants comes from the *Chinese Statistical Yearbook*, and we used the China's GDP deflator to eliminate price trends. Rauch (1995) once used the data of to what extent to use the civil service system (to have improved the professional level of government) to measure the impact of governance by government on infrastructure investment, and reached a significant conclusion.

Regarding the official corruption index, we have no way to obtain the provincial data on official corruption in the existing statistical data, but we have got hold of the provincial data of the number of cases of corruption of local government officials. However, according to our previous discussion, if the corruption opportunities may have a positive impact on infrastructure investment, then the willingness and intensity of the government to strike corruption naturally will help reduce the probability of official corruption, because the anti-corruption measures to punish corrupt officials have raised the cost of corruption of officials. As a result, as far as the incentive for infrastructure investment is concerned, the impact of corruption can be indirectly identified from the impact of anti-corruption. Given the differences in the intensity of fighting against corruption among local governments in China, we expect this difference is likely to affect the growth of local infrastructure investment.

We used the "number of corruption and bribery cases per 10,000 public officials" to measure the anti-corruption efforts in each province. Is it possible that the larger per capita number of cases means that the anti-corruption effort is more intense or the degree of corruption is greater in a region? We believe the former

---

[64] In fact, the administrative costs provided in *A Collection of Statistics of New China in Fifty Years* also do not include public security, procuratorial, and courts expenditures, even the expenditure records of those organs are not available. *Chinese Financial Yearbook* listed the two statistics separately, but only the data after 1992 was included. Therefore, the seriously inadequate data made us unable to cover expenditure of public security organs, procuratorial organs and people's courts in the administrative expenses.

is true. Xie Ping and Lu Lei (2005)[65] published Chinese financial corruption index which shows the order of corruption in various regions: the western region (5.85), southern China (5.79), northern China (5.74), central China (5.32), eastern China (5.00), northeastern China (4.45). This conclusion is consistent with our interpretation of the data. For example, according to our data, the per capita cases on file in three provinces in "southern China"—Guangdong, Hainan, Guangxi—are very low, and the anti-corruption efforts there should be understood as weak, which is consistent with the conclusion of Xie Ping and Lu Lei (2005) that there is a higher level of financial corruption in southern China. East and Northeast China have the highest number of per capita cases, and their corresponding financial corruption is also the lowest. In addition, the 1988–1992 corruption index in China released by International Transparency (IT) was higher than that after 1992, indicating that the anti-corruption effort of this period was greater.[66] Our data also revealed that in this period the per capita number of cases on file in provinces was highest in all years. Therefore, we think that the number of per capita cases can partly represent the intensity of local government's efforts to curb the corruption of officials.

For the data, we need to make the following explanations. First of all, the "number of cases involving corruption and bribery cases" is derived from the Annual Report of the People's Procuratorate (per province) of *Chinese Procuratorial Yearbook* (1989–2003). The "number of public servants" comes from the category of "number of employees in sub-sectors" (per year) of *Chinese Statistical Yearbook*. To divide these two items with each other, and the "number of corruption and bribery cases of public officials per 10,000 person" is obtained. Moreover, in the 1997 provincial Annual Report of the People's Procuratorate, most provinces reported only the total number of economic cases in five years (1993–1997). Although we have got the data of the first four years out of the five, the data obtained by backward deduction differed so greatly with the previous four years that the 1997 data we got in this way cannot be trusted and therefore was not included in our data. Finally, in some years, some provinces provided only the total number of economic cases, but no specific number of corruption and bribery cases. If we assume that the proportion of corruption cases to the total economic cases in adjacent years remained unchanged, then we can use the total economic cases of current year to be multiplied by the proportion of corruption cases to the total economic cases in adjacent years to calculate the corruption and bribery cases in the current year. In the total observed values, the observed value calculated by this method only accounted for only 15%.

Apart from the above three key explanatory variables, we also placed some other variables into the regression such as the initial value of per capita infrastructure investment period, per capita urban and rural savings and per capita GDP. The initial value of the per capita infrastructure investment period is the amount of infrastructure investment in the previous year. This variable examines whether there is a catch-up

---

[65] Xie Ping, Lu Lei (2005).

[66] After 1992, China's honest index was on the decline, and investment in China's infrastructure began to accelerate after 1992. It seems that the relationship between the two is not accidental.

effort on investment in infrastructure targeted at developed regions by underdeveloped regions. The per capita savings deposits in urban and rural areas are meant to investigate whether the financial resources owned by provinces will have a significant impact on infrastructure investment. All these data are from *Chinese Statistical Yearbook*. We used the China's GDP deflator to remove price trends. The actual per capita GDP measures per capita income, in order to examine whether infrastructure investment has an income effect (lower income areas receive more transfer payments from the state, so they have more investments); this index were used by Kemmerling and Stephan (2002)[67] in their studies. We also used China's GDP deflator to eliminate the price trends in the per capita GDP.

Finally, we also added dummy variables of four years in the regression (Dummy 89, Dummy 90, Dummy 93, Dummy 94). These variables were valued at 1 in the current year and 0 in other years. Dummy 89 and Dummy 90 were used to control the negative effect of the political turmoil in the first half of 1989 on infrastructure investment. Dummy 93 was meant to examine whether the overheated economy of the 1993 had led to higher infrastructure investment. In view of the time lag effect of overheated infrastructure investment, we have also thrown in Dummy 94.[68] At the same time Dummy 99 was also added. This variable was 1 before 1999, and 0 in subsequent years, because 1999 was the first year of the western development strategy and also the period when the East Asian financial crisis had an impact on China, so we want to see whether it had a positive or negative impact on the investment in infrastructure.

The estimation results reported is in Table 11.3. The first column includes all the systematic GMM estimation of explanatory variables, and the two variables of the actual per capita GDP and the per capita urban and rural savings are not significant.[69] In the second column, we removed the non-significant variables and re-estimated the systematic GMM. The third column is differential GMM estimation. The fourth column is the random effect estimation of instrumental variables. As can be seen from the estimation results, the coefficients of the various estimation methods are consistent, which is in line with our theoretical explanation. But the optimal estimation system is obviously systematic GMM method, which produced the best results and its core variable coefficients were significant and passed the Sargan test and the original assumption that the error item itself in differential equation is related with first-order sequence but not related to the second order sequence. Differential GMM method is not significant in the anti-corruption indicator because of the reasons mentioned above—the changes of anti-corruption index are not obvious and it is not very effective to designate lag variable as the instrumental variable of difference variable; to make matters worse, it cannot pass the Sargan test, indicating that it

[67] Kemmerling and Stephan (2002).

[68] From the statistical point of view, the growth rate of capital construction investment of the national total level reached its peak in 1993 and 1994, respectively at 53.2% and 39.5%, which did not fall back to below 15% till 1995.

[69] We put either of the two variables into the equation, and found that the coefficients were still not significant and did not change the results of other variables.

rejected the original hypothesis that tool variables and the error term are not related, so it failed to solve the endogeneity problem. The IVRF method is not significant in the per capita administrative expenditure variable, and its anti-corruption index is not as significant as systematic GMM method. These results show that the systematic GMM estimation method we have adopted has well solved the endogeneity problem and the validity of estimation.

Let's make some explanations regarding the regression results of the second column.

First, the infrastructure investment has a significant catch-up effect and the four methods of estimation have shown it at a significant level of 1%. The areas with less investment in infrastructure (western and central regions) have surpassed the eastern region in investment growth rate, which means that local governments in the central and western regions attached great importance to infrastructure investment and that the west development measures are effective.

Second, foreign direct investment on infrastructure growth is significantly positive, which verified our observation and theoretical hypothesis. The existing infrastructure can attract foreign direct investment enterprises to a certain extent and after foreign-invested enterprises entered this field, they would consider the government performance on infrastructure construction as one of the important factors for further investment. This has prompted the local government where the investment was made to honor their commitment and continue improving the local infrastructure in order to retain the enterprises and attract more foreign enterprises to enter, thus creating a virtuous circle.

Third, we find that the per capita administrative costs of public servants have significantly affected investment in infrastructure. Evans (1992) believes that the level of professionalism of government institutions is a necessary condition for a country to have a "developmental" government. Rauch and Evans (2000)[70] pointed out that the introduction of the civil service system, raising the civil service wages and promotion to higher office are all ways to improve the professional level and efficiency of the government. The rise of public officials' administrative expenses has increased civil servants' wages and benefits, and improved the government's professional level to a certain extent, and this "developmental" government is willing to develop more infrastructure construction to promote economic growth.

Fourth, the impact of anti-corruption indicators on infrastructure investment is interestingly negative, suggesting that an increase in anti-corruption efforts will reduce marginal investment in infrastructure. Tanzi and Davoodi (1998), in their transnational empirical studies, show that corruption has a positive impact on infrastructure investment, and explain that infrastructure investment could be easily manipulated by rent-seeking officials.[71] Mauro (1998) also pointed out in his writing that government officials will spend more on public investment projects that are vulnerable to bribery, and argued that infrastructure investment is more likely to be rent-seeking than public spending such as education. Tanzi and Davoodi (1998) held in

[70] Rauch and Evans (2000).

[71] Tanzi and Davoodi (1998).

Table 11.3 Estimation of determinants of infrastructure investment (interpreted variables: growth rate of infrastructure investment)

	(1) SYS-GMM	(2) SYS-GMM	(3) DIF-GMM(2)	(4) IVRE(3)
Logarithm of the initial value of the per capita infrastructure investment period/loginfinvpc_1	−0.140***	−0.119***	−0.465***	−0.107***
	0.0394(1)	0.0304	0.0649	0.0380
Logarithm of foreign direct investment per capita/logrfdipc	0.0349**	0.0395***	0.0996***	0.0372**
	0.0161	0.0124	0.0241	0.0167
Logarithm of administrative costs of public servants per capita/logdmexpp	0.100**	0.0932*	0.304**	0.0649
	0.052	0.0496(4)	0.104	0.0576
The number of cases of corruption and bribery of public servants per capita/anticorrpp	−0.0027**	−0.003***	−0.0008	−0.0032**
	0.0013	0.0012	0.0019	0.0014
Logarithm of the actual per capita GDP/logrgdppc	−0.0580			
	0.100			
Per capita urban and rural savings/loglocalsavpc	0.0831			
	0.0794			
Dummy 89	−0.0181	−0.0323	−0.0567	
	0.0837	0.0826	0.0873	
Dummy 90	0.0081	0.0072	−0.0203	0.0064
	0.0786	0.0786	0.0796	0.0850
Dummy 93	0.164**	0.157**	0.0906	0.163**
	0.0711	0.0709	0.0647	0.0742
Dummy 94	0.124*	0.119*	0.0921	0.125*
	0.0710	0.0704	0.0644	0.0735
Dummy 99	−0.0693	−0.0562	−0.147**	−0.0509
	0.0597	0.0582	0.0699	0.0628
Constant term	0.318	0.128		0.341*
	0.709	0.328		0.388
Sargan test value	0.175	0.194	0.000	
The error item $\varepsilon_{i,1}$—$\varepsilon_{i,t-1}$ with the first-order sequence tests	0.000	0.000	0.000	

(continued)

Table 11.3 (continued)

	(1) SYS-GMM	(2) SYS-GMM	(3) DIF-GMM(2)	(4) IVRE(3)
With the second-order sequence tests	0.989	0.972	0.902	
Observed value	341	341	281	310

Note ① The value below the coefficient is the standard deviation, *** Means significant at the 1% level, ** Means significant at 5% level, and * Means significant at the 10% level; ② In the GMM estimation, we only specify the number of cases of corruption and bribery of public officials and dummy variables as exogenous variables, the other variables are considered as endogenous variables in order to control the endogenity problem; ③ Hausman tested the P value and the result is 0.11, so it does not reject the original hypothesis that the coefficients IVFF and IVRF do not differ systematically, so we adopted IVRF and reported its results. Instrumental variables lag phase I was done here for infrastructure investment, foreign direct investment and administrative expenses; ④ The P value of the number of the corruption and bribery cases of public officials is 0.046 in the first column and 0.06 in the second column and are not significant in difference

further analysis that corruption will reduce the original infrastructure maintenance costs, cause the quality of infrastructure investment to decline and the investment in infrastructure project expenditures rise. It will also cause the costs of corruption to be included in the infrastructure investment. Therefore, in this sense, the strengthening of anti-corruption effort may also curb some of the infrastructure investments driven by corruption opportunities, and may have a positive effect on infrastructure as a whole. The problem is complex and needs further study.

Finally, we find that the symbols of all dummy variables are in line with our expectations, indicating that these dummy variables can control the effects of those macro fluctuations. Of course, only the dummy variables in the 1993 and 1994 are statistically significant, while the regression coefficients of the remaining dummy variables are not significant, but are still consistent with the economic logic in coefficient symbols.

11.6 Conclusion

In the literature of economic development, the contribution of infrastructure to economic growth has been paid attention to. How to measure the marginal contribution of infrastructure to economic growth or productivity has attracted economists' attention. But another economic issue that deserves attention and research is that, what determines or influences the continued investment of infrastructure which is a public product with significant spillover effects? Why is it that some governments are better at building infrastructure than other governments? These issues naturally need us to shift our attention to government and political governance. In most Western countries, because the construction and updating of infrastructure investment and financing involve the finance of government, inter-governmental fiscal relationship, nature of democratic political system and the complex political system and behavior of voters that impose restrictions on government actions, so this research often becomes a typically empirical study of political economics in the existing literature.

Based on the existing research literature and using Chinese experience as a case study, we try to describe and explain the changes in China's physical infrastructure over the past 20 years in this article. As far as the existing literature is concerned, the experience of China since its reform and opening to the outside world contains almost all the information in the existing literature of development economics in varying degrees. This is not only because of the implementation of the fiscal system reform and decentralization in the middle of the 1980s in China, but also because the political pattern and governance of Chinese government has undergone interesting changes during this period. China has 31 provincial governments (nearly 3,000 county-level governments), and the size of such a sample allows us to use China's data to do research that also involve the situation of other countries. China's existing statistics and their quality have basically provided what we need in our studies. In contrast to transnational studies, the only downside is that the accumulation and construction of quantitative databases involving qualitative concepts of government and politics are still very backward. This tends to have prevented us from doing some valuable basic research work.

Even if there are still incomplete data and other technical problems, many studies can be carried out based on China's provincial data. This paper makes full use of the existing data and tries to make up for the lack of research in the economic literature on the changes of China's infrastructure level and its investment decisions since the reform and opening up. The basic conclusions that can be drawn from our research include:

(1) Since the reform and opening up, especially after the 1990s, great changes have taken place in the level of infrastructure in China and its mode of investment in infrastructure and the local government plays a very important role in infrastructure investment. Our research shows that without decentralization and correct incentives for local governments, it would be difficult to imagine China being able to achieve such a good level of infrastructure. There is no doubt that good infrastructure has supported China's direct productive investment and economic growth.
(2) Over the past 20 years, the level of Chinese infrastructure showed a significant gap between the coastal and inland areas, especially the "backward" status of the central area which basically did not change at all since the first half of the 1990s. This may be because the west region has been supported by the central government's transfer payments and investment in infrastructure, and the reform and opening up have enabled the east to better form a benign interaction between infrastructure construction and economic growth. However, we find that infrastructure investment has a significant "catch-up effect". As long as the central and western governments continue to make effort, the relative gap will gradually be narrowed.

(3) After the level of economic development, financial deepening and other factors have been controlled, the competition among local governments in attracting foreign investments and the transformation of government's governance are important factors to explain the investment decisions of infrastructure in China. This means decentralization, opening-up, government system reform and improvement of professionalism in government are very important for the government to commit itself to the construction and improvement of infrastructure. This conclusion is not only in line with the findings of other economic or transnational studies in the existing economic literature, but also has reference value for other transitional and developing economies.
(4) It is generally believed that, as infrastructure investment may offer a greater chance of official corruption than other social services provided by the government such as education, so in the existing literature, the degree of corruption of government officials and infrastructure investment performance have a positive correlation. This study did find that the anti-corruption index we used has a negative marginal impact on infrastructure investment, which indicates that the intensity of the anti-corruption effort by the government will reduce the investment in infrastructure at the margin. This means that the opportunity of official corruption has a positive impact on the growth of investment for infrastructure (such as transportation and city construction). However, considering that corruption may also have a positive impact on improving the quality of infrastructure construction, the implications of this conclusion may need further consideration and research.

Author's Note

I wrote this article in collaboration with my students Fu Yong, Gao Yuan and Zhang Hong. Although I had the urge to write this article long time ago, I have delayed studying the subject repeatedly. When we started collecting literature and data in 2006, I found it more difficult than I had expected. In a sense, this is an article that we have spent the most energy on. Not only did we check and discuss the little progress of the article every week, but overstrain in the writing of this article caused serious problems in my eyes. The condensed edition of this article was published as the top piece in the No. 3 issue of *Economic Research* in 2007.

Within the framework of China's political and economic system, the article explains the remarkable achievements China has made in building and improving its physical infrastructure since the reform, especially in the1990s. On the basis of the existing literature and provincial panel data, we not only measured the stock change and regional disparity of infrastructure in China since the reform and, by using GMM method, tested the important variables that can explain the changing pattern of infrastructure investment expenditure. We find that after the level of economic development, financial deepening and other factors have been controlled, the yardstick competition among local governments in attracting foreign investments and the transformation of governance are important factors to explain the investment decisions of infrastructure in China. This means decentralization, Tiebout competition, the transition toward a developmental government are essential in improving the stimulus for infrastructure investment by the government.

References

Arelano, M., O. Bover, Another Look at the Instrumental Variable Estimation of Error-Component Models, *Journal of Econometrics*, 1995, 68, pp. 29–51.

Arelano, M., S. Bond, Some Tests of Specification for Panel Data: Monte Carlo Evidence and an Application to Employment Equations, *Review of Economic Studies*, 1991, pp. 277–297.

Arrow, K.J., M. Kurz, *Public Investment, the Rate of Return and Optimal Fiscal Policy*, Johns Hopkins University Press, 1970.

Aschauer, D.A., Does Public Capital Crowd out Private Capital? *Journal of Monetary Economics*, 1989a, 24, pp. 178–235.

Aschauer, D.A., Is Public Expenditure Productive? *Journal of Economic Literature*, 1989b, 23, pp. 177–200.

Aschauer, D.A., Public Investment and Productivity Growth in The Group of Seven, Economic Perspectives, Federal Reserve Bank of Chicago, 1989c, 13, pp. 17–25.

Aschauer, D.A., Infrastructure and Macro Economic Performance: Direct and Indirect Effects, in: The OECD Jobs Study: Investment, Productivity and Employment, 1995.

Bardhan, P., Awakening Giants, Feet of Clay: A Comparative Assessment of the Rise of China and India, Paper presented at International Conference on the Dragon and the Elephant: China and India's Economic Reforms, 2006.

Barro, R.J., Economic Growth in a Cross Section of Countries, *Quarterly Journal of Economics*, 1991, 106 (2), pp. 407–443.

Blanchard, O., A. Shleifer, Federalism with and without Political Centralization: China versus Russia, Working Paper 7616, NBFR, 2000.

Blundel, R., S. Bond, Initial Conditions and Moment Restrictions in Dynamic Panel Data Models, *Journal of Econometrics*, 1998, 87, pp. 115–143.

Bond, S., Dynamic Panel Data Models: A Guide to Micro Data Methods and Practice, *Portuguese Economic Journal*, 2002, 1, pp. 141–162.

Cao, Y., Y. Qian, B.R. Weingast, From Federalism, Chinese Style, to Privatization, Chinese Style, *Economics of Transition*, 1999, 7 (1), pp. 103–131.

Cheng Shiyi, Zhang Jun: *A Study of the Efficiency of Fiscal Expenditure of China's Local Government: 1978–2005*, Chinese Social Sciences, 2008 (4).

Demurger, S. Infrastructure Development and Economic Growth: An Explanation for Regional Disparities in China, *Journal of Comparative Economics*, 2001, 29.

Démurger, S. Infrastructure, Development and Economic Growth: An Explanation for Regional Disparities in China, *Journal of Comparative Economics*, 2001, 29, pp. 95–117.

Evans, P.B., The State as Problem and as Solution: Predation, Embedded Autonomy and Structural Change, in: Haggard, Stephan, Robert R. Kaufman, *The Politics of Economic Adjustment: International Constraints, Distributive Conflicts, and the State*, Princeton University Press, Princeton, 1992.

Fan Jiuli, Bai Baoli: A Study on the Regional Differences of Infrastructure Investment and Economic Growth in China, *Human Geography*, 2004a (19), pp. 25–30

Fan Jiuli, Bai Baoli: Effect of Infrastructure Capital on Economic Growth—Level Two and Three Factor CES Production Function Estimation, *Economic Forum*, 2004b (11), 10–13.

Fan Jiuli, Bai Baoli, Pan Quan: Literature Review on the Relationship between Infrastructure Capital and Economic Growth, *Shanghai Economic Research*, 2004c (1), 36–43.

Fan, S., X. Zhang, Infrastructure and Regional Economic Development in Rural China, *China Economic Review*, 2004, 15, pp. 203–214.

Fasterly, W., R. Levine, Africa' s Growth Tragedy: Policies and Ethnic Divisions, *Quarterly Journal of Economics*, 1997, 112, pp.1203–1250.
Haggard, Stephan, *Pathways from Periphery: The Politics of Growth in the Newly Industrializing Countries*, Cornell University Press, Ithaca 1990.
Henisz, W.J., The Institutional Environment of Infrastructure Investment, *Industrial and Corporate Change*, 2002, 11 (2), pp. 355–389.
Hu Shudong: *Central and Local Relation in Economic Development*, Shanghai, Shanghai DXS Joint Company, Shanghai People's Publishing House, 2001.
Kemmerling, A., A. Stephan, The Contribution of Local Public Infrastructure to Private Productivity and Its Political Economy: Evidence from a Panel of Large German Cities, *Public Choice*, 2002, 113 (3–4), pp. 403–424.
LaPorta, R., F. Lopez-De-Silanes, A. Shleifer, R. Vishny, The Quality of Government, *Journal of Law, Economics and Organization*, 1999, 15 (1), pp. 1113–1155.
Li Boxi, Liu Deshun: A Regional Comparative Analysis of Infrastructure and Economic Growth in China, *Management World*, 1995 (2), 106–111.
Li, Hongbin, Li, Anzhou, Political Turnover and Economic Performance: Incentive Role of Personnel Control in China, *Journal of Public Economics*, 2005, 89, pp. 1743–1762
Lin, J.Y., Z. Liu, Fiscal Decentralization and Economic Growth in China, *Economic Development and Cultural Change*, 2000, 49, pp. 1–22.
Lu Minghong: Evaluation and Comparison of Investment Environment in Different Regions of China: 1990–2000. *Management World*, 2002 (11), 42–49.
Mauro, P., Corruption and the Composition of Government Expenditure, *Journal of Public Economics*, 1998, 69, pp. 263–279.
North, D.C., R.P. Thomas, *The Rise of Western World: A New Economic Theory*, Cambridge University Press, Cambridge, 1973.
Oates, Walace, *Fiscal Federalism*, Harcourt Brace Jovanovic, New York, 1972.
Perkins: China's Economic Growth, China *Economics Quarterly*, 2005, 4 (4), 891–912.
Przeworski, A., F. Limongi, Political Regimes and Economic Growth, *Journal of Economic Perspectives*, 1993, 7, pp. 51–69.
Qian Y., B. Weingast, Federalism as a Commitment to Preserving Market Incentives, *Journal of Economic Perspectives*, 1997, 11 (4), pp. 83–92.
Qian, Y., G. Roland, Federalism and The Soft Budget Constraint, *American Economic Review*, 1998, 88 (5), pp. 143–149.
Randolph, S., Z. Bogetic, D. Hefley, Determinants of Public Expenditure on Infrastructure, Transportation and Communication, The World Bank Policy Research Working Paper, Washington D.C., 1996.
Rauch, J.F., Bureaucracy, Infrastructure, and Economic Growth: Evidence from US Cities during the Progressive Era, *American Economic Review*, 1995, 85 (4), pp. 968–979.
Rauch, J.F., P.B. Evans, Bureaucratic Structure and Bureaucratic Performance in Less Developed Countries, *Journal of Public Economics*, 2000, 75, pp. 49–71.
Shleifer and Vishiny: *Grabbing Hand*, tr. Zhao Hongjun, Beijing, CITIC Publishing House, 2004.
Shleifer, A., Government in Transition, *European Economic Review*, 1997, 41, pp. 385–410.
Tanzi, V., H. Davoodi, Corruption, Public Investment and Growth, IMF Working Paper, Washington D.C, 1997.
Tanzi, V., H. Davoodi, Roads to Nowhere: How Corruption in Public Investment Hurts Growth, IMF Working Paper, Washington D.C., 1998.
Tiebout, C., A Pure Theory of Local Expenditures, *Journal of Political Economy*, 1956, 64 (5), pp. 416–424.
Treisman, D., Decentralization and the Quality of Government, Working Paper, University of California, Los Angeles, 2000.
Wei Houkai: Influence of Foreign Direct Investment on China's Regional Economic Growth. *Economic Research*, 2002 (4), 19–26.

Wei Xinya: Regional Differences in Investment in China's Infrastructure Construction. *Shanghai Economic Research*, 2002 (12), pp. 20–25.
World Bank: *World Development Report of 1994*, pp. 2, 13, Beijing, Chinese Finance and Economics Press, 1995.
Xie Ping, Lu Lei: *Economics Analysis of Financial Corruption in China*, Beijing, CITIC Publishing House, 2005.
Yang Yongheng: Human Development Index Substitution Technology based on Principal Component Analysis, *Economic Research*, 2005 (7), 4–17.
Zhang Jun, Jin Yu: Re-Testing the Correlation between Financial Deepening and Productivity in China: 1987–2001, *Economic Research*, 2005 (11).
Zhang Jun, Wu Guiying, Zhang Jipeng: Estimation of Chinese Provincial Physical Capital Stock: 1952–2000, *Economic Research*, 2004 (10).
Zhang Jun: Political Economy of India and China's Growth, *Peking University Business Review*, 2006 (22).
Zhang Yan, Xia Jijun: Evaluation of Tax Competition Theory—An Analysis of Tax Relief Competition among China's Local Governments, *Economics Perspectives*, 2006.
Zhuravskaya, E.V., Incentives to Provide Local Public Goods: Fiscal Federalism, Russian Style, *Journal of Public Economics*, 2000, 76, pp. 337–368.

Chapter 12
Irregular Financial Sector in Rural China After the Reform: A Case Study of Wenzhou

12.1 Introduction

In the rural financial (credit) market, the irregular sector refers to the spontaneous formation of the private credit sector relevant to the official financial system and the banking organization. Compared with the official financial sector, the irregular credit has a long history, because what we call the formal banking sector and financial markets today are only the innovation and development of modern system. However, in many countries in the world, especially in developing countries, we find that this old, spontaneously formed credit market still exist in some rural areas, constituting a significant part of the rural financial (credit) market.

In the period of planned economy in China, although the rural private capital market was almost banned, it has been always in existence in a variety of flexible and covert forms.[1] The change of the non collectivization agricultural production system started in 1978 and the rural reform led to the unprecedented development of the economy and non-governmental credit of the rural areas in China. In some economically developed rural areas and towns, many private economies such as village enterprises, family enterprises and families that went in for a special kind of production gradually appeared. Since they could not get the credit they needed from the official financial departments, their demand for a considerable amount of money was met by private capital market financing. Moreover, in rural areas throughout the country there also appeared a variety of folk credit organizations, such as savings societies, foundations, credit services, credit cooperatives, partnership private financial organizations, which developed rapidly after 1978.

In Wenzhou of Zhejiang province, the private credit in rural areas has always been highly developed. In recent years, with the development of family-based production and exchanges, the demand for funds has been expanding day by day and the folk credit is booming because farmers have more cash at their disposal. It is estimated that

[1] I failed to collect information about non-governmental finance before the economic reform (1949–1978), nor any data. But I did hear something introduction about it in Wenzhou.

J. Zhang, *Reform, Transformation and Growth*, Understanding China,
https://doi.org/10.1007/978-981-99-5712-5_12

in 1985, the funding needs of the city's rural self-employed households and township enterprises reached 650–700 million *yuan*, of which bank (credit cooperative) loans accounted for about 30% of the total demand, private lending accounted for 36%, and the rest was owned by enterprises themselves. In economically developed coastal plain areas of Wenzhou, the proportion of private lending was even larger. In Qianku Town, Cangnan county of Wenzhou, 10 big wholesale households, 26 large shops and 9 companies needed a total capital of 3.664 million *yuan*. Apart from their own money, loans from credit cooperatives could only make up for 38% of the funding, so 62% was from the non-governmental or folk credit; township enterprises and the family businesses in Liuchi, Leqing county borrowed 50% of their circulating fund from folk credit[2] (Zhang and Li 1990).

However, the development of the rural irregular financial sector and its scale caused a strong reaction from local governments and formal financial sectors (especially the official banking sector).[3] They usually defined the folk credit as illegal "usury", arguing that the irregular credit was an adverse current in the financial markets, a huge latent financial risk, seriously disrupting the financial order. They were trying to put pressure on the government to try to crack down on the existence of the irregular credit sector through policy intervention, or at least to curb its expansion.[4] However, this effort often caused the choice of policy to be in trouble because of the excessive cost of regulation.

The plight of the policy reflected, to a large extent, the misunderstanding of the structure of the rural financial (credit) market and the way it was operated by the regulatory authorities. For example, they saw the rural financial sector as a unified rather than a segmented entity and defined the folk credit as "usury". For the case of Wenzhou, almost all researchers of financial problems have invariably resorted to "dialectics" in their understanding of non-formal financial sector: on the one hand, they think the irregular financial sector complemented formal financial sector to a certain extent which has promoted the development of productivity; on the other hand, the rural irregular credit activity has the nature of usury, thus it has hampered the development of production. Frankly, these ambivelent explanations are not helpful to provide correct policy guidance and valuable policy options for the government, nor does it improve our deep understanding of the rural irregular financial sector in theory, which largely makes our theoretical research on rural non-formal financial sector far lag behind its development.

---

[2] Zhang and Li (1990).

[3] I was deeply impressed by this in Wenzhou. On the one hand, the offcial financial sector had a negative attitude towards the development of rural irregular finance; on the other hand, some officials of the relevant government departments seemed to show a supportive attitude.

[4] And yet, when the bank departments wanted the government to intervene and ban the rural folk credit market, the commission of structuring reform and other departments (such as agriculture bureau, agriculture committee and industrial and commercial bureau) all supported development of private credit in different degrees. In fact, many non-governmental credit institutions were often examined and approved by the authorities of the government and registered by the industrial and commercial bureau without approval from the local people's Bank of China.

The purpose of this paper is to provide an economic explanation for the irregular financial sector in China's rural areas after the reform. For this purpose, first, I chose Wenzhou in Zhejiang as an empirical case, although rural credit is a common phenomenon in many rural areas throughout the country. Second, I will develop an analysis framework in this paper, analyze the structure and nature of rural financial sector by using the theory of information economics, try to answer why the rural financial market is a segmented one, why the irregular sector may not be expelled from the rural financial market by the formal sector, and in what ways can we to explain the interest rate difference between the formal and irregular sectors. Through the explanation of these problems and the analysis of the case in Wenzhou, I hope this article will provide some reference for policy choices.

12.2 A Survey of Rural Nongovernmental Credit Sector in Wenzhou

Since the economic reform and opening up in 1978, the economy of Wenzhou formed a unique pattern, especially in the rural regions where a flexible market mechanism was been established and the private sector was rapidly expanding in rural areas which is known as the "Wenzhou model" (Zhang and Li 1990). From 1978 to 1991, the total output value of the city increased by 5.2 times, the total output value of industry and agriculture increased by 4.6 times, the fiscal revenue increased by 6.4 times, and the per capita income of farmers increased by 8.2 times. A total of 454 commodity markets came into being in the city, of which 35 had an annual turnover of more than 10 million *yuan*, 12 had more than 50 million *yuan*, 12 more than 100 million *yuan*. In the process of market transaction, 140,000 marketing salesmen were engaged in the purchase and sale of goods and raw materials, more than 85% of the products and raw materials were sold through the market, 78% of steel, 80% of cement and 87% of coal of the city were allocated through market.[5] This production and economic organization and form that were mainly distributed in rural areas were in increasing need of the small-scale and short-term funding. However, the total amount of credit and credit structure provided by official financial sector were far from being able to meet this demand,[6] thus providing the opportunity for the development of rural private finance sector in the market.

(1) Free Borrowing

In rural areas, free lending is typically a free credit activity between friends or relatives with less amount of money and short period. In recent years, with the development of

---

[5] Zhang and Mao (1993).

[6] Zhang Zhenyu and Mao Chunhua noted in their book *A Survey of the Wenzhou Financial Phenomenon under the Condition of Socialist Market Economy* that at the beginning of the 80s, the demand of the rural township enterprises and private sector for funds amounted to 700 million *yuan*, while the funds the official banks and rural credit cooperatives could provide were only 200 million *yuan*.

the rural economy, the scale of this kind of lending has expanded and the use of funds has shifted from daily necessity to production, so it has become the main channel for individual proprietor to make up for his capital shortage and constituted a free credit market. According to an observation survey in 1993 of 50 fixed households in Jinhou village, Ruian city under Wenzhou (one of the country's rural fixed observation sites), 26 peasant households borrowed money via free credit, accounting for 52% of the total amount and, at the end of that year, the cumulative borrowing amount was 614,500 *yuan*, accounting for 92.5% of the total loans with the average household loan amounting to 12,300 *yuan* (among 50 households). If calculated according to the city's total 710,000 households, the amount of free credit reached as high as 31.6%; even if at a discount of 50%, the amount was still as high as 1.58 billion *yuan* (Chen Jianguang 1995). According to a survey conducted in August 1992, people in Cangnan county had 420 million *yuan* in cash, 350 million of which was involved in private lending activities, and the number of households and the amount of financing in private lending in Oubei and Qiaotou towns of Yongjia county accounted for more than 40%.[7] Most of the free private lending funds were invested in production. In the private loans of the aforementioned 50 households, 106,500 *yuan* was used for daily life, accounting for only 17.3% while 508,000 *yuan* was used in production accounting for 82.7%. In the same year, the total loans borrowed by these 50 households from banks and credit cooperatives were 50,000 *yuan*, accounting for only 8.1% of the private loans (Chen Jianguang 1995). This shows that the funds for the farmers' production and operation in Jinhou village were mainly from the irregular financial sector rather than the official financial sector. According to Chen Jianguang's same survey, private free lending was also the major source of corporate liquidity. According to a survey of 10 private, joint-stock and partnership enterprises, the floating capital borrowed by these 10 companies in 1993 was 679,300 *yuan*, out of which 449,300 *yuan* was from private sector, accounting for 66.1% (Chen Jianguang 1995).

According to the survey, there were two main forms of free lending. ①Direct borrowing. It refers to a form of direct borrowing whereby both sides agreed on the amount of loan, duration and interest rate. It was based on mutual understanding and trust of both sides, including short-term lending with interest among relatives and friends. According to statistics, in 1988, 779,000 *yuan* of direct loans was transacted in Litou village, Ruian among the total loans, accounting for 86.2%. ②Intermediary. It is a form of indirect capital borrowing with profit. Lenders use the intermediary who then lend and recover the money. An intermediary does not have a lot of money, but is well aware of the lenders in the surrounding regions and has established his credibility. It is essentially a kind of capital borrowing activity. An intermediary has to pay a monthly interest rate of 20–25‰ to the lender and receive an interest rate of 25–30‰ from borrowers, with a margin of 5‰. A survey conducted for Cuiteng district of Ruian city in August 1992 found that there were nearly 30 administrative villages in the district and each village had an intermediary on average. The average credit loan was 1 million *yuan* with the total amount reaching 30–4000 million *yuan*

[7] Zhang and Mao (1993).

which was close to the amount of credit loans released by local banks and credit cooperatives in 1991, according to Chen Guoxing of Wenzhou Agricultural Bank.

The main period of the formation and development of the rural nongovernmental credit sector in Wenzhou was during 1978–1987. In 1978–1982, rural household industry began to start in Wenzhou. As the equipment was crude and needed less money, the farmers could operate their business by borrowing a small amount of money to purchase production equipment and raw materials. As a result, the capital turnover was extremely fast. At that time, the income and accumulation of farmers of Wenzhou from agriculture were very low, and banks and credit cooperatives did not provide loans to non-agricultural self-employed business. Therefore, the private lending for production was born at the right moment and developed rapidly. The folk credit at this stage took the various forms of direct loans. During 1983–1987, after several years of operation, rural family business in Wenzhou had accumulated a huge amount of money, so apart from the funds used for operation in the process of production and circulation, there were also a large amount of idle funds. On the other hand, as the rural household industry expanded rapidly, and the specialized market continued to emerge, the demand for funds increased rapidly as well. By the end of 1986, the number of individual industrial and commercial households in Wenzhou had reached 138,400 with 350,000 people. The city's rural trade markets reached nearly 400, of which there were more than 130 specialized markets and the annual turnover of the 10 largest specialized markets was about 1 billion *yuan*. If turnover is calculated as 4 times a year, more than 250 million *yuan* worth of circulating funding was needed. The accumulation of rural money therefore provided more and more funds for nongovernmental credit. The development of rural household industry and commerce and the expansion of specialized markets generated a demand for a great deal of short-term funds, thus further promoting the development of rural credit. During this period, the scale of private credit expanded, and the form of indirect financing appeared. According to the 1993 statistics, in the amount of money in circulation on the market in rural areas of Wenzhou, the funds from the national banks and credit cooperatives accounted for only 20%, borrowings from private capital market accounted for 40%, and funds raised by the private proprietors accounted for 40%. In other words, the amount of private lending was 2 times as much as loans from banks and credit cooperatives according to Chen Guoxing of Wenzhou Agricultural Bank.

There were three main types of credit in rural credit market in Wenzhou. First, free lending, which can be directly traded by both sides of the lender and borrower, or through intermediary agencies. Second, "rotating savings and credit association" (ROSCA). A few people set up a group, each person contributes a certain amount of money per month which is loaned to a member of the group to meet the temporary funding requirements of the borrower. The third were the local credit organizations, such as private money lending organizations, pawnshops and mutual funds. The funds borrowed by rural individuals and private enterprises directly from private credit organizations were usually short in time, large in amount and higher in interest rates. In addition, there were various forms of fund-raising. For example, in order to solve the problem of insufficient funds for production, some township and village enterprises would employ workers who would bring money to the plant, the principal and interest of which would be paid back on a regular basis. Or, a collective and individual enterprise would absorb individual shareholders and distribute profits according to shares. These forms existed in Wenzhou and, according to the survey, these irregular folk credits had constituted more than 1/3 of the total rural credit in Wenzhou, becoming a fairly large irregular financial sector.[8] With regard to the interest rate level, the interest rates of the rural private sector were generally higher than the level of the official sector. In Wenzhou, private credit interest rates had become stable at the monthly interest rate of around 30‰, though the credit funds were still in short supply, which meant that in the folk credit market there was an excess demand.[9]

(2) Rotating Savings and Credit Association

Also called "gathering", it is a popular form of credit in China, usually formed by relatives and friends (commonly known as "members") invited by a sponsor (called "master"). They meet at the agreed time, collect a certain amount of money and lend it to one member to use in turn as a form of mutual help.[10] The master receives the first payment, and then lent it to the members in rotation. There are three ways of getting the money: according to the order arranged in advance ("lending by rotation"); through throwing dice ("dice throwing)[11]; and submit a tender (bidding). In Wenzhou, the rotating association is mainly divided into two categories—"rotating" and "bidding" which spawned more varieties later on.

A few years ago, a popular rural "association" in Wenzhou usually had more than 10 or dozens of members ranging from 2 to 101. The duration of the association lasted at least about one year; some could last for 5 years with the longest for 8 years and 4 months. The amount of money involved in each association ranged from several thousand *yuan*, ten thousand *yuan* or hundreds of thousands of *yuan* (such as "tai association"). In general, the majority of associations would have 10 thousand *yuan* available for lending and their scale would gradually develop larger and more members would join in. Most of the participants were farmers or cadres with more income, and some would even join three or four associations at the same time. According to the investigation and analysis in the second half of 1985, various "associations" were quite common in Wenzhou area with the amount of money transacted reaching as high as 150 million *yuan*, so, it has become one of the main forms of credit in the private capital market in the rural areas of Wenzhou.

---

[8] The data on the scale of Wenzhou's private credit comes from my survey in Wenzhou in August 1996.

[9] My survey in Wenzhou also showed that the current rate of private credit in Wenzhou is generally stable at around 30‰.

[10] This kind of credit association still existed in the rural areas after the founding of new China, although it was cracked down and banned by the government at that time. The government even advocated "workers mutual savings association" to replace "rotating savings credit association" which was considered to have the "usury" nature.

[11] Relatively speaking, the loan interest rate of dice throwing is slightly higher, also at 30‰ (monthly), but the period of this loan is longer.

(3) Private Financing

A survey in 1985 showed that, in 1985, there were 2,301 self-funded rural enterprises accounting for 79.45% of the total number of households engaged in self funding business in urban and rural areas with pooled money amounting to 136 million 160 thousand *yuan*. It accounted for 78.48% of the funds loaned to township enterprises and collective businesses by banks and credit cooperatives of that year, or 84.59% of the total funds raised by urban and rural enterprises. Seventy percent of the funds raised was used as working capital of the enterprises, and 30% for construction.[12]

According to the survey of social fund-raising of township enterprises in Ouhai,[13] the funds raised from sectors of society by the region's township enterprises accounted for 38% of the total number of households, and the amount raised accounted for 80% of the fixed and floating capital of these enterprises over the same period and 42.5% of all their funding sources (excluding the settlement fund and undistributed profits). It was also 2.3 times higher than the loans granted to township enterprises by banks and credit cooperatives in the same period. There were only 28 self-funded enterprises in Hongqiao district, Yueqing county by the end of 1983 which employed 190 people; by the end of 1984 the enterprises there reached 109, employing 730 people; by the end of 1985, the number of enterprises totaled 388 with 2,620 permanent employees and 5,000 temporary workers totaling 7,620 people. 130 self-funded enterprises opened accounts at the Hongqiao Agricultural Bank, and their raised funds were 380 million *yuan*, while the loans they borrowed from the bank was only 80,000 *yuan*, accounting for only 17.4% of the total funds raised by the enterprises according to Qian Linsen's survey in 1986.

There were many sources for private financing, and the funds raised were mainly invested to replenish circulating funds. For example, a survey of 595 enterprises which had opened accounts at an industrial and commercial bank of China in Wenzhou city revealed that the funds raised by these enterprises totaled 24.802 million *yuan*, of which 7.450 million *yuan* was from savings deposits, accounting for 30% of the total; and the individual funds were10.83 million *yuan*, accounting for 43.7%. According to a survey of the city of Ruian, 18.3% of the raising funds was from the savings deposits; 62.7% from individual money, and the rest accounted for 19% of the total. The funds raised were mainly used to replenish the floating capital. According to a survey conducted by a local industrial and commercial bank, 71.9% self raised funds were used for floating capital; those for technical renovation accounted for only 4.7%, and those for other uses accounted for 23.4%.

At present, the main forms of rural private financing in Wenzhou are as follows. ①Joint venture. This is a fund-raising form by which the investor sets up factories which comes in two types: one is for a few investors to invest and manage a company by hiring temporary workers to engage in production who earn hourly or piece wages. This kind of enterprise is large in production scale, has a large army of laborers but

[12] Zhang and Li (1990).

[13] The survey report was provided by Zhang Lidong of the Ouhai branch of Wenzhou Agricultural Bank, which was included in a book entitled *A Preliminary Study of Wenzhou Capital Market* edited by Wenzhou Finance Society.

has to borrow a large amount of loans from the banks. Another type is real joint venture, for the scale of production is dependent on the amount of investment. This kind of operation is also called "capital takes care of production" because the vast majority of funds for production is provided by the investors themselves and interest for their shares are either calculated or not calculated. ② Employee investment. This kind of fund raising occurs when an enterprise in transition lacks funds or bank loans cannot meet its needs. It is stipulated that enterprise employees must invest a certain amount of money as an obligation to the enterprise, and the latter generally pays dividends on the shares contributed, or distribute dividends from the profits after tax is paid. This type of social fund raising accounted for a great proportion in Wenzhou. ③Introduction of funds from outside. This is a form thereby new enterprises introduce funds from other parts of the country for the development of production in the case of insufficient investment by their workers. ④ Investment management. This is a fund-raising in the form of the horizontal economic cooperation between township and urban industries. ⑤ Special and temporary fund-raising. It is a one-time funding to meet the specific needs of an enterprise, mainly for the purchase of an piece of equipment and materials, as well as the purchase of raw materials for temporary, seasonal use.

Private financing is generally short term and paid back on time. The period is generally 1–3 years and most of the temporary fund raising abides by the principle of "voluntary buying and withdrawing of shares". The dividend or interest rate is generally high, close to that of the free credit at a monthly interest rate of 20–30‰, more than doubled the interest rate of the savings deposit for the same period of time.[14]

(4) Foundation

In recent years, in the process of rural reform, a large number of towns and villages have gradually established rural cooperative foundations under the guidance of local party and government leaders and rural cooperative economic management departments.[15] The management and business scope of these institutions all followed that of the local rural credit cooperatives, but they have far more greater degree of flexibility than credit cooperatives; therefore, their scale of business continued to expand. By the end of 1992, 38 rural foundations were established in Wenzhou–8 in Pingyang, 17 in Cangnan, 10 in Ruian and 3 in Yongjia. By the end of August, 1993, the number grew to 88 with 27 million *yuan* in asset, 438.56 million *yuan* in deposits and 410.07 million *yuan* in loans, employing 572 people. Out of these 88 foundations, 75 was examined and approved by the Commission of Structural Reform of Wenzhou, 11 was approved by Agricultural Committee of Wenzhou, and the other

[14] For example, according to a survey (1986) conducted by Qian Shusen in Wenzhou, the fund-raising period in Hongqiao district, Yueqing county of Wenzhou was generally 1–3 years, and the dividend was generally 20–25‰ per month.

[15] Seen from the national level, the rural cooperative foundation appeared as early as 1984 according to the survey of Cui Liukang in 1996.

2 borrowed loans amounting to 600 million *yuan* in December 1993.[16] As the foundations continued to expand their scale of business, the local agricultural banks and credit cooperatives felt a lot of pressure and the People's Bank was also ambivalent in its attitude as to how to regulate the foundations.[17] The rural foundations in Wenzhou have the following characteristics: first, they can raise a large amount of financing; second, their interest rate, which kept fluctuating, doubled that of bank deposits, only slightly lower than the interest rate of private lending[18]; thirdly, the capital was pooled by private individuals or contributed by rural cooperatives; fourth, the capital was loaned primarily to individual entrepreneurs, township enterprises, collective and private enterprises.

(5) Pawn Shops[19]

After Huamao Pawn Firm—the first pawn shop ever established after new China was founded—appeared in Chengdu, Sichuan in January 1981, Wenzhou also witnessed the opening of its first pawn shop–Wenzhou Jincheng Pawn Shop in February 9. In less than a year, 42 pawnshops were approved in the city of Wenzhou, accounting for about 1/5 of the country's total. Except Dongtou county, Wenzhou's pawn shops could be found in eight counties (cities) and two districts, of which 12 were opened in Wenzhou proper, and the rest were scattered in rural areas.

According to the statistics provided by Zhang Zhenyu and Mao Chunhua (1993),[20] the sources of operating capital of pawn firms mainly came from three aspects. First, borrowing money from financial institutions. The 34 pawn business borrowed more than 36 million *yuan* from all kinds of financial institutions, of which about 30 million *yuan* from banks and more than 6 million *yuan* from urban credit cooperatives and rural financial services, accounting for 58.9% of the total assets of the pawn industry. According to the statistics by the end of 1989, 10.20 million *yuan* of loans had yet to be collected by the 12 pawn business in Wenzhou City. Second, "self fund-raising" or borrowing money from higher authorities and enterprises and institutions. The 34 pawn firms borrowed 9.34 million *yuan* in this way, accounting for 15.4% of the total assets. Third, ones' own capital. The 34 pawn shops owned 15.78 million *yuan* (3 million were collective stocks), accounting for 25.70% of total assets. The pawn

[16] The data provided by Chen Guoxing from the agricultural bank of Wenzhou show that since the Commission of Restructuring Reform of Cangnan County in Wenzhou issued the Notice on the Experiment of Rural Stock Cooperative Foundation in August 1992, 15 foundations were approved the county's Commission of Restructuring Reform in February 1993, of which 11 commenced their business.

[17] According to my survey in Wenzhou, the people's bank of Wenzhou was trying to rectify the rural cooperative foundations, but, because of disagreements among government's leaders, the banking sector could do nothing but complain.

[18] Seen from the national level, the lending rate of the rural cooperative foundation is about 2–3 times higher that that of the rural credit cooperatives.

[19] Pawn is a private financing system providing small amount of loans by using clients' articles as collateral.

[20] The basic information of the pawn industry in Wenzhou was provided by Zhang Zhenyu and Mao Chunhua (1993).

shop with the largest amount of capital had 1.5 million *yuan*, while the one with the minimum capital had of 300,000 *yuan*.

The business range of pawn firms is divided into two categories: movable property and immovable property. The former includes daily necessities, household appliances, jewelry, securities, surplus raw materials, idle equipment and vehicles; the latter mainly includes housing. The service fee of pawn business is calculated according to the monthly amount of pawn rate of 24–48%, warehouse fee and insurance fee are calculated at 3–9‰ respectively according to the item's value and size; its comprehensive rate is higher than lending rates of the urban credit cooperatives and lower than the interest rate of private lending. Evaluation method of pawn items is as follows: real estate in general is valued at around 50% of the market price; pledge of movables is valued depending on the market situation; for instance, gold jewelry is generally valued at 70–75% of the market price.

12.3 Why Irregular Sector Exist?

Economically, the existence of irregular financial markets in rural areas is associated with excessive regulation and repression by the official financial markets. Therefore, the emergence and development of the private credit market is only a reflection of the general market distortion. The Wenzhou case is no exception.

The usual explanation for the development of Wenzhou rural credit market is that, after the economic reforms in 1978, Wenzhou's economic structure has brought about the close relation between its economic development and private capital. There is no foundation of big industry in Wenzhou, and family and private business run by farmers is the main part of the economy. Whether in production, circulation and other areas, individual, private, joint-stock and township enterprises account for a large proportion (see Table 12.1). According to the data of the Bureau of Statistics of Wenzhou, in the industrial output value of the first half of 1991, the state sector accounted for 17.1%, collective sector accounted for 51.3%, individual and private businesses accounted for 31.6%; with regard to retail sales, state sector accounted for 38%, collective sector accounted for 14%, individual and private businesses accounted for 48%. Due to the fact that non-state sector in the economy of Wenzhou constitutes a larger proportion, it is extremely difficult for this sector to access credit from the regular financial sector in order to meet its development needs. This is mainly because there has not been a mature and complete financial market in the process of economic transition, and the official finance is completely arranged by relying on government intervention and the allocation of financial resources is completely influenced by the preferences of local government for ownership. In other words, the official financial sector is mainly focused on state-owned and collective sectors in granting their loans. The data of Wenzhou's Industrial and commercial bank of China and agricultural bank of China released in July 1991 show that, in terms of the industrial working capital loans, state sector accounted for 58.05%, collective sector accounted for 41.1% and the individual and private businesses accounted for 0.81%; as far as commercial

Table1 Proportion of output value of Wenzhou's private enterprises, individual businesses and state-owned, collective enterprises. Unit: %

Year	Industrial system			Business system		
	The whole people	Collective	Private-individual	The whole people	Collective	Private-individual
1980	31.49	54.67	13.84	38.54	59.30	2.16
1985	18.36	56.23	23.41	27.52	44.98	27.50
1987	13.95	54.49	31.57	28.26	38.97	32.82
1990	12.07	52.50	33.75	21.89	21.94	40.05
1991	16.50	51.88	31.62	23.74	24.22	52.04
1992	13.08	51.29	35.63	33.62	13.51	52.81

Source Huang Chonghu: *Practice and Exploration of Finance in Wenzhou*, Wenzhou Social Federation and Wenzhou Financial Society, 1995

loans go, state-owned sector accounted for 86.24%, the collective sector accounted for 7.53% and individual and private businesses accounted for 6.23%. The above shows that although the private economy, in the form of the family and private business, constitutes a large proportion in the production and circulation, it is not favored by the government because of its ownership nature, nor does it have a credit records in the country's regular financial sector, so it is impossible for it to get a large amount of loans from official financial institutions as the start-up capital. The private entrepreneurs can only resort to irregular loans to raise capital because the money at their disposal is very limited. With the development of family industry, a large number of joint-stock and private enterprises sprung up in rural areas, but the nature of these enterprises determines that the investors are entrepreneur themselves, who, apart from their own capital accumulation, mainly seek large amount of capital to fill in the gap from private lending. Secondly, in the non-state sector in Wenzhou, because the private economy run by individual farmers accounts for a large share, far higher than the national average, especially in non production areas where this share has an absolute advantage, the farmer-turned-proprietors in non-production areas have a large demand for short term funds, although the average loan (the amount loaned each time) is relatively small. This also has led to the dependence of peasant households on the credit of unofficial financial sector in rural area.

Another more common reason is that, due to the underdevelopment and incompleteness of the financial markets, the official financial sector has left a lot of gaps which is filled by the unofficial financial sector. As a matter of fact, the existence of the regular and irregular sectors in the rural financial markets in developing countries is a widespread empirical phenomenon.[21] We can see from the international experience that in the past 40 years, governments in many countries have tried to introduce regular financial system and institutions in order to provide cheap credit in rural areas, but did not seem to have produced the expected results. Although the government

[21] Von Pischke et al. (1990).

Table 12.2 Informal financial sector in rural areas: cases in developing countries

Survey regions and period	Share of formal sector in total	Average interest rate		Average transaction volume	
		Formal sector	Informal sector	Formal sector	Informal sector
Zaria, Nigeria					
1987–1988	8	-3.6	7.5	266	51
Nakhon Ratchasima province, Thailand:					
1984–1985	44	12–14	90	254	440
India:					
1951	7	3.5– 12.5	7–35	400	200
1961	17	–	–	–	–
1971	30	–	–	–	–
1981	61	10–12	22	–	80–345
Chambar, Pakistan					
1980–1981	25	12	79	–	284

Source K. Holff, J. Stiglitz, Introduction: Imperfect Information and Rural Credit Market Puzzles and Policy Perspectives, *World Bank Review* 1990,4 (3), pp.235–250

has spent a lot of resources on building up the rural credit market system through the establishment of regular financial departments (such as rural credit cooperatives and agricultural banks), the unofficial financial sector (such as private credit) still exists and has developed continuously. Even though in most cases, the unofficial interest rate is much higher than that of the regular rural financial sector (see Table 12.2), the cheap official credit has not been able to drive the unofficial credit from the rural financial market. This has really provided much food for thought.

As mentioned above, the formal rural financial sector is generally arranged by relying on government intervention and the mobilization of financial credit, the purpose of which is to put the financial markets in rural areas completely under the control of the financial policy of the government, or the so-called "supervised credit". For a long time, this kind of policy reflects the traditional view of the rural financial theory. The rural finance school (FF) argues that farmers in rural areas are irrational and lack the ability to save, and that rural financial markets cannot exist without the subsidies provided by the government. In their view, the existence of the irregular sector in rural financial markets is a form of usury that adversely affects farmers and must be replaced by regular institutions.[22] The policy implications of this theory in the 1960s–70s led many developing countries to completely imitate the formal financial system of developed countries and support the development of agriculture through low interest rates and credit subsidies. But the fact proved that this effort was not successful.

[22] Luo and Yang (1995).

Table 12.3 Different views of rural financial market school and rural financial school on irregular financial sector

View	Rural Financial Theory	Rural Financial Market
Existence value	None	Contribution to some extent
Reason	The farmers in rural areas are irrational and lack the ability to save, and the rural financial markets cannot exist without the subsidies provided by the government. The existence of the irregular sector in rural financial markets is a form of usury that adversely affects farmers and must be replaced by regular institutions	The existence of the irregular sector is not a pernicious act of usury. In fact, if the transaction costs and risks are taken into account, the cost of obtaining loans from the formal sector does not necessarily lower than that of the non formal sector. Moreover, in developing countries, no mature financial market has been in existence, so the irregular sector can make up for the gaps in rural finance

Source Adapted from the literature provided by Luo Mingzhe and Yang Kunfeng (1995)

However, since the 1980s, the rural financial market theory (RFM) developed by scholars such as Adams has challenged the traditional theory of subsidized credit.[23] They believe that the existence of the irregular sector is not a pernicious act of usury. In fact, if the transaction costs and risks are taken into account, the cost of obtaining loans from the formal sector does not necessarily lower than that of the non formal sector. Moreover, in developing countries, no mature financial market has been in existence, so the irregular sector can make up for the gaps in rural finance. Take the interest rate level as an example. Usury theory regards the irregular sector as the usurer, holding that the monopoly power of rural lenders is the main cause of the high level interest rates of irregular sector. In the view of the transaction cost theory, however, this high rate reflects the rural lenders' consideration of the default risk that might be caused by borrowers. while the theory of usury claims to replace the irregular sector with the formal sector, the other theory obviously requires that policy intervention be reduced to the minimum degree (see Table 12.3).

12.4 Interest Rate and Market Characteristics of the Private Sector

Figure 12.1 shows the big differences in the level of interest rates and their pattern of change between the irregular and official financial sectors in Wenzhou. With regard to the experience of Wenzhou, the current average monthly interest rate of rural free private lending rate is 25‰, with some higher than 30‰; and the average monthly interest rate of private loan for enterprises was 20‰ to 26‰, much higher than that of

[23] Adams (1984).

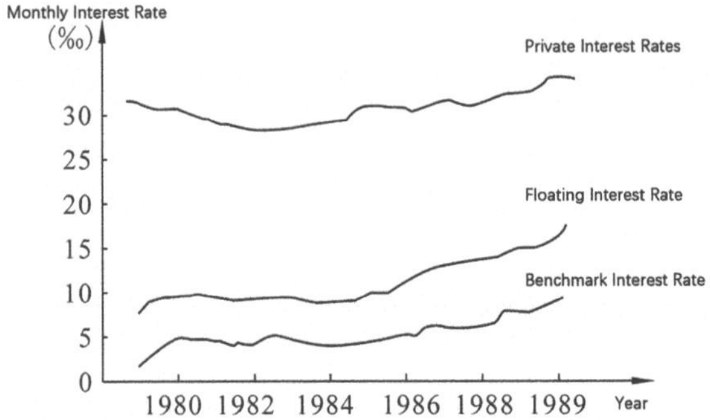

Fig. 12.1 Changes of private interest rates and official interest rates (1979–1989)

the official financial sector.[24] From Fig. 12.1, we can see that the average interest rate of private credit is higher than that of the official interest rate by 2–3 times. Although the state financial institutions have raised interest rates several times, the interest rates of private credit have remained stable, and there seemed to be no obvious reaction to the interest rate adjustment by the official sector.

Thus, Fig. 12.1 may signify a very important feature of the private credit market, that is, the official and private sectors were separated. Moreover, as we have noticed in Fig. 12.1, the changes in private interest rates were not obvious with the passage of time, which may reflect another characteristic–the rural private financial market does not entirely have the classical free market structure. If this is correct, then, as we have mentioned earlier, the phenomenon that there is an excess demand in the irregular credit market in rural Wenzhou is understandable. If prices can make demand equal supply in the rural financial (credit) markets, we should be able to see higher private interest rates in the case of Wenzhou. And if the structure of rural financial market is not a classical structure, the interest rate level may not let prices make demand equal supply in the rural credit market, so even if there is an excessive demand in this market, interest rates may not be adjusted upwards. Therefore, we have encountered some important issues to be discussed: why can private financial sector maintain a higher interest rate than the official sector? In particular, why is the interest rate of irregular sector not sensitive to the changes of interest rate of the official sector? Why cannot private interest rate let the prices make demand equal supply in the private market?

In the past 30 years, especially in the last 10 years, many economists have done a lot of pioneering studies on incomplete information theory, and gradually developed a market structure information model.[25] By Using this model, economists have improved their understanding of the characteristics of many markets. The application of this information-based analysis paradigm to the study of credit markets has become one of the most significant fields of economic development since the

[24] I was told by the staff of the financial department of Wenzhou that the interest rate of the rural private financial market in Wenzhou is still stable at 30‰.

[25] Information economics is undoubtedly one of the most important fields of mainstream economics.

80 s.[26] The most important findings from this application are as follows. ① In market transactions, certain key yet often difficult to be observed information about qualities (quality of goods or human behavior) is asymmetrically distributed between the two parties on the market. Just as in a commodity transaction where the buyer has much less information about the quality of the goods than the seller,[27] in credit market, lenders usually do not have complete information about the default risk of the borrowers. ② If the information on default risk is seriously asymmetrical among the lender and borrower, then the role of interest rates in the lending market, as a price parameter of borrowed capital, is not only to adjust the supply and demand of the capital, but also becomes a signal, assuming the function of "selection" which is used to screen the default risk of different borrowers, just as education plays the role of filtering human talents. ③ If the interest rate is not only the price lever to adjust the supply and demand of capital, but also assumes a special function to filter the risk of repayment, then the change of interest rate of the credit market has become the risk portfolio tool by the lenders to adjust their credit selection. ④ If the interest rate has the function of changing the default risk combination, the credit market cannot be operated like a classical market. That is to say, the interest rate in equilibrium may not be able to let prices make demand equal supply in the market, even if the credit market is completely competitive. For example, when there is an excessive demand in this market, interest rates may have a slow response and not necessarily increase.

Based on these theoretical backgrounds, we can further analyze the segmentation characteristics of rural credit market in Wenzhou and some empirical observations on irregular credit sector. To look at private credit interest rate in part as regulating the credit risk portfolio or a function of screening the default risk from the perspective of information asymmetry is the key to understanding the rural credit market structure and interpreting the private interest rate. Based on this theory, we believe that the segmentation of rural credit market and the fact that its interest rate can maintain a stable level higher than the official credit sector is a rational response of farmers and farmers' organizations to the imperfect distribution of default risk information in the rural financial market. Let's make a brief analysis to illustrate this point. According to the survey, in the rural credit market of Wenzhou, the credit that cannot be provided by the banking departments of the state is mainly short-term credit of small amount (mostly tens of thousands or several hundred thousand *yuan*). In rural areas, however, the demand for such credit is very strong, which provides the potential for the development of the private credit market. However, the private credit sector is different from the official one, because the private credit lacks the institutional arrangements of the official sector, so that the lenders will face the more serious problems of risk screening and the effective implementation of the terms of the loan contract (whether written or tacit). For a short-term credit, how to screen the risk of loan repayment and ensure the effective implementation of the terms of the loan contract may be the most important issue faced by private lenders. Therefore, on the one hand, as long as there is the regulation and repression by the official

[26] Stiglitz and WFiss (1981).

[27] Akerlof (1973), Spence (1973).

financial sector, and the interest rate of official finance is distorted, we can observe the higher interest rates of irregular financial sector; on the other hand, different from the general commodity market, financial market is a high-risk market, so the higher interest rates we have observed in the rural private financial market also contains the private lenders' "premium" on the greater risk expectations. These can explain why interest rates in irregular credit markets are higher than those in the formal financial sector.

But how can we explain the fact that the interest rate of private credit market is not sensitive to the interest rate adjustment of formal financial sector? In this paper, we will consider the problem of imperfect information in private credit market and try to explain the stability of the private interest rate with this consideration. Generally speaking, whether the principal and interest of a loan can be repaid depends on how many net returns the borrower can get after deducting the loan's principal and interest, and the latter, in turn, depends on the risk of the business the borrower engages in with the loan he borrowed. For borrowers, the greater the risk of a business is, the greater the expected value of his return on investment. Therefore, the expected profit function of the borrower is a rapidly upward curve. In Fig. 12.2, we represent it with EV_d. For lenders, under certain operating risk conditions, his expected return on the credit provided depends on the possible net return of the borrower obtained from the loan. However, with the risk of business of the borrower increases, that is to say, when the probability of a borrower to obtain very high or very low return is greater than the probability of modest gains, the risk of default on the part of the borrower will be increased. So, for the lender (creditor), the greater the risk of the project selected by the borrower (debtor) is, the greater the risk of default will be, so the lender's return expectations may decrease with the increase of risk of borrower's business. It is clear that there is an "inverted U" curve EV_c between the lender's expected return and the risk scope of the borrower's business projects, and this curve is the expected return function of the lender.

Now let us take into account imperfect information in the lending market. We assume that the lender does not have sufficient information about the borrower's loan

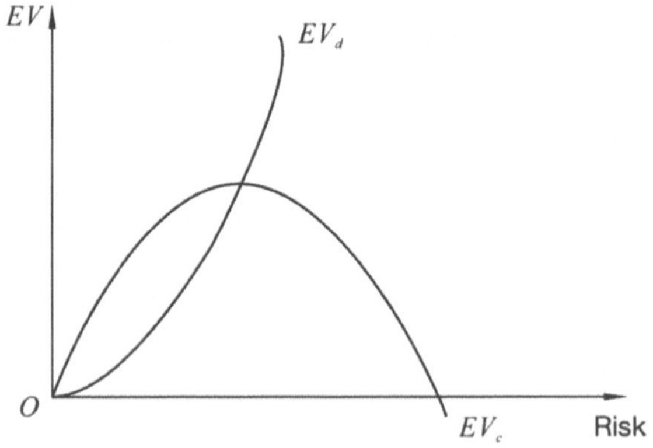

Fig. 12.2 Risk selection and expected return function

risk. Because of the asymmetric information, according to our theory, the interest rates will play the role of filtering the default risk of borrower for the lender, so that in the credit market, the interest rate level and adjustment will regulate the risk portfolio of the credit market. But, how does interest rate filter the borrower's default risk?

We can see from Fig. 12.3 that, as long as EV_d curve can be determined, the interest rates of credit market will be determined by the intersection of EV_c and the upward-going EV_d. Of course, in this case, an optimal equilibrium interest rate, γmax, can only be reached when the curve EV_d intersects with the curve EV_c. at the highest point. The problem is that the lender in general does not know exactly the location of the curve EV_d because of the imperfect information, so even if there is a demand pressure on increasing the interest rate in the private credit market, the level of interest rates is not likely to continue to be adjusted to the right side of $\gamma_{\max}$ as seen in Fig. 12.3. The reason is that when information is imperfect, the only way to ensure that the lender's expected returns are not rapidly diminishing is to keep the interest rates at $\gamma_{\max}$ or on its left side. Therefore, even if there is excessive demand for credit on the right side of $\gamma_{\max}$, lenders will not set interest rates above the $\gamma_{\max}$. This shows that in the credit market, because the interest rate–as a signal of price–also acts as a "filter" of default risk, it cannot be increased even when there is an excessive demand; instead, it will tend to be relatively stable compared with credit demand in order to overcome the "adverse selection" in the private market. As a result, the great demand for credit does not necessarily boost the further increase of interest rate. This provides a feasible explanation for the relatively high level and a more stable trend of interest rates in the private credit market in Wenzhou.

The analysis of the high interest rates in the private credit market made by us from the perspective of information economics is very different from the previous interpretations of the phenomenon of "usury" in rural areas. For a long time, people generally believe that the existence of the high private interest rates in rural regions is because of the monopoly power held by lenders in the rural financial market; therefore, to reduce the rural usury, the government must introduce the modern official financial system into the rural areas to "crowding out" the loan sharks from the rural financial market. However, the economy of developing countries over the past

Fig. 12.3 Interest rate decisions in the private credit market

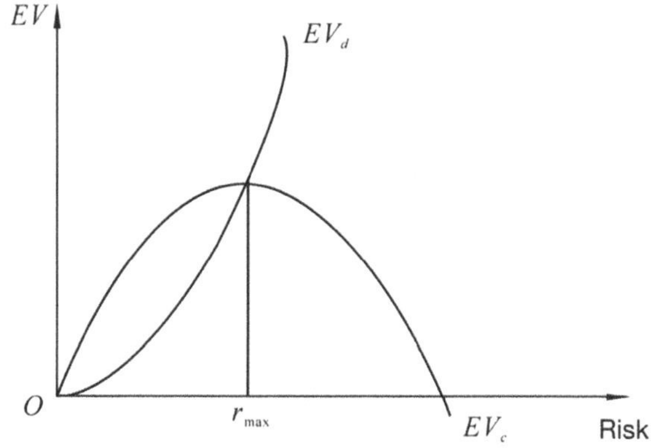

40 years show that the financial intervention of the government did not succeed, and that the establishment of formal financial institutions in rural areas did not completely replace the irregular sector whose interest rates are still maintained at higher price than that of the formal sector.

This shows that the old interpretation of usury is doubtful. In contrast, we approached the relatively stable and high interest rates of the irregular financial sector from the perspective of information economics and regarded it as a rational response to the imperfect information about the default risk in the rural financial market. Default risk faced by each lender is different, but because of incomplete information, it is extremely difficult for lenders to ascertain the degree of default risk of each borrower in advance, so the interest rate becomes a tool to screen or filter the default risk of borrowers in order to alleviate the "adverse selection" of private credit market. We show In Fig. 12.3 that in the case of insufficient information, when the credit demand is very strong, interest rates will still remain at a stable level to filter the risk types of the borrowers, but it will not be high enough to eliminate all the excess demand for credit. As a result, we observed that private interest rates in Wenzhou were almost 3 times higher than the official rates. But it cannot let the price make demand equal supply in the rural credit market with the result that credit is still in great demand in the rural private credit market.

It should be said that in addition to overcoming the problem of imperfect information by using the interest rate as a mechanism to filter the default risk, the lender can also directly "buy" information. "Buying" or investing in information means that the lender filters the borrower directly through a "non-market" approach and directly monitors the latter's implemention of the terms of the credit contract. The so-called non marketization refers to the fact that the lender "filters" the borrower not by interest rates, but through interpersonal relationship, regional relationship and even "associations" to overcome the problem of the imperfect information of credit market. It is so because the problem of imperfect information tends to be less serious in the following circumstances: ① lending and borrowing occur among relatives and friends or expanded interpersonal relationships; ② lending and borrowing occur among people living in the same (such as village or neighborhood) or nearby areas; ③ lending and borrowing occur by borrower offering pledged goods to the lender; ④ lending and borrowing occur through small community organizations and so on. All these non-market arrangements make the issue of insufficient information in the lending and borrowing relationship less serious and implementation and monitoring of the terms of the credit contract easier. But interest rates on lending are not always becoming lower because of this, for, on some occasions, the costs of these non-market arrangements may be taken into account in the interest rates. Therefore, in this case, the high private interest rates reflect the resource cost of information investment. This provides a feasible explanation for the various forms of credit that we have observed in the rural financial market in Wenzhou such as the appearance of pawn firms and various "associations".

In fact, in other developing regions, or in China's Wenzhou, private lending was initially extended from friends, family members and neighborhood, because the problems of imperfect information and keeping an agreement among friends and neighbors are generally not serious. In terms of contract, form is not important, even if there is only a tacit understanding due to the long-standing affection and friendship among friends and family members. This kind of tacit or implicit contract can be self-enforcing. In the credit relationship of relatives and friends, borrowing is often cheap and interest-free because the screening problem is not serious. With the continuous expansion of the lending chain, the irregular credit gradually developed as a market, in the process of which interest rates began to gradually play the function of screening. As far as the case of Wenzhou is concerned, we have mentioned before that the private credit based on mutual understanding and mutual trust is only restricted to family members and friends, and most of the credit is interest-free. But the private credit as a market gradually developed through intermediary organizations with the monthly interest rate set as high as 20‰ to 30‰. The interest rates also play the "screening" function in the private lending market. In this sense, the development of rural private financial market in Wenzhou since the reform has also provided us with a more general experience of the evolution and development of the market.

12.5 Conclusion

The growth of the rural nongovernmental financial sector in Wenzhou provides us with a case for understanding the development pattern of China's rural financial market after the reform. The study of this case also provides us with some policy implications which should be emphasized in the market-orientation process.

For a long time, we have not really understood the segmented features and structure of rural financial market when this market was regulated and restricted by official departments. People always believe that private credit activities will continue to pose a "challenge" to the official banking, and financial authority has been trying to crack down on the private credit activities and drive them underground. Some financial theorists have realized the high cost of controlling the nongovernmental sector, but, probably due to the same understanding mentioned above, many of them still believe that the private credit market can be "squeezed out" by means of a series of reform on interest rate and attracting deposits. One of the most typical theories is the implementation of floating interest rate (basically floating-up tendency) to attract a lot of deposits and turn the capital from "external circulation" to "internal circulation", so that the banks will have more strength to implement their own credit policy. But one of the conclusions of our analysis is that, it is virtually impossible to completely curb the development of the rural irregular financial sector under the condition that the whole financial system is still being suppressed and the financial market is underdeveloped. Because of the segmentation characteristics of rural financial market, we can be sure that the rural financial system controlled by the state has not and will not be able to mobilize more financial resources because of the repression of irregular financial markets.

Since the 1980s, the focus of rural financial reform has been focused on the reform of rural credit cooperatives, but it has never gone beyond the control of agricultural banks. In the face of the strong challenges of irregular financial sector, credit cooperatives began to decline under strict control. This pattern has posed a challenge to our financial control policy. From the present point of view, in the face of such a development, the policy of control has been in trouble. With the development of market-orientated reform in economy, the market-oriented reform of the whole financial system is inevitable. The analysis of this article implies that, while reforming the formal financial sector, we should actively guide rather than restrain the rural irregular financial sector from entering the market. At the same time, when opening the rural financial market step by step, we should also relax the control over the rural credit cooperatives and let them enter the market as independent financial organizations. The role of government is to regulate the whole rural financial market, and make it evolve into a more orderly competition.

Author's Note

This is one of the few articles I have published in the field of financial economics. The design of it was probably conceived in 1996. In that year, with the funding from the Beijing Tianze Economic Institute, I carried out an investigation on the institutional changes of Chinese rural financial market and wrote cases. With the assistance of Dr. Qian Yanmin from Agricultural University in Zhejiang (now merged with Zhejiang University), I went to Wenzhou to investigate the private lending market two times. I called on the agricultural bank of Wenzhou, the people's bank of Wenzhou and the Economic Restructuring Office, as well as read the local policies and regulations and a lot of first-hand information of private lending cases. I also met with scholars in Zhejiang province and city of Wenzhou who are engaged in the study of Wenzhou private lending such as Zhang Renshou and Chen Guoxing. From them, I learned more details of the story, and also got hold of books and articles they wrote.

Like in other developing countries, "irregular finance" or "private credit markets" exists in many rural and urban areas of China. I have been to the south of Jiangsu to investigate and noticed the importance of private lending for the development of local private enterprises. Of course, the most typical private financial market is in Wenzhou, Zhejiang. Therefore, as long as the private lending is concerned, Wenzhou must be mentioned. The "Wenzhou model" widely accepted by economists is in fact largely determined by the historical tradition of Wenzhou's private financial market. And in my article I have provided a case of Wenzhou's private lending market mainly from the point of view of economics, which was not consistent with the control concept of the banking authorities at that time. This article focuses more on observation and explanation, and less on the popular discussion of financial regulatory policy at that time.

This article was included in the collection of cases edited by Beijing Tianze Economic Institute, and published in the 20th volume (Autumn) of *Chinese Social Science Quarterly* (Hong Kong) in 1997. It was widely quoted for many years.

References

D. W. Adams, Why Agricultural Credit Program in low Income Countries Perform Poorly? Farm Credit Situation in Asia, APO, 1984.

G. Akerlof, The Market for "Lemons": Quality, Uncertainty and The Market Mechanism, *Quarterly Journal of Economics,* 1970, 86.

Luo Mingzhe, Yang Kunfeng: An Investigation of the Rural Financial Market Theory, see Jiang Heping: *China's Agriculture towards Twenty-First Century*, Beijing, Chinese Agricultural Press, 1995.

A. M. Spence, Job Market Signaling, *Quarterly Journal of Economics*, 1973, 87.

J. Stiglitz, A. WFiss, Credit Rationing in Markets with Imperfect Information, *American Economic Review*, 1981, 71.

J. D.Von Pischke et al.: *Rural Finance in Developing Economies*, tr. Tang Shisheng, et al., Beijing, Chinese Finance Press, 1990.

Zhang Renshou, Li Hong: *A Study of Wenzhou Model*, Beijing, Chinese Social Science Press, 1990.

Zhang Zhenyu, Mao Chunhua: *A Survey of the Wenzhou Financial Phenomenon under the Condition of Socialist Market Economy*, Hangzhou, Zhejiang University Press, 1993.

Postscript

It is gratifying to be invited by the press to select my own articles and edit them into an academic book. Although I have published about 100 research papers in the past 20 years, it is not an easy task to compile a book with an overriding theme. It has to be evaluated by my peers and readers, which gives me a lot of pressure.

Since my area of study is the reform and growth of Chinese economy, I decided to select articles around the theme "reform, transformation and growth: observation and interpretation". Some of the articles were first published in 1989 and some were recently published in 2009, which had a span of 20 years. The contents of these articles can be divided into five distinct sections, so the book is structured in five major parts accordingly. It must be admitted that the early and later articles are very different in subjects and research methods due to my own interest and the impact of the Chinese economic reform stages at that time. But for a growing young economist, it is inevitable for him to go through the process of starting, growth and transformation like the development of the Chinese economy.

For various reasons, what I did was only to choose the articles. And the whole editorial process of this book was aided greatly by my doctoral student Tang Dongbo and Ms. Chen Mei of the Office of Chinese Economic Research Center of Fudan University. My master's degree students, Zhang Xiaomu and Huang Bo, helped translate two papers from English into Chinese, and I am grateful to them. My thanks also go to Professor Li Xiaoxi of the Beijing Normal University, Beijing Normal University Press's director Yang Geng, deputy editor-in-chief Ye Zi and editor Ma Hongli for their care and support for the publication of the book.

A large part of the book has been funded by research projects, especially the city key project of Shanghai (Western Economics B101), "Research on International Competitiveness of Chinese Economy", a project of 985 state philosophy and social sciences innovation base of Fudan University, and the Yangtze River Scholar/Distinguished Professor Project of Education Ministry. I appreciate these organizations for funding my studies.

J. Zhang, *Reform, Transformation and Growth*, Understanding China,
https://doi.org/10.1007/978-981-99-5712-5

I also want to thank my parents, the parents of my wife and my sisters and brothers for heir selfless and consistent support for my family and me. Last but not least, the love from my wife and son made me look forward to the future with great expectations.

Jun Zhang
2010 in Shanghai

The manufacturer's authorised representative in the EU is Springer Nature Customer Service Centre GmbH, Europaplatz 3, 69115 Heidelberg, Germany. If you have any concerns regarding our products, please contact ProductSafety@springernature.com

Printed and bound by CPI Group (UK) Ltd, Croydon, CR0 4YY
01/10/2026
02225849-0013